Hampshire Record Series Volume XIV

The Pipe Roll of the Bishopric of Winchester 1301-2

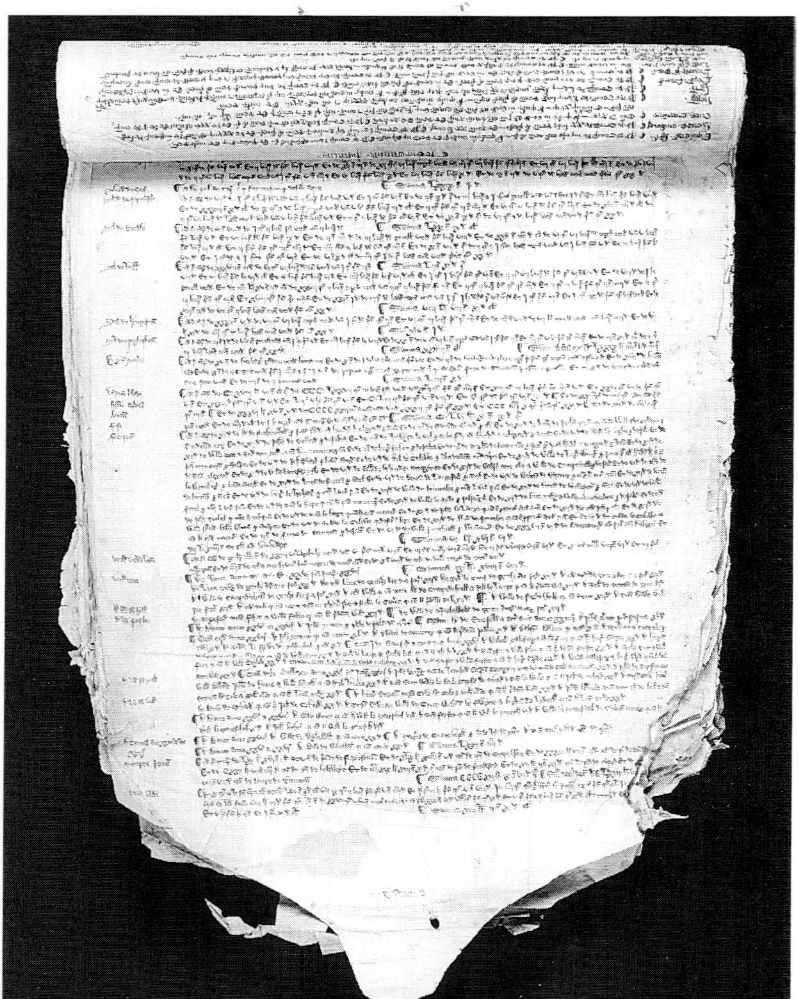

First membrane of the Winchester pipe roll for 1301-2 showing the beginning of the account for Taunton.
(Hampshire Record Office, 11M59/B1/58, m. 1)

Hampshire Record Series Volume XIV

The Pipe Roll of the Bishopric of Winchester 1301-2

Edited by
Mark Page

Hampshire County Council
Winchester
1996

Hampshire Record Series

General Editor
S. J. Lewin
Technical Adviser
B. J. Iles

Published in 1996 by Hampshire County Council
The Castle, Winchester, SO23 8UJ

Distributed by Hampshire Record Office
Sussex Street, Winchester, SO23 8TH

Printed by Hobbs the Printers of Southampton

ISSN 0 267 9930
ISBN 1 85975 108 3

Contents

Illustrations, Maps and Tables

ILLUSTRATIONS

MAPS

TABLES

Preface

This volume is the first to be published as a result of the Winchester Pipe Rolls Project, a three-year project funded by Hampshire County Council and begun in September 1993. From the first the aim of the project has been to make the Winchester pipe rolls more accessible, both to the specialist and non-specialist alike, and it is hoped that this volume will go some way towards the fulfilment of that aim. It is envisaged that at least one other volume will be published by Hampshire Record Series to accompany the first. This will be a translation of the pipe roll from 1409-10, a very different document from that translated for the present volume.

My principal thanks then are to the generosity of Hampshire County Council for funding the project, and to Councillor F A J Emery-Wallis DL, the chairman of Hampshire Archives Trust, and Miss Rosemary Dunhill, the County Archivist of Hampshire, for their work to establish the project in the first place.

The project has been supervised by a Steering Group chaired by Councillor Emery-Wallis. To the members of that group, Dr Richard Britnell, Rosemary Dunhill, Dr Brian Golding, Miss Barbara Harvey, Professor Paul Harvey, Dr Derek Keene, Miss Sarah Lewin and Dr Christopher Woolgar, I offer grateful thanks. All have offered much critical advice and guidance from which I and the volume have benefited greatly. I must particularly acknowledge the help of Professor Harvey, Dr Keene, and Dr Woolgar, the out-going general editor of Hampshire Record Series, for saving me from numerous errors of translation. The in-coming general editor, Sarah Lewin, has offered unstinting help at every stage of the project.

I would also like to thank for their comments at various stages of the project Professor Christopher Dyer, Dr Harold Fox, Dr James Galloway, Dr John Hare, Professor John Langdon, Mr Edward Roberts, Dr Christopher Thornton and Dr Jan Titow. All have offered welcome advice and encouragement.

Members of staff at Hampshire Record Office have been characteristically helpful throughout the project. The microfiche were prepared by Mr Martin Bray.

Abbreviations

AHEW, ii	*The Agrarian History of England and Wales*, ii, *1042-1350*, ed. H. E. Hallam (Cambridge, 1988)
AHEW, iii	*The Agrarian History of England and Wales*, iii, *1348-1500*, ed. Edward Miller (Cambridge, 1991)
BL	British Library
CPL, i	*Calendar of Papal Letters*, i, *1198-1304*, ed. W. H. Bliss (HMSO, 1893)
DMLBS	*Dictionary of Medieval Latin from British Sources*, ed. R. E. Latham and D. R. Howlett (4 vols., Oxford UP, for British Academy, 1975-89)
EcHR	*Economic History Review*
EHR	*English Historical Review*
HRO	Hampshire Record Office
OED	*The Oxford English Dictionary*
Reg. Pontissara	*Registrum Johannis de Pontissara, Episcopi Wyntoniensis, A.D. MCCLXXXII-MCCCIV*, ed. C. Deedes (2 vols., Canterbury and York Soc., 19, 30, 1915-24)
VCH Hants.	*Victoria County History of Hampshire & The Isle of Wight* (5 vols. in 6, London, 1900-14)

Introduction

Throughout the middle ages the diocese of Winchester was the wealthiest see in England and was, it is claimed, second only to the diocese of Milan in Europe as a whole.[1] Most of this wealth derived from the enormous estate of the bishopric, which extended far beyond the spiritual boundaries of the see. The diocese comprised the counties of Hampshire, including the Isle of Wight, and Surrey. The estate, on the other hand, included lands in a further five southern counties: Somerset, Wiltshire, Berkshire, Oxfordshire and Buckinghamshire; however, the bulk of the manors was located in Hampshire. Most of this vast territory came to the bishops before the Norman Conquest, through the pious gifts of West Saxon kings from the seventh century to the tenth, although this by no means guaranteed the inalienability of the estate. In 1284 Edward I appropriated to the crown the episcopal properties on the Isle of Wight, allowing in return the cession of certain manors in Hampshire belonging to the priory of St Swithun's to the bishop.[2] The composition of the bishopric estate was thus not entirely stable. Its structure too fluctuated greatly over the centuries, as manors were leased, either on a temporary or a permanent basis, merged together or split into their constituent parts.

These changes can often be discerned by reference to the records of the estate, and in particular to the Winchester pipe rolls. Much ink has been spilt eulogising the pipe rolls since Maitland first drew attention to them in 1889.[3] That this is not simply hyperbole is indicated by the vast historiography that has built up around the rolls, with scholars in a number of disciplines and with a wide variety of interests continuing to plunder them to this day. The Winchester pipe rolls are enrolled accounts, a fair copy of the year's account, from Michaelmas to Michaelmas, for the whole of the bishopric estate, which were drawn up from the individual manorial account rolls after these had been corrected at audit. In all, 191 rolls survive in broken series from 1208-9 until 1455-6. Thereafter, the accounts continue from 1457-8 until 1710-11 in the form of 137 parchment volumes. The roll which has been

1 T. W. Mayberry, *Estate Records of the Bishops of Winchester in the Hampshire Record Office* (Hampshire County Council, 1988), p. 4. According to J. C. Dickinson, *An Ecclesiastical History of England: The Later Middle Ages* (London, 1979), p. 47, 'the bishopric of Winchester became the most lucrative in England, a fourteenth-century magnate noting "Canterbury hath the finer stable but Winchester the deeper manger"'. For an estimate of the bishop of Winchester's income in 1301-2, see below, pp. xx–xxi.

2 Mayberry, *Estate Records*, pp. 4, 17; *VCH Hants.*, iii, p. 285; v, p. 218; *Reg. Pontissara*, ii, pp. 426-31. The bishop received Alverstoke, Droxford, Gosport and Havant.

3 *Select Pleas in Manorial and Other Seignorial Courts*, ed. F. W. Maitland (Selden Soc., 2, 1889), p. xiv; Mayberry, *Estate Records*, pp. 4, 6.

translated for this volume is the fifty-eighth of this series of 191, the seventeenth of the 18 rolls to survive for the episcopate of John of Pontoise (1282-1304).[1]

The Document

The document consists of 32 parchment membranes of unequal length, varying between 650mm and 740mm from the head to the tip of the tapered end. The average width of the membranes is 430mm. The foot of each membrane is tapered off slightly to a blunt end, on the face of which the consecutive numbers of the membranes have been written in arabic numerals in a modern hand. Above them are written the names of the manors in the same hand as the text of the roll (Plate 1). The tapered ends allow simple and speedy searches to be made for the accounts of particular manors without the necessity of having to unroll the entire document. The membranes are single pieces of parchment rather than two pieces stitched together, the strict definition of a 'pipe' in the Exchequer sense, although it is clear that the Winchester accounts were called pipe rolls (*pipas*) by contemporaries.[2] The membranes were probably originally stitched together at the head by leather thongs, but are now held in place with string. At the head of each membrane, on both face and dorse, the scribe wrote the name of the manor of which he was then copying the account. There is on average 80 lines of writing on each side of the membranes, apart from the dorse of the last membrane, on which 17 lines have been written. The rest has been left completely blank, except that at the foot the scribe has written 'Compotus E*pisco*patus Winton*iensis* cons*ecrationis* d*omi*ni Johannis e*pisco*pi vicesimo p*ri*mo', as he had done at the head of the first membrane, to serve as a label when the manuscript was rolled up. On most of the membranes faint ruled lines, about 7mm apart, can be discerned. Each membrane also has two margins. The right-hand margin, on average 50mm wide, has been left blank. In the left-hand margin, on average 60mm wide, the scribe has written the sub-headings of the cash, corn and stock accounts. The names of the manors, at the beginning of each account, and usually too the headings at the beginning of the corn and stock accounts, were written in the centre of the line, rather than in the margin.

The general condition of the manuscript is excellent and very little text is missing. There are jagged tears at the foot of membranes 1 to 5 and a little higher up in the right-hand margin on the face of membranes 18 to 32, but usually this has meant the loss of just a few letters. There is too some slight discoloration in the right-hand margins on the face of membranes 7 to 29 which has also affected the left-hand margins on the dorse, but there is nothing in the manuscript that is unreadable. The manuscript is very neat, with few interlineations, crossings out or erasures, and is written in a single hand. In the right-hand margin on the face of membrane 10 is the drawing of a head in profile wearing a Phrygian cap (Plate 2). There is also a drawing of a foliated cross at the beginning of the grange account on the face of membrane 26. Other less elaborate drawings serve to mark later additions to the text.[3] On the face of membrane 29 the heading has been given some modest decoration (Plate 3), but there are none of the highly decorated initial letters to be found in some rolls.[4] Nor are

1 For a brief biography of Bishop John, see J. H. Denton, 'John of Pontoise', in *The Dictionary of National Biography: Missing Persons*, ed. C. S. Nicholls (Oxford, 1993), pp. 357-8.

2 *The Pipe Roll of the Bishopric of Winchester 1210-1211*, ed. N. R. Holt (Manchester, 1964), pp. ix-x; Mayberry, *Estate Records*, p. 6. The references below, on p. 353, are to Exchequer pipe rolls. The origin of this use of 'pipe' is uncertain, for which see *OED*, xi, p. 886.

3 There are two of these on the face of membrane 10.

4 For example, the portrait of the king, presumably Edward III, at the beginning of the roll for 1335-6, and the fox or hare at the beginning of the roll for 1336-7: HRO 11M59/B1/88-9.

there any rubrics in the pipe roll of 1301-2, as can be found in several other rolls from about this time.[1] It is unclear how long the scribe spent compiling the pipe roll, although it appears that he wrote no more than one or two membranes at a time. There is no discernible pattern to the scribe's pen-breaks, which occur not only at the end of membranes and at the end of the accounts of particular manors, but also within sub-sections of the accounts. The identity of the scribe is not known.

The pipe rolls were engrossed from a large number of subsidiary documents which were drawn up by the reeves and other manorial officials. The most important of these documents were the compotus rolls, on which was recorded the bulk of each manor's account. Substantial numbers of these documents survive from the late fourteenth and fifteenth centuries but not for 1301-2. Court rolls similarly survive in considerable numbers from the late fourteenth and fifteenth centuries. These listed the fines and amercements levied in the bishop's courts, often in more detail than the abbreviated versions found in the pipe rolls, in the entry and marriage fines and perquisites sub-sections. There are a number of references to court rolls in the pipe roll of 1301-2.[2] Reference can also be found to more detailed accounts of particular items. These include the numbers of pigs liable for pannage, the labour services of customary tenants, and the costs of building repairs.[3] It is likely that these accounts were originally separate from the compotus rolls and were among the many different types of document used by the reeves. The fourteenth-century compotus rolls nevertheless indicate that the contents of some of these documents were copied up before the audit so that the scribe who compiled the pipe roll may not have seen them. Other documents referred to in the pipe roll of 1301-2 include the account of the bishop's chamberlain and letters of the bishop and of his constable, steward and treasurer.[4] None of these subsidiary documents survive.

For most of their existence the pipe rolls were kept in the episcopal palace at Wolvesey, and were occasionally used by the bishop's officers as a source for manorial custom and precedent.[5] Tenants too recognised the usefulness of the rolls in this respect. In 1302 a tenant of the Somerset manor of Holway paid 3*d.* for a 'search of the rolls', whilst an agreement reached at the Pavilion Court, the bishop's court at St Giles's Fair, was recorded on the pipe roll, presumably as a means of securing its public confirmation and authenticity.[6] In 1869 the bishopric estates and their records were surrendered to the Ecclesiastical Commissioners. The bulk of these records, including the pipe rolls, was then transferred to the Public Record Office in 1892. Ownership of the collection passed to the Church Commissioners on their creation in 1948, and in 1959, in accordance with the policy of the Commissioners of transferring records to appropriate local centres, the greater part of the bishopric collection was deposited at Hampshire Record Office.[7]

1 For example, the first four rolls of the episcopate of John of Pontoise (1282-6): HRO 11M59/B1/42-5.

2 Below, pp. 58, 67, 87.

3 Below, pp. 77, 223, 359.

4 Below, pp. 213, 362-3.

5 Mayberry, *Estate Records*, pp. 4-5; below, p. 160, which perhaps refers to a Winchester pipe roll.

6 Below, pp. 30, 347-9; D. Keene, *Survey of Medieval Winchester* (2 vols., Oxford, 1985), i, p. 13-14.

7 Mayberry, *Estate Records*, p. 5. In the PRO the pipe roll of 1301-2 had the reference Eccles. 2-159448.

The Estate of the Bishopric of Winchester

At the beginning of the fourteenth century the bishop of Winchester held an estate consisting of nearly 60 manors and 10 boroughs spread over seven southern counties. In the pipe roll of 1301-2 separate accounts were given of 57 manors and eight boroughs, together with those of the bishop's marshal and warrener, and the Fair of St Giles. Of these, 29 manors and five boroughs were located in Hampshire, one of which, Cams in Fareham, was held in wardship by the bishop between 1300 and 1303.[1] The accounts of another two boroughs, Farnham and Fareham, were incorporated into the accounts of their respective manors. In addition, the accounts of a number of manors which would later be accounted for separately were also incorporated into the accounts of their larger neighbours. Marwell, for example, which appeared under a separate heading for the first time in the pipe roll of 1347-8 was subsumed within Twyford manor in 1302. Similarly, Charlton, a part of Downton manor in 1302, was given its own account for the first time in the roll of 1379-80. There was a tendency for manors to split into their constituent parts over the course of the thirteenth and fourteenth centuries, thereby giving the false impression that the bishop's estate was being enlarged. Thus, in the first five pipe rolls the manors of Highclere and Burghclere were accounted for together under the heading *Clera*. Thereafter they were always accounted for separately.[2] This development was almost certainly a response to the increasing amount of detail included in the accounts, which led to a growing number of specialist subdivisions amongst the receipts and expenses and increasingly long manorial entries.[3]

A number of the manors which began to be accounted for separately during the thirteenth century nevertheless remained subordinate to their capital manors. Of the 57 manors given separate headings in the roll of 1301-2, six were sub-manors of Taunton and four were sub-manors of Wargrave. One effect of this was that money collected on these manors was delivered to the reeve of the capital manor, rather than directly to the bishop's treasurer at Wolvesey, as practised on the rest of the estate. Another was that grain and livestock were regularly transferred between the manors. Other manors were also linked in this way. The five North Hampshire manors of Ashmansworth, Burghclere, Ecchinswell, Highclere and Woodhay, for instance, transferred oxen, sheep, wool and cheese, but otherwise retained their independence.[4] Occasionally the accounts of manors given separately in one roll were merged in another, particularly if one of those manors was at farm. Thus, the manor of Bishops Fonthill in Wiltshire, intermittently at farm between 1208-9 and 1232-3, was accounted for separately in 1208-9 and with neighbouring East Knoyle in 1210-11, and fluctuated between the two practices until it was taken back into direct management. A slightly different example is that of Pavymor, a part of Bitterne manor, which was given its own account for much of the mid-thirteenth century, even though this usually amounted to only four or five lines. By 1302, however, it was accounted for within the stock account of Bitterne manor, although its profits continued to be sent directly to Wolvesey. These few examples illustrate how the

1 The manor was held by the family of Oysell: *VCH Hants.*, iii, p. 214.

2 For other examples of this practice, see J. Z. Titow, 'Land and Population on the Bishop of Winchester's Estates 1209-1350' (unpublished PhD thesis, University of Cambridge, 1962), pp. 4-5.

3 Below, p. xx.

4 Below, pp. 110-11, 117, 122, 127, 131; E. Miller, 'Farming practice and techniques: the southern counties', *AHEW*, iii, pp. 292-3.

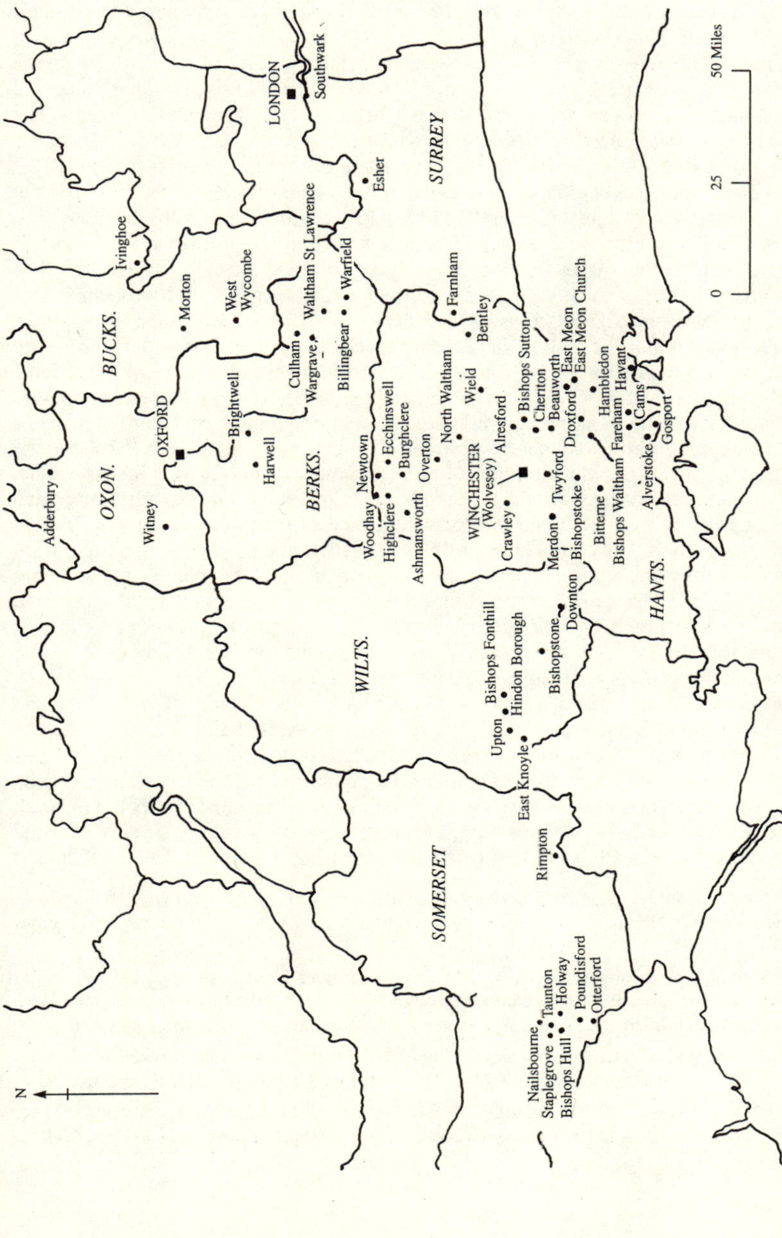

The Estate of the Bishopric of Winchester, *c.*1300

structure of the bishop's manorial administration was constantly being modified, probably in response to the instructions of the auditors.[1] The format of the roll of 1301-2 should thus in no way be regarded as a blueprint for all the pipe rolls in the bishopric collection. Similarly the order in which the manors appear in this roll is not the same as in all the others.

One other variable that should be noted is that the various manors of the estate did not always measure the land in the same way. Thus, on some manors the standard acre was used. This was measured by the perch (*acra per perticam*), was of constant size and did not vary over time. On other manors, however, the customary acre, or the acre as it lies (*acra sicut jacet*), was employed. This varied in size both over time and from manor to manor and seems to have been an estimated measurement. The customary acre was used by virtually the whole estate for the first two decades of the pipe rolls series. Twyford was the only consistent exception. Then, between 1231-2 and 1277-8 almost every manor switched to using standard acres. After the gap in the pipe rolls series between 1278 and 1282 six manors are found to have reverted to using customary acres and were joined in this practice by a further 13 manors in 1301-2. The entire estate then reverted again to standard acres in 1320-1. The customary acre was usually smaller than the standard acre, often by as much as a half, although exact correlations cannot always be made. The change by so many manors to customary acres in 1301-2 means that direct comparison with the acreages recorded in the pipe roll of 1300-1 are difficult and have to be made with caution.[2]

The pipe roll of 1301-2 reveals that most of the bishop of Winchester's estate was in direct management at the beginning of the fourteenth century. Only Otterford, a sub-manor of Taunton, the manors of Freefolk in Overton and Seale in Farnham, the borough of Farnham, and a number of mills and other resources were at farm. This was the situation for much of the thirteenth and fourteenth centuries, when grain and livestock prices were high and profits were greater if the land was farmed directly rather than leased. Only from about 1400 did the increasingly uncertain returns from direct management lead the bishop to begin leasing his manors, thereby guaranteeing a fixed rent and passing on the risks of farming to the lessee.[3] When this occurred the pipe rolls lose much of their historical value because unlike the reeve, who was accountable for everything produced and consumed on the manor, the lessee accounted for just his annual farm, the profits of the manorial courts, and the money spent repairing the manorial buildings, together with details of the lands and livestock leased. Even from about 1350 certain assets were being leased, so that the rolls cease to reflect the economic reality and record instead the lessee's liability. For example, the yield of a particular grain or the number of piglets farrowed might be leased at a set figure, the lessee being allowed to keep the remainder or being liable to make up the shortfall. The rolls would then record this set figure, rather than what was actually produced, because this is what the bishop received.[4] Thus at Rimpton

1 E. Swift, 'The Machinery of Manorial Administration with special reference to the Lands of the Bishopric of Winchester 1208-1454' (unpublished MA thesis, University of London, 1930), pp. 15, 62.

2 This paragraph is largely based upon Titow, 'Land and Population', pp. 145-64, which includes conversion tables from customary to standard acres. For the type of acre employed by individual manors, see J. Z. Titow, *Winchester Yields* (Cambridge, 1972), pp. 150-1 (Table Q).

3 E. Miller and J. Hatcher, *Medieval England: Rural Society and Economic Change 1086-1348* (London, 1978), pp. 210-12; J. M. W. Bean, 'Landlords', *AHEW*, iii, pp. 580-2.

4 P. D. A. Harvey, *Manorial Records* (British Records Association, Archives and the User, no. 5, 1984), p. 34; J. S. Drew, 'Manorial accounts of St Swithun's Priory, Winchester', *EHR* 62 (1947), pp. 31-4.

after 1362 the rolls record the same number of adult pigs each year, the same number of piglets born and no mortalities.[1]

It is not clear whether any such assets were leased in 1301-2. A whole series of rolls would need to be checked before a definitive answer could be given. However, judging by the number of auditorial additions copied onto the roll, it is probable that at this time the bulk of the estate remained in direct management. The audit was one of the chief ways in which the bishop controlled the running of his estate. It took place annually after the end of the financial year at Michaelmas, usually at Wolvesey Castle. There the reeves of each of the bishop's manors and boroughs would present their accounts and hand over whatever money they owed to the bishop's treasurer. The auditors would examine the accounts and frequently queried or disallowed what the reeve claimed, probably on the basis of past accounts or the view which was sometimes made about halfway through the accounting year. When everything had been settled, the reeve's account and the auditors' additions were then copied onto the pipe roll, which thus provides a record of the debate which had taken place between the local and the central official (Plate 4).[2]

The rigour with which the auditors examined the reeve's account is revealed by a survey of the bishopric's compotus rolls. The earliest surviving compotus roll—the roll brought by the reeve to the audit—dates from 1345-6 for the manor of Hambledon.[3] This is thus the first time that the pipe roll can be checked against the original roll. There are a multitude of crossings out on the compotus, presumably made by the auditors, disallowing the claims of the reeve. For example, the reeve claimed to have sold just over 67 quarters of barley for £10 6*s.* 1½*d.* The auditors, however, thought it worth £11 3*s.* 6½*d.* and this was the amount recorded on the pipe roll (Plate 5). The auditors' instructions to the reeves were also copied onto the rolls. In 1302 these ranged from the parsimonious 'henceforth the dairymaid should receive a quarter [of barley] every 12 weeks' rather than every 10, to the pedantic 'from now on the age of the piglets should be distinguished', to the vacillating 'henceforth there should only be one horse there and no cart if that seems to be right'.[4] An examination of subsequent rolls would show whether or not the auditors' advice had been taken.

The Estate Officials

It is not entirely clear who carried out the audit during the thirteenth and fourteenth centuries, but it seems likely that the bishop's steward, treasurer and the clerk of the bishopric were among the officials involved.[5] In 1302 these offices were filled by Robert de Harwedon, Geoffrey de Farham and Simon de Farham respectively. They are frequently mentioned in the roll. Money sent from the manors to the treasury at Wolvesey was usually said to have been delivered to Geoffrey de Farham. Whilst he was at Farnham the treasurer dispatched a number of letters to Wargrave and Esher,

1 C. Thornton, 'Efficiency in medieval livestock farming: the fertility and mortality of herds and flocks at Rimpton, Somerset, 1208-1349', in *Thirteenth Century England IV*, ed. P. R. Coss and S. D. Lloyd (Woodbridge, 1992), p. 43.

2 Harvey, *Manorial Records*, p. 33.

3 HRO 11M59/B2/20/1.

4 Below, pp. 84, 212, 257, 302. Auditors' instructions to the reeves only began in 1300-1, for which see M. Page, 'Challenging Custom: the auditors of the bishopric of Winchester *c.*1300-*c.*1310', *Thirteenth Century England VI* (forthcoming).

5 The title *clericus episcopatus* was not used in the roll of 1301-2, but for contemporary use of the term, see Swift, 'Machinery of Manorial Administration', p. xxvii.

making enquiries about rents and arrears due, and presumably also about the cost of the building work taking place there. He and the steward together authorised the payment of funds from Crawley manor to expedite certain business of the bishop in Buddlesgate hundred. Geoffrey alone ordered the purchase of wax with which to make candles for the chapel at Bitterne, and similarly authorised the bestowal of gifts on Twyford manor.[1] Finally, the treasurer was also recorded as having travelled to Merdon to supervise the carpenter during the sale of bark and timber there and was similarly involved at Bishopstoke. The receipts from these sales were not recorded in the pipe roll and it is likely that they went directly into the bishop's coffers. After his death John of Pontoise was accused of selling and destroying the woods of the bishopric for his own profit and these entries may perhaps go some way towards substantiating the charge.[2]

The treasurer was thus in charge of the estate's finances; he was in consequence one of the bishop's most important officials. Geoffrey de Farham occupied the position between 1293 and 1303 and was one of the men most often appointed to oversee the temporal and spiritual administration of the see during Bishop John's absences abroad.[3] He was also responsible for the running of the household at Wolvesey Castle, for which he received an annual allowance of 20 marks in 1293, and it is likely that he spent most of the year at Wolvesey.[4] The steward, by contrast, who stood at the apex of the bishop's manorial administration, was a much more peripatetic official. He was responsible, *inter alia*, for presiding at the hundred-courts which took place on each manor during the semi-annual tourns at Martinmas and Hockday. In this he was assisted by the clerk of the bishopric, Simon de Farham, who frequently served in his place. Between them the two men managed to visit almost every manor on the estate. Only at Bishopstone did the bailiff preside at both hundred-courts in 1301-2, whilst at Downton the bailiff was granted expenses for holding the tourn at Hockday.[5] Simon de Farham held the tourn 'in the place of the steward' on nine manors at Martinmas and ten at Hockday. His itinerary took him from Hampshire into Wiltshire, Berkshire, Oxfordshire and Buckinghamshire and at each manor he received a provision of wheat, and oats for his horses, as well as his expenses in cash. An indication of the length of time it took to complete the tourns is provided by the dates of the hundred-courts held at Adderbury, both of which were presided over by Simon. The Martinmas court took place on Sunday 10 December 1301, whilst the Hockday court began on Thursday 28 June 1302, even though Martinmas fell on 11 November and Hockday on 1 May.[6] The steward's circuits must have taken even longer, requiring his presence at some 20 manors, and this was only one of his responsibilities.

The range of the steward's duties is indicated in brief by an entry in the Rimpton account recording his expenses for visits there 'to view the state of the manor, to hold

1 Below, pp. 88, 213, 246, 273.

2 Below, pp. 77, 81, 277; J. H. Denton, 'Complaints to the apostolic see in an early fourteenth-century memorandum from England', *Archivum Historiae Pontificiae* 20 (1982), p. 392; cf. D. L. Farmer, 'Woodland and pasture sales on the Winchester manors in the thirteenth century: disposing of a surplus, or producing for the market?', in *A Commercialising Economy: England 1086 to c.1300*, ed. R. H. Britnell and B. M. S. Campbell (Manchester, 1995), pp. 111-14.

3 *Reg. Pontissara*, i, pp. 87, 152-5, 331-2; ii, 640, 779-80, 782-3, 801-3, 833.

4 *Reg. Pontissara*, i, p. 59.

5 Below, pp. 66, 74.

6 Below, pp. 147, 149.

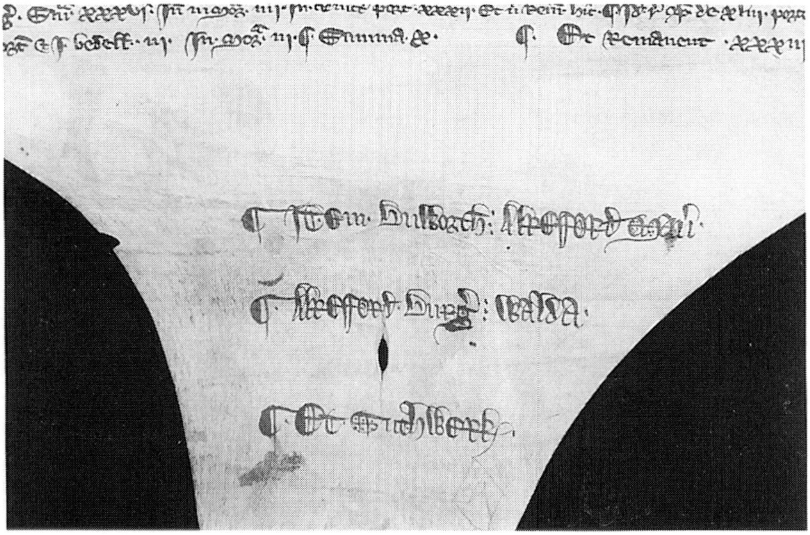

Plate 1. 1301-2 pipe roll showing the tapered end of one of the membranes. (Hampshire Record Office, 11M59/B1/58, m. 29)

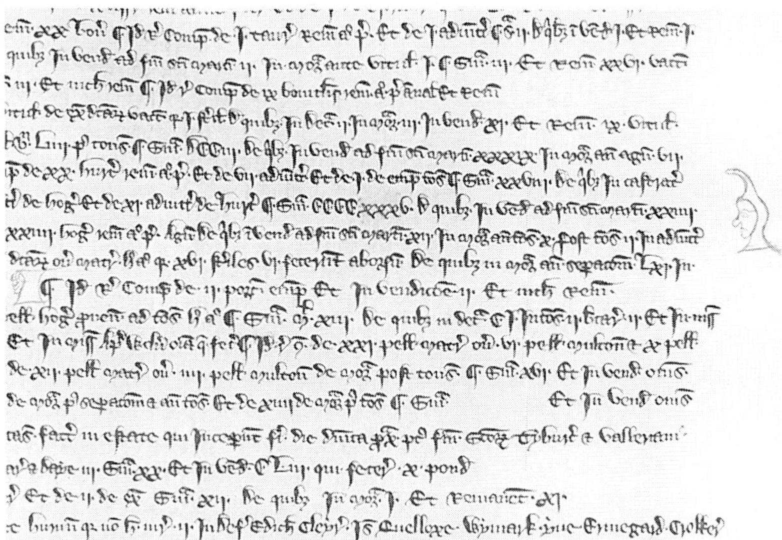

Plate 2. 1301-2 pipe roll account for Overton showing illustrations in the margin and the text, presumably to mark an interlineation in a later hand on the left hand side of the membrane.
(Hampshire Record Office, 11M59/B1/58, m. 10)

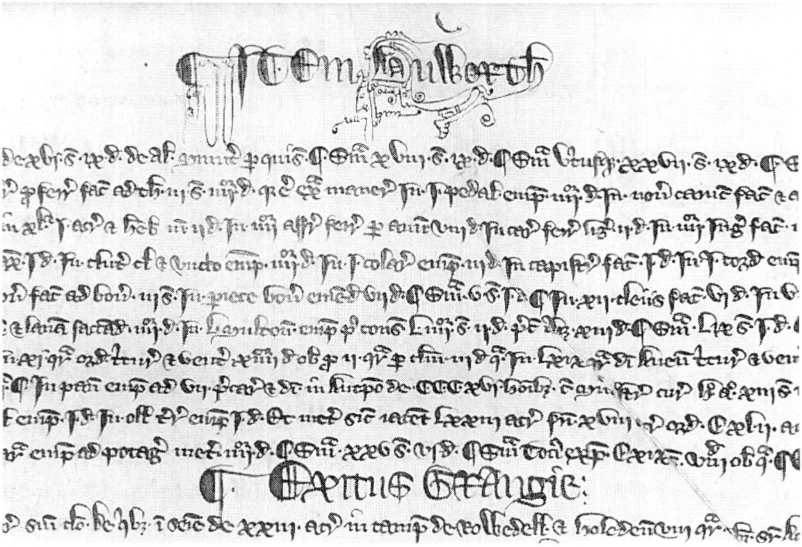

Plate 3. 1301-2 pipe roll account for Beauworth showing some modest decoration of a membrane heading.
(Hampshire Record Office, 11M59/B1/58, m. 29)

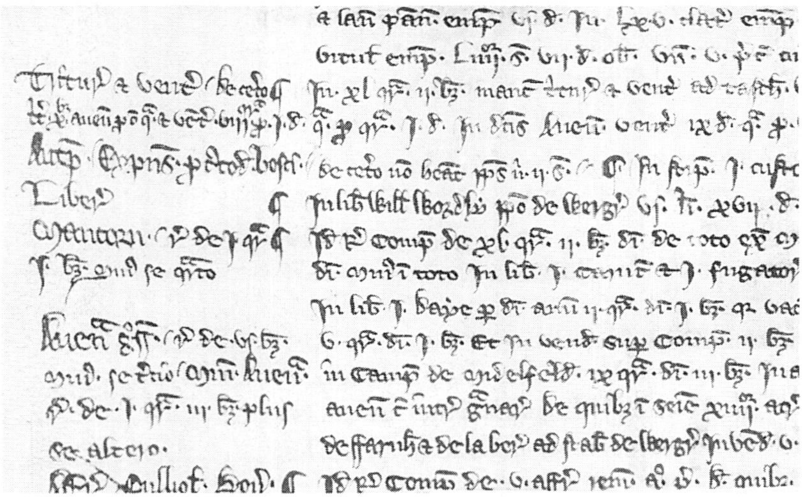

Plate 4. 1301-2 pipe roll account for Billingbear showing comments and yield figures made by the auditors.
(Hampshire Record Office, 11M59/B1/58, m. 18d)

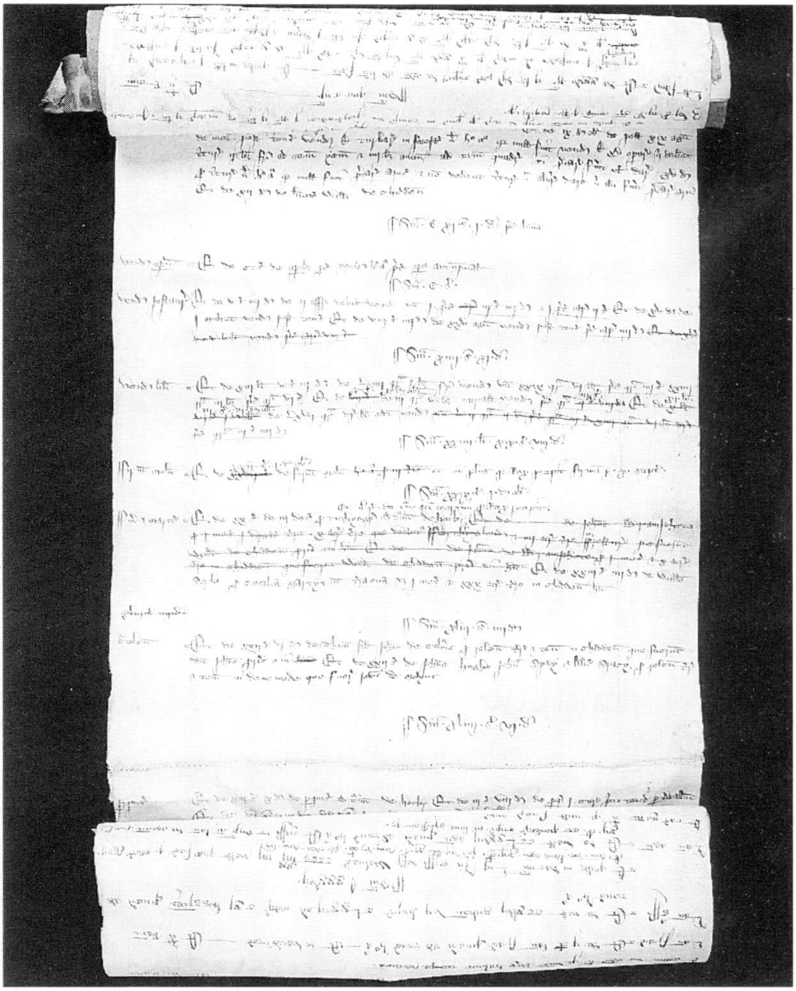

Plate 5. The earliest surviving compotus roll, dating from 1345-6 for the manor of Hambledon, showing a number of crossings out made by the auditors. (Hampshire Record Office, 11M59/B2/20/1)

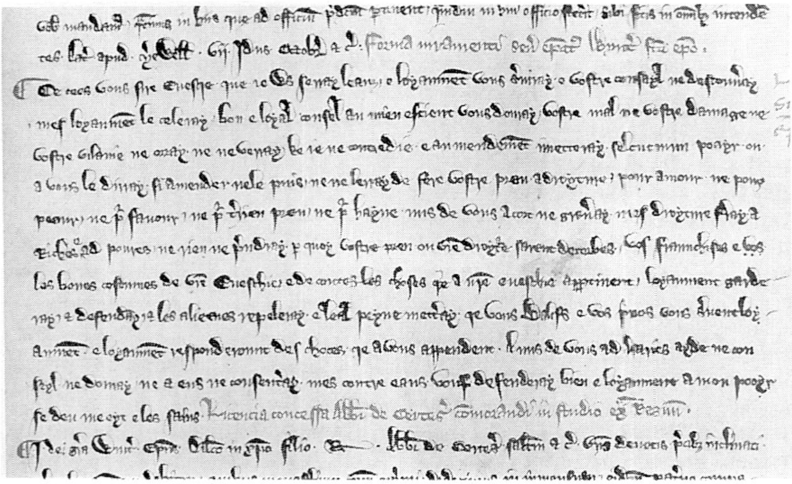

Plate 6. Steward's oath from the register of John of Pontoise.
(Hampshire Record Office, 21M65/A1/1, fo. 65r)

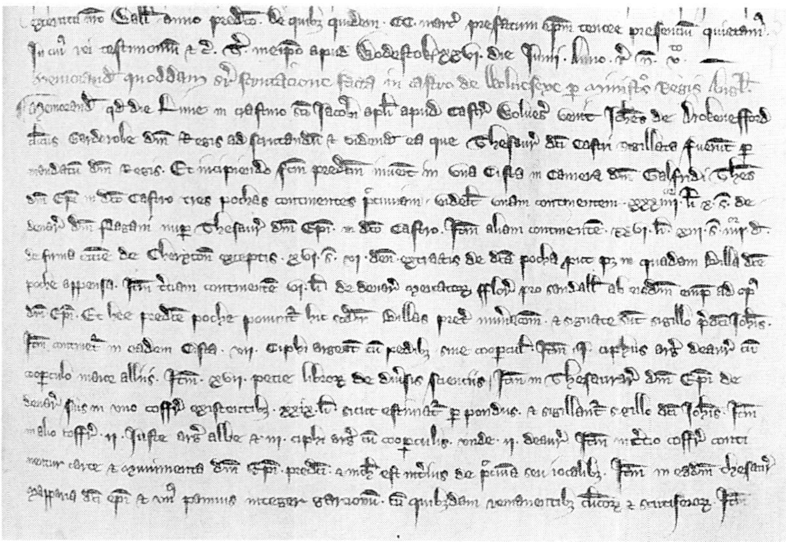

Plate 7. Inspection of John of Pontoise's treasury at Wolvesey Castle made by an official of the king in 1294.
(Hampshire Record Office. 21M65/A1/1, fo. 126r)

court, and to expedite other business of the lord'.[1] This business included acting as the bishop's attorney in the king's court, a common duty of the thirteenth-century steward, although in 1302 Robert de Harwedon delegated the responsibility to one of his servants. He also authorised the delivery of oats from Downton to Hugh Despenser, one of the king's most trusted ambassadors in the 1290s.[2] In addition, according to his oath, the steward was 'loyally to preserve and defend all those things pertaining to your bishopric, to repel aliens, and to spare no pains to ensure that your bailiffs and reeves serve you loyally' (Plate 6).[3] There is little doubt that in fulfilling these obligations the steward travelled widely throughout the estate and occasionally the roll provides more substantial details of his itinerary. For example, the reeve of Witney recorded that Robert de Harwedon was in residence there between Friday 5 January and Friday 26 January 1302. He then visited Ivinghoe at the beginning of February and Overton on Thursday 14 June. Simon de Farham travelled between Downton and Taunton twice in this year and once between Taunton and Merdon, whilst at West Wycombe he stayed for nine nights.[4] Steward, clerk and treasurer all dispatched letters from Farnham and so must have spent time at the bishop's castle there and the Wolvesey account reveals that both steward and treasurer had permanent accommodation in the bishop's palace.[5] All three officers were paid directly from the wardrobe, so that their salaries do not appear on the pipe rolls, although the steward and clerk each received expenses from the manors which they visited.

Below the steward in the hierarchy of the estate's officials were the bailiffs. During the thirteenth century an ever-growing corps of professional bailiffs emerged in England to fulfil the increasingly complex demands of manorial administration.[6] The bailiffs of the Winchester estate were each in charge of a group of manors, usually defined along geographical lines. Thus, the Wiltshire manors were the responsibility of one bailiff, the seven manors in the north of Hampshire of another. It was not, however, until the later fourteenth century that the various manors of the bishopric estate were formally organised into bailiwicks and in 1302 there was still a degree of fluidity. For example, the bailiwicks of Bishops Sutton and East Meon were not yet differentiated and the Soke of Winchester shared a bailiff with the bailiwick of Twyford.[7] In addition, the manors of Bitterne and Havant were each in the hands of a sergeant (*serviens*), a somewhat lesser official, and both were visited by the bailiffs of neighbouring manors. Finally, at Taunton and Farnham the constables of the castles took the place of a bailiff, although the constable of Farnham also served as the bailiff of Wargrave and Bentley.

The duties of the bailiff were to oversee the administration of the manors in their bailiwicks, to hold court in between the sessions of the tourn, and to assist the reeves

1 Below, p. 43.

2 Below, pp. 67, 197. For Hugh Despenser, see M. Prestwich, *Edward I* (London, 1988), pp. 387, 391, 491.

3 *Reg. Pontissara*, i, p. 262.

4 Below, pp. 66, 81, 96, 141, 156, 166. The evidence for Robert's stay at Witney and Simon's stay at West Wycombe derives from allowances of fodder for their horses, which does not necessarily imply that they themselves were at the manors for the periods of time specified.

5 Below, pp. 213, 359.

6 A. Harding, *England in the Thirteenth Century* (London, 1993), p. 150.

7 The composition of the late fourteenth-century bailiwicks is set out in Mayberry, *Estate Records*, pp. 17-18.

in the drawing up of their accounts. In particular, bailiffs were required to oversee the ploughing of the demesne and the reaping of the harvest, although it was not always possible for them to be in direct attendance. Thus, at Wargrave the hayward took charge of the grange and the ploughing because the bailiff was unable to be there, whilst at Fareham the reeve and the beadle oversaw the harvest.[1] At Havant the bailiff took charge of the rebuilding of a mill, and at Witney purchased items for the repair of another. At Witney Borough he was responsible for the sale of licences to buy and sell merchandise, and at Brightwell for licences to sell demesne property.[2] On a number of manors the bailiff had his own room, on others his own stables, and each bailiff probably also had his own clerk and servant.[3] Bailiffs were paid expenses from the revenues of those manors which they visited, and annual fees and fur for their robes from the capital manors of the bailiwicks. Thus Nicholas de Itchen took £6 15*s*. 6*d*. from East Meon and £5 17*s*. from Bishops Sutton. Henry la Wayte received £5 for himself and his *familia* from Highclere, and John de Herierd took £4 15*s*. from Twyford and £3 10*d*. from the Soke of Winchester.[4]

Although the bailiff presented the accounts of his bailiwick jointly with the reeves of the manors, the financial responsibility for those manors ultimately rested with the reeve alone. The reeve was the most important official on the manor, responsible for everything produced and consumed. He was an unfree tenant of the bishop and was chosen for the post by the lord or, more often, by his own fellow-tenants.[5] His duties were manifold: organising the tilling of the demesne lands and the care of the livestock, with the help of hired workers and of whatever labour services were due from the tenants; buying and selling livestock and corn to best advantage; seeing that the grain was effectively threshed and properly stored; and looking to the good order of the farm buildings and implements. He also collected the rents due from the bishop's tenants and the fines imposed in the manorial court. He distributed wages both in cash and kind, and finally, at the end of the year, handed over the profits of the manor to the bishop's treasurer.[6] In return he was spared payment of some of his rent. This might be as little as one shilling or as much as five, but the amount was fixed and in most cases was the same in 1301-2 as it had been in 1210-11, despite the fact that the price of grain more than doubled over the same period.[7] On some manors he was also granted an allowance of grain, on others a cheese, piglet or lamb. He might also be relieved of other obligations, such as the reeve of Bishopstone who was granted 1*s*. 6*d*. for making a plough which ordinarily he was obliged to do without payment as part of the customary service for his land, but which he was quit of whilst he was reeve.[8] Although contemporary treatises on estate management recommended that reeves should serve for no more than a year, this advice was frequently ignored. On the Winchester estate, like so many others, reeves could stay in office for many years.

1 Below, pp. 177, 228.

2 Below, pp. 139, 145, 195, 240.

3 For examples, see below, pp. 67, 137, 150, 186, 245, 272, 299.

4 Below, pp. 108, 272, 287, 307, 346.

5 Harvey, *Manorial Records*, p. 5; A. E. Levett and A. Ballard, *The Black Death on the Estates of the See of Winchester* (Oxford Studies in Social and Legal History, v, 1916), p. 14.

6 Harvey, *Manorial Records*, p. 5; Miller and Hatcher, *Medieval England*, p. 193; *Winchester Pipe Roll 1210-11*, p. xliv.

7 *Winchester Pipe Roll 1210-11*, p. xliv; D. L. Farmer, 'Prices and wages', *AHEW*, ii, pp. 718-19, 760-1.

8 Below, p. 73.

David Martin, for instance, who served as reeve of Crawley in 1301-2, was still in office in 1309-10, as were Thomas Swon, reeve of Highclere, and Richard le Young, reeve of Ecchinswell, and other examples could no doubt be found.[1]

The reeve was assisted in the running of a manor by a number of his fellow-tenants who were appointed to the various manorial offices. The Winchester estate was marked by the extent to which it employed customary rather than hired labour to fill many of these positions. Tenants were often obliged to serve as beadles, carters, cowherds, haywards, park-keepers, ploughmen, shepherds, smiths and swineherds, offices which many lords in thirteenth and fourteenth-century England filled with hired workers.[2] The number of manorial servants employed by the bishop of Winchester varied from manor to manor, depending on its size and resources, and ranged from about half a dozen to more than twenty.[3] The means of their reward also varied considerably across the estate. At Crawley, for example, the smith was remitted 2*s*. 8*d*. of his rent and received a lamb and a cheese for his service, whilst at Brightwell he was quit of 2*s*. 6*d*. of rent and was paid a 4*s*. stipend and a 2*d*. corrody. Similarly, at Woodhay, the hayward was remitted 2*s*. of his rent, was paid a 6*s*. 8*d*. stipend, and received half a quarter of wheat, six-and-a-half quarters of bere and a bushel of oats, whilst at Overton he was quit of 3*s*. of rent and received half a quarter of bere, a lamb and a cheese.[4] On other manors, such as Bentley and Fareham, a hayward was not employed at all. The pattern of manorial offices and the patterns of reward were thus subject to almost limitless variation, both geographically and over time. For example, the manorial servants granted quittances of rent at Downton in 1301-2 were not exactly the same as those in 1324-5, and nor were they identical at Crawley in 1301-2 and 1355-6.[5] The only generalisation that can be made with certainty is that at the beginning of the fourteenth century the bishop of Winchester employed relatively little hired labour on his demesne.

The Income and Expenditure of the Estate

The Winchester pipe rolls take the form of a charge-discharge account, and deal first with cash, then with corn, and then with stock. This was the standard pattern of manorial accounting in England in the middle ages and the pipe rolls vary only slightly from the norm. For example, the inclusion of quittances and defaults of rent in the charge section of the cash account, immediately after the total of the tenants' rents, was peculiar to the bishopric and one or two other estates. In most accounts these entries were placed in the discharge, among the manor's expenses.[6] In the cash account the reeve listed the income of the manor first. This derived partly from rents, partly from the sale of produce, and partly from fines imposed in the manorial court. From these receipts were deducted the running costs of the manor, as expended by

1 *Walter of Henley and Other Treatises on Estate Management and Accounting*, ed. D. Oschinsky (Oxford, 1971), p. 279; HRO 11M59/B1/65, mm. 6, 7d, 8d.; cf. P. D. A. Harvey, *A Medieval Oxfordshire Village: Cuxham, 1240-1400* (Oxford, 1965), pp. 64-5.

2 M. M. Postan, *The Famulus: The Estate Labourer in the Twelfth and Thirteenth Centuries* (*EcHR*, Supplement 2, 1954), pp. 16-17, 26-8, 33, 37, 43, 45-7.

3 Compare, for example, the manors of Bishopstone and Downton: below, pp. 61-2, 71.

4 Below, pp. 85, 90-1, 97-9, 123, 126-7, 192, 195, 197.

5 J. Z. Titow, *English Rural Society 1200-1350* (London, 1969), p. 116; N. S. B. and E. C. Gras, *The Economic and Social History of an English Village (Crawley, Hampshire) A.D. 909-1928* (Cambridge, Mass., 1930), p. 270.

6 Harvey, *Manorial Records*, pp. 27, 30.

the reeve, bailiff and other officials. Money was spent on repairs to ploughs, carts and buildings, the purchase of corn and stock, and the hire of labour. Each of these different types of expense was given its own sub-section: cost of ploughs, cost of carts, cost of buildings and so on. This practice had developed over the course of the thirteenth century as more and more detail was included in the accounts. For example, at Merdon in 1208-9 all the manor's expenses were included in a consolidated account headed *Expensa*, which did not itemise individual pieces of expenditure. Thus, the costs associated with the dairy were given as a single lump sum.[1] In 1301-2, by contrast, each individual item—cloth for the dairy, grease for the sheep, canvas for the wool and so on—was accounted for separately in a sub-section devoted solely to dairy expenses. Such an increase in the amount of detail recorded on the rolls adds greatly to their historical value.

Once the receipts and expenses were totalled up the remainder was owed by the reeve to the treasurer at Wolvesey. There was a tendency not to leave money in the reeve's hands and often income collected on the manors was sent to Wolvesey during the year before the audit at Michaelmas. Thus, the £103 said to have been in the possession of the coroner of Wiltshire in 1302 was undoubtedly on its way from Taunton to Wolvesey when its keeper met an untimely end.[2] The total of these 'cash deliveries' gives an idea of the bishop's immediate profit from the estate. In 1301-2 they amounted to almost £2,405, a sum equivalent to the annual income of a middle-ranking earl.[3] These accounts were not primarily designed to indicate profit. Their purpose was to show the state of account between the official and his lord, to show how much was owing to one or the other once every transaction had been allowed for. Nevertheless, it is possible to calculate the level of income generated by the estate, to assess the various sources of this income, and to estimate the profit made therefrom.

In 1301-2 gross receipts exceeded £5,188.[4] Of this, £2,405 (46%) was delivered to Wolvesey; a further £1,425 (28%) was owed at the audit and was carried over as arrears into the following year; and the remaining £1,358 (26%) was spent by the reeves and bailiffs of the manors and boroughs of the estate. These figures exclude any profit made by the bishop from the sale of the estate's wool which was not recorded on the pipe roll and which in 1301-2 exceeded £291.[5] An examination of the pipe roll from 1302-3, moreover, reveals that the whole of the £1,425 arrears

1 *The Pipe Roll of the Bishopric of Winchester 1208-9*, ed. H. Hall (London School of Economics and Political Science, 1903), p. 34.

2 Below, p. 5.

3 For example, John de Warenne, earl of Surrey, Henry de Lacy, earl of Lincoln, or Isabella de Fortibus, dowager countess of Devon and Aumale (d. 1293), who had an income of over £2,500 a year: M. Altschul, *A Baronial Family in Medieval England: The Clares 1217-1314* (Baltimore, 1965), p. 206.

4 The gross receipts of each manor are given at the end of the charge of the cash account, before the expenditure of the manor is listed. They do not include arrears.

5 In 1301-2 16,607 adult sheep fleeces and 4,574 lambs' fleeces were sent to Wolvesey. An average adult fleece weight of 1.16 lb and lamb's fleece weight of 0.44 lb have been derived from figures in M. J. Stephenson, 'The Productivity of Medieval Sheep on the Great Estates, 1100-1500' (unpublished PhD thesis, University of Cambridge, 1986), pp. 315-16. Assuming a stone of 14 lb and that both adult fleeces and lambs' fleeces fetched 3.84*s*. a stone, the price given in T. H. Lloyd, *The Movement of Wool Prices in Medieval England* (*EcHR*, Supplement 6, 1973), p. 40, then the adult fleeces were worth £264 4*s*. and the lambs' fleeces £27 12*s*., a total of £291 16*s*.

carried forward from the previous year were paid into the treasury at Wolvesey by Michaelmas 1303 at the latest.[1] This means that the bishop's total income from his estate between the end of 1301 and Michaelmas 1303 amounted to the very considerable sum of £4,121. Add to this the bishop's spiritual revenues, the dues and fees collected for the performance of his pastoral work, from institutions, consecrations, probate cases and visitations, which Virginia Davis has estimated could have amounted to around £300 a year at the time of the Reformation,[2] and the bishop of Winchester's annual income at the beginning of the fourteenth century was equivalent to that of a high-ranking earl.[3]

There is little reason to suppose that the receipts collected in 1301-2 were untypical of the late thirteenth and early fourteenth centuries as a whole. Titow has calculated that between 1299 and 1308 gross receipts ranged between about £4,500 and £5,250 a year.[4] There were, of course, considerable variations in the value of the different bailiwicks of the estate and of the individual manors within those bailiwicks. Table 1 reveals that the bailiwicks of East Meon and Taunton were by far the most valuable on the estate, generating an income almost double that of most of the others. These were large and fertile areas of land. The Vale of Taunton has been described as the 'paradise of England' and 'the granary of the west',[5] and throughout the period 1300-24 the bailiwick achieved the largest average area under seed and the highest average yields per seed.[6] It was too the most populous area of the estate.[7] The bailiwick of East Meon also contained some of the bishopric's most fertile and populous manors. In addition, its income was swelled by the tithes collected from East Meon Church and Hambledon Church, which at the beginning of the fourteenth century were the only tithes appropriated directly by the bishop.

Table 1. *Gross receipts of the Winchester bailiwicks, 1301-2*

	Receipts	*(with wool)*		*Receipts*	*(with wool)*
Taunton	£801-11-½	(£801-11-½)	Bishops Sutton	£421-18-11¼	(£461-3-11¼)
Downton	£415-1-1½	(£480-19-1½)	East Meon	£815-3-1½	(£861-8-1½)
Wargrave	£412-10-2	(£423-13-2)	Bishops Waltham	£348-11-8¾	(£369-17-8¾)
Witney	£428-16-9	(£438-13-9)	Twyford	£583-17-8¾	(£631-17-8¾)
Farnham	£316-12-7½	(£321-9-7½)	Soke	£178-0-¼	(£178-0-¼)
Highclere	£465-1-2¼	(£510-5-2¼)			

It is possible to discern from the accounts the relative importance of different sources of income on different parts of the estate. The manors of East Meon and

1 HRO 11M59/B1/59.

2 V. Davis, *William Waynflete, Bishop and Educationalist* (Woodbridge, 1993), pp. 117-18.

3 For example, Gilbert de Clare, earl of Gloucester, who commanded an income of between £4,500 and £5,000 in 1295, or Roger Bigod, earl of Norfolk, who had about £4,000 in 1306: Altschul, *The Clares*, pp. 205-6. For estimates of the bishop of Winchester's income in the early and late fifteenth century, see G. L. Harriss, *Cardinal Beaufort* (Oxford, 1988), pp. 411-13; Davis, *William Waynflete*, pp. 119-20.

4 Titow, 'Land and Population', p. 67. These figures are almost certainly too low because Titow excluded receipts from several manors and all the boroughs in his calculations (p. 8).

5 S. Harvey, 'Domesday England', *AHEW*, ii, p. 105; E. Miller, 'The occupation of the land: the southern counties', *AHEW*, iii, p. 137.

6 Titow, *Winchester Yields*, pp. 121-39.

7 Titow, 'Land and Population', pp. 96, 100.

Taunton, for example, which in 1301-2 generated the largest gross receipts, owed their prominence principally to the size and fertility of their arable lands.[1] Both manors derived the bulk of their income from the sale of corn.[2] Farnham, by contrast, derived most of its income from rents and possessed very little land under seed.[3] Other manors, such as Downton, Bishops Waltham and Twyford, achieved a more even spread of resources.[4] Each manor thus possessed its own unique make-up, a result of its size, fertility, topography, population and custom, even though all six manors generated fairly similar levels of income.[5]

Of the £5,188 generated by the Winchester estate in 1301-2, over £3,028 (58%) derived from the sale of demesne produce, including corn; over £1,590 (31%) came from rents; and nearly £570 (11%) derived from fines imposed in the manorial and borough courts.[6] As Titow has commented, 'the lord's own farming of the demesne constituted a much greater share of the total profits of the Winchester estates than the various dues and revenues received from the tenants'.[7] Every conceivable manorial resource was sold on the bishopric estate, from pannage and timber, cheese and butter, skins and hides, to every kind of livestock, to nuts, honey, bark and turf. Long lists of the sale of pasturage can also be found, an excellent source of field names for the local historian and evidence of the pressure upon pasture during the thirteenth and early fourteenth centuries, which made it profitable for the bishop to sell any odd scrap of grazing that was going spare. Thus, at Witney in 1302 2*s*. was paid for the pasturage on the road to 'Waylesmull', whilst at Downton the reeve received 2*s*. for the pasturage beside a ditch.[8] In some places the pasture was so poor that no buyers could be found, whilst at Winchester the land was affected in a way reminiscent of the recent construction of the motorway through Twyford Down, which caused a layer of chalk-dust to settle over much of the surrounding area. In 1302 the foundation of the chapel of St Elizabeth below the meadow of St Stephen just south of Wolvesey Castle led the reeve of Wolvesey manor to record that only 4*s*. was received from the pasturage of the meadow in this year, instead of the usual 5*s*. for six

1 In 1301-2 Taunton had 1,444 acres under seed and East Meon 555¼ acres. These were the largest acreages under seed, apart from Merdon (699 acres) and Downton (555¾ acres), but the yields per seed on these manors were generally poorer than those achieved at Taunton and East Meon: Titow, 'Land and Population', Table 1; Titow, *Winchester Yields*, pp. 123, 126, 133-4.

2 60.5% of gross receipts derived from the sale of demesne corn at Taunton (i.e. excluding the sale of mill corn) and 41.4% (37.9% if sales of wool are taken into consideration) at East Meon. Taunton did not produce any wool in 1301-2.

3 61.6% of gross receipts derived from rents at Farnham (including the farm of the borough). In 1301-2 the manor possessed only 64½ acres under seed (Titow, 'Land and Population', Table 1) and produced very little wool.

4 At Downton 23.6% of gross receipts derived from rents, 31% from the sale of demesne produce (excluding corn but including wool), 36.6% from the sale of corn (including mill corn), and 8.8% from fines. At Bishops Waltham the figures were 31.3%, 35.5%, 16.7%, and 16.5% respectively. At Twyford they were 28.4%, 47.3%, 28.5%, and 5.8% respectively.

5 Including sales of wool, East Meon produced roughly £295, Taunton £259, Twyford £256, Bishops Waltham £237, and Downton and Farnham £220 in 1301-2.

6 I have included the sale of surplus villein services with demesne produce, as argued by Titow, 'Land and Population', p. 11; farms and annual gifts with rents; and annual recognizances with fines. If sales of wool were included the percentages would be 61%, 29%, and 10% respectively.

7 Titow, 'Land and Population', p. 9.

8 Below, pp. 62, 133.

months, because the construction of the chapel had resulted in the pasture there becoming chalky on all sides.[1]

The most important sales, however, were those of grain. In 1301-2 nearly £1,900 derived from this source, some 63% of the total sale of demesne produce and 37% of gross receipts.[2] According to Titow, 'grain production was by far the most important aspect of demesne farming right up to the Black Death, and the most important single source of manorial revenue almost to the very end of the period 1209-1350 when it was overtaken by the rents'.[3] In 1301-2 oats was the most common crop on the estate as a whole, as it had been throughout the thirteenth century. Only in the 1330s or 1340s did the total arable under wheat finally overtake that under oats, and the acreages of both declined slightly over the course of the thirteenth and early fourteenth centuries to make way for an increase of barley and legumes.[4] This general picture of course masks considerable regional and manorial variation. On East Meon, for example, legumes were hardly grown at all and oats remained by far the most important crop. On Brightwell wheat was dominant at the beginning of the thirteenth century, but gradually lost ground to rye, barley and dredge. On Overton the arable under wheat and barley increased at the expense of bere and oats. On Taunton the percentage of wheat and oats sown remained fairly constant over the whole period 1209-1350.[5] The emergence of wheat as the estate's dominant crop was thus by no means a uniform development.

The gradual supersession of oats by wheat coincided with a marked contraction of the demesne, which reduced the income from sales of grain and enhanced the relative importance of rents as a source of manorial revenue.[6] Rents, according to Titow, 'constituted the most stable and ever-increasing element of manorial economy'.[7] They were owed by the tenants for their holdings on the manor, and were usually paid quarterly. The rate at which a tenant paid varied from manor to manor and can often be determined by reference to the mid-thirteenth century custumals of the estate, now in the keeping of the British Library. On the Taunton manors, for example, the rate was set at 10*s*. a virgate, on Crawley it was most often 8*s*. a virgate.[8] The gradual rise in the total of these rents during the thirteenth and early fourteenth centuries was the result, at first, of increases in the amount of land taken into cultivation, and later of large-scale leasing of the demesne. It is clear too that some rents included an increment for the commutation of labour services which also caused them to rise.[9]

1 Below, p. 357.

2 If sales of wool are included these percentages would be 57% and 35% respectively.

3 Titow, 'Land and Population', p. 11.

4 Titow, 'Land and Population', pp. 34-5, Table 6; cf. H. E. Hallam, 'Farming techniques: southern England', *AHEW*, ii, p. 356.

5 Titow, 'Land and Population', Table 6.

6 Titow, 'Land and Population', pp. 21-35, 55-7; Miller and Hatcher, *Medieval England*, pp. 201-2.

7 Titow, 'Land and Population', p. 57.

8 BL Egerton MS 2418. I have used the microfilm of this manuscript kept at Hampshire Record Office (M405). For a translation of the custumal relating to Taunton and a transcription of that for Crawley, see *The Medieval Customs of the Manors of Taunton and Bradford on Tone*, ed. T. J. Hunt (Somerset Record Soc., 66, 1962), pp. 31-82; Gras and Gras, *Economic and Social History of an English Village*, pp. 232-8.

9 Titow, 'Land and Population', pp. 58-61.

Together, rents and the sale of demesne produce, including corn, accounted for some 89% of gross receipts in 1301-2.[1] The remaining 11% derived from the fines imposed in the bishop's courts. These derived both from amercements levied for the many and various transgressions committed by the tenants, and from entry and marriage fines. Entry fines were paid to the bishop by the incoming tenant of a piece of land on the death or withdrawal of the outgoing tenant. The level of these fines rose considerably during the thirteenth and early fourteenth centuries as increasing land-hunger led to more and more colonisation and sub-letting and the bishop took advantage of rising prices to compensate himself for the fixed rate of rents.[2] Marriage fines were payable when an unfree female tenant of the bishop was married. They usually specify whether the marriage took place within or outside the manor and can thus be used to study female marriage patterns and migration. In 1301-2, for example, 32 marriages took place within the manor and 41 outside, out of a total of 81 marriages recorded. The fines were most often paid by the woman's father (46 times in 1301-2) or mother (20 times), but occasionally a brother (three times), guardian (twice), stepfather (once), bridegroom (once), or even the woman herself (eight times), paid the fee.[3]

The bishop of Winchester thus collected a very substantial income in 1301-2, certainly more than any of his episcopal contemporaries.[4] But whilst the pipe rolls allow us to assess the various sources of his income, they are silent about how the bishop spent his money. There is clear evidence that John of Pontoise was a very wealthy man. For example, he owned large amounts of silver plate and jewels, and he spent many thousands of pounds in support of St Augustine's Abbey, Canterbury.[5] The inspection of the treasury at Wolvesey made by officers of the king in 1294 revealed, *inter alia*, a silver crozier, silver goblets and spoons, and money for sandals bought from Florentine merchants (Plate 7).[6] Furthermore, in June 1298 Philip of France was requested by the pope to restore gold, silver, vessels, books, vestments, jewels and money belonging to the bishop, which he had deposited at various monasteries in Paris and which the king of France had seized.[7] But the lack of any household or wardrobe accounts makes it very difficult for us to provide any details about the bishop's average annual expenditure, his household or his way of life.[8] The only reference to the wardrobe on the pipe roll of 1302 is in an entry recording the payment of £1 to the reeve of Southwark.[9] The expenditure recorded on the rolls is concerned almost exclusively with the money spent by the reeves and other officials on the running costs of the manors and the estate. There are thus a few references to

1 90% if sales of wool are included.

2 Titow, *English Rural Society*, pp. 73-8.

3 For references, see entries under 'marriage' in index.

4 The estate of the see of Canterbury was worth about £2,616 a year at the end of the thirteenth century: F. R. H. DuBoulay, *The Lordship of Canterbury* (London, 1966), p. 243. In 1086 the archbishopric lands had been worth more than the Winchester estate: Miller and Hatcher, *Medieval England*, p. 16.

5 Denton, 'Complaints to the apostolic see', p. 393.

6 *Reg. Pontissara*, i, pp. xlv-xlvi; ii, pp. 495-6.

7 *CPL*, i, p. 576; *Reg. Pontissara*, i, pp. cxi-cxii.

8 The Register occasionally provides a few details, such as the annual allowance of 50 marks granted for the maintenance of the household of Wolvesey Castle in 1291 and 20 marks in 1293: *Reg. Pontissara*, i, p. 59; ii, p. 473.

9 Below, p. 335.

the preparations made for the bishop's visits to certain manors, of his hospitality there to other lords, of swans and peacocks being sent from the manors to his residences at Wolvesey and in London.[1] But there is nothing about the bishop's private expenses.[2]

The expenditure of the estate in 1301-2 appears to have included little that was out of the ordinary. The sub-headings of the expense accounts—costs of ploughs, carts, buildings, dairy, mills, parks, harvest, threshing, winnowing, weeding, mowing—can be found in many other rolls. Amongst the purchases made by the reeves in 1301-2 were sufficient iron, steel and timber for the construction or repair of over 250 ploughs, an average of about five ploughs for each of the 51 manors on which they were found.[3] Harrows, carts, wagons and wains were also made and repaired in considerable numbers and these, together with the ploughs, were hauled by the 1,424 oxen, 214 plough-horses, 78 cart-horses, 22 mares and four asses which remained on the estate at the end of the financial year in 1302. The draught stock of the bishopric also included a number of mill-horses which were used to power those mills temporarily without access to water or wind power, as at Farnham and Southwark.[4] The bishop held over 70 mills in 1302, both at farm and in demesne. The pipe roll records the myriad expenses associated with these and other types of building. At Havant, for example, the bailiff spent over £12 rebuilding the mill of Brockhampton, including the purchase of a new millstone, whilst at Marwell the reeve was responsible for the construction of a new dairy building. Like a number of large building projects in this year, a detailed account of the reeve's expenses was not given in the pipe roll. Only at Wargrave was a full account of new building work recorded, for the stable which burned down one night and was rebuilt at a cost of nearly £26.[5] The dry summer of 1302 no doubt heightened the risk of fire, although the roll suggests that the wind was by far the greater hazard to manorial buildings. Many structures were damaged by high winds in this year, which at Farnham were described as stormy (*tempestate*m), although it appears that this was not particularly unusual.[6] The estate experienced no abnormal weather conditions in 1301-2. Nor was the year characterised by unusual levels of animal mortality, by any marked fluctuation in the size of the demesne, or by unusual levels of rents, fines and profits.[7] In short, the pipe roll of 1301-2 provides a reasonably representative picture of the Winchester estate in the late thirteenth and early fourteenth centuries, of both its income and its expenditure.

The Winchester pipe rolls are a rich source for the historian of rural society in southern England in the later middle ages. For over two hundred years, between the

1 For examples, see below, pp. 111, 207, 215, 276, 359.

2 Before 1500 only three household accounts survive for bishops of Winchester, dated November 1319, September 1351, 1356 or 1362, and April to September 1393: *Household Accounts from Medieval England*, ed. C. M. Woolgar (2 vols., Records of Social and Economic History, new ser., 17-18, 1992-3), ii, pp. 701, 712, 721.

3 The accounts do not always record the exact number of ploughs on each manor, just those that were made or repaired in a particular year. In 1301-2 there were no ploughs recorded at Alverstoke, Gosport, Otterford, Southwark, Taunton and Warfield.

4 Below, pp. 212, 216, 335-6.

5 Below, pp. 177-8, 240, 273.

6 For examples, see below, pp. 155, 214. References to wind damage can be found in many other rolls.

7 J. Z. Titow, 'Evidence of weather in the account rolls of the Bishopric of Winchester, 1209-1350', *EcHR*, 2nd ser., 12 (1960), pp. 381, 403; Titow, 'Land and Population', pp. 21a, 63, 67, Tables 2-5.

beginning of the pipe rolls series in 1208 and the leasing of the bishopric demesnes after 1400, these manuscripts contain an enormous variety of information about the economic and social conditions of this great estate, about its agriculture and administration, its lands and buildings, and the peasantry who ploughed and harrowed, reaped and sowed on behalf of their often distant lord. Even after the last manors were leased late in the fifteenth century the pipe rolls continue to record valuable information regarding the manorial courts and the buildings of the estate. The roll translated for this volume offers an example of the diversity of information to be found in the series as a whole.

Method of Editing

The decision to publish a translation, rather than a transcription, of a Winchester pipe roll was taken to promote the accessibility of these important documents. The rolls are written in highly abbreviated Latin and employ idioms and expressions which are sometimes difficult to translate or to understand from the context of the document alone. Inevitably, therefore, some of the subtleties and ambiguities of the original have been lost in attempting to make this volume as readable and as comprehensible as possible to readers who may be unfamiliar with the language and content of medieval manorial account rolls. More specialist readers ought to be aware that whilst every attempt has been made to equate each Latin term with an English equivalent, in a minority of cases this has proved impossible. A number of words used in the roll have mutiple meanings in English. Equally some Latin words cannot be adequately distinguished and have been translated in exactly the same way. An example of the former is provided by *domus* which has been translated as 'building', 'house' or 'room' according to context. An example of the latter is 'boar', which is usually given as *verrus* but also occasionally as *aper*. The Latin has been included in the text for many doubtful or unusual translations, but a microfiche of the manuscript is provided with the view that no translation can compete with the original.

Place-names have been modernised where a modern form is known with the manuscript variations given in the index. The principal sources used to identify place-names have been R. E. Glasscock, *The Lay Subisdy of 1334* (London, 1975) and the relevant volumes of the *English Place-Name Society* and *Victoria County History*. Forenames have also been modernised wherever possible, whilst surnames have been transcribed as they appear in the roll, with variants brought together under a standard form in the index. It is often impossible to distinguish the letters *c* and *t* in the manuscript, and *u* and *v* were also used interchangeably by the scribe. Where these letters appear in personal and place-names the most likely form has been given. For personal names P. H. Reaney, *A Dictionary of British Surnames* (London, 1958) has been used as a guide.

Arabic numerals have replaced the Roman numerals of the manuscript. Numbers have been given in words rather than figures only where this is so in the roll. No systematic attempt has been made to add up the totals of each paragraph. Where mistakes in the arithmetic have been spotted, however, a note of the correct figure is given.

Although very neat the manuscript contains many scribal errors. The commonest are erasures of single letters or figures caused by slips of the pen and, apart from one or two doubtful cases, these have been passed over without comment. The accidental repetition of words has also generally been ignored. Cancellations, omissions and interlineations, on the other hand, have usually been footnoted or noted in the text by means of the following conventions:

⌈ ⌉ : interlineations in the same hand as the surrounding passage

⌠ ⌡ : interlineations in a different hand from the surrounding passage

{ } : auditorial additions

⟨ ⟩ : words or letters cancelled in any way

... : letters lost or illegible

[ ] : editorial reconstructions of missing words or letters

bold denotes marginal headings and auditorial additions. These have been centred if they appear centred in the manuscript.

italics denote editorial additions, such as membrane numbers and extensions to personal and place-names which are abbreviated in the roll. Latin forms after the translation are given in italics in round brackets. Round brackets have also been used to give the dates of feast days and regnal years.

Abbreviations employed in the text are ‘qr’ for ‘quarter’ and ‘bus.’ for bushel.

The translation is for the most part literal. Liberties have been taken with the original only to increase comprehensibility or to avoid tedious repetition. The translation of the stock accounts, for example, omit the opening ‘the same render account for’ of each item which are found in the manuscript. Occasionally it is unclear from the roll whether a noun is meant to be singular or plural and the translation has been made on contextual grounds. In all cases of doubt, however, concerning this and other matters, the reader is advised to consult the microfiche.

The Pipe Roll
(HRO 11M59/B1/58)

Manors

Winchester Pipe Roll 1301–2

m.1

Account of the Bishopric of Winchester for the twenty-first year of the consecration of the lord bishop John

Taunton

Arrears

Philip de Paunton', constable of Taunton, and the reeve render account for £514 of arrears from the previous year. All delivered to Sir G*eoffrey de Farham*, treasurer of Wolvesey, by 2 tallies, one of which tallies, which totalled £103, was not handed over at the account, but is in the hands of the coroner of Wiltshire because it was found on a certain slain man, which tally henceforth becomes of no importance.

Farms of mills

The same render account for £1 11*s*. 6*d*. for the farm of the mills of Otterford and Wateleghe together with two shillings of land adjacent to the same mills; £2 13*s*. 4*d*. for the farm of the fulling mill which J*ohn* Fullo holds this year.[1] Total, £4 4*s*. 10*d*.

Mills of Taunton[2]

The same render account for £8 10*s*. 6½*d*. from 29½ qrs of wheat sold from the issue of the same mill, at 4*s*. a qr for 5½ qrs, 5*s*. a qr for 2 qrs 5 bus., 6*s*. a qr for 10 qrs 5 bus., and 6*s*. 8*d*. a qr for 10 qrs 6 bus.; £2 10*s*. 9½*d*. from 14 qrs 1½ bus. of maslin sold, at 2*s*. a qr for 2 qrs ½ bus., 3*s*. 4*d*. a qr for 2 qrs 6 bus., and 4*s*. a qr for 9 qrs 3 bus.; £11 12*s*. from 38 qrs 2½ bus. of first-grade malt sold from the issue of the same mill, at 5*s*. 4*d*. a qr for 12 qrs 6½ bus., 6*s*. a qr for 9½ qrs, and 6*s*. 8*d*. a qr for 16 qrs; £7 5½*d*. from 83 qrs 7 bus. of second-grade malt sold from the issue of the same mill, at 1*s*. 8*d*. a qr for 81 qrs 7 bus., and 2*s*. a qr for 2 qrs. Total, £29 13*s*. 9½*d*.

Mills of Obridge

The same render account for £4 4*s*. 1½*d*. from 15 qrs 2 bus. of wheat sold from the issue of the same mill, at 4*s*. a qr for 5 qrs, 5*s*. a qr for 1 qr 1 bus., 6*s*. a qr for 3½ qrs, and 6*s*. 8*d*. a qr for 5 qrs 5 bus.; £1 1*s*. from 4 qrs of oatmeal (*gruell'*) sold, at 6*d*. a bus. for 2 bus., and 5*s*. 4*d*. a qr for 3 qrs 6 bus.; £5 5*s*. 8*d*. from 31 qrs 6 bus. of maslin sold, at 2*s*. a qr for 9 qrs 6 bus., 3*s*. 4*d*. a qr for 2 qrs 6 bus., and 4*s*. a qr for 19 qrs 2 bus.; £3 10*s*. 11*d*. from 11 qrs 5 bus. of first-grade malt sold, at 5*s*. 4*d*. a qr for 3 qrs 3

1 John Fullo held this mill between *c*.1296 and 1323.

2 For a discussion of the number and location of the bishop's mills at Taunton, see *Medieval Customs of Taunton*, pp. xlv-l.

bus., 6*s.* a qr for 3 qrs 1 bus., and 6*s.* 8*d.* a qr for 5 qrs 1 bus.; £2 2½*d.* from 24 qrs 1 bus. of second-grade malt sold, at 1*s.* 8*d.* a qr. Total, £16 1*s.* 9*d.*

Poullemull'

The same render account for £1 14*s.* 6*d.* from 5 qrs 7 bus. of wheat sold, at 4*s.* a qr for 1 qr 3 bus., 6*s.* a qr for 1½ qrs, and 6*s.* 8*d.* a qr for 3 qrs; 5*s.* 4*d.* from 1 qr of oatmeal sold; £2 3*d.* from 11 qrs 1 bus. of maslin sold, at 2*s.* a qr for 2 qrs, 4½*d.* a bus. for 2 bus., and 4*s.* a qr for 8 qrs 7 bus.; £1 17*s.* 11*d.* from 5 qrs 7½ bus. of first-grade malt sold, at 6*s.* a qr for 2½ qrs, and 6*s.* 8*d.* a qr for 3 qrs 3½ bus.; £1 2½*d.* from 12 qrs 1 bus. of second-grade malt sold, at 1*s.* 8*d.*[1] a qr. Total, £6 18*s.* 2½*d.*

Mill of Langford

The same render account for 10*s.* 11½*d.* from 2 qrs ½ bus. of wheat sold, at 6*d.* a bus. for 7 bus., 9*d.* a bus. for 5½ bus., and 10*d.* a bus. for 4 bus.; 2*s.* ½*d.* from 3 bus. 1 peck of oatmeal sold, at 6*d.* a bus. for ½ bus. 1 peck, and 8*d.* a bus. for 2½ bus.; £2 1*s.* 3*d.* from 12 qrs 6 bus. of maslin sold, at 2*s.* a qr for 4 qrs 7 bus., and 4*s.* a qr for 7 qrs 7 bus.; 15*s.* 8*d.* from 2 qrs 5 bus. of first-grade malt sold, at 5*s.* 4*d.* for 1 qr, 9*d.* a bus. for 6 bus., and 10*d.* a bus. for 7 bus.; 9*s.* 2*d.* from 5½ qrs of second-grade malt sold, at 1*s.* 8*d.* a qr. Total, £3 19*s.* 1*d.*

Mill of Corfe

Nothing from the mill of Corfe because it stands idle from a want of water.

Mill of Pitminster

The same render account for 7*s.* from 1 qr 2 bus. of wheat sold, at 6*d.* a bus. for 2 bus., and 6*s.* for 1 qr; 2*s.* 9¼*d.* from 4 bus. 1 peck of oatmeal sold, at 1¼*d.* for 1 peck, and 8*d.* a bus. for 4 bus.; £1 13*s.* 10½*d.* from 9 qrs ½ bus. of maslin sold, at 3½*d.* a bus. for 5 bus., 3*s.* 4*d.* a qr for 2 qrs, and 4*s.* a qr for 6 qrs 3½ bus.; 16*s.* 4½*d.* from 2 qrs 7½ bus. of first-grade malt sold, at 6*d.* a bus. for 5 bus., and 6*s.* a qr for 2 qrs 2½ bus.; 11*s.* 9¼*d.* from 7 qrs ½ bus. of second-grade malt sold, at 1*s.* 8*d.* a qr. Total, £3 11*s.* 9½*d.*

Mill of Trull

The same render account for 6*s.* 8*d.* from 1 qr 2 bus. of wheat sold, at 5*d.* a bus. for 2½ bus., and 9*d.* a bus. for 7½ bus.; 2*s.* 4*d.* from 3½ bus. of oatmeal sold, at 8*d.* a bus.; £1 5*s.* 4½*d.* from 6 qrs 7½ bus. of maslin sold, at 3½*d.* a bus. for 5 bus., 3*s.* 4*d.* a qr for 2 qrs, and 4*s.* a qr for 4 qrs 2½ bus.; 11*s.* 8¼*d.* from 2 qrs 1 peck of first-grade malt sold, at 6*d.* for 1 bus., 8*d.* a bus. for 3 bus., and 6*s.* a qr for 1½ qrs 1 peck; 6*s.* 10½*d.* from 4 qrs 1 bus. of second-grade malt sold, at 1*s.* 8*d.* a qr. Total, £2 12*s.* 11¼*d.*

Mills of Bishops Hull

The same render account for £1 18*s.* 3*d.* from 6 qrs 7½ bus. of wheat sold, at 3*s.* 8*d.* for 1 qr, 6½*d.* a bus. for 6 bus., 6*d.* a bus. for 5 bus., 7½*d.* a bus. for 4 bus., 6*s.* a qr for 1 qr 1 bus., and 6*s.* 8*d.* a qr for 2 qrs 7½ bus.; 8*d.* from 1 bus. of oatmeal sold; £4 15*s.* 2½*d.* from 27 qrs 2 bus. of maslin sold, at 2*s.* a qr for 2 qrs 2 bus., 2*s.* 4*d.* a qr for 2 qrs 2 bus., 2*s.* 8*d.* a qr for 2 qrs 3 bus., 3*s.* a qr for 2 qrs 3 bus., and 4*s.* a qr for 18 qrs; £1 1*s.* 1*d.* from 3½ qrs of first-grade malt sold, at 5*s.* 4*d.* a qr for 1 qr 1½ bus., 6*s.* for 1 qr, and 6*s.* 8*d.* a qr for 1 qr 2½ bus.; 13*s.* 9*d.* from 8 qrs 2 bus. of second-grade malt sold, at 1*s.* 8*d.* a qr. Total, £8 8*s.* 11½*d.*

1 MS omits '*d.*'

Mill of Kingston St Mary

The same render account for £1 12*s*. 6*d*. from 8 qrs 7 bus. of maslin sold, at 2*s*. a qr for 1½ qrs, and 4*s*. a qr for 7 qrs 3 bus.; 4*s*. 8*d*. from 7 bus. of oatmeal sold, at 8*d*. a bus.; 7*s*. 11*d*. from 4 qrs 6 bus. of second-grade malt sold, at 1*s*. 8*d*. a qr. Total, £2 5*s*. 1*d*.

Mill of Nailsbourne

The same render account for 3*s*. 1*d*. from 5 bus. of oatmeal sold, at 5*d*. for 1 bus., and 8*d*. a bus. for 4 bus.; £1 1*s*. from 5 qrs 6 bus. of maslin sold, at 2*s*. for 1 qr, and 4*s*. a qr for 4 qrs 6 bus.; 3*s*. 11½*d*. from 2 qrs 3 bus. of second-grade malt sold, at 1*s*. 8*d*. a qr. Total, £1 8*s*. ½*d*.

Total of all the mills, £79 4*s*. 5¾*d*.

Issues of the manor

The same render account for 15*s*. from the herbage (*herbag'*) of the garden sold this year; 10*s*. from 1 cask of cider sold apart from the vessel; 2*s*. from the herbage of a certain plot beside the ditch outside the west gate of the castle sold; 14*s*. from reeds sold; 9*s*. from 2 swans sold, at 4*s*. for 1, and 5*s*. for 1; nothing from the pasturage beside the fishpond on the west side because it is granted to the Prior of Taunton by the bishop forever; 10*d*. from one pair of old wheels without the ironwork sold; 4*s*. from 2 posnets sold. Total, £2 14*s*. 10*d*.

Sale of corn

The same render account for £118 5*s*. ¾*d*. from 377 qrs 3 bus. of wheat sold, at 4*s*. a qr for 14 qrs, 4*s*. 6*d*. a qr for 13 qrs 3 bus., 5*s*. a qr for 26 qrs 7 bus., 5*s*. 6*d*. a qr for 19 qrs, 6*s*. a qr for 50 qrs 5 bus., 6*s*. 8*d*. a qr for 153 qrs, and 6*s*. 10*d*. a qr for 100½ qrs; £1 4*s*. from 8 qrs of barley sold, at 3*s*. a qr; £36 15*s*. 10*d*. from 422 qrs of oats sold, at 1*s*. 8*d*. a qr for 32 qrs, and 1*s*. 9*d*. a qr for 390 qrs; 1*s*. from 4 bus. of peas sold; 4½*d*. from 1 bus. of maslin sold at the audit (*s*upe*r* *comp*otum); 4*s*. from 2 qrs of peas sold. Total, £156 10*s*. 9¼*d*.

Perquisites

The same render account for 1*s*. from Adam de Nutherethot' for release from suit which he owes to the hundred-court for the year; 2*s*. from Edmund Ev*er*ard for the same; 1*s*. from the tithing of Vennhampton because they did not produce in court (*h*abuerunt) William Chapelayn who is in their tithing; 1*s*. from John de Orchard for default; 2*s*. from Hawis le Vel for release from suit which she owes to the hundred-court for the year; 6*d*. from Henry le Leghe for default; 1*s*. from William Prat and Ralph atte Med' because they did not produce in court the individual (*q*ue*m*) whom they had bailed; 2*s*. from Hugh Fichet for default; 2*s*. from Stephen de Beaumu*n*t for release from suit which he owes to the hundred-court for the year; 1*s*. from John atte Ston' for contempt; 6*d*. from John Ev*er*ard for licence to come to an agreement; 6*d*. from Robert le Calewe for unjustly withholding a certain writing (*scripti*); 1*s*. from William de Lugdeburg' for release from suit which he owes to the hundred-court for ½ year; 1*s*. from William Bonefaȝ for the same; 6*d*. from Gilbert de la Hurn' because he withdrew his suit; 1*s*. from Geoffrey atte Oke and William de Cnappehall' for default; 6*d*. from Thomas de la Wyteheg' for licence to come to an agreement; 1*s*. from the tithing of Norton Fitzwarren for concealment; 6*d*. from the tithing of Langford for concealment; 6*d*. from Walter de Vygmur for transgression (*t*ra*ns*gressione) against his neighbour; 1*s*. from the tithing of Hoccombe for concealment; 6*d*.

from Hugh le Helyar' for transgression against his neighbour; 1*s*. from William de Huntalre for transgression against his neighbour; 1*s*. from the tithing of Hillfarance for concealment; 6*d*. from William Potel for transgression against his neighbour; 3*d*. from Richard le Hope because he did not produce in court the individual whom he had bailed; 1*s*. from William le Ryde for false complaint; 1*s*. from Luke Mody and William Punchardon for default; 3*d*. from John Rochel for transgression against his neighbour; 6*d*. from Richard le Hop*ere* because he did not produce in court the individual whom he had bailed; 1*s*. from John le Lange because he is not proceeding with his complaint; 1*s*. from the same John for the same; 1*s*. from William, attendant (*garcio*n*em*) of the bailiff of the liberty, for contempt; 6*d*. from Robert le Calewe because he defaulted at law; 1*s*. from Alice de Pyntelye because she is not proceeding with her complaint; 6*d*. from Robert le Calewe because he did not produce in court the individual whom he had bailed; 2*s*. from the Prior of Taunton for default; 6*d*. from William Punchard' for licence to come to an agreement; £1 17*s*. 6*d*. from those who brewed ale on the feast of St Calixtus (14 October); £3 4*s*. from the same on Hockday (1 May). Total, £6 16*s*. 6*d*.

Sale of old oxen
The same render account for £9 4*s*. from 23 old oxen sold, at 7*s*. each for 5, 7*s*. 4*d*. each for 3, 7*s*. 6*d*. each for 2, 8*s*. 6*d*. each for 10, and 9*s*. each for 3; 4*s*. from the hide and flesh sold of one ox dead from murrain; 10*s*. 8*d*. from the hides sold of 5 oxen dead from murrain. Total, £9 18*s*. 8*d*.

Green wax
From the Bench for the year ending 26 Edward I, beginning 27 Edward I (1298-9): 1*s*. 8*d*. from Luke Mody from the issues of his land outside the manor (*t*e*rre sue for*'); 1*s*. from the same Luke from the issues of his land outside the manor; 1*s*. from Robert le Cauf from the issues of land outside the manor; 1*s*. from the same Robert from the issues of his land outside the manor; 1*s*. from William de Caupedehall' from the issues of his land outside the manor; 1*s*. from the same William because he did not come and from Adam de Cnappedehall' and John le Lange because they did not produce in court the aforesaid William; 1*s*. from Robert de Tetton' from the issue of his land outside the manor; 1*s*. from the same Robert because he did not come and from Richard in the M*er*she and Nicholas le Com*ere* because they did not produce in court the aforesaid Robert.

From Hilary term: 1*s*. from William de Norhtwold because he did not come; 1*s*. from Richard Godde, William de Roreford', Richard P*ar*fet and William Fab*er* because they did not produce in court the aforesaid William.

From Easter term: 1*s*. from William de Norhtwold' from the issue of his lands outside the manor.

From the Bench for the years 25 and 26 Edward I (1297-8): ½ mark from John Meriet for many defaults.

Court of H*enry* de Enefeld and his fellows for the year 24 Edward I (1296): 3*s*. 4*d*. from John M*er*iet for disseisin.

The same court for the year 27 Edward I (1299): 3*s*. 4*d*. from John Meriet because he did not come; 10*d*. from Thomas le Someter because he did not produce in court the aforesaid John; 3*s*. 4*d*. from Geoffrey Blome for the same; 10*d*. from Robert atte Stapele for the same; 10*d*. from Robert le Nywe de Middenhal' for the same.

Court of J*ohn* de Bateford and his fellows for the year 26 Edward I (1298): 1*s*. 8*d*. from Walter Malefray and William Punȝ because they did not produce in court Hugh Gregori; 1*s*. 8*d*. from Hugh Gregory and Roger Malefray because they did not produce in court William Punȝ; 1*s*. 8*d*. from Robert le Lange and Nicholas Hod because they did not produce in court Thomas Hod; 1*s*. 8*d*. from Richard P*ar*fet and William Fab*er* because they did not produce in court William Parfet; 1*s*. 8*d*. from Nicholas Trot and William Punȝ because they did not produce in court William Caylok; 1*s*. 8*d*. from Thomas Red and William Hod because they did not produce in court Walter Malefray; 1*s*. 8*d*. from Richard Parfet and William Parfet because they did not produce in court Hugh Glyde; 1*s*. 8*d*. from Walter Malefray and Hugh Glyd' because they did not produce in court William atte Wll'.

From Michaelmas term: Court of Roger Brabazon for the year ending 26 Edward I, beginning 27 Edward I (1298-9): 1*s*. 8*d*. from John Wyry*ng*, Robert de Hamwod', Geoffrey Benayt and Richard Lel because they did not produce in court Gilbert de Borh*a*m; 1*s*. 8*d*. from John de Suyffemore, William Bolt*ere*, John de Hurne and William Broch' because they did not produce in court Thomas Lambre; 1*s*. 8*d*. from Richard Stot', Walter le Bule, Stephen de O*r*chard and Richard le Bule because they did not produce in court John de O*r*chard; 1*s*. 8*d*. from Roger Cole, Henry Steven', Adam Cole and Robert Cl*ericus* because they did not produce in court Luke Mody.

From Hilary term: 1*s*. 8*d*. from Henry Steven', Roger Cole, Adam Cole and Robert Cl*ericus* because they did not produce in court the aforesaid Luke; 1*s*. 8*d*. from John le Bule, Richard Stot', Thomas de Hel' and Richard le Bule de Orchard because they did not produce in court John de Orchard; 1*s*. 8*d*. from Roger Godman, William de Cruce, Walter le Sweyte and Augustine de Lydiard because they did not produce in court Luke Mody.

From the Bench for the years 26 and 27 Edward I (1298-9): 6*d*. from Thomas de Wones because he did not produce in court William le Mareschal; 6*d*. from Richard Parfet because he did not produce in court William le Maresch*al*; 10*d*. from William le Mareschal de Cheden' the younger because he did not produce in court William le Mareschal; 6*d*. from John Lochel because he did not produce in court William le Maresch*al*.

From Chancery for the years 27 and 29 Edward I (1299-1301)
From the Bench for the year 28 Edward I (1300): 1*s*. 8*d*. from William de Wybewll' because he did not come.
½ mark from Margery de Suetehegh' to have a writ; ½ mark from Richard Trul to have an assize.
From the Bench for the years 25 and 26 Edward I (1297-8): 1*s*. 8*d*. from William de Wibewll' because he did not come.

Total, £3 12*s*. 4*d*.

Foreign receipts
The same render account for £61 16*s*. 2*d*. from the reeve of Nailsbourne; £49 14*s*. 5*d*. from the reeve of Staplegrove; £33 7*s*. 3*d*. from the reeve of Trull; £122 6*s*. 4*d*. from

the reeve of Holway; £99 13*s*. 10¼*d*. from the reeve of Poundisford; £12 2*s*. 11*d*. from the reeve of Otterford; [£34] 8*s*. 8*d*. from the borough of Taunton. Total, £413 9*s*. 7¼*d*.

Total of all receipts, £672 7*s*. [2¼*d*.]

Purchase of corn
In 10 qrs 5 bus. of wheat bought for sowing £2 17*s*. 1½*d*., at 5*s*. 4*d*. a qr for 9 qrs 2 bus., and 5*s*. 8*d*. a qr for 1 qr 3 bus. In 4 qrs of rye bought for sowing £1, at 5*s*. a qr. In 40 [qrs ½ bus.] bought for the liveries of the manorial servants (*ad lib' fam'*) £8 3*d*., at 4*s*. a qr. In 27 qrs 6 bus. of mixed oats bought for fodder £1 5*s*. 6*d*., at 10*d*. a qr for ⌈12⌉ qrs, 11*d*. a qr for 5 qrs 1 bus., plus 1*d*. in all, [1*s*. a qr for 9 qrs], 2*d*. a bus. for 5 bus., and 11½*d*. for 1 qr. Total, £13 2*s*. 10½*d*.

m.1d
Cost of carts
In fitting the cart with axles three times during the year 3*d*. In 24 clouts with nails for the cart 2*s*. In grease for the cart for the year 10*d*. In repairing the cart many times during the year 7*d*. In repairing harnesses for the year 7½*d*. In one pair of traces 7*d*. In one crupper ¾*d*. In shoeing two cart-horses for the year by fixed agreement 5*s*. In stipend of one carter and one gardener for the year 5*s*. 9*d*. In one horse bought for the cart 17*s*. Total, £1 12*s*. 8¼*d*.

Repair of buildings with small expenses
In hiring a carpenter to raise (*erigend'*) the west barn which was nearly in ruins 5*s*. 2*d*. In repairing the foundations under two posts in the same barn 6*d*. In re-roofing in places the aforesaid barn, bishop's hall, granary, and 4 turrets round the great tower, 4*s*. 6*d*. In 4,000 slates bought for this 4*s*. 4*d*., at 1*s*. 1*d*. a 1,000. In roofing the whole of the barley-barn with straw 1*s*. 4*d*. In roofing one privy for the household within the inner bailey with straw 2*d*. In roofing anew the building adjoining the lord's press 1*s*. 2*d*. In one basket bought 5*d*. In one shovel and 2 spades bought and the same fitted with iron 7*d*. In one new pick-axe bought 6*d*. In mending one hoe 1½*d*. In mending the lock of the door to the great tower 1*d*. In one key bought for the garden-gate to the meadow and mending the lock of the same 1½*d*. In timber sawn for two ladders and two dung-carts (*scenevector'*) 4*d*. In cleaning and deepening one well beside the constable's kitchen 10*d*. In 1 hemp rope for drawing water from the aforesaid well 3*d*. In clearing dung from the castle and sheepcote (*berc'*) of Holway to the fields £3 19*s*. 10¼*d*. In parchment bought 3*s*. Total, £5 3*s*. 3¼*d*.

Purchase of old oxen
In 29 old oxen bought for fattening £9 12*s*. 2*d*., at 6*s*. 5*d*. each for 17, 7*s*. each for 10, and 6*s*. 6*d*. each for 2, plus 1*d*. in all. Total, £9 12*s*. 2*d*.

Threshing of corn
In threshing 289 qrs 3 bus. of wheat by piece-work £3 3½*d*., at 2½*d*. a qr. Total, £3 3½*d*.

Steward's expenses
In expenses of the steward holding his tourn at Martinmas (11 November), £1 11*s*. 10*d*. by one tally. In expenses of Simon de Farham holding the tourn at Hockday (1 May) 11*s*. Total, £2 2*s*. 10*d*.

Constable's expenses
In expenses of the constable, castle household, and other visitors for the year, £9. In fur for the summer robes of the constable and clerk of the castle 6*s*. Total, £9 6*s*.

Costs of mills
Mills of Taunton: In two French millstones bought for the corn mill £4 5*d*. In transporting the same 8*d*. In carrying the same from Wareham to Taunton £1 10*s*. In expenses of one miller going to and returning from Wareham in order to choose and settle for (*emen*d') the said millstones 2*s*. In iron bought to lengthen the spindle for the said millstones 10*d*. In iron and steel bought to repair the bills for perforating the aforesaid millstones 1*s*. 4*d*. In one Welsh millstone bought for the malt mill 9*s*. In iron bought to lengthen the spindle of the same mill for the same millstone 6*d*. In iron bought to renew the mill-rind of the millstone for corn 9*d*. In iron bought to mend the collars of the spindles of both mills 5*d*. In iron and steel to renew the bills of both mills and to sharpen and repair the same frequently during the year 1*s*. In one band made to hoop the head of the driving-shaft with iron bought for the same 5*d*. In nails bought to mend the wall of the mill 5*d*. In hiring a carpenter to mend the sluice at la Fre*n*shewere £1 5*s*. 4*d*. In timber sawn for the same sluice 3*s*. In large nails for the same 1*s*. Total, £7 17*s*. 1*d*.

Mills of Obridge: In two Welsh millstones bought for the malt mill 18*s*. In iron bought to lengthen the spindle for the aforesaid millstones 3*d*. In hooping one head of the driving-shaft with iron 6*d*. In iron bought to repair the collar of the spindle of the malt mill 3*d*. In iron and steel bought to renew the bills of both mills and to sharpen and repair the same frequently during the year 1*s*. 3*d*. In mending the wall of the mill 1*d*. In two boards for mending the sluice 5*d*. In nails for the same 9*d*. In one key bought for the maslin chest ½*d*. Total, £1 1*s*. 6½*d*.

Poulmulle: In two Welsh millstones bought 18*s*. In iron bought to lengthen the spindle for the aforesaid millstones 6*d*. In hooping two rundles for the spindle with iron bought for this 1*s*. In hooping one head of the driving-shaft with iron 6*d*. In making one ring to put in the eye of the other millstone with iron bought for this 6*d*. In iron bought to repair the collar of the spindle 3*d*. In iron and steel bought to renew the bills and to sharpen and repair the same frequently during the year 9*d*. Total, £1 1*s*. 6*d*.

Mill of Langford: In one Welsh millstone bought 10*s*. In iron bought to lengthen the spindle for the same millstone 3*d*. In iron bought to renew the mill-rind 6*d*. In hooping one head of the driving-shaft with iron 5*d*. In iron and steel to renew the bills and to sharpen and repair the same frequently during the year 11½*d*. In stipend of the smith repairing the ironwork of the aforesaid 4 mills for the year by fixed agreement 8*s*. Total, £1 1½*d*.

Total of all expenses of all the mills, £11 3*d*.

Total of all expenses, £55 4½*d*.

And he owes, £617 6*s*. 9¾*d*.

In allowance of the reeve for expediting certain business of the lord by order of the same lord £5. In allowance of the same for marling 12½ acres of land at Nailsbourne and 12 acres of land at Poundisford £6 5*d*. In allowance of the same for constructing anew the building for the press, for all costs, £2 18*s*. 7*d*. In allowance of the same for constructing 1 new bridge at St Paul and another at Madebrok' £1 9*s*. 1*d*. In allowance of the same for roofing anew the great tower in places and for mending the old roof in places, for all costs, £1 16*s*. 6*d*. In allowance of the same for mending the round tower £1 17*s*. 3*d*. In allowance of the same for making gifts to the sheriff and for the expenses for certain justices and for holding the hunt £3 4*s*. 10¼*d*. Total of all allowances, £22 6*s*. 8¼*d*.

Cash deliveries
Delivered to Sir *Geoffrey*, treasurer of Wolvesey, by 1 tally, £365.

Total of all allowances and cash deliveries, £387 6*s*. 8¼*d*.

And thus he owes clear, £230 1½*d*.

Issues of the grange in the castle
Wheat
{yield: five-fold plus 2 qrs 6½ bus.}
The same render account for 520 qrs 7½ bus. from the whole issue of wheat this year by struck measure; 10 qrs 5 bus. bought. Total, 531 qrs 4½ bus.
Sown over 181 acres at Holway, 41 qrs 3 bus.; that is, 2 bus. an acre, less 3 qrs 7 bus. in all. Sown over 145 acres at Bishops Hull and Trull, 27 qrs 7 bus.; that is, 2 bus. an acre, less 8 qrs 3 bus. in all. Sown over 130½ acres at Staplegrove, 28 qrs 5 bus.; that is, 2 bus. an acre, less 4 qrs in all. Delivered to the Prior of Taunton for the tithe of all the mills, 5 qrs. Delivered to the door-keeper of the castle for the year, 4 qrs 2½ bus. In provision of the steward for his two tourns, 1 qr 6 bus. In provision of the constable, castle household, and other visitors for the year, 23½ qrs. Mixed below for the liveries of the manorial servants, 21 qrs 6 bus. Sold, 377 qrs 3 bus. Total, 531 qrs 4½ bus. It balances.

Rye
The same render account for 4 qrs of rye bought.
Sown over 4 acres at Bishops Hull, 1 qr; that is, 2 bus. an acre. Sown over 11½ acres at Staplegrove, 2 qrs 7 bus.; that is, 2 bus. an acre. Mixed below for the liveries of the manorial servants, 1 bus. Total, 4 qrs. It balances.

Barley
{yield: four-fold less 1 qr 1 bus.}
The same render account for 15 qrs 3 bus. from the whole issue of barley by struck measure.
Sown over 5½ acres at Holway, 2 qrs 3 bus.; that is, 4 bus. an acre, less 3 bus. in all. Delivered to the prior for the tithe of all the mills, 5 qrs. Sold, 8 qrs. Total, 15 qrs 3 bus. It balances.

Oats
{yield: three-and-a-half-fold less 2 qrs 6 bus.}
The same render account for 664 qrs 7 bus. from the whole issue of oats by struck measure; 27 qrs 6 bus. bought. Total, 692 qrs 5 bus.
Sown over 196 acres at Holway, 90 qrs 1 bus.; that is, 4 bus. an acre, less 7 qrs 7 bus. in all. Sown over 127 acres at Trull and Bishops Hull, 46 qrs 2 bus.; that is, 4 bus. an

acre, less 17 qrs 2 bus. in all. Sown over 137½ acres at Staplegrove, 61 qrs 3 bus.; that is, 4 bus. an acre, less 7 qrs 3 bus. in all. Delivered to the Prior of Taunton for the tithe of all the mills, 5 qrs. In fodder of two cart-horses in the castle for the year, 12 qrs. In fodder of the steward's horses for his two tourns, 3 qrs 7 bus. In fodder of the horses of the constable, castle household, and other visitors for the year, 52 qrs. Sold, 422 qrs. Total, 692 qrs 5 bus. It balances.

Peas
{yield: nine-fold less 2 bus., with 20 qrs by estimation remaining in one stack}
The same render account for 4½ qrs from the issue of peas by struck measure. Sown over 4 acres at Holway, 1 qr; that is, 2 bus. an acre. Sown over 4 acres at Bishops Hull, 1 qr; that is, 2 bus. an acre. Sold, 2 qrs 4 bus. Moreover, 18 qrs by estimation remain in the stacks from the previous year; 20 qrs from this year.

Proof of liveries
The same render account for 21 qrs 6 bus. received above from wheat; 1 bus. received above from rye; 40 qrs ½ bus. bought. Total, 61 qrs 6½ bus.
Delivered to 4 oxherds at Holway for the year, 17 qrs 2 bus., taking a quarter every 12 weeks. Delivered to 3 oxherds at Trull and Bishops Hull for the year and a fourth oxherd for three terms, 16 qrs 2 bus., taking a quarter every 12 weeks. Delivered to two oxherds at Staplegrove for the year, 8 qrs 5 bus., taking a quarter every 12 weeks. Delivered to one watchman, one carter and one gardener in the castle for the year, 12 qrs 7½ bus., taking a quarter every 12 weeks. In customary payment for the boon-reaping at Holway, 3 qrs 2 bus. In customary payment for the boon-reaping at Trull and Bishops Hull, 2 qrs 2 bus. In customary payment for the boon-reaping at Staplegrove, 1 qr 2 bus. Sold at the audit, 1 bus. Total, 61 qrs 7½ bus. It balances.

Issues of the mills

Mills of Taunton
Wheat: 29½ qrs from the issue of the mill; all sold.
Maslin: 14 qrs 1½ bus. from the issue of the mill; all sold.
First-grade malt: 38 qrs 2½ bus. from the issue of the mill; all sold.
Second-grade malt: 83 qrs 7 bus. from the issue of the mill; all sold.

Mills of Obridge
Wheat: 15 qrs 2 bus. from the issue of the mill; all sold.
Oatmeal: 4 qrs from the issue of the mill; all sold.
Maslin: 31 qrs 6 bus. from the issue of the mill; all sold.
First-grade malt: 11 qrs 5 bus. from the issue of the mill; all sold.
Second-grade malt: 24 qrs 1 bus. from the issue of the mill; all sold.

New Mill
Wheat: 5 qrs 7 bus. from the issue of the mill; all sold.
Oatmeal: 1 qr from the issue of the mill; all sold.
Maslin: 11 qrs 1 bus. from the issue of the mill; all sold.
First-grade malt: 5 qrs 7½ bus. from the issue of the mill; all sold.
Second-grade malt: 12 qrs 1 bus. from the issue of the mill; all sold.

Mill of Langford
Wheat: 2 qrs ½ bus. from the issue of the mill; all sold.

Oatmeal: 3 bus. 1 peck from the issue of the mill; all sold.
Maslin: 12 qrs 6 bus. from the issue of the mill; all sold.
First-grade malt: 2 qrs 5 bus. from the issue of the mill; all sold.
Second-grade malt: 5½ qrs from the issue of the mill; all sold.

Nothing from the mill of Corfe because it stands idle from a want of water.

Mill of Pitminster
Wheat: 1 qr 2 bus. from the issue of the mill; all sold.
Oatmeal: 4 bus. 1 peck from the issue of the mill; all sold.
Maslin: 9 qrs ½ bus. from the issue of the mill; all sold.
First-grade malt: 2 qrs 7½ bus. from the issue of the mill; all sold.
Second-grade [malt]: 7 qrs ½ bus. from the issue of the mill; all sold.

Mill of Trull
[Wheat]: 1 qr 2 bus. from the issue of the mill; all sold.
Oatmeal: 3½ bus. from the issue of the mill; all sold.
[Maslin]: 6 qrs 7½ bus. from the issue of the mill; all sold.
[First-grade malt]: 2 qrs 1 peck from the issue of the mill; all sold.
[Second-grade malt]: 4 qrs 1 bus. from the issue of the mill; all sold.

Mills of Bishops Hull
[Wheat]: 6 qrs 7½ bus. from the issue of the mill; all sold.
[Oatmeal]: 1 bus. from the issue of the mill; all sold.
[Maslin]: 27 qrs 2 bus. from the issue of the mill; all sold.
[First-grade malt]: 3½ qrs from the issue of the mill; all sold.
[Second-grade malt]: 8 qrs 2 bus. from the issue of the mill; all sold.

Mill of Kingston St Mary
[Oatmeal]: 7 bus. from the issue of the mill; all sold.
[Maslin]: 8 qrs 7 bus. from the issue of the mill; all sold.
[Second-grade malt]: 4 qrs 6 bus. from the issue of the mill; all sold.

Mill of Nailsbourne
[Oatmeal]: 5 bus. from the issue of the mill; all sold.
[Maslin]: 5 qrs 6 bus. from the issue of the mill; all sold.
[Second-grade malt]: 2 qrs 3 bus. from the issue of the mill; all sold.

[The same render] account for 1 cask of cider remaining from the previous year; 3 casks of cider from the issue of the garden this year. Total, 4. 1 sold; 3 full casks remain.

m.2

Stock

Plough-horses: 2 remain from the previous year; 1 bought. Total, 3. They remain.
Oxen: 29 old oxen bought for fattening. 6 in murrain; 23 sold. Total, 29. None remain.
Swans: 9 remain from the previous year; 14 offspring this year. Total, 23. 2 sold; 21 remain, 8 of them old, 13 young.
Salt: 7 qrs 5 bus. remain from the previous year; they remain.

Weapons: 990 crossbow bolts, 2 hauberks, 1 roll for burnishing arms, 10 iron helmets, 10 padded tunics, 10 painted shields, 12 crossbows of which two have two feet, 5 crossbow belts and 34 lances remain from the previous year; they remain. **Utensils:** two chests and 1 great lead vessel remain from the previous year; they remain. Brass pots remain from the previous year; they remain. 3 brass posnets remain from the previous year; 2 sold; 1 remains. 1 tripod, 2 copper pans and 1 grid-iron remain from the previous year; they remain. 9 casks and 9 tubs remain from the previous year; they remain. 11 barrels and 3 tuns, 1 coffer bound with iron to put treasure in, 2 axes, 2 carts with iron tyres, 3 wagons, 1 ewer and 1 basin remain from the previous year; they remain.

Kingston St Mary and Nailsbourne

The account of Roger Uppehull', reeve of this place.

Rents

The same renders account for £21 3*s*. 9½*d*. for rents of assize at Christmas, Easter (22 April), the Nativity of the blessed John the Baptist (24 June), and Michaelmas (29 September), in equal portions. Total, £21 3*s*. 9½*d*.

Quittances

In quittance of one worker for the year 1*s*. 6*d*.; 4 workers working two days a week for three terms of the year and everyday at harvest-time except Saturday at Nailsbourne 8*s*., or 2*s*. each; two ploughmen for the year 4*s*.; 4 workers working at Fulford in the same way as the 4 workers at Nailsbourne 8*s*.; one beadle for the year 2*s*. 6*d*.; one ploughman for the year 3*s*.; five workers working one day a week for three terms of the year and a second day at harvest-time at Kingston St Mary 5*s*. Total, £1 12*s*.

Defaults of rent

In default of two small holdings (*bordell'*) drawn into demesne at Nailsbourne 2*s*.; the curtilage of the widow Wluron' drawn into demesne 6*d*.; the land and mill of Pleycroft in Fulford surrendered to Robert Mannsel by Bishop Richard 4*s*. 7½*d*. Total, 7*s*. 1½*d*.

Total of quittances and defaults of rent, £1 19*s*. 1½*d*.

Total of rents remaining, £19 4*s*. 8*d*.

Issues of the manor

The same renders account for 19*s*. 4½*d*. from pannage of pigs this year; 12*s*. 11*d*. from hundredpenny; nothing from the pasturage of Lipwellesmed' this year because it was pastured with the lord's oxen; nothing from the pasturage of Slapemed' this year because it was pastured with the lord's oxen; 8*s*. from the pasturage of Illbeare and the pasturage of Horewes near the same field sold in winter and summer; 1*s*. from the pasturage of Edwynesrigge sold in winter and summer; nothing from the pasturage of Estbradehenlegh' this year for a want of buyers; 1*s*. from the pasturage of Lipwlleslak' and of a certain small parcel of pasture in the same field sold in summer; nothing from the pasturage of la Done this year because it was sown with rye; 1*s.* from the pasturage of the way (*itineris*) to la Done sold; nothing from the pasturage in the waterlete after mowing this year because it is marled and lies fallow; nothing from the pasturage of Dodhullemed' after mowing this year because it was pastured with the lord's oxen; nothing from the pasturage of Dodhull*e*wod' here because the wood pertains to Staplegrove and the reeve of Staplegrove is answerable; 2*s.* from the pasturage of Lyttlelangelond sold in summer; 1*s.* 6*d.* from the pasturage of Westbradehenligh' sold in winter and summer; £2 8*s.* from 4 old oxen sold, at 11*s.* each; 6*s.* from the hide and flesh sold of one ox dead from murrain; 7*s.* 6*d.* from 10 old wethers sold before shearing, at 9*d.* each; £2 3*s.* from 21½ cloves of coarse wool sold, at 2*s.* a clove; 2*s.* 10½*d.* from the skins sold of 12 wethers, one hogg, and 2 lambs before shearing, and of 4 wethers after shearing; 8¼*d.* from the fleeces of 8 lambs sold; 11*s.* 1½*d.* from 53 cheeses made in winter from accumulated milk (*de coll'*) sold by warrant (p*er manu'*); £4 12*s.* 7*d.* from 11 weys of summer cheese sold, at 8*s.* 5*d.* a wey; 9*s.* 1½*d.* from butter sold; nothing from bark and loppings this year; 2*s.* 6*d.* from the residue of Peter's pence at Nailsbourne and Fulford; 2*s.* 1*d.* from 25 hens from churchscot sold; £3 6*s.* 10½*d.* from portions of labour services sold; 1*s.* 3*d.* from 2½ lb of wax from recognizances sold; 7*d.* from 1 ploughshare from a recognizance sold; 5*s.* 6*d.* from woodway; 15*s.* 2*d.* from dairy produce (*lactag'*) sold at the audit. Total, £18 1*s.* 7¾*d.*

Sale of corn
The same renders account for £19 6*s.* 8*d.* from 59 qrs 2 bus. of wheat sold, at 6*s.* a qr for 6 qrs, 5*s.* a qr for 4 qrs 6 bus., 6*s.* 8*d.* a qr for 27 qrs, and 6*s.* 10*d.* a qr for 21½ qrs sold to customary tenants; £3 9*s.* 4½*d.* from 13 qrs 7 bus. of rye sold, at 5*s.* a qr; £7 7*s.* from 84 qrs of coarse oats sold to customary tenants, at 1*s.* 9*d.* a qr; £1 5*s.* from 12½ qrs of peas sold, at 2*s.* a qr. Total, £31 8*s.* ½*d.*

Entry and marriage fines
The same renders account for £2 10*s.* from Richard le Smyht to have Matilda in the M*e*rsch' who holds 1 messuage ½ virgate of land and 1 acre of meadow; 2*s.* from Joan atte M*er*she to have 1 house in Staplegrove by surrender of Richard le Smyht; 4*s.* from William le Vythelere to have 1 ferling of land in Kingston St Mary by surrender of Agnes atte Crosse; 10*s.* from the communal fine on Hockday (*hockedayeswyte*) at Kingston St Mary; 6*s.* 8*d.* from the same at Nailsbourne; 4*s.* from the same at Fulford. Total, £3 16*s.* 8*d.*

Perquisites
The same renders account for 6*d.* from Edith de Westehegh' for trespass (*delicto*) of pasture; 3*d.* from William son of Mab*el* for the same; 3*d.* from Robert atte Mull' of Kingston St Mary for the same; 3*d.* from Sevarus de Kyng*ston* for the same; 1*s.* from Stephen atte Sclape for trespass of wood; 3*d.* from William Wynt' for trespass of pasture; 1*s.* 6*d.* from William Curvays and 5 of his neighbours for attaching their pigs in the lord's wood at the time of mast; 1*s.* 6*d.* from John le Butelyr for having his pigs in the lord's park at the time of mast; 1*s.* 10*d.* from William Havelyng and Robert atte Mull' for the same; 3*d.* from Stephen atte Slape for the same; 3*d.* from Margery Wynt' for the same; 3*d.* from Sevarus de Kyng*ston* for trespass of corn; 6*d.* from John Bonecors and Ralph Sweyt for breaking and carrying off the fencing of the park; 3*d.* from Adam Bryce for withholding a debt; 3*d.* from Walter, son of Walter de Buveweye, for transgression against his neighbour; 3*d.* from Walter le Westren' for false complaint; 3*d.* from Richard Garlaund for transgression against the lord; 3*d.*

from Adam Bryce for trespass of pasture; 3*d*. from Adam Warman for the same; 3*d*. from William son of Mab*el* for the same; 6*d*. from Thomas Clode for the same; 6*d*. from John Aylard for transgression against the lord; 3*d*. from Robert le Cras for unjustly withholding a debt; 6*d*. from Adam Brice and Adam Warman for transgression against their neighbour; 3*d*. from William Pylebred for unjustly withholding a debt; 3*d*. from Robert le Cras for false complaint against Roger Uppehull'; 6*d*. from William Wynt' for transgression against his neighbour; 6*d*. from William Clod*e* and Sevarus de Kyng*ston* for transgression against the lord; 3*d*. from William Frenshe in the M*er*she for trespass of corn; 3*d*. from Richard in the M*er*sh' for the same; 6*d*. from John le Bule for transgression against his sister; 6*d*. from the tithing of Kingston St Mary for concealment; 3*d*. from Richard Gaurlaund for transgression against his neighbour; 1*s*. from Richard le Tressher' and William Mess*or* for transgression against their neighbour; 9*d*. from Margery Brice and two of her neighbours for trespass of the park-fence; 7*d*. from Walter Buveweye and Agnes Leggele for trespass of corn and pasture; 3*d*. from William Wytchild for trespass of wood; 1*s*. 6*d*. from three of the lord's oxherds for keeping the oxen badly; 3*d*. from Margery Wynt' for transgression against her neighbour; 3*d*. from Hugh Punȝ because he withdrew his suit; 6*d*. from William son of Mab*el* for transgression against his neighbour; 6*d*. from Richard Luv*er*ih for trespass of pasture; 6*d*. from Thomas Pyek for the same; 1*s*. from Nicholas le Combar' for trespass of corn and pasture; 3*d*. from William Luv*er*ihc for transgression against his neighbour; 3*d*. from Walter Curvays for trespass of pasture; 6*d*. from William Bryce for contempt; 3*d*. from Nicholas atte Bernne and Nicholas Luv*er*ich, the lord's ploughmen, for bad ploughing; 3*d*. from Ralph atte Wat*ere* because he is not proceeding with his complaint; 3*d*. from John le Bule for breaking an agreement; 2*s*. from William le Westehegh' for various transgressions against the lord; 3*d*. from William Frensh' in the M*er*sh' for contempt; 1*s*. 3*d*. from Richard in the M*er*sh' and 4 of his neighbours for mowing the meadow badly; 1*s*. from Walter Kene for default of carrying-service at harvest-time; 3*d*. from William Frensh' in the M*er*sh' for reaping and gathering corn badly at harvest-time; 6*d*. from William Luv*er*ich of Vennhampton because he did not come to the boon-reaping as he was summoned; 6*d*. from Robert atte Mull' for the same; 1*s*. 10*d*. from Richard in the M*er*sh' and 10 of his neighbours for reaping and gathering corn badly at harvest-time; 2*s*. from Jordan le Bul' and 7 of his neighbours because they did not come to reap rye as they were summoned; 3*d*. from the tithing of Kingston St Mary because it comes less of late; 3*d*. from William Baldewyn' for transgression against his neighbour; 6*d*. from Thomas and Richard, sons of Robert atte Mull', for the same; 1*s*. from Roger Uppehull' because he neglected to perform his office; 6*d*. from William de Westeh', beadle, for the same; 3*d*. from the tithing of Kingston St Mary because it comes less of late; 6*d*. from Adam Bryce for transgression against his neighbour; 6*d*. from Richard Pal for the same; 3*d*. from William Clode because he did not produce in court the individual whom he had bailed; 1*s*. from the tithing of Fulford for concealing landless men (*garcionum*) outside the tithing; 2*d*. from Baldwin atte Wat*ere*, beadle, because he performed his office less well in the presence of the steward; 2*s*. 8*d*. from the whole hundred of Nailsbourne for false complaint; £1 9*s*. 3*d*. from those who brewed ale this year for breaking the assize of ale. Total, £3 10*s*. 10*d*.

Total of both, £7 7*s*. 6*d*.

Total of all receipts, £76 1*s*. 10¼*d*.

Cost of ploughs
In iron and steel for making and repairing the ironwork of 3 ploughs for the year 12*s*. In stipend of the smith making and repairing the aforesaid ironwork for the year 2*s*. 6*d*. In 3 ploughshares bought 1*s*. 9*d*. In boon-works of 15½ ploughmen ploughing 2 full days in winter and as many ploughmen in Lent ploughing in the same way 2*s*. 7*d*., at ½*d*. a ploughman a day. In making 6 new ploughs 9*d*. In repairing the old ploughs many times during the year 8½*d*. In trimming and sawing timber for yokes and wooden halters (*lannos*) of ploughs 6*d*. In making yokes and wooden halters 5*d*. In food for 3 ploughmen, one beadle and one smith according to custom at Christmas and Easter 10*d*. In food for 14 workers according to the same custom 1*s*. 2*d*. In stipend of 3 oxherds for the year 7*s*. 6*d*. In quittance of a ploughman and beadle for 15 Saturday ploughings 1*s*. 10½*d*., at 1½*d*. a Saturday. In 3 oxen bought £2 4*d*., at 13*s*. 4*d*. for one, and 13*s*. 6*d*. each for 2. In shoeing one plough-horse harrowing at two sowings 5*d*. In 16 qrs of charcoal made for making and repairing the ironwork of 3 ploughs for the year 2*s*., at 1½*d*. a qr. In 18 qrs of oats bought for forage from customary tenants for a want of forage 1*s*. 6*d*., at 1*d*. a qr. Total, £3 16*s*. 10*d*.

Purchase of corn
In 3 qrs 2 bus. of rye bought 13*s*., at 4*s*. a qr. In 9½ qrs of maslin bought for the liveries of the manorial servants £1 18*s*., at 4*s*. a qr. In 50 qrs of coarse oats bought £4 4*d*., at 1*s*. 6*d*. a qr for 18 qrs, and 1*s*. 8*d*. a qr for 32 qrs. Total, £6 11*s*. 4*d*.

Cost of wagons
In 100 large nails for repairing the old wagons 1*s*. 10*d*. In fitting 3 wagons with axles 3*d*. In 18 clouts with nails bought 2*s*. 8*d*. In grease for the wagons 3*d*. In repairing wagons in preparation for harvest-time 5*d*. In 1 hemp rope 1*s*. Total, 6*s*. 5*d*.

Repair of buildings with small expenses
In re-roofing the barn and granary in part 1*s*. In mending the outside gate of the curia with nails bought for the same 2*d*. In 1 billhook for cutting hedges 2*d*. In 1 dung-fork fitted with iron 3½*d*. Total, 1*s*. 7*d*.

Dairy and sheepcote
In grease for diseased sheep 2*s*. 2*d*. In 5½ bus. 1 peck of salt 1*s*. 7*d*., at 3½*d*. a bus. for 5 bus., and 1½*d*. for ½ bus. 1 peck. In a press 8*d*. In linen and woollen cloth for cheese 7*d*. In earthenware pots and pans 3½*d*. In roofing the whole of the sheepcote 1*s*. 3*d*. In stipend of 1 shepherd and 1 dairymaid for the year 5*s*. In 7 wethers bought before shearing 8*s*. 9*d*., at 1*s*. 3*d*. each. In 2 ewes bought after breeding and before shearing 2*s*. 6*d*. Total, £1 2*s*. 9½*d*.

Threshing of corn
In threshing 39 qrs of wheat and 14 qrs 7 bus. of rye by piece-work 11*s*. 2¾*d*., at 2½*d*. a heaped quarter. Total, 11*s*. 2¾*d*.

Harvest-time
In customary payment for the mowing of 16 acres of meadow at Nailsbourne 4*d*. In customary payment for the mowing of 12 acres of meadow at Fulford 4*d*. In customary payment for the mowing of 17 acres of meadow at Kingston St Mary 8*d*. In customary payment for the boon-reaping at Nailsbourne 6*d*. In customary payment for the boon-reaping at Fulford 7*d*. In customary payment for the boon-reaping at Kingston St Mary 7*d*. In covering one haycock 6*d*. Total, 3*s*. 6*d*.

Mills

In one Welsh millstone for the mill at Nailsbourne 10*s*. In sawing timber for the inner wheel of the mill at Kingston St Mary and the outer wheel of the mill at Nailsbourne 1*s*. 8*d*. In 50 Welsh boards bought to cover the outer wheel of the mill at Nailsbourne 6*s*. 1*d*. In 1,000 nails for covering the same wheel 4*s*. 2*d*. In hooping one head of the driving-shaft of the mill at Nailsbourne with iron 3¼*d*. In iron and steel for repairing and sharpening the bills at both mills for the year 1*s*. 3½*d*. In stipend of the smith sharpening the aforesaid bills for the year 6*d*. In allowance of the reeve for selling oxen as charged above because they were sick 8*s*. Total, £1 11*s*. 11¾*d*.

Total of all expenses, £14 5*s*. 8*d*.

Cash deliveries

Delivered to Walter de Buddeligh', reeve of Taunton, £61 16*s*. 2¼*d*.

Wheat

{yield: three-and-a-half-fold plus 1 qr}

The same renders account for 88½ qrs from the whole issue of wheat by struck measure.

Sown over 57½ acres, 13 qrs 1 bus.; that is, 2 bus. an acre, less 1 qr 2 bus. in all. Mixed below with rye to make maslin for sowing, 1 qr. Mixed below for the liveries of the manorial servants, 15 qrs 1 bus. Sold, 59 qrs 2 bus. Total, 88½ qrs. It balances.

Maslin

The same renders account for 1 qr received above from wheat; 1 qr 1 bus. received below from rye. Total, 2 qrs 1 bus.

All sown over 10 acres; that is, 2 bus. an acre, less 3 bus. in all.

Rye

{yield: three-fold plus 5 bus.}

The same renders account for 19 qrs 6 bus. from the whole issue of rye by struck measure; 3 qrs 2 bus. bought. Total, 23 qrs.

Sown over 22½ acres, 4 qrs 6 bus.; that is, 2 bus. an acre, less 7 bus. in all. Mixed above to make maslin for sowing, 1 qr 1 bus. In customary payment for the boon-reaping, 3 qrs 2 bus. Sold, 13 qrs 7 bus. Total, 23 qrs. It balances.

Coarse oats

{yield: 26 qrs 7 bus. more than was sown}

The same renders account for 69 qrs 2 bus. from the whole issue of coarse oats by struck measure; 7 qrs received from small oats for sowing; 50 qrs bought. Total, 126 qrs 2 bus.

Sown over 88½ acres, 42 qrs 2 bus.; that is, 4 bus. an acre, less 2 qrs in all. Sold, 84 qrs. Total, 126 qrs 2 bus. It balances.

Small oats

{yield: two-fold less 1½ qrs}

The same renders account for 20½ qrs from the whole issue of small oats by struck measure.

Sown over 30 acres, 13½ qrs; that is, 4 bus. an acre, less 1½ qrs in all. Mixed above with coarse oats for sowing, 7 qrs. Total, 20½ qrs. It balances.

Peas
{yield: six-and-a-half-fold plus 6 bus.}
The same renders account for 13 qrs 6 bus. from the whole issue of peas by struck measure.
Sown over 5½ acres, 1 qr 2 bus.; that is, 2 bus. an acre, less 1 bus. in all. Sold, 12½ qrs. Total, 13 qrs 6 bus. It balances.

Proof of liveries
The same renders account for 15 qrs 1 bus. received above from wheat; 9½ qrs bought. Total, 24 qrs 5 bus.
Delivered to 3 oxherds, one shepherd and one hayward for the year, 21 qrs 4½ bus., taking a quarter every 12 weeks. Delivered to one cowherd for 37 weeks, 3 qrs ½ bus., taking a quarter every 12 weeks. Total, 24 qrs 5 bus. It balances.

m.2d

Stock

Plough-horses: 2 remain from the previous year; 1 added from colts. Total, 3. They remain.
Colts: 1 three-year-old male added to plough-horses; none remain. 1 two-year-old male remains from the previous year's 1-year-olds; it remains. 1 one-year-old male remains from the previous year's offspring; it remains.
Oxen: 26 remain from the previous year; 3 bought. Total, 29. 1 in murrain; 4 sold. Total, 5. 24 remain.
Cows: 1 remains from the previous year which is delivered to the reeve of Poundisford before breeding; none remain.
Bullocks: 2 remain from the previous year's yearlings; they remain, 1 of them male.
Wethers: 159 remain from the previous year; 3 added from hoggs; 1 from the reeve of Poundisford before shearing; 7 bought before shearing. Total, 170. 12 in murrain before shearing, 4 after shearing; 10 sold before shearing. Total, 26. 144 remain.
Ewes: 11 remain from the previous year; 3 added from hoggs; 2 bought after breeding and before shearing; 1 from the heriot of Agnes atte Crosse after shearing. Total, 17. They remain.
Hoggs: 7 remain from the previous year's lambs; 1 in murrain before shearing; 3 added above to wethers, 3 to ewes; none remain.
Lambs: 11 produced by the said ewes this year. 1 in tithe; 2 in murrain before shearing. Total, 3. 8 remain.
Coarse wool {yield of fleece 3½*d.* less 2*d.* in all}: 145 fleeces from wethers, 13 from ewes and 6 from hoggs produced at the shearing this year. Total, 164. 16 in tithe; 148 sold, which made 21½ cloves. Total, 164. It balances.
Lamb's-wool {fleeces yield 1 more in all}:[1] 8 fleeces produced at the shearing this year; all sold, which made 3 lb.
Hides: the hide and flesh of one ox dead from murrain sold; none remains.
Skins: 12 from wethers and 1 from a hogg dead from murrain before shearing; 4 from wethers dead from murrain after shearing. Total, 19. All sold; none remain.
Winter cheese: 53 made in winter from accumulated milk; all sold by warrant; none remain.
Summer cheese {yield of cow 4*s.* because 3 were not in milk on account of being sick}: 26 small cheeses made from accumulated milk before beginning to make cheese everyday; 147 produced by the dairy this year between the day before the

1 MS 'vell' r' de j pl*us* i*n* toto q*uam*'.

nones of May (6 May) and Michaelmas (29 September), both days included. Total, 173. 17 in tithe; 156 sold, which made 11 weys. Total, 173. It balances.
Hens: 25 from churchscot; all sold; none remain.
Recognizance wax: 1 lb from John Trappe; ½ lb from William Godman; ½ lb from William son of Roger; ½ lb from Briton de Yaford. Total, 2½ lb, which were sold as made clear within; none remains.
Ploughshares: 1 from the recognizance of Ralph Britor which was sold as made clear within; none remain.
Charcoal: 16 qrs made this year which were used in making and repairing the ironwork of 3 ploughs; none remains.

Staplegrove

The account of William atte Mull', reeve of this place.

Rents

The same renders account for £30 2*s*. 8*d*. for rents of assize at Christmas, Easter (22 April), the Nativity of the blessed John the Baptist (24 June), and Michaelmas (29 September), in equal portions. Total, £30 2*s*. 8*d*.

Quittances

In quittance of two ploughmen and one beadle for the year 3*s*. 9*d*., or 1*s*. 3*d*. each; 7 workers working one day a week for three terms of the year and everyday at harvest-time except Saturday 12*s*. 3*d*., or 1*s*. 9*d*. each. Total, 16*s*.

Defaults of rent

In default of 1 acre of meadow drawn into demesne at Mill Lane 6*d*.; 2 small holdings drawn into demesne 1*s*. 6*d*. Total, 2*s*.

Total of quittances and defaults of rent, 18*s*.

Total of rents remaining, £29 4*s*. 8*d*.

Issues of the manor

The same renders account for £1 12*s*. 2½*d*. from pannage of pigs this year; 19*s*. from hundredpenny this year; 5*s*. from the pasturage in Mytheghemed sold in winter; nothing from the pasturage of Dodhill this year because it was pastured with the lord's oxen; nothing from the pasturage of Burm*er*hs this year because it was sown with wheat; nothing from the pasturage of Clehull' this year because it was pastured with the lord's sheep; 4*s*. 6*d*. from the pasturage of Syndercroft sold in winter and summer; 2*s*. from the pasturage of Brad' sold in winter; 3*s*. from the pasturage of Bihsshoplo*n*d' sold in winter; 6*s*. from the pasturage in the waterlete sold after mowing; nothing from the pasturage of the way to Nailsbourne this year because the field beside which it lay was waterlete; 5*s*. from the pasturage of Dodhill sold in summer; 1*s*. from the pasturage of the way to Staplegrove beside Langeforurch' sold; 1*s*. from the pasturage of the way to Wytemor in the north field of Langefor' sold in summer; nothing from the pasturage of the way beside Syndercroft this year because the field lay fallow; nothing from the pasturage in Langeforurch' this year because it was sown with wheat; 5*s*. from 1 plough-horse sold; £2 17*s*. 6*d*. from 5 old oxen sold, at 11*s*. 6*d*. each; £2 5*s*. 9½*d*. from portions of labour services sold; 2*s*. 9*d*. from 5½ lb of wax from recognizances sold, at 6*d*. a lb; 8*s*. 9*d*. from woodway; £1 12*s*. 8*d*. from 12 workers of Mill Lane, who were accustomed to maintain the quay beside the water which runs to the town mill of Taunton, which is called Frenshewer', to be released from these works for the year, which are commuted for 8*d*. a week, excepting the three weeks of Christmas, Easter and Pentecost, during which they are not bound nor are accustomed to work, and this work is commuted because there are not sufficient tenants to do the same work; 1*s*. from Michael Lu*ver*ich so that he may remain outside the liberty and pay suit of court for his tithing at the two tourns; 8*s*. 5*d*. from the market tolls of Mill Lane this year; 6*d*. from the heriot of Adam Chek because he did not have 1 beast (*averi*um); 6*d*. from the heriot of Benedict Sygar for the same; 3*s*. 4*d*. from the moiety of 1 cow from the heriot of John Luverich sold; 6*d*. from the heriot of Matilda la Cartar' because she did not have one beast. Total, £12 5*s*. 5*d*.

Entry and marriage fines
The same renders account for 4*s*. from Alice, daughter of Nicholas Kynele, to have 1 messuage and 3 acres of land by surrender of Adam Chek; £1 from John Kynele to have 1 messuage and 10 acres of land which belonged to Benedict Sygar; 13*s*. 4*d*. from Juliana, who was wife of John Cullyng of Dodhill, to retain 1 messuage and 1 ferling of land which belonged to the aforesaid John her husband; 10*s*. from Nicholas P*ersone* to have ½ ferling of land by surrender of Agnes his mother; 10*s*. from the same Nicholas to have ½ ferling of land by surrender of Matilda P*er*sone; 6*s*. 8*d*. from John le Palm*ere* to have 1½ acres of land by surrender of Adam Kempe; 3*s*. from Agnes, daughter of Thomas le Kyng, for marrying within; 2*s*. from Walter Cole for marrying Agnes his daughter outside; 1*s*. from Gilbert atte Cruche for himself marrying Agnes P*er*sone; 4*s*. from John de Cothagh' to have two houses beside the house of Nicholas Kynele by surrender of Matilda la Cart*ere* his mother; 10*s*. from Juliana, daughter of John Lu*ve*rich, to have 1 messuage and 5 acres of land by surrender of the aforesaid John her father; 6*s*. 8*d*. from Adam Cole By Northeton' for marrying Alice his daughter outside; £1 10*s*. from the communal fine on Hockday (*hockedayeswyte*). Total, £6 8*d*.

Perquisites
The same renders account for 6*d*. from Richard Austyn for trespass of pasture; 2*d*. from Nicholas atte Wythege for the same; 2*d*. from Nicholas Pyek for trespass of wood; 6*d*. from John atte Crosse for trespass of pasture; 8*d*. from Gilbert Dauwe for the same; 2*d*. from Nicholas Pyek for attaching his pigs in the park of Nailsbourne at the time of mast; 1*s*. 6*d*. from Robert de Eggebury and 3 of his neighbours for attaching their pigs in Dodhullewod' at the time of mast; 3*d*. from Gilbert Dauwe for trespass of pasture; 6*d*. from John Passage for the same; 6*d*. from Nicholas Kynele for the same; 3*d*. from Richard Austyn for the same; 9*d*. from Richard Kyng of Illbeare and two of his neighbours because they did not come to the threshing in the castle as they were summoned; 1*s*. from William le Knyg' de Pykenhegh' and two of his neighbours for trespass of pasture; 1*s*. from Richard Wynt' for the same; 6*d*. from Ellen de Pyrilond for transgression against her neighbour; 3*d*. from Thomas Fulkem*ere* for trespass of pasture; 6*d*. from Margery de Burlo*nd*' for unjustly withholding a debt; 3*d*. from Robert Uppehull' for transgression against the lord; 1*s*. from Richard Wynt' and other executors of Thomas le Kyng for transgression against the lord; 1*s*. from William le Knygȝ de Pykenhegh' for trespass of pasture;

6*d.* from John de Chelewardeswod' for transgression against the lord; 3*d.* from Robert de Dodh*u*ll' for trespass of corn; 3*d.* from Walter Cullyng for the same; 3*d.* from Nicholas Pyek for trespass of pasture; 3*d.* from William Knygȝ de Pykeh' for the same; 6*d.* from Thomas Cole of Dodhill because he carried off fencing of the park of Nailsbourne; 6*d.* from Thomas Trot for unjustly withholding a debt; 3*d.* from Nicholas Cully*ng* because he is not prosecuting a certain assault made before his tithing; 3*d.* from Margery Luv*er*ich for threshing corn badly; 3*d.* from John Gileb' for transgression against the lord; 6*d.* from the tithing of Obridge because it did not attach disturbers of the peace in its tithing; 6*d.* from Hugh Bytheweye, beadle, because he neglected to perform his office; 6*d.* from Richard le Knygȝ of Illbeare for trespass of wood; 1*s.* from John le Palm*ere* atte Yerd for the same; 3*d.* from Margery Luv*er*ich for trespass of pasture; 6*d.* from Walter Burlo*nd*' for the same; 3*d.* from Richard Luv*er*ich for trespass of corn; 9*d.* from John Passag' and two of his neighbours for transgression against the lord; 1*s.* from Ellen de Pyrilond for trespass of pasture; 2*s.* from William atte Mull' of Staplegrove for the same; 6*d.* from Hugh Bytheweye because he bore false witness in court; 6*d.* from Walter Shern' because he did not come to an inquest; 3*d.* from John atte Oke for transgression against his neighbour; 6*d.* from William Ma*n*nsel for unjustly withholding a debt; 6*d.* from Henry de Apfle for trespass of pasture; 3*d.* from Gilbert Dauwe for the same; 6*d.* from Robert Uppehulle for the same; 1*s.* from 2 of the lord's oxherds of Staplegrove for keeping the lord's oxen badly; 3*d.* from Gilbert Tresor for trespass of corn; 6*d.* from William Luv*er*ich for transgression against his neighbour; 3*d.* from Nicholas le Knytȝ for transgression against the lord; 6*d.* from Ellen Pyrilond for trespass of pasture; 3*d.* from William Mannsel for transgression against the lord; 3*d.* from Richard Wynt' for default; 10*d.* from Benedict de Whytemor and 4 of his neighbours for winnowing corn badly; 3*d.* from Benedict de Wytemor for trespass of pasture; 3*d.* from Nicholas Cullyng of Staplegrove for the same; 6*d.* from Nicholas Kynele for trespass of corn; 3*d.* from Walter Cole of Pyrland for the same; 3*d.* from Benedict de Whytemor for the same; 2*d.* from Walter Cully*ng* for the same; 6*d.* from Henry, son of Thomas le Baker', for transgression against Matilda la Webbe; 6*d.* from Roger Cole for trespass of corn and pasture; 6*d.* from John Budd' for transgression against Juliana la Pur; 3*d.* from Gilbert T*re*sor for trespass of corn and pasture; 6*d.* from William atte Wat*ere* because he did not produce in court Robert le Frye whom he had bailed; 1*s.* 6*d.* from Adam atte Ston' and 8 of his neighbours because they did not come to the boon-reaping at harvest-time; 6*d.* from John atte Crosse for trespass of pasture; 1*s.* from John Warma*n* for enrolling a certain agreement; 3*d.* from the tithing of Obridge because it comes less of late; 1*s.* from the tithing of Staplegrove for concealing landless men outside the tithing; 1*s.* from the tithing of Pyrland for the same; 2*s.* from the tithing of Obridge for the same; 1*s.* from the tithing of Mill Lane for the same; 6*d.* from the tithing of Obridge because it did not produce in court the individual whom it had bailed; 1*s.* from the tithing of Burlands for concealing certain honey; 1*s.* from the tithing of Holway for the same; 2*d.* from Hugh Bytheweye because he performed his office inadequately in the presence of the steward; £2 16*s.* 6*d.* from those who brewed ale for breaking the assize of ale; 4*s.* from those who are declared outlaws by false complaint; 8*s.* from the small perquisites of the court. Total, £5 13*s.* 1*d.*

Total of both, £11 12*s.* 9*d.*

Total of all receipts, £53 2*s.* 10*d.*

Cost of ploughs
In iron and steel for the ironwork of 2 ploughs for the year 8*s*. 2*d*. In stipend of the smith making and repairing the aforesaid ironwork for the year 2*s*. In 2 ploughshares bought 1*s*. 2*d*. In boon-works of 27½ ploughmen ploughing 2 full days in winter and as many ploughmen in Lent ploughing in the same way 4*s*. 5*d*., at ½*d*. a ploughman a day. In timber sawn for ploughs 3*d*. In making 5 new ploughs 7½*d*. In mending the old ploughs many times during the year 6*d*. In 5 new yokes made 1*d*. In food for 1 beadle and 2 ploughmen according to custom at Christmas and Easter 6*d*. In food for 19 workers according to the same custom 1*s*. 7*d*. In stipend of 2 oxherds for the year 5*s*. In quittance of a ploughman and beadle for 16 Saturday ploughings 2*s*., at 1½*d*. a Saturday. In 13 qrs of charcoal made for making and repairing the ironwork of 2 ploughs for the year 1*s*. 7½*d*., at 1½*d*. a qr. In 3 oxen bought £1 14*s*.[1] 6*d*., at 11*s*. 6*d*. each. In shoeing one plough-horse harrowing at both sowings 6*d*. Total, £3 12*s*. 11*d*.

[Cost of wagons]
In fitting one wagon with axles 1*d*. In 8 clouts with nails bought for the wagons 1*s*. 1*d*. In grease for the wagons and dung-carts (*carm'*) 3*d*. In repairing wagons in preparation for harvest-time 3*d*. Total, 1*s*. 8*d*.

[Repair of buildings]
In building one earthen wall between the byre and wagon-shed 4*d*. In timber sawn for making a new gate for the hay barton 5*d*. In nails, hooks and hinges for the same gate 1*s*. 1*d*. Total, 1*s*. 10*d*.

[Harvest-time]
In customary payment for the mowing of the third part of a certain meadow which is usually mowed for 1*s*., 4*d*., because two parts of the same meadow are leased for a fixed rent. In customary payment for the mowing of a certain meadow leased for the customary tenants to mow in place of the two parts of meadow leased for a fixed rent 8*d*. In customary payment for the boon-reaping 9*d*. In covering one haycock 3*d*. Total, 2*s*.

Total of all expenses, £3 8*s*. 5*d*.

[Cash deliveries]
Delivered to Walter de Buddelye, reeve of Taunton castle, £49 14*s*. 5*d*.

Stock

[Plough-horses]: 1 remains from the previous year; 1 from the heriot of John Cullyng of Dodhill; 1 sold; 1 remains.
[Oxen]: 21 remain from the previous year; 3 bought. Total, 24. 5 sold; 19 remain.
[Cows]: one remains from the previous year which is delivered to the reeve of Poundisford before breeding; none remain. The moiety of 1 cow from the heriot of John Luv*e*rich is sold; none remain.
[Recognizance wax]: ½ lb from Nicholas de Lambrot; ½ lb from Walter le Tayllur; ½ lb from Thomas le Brekker'; ½ lb from William le Tayllor; ½ lb from Walter atte Pyle; ½ lb from William Wrkman; ½ lb from Jordan Godefray; ½ lb from William le Blake; ½ lb from Walter le Yonge; ½ lb from Richard atte Wat*ere*; ½ lb from Robert de Bladkedon', for the first time this year. Total, 5½ lb, which were sold as made clear within; none remains.

1 MS omits '*s*.'

[Charcoal]: 13 qrs made this year which were used in making and repairing the ironwork of two ploughs for the year; none remains.

m.3

Trull and Bishops Hull

Rents
The same renders account for £21 4*s.* ¼*d.* for rents of assize at Christmas, Easter (22 April), the Nativity of the blessed John the Baptist (24 June), and Michaelmas (29 September), in equal portions. Total, £21 4*s.* ¼*d.*

Quittances
In quittance of 4 ploughmen and 1 beadle at Trull and Bishops Hull 6*s.* 3*d.*, or 1*s.* 3*d.* each; 6 workers at Trull and 7 workers at Bishops Hull working 2 days a week for 3 terms of the year and everyday at harvest-time except Saturday 3*s.* 3*d.*, or 3*d.* each. Total of quittances, 9*s.* 6*d.*

Total of rents remaining, £20 14*s.* 6¼*d.*

Issues of the manor
The same renders account for £1 2*s.* 3*d.* from pannage of pigs this year; 15*s.* 1*d.* from hundredpenny this year; 4*s.* from the pasturage in Trendlemor sold after mowing in winter; nothing from the pasturage of Holtfurlang this year because it was sown with wheat; 8*s.* from the pasturage of Langed', Orchardmed and Bromd' sold; 3*s.* from the pasturage in Hayg*ro*ve sold after mowing; 5*s.* from the pasturage of Pyrih' sold in winter and summer; 2*s.* 6*d.* from the pasturage of Mullesg*ro*vesmed' sold in winter; 5*s.* from the pasturage of Hodecu*m*be sold in winter and summer; 3*s.* from the pasturage of Loscu*m*b' sold in winter; 6*s.* from the pasturage of Horsweye and Ryhsh*a*m sold in winter; 8*s.* from the pasturage of the fields on the near side of Bishops Hull sold in winter; nothing from the pasturage of Burywey because the road was so narrow that no pasture grew there; 2*s.* from the pasturage of Langed' sold in winter; 1*s.* from the pasturage of the way to Bishops Hull sold in summer; 5*s.* from the pasturage of Castelmed sold in winter; 2*s.* 6*d.* from Walter Piris for the pasturage on both sides of the alder wood beside Loscu*m*b' and Pyriheye just as Nicholas de Chelewardeswod' held the same and for the pasturage around the fields of Loscu*m*b' and Pyrih' when they were sown with winter or summer corn (*yvernag' vel' tremays*); 2*s.* 6*d.* from John Sprut to have the pasturage of Tukyngdih for the year by fine which he has made for the same; 6*d.* from the same John to have 2 pieces of pasturage, that is, Kenesplot and Mulleheye, for the year by fine which he has made for the same; 6*s.* 8*d.* from 1 feeble plough-horse sold; £2 8*s.* from 4 sick oxen sold, at 12*s.* each; 3*s.* from the moiety of 1 cow sold; £1 1*s.* from the hides and flesh sold of 3 oxen dead from murrain, at 7*s.* each; nothing from stubble this year because there is none; £1 6*d.* from hay sold; 3*s.* from loppings in Hayg*ro*ve sold; £2 18*s.* 9*d.* from portions of labour services sold; 3*s.* 3*d.* from 6½ lb of wax from recognizances sold, at 6*d.* a lb; 3*d.* from Thomas le Frye for recognizance; 8*s.* 4*d.* from woodway; 1*s.* from mast sold in Hodecu*m*b'; 1*s.* from mast sold in Hayg*ro*ve; 2*s.* from mast sold in Chelewardeswod'; 2*s.* 4*d.* from two ash trees blown down by the wind on the street of Bishops Hull sold. Total, £13 14*s.* 11*d.*

Mills
He does not answer for the mills because they are answered for in the castle account.

Entry and marriage fines

The same renders account for 6*s*. 8*d*. from Richard, son of William Shaldon, to have 1 acre of meadow by surrender of Roger de Upkot'; £1 from Alice, who was wife of John le Goude, to retain 1 messuage and 10 acres of land which belonged to the aforesaid John her husband; £1 from Richard Babbe to have the aforesaid Alice with her land; 3*s*. from John, son of Walter Sprut, to have 1 house in Cokhagh' by surrender of the aforesaid Walter his father; 3*s*. from Walter Godman for marrying Alice his daughter outside; 1*s*. from Adam Tursyn for marrying Avice his daughter outside; 2*s*. from Walter Bagh' for marrying Margery his sister outside; 2*s*. from Thomas Byllyng for marrying Joan his daughter within; 2*s*. from Richard, son of Thomas Jordan, for 3 day-works (*daenis*) of land by surrender of the aforesaid Thomas his father; 5*s*. from Robert Uppecleyve for marrying Alice his daughter outside; 13*s*. 4*d*. from the communal fine on Hockday (*hockdayeswyte*) at Trull; 10*s*. from the same at Bishops Hull. Total, £4 8*s*.

Perquisites

The same renders account for 6*d*. from William de Norton' for trespass of pasture; 2*s*. from a certain stranger for the same; 6*d*. from Adam de Choleward' for transgression against his neighbour; 1*s*. from Thomas Trot, Ralph de Gilmeto*n* and Nicholas Cade for the same; 6*d*. from Thomas Kene and Walter Kene because they did not come to an inquest; 6*d*. from Walter Godm*an* for unjustly withholding a debt; 3*d*. from John Pare for trespass of pasture; 3*d*. from John Prior for transgression against the lord; 3*d*. from John Wara*n*t for the same; 3*d*. from John Cap*ellanus* of Bishops Hull for the same; 3*d*. from John, son of John de Fryth' the younger (*inferior'*), for the same; 1*s*. from Walter and Roger, sons of Walter Will', for transgression against their mother; 6*d*. from John Cade because he is not proceeding with his complaint; 3*d*. from Margery de Tottewrch' for threshing oats badly in the castle; 6*d*. from Thomas Kene for unjustly withholding a debt; 2*d*. from John Gileb' of Bishops Hull for threshing corn badly; 1*s*. from Thomas Bylly*ng* for unjustly withholding a debt; 4*s*. from John Bord' for transgression against the clerk of the castle; 3*d*. from William Stilh*am* for transgression against the lord; 1*s*. from William Shalden because he allowed the lord's oxherds to be idle; 6*d*. from Walter Kene for trespass of pasture; 6*d*. from 2 of the lord's oxherds of Bishops Hull because they drove the lord's oxen less well; 6*d*. from John in the Wynhus' for trespass of pasture; 6*d*. from William Bat for contempt; 3*d*. from John in the Wynh' for trespass of pasture; 6*d*. from Thomas Bylly*ng* for unjustly withholding a debt; 6*d*. from the same Thomas for transgression against the lord; 6*d*. from Walter, beadle, for the same; 6*d*. from the same Walter for the same; 6*s*. from Richard atte More and 5 of his neighbours for the same; 6*d*. from Walter Kene and Robert Uppeclyve because they did not come to carry hay; 1*s*. from 4 of the lord's oxherds for transgression against the lord and for trespass of pasture; 1*s*. from John Turpyn for trespass of corn at harvest-time; 1*s*. from Richard Cole of Bishops Hull for the same; 3*d*. from William Maystr' de Fritheh' for unjustly withholding a debt; 6*d*. from John Sprut of Rumwell for trespass of pasture; 1*s*. from John in the Wynh' and Jordan Culy*ng* for transgression done in the castle; £1 from William in the Wynh', the lord's gardener, for various transgressions done in the castle and outside; 1*s*. from Roger le Baller' for trespass of corn at harvest-time; 6*d*. from Henry, son of Thomas le Baker', for transgression against Matilda la Webbe; 1*s*. from the tithing of Dipford because it did not produce in court Robert Gone whom it had bailed; 2*d*. from Walter, beadle, because he performed his office inadequately in the presence of the steward; £1 14*s*.

9*d*. from those who brewed ale this year for breaking the assize of ale. Total, £4 7*s*. 10*d*.

Total of both, £8 15*s*. 10*d*.

Total of all receipts, £43 5*s*. 3¼*d*.

Cost of ploughs
In iron and steel for the ironwork of 4 ploughs for the year 14*s*. 5*d*. In stipend of the smith making and repairing the aforesaid ironwork for the year with the lord's charcoal 4*s*. In 4 ploughshares bought 2*s*. 4*d*. In boon-works of 19 ploughmen in winter at Bishops Hull and Trull ploughing 2 full days and as many ploughmen in Lent ploughing in the same way 3*s*. 2*d*., at ½*d*. a ploughman a day. In food for 1 beadle and 4 ploughmen according to custom at Christmas and Easter 10*d*. In food for 5 workers and 1 maidservant at Trull and 7 workers at Bishops Hull according to the same custom 1*s*. ½*d*. In trimming and sawing timber for ploughs 1*s*. 1*d*. In making 4 new ploughs from the same timber 6*d*. In restoring and repairing (*emend' & reparand'*) the old ploughs many times during the year 6½*d*. In making yokes and wooden halters 6*d*. In stipend of 3 oxherds for the year and a fourth oxherd for three terms 9*s*. 4½*d*. In quittance of a ploughman and beadle for 60 Saturday ploughings 7*s*. 6*d*., at 1½*d*. a Saturday. In 10 oxen bought £6 7*s*. 1*d*., at 11*s*. 4*d*. each for 3, 13*s*. 4*d*. each for 6, and 14*s*. 1*d*. for 1. In shoeing 1 plough-horse harrowing at both sowings 5*d*. In mending the teeth of the harrow 3*d*. In 20 qrs of charcoal made for the ironwork of 4 ploughs for the year 2*s*. 6*d*., at 1½*d*. a qr. In 1 shovel bought and the same fitted with iron 3*d*. Total, £8 15*s*. 9½*d*.

Cost of wagons
In 60 large nails for repairing the wagons 10*d*. In fitting 2 wagons with axles 2*d*. In 22 clouts with nails for the wagons and dung-carts (*carm'*) 2*s*. 10*d*. In nails for frequently fastening clouts 6*d*. In grease for the wagons and dung-carts 6*d*. In repairing wagons in preparation for harvest-time 7½*d*. Total, 5*s*. 5½*d*.

Repair of buildings
Nothing in building repairs this year.

Cost of the harvest
In mowing 13 acres of meadow according to custom at Trull 6*d*. In mowing 50 acres of meadow according to custom at Bishops Hull 1*s*. In customary payment for the boon-reaping at Bishops Hull and Trull 1*s*. In mowing 7 acres of meadow in Horsweye and ox-pasture by piece-work 2*s*. 7½*d*., at 4½*d*. an acre. In covering 1 haycock 8*d*. Total, 5*s*. 9½*d*.

Cost of the mill
In 25 Welsh boards bought for covering the outer wheel 6*s*. In 200 nails for covering the same wheel 10*d*. In hooping the old outer wheel with iron before the new one was made 9*d*. In 1 band made to hoop the head of the driving-shaft with iron bought for the same 6*d*. In iron bought to lengthen the spindle and repair the collar of the same spindle with the stipend of the smith 7*d*. In renewing the bills with iron and steel bought for the same 4¾*d*. In 1 basket bought in which to measure corn 3½*d*. In another smaller basket to carry corn at the mill 1½*d*. In mending the roof of the mill-building 2*d*. In sharpening the bills for the year 6*d*. Total, 10*s*. 11¾*d*.

Total of all expenses, £9 18*s*. ¼*d*.

Delivered to Walter de Buddelye, reeve of Taunton castle, £33 7*s*. 3*d*.

Stock

Plough-horses: 2 remain from the previous year; 1 sold; 1 remains.
Oxen: 32 remain from the previous year; 10 bought. Total, 42. 3 in murrain before Christmas; 4 sold. Total, 7. 35 remain.
Moiety of one cow: the moiety of 1 cow from the heriot of John le Goud' is sold; none remain.
Recognizance wax: ½ lb from John Seman for annual recognizance; ½ lb from Richard Sagge for the same; ½ lb from William Holema*n* for the same; ½ lb from William de Frethehegh' for the same; ½ lb from Nicholas Cole for the same; ½ lb from Adam Montekyn for the same; ½ lb from Richard le Saghyar' for the same; ½ lb from John Fab*er* of Bishops Hull for the same; nothing from Adam Wade because he is dead; ½ lb from Robert Hokkeday for the same; ½ lb from William le Char' for the same; ½ lb from John Scardelayn for the same; ½ lb from Peter le Hop*ere* for the same; ½ lb from Roger le Baller' for the same. Total, 6½ lb, which were sold as made clear within; none remains.
Charcoal: 20 qrs made this year which were used in making and repairing the ironwork of 4 ploughs for the year; none remains.

Holway

The account of Richard Wodekot, reeve of this place.

Rents
The same renders account for £63 4*s*. 3*d*. for rents of assize at Christmas, Easter (22 April), the Nativity of the blessed John the Baptist (24 June), and Michaelmas (29 September), in equal portions. Total, £63 4*s*. 3*d*.

Quittances
In quittance of 4 ploughmen for the year 5*s*., or 1*s*. 3*d*. each; 9 workers working three days a week for 3 terms of the year and everyday at harvest-time except Saturday 11*s*. 3*d*., or 1*s*. 3*d*. each; 1 smith for the year 1*s*. 3*d*.; 1 beadle for the year 6*d*.; 12 cottars working 2 days a week for three terms of the year and three days a week at harvest-time 3*s*., or 3*d*. each. Total, £1 1*s*.

Defaults of rent
In default of the land of Swyt drawn into demesne 1*s*.; the land of Robert de Legh' 8*s*. 6*d*.; the land of Pyxton' given to Baldwin son of Gerard in exchange for Corfe, Nailsbourne and Fulford by Bishop Richard £2 5*s*.; the land of Jordan de Fidekot' granted by Bishop Godfrey 4*s*. 11*d*.; the land of Bridgwater stolen (*ablate*) by William le Bru*ere* in the time of Bishop Godfrey 3*s*. Total, £3 2*s*. 5*d*.

Total of quittances and defaults of rent, £4 3*s*. 5*d*.

Total of rents remaining, £59 10*d*.

Issues of the manor
The same renders account for £1 19*s*. 8½*d*. from pannage of pigs this year; £1 2*s*. 7*d*. from hundredpenny; 5*s*. 6*d*. from the pasturage of Hayedemed sold after mowing in

winter; 13*s*. 4*d*. from the pasturage of M*er*swllelake and Smetheh*a*m sold in winter; 2*s*. from the pasturage of Wydemed sold after mowing in winter; 5*s*. from the pasturage of Pytmed sold in winter; 8*s*. from the pasturage of Baldewynesmed sold in winter; 8*s*. from the pasturage in Suthtrademor sold after mowing in winter; 19*s*. 5¼*d*. from Leffon this year; 13*s*. 4*d*. from unenclosed pasturage sold during the year; nothing from the pasturage of la M*er*sch' this year for a want of buyers; 6*s*. from the pasturage of la Flor sold; 2*s*. 6*d*. from the pasturage of Blaked' sold in winter and summer; 4*s*. from the pasturage of la Dych' beside la Wynyerd' and other parcels of pasture beside the east side of the fishpond sold in summer; nothing from the pasturage of Langebroc this year for a want of buyers; 6*s*. from the pasturage of Tu*n*feld' sold in winter; nothing from the pasturage of la Flordych and other pasturage around the same field this year for a want of buyers; 6*s*. 8*d*. from the pasturage of la Ryded' sold in winter; nothing from the pasturage of Westfurl', Estfulelo*n*d, Dustrel' and the fields beside the fishpond this year because they were sown with wheat; 2*s*. 6*d*. from the pasturage of the way between Taunton and Shoreditch sold in summer; 1*s*. 8*d*. from the pasturage of a certain plot between the sluice and the pasturage which the bishop granted to the Prior of Taunton sold in winter and summer; 3*d*. from the pasturage of the sheepcote of Holway sold; 6*s*. from the fishery of Tappyngewer', and not more because the Abbot of Glastonbury encroached on the waters of the fishery by ditches so that the fishery was almost destroyed, on account of which the old rent was not able to be paid; 7½*d*. from a certain messuage, part of the same fishery; £4 9*s*. 6*d*. from 6 old oxen sold, at 13*s*. 6*d*. for one, 14*s*. 6*d*. each for 4, and 18*s*. for 1; 4*s*. 6*d*. from 1 feeble cow from the heriot of Walter Cok sold before breeding; £3 5*s*. 6*d*. from hay sold; 6*s*. from bark and loppings sold; nothing from wood blown down by the wind this year; £6 6½*d*. from portions of labour services sold this year; 3*s*. from 6 lb of wax from recognizances sold, at 6*d*. a lb; 7*d*. from 1 ploughshare from a recognizance sold; 17*s*. 6*d*. from woodway; 3*d*. from John Tredegold' for annual recognizance; 6*s*. from mast sold in Haywod'; 3[*s*.] from mast sold in Cnollwod'; 2*s*. from mast sold in H*a*mwod'; 1*s*. 6*d*. from 1 poplar sold at Shyreford; 6*d*. from the heriot of German le Hop*er*e because he did not have 1 beast; 6*d*. from the h[eriot] of Richard Moriȝ because he did not have 1 beast; 6*d*. from the heriot of William Fleke because he did not have 1 beast; 6*d*. from the heriot of Walter le Bule because he did not have 1 beast; 6*d*. from the heriot of Roger Upkote because he did not have 1 beast. Total, £24 15*s*. 5¾*d*.

m.3d

Entry and marriage fines

The same renders account for 6*s*. 8*d*. from Alice, who was wife of Walter le Cok, to retain 1 messuage and 6 acres of land which belonged to the aforesaid Walter her husband; 6*s*. 8*d*. from John Elyot to have the aforesaid Alice with her land; 3*s*. from Agnes Cutebold to have 1 acre of land in Burnȝyvel' by surrender of Nicholas Cutebold; £2 10*s*. from Robert de Norton' to have 1 messuage and 10 acres of land which belonged to John de Nort*on* his father; £2 6*s*. 8*d*. from William, son of Randolph de Hayd', to have 1 messuage and 10 acres of land which belonged to the aforesaid Randolph; 13*s*. 4*d*. from Edmund P*arcarius* to have 1 house and 3 acres of land by surrender of German le Hop*er*e; 3*s*. from Alice, who was wife of Walter le Bule, to retain 1 messuage and 5 acres of land which belonged to the aforesaid Walter her husband; £5 from William, son of Adam atte More, to have 1 messuage and 1 virgate of land in Stoke St Mary by surrender of Richard Moriȝ; £1 from William, son of Edmund P*arcarius*, to have 1 messuage and 1 ferling of land by resignation of

William Fleke; 6*s*. 8*d*. from Peter Moriȝ for marrying Alice his daughter within; 2*s*. from Henry de Cutlesheye for marrying Agnes his sister within; £2 from Christina, who was wife of William Moriȝ, to retain 1 messuage and ½ virgate of land which belonged to the aforesaid William her husband; 10*s*. from Walter le Bolt to have 3 acres of land in Burnȝyveley by surrender of Roger de Upkote; £10 from John Lambard to have 1 messuage and 1 virgate of land in Brockton' by surrender of Christina his mother; £1 from John le Archer to have 1 acre of meadow which he recovered from Richard Gone; 4*s*. from Edith, relict of Walter Willi', for marrying Alice her daughter within; 6*s*. 8*d*. from William atte Mor' for marrying Agnes his daughter outside; £2 from the communal fine on Hockday (*hockedayswyte*); £5 from William, son of William Russel, as the lord allowed him to hold 1 messuage five acres of land and 1 acre of meadow which belonged to Emma his grandmother, saving whatever rights. Total, £33 18*s*. 8*d*.

Perquisites

The same renders account for 2*s*. from Nicholas atte Slad' for trespass of corn at harvest-time; 1*s*. 10*d*. from a certain stranger for trespass of pasture; 6*d*. from William atte More for the same; 11*d*. from Thomas Trese and his neighbours for the same; 6*d*. from Stephen de Shyreford for an inadequate count against John de Chelewardwod'; 6*d*. from Robert Mude and 2 of his neighbours for trespass of pasture; 6*d*. from Ralph Dauwe for bad ploughing; 3*d*. from William atte Poul' for unjustly withholding a debt; 6*d*. from Gilbert de Helfnaked' for keeping 2 of his pigs in the castle for 4 days; 2*s*. from Henry de H*a*mme for transgression against the lord; 3*d*. from Nicholas Cade for default; 6*d*. from Robert Purs and Elias de Halghewll' for trespass of pasture; 6*d*. from Thomas le Leth' for the same; 3*d*. from Richard Wodekoc for the same; 2*s*. from Adam de Stok' and John Gon' of Henlade for transgression against the lord; 3*d*. from John Wally*n*g for trespass of corn; 6*d*. from Peter Moriȝ for false complaint; 1*s*. from the same Peter for transgression against his neighbour; 3*d*. from Richard Moriȝ for unjustly withholding a debt; 3*d*. from John Du*n*hol for the same; 3*d*. from Richard Gauty*n*g for contempt; 3*d*. from Roger de Shordyhc for trespass of pasture; 3*d*. from John Frenhs for the same; 1*s*. 2*d*. from Adam Jude and his neighbours for transgression against the lord; 3*d*. from Robert Hugȝe for searching the rolls; 1*s*. from John Pare for performing his office less well; 1*s*. 3*d*. from Walter Kynel' and 3 of his neighbours for bad ploughing; 6*d*. from Hugh atte Poul' for contempt; 13*s*. 4*d*. from Thomas de Shyreford for negligence whilst he was reeve; 6*d*. from Richard Gauty*n*g for contempt; 1*s*. 4*d*. from Peter Moriȝ and his neighbours for inadequate harrowing; 1*s*. 3*d*. from Thomas de Mulesg*ro*ve and his neighbours for the same; 3*d*. from Thomas le Leth' for a want of ploughing; £1 6*s*. 8*d*. from Hugh de Poul' because he was convicted of a certain false tally made against John le Michele; £1 from John Gone of Henlade for manifest contempt against the lord; 2*s*. from the tithing of Holway for concealment; 1*s*. from Ralph Dauwe for arraigning a certain neighbour; 1*s*. from Adam Jordayn the younger for transgression against his father; 2*s*. for false complaint against his tithing; 13*s*. 4*d*. from Thomas de Shireford because he withheld the lord's silver in his possession when he was reeve after being warned; 3*d*. from Thomas Prut for unjustly withholding a debt; 6*d*. from Hugh de Hayd' for licence to carry his dung beyond the lord's land; 6*d*. from John de Chelewardeswod' for licence to come to an agreement with John Rochel; 2*s*. from John Gone of Henlade and Richard his brother for transgression against the lord; 2*s*. from William atte Mor' for contempt; 3*d*. from Richard Wodekot for trespass of pasture; 2*s*. from Richard le Kyngȝ of West

Bagborough for trespass of corn; 3*s*. 4*d*. from William atte Mor' for contempt; 2*s*. from Adam de Stoke for transgression against Juliana le Hop*ere*; 6*d*. from William Godday for the same; 6*d*. from Edmund La*n*brigȝ for trespass of corn; 6*d*. from John G*r*ey for transgression against his neighbour; 1*s*. from Henry Hugh' for transgression against the lord; 6*d*. from Hugh atte Poul' for a bad attachment; 6*d*. from John Dun for transgression against the lord; 6*d*. from John Gone of Henlade for transgression against his neighbour; 2*s*. from Adam de Rihsh*a*m to have an inquest; 1*s*. from the tithing and the tithing outside the east gate for contempt; 6*d*. from Robert de Mulesg*ro*ve and Walter H*ab*uoyt for mowing the meadow badly; 6*d*. from William Gone for transgression against his neighbour; 3*d*. from William le Wop for contempt; 3*d*. from the hayward of Holway for trespass of pasture; 4*d*. from William Sharp and Benedict Pye for the same; 6*d*. from Walter Kenele and Walter H*ab*uoht for default; 3*d*. from John le Michele and Robert Purs for weeding corn badly; 2*d*. from Thomas Trese for trespass of pasture; 1*s*. from 4 of the lord's oxherds of Holway for trespass of corn; 3*d*. from William le Hurt for transgression against his neighbour; 3*s*. 6*d*. from William atte Mor' and 6 of his neighbours because they did not come to an inquest; 3*d*. from Gilbert atte Byken' for transgression against the lord; 3*d*. from Richard Gauty*ng* for gathering corn badly at harvest-time; 3*d*. from Simon le Smyht of Henlade for the same; 6*d*. from Joan de Insul*a* for trespass of pasture; 6*d*. from Nicholas Curenoghel for trespass of corn; 1*s*. from Richard Haward' of Holway and William le Palm*ere* for keeping the corn badly at harvest-time; 6*d*. from Richard Wodekoc and Richard, beadle, for negligence at harvest-time; 6*d*. from the same Richard and William, beadle of Wudelo*nd*, for transgression against the lord; 6*d*. from Thomas de Shireford for trespass of corn; 6*d*. from Henry de Cutlesheye for licence to come to an agreement; 6*d*. from Richard de Buddelye for transgression against his neighbour; 6*d*. from Christina atte Castele and Christina Moriȝ for reaping corn badly; 6*d*. from John Wally*ng* to have an inquest; 6*s*. 8*d*. from William Luffey for bad purchasing of corn at harvest-time; 6*d*. from Thomas le Kyngȝ because he defaulted at law; 3*d*. from Peter le Clut*ere* for transgression against his neighbour; 2*d*. from Walter Bryce for trespass of corn; 6*d*. from Gilbert de Helfnaked' and Elias Cole for transgression against the lord; 8*d*. from Christina Brice and 3 of her neighbours for insufficient workers sent to stack corn in the castle; 3*d*. from Thomas Trese for trespass of corn; 6*d*. from Walter le Man for the same; 3*d*. from Thomas Trese for breaking the lord's pound (*pundbruch'*); 6*d*. from Henry de Cutlesheye and Gorwyd' his brother for unjustly withholding a debt; 6*s*. 8*d*. from Henry Hugh' for various transgressions against the lord; 2*s*. from Roger de Halghewll' for levying his debt; 2*s*. from the tithing of Holway for concealing landless men outside the tithing; 2*s*. from the tithing of Ruishton for the same; 6*d*. from Adam Jude because he built a certain wall too near the king's highway; 6*d*. from William le Ryde for building a dunghill on the king's highway; 6*d*. from Justina Fr*a*nceys for the same; 3*s*. from the tithing of Henlade for concealing landless men outside the tithing; 1*s*. from the same tithing for concealing the raising of the hue; 2*s*. from the tithing of Stoke St Mary for concealing landless men outside the tithing; 6*d*. from Stephen de Shireford' for unjustly raising the hue; 6*d*. from Richard, beadle, because he neglected to perform his office; 4*d*. from the same Richard and William, beadles, because they performed their offices less well in the presence of the steward; 1*s*. from Gilbert Drin for licence to withdraw from the tithing; £2 10*s*. 9*d*. from those who brewed ale this year for breaking the assize of ale; 8*s*. 5*d*. from other small perquisites. Total, £11 7*s*. 5*d*.

Total of both, £45 6*s*. 1*d*.

Total of all receipts, £129 2*s.* 4¾*d.*

Cost of ploughs
In iron and steel for making and repairing the ironwork of 4 ploughs for the year 15*s.* 5*d.* In 4 ploughshares bought 2*s.* 5*d.* In boon-works of 37½ ploughmen ploughing 2 full days in winter and as many full days in Lent 6*s.* 3*d.*, at ½*d.* a ploughman a day. In food for one beadle, 1 smith and 4 ploughmen according to custom at Christmas and Easter 1*s.*, or 2*d.* each. In food for 23 workers according to the same custom 1*s.* 11*d.*, or 1*d.* each. In quittance of 4 ploughmen for 12 Saturday ploughings 6*s.*, at 1½*d.* a ploughman a Saturday. In stipend of 4 oxherds for the year 10*s.* In 20 qrs of charcoal for making and repairing the ironwork of 4 ploughs for the year 2*s.* 6*d.*, at 1½*d.* a qr. In sawing timber for ploughs 1*s.* In shoeing 1 plough-horse harrowing at both sowings 3*d.* In 5 oxen bought £3 10*s.* 4*d.*, at 13*s.* 4*d.* for 1, 14*s.* each for 2, and 14*s.* 6*d.* each for the other two. In quittance of the Prior of Montacute for the pasturage of Crih 2*s.* 6*d.* Total, £5 19*s.* 7*d.*

Cost of wagons
In fitting the wagons and dung-carts (*carm'*) with axles 5*d.* In 16 clouts with nails bought 2*s.* 2½*d.* In grease for the wagons and dung-carts 2½*d.* In repairing wagons in preparation for harvest-time with timber sawn for this 3½*d.* Total, 3*s.* 1½*d.*

Repair of buildings
In stipend of 1 carpenter repairing the wall between the wagon-shed and charcoal-house 4*d.* In laths bought for covering part of the same building 9*d.* In 250 nails for laths for the same building 2½*d.* In roofing nearly the whole of the same building 10*d.* In 4 boards bought for making one door to the byre 4*d.* In nails for the same door 1¾*d.* In two dung-forks fitted with iron 6*d.* Total, 3*s.* 1¼*d.*

Cost of the harvest
In customary payment for the mowing of 180 acres of meadow 1*s.* 6*d.* In customary payment for the mowing of the meadow which belonged to Robert le Leth' 1*s.* 6*d.* In mowing the meadow which belonged to Robert de Totton' 5*d.* In customary payment for the boon-reaping 2*s.* 8*d.* In mowing 5½ acres of ox-pasture by piece-work and tossing (*levand'*) the said hay 3*s.* 8*d.* In covering 1 haycock 6*d.* Total, 10*s.* 3*d.*

Total of all expenses, £6 16*s.* ¾*d.*

Delivered to Walter de Buddelye, reeve of Taunton castle, £122 6*s.* 4*d.*

Stock

Plough-horses: 1 remains from the previous year; it remains.
Oxen: 38 remain from the previous year; 1 from the heriot of John de Norton'; 1 from the heriot of William Moriȝ; 5 bought; 1 from the heriot of Christina de Brokton'. Total, 46. 6 sold; 40 remain.
Cows: one from the heriot of Walter le Cok is sold; none remain.
Yearlings: one male from the heriot of Ralph de Hayd'; it remains.
Recognizance wax: 1 lb from Adam le Michele; ½ lb from Gilbert Capel; ½ lb from Roger Her*ing*; ½ lb from Ralph le Tayllur; nothing from Richard, son of Walter de Buddelye, because he holds land of the lord and gives hundredpenny; ½ lb from Adam Tette; ½ lb from Nicholas Godman; ½ lb from Gilbert Gone; ½ lb from

Richard Scoyt; ½ lb from Richard Tredegold; 1 lb from Walter, son of Walter Wille, for the first time this year. Total, 6 lb, which were sold as made clear within; none remains.

Charcoal: 20 qrs made this year which were used in making and repairing the ironwork of 4 ploughs for the year; none remains.

Poundisford

Rents

The same renders account for £38 13*s*. 3¼*d*. for rents of assize at Christmas, Easter (22 April), the Nativity of the blessed John the Baptist (24 June), and Michaelmas (29 September), in equal portions. Total, £38 13*s*. 3¼*d*.

Quittances

In quittance of one ploughman at Corfe for the year and six workers working 2 days a week for three terms of the year and everyday at harvest-time except Saturday 14*s*., or 2*s*. each; 1 ploughman and 1 worker working for ½ year as above 2*s*.; 1 worker working 1 day a week for 3 terms of the year and two days a week at harvest-time 1*s*.; 2 ploughmen, 1 beadle and 4 workers at Poundisford working 2 days a week for 3 terms of the year and everyday at harvest-time except Saturday 8*s*. 9*d*., or 1*s*. 3*d*. each; 3 cottars working 1 day a week for 3 terms of the year and 3 days a week at harvest-time 1*s*. 10½*d*., or 7½*d*. each; 1 cottar working 1 day a week for 3 terms of the year and two days a week at harvest-time 3¾*d*. Total, £1 7*s*. 11¼*d*.

Defaults of rent

In default of the land drawn into the park, that is, 104 acres and one perch, which the Prior of Taunton, Adam Sydewyn', Richard Cadel, Aeln*er*ius, Richard le Wastur, Ingolf, Walter Totty*ng*, German Mol*endinarius*, Hugh de Clyve, William Faber, William Cnap, Richard Gore, Richard Suvenoke, William Cutty*ng*, Cng*er*mins de Fuleford, Osbert de Amnyngeford, Roger Cherd', Robert Dun, Richard Brice, Roger Spyry*ng*, William Fre*n*sh', Philip Spyry*ng*, Roger Cherd, Stephen de Canesg*ro*ve, Robert Fab*er*, Christina, widow of Roger de Annyngeford, and Adam de Annyngeford held, 15*s*. 9½*d*.; 2 cottages (*cotell'*) similarly drawn into the park 2*s*. 6*d*.; the land of Adam de Dudeleston', that is, 9 acres, similarly drawn into demesne 1*s*. Total of defaults of rent, 19*s*. 3½*d*.

Total of quittances and defaults of rent, £2 7*s*. 2¾*d*.[1]

Total of rents remaining, £36 6*s*. ½*d*.

m.4

Issues of the manor

The same renders account for £1 16*s*. 9½*d*. from pannage of pigs this year; £1 3*s*. 10*d*. from hundredpenny; 12*s*. from the pasturage of Holem*ere* and Rededon' sold in winter and summer; nothing from the pasturage of Dyhfulrlo*ng*, Esterdon' and Westeredon' this year because they were sown with wheat; 3*s*. from the pasturage of Corfmor sold in winter; nothing from the pasturage of Lakemed this year because it was pastured with the lord's livestock; 1*s*. 6*d*. from the pasturage of Fenalre and

1 MS 'ij d. ob. {q.}'.

Fenhurst sold in winter; £3 1*s*. from 5 oxen sold, at 12*s*. 3*d*. each for 4, and 12*s*. for one; £3 18*s*. from 13 cows sold before breeding, at 6*s*. each; 2*s*. 6*d*. from the moiety of 1 cow from the heriot of Henry Abel sold; 4*s*. from 1 steer sold; £1 2*s*. from 22 suckling calves sold, at 1*s*. each; £11 9*s*. from 69 pigs sold, at 2*s*. each for 15, 2*s*. 6*d*. each for 10, 3*s*. 6*d*. each for 4, and 4*s*. each for 40; 4*s*. 9*d*. from the hides sold of two oxen dead from murrain soon after Christmas; 3*s*. 6*d*. from the hide and flesh sold of 1 cow dead from murrain before breeding; 1*s*. from the hide sold of 1 cow dead from murrain before breeding; 1*s*. 5*d*. from the hide sold of 1 cow dead from murrain after breeding; 1*s*. 11*d*. from the hides sold of 2 steers dead from murrain; 1*s*. 1*d*. from the hide sold of 1 ox dead from murrain; nothing from bark and loppings this year; 1*s*. 2*d*. from the residue of Peter's pence at Corfe; £6 4*s*. 5½*d*. from portions of labour services sold this year; 1*s*. 9*d*. from 3½ lb of wax from recognizances sold, at 6*d*. a lb; nothing from cheese and butter this year because the dairy is at Nailsbourne; 12*s*. 6*d*. from woodway; 6*d*. from the heriot of Edith la Webbe because she did not have 1 beast; 6*s*. from the moiety of 1 ox sold. Total, £31 13*s*. 8*d*.

Sale of corn

The same renders account for £15 16*s*. 3½*d*. from 46½ qrs of wheat sold, at 6*s*. 8*d*. a qr for 8 qrs 6 bus., and 6*s*. 10*d*. a qr for 37 qrs 6 bus. sold to customary tenants; £13 9*s*. 6*d*. from 154 qrs of oats sold to customary tenants, at 1*s*. 9*d*. a qr. Total, £29 5*s*. 9½*d*.

Entry and marriage fines

The same renders account for £1 13*s*. 4*d*. from John Goddey to have Gunilda attare Balke with her land; 6*s*. 8*d*. from Gunilda, who was wife of Henry Abel, to retain 1 messuage and 5 acres of land which belonged to the aforesaid Henry her husband; 6*s*. 8*d*. from John, son of Walter de Fuleford, to have 1 house which belonged to Henry de Fuleford in South Trendle; £1 6*s*. 8*d*. from Walter de Fuleford' to have 5 acres of land and 1 plot containing about 3 perches which belonged to the aforesaid Henry; 6*s*. 8*d*. from Walter Bach' to have ½ acre of meadow which belonged to Henry de Fuleford'; 1*s*.[1] from Edmund P*arcarius* to have the moiety of 1 house which belonged to Adam le Whytt*ere* in Poundisford; 4*s*. from Matilda, who was wife of Stephen le Hop*ere*, to retain 1 messuage and 7 acres of land which belonged to the aforesaid Stephen her husband; £6 from Roger Aylwyn' to have 1 messuage and ½ virgate by surrender of Alice his mother; 2*s*. from Hugh Dun to have one house in South Trendle by surrender of Geoffrey Pope; £1 10*s*. from Stephen le Kyng to have 1 messuage and 1 ferling of land by surrender of Lucy his mother; 3*s*. from Richard de Canesg*ro*ve to have Agnes, who was wife of William Roberd, with her land; 4*s*. from John Sweyt to have 1 house in Canesg*ro*ve; 5*s*. from Hugh de Annyngeford to have 1 house in Annyngeford by surrender of William de Annyngeford; 6*s*. 8*d*. from Walter de Suvenok' for marrying Matilda his daughter outside; 2*s*. from Christina de Suvenok for marrying Christina her daughter within; 10*s*. from William Gulye to have the moiety of a certain house in South Trendle which came into the lord's hands for want of an heir; 1*s*. from John Gor' to have 1 day-work (*daena*) of land by surrender of John Hataȝ; 5*s*. from Walter de Suvenok to have 5 acres of land by surrender of John le Archer; 13*s*. 4*d*. from John Weu for marrying Agnes his daughter outside; 2*s*. from Gunilda de Suetehegh' for marrying Edith her daughter within; 2*s*. from Walter le White for marrying Christina his daughter within; 2*s*. from Juliana, daughter of John le Suytht of Leigh, to have 1 day-work of land by surrender

1 MS 'Et de x. xij d.'.

of William le Suyht; 5*s*. from the communal fine on Hockday (*hockedayeswyte*) at Corfe; £2 from the same at Poundisford. Total, £16 18*s*.

Perquisites

The same renders account for 6*d*. from John de Orchard for trespass of pasture; 6*d*. from William Coffyn for the same; 8*d*. from Margery de Orchard for the same; 1*s*. from John de Treyburth' for the same; 1*s*. from Richard Polruel for the same; 6*d*. from John Godard for trespass of wood; 6*d*. from John Amnuret because he did not produce in court the individual whom he had pledged; 3*d*. from John de Swetehegh' for false complaint; 1*s*. from Simon de Ralegh' for licence to come to an agreement; 3*d*. from William de Hughelegh' because he did not come to an inquest; 6*d*. from William Hardgrey for trespass of pasture; 3*d*. from John de Chilkepath' for contempt; 6*d*. from Henry le Sweyn for trespass of wood; 3*d*. from Roger atte Wuderne for unjustly withholding a debt; 6*d*. from Richard de Apsweye for trespass of wood; 6*d*. from Christina atte Heggy*n*ge for the same; 6*d*. from Richard Mouf for the same; 2*s*. from Henry Swey*n* and 3 of his neighbours for the same; 1*s*. from Adam le Mounk for the same; 3*d*. from John Goddey for contempt; 3*d*. from John Puke for trespass of corn; 1*s*. from the tithing of Leigh for an inadequate presentment; 3*d*. from Roger Aylwyn' for unjustly withholding a debt; 6*d*. from Richard, the lord's swineherd, for keeping the pigs badly; 5*s*. from Nicholas Aylm' and 9 of his neighbours for trespass of wood; 1*s*. 6*d*. from Thomas Aylm' for attachment of his goats in Pykeryge; 1*s*. from Gilbert le Mounk for the same; 1*s*. from William Fryn for the same; 1*s*. from Walter de Foxg*ro*ve for the same; 3*d*. from Bricell' de Blaked' for attachment of his goats in Abbecu*m*b'; 3*d*. from William Godard for licence to come to an agreement; 1*s*. from the reeve of Poundisford because he often allowed the oxherds to be idle after dinner; 2*d*. from Walter Bagh' and Walter Sprut for transgression against their neighbour; 2*s*. from John Goddey for trespass of corn; 6*d*. from Roger Gilly*n*g for the same; 3*d*. from Walter le Whyte because he did not come to carry hay; 6*d*. from the reeve and beadle for their negligence; 1*s*. from Walter de Fuleford and William Gulye for transgression against their neighbour; 6*d*. from the lord's oxherds for their negligence; 2*s*. from the tithing of Dudeleston' for a bad presentment; 1*s*. from the same tithing for concealing landless men outside the tithing; 1*s*. from the tithing of South Trendle for the same; 1*s*. from the tithing of South Fulford for the same; 2*d*. from Walter Hatherich, beadle of Corfe, because he performed his office less well in the presence of the steward; 17*s*. from those who brewed ale this year for breaking the assize of ale. Total, £2 13*s*. 4*d*.

Total of both, £19 11*s*. 4*d*.

Total of all receipts, £116 16*s*. 10*d*.

Cost of ploughs

In iron and steel for making and repairing the ironwork of 4 ploughs for the year 15*s*. 11*d*. In stipend of the smith making and repairing the said ironwork for the year 3*s*. 10*d*. In 4 ploughshares bought 2*s*. 4*d*. In boon-works of 42 ploughmen ploughing 2 full days in winter and as many full days in Lent at Corfe and Poundisford 7*s*., at ½*d*. a ploughman a day. In trimming and sawing timber for ploughs, yokes and wooden halters 1*s*. 6½*d*. In making 4 new ploughs 6*d*. In repairing the old ploughs many times during the year 1*s*. 2*d*. In making yokes and wooden halters 5*d*. In food for two beadles and 4 ploughmen according to custom at Christmas and Easter 1*s*. In food for 8 workers according to the same custom 8*d*. In stipend of 4 oxherds and 1 swineherd for the year 12*s*. 6*d*., or 2*s*. 6*d*. each. In stipend of 1 park-keeper and hayward for the year 6*s*. 8*d*. In quittance of the ploughmen of Corfe for 10 Saturday ploughings 1*s*. 3*d*., at 1½*d*. a Saturday. In quittance of the ploughmen and beadle of Poundisford for 32 Saturday ploughings 4*s*., at 1½*d*. a Saturday. In 21 qrs of charcoal made for making and repairing the ironwork of 4 ploughs for the year 2*s*. 7½*d*. In shoeing 1 plough-horse harrowing at two sowings 5*d*. In 37 qrs 6 bus. of wheat bought for forage from customary tenants 6*s*. 3½*d*., at 2*d*. a qr of forage. In 64 qrs of oats bought for forage from the same customary tenants 5*s*. 3½*d*., at 1*d*. a qr of forage. Total, £3 13*s*. 5½*d*.

Purchase of corn
In 19 qrs 6½ bus. of maslin bought £3 16*s*. 7*d*., at 3*s*. 4*d*. a qr for 4 qrs, and 4*s*. a qr for 15 qrs 6½ bus. In 75 qrs of oats bought from customary tenants according to custom £5 12*s*. 6*d*., at 1*s*. 6*d*. a qr. Total, £9 9*s*. 1*d*.

Cost of wagons
In 1 pair of wheels 4*s*. 11*d*. In fitting 1 new binding (*ligatura*) to the same wheels 8*s*. ¼*d*. In stipend of the smith fitting the aforesaid wheels with the aforesaid binding 6*d*. In 60 large nails for mending the old wagons 10*d*. In fitting the wagons and dung-carts (*carm'*) with axles 4*d*. In 20 clouts with nails bought 2*s*. 8*d*. In grease for the wagons and dung-carts 4*d*. In trimming and sawing timber for wagons and axles 6*d*. In making one new pair of cart-shafts and repairing wagons in preparation for harvest-time 6*d*. In 1 hemp rope bought 1*s*. Total, 19*s*. 7¼*d*.

Purchase of stock
In 3 cows bought before breeding £1 6*s*. 3*d*., at 8*s*. 9*d*. each. In two cows bought after breeding 16*s*. 9*d*., at 8*s*. for one, and 8*s*. 9*d*. for the other. Total, £2 3*s*.

Repair of buildings with small expenses
In re-roofing the larger barn in places 10*d*. In 1 lock bought for the door of the same barn 4*d*. In one three-pronged dung-fork fitted with iron 3*d*. In making well (*sanand'*) 32 female piglets 10*d*. In clearing dung from the curia to the fields 2*s*. 10*d*. In digging 12 perches of ditches beside la Westered' 9*d*., at ¾*d*. a perch. In digging 20 perches of ditches there 1*s*. 8*d*. Total, 7*s*. 6*d*.

Threshing of corn
In threshing 20 qrs 6 bus. of wheat by piece-work 4*s*. 4*d*., at 2½*d*. a heaped quarter. Total, 4*s*. 4*d*.

Cost of mills
In repairing the collar of the spindle of the mill of Pitminster with iron bought for the same 6½*d*. In 1 iron hoop for putting in the hole of the millstone lying in the same mill 4½*d*. In 2 baskets bought in which to measure corn at both mills 4*d*. In toll of one sester of ale (*uno tolsester*) at the mill of Trull 1*d*. In iron and steel for renewing the bills of both mills with the stipend of the smith 1*s*. 1*d*. In sharpening the same bills for the year 6*d*. Total, 2*s*. 11*d*.

{Henceforth answer for capons}

Cost of the harvest
In customary payment for the mowing of 17 acres of meadow at Corfe 6*d*. In mowing 1 acre of meadow which belonged to the Prior of Taunton there 5*d*. In customary payment for the mowing of 13 acres of meadow at Poundisford 6*d*. In customary payment for the boon-reaping at Corfe 5*d*. In customary payment for the boon-reaping at Poundisford 9*d*. In covering one haycock 6*d*. Total, 3*s*. 1*d*.

Total of all expenses, £17 2*s*. 11¾*d*.

Cash deliveries
Delivered to Walter de Buddelye, reeve of Taunton, £99 13*s*. 10¼*d*.

Issues of the grange

Wheat
{yield: two-and-a-half-fold less 5½ bus.}
The same renders account for 83 qrs ½ bus. from the whole issue of wheat by struck measure.
Sown over 111½ acres at Poundisford and Corfe, 26 qrs 2 bus.; that is, 2 bus. an acre, less 1 qr 5 bus. in all. Also sown at Poundisford by the villeins according to custom, 26½ acres.[1] Delivered to the park-keeper for the year, 4 qrs 2½ bus., taking a quarter every 12 weeks. Mixed below for the liveries of the manorial servants, 6 qrs. Sold, 46½ qrs. Total, 83 qrs ½ bus. It balances.

Oats
{yield: two-fold plus 6 qrs 6 bus.}
The same renders account for 127 qrs 6 bus. from the whole issue of oats by struck measure; 75 qrs bought. Total, 202 qrs 6 bus.
Sown over 119½ acres at Poundisford and Corfe, 48 qrs 6 bus.; that is, 4 bus. an acre, less 11 qrs in all. Also sown at Poundisford by the villeins according to custom, 26½ acres.[2] Sold, 154 qrs. Total, 202 qrs 6 bus. It balances.

Proof of liveries
The same renders account for 6 qrs received above from wheat; 19 qrs 6½ bus. bought. Total, 25 qrs 6½ bus.
Delivered to 4 oxherds and one swineherd for the year, 21 qrs 4½ bus., taking a quarter every 12 weeks. Delivered to one cowherd for 15 weeks, 1 qr 2 bus., taking a quarter every 12 weeks. In customary payment for the boon-reaping at Poundisford and Corfe, 3 qrs. Total, 25 qrs 6½ bus. It balances.

Stock

Plough-horses: 1 female remains from the previous year; it remains.
Colts: 1 one-year-old female remains from the previous year's offspring; it remains. 1 male from the offspring of the said plough-horse this year; it remains.
Oxen: 44 remain from the previous year; 3 added from steers; 1 from the heriot of Alice, who was wife of Alwyn de Esttrete; the moiety of 1 from the heriot of Lucy le Kyng. Total, 48 and a moiety. 2 in murrain; 5 and a moiety sold; 41 remain.
Cows: 47 remain from the previous year; 3 added from steers; 1 from the reeve of Nailsbourne before breeding; 1 from strays before breeding; 3 bought before

1 MS 'It*em* ⟨se*m*inant*ur*⟩ ⌈de se*m*i*ne* villan*orum*⌉ ap*u*d Pundeford de cons*uetudine* vill*anorum*'.

2 MS 'It*em* se*m*inant*ur* ap*u*d Pund*eford* de cons*uetudine* ⌈de se*m*i*ne*⌉ villano*rum*'.

breeding; 1 from the reeve of Staplegrove before breeding; 1 from the heriot of Stephen le Hop*ere* after breeding; 2 bought after breeding; the moiety of 1 from the heriot of Henry Abel. Total, 59 and a moiety. 2 in murrain before breeding, 1 after breeding; 13 before breeding and a moiety sold. Total, 16 and a moiety. 43 remain.
Bulls: 3 remain from the previous year; they remain.
Steers: 10 remain from the previous year's bullocks; 3 in murrain; 1 sold; 3 added to oxen, 3 to cows; none remain.
Bullocks: 16 remain from the previous year's yearlings; 16 remain.
Yearlings: 8 remain from the previous year's calves; 1 in murrain; 7 remain.
Calves: 35 produced by the said cows this year, and not more because 6 were sterile. 3 in tithe; 22 sold. Total, 25. 10 remain.
Wethers: 1 from the heriot of Henry de Fuleford which is delivered to the reeve of Nailsbourne before shearing; none remain.
Pigs: 82 remain from the previous year; 40 added from hoggets. Total, 122. 69 sold; 53 remain, 3 of them old sows.
[Hoggets]: 46 remain from the previous year's piglets; 6 in murrain; 40 added to pigs; none remain.
[Piglets]: 18 farrowed before Christmas; 22 farrowed in Lent; 18 farrowed in autumn. Total, 58. 5 in murrain; 5 in tithe. Total, 10. 48 remain.
[Hides]: 2 from oxen, 3 from cows, 3 from steers, and 1 from a yearling, dead from murrain. Total, 9. 8 sold as made clear within; 1 from a yearling of no value in repair of 1 cart saddle; none remain.
[Recognizance wax]: ½ lb from Robert Tudema*n*; ½ lb from Richard, son of Walter de la Quarere; 1 lb from Richard Smorenoghel; ½ lb from Walter son of Clarice; ½ lb from William Baco*n*; ½ lb from Roger le Coliar'. Total, 3 lb, which were sold as made clear within; none remains.
[Charcoal]: 21 qrs made from the manor's own wood (*de proprio bosco*) this year which were used in making and repairing the ironwork of 4 ploughs for the year; none remains.

m.4d

Otterford

The account of Hugh atte Poule, farmer of this place.

Rents
The same renders account for £11 for the farm of the hamlet of Otterford this year. Total, £11

Issues of the manor
The same renders account for 4*s*. 8*d*. from pannage of pigs this year; 3*s*. from hundredpenny this year. Total, 7*s*. 8*d*.

Entry and marriage fines
The same renders account for 1*s*. from Richard, son of John de Fyfid', to have 1 ferling of land in Otterford; 4*s*. from woodway; 1*s*. from Joan Water' for marrying herself within. Total, 6*s*.

Perquisites
The same renders account for 1*s*. from the whole tithing of Otterford for release from their suit to him for the year, so that they may come to the two law-days; 6*d*. from

Warin Lansp' because he is not proceeding with his complaint; 1*s*. from Roger de Luggeston' for transgression against Richard le Smyht of Yarcombe; 6*s*. 3*d*. from those who brewed ale this year for breaking the assize of ale; 6*d*. also from those who brewed ale. Total, 10*s*. 3*d*.

Total of both, 15*s*. 3*d*.

Total of all receipts, £12 2*s*. 11*d*.

Delivered to the reeve of Taunton castle, £12 2*s*. 11*d*.

Taunton Borough

Rents

The same renders account for £22 16*s*. 2*d*. for rents of assize at Christmas, Easter (22 April), the Nativity of the blessed John the Baptist (24 June), and Michaelmas (29 September), in equal portions. Total, £22 16*s*. 2*d*.

Quittances

In quittance of two reeves for the year 4*s*. Total, 4*s*.

In default of a certain tenement which belonged to Roginald le Dygher' beside la Poule because it lies empty 6*d*.; one plot which belonged to Walter Pokoc because it lies empty 6*d*. Total, 1*s*.

Total of quittances and defaults of rent, 5*s*.

Total of rents remaining, £22 11*s*. 2*d*.

Perquisites

The same renders account for 13*s*. from stallage this year; £3 1*s*. from those who brewed ale at Hockday (1 May) for breaking the assize of ale; £3 6*d*. from those who brewed ale at Michaelmas for the same; 8*s*. from toll-corn sold this year and not more because the tenants of the Prior of Montacute, of Crih, H*a*mme and Tattesburch', who are accustomed to give toll are now quit by order of the bishop; £3 10*s*. from tolls of the market and fair of St Botulph this year; 3*d*. from Thomas Segar because he is not proceeding; 6*d*. from Thomas le Norays for licence to come to an agreement; 6*d*. from Robert le Rop*ere* for transgression against the lord; 3*d*. from John Churihma*n* for transgression against his neighbour; 1*s*. from the bailiff of the borough for contempt; 6*d*. from Richard de la Lake because he did not produce in court the individual whom he had pledged; 3*d*. from Thomas le Lorm' for transgression against his neighbour; 6*d*. from John de Orchard' because he is not proceeding with his complaint; 6*d*. from John Balke for licence to come to an agreement; 3*d*. from John le Frye for unjustly raising the hue; 6*d*. from Robert le Large for transgression against his neighbour; 3*d*. from a certain stranger for transgression against John Balk; 6*d*. from John Balk for default; 3*d*. from John Boveney because he withdrew his suit; 6*d*. from John Balk for transgression against his neighbour; 3*d*. from William Cridewey for transgression against his neighbour; 3*d*. from Alice la Chalon*ere* because she is not proceeding with her complaint; 3*d*.

from Adam Akewombe for unjustly withholding a debt; 3*d.* from William le Flett*ere* for the same; 2*s.* 6*d.* from Adam Akewomb' and another regrater for regrating; 3*d.* from Adam Akewo*m*be for transgression against his neighbour; 3*d.* from John le Frye for unjustly withholding a debt; 3*d.* from William Galpy*n* for the same; 6*d.* from John Elys for transgression against his neighbour; 1*s.* from Nicholas le Whyte of Devon for unjustly raising the hue; 3*d.* from Walter de Buddelye because he did not produce in court the individual whom he had bailed; 3*d.* from Gilbert Dauwe for the same; 6*d.* from John Gulye for transgression against his neighbour; 4*d.* from Philip Leg for false complaint; 2*d.* from Sevarus de Torre for transgression against his neighbour; 6*d.* from Joan atte Mor' because she withdrew her suit; 6*d.* from Richard le Dygher' for transgression against his neighbour; 3*d.* from John Balk for the same; 3*d.* from Roginald Tatkelake for unjustly withholding a debt; 3*d.* from Matilda la Fatte for the same; 1*s.* from Roger Elyot of Tiverton for transgression against his neighbour; 3*d.* from Thomas Segar for the same; 3*d.* from William Byhsshop for the same; 1*s.* from Roger de Tyv*er*ton' because he is not proceeding; 3*d.* from Richard Spyri*ng* for default; 3*d.* from John Russel for transgression against his neighbour; 5*s.* from a certain house beside the north gate of Taunton which is in the lord's possession; 1*s.* 6*d.* from a certain forge in the north street of Taunton which is in the lord's possession through the death of a certain woman who held the same forge in dower of the heir of the aforesaid Thomas le M*a*reschal. Total, £11 17*s.* 6*d.*

Total of all receipts, £34 8*s.* 8*d.*

Delivered to the reeve of Taunton castle, £34 8*s.* 8*d.*

Rimpton

Rents of assize

Henry le Whyte and Robert Boye, reeve of Rimpton, render account for £1 4*s.* 6*d.* for rents at Christmas; £1 4*s.* 6*d.* at Easter (22 April); £1 4*s.* 6*d.* at the Nativity of the blessed John the Baptist (24 June); £1 4*s.* 6*d.* at Michaelmas (29 September). Total, £4 18*s.*

Quittances

In quittance of 1 reeve for the year 3*s.*; 4 ploughmen, 2 ox-drovers for the year 12*s.*; 18 workers who harrowed, gripped, dug, threshed corn, mowed meadows, tossed and carried hay, reaped and carried corn at harvest-time, and did other necessary work, £1 16*s.* for the year, or 2*s.* each. Total, £2 11*s.*

Defaults of rent

In default of the house and curtilage of John de Molend*ino* because it is in demesne 1*s.* Total, 1*s.*

Total of quittances and defaults of rent, £2 12*s.*

Total of rents remaining, £2 6*s.*

Issues of the manor

The same render account for 4*s.* 9½*d.* from pannage of 48 pigs and 19 hoggets this year, at 1*d.* a pig and ½*d.* a hogget; 3*s.* from churchscot at Martinmas (11

November); 8*s*. 6*d*. from the pasturage of 17 oxen sold in winter; 9*s*. 4*d*. from the pasturage of 24 plough-horses and 8 colts sold after Martinmas, at 4*d*. a plough-horse and 2*d*. a colt; nothing from the pasturage of la Grutte for the lord's stock; 2*s*. from the pasturage of Alsyesh*a*m sold in summer; 6*d*. from the pasturage sold at Oclefurlo*n*g and not more because the field was sown with summer corn (*tremes'*) this year; 1*s*. 2*d*. from the pasturage of la Portweye this year; 1*s*. 6*d*. from the pasturage of Wetenegarston'; 10*d*. from the pasturage of P*ar*va Sterte sold this year; 1*s*. 2*d*. from the pasturage of Mag*na* Sterte; nothing from the pasturage beside la Marlygputte this year because it is fallow; 1*s*. 4*d*. from the pasturage of Barweyerewe; 8*d*. from the pasturage of H*am*stedereweye sold; nothing from the pasturage beside the dovecote because it is fallow; 6*d*. from the pasturage beside the house of John de Mol*endino*; 6*s*. 10*d*. from the herbage for 68 plough-horses and 28 bullocks sold in the wood between Hockday (1 May) and Lammas (1 August), at 1*d*. a plough-horse, ½*d*. a bullock; 9*s*. 3*d*. from 1 male colt aged 2 years sold in summer; 6*s*. 4*d*. from 1 female plough-horse from strays; £1 14*s*. from 3 oxen sold in Lent, at 11*s*. 4*d*. each; £1 16*s*. from 4 oxen sold in summer, at 9*s*. each; £2 9*s*. from 6 oxen sold because sick, at 8*s*. 2*d*. each; 3*s*. 10*d*. from 1 young heifer (*boviculo fem'*) sold in Lent; £3 from 20 pigs sold at Martinmas, at 3*s*. each; 13*s*. 4*d*. from 5 pigs sold, at 2*s*. 8*d*. each; 9*s*. 4*d*. from the hides sold of 3 oxen in murrain; 5*s*. 6*d*. from the hides sold of 4 cows in murrain; 3*s*. 4*d*. from the hides sold of 3 heifers (*juvenc'*) in murrain; 1*s*. 10*d*. from the hides sold of 2 young heifers in murrain; 6*d*. from the hides sold of 3 calves in murrain; 6*d*. from the hides sold of 4 calves in murrain; £1 from 2 casks of cider which remained, sold wholesale apart from the vessels; 1*s*. 2½*d*. from 19 rowen cheeses (*cas' de rewayn*) sold without weighing; £1 4*s*. 3*d*. from 141 cheeses from the issue of the summer sold, weighing 2½ weys and 3 stone, at 9*s*. a wey and 7*d*. a stone; 3*s*. 2*d*. from butter sold by the dish; 1*s*. 9*d*. from the residue of Peter's pence according to custom; 6*s*. 6½*d*. from dairy produce sold at the audit. Total, £16 11*s*. 9½*d*.

Sale of corn

The same render account for £32 7*s*. from 121 qrs 2½ bus. of wheat sold, at 5*s*. 4*d*. a qr; £1 3*s*. 5¾*d*. from 6 qrs 1 bus. of curall sold, at 3*s*. 10*d*. a qr; £3 1*d*. from 12 qrs 7 bus. of maslin sold, at 4*s*. 8*d*. a qr; 4*s*. 7*d*. from 1 qr 3 bus. of barley sold, at 3*s*. 4*d*. a qr; £1 12*s*. 6*d*. from 16 qrs 2 bus. of beans sold, at 2*s*. a qr; 11*s*. 9*d*. from 5 qrs 7 bus. of peas sold, at 2*s*. a qr; 1*s*. 10*d*. from 1 qr 3 bus. of vetches sold, at 2*d*. a bus.; £5 18*s*. 7½*d*. from 54 qrs 6 bus. of oats sold, at 2*s*. 2*d*. a qr; 8*s*. 9*d*. from 2 qrs 5 bus. of barley sold at the audit. Total, £45 8*s*. 7¼*d*.

From the issue of the mill

The same render account for 8*s*. 1½*d*. from 1 qr 5 bus. of wheat from the issue of the mill sold, at 5*s*. a qr; 10*s*. 5½*d*. from 3 qrs 5½ bus. of first-grade and second-grade malt from the issue of the mill sold, at 2*s*. 10*d*. a qr. Total, 18*s*. 7*d*.

Entry and marriage fines

The same render account for 8*s*. from the whole tithing of Rimpton for tithingpenny at the two hundred-courts; 13*s*. 4*d*. from the fine of William le Nottey to have Joan Kage with 1 ferling of land; £5 6*s*. 8*d*. from the fine of William le Denays to have 1 virgate of land with Albreda, relict of Richard de Bosco; £4 13*s*. 4*d*. from John de Wolmynton' to have Alice, relict of Henry Alayn, with 1 virgate of land; 6*s*. from Albreda, the relict of de Bosco, to retain 1 virgate of her husband's land. Total, £11 7*s*. 4*d*.

Perquisites

The same render account for 8*d.* from William de Staford and Richard de Holeweye for trespass (*transgressione*) of pasture; 6*d.* from John de Crawthorn' for the same; 3½*d.* from Roger Puphorn and his fellow for the same; 1*s.* 9*d.* from Henry le Takeler', Henry Petyr, John Nob' and Robert Blakesol' for breaking the assize of ale; 1*s.* from Robert de Quercu, Henry Gille, Henry Takeler' and John Nob' for the same; 2*s.* from Henry Gill', John Nob', Jordan Burrich and Agnes Pet*ra* for the same; 6*d.* from Richard le Cok for trespass of pasture; 6*d.* from Richard atte Wude and William Woderis for the same; 1*s.* from the whole tithing because it did not produce William atte Wod' at the law-day; 2*s.* from Henry Gill' for breaking the assize of ale; 1*s.* 6*d.* from Henry le Takeler' for the same; 9*d.* from Agnes Pet*ra* and Albreda atte Wud' for the same; 2*s.* from Robert de Quercu and Henry Kyggel for transgression against John Datyn; 1*s.* from William Mol*endinarius* and his neighbours for trespass of pasture; 1*s.* from Peter de Bosco, John atte Brok and Henry Kyggel for the same; 1*s.* 3*d.* from William Hardy*ng*, Robert atte Hok', Albreda atte Wod' and William Woderys for the same; 2*s.* 3*d.* from John de Crawthorn', Robert Blakesole, William Hardy*ng*, John Hamu*nd*, William Silvestr', Alice Alayn, Peter atte Wude, William Woderys and William de Wolmyngton' for trespass of pasture. Total, £1 5½*d.*

Total of both, £12 7*s.* 9½*d.*

Total of all receipts, £77 12*s.* 9¼*d.*

Cost of ploughs

In iron bought to maintain the ironwork of 4 ploughs for the year 4*s.* 1¾*d.* In stipend of the smith repairing and restoring the ironwork of the said ploughs for the year 3*s.* 6½*d.* In 8 yokes bought for ploughs 5½*d.* In 5 yokes bought 9*d.* In expenses of 1 boon-work of 36 ploughmen and 24 harrowers, ploughing and harrowing 37 acres for the winter sowing, besides bread from stock: ale bought 2*s.* 2*d.*; meat bought 2*s.* 3*d.*; cheese bought 3*d.* In 1 boon-work of 11 ploughmen working on the fallow according to custom 11*d.* In 4 oxen bought £2 9*s.* 2*d.*, at 12*s.* 3½*d.* each. In 3 oxen bought £1 13*s.* ¾*d.*, at 11*s.* ¼*d.* each. In 5 oxen bought £2 14*s.* 7*d.*, at 10*s.* 11*d.* each. In blood-letting of oxen 3*d.* In hiring 2 men for 6 days to hold the ploughs whilst the ploughmen of the vill mow the meadows 6*d.* In stipend of 2 ox-drovers for the year 10*s.* Total, £8 2*s.* ½*d.*

[Cost of] wagons [and carts]

In dowels bought for the wagons for the year 6½*d.* In 6 tacks with nails bought for the wagons 10*d.* In 1 pair of wheels bought for the cart 2*s.* 10*d.* In 1 collar bought for the cart 4½*d.* In grease bought for the wagons for the year 4*d.* In shoeing and tethering 2 plough-horses for the year 1*s.* 4*d.* In 4 halters bought for plough-horses for the year 2*d.* In stipend of 1 carter for the year holding the place of the hayward 5*s.* Total, 11*s.* 5*d.*

[Repair of buildings and allowance of food] for customary tenants

In sand and lime bought for roofing the hall 8*d.* In tiles bought for the same 8*d.* In nails bought for the same 1¾*d.* In stipend of 1 tiler roofing the said hall beside the latrine 6*d.* In stipend of 1 carpenter mending the walls of the small barn 6*d.* In roofing the great stable by piece-work 2*s.* 6*d.* In allowance of food (*potura*) for the customary tenants of the vill at Christmas according to custom 4*s.* Total, 8*s.* 11¾*d.*

Sheepcote (*bercar'*) and dairy
In 13 hurdles bought for the fold (*fald'*) 1*s*. 2*d*. In stipend of one shepherd for the year 4*s*. In 4 bus. of salt bought for the dairy for the year 1*s*. 3*d*. In 1 ell of linen cloth bought for the dairy 3*d*. In clay pots and pans bought for the dairy 2¼*d*. In stipend of 1 cowherd for the year 2*s*. 6*d*. In stipend of 1 dairymaid for summer and autumn 2*s*. Total, 11*s*. 4¼*d*.

Small and necessary [expenses]
In castrating 12 piglets 4*d*. In quittance of the tithe of 1 foal 1*d*. In mending 1 three-pronged fork 1*d*. In 1 sack bought for corn 10*d*. In 1 piece of iron bought for the beam 1*d*. In stone bought to mend the bridge which is called Wodebrigge 9*d*. In stipend of the mason mending the said bridge 10½*d*. Total, 3*s*. ½*d*.

[Cost of] the mill
In one stone millstone bought for the mill 8*s*. 3*d*. In making one mill-spindle 5*d*. In nails bought for the mill-wheel 2½*d*. In stipend of the miller for the year 5*s*. In quittance of the tithe of the mill 2*s*. Total, 15*s*. 10½*d*.

m.5
Weeding corn and mowing the meadow
In weeding corn 3*s*. 6*d*. In covering 1 haycock 3*d*. In expenses of 1 reap-reeve (*rypereve*) for 6 weeks at harvest-time 3*s*. 6*d*., at 1*d*. a day. In stipend of the same 2*s*. In covering 1 stack of beans by piece-work 4*d*. Total, 9*s*. 7*d*.

Steward's expenses
In expenses of the steward and his clerk for their visits to view the state of the manor, to hold court, and to expedite other business of the lord, 8*s*. 8*d*. by 2 tallies. Total, 8*s*. 8*d*.

Bailiff's expenses
In expenses of the bailiff for the year £3 10*d*., at 2*d*. a day. Total, £3 10*d*.

Total of all expenses, £14 11*s*. 9½*d*.

And thus he owes, £63 11¾*d*.

Cash deliveries
Delivered to Sir G*eoffrey*, treasurer of Wolvesey, by 1 tally, £38. Total, £38.

And thus he owes clear, £25 11¾*d*.

Issues of the grange
Wheat
{yield: 5½-fold plus 6½ bus. in all with the issue of maslin below}
The same render account for 144½ qrs of wheat from the issue of the grange threshed by the customary tenants of the vill by struck measure. Total, 144½ qrs.
Sown over 117 acres, 22 qrs ½ bus.; that is, 1½ bus. an acre, plus 1 bus. in all. In bread baked for the provision of one boon-work for winter sowing, 6 bus. In provision of the steward for his visits, 3 bus. Sold within, 121 qrs 2½ bus. Total as made clear. It balances.

Curall

The same render account for 20 qrs 1 bus. of curall from the issue of the grange threshed like wheat above. Total, 20 qrs 1 bus.

Mixed for the liveries of the manorial servants, 14 qrs. Sold within, 6 qrs 1 bus. It balances.

Maslin

{yield: 5½-fold with wheat above}

The same render account for 12 qrs 7 bus. of maslin from the issue of the grange threshed as above. Total, 12 qrs 7 bus. Sold within. It balances.

Barley

{yield: seven-fold less ½ qr}

The same render account for 10 qrs of barley from the issue of the grange. Total, 10 qrs.

Sown over 3 acres, 7½ bus.; that is, 2½ bus. an acre. In supporting piglets, 5 bus. Mixed for the liveries of the manorial servants, 4 qrs 3½ bus. Sold within, 1 qr 3 bus. Sold at the audit, 2 qrs 5 bus. It balances.

Beans

{yield: seven-fold less 1 qr with 35 qrs by estimation remaining in the stack}

The same render account for 1 qr 2 bus. of beans remaining from the previous account; 27 qrs from this year's issue. Total, 28 qrs 2 bus.

Sown over 15 acres, 7 qrs 2 bus.; that is, ½ qr an acre, less 2 bus. in all. In feeding pigs, 2½ qrs. Mixed for the liveries of the manorial servants, 2 qrs 2 bus. Sold within, 16 qrs 2 bus. Total as above. 35 qrs by estimation remain in a certain stack.

Peas

{yield: 7½-fold less ½ bus. with the remainder in the stack}

The same render account for 6 qrs of peas remaining from the previous account; 1 qr 5 bus. from this year's issue. Total, 7 qrs 5 bus.

Sown over 2 acres, 2 bus. In supporting pigs in winter, 1½ qrs. Sold within, 5 qrs. Total as above. 3 qrs by estimation remain in the stack.

Vetches

{yield: 10½-fold plus 1½ bus.}

The same render account for 1 qr 6 bus. of vetches from the issue. Total, 1 qr 6 bus.

Sown over 3 acres, 3 bus. Sold within, 1 qr 3 bus. Total as above. 5 qrs by estimation remain in the stack.

Oats

{yield: 3-fold plus 7 qrs 6 bus.}

The same render account for 107 qrs 7 bus. of oats from the issue. Total, 107 qrs 7 bus.

Sown over 129 acres, 48 qrs; that is, 3 bus. an acre. In customary payment of the manorial servants in Lent, 1 qr. In fodder of the plough-horses in winter, 1½ qrs. In fodder of the horses of the steward and his clerk for their visits, 1 qr, by 2 tallies of 2 bus., within with expenses. In a gratuity made to the beadle of the hundred of Horethorne of fodder for his horse, 1 qr. Sold within, 54 qrs 6 bus.

Issues of the mill

The same render account for 1 qr 5 bus. of wheat from the issue of the mill for the year. Total, 1 qr 5 bus. All sold within. It balances.

The same render account for 9 qrs 2 bus. of maslin from the issue of the mill for the year. Mixed for the liveries of the manorial servants, 9 qrs 2 bus. Total, 9 qrs 2 bus. It balances.
The same render account for 3 qrs 5½ bus. of first-grade and second-grade malt from the issue of the mill for the year. Total, 3 qrs 5½ bus. Sold within.

Proof of liveries
The same render account for 14 qrs of curall, 4 qrs 3½ bus. of barley, 2 bus. of beans, and 9 qrs 2 bus. of maslin from the mill above, mixed for the liveries of the manorial servants. Total, 29 qrs 7½ bus.
Delivered to 1 carter holding the place of the hayward, 2 ox-drovers, 1 miller and 1 shepherd for the year, 21 qrs 4½ bus., each taking 1 qr every 12 weeks. Delivered to 1 woman keeping the hearth in winter, ½ qr. Delivered to 1 cowherd and 1 swineherd for the year, 6½ qrs, both taking ⌈1⌉ qr every 16 weeks. Delivered to 1 dairymaid for 22 weeks before Michaelmas, 1 qr 3 bus., taking 1 qr every 16 weeks. Total, 29 qrs 7½ bus.

Stock
Plough-horses: 2 females remain; 1 female from strays. 1 from strays sold within. Total, 1. 2 females remain.
Colts: 2 remain, one male aged 1½ years, the other female aged ½ year; 1 female from this year's offspring. Total, 3. 1 fully-grown male aged 2 years sold within; 2 females remain, 1 aged 1½ years, the other ½ year.
Oxen: 36 remain; 2 added from steers below; 1 from the heriot of Richard de Bosco; 12 bought within. Total, 51. 3 in murrain; 13 sold within. Total, 16. 35 remain.
Bulls: 1 remains. Total, 1. 1 remains.
Cows: 18 remain. Total, 18. 2 in murrain before calving, 2 after calving. Total, 4. 14 remain.
Steers: 5 steers and heifers (*juvenc'*) remain from the previous year's bullocks. Total, 5. 2 added to oxen above; 3 in murrain. Total, 5. None remain.
Bullocks: 6 remain from the previous year's yearlings, 2 of them male. 2 young heifers (*bovicul' fem'*) in murrain; 1 young heifer sold within. Total, 3. 2 bullocks and 1 heifer (*juvenc'*) remain.
Yearlings: 9 remain from the previous year's calves, 5 of them male. Total, 9. 9 remain, 5 of them male.
Calves: 14 from the offspring of the aforesaid cows and not more because 2 cows sterile and 2 in murrain before calving. Total, 14. 1 in tithe; 7 in murrain. Total, 8. 6 remain, 2 of them male.
Pigs: 16 remain; 38 added from hoggets below. Total, 54. 2 in murrain in autumn; 25 sold within. Total, 27. 27 remain.
Boars (*Aper*): 1 remains.
Sows: 3 remain.
Hoggets: 38 remain from the piglets of the previous account. Total, 38. 38 added above to pigs. Total as above. None remain.
Piglets: 14 farrowed in October; 13 farrowed in February; 17 farrowed in June. Total, 44. 4 in tithe; 8 in murrain. Total, 12. 32 remain.
Hides: 3 from oxen, 4 from cows, 3 from heifers, 2 from bullocks and 7 from calves in murrain above. Total, 19. All sold.
Cider: 2 casks remain from the previous account; 2 casks from the issue of the garden this year. Total, 4. 2 casks sold within. Total, 2. 2 casks remain.

Cheese {yield of cow 3*s*. this year and not more on account of the sickness of others this year}: 19 rowen cheeses; 162 from the issue of the dairy between Saturday before the feast of St George (21 April) and Michaelmas (29 September), at 1 cheese a day, the first and last day included. Total, 181. 16 in payment of tithe; 1 in customary payment to the dairymaid; 1 in provision of the steward; 3 in provision of the bailiff and others at harvest-time; 19 rowens sold within without weighing; 141 from the issue of the summer, weighing 2½ weys and 3 stone. Total as above. None remain.
Butter: all sold within by the dish.
Plough feet: 1 remains; 3 from the chevage of John Batyn, William P*r*igge and John Bercar*ius*. Total, 4. 4 used for 4 ploughs during the year. Total as above. None remain.
Vessels and utensils: 6 casks, 4 barrels, 3 tubs, 1 brass ewer, 1 basin, 1 bucket, 4 wains (*plaustr'*) and 1 cart with iron tyres, 5 ropes for wagons and carts, 1 saddle for the cart with saddle-pads, 1 swingletree with 2 collars, 1 pot, 1 brass posnet, 1 ½-bushel measure, 1 winnowing-fan, 1 sack, 1 tripod, 1 trough, 5 buckets, 6 cheese-baskets, 1 large bowl and 1 basket (*sporta*) remain; 1 pair of cart-wheels bought within; 2 buckets, 2 cheese-baskets and 1 basket (*sportu*m) used; all the rest remains.

East Knoyle

Arrears

Theobald de Thedgden', bailiff, and John de Legh', reeve, render account for £27 11*s*. 7½*d*. of arrears from the previous year. Delivered to Sir G*eoffrey*, treasurer of Wolvesey, by 1 tally, £22 13*s*.

Rents of assize

The same render account for £18 6*s*. for all rents of assize from the manor of East Knoyle for the year, that is, £4 17*s*. 1½*d*. at the feast of St Andrew (30 November), Palm Sunday (15 April) and Lammas (1 August), and £3 14*s*. 7½*d*. at Michaelmas (29 September). Total, £18 6*s*.

Quittances

In quittance of 1 reeve for the year 5*s*.; 1 shepherd for the year 1*s*. 6*d*.; 1 beadle who is overseer of the harvest (*messor*) for the year 3*s*.; 1 smith making the ironwork of 7 ploughs for the year 3*s*.; 1 cowherd for the year 1*s*. 6*d*.; 1 shepherd of wethers for the year 3*s*.; 1 shepherd of ewes for the year 3*s*.; 1 keeper of hoggs for the year 1*s*. 6*d*.; 1 woodward who kept the pigs for the year 1*s*. 6*d*.; 10 ploughmen for the year 15*s*., or 1*s*. 6*d*. each. Total, £1 18*s*.

Defaults of rent

In default of 2 virgates of wheat drawn into demesne, 6*s*. for the year; 1 croft of John Blakeman drawn into demesne, 1*s*. for the year; 1 virgate of land of Osbert de Kyngestwod' drawn into demesne, 4*s*. 3*d*. for the year; 1 virgate of land of Geoffrey Philep drawn into demesne, 3*s*. 3¼*d*. for the year; 1 virgate of land of John de la Hale drawn into demesne, 3*s*. 3¼*d*. for the year; 1 croft of Geoffrey drawn into demesne, 6½*d*. for the year; 1½ virgates of land of Hugh Baroun drawn into demesne 6*s*. 2½*d*.; 1 virgate of land of Roger drawn into burgage 3*s*. 3½*d*.; ½ virgate of land of Adam drawn into demesne 2*s*. 7½*d*.; the land of Roger drawn into burgage 1*s*. 1*d*.; 3 acres of land on the site of the mill of Lucsselye 4*s*.; ½ virgate of land of Geoffrey Terry drawn into demesne within the wheat enclosure 1*s*. 6*d*.; 1 croft of John Blake*man* drawn into demesne 1*s*. 1*d*.; the manor of Upton which is in the lord's hands £3 5*s*. 8¼*d*.; a third part of 1 acre of land in the wheat enclosure which John Herb*ert*' held drawn into demesne, 8*d*. for the year; 12 acres of land in the wheat enclosure which John de Halwell' held drawn into demesne, 6*s*. for the year. Total, £5 10*s*. 5¾*d*.

Total of quittances and defaults of rent, £7 8*s*. 5¾*d*.

Total of rents remaining, £10 17*s*. 6¼*d*.

Wax
The same render account for ½ lb of wax from William atte Ford' for annual recognizance. Delivered to Wolvesey. Nothing from the rent of cumin of John de Lussely this year because he is dead.

Annual recognizance
The same render account for 3*d*. from Henry de Fonte for annual recognizance; 3*d*. from Robert Towy for the same; 6*d*. from John Gill' for the same; 6*d*. from John Osegod for the same so that he will do suit to the 2 courts and notwithstanding will do the service pertaining to his land; 3*d*. from Hugh Doun for annual recognizance; 6*d*. from John de la M*er*she for the same so that it is granted to him that he should not give tithingpenny (*ththingfelu'*) nor be chosen on other land which he holds in tenure nor be chosen to be a manorial servant in the curia, but that he should remain a villein (*nat'*) as before in all other things. Total, 2*s*. 3*d*.

Issues of the manor
The same render account for 4*s*. 6*d*. from pannage of pigs at Martinmas (11 November), at 1*d*. a pig over a year old, and ½*d*. a younger pig; nothing from pasturage this year for the lord's livestock; 7*s*. 6*d*. from the agistment of oxen and cows in ox-pasture this year, at 10*d*. a head; 2*s*. 6*d*. from droving in the wheat enclosure; 1*s*. 6*d*. from droving in the park; 15*s*. from the pasturage of Estcu*m*b' sold to Hindon Borough this year; 1*s*. 2*d*. from the residue of Peter's pence and not more because the officials of the curia are quit and besides this the church seized 1*s*. from churchscot; 5*s*. 5*d*. from the land which William Husey and Walter Boll' hold in villeinage for release from labour service; 4*s*. from the land which belonged to Alexander le Cath for release from labour service this year; 4*s*. from Joan Noteky*n* and Geoffrey Lyndenyes for release from labour service at harvest-time; 4*s*. from Robert le Palm*ere* for release from service for ½ virgate of land in villeinage this year; £1 9*s*. from 3 oxen sold at Martinmas, at £1 for 2, and 9*s*. for 1; £1 11*s*. 2*d*. from 5 sick oxen sold, at 15*s*. for 2, and 5*s*. 4½*d*. each for 3, plus ½*d*. in all; £1 13*s*. from 6 old cows sold, at 13*s*. 4*d*. for 2, 5*s*. each for 3, and 4*s*. 8*d*. for 1; £2 9*s*. from 49 wethers sold at Martinmas, at 1*s*. each; £1 1*s*. 8*d*. from 26 ewes sold, at 10*d*. each; £1 10*d*. from 50 feeble lambs sold before shearing, at 5*d*. each; £4 4*s*. 6*d*. from 34 pigs sold, at 2*s*. 6*d*. each apart from 1 at 2*s*.; £1 17*s*. 6½*d*. from the skins sold of 199 wethers, rams, ewes and hoggs in murrain before shearing, at 3*d*. a skin of wethers, 2¼*d*. of ewes, and 1¾*d*. of hoggs; 10*s*. 11¾*d*. from the skins sold of 137 lambs before shearing, at 1*d*. a skin for 116, and ¾*d*. each for 21, plus 1*d*. in all; 3*d*. from the skins sold of 6 lambs in murrain after shearing; 1*d*. from the skins sold of 6 rotted sheep; 2*s*. from the skins sold wholesale of 16 wethers, 1 ram, 19 ewes after shearing;

7*s*. 2*d*. from the hides sold of 3 oxen in murrain, at 4*s*. 2*d*. for 2, and 3*s*. for 1; 5*s*. 2*d*. from the hides sold of 4 cows in murrain, at 1*s*. 3½*d*. each; 1*s*. 2*d*. from the hide sold of 1 heifer in murrain; 8*d*. from the hide sold of a certain other heifer in murrain; 2*s*. 6*d*. from the hides sold of 10 yearling calves in murrain, at 3*d*. a hide; 10*s*. from 10 of this year's calves sold, at 1*s*. each; 6*d*. from the hides sold of 6 calves in murrain; nothing from coarse wool and lamb's-wool this year because it is sent to Wolvesey; £1 19*s*. from 26 stone of wool locks sold, at 1*s*. 6*d*. a stone; nothing from winter cheese this year; £9 18*s*. from 22 weys of summer cheese sold, at 9*s*. a wey; £1 12*s*. from 3½ weys, 1 clove, 4 lb of butter sold, at 9*s*. a wey; 5*s*. from 60 hens from churchscot sold; 11*d*. from cider sold; £3 15*s*. 2*d*. from profit (*lucro*) on livestock bought and sold which were bought the previous year for the agistment of pasture. Total, £37 6*s*. 11¼*d*.

Sale of corn

The same render account for £16 10*s*. from 66 qrs of wheat sold, at 5*s*. a qr; £2 6*s*. 8*d*. from 20 qrs of curall sold, at 2*s*. 4*d*. a qr; £5 1*s*. 6*d*. from 34½ qrs of barley sold, at 3*s*. a qr for 32½ qrs, and 2*s*. a qr for 2 qrs; £4 3*s*. 8*d*. from 51 qrs of oats sold, at 1*s*. 8*d*. a qr for 45 qrs, 1*s*. 6*d*. a qr for 4 qrs, and 1*s*. 4*d*. a qr for 2 qrs; 1*d*. from ½ bus. of oats sold; £1 15*s*. 8*d*. from 12 qrs 2 bus. of peas sold, at 3*s*. a qr for 10 qrs 5 bus., and 2*s*. 4*d*. a qr for 1 qr 5 bus. Total, £29 17*s*. 6*d*.

Entry and marriage fines

The same render account for 5*s*. from Alice le Cras to retain 1 virgate of land which belonged to Walter le Cras; 10*s*.[1] from William Fab*er* to have 1 virgate of land which belonged to Matilda le Neywe; £1 10*s*. from John Elys for the entry fine for the tenement and land which belonged to Roger his father; 5*s*. from Stephen de Wyk' to retain ½ virgate of land which belonged to John his father; 4*s*. from John Boll' to have ½ virgate of land with Matilda, formerly wife of William atte Toneshe*nd*'; £1 from John de Lusschleye for 1 messuage with a croft which belonged to John i*n* le Mers; 3*s*. 4*d*. from the tithing of East Knoyle for tithingpenny at the hundred-court of Martinmas; 3*s*. 4*d*. from the tithing of Milton for the same; 3*s*. 4*d*. from the tithing of East Knoyle at the hundred-court of Hockday for the same; 3*s*. 4*d*. from the tithing of Milton for the same. Total, £4 7*s*. 4*d*.

m.5d

Pleas and perquisites

The same render account for £3 18*s*. 10*d*. from the pleas and perquisites of the court this year. Total, £3 18*s*. 10*d*.

Total of both, £8 6*s*. 2*d*.

Total of all receipts, £86 10*s*. 4½*d*.

Cost of ploughs

In ironwork of 6 ploughs with ploughshares and coulters repaired and made anew by fixed agreement 17*s*. In 6 plough feet bought for ploughs 1*s*. 6*d*. In 6 pairs of wheels bought for ploughs 2*s*. In 14 yokes bought 1*s*. 2*d*. In stipend of 1 man making and repairing timber for ploughs 1*s*. In iron spikes bought for harrows 1*s*. 3*d*. In 2 harrows made from the lord's own timber and others mended 5*d*. In 1 seed-basket

1 MS omits '*s*.'

bought 1*d*. In boon-works of 10 ploughmen 1*s*. In 6 oxen bought for ploughs £2 14*s*. 5*d*., at 19*s*. for 2, 18*s*. 6*d*. for 2, 10*s*. 4*d*. for 1, and 6*s*. 7*d*. for 1. In stipend of 2 oxherds for the year 6*s*. Given to the smith in place of 2 trunks which he is accustomed to have for making ploughs 2*s*. Total, £4 7*s*. 10*d*.

Purchase of corn
In 30 qrs of oats bought for sowing £3 6*s*. 8*d*., at 2*s*. 8*d*. a qr for 10 qrs, and 2*s*. a qr for 20 qrs. Total, £3 6*s*. 8*d*.

Cost of carts and wagons
In 1 pair of wheels bought for the carts 2*s*. In 1 binding bought anew and fitted to the said wheels with clamps and large and small nails, and the stipend of the smith, 8*s*. 10*d*. In 2 axles bought and fitted to the carts with the stipend of the carpenter who made 1 new cart-body 10*d*. In clouts and nails bought for the carts and wagons 1*s*. 6*d*. In grease bought for the carts and wagons 1*s*. ½*d*. In 2 saddles bought for the carts 2¼*d*. In repairing saddle-pads for the same with the lord's leather, and for 5 collars with the stipend of 1 man who made them, 1*s*. In hoops made from the lord's iron for hooping the hubs of the wagons 4*d*. In 1 cart-rope bought 1*s*. 3*d*. In 1 pair of traces bought 5*d*. In white leather bought for mending harnesses 5*d*. In 3 halters made from hair ¾*d*. In shoeing 6 plough-horses for the year 9*s*. 8*d*. In 4 sacks bought 2*s*. 9½*d*. In stipend of 2 carters for the year 6*s*. Total, £1 16*s*. 6*d*.

Cost of the dairy
In 2 qrs 2 bus. of salt bought 6*s*., at 2*s*. 8*d*. a qr. In woollen and linen cloth bought for straining milk and wrapping cheese 1*s*. In a press bought 1*s*. 1½*d*. In earthenware pots and pans bought and the repair of 1 brass pan 11½*d*. In 4 new buckets bought and 2 cheese-vats 2*s*. 8*d*. In stipend of 1 dairymaid for the year 2*s*. Total, 13*s*. 9*d*.

Purchase of stock
In 2 cows bought 16*s*., at 8*s*. each, and 2 for 14*s*., at 7*s*. each, and 2 for 13*s*. 9*d*. Total, £2 3*s*. 9*d*.

Sheepcote
In grease and verdigris bought for greasing sheep £1 14*s*. In 1 iron stake bought 9*d*. In stipend of 1 man re-roofing the ewe-house in places 1*s*. In washing and shearing sheep 2*s*. In 38 ells of canvas bought for packing wool 10*s*. 3½*d*., at 3¼*d*. an ell. In making 6 sacks and packing the said wool, with thread bought for the same, 2*s*. 6*d*. Total, £2 10*s*. 6½*d*.

Cost of buildings
In re-roofing the hall, kitchen, dairy, byre, barn, and the room (*camer'*) above the gate, 14*s*. 10*d*. In stipend of 1 man making anew 2 gates, 1 to the park and the other in front of the barn, 1*s*. 6*d*. In hooks and hinges, large and small nails bought, with the stipend of the smith, 1*s*. 8*d*. In stipend of 1 man building the gable of the hay-barn 2*s*. 6*d*. In stipend of 1 man repairing and plastering (*plast*rant*'*) the walls of the cow-shed 8*d*. In stipend of 1 man planting a coppice around the park and repairing the gate of the same 6½*d*. In stipend of 1 man repairing the press and 1 cask 7*d*. In castrating 21 pigs 7*d*. In mending 1 lock to the cellar and 1 axe 3*d*. In fitting 1 shovel bought with iron 1*d*. In enclosing 36 perches around Frere*n*heyth' 1*s*., at 1*d*. per 3 perches. In enclosing 30 perches around the park 1*s*. 10½*d*., at ¾*d*. a perch. Total, £1 6*s*. 1*d*.

Threshing
In threshing 105 qrs of wheat, 2 bus. of curall, by piece-work by struck measure, £1 10½*d*., at 2*d*. a qr. In winnowing the same 2*s*. 1*d*., at 1*d*. per 5 qrs. In threshing and winnowing 97 qrs 4 bus. of barley by piece-work, 9*s*. 9*d*., at 1½*d*. per 10 struck bushels. In threshing and winnowing 98 qrs of oats by piece-work, 6*s*. 6¾*d*., at 1*d*. a heaped quarter. In threshing and winnowing 22 qrs of peas by piece-work, 2*s*. 2¼*d*., at 1½*d*. a qr of 10 struck bushels. Total, £2 1*s*. 5½*d*.

Expenses of the harvest
In weeding 333 acres of every kind of corn 9*s*. 3*d*., at 1*d*. per 3 acres. In mowing and tossing 52 acres of meadow because it was neither mowed nor tossed by customary tenants £1 1*s*. 3*d*., at 5*d*. an acre, plus 1 acre in all. In boon-works, nothing, because all the corn was reaped for sheaves. In provision of the reeve, 1 rider going round with the overseer of the harvest at harvest-time, 1 overseer of the harvest, and 1 granary-keeper, who were at table at harvest-time, 9*s*. 4*d*., because the beadle did not remain there continually. In stipend of the said rider 5*s*. In stipend of two stackers at harvest-time 4*s*. Total, £2 8*s*. 10*d*.

Steward's expenses
In expenses of the steward and Simon, clerk, for their visits, 8*s*. 8*d*. In expenses of Peter de Schipton from Michaelmas until Hilary (13 January) £1 9*s*. 9*d*. In expenses of Theobald, now bailiff, for his visits, £1 3*s*. 2*d*. Total, £3 1*s*. 7*d*.

Total of all expenses, £23 17*s*.

And thus he owes, £62 13*s*. 4½*d*.

Delivered to Sir G*eoffrey*, treasurer of Wolvesey, by 1 tally, £40 11*s*. 4*d*.

And thus he owes clear, £22 2*s*. ½*d*.

Hindon Borough

Rents of assize
Theobald de Theygden', bailiff, and Walter Mossel render account for £6 9*s*. 2½*d*. for all rents of assize from the vill of Hindon for the year at Michaelmas (29 September). Total, £6 9*s*. 2½*d*.

Quittances
In quittance of 1 reeve for the year 1*s*. Total, 1*s*.

Defaults of rent
In default of 8 acres of land and 1 burgage which Andrew de la Mar' held during the time of Peter, formerly bishop of Winchester, 4*s*. 8*d*., of which Robert de la Mar' holds the land and pays 4*d*. a year which is included above in the rents. Total, 4*s*. 8*d*.

Total of quittances and defaults of rent, 5*s*. 8*d*.

Total of rents remaining, £6 3*s*. 6½*d*.

Stallage

The same render account for 1*s*. from Thomas le Hop*ere* for stallage in the market for the year; 6*d*. from Hamo Dev*ere*l for the same; 6*d*. from John le Hackar' for the same; 1*d*. from Philip Tette for the same; 1*s*. from John Tryllawey for the same; 6*d*. from Robert Pycok for the same; 9*d*. from Walter Juvedy and Robert le Palm*ere* for the same; 4*d*. from Mericia, widow, for the same. Total, 4*s*. 8*d*.

Pleas and perquisites

The same render account for 19*s*. 2*d*. from the pleas and perquisites of the court of Hindon this year. Total, 19*s*. 2*d*.

Total of all receipts, £7 7*s*. 4½*d*.

And he owes it all.

Delivered to Sir G*eoffrey*, treasurer of Wolvesey, by 1 tally, £7 7*s*. 4½*d*.

And he is quit.

Issues of the grange
Wheat
{yield: 5-fold less 7 qrs}

The same render account for 105 qrs from the whole issue of wheat by struck measure; 9 qrs by estimation in sheaves given to the reapers at harvest-time; 1½ qrs by estimation in 2 acres which the smith and beadle receive according to custom, because they receive at a better rate (*de melior'*), besides manure and folding, according to their choice. Total, 115½ qrs.

Sown over 81½ acres measured by the perch (*p*er *p*er*tic'*) in the fields of Crabewyke and Alphesheyeth', 30½ qrs; that is, 3 bus. an acre. Delivered to 1 attendant who is through the bailiff to oversee the threshing by the ploughmen and other officials of the curia, 1 qr 5 bus., because he takes the rest in barley. Delivered to 1 warrener for the same time, 1 qr 5 bus., taking the rest in barley, at a bushel a week. In provision of the steward for 1 visit, 2 bus. In provision of Peter de Schypton', bailiff from Michaelmas until Hilary, 2½ qrs. In provision of the bailiff now for his visits, 1 qr 2 bus. In provision of the harvest, 1 qr. In customary payment to 1 beadle who sowed all the corn, 2 bus., taking the rest in barley. Given to the reapers by estimation in sheaves for reaping corn at harvest-time, 9 qrs, because they take the fifteenth sheaf. Delivered to the smith and beadle by estimation in 2 acres, 1½ qrs. Sold, 66 qrs. It balances.

Curall

The same render account for 20 qrs of curall from the whole issue by struck measure. And sold.

Barley
{yield: 4-fold less 6 qrs}

The same render account for 97½ qrs from the whole issue of barley by struck measure; 8½ qrs by estimation in sheaves given to the reapers at harvest-time. Total, 106 qrs.

Sown over 57 acres measured by the perch, of which 40 acres lie beside the ewe-house, and 17 lie in Garstonselylo*n*d' and Heled', 28½ qrs; that is, ½ qr an acre.

Delivered to 2 carters and 2 oxherds, 24 qrs, each taking a quarter every 8 weeks, and taking the rest, that is, 2 qrs, in peas. Delivered to 1 attendant who kept the oxen in winter, harrowed at both sowings, and spread dung, 2½ qrs. In customary payment to 1 beadle who sowed the seed, 2 bus., because 2 bus. are subtracted from the wheat which he was accustomed to receive before. In customary payment for food and drink at Christmas and Easter, 2 qrs. Delivered to 1 dairymaid for ½ year, 2½ qrs. Delivered to 1 attendant who is through the bailiff to oversee the ploughmen threshing and winnowing at East Knoyle, Upton and Bishops Fonthill from the Purification (2 February) until Lammas (1 August), 1 qr 5 bus., because he takes the rest in wheat, at 1 qr every 8 weeks. Delivered to 1 warrener for the same time, 1 qr 5 bus. **{Henceforth the warrener will take a quarter every 10 weeks, half of wheat and half of barley}** Given to the reapers by estimation in sheaves at harvest-time, 8½ qrs. Sold, 34½ qrs. It balances.

Oats
{yield: two-fold less 6 qrs}
The same render account for 98 qrs of oats from the whole issue by struck measure; 8 qrs by estimation in sheaves given to the reapers for reaping corn at harvest-time; 30 qrs bought. Total, 136 qrs.
Sown over 87 acres which lie in Kygwoderigg' and le Brech', 65 qrs 2 bus.; that is, 6 bus. an acre. In fodder of 6 horses at the time of both sowings, 5½ qrs. In fodder of the horses of Peter de Scypton' from Michaelmas until Hilary, 1½ qrs. In fodder of the horses of the bailiff now for his visits, 1½ qrs. Given to the reapers by estimation in sheaves for reaping corn at harvest-time, 8 qrs, because they take as much from other corn. In making meal (*farina*) for the pottage of the manorial servants, 1 qr. In fodder of the steward's horses, 6 bus. In fodder of the horses of Simon de Farh*am*, 3½ bus. Sold, 51 qrs ½ bus. It balances.

Peas
{yield: 5-fold plus 1 qr}
The same render account for 22 qrs from the whole issue of peas by struck measure; 1½ qrs by estimation in sheaves given to the reapers at harvest-time. Total, 23½ qrs.
Sown over 13 acres which lie in Cu*m*be, 3 qrs 2 bus.; that is, 2 bus. an acre. Given to the reapers by estimation in sheaves at harvest-time, 1½ qrs. Mixed with barley for the liveries of the manorial servants, 2 qrs. In supporting pigs in winter, ½ qr. Sold, 12 qrs 2 bus. Total, 18 qrs. 4 qrs remain in the granary.

Vetches
{yield: two-and-a-half-fold less ½ bus.}
The same render account for 14 qrs of vetches by estimation in the stack. They remain in the stack.

Stock

Plough-horses: 6 remain from the previous year. Total, 6. 1 in murrain; 5 remain.
Oxen: 47 remain from the previous year; 8 additions; 6 bought; 1 from the heriot of John de Wyk'. Total, 62. 8 sold at Martinmas and afterwards because they were sick; 4 in murrain. Total, 12. 50 remain.
Bulls: 1 remains from the previous year; 1 addition. Total, 2. 2 remain.
Cows: 34 remain from the previous year; 9 additions; 6 bought after calving about the feast of St John (24 June). Total, 49. 4 in murrain before calving; 6 sold, 3 after calving. Total, 10. 39 remain.

Steers: 20 remain from the previous year's bullocks. Total, 20. 8 added to oxen, 1 to bulls, and 9 to cows; 2 in murrain. Total, 20. None remain.
Bullocks: 19 remain from the previous year's yearlings, now 2 years old; 1 from the heriot of John atte Mers. Total, 20. 20 remain, 7 of them male.
Yearlings: 20 remain from the previous year's calves, now a year old. 10 in murrain. Total, 10. 10 remain.
Calves: 34 from the offspring of the said cows this year because 2 sterile. 3 in tithe; 10 sold; 6 in murrain. Total, 19. 15 remain.
Wethers: 562 remain from the previous year; 90 added from stock. Total, 652. 49 sold, 20 after shearing; 53 in murrain before shearing, 16 after shearing; 10 delivered to the reeve of Bishops Fonthill after shearing. Total, 128. 524 remain.
Rams: 12 remain from the previous year; 9 added from stock. Total, 21. 2 in murrain before shearing, 1 after shearing. Total, 3. 18 remain.
Ewes: 801 remain from the previous year; 102 added from stock; 10 from Bishops Fonthill after shearing. Total, 913. 26 sold at Martinmas; 1 in customary payment to the shepherd; 22 in murrain before lambing, 47 after lambing and before shearing, and 19 after shearing. Total, 115. 798 remain.
Hoggs: 276 remain from the previous year's lambs; 75 in murrain before shearing; 90 added to wethers, 9 to rams, and 102 to ewes. None remain.
Lambs: 705 from the offspring of the said ewes this year and not more because 47 were sterile, 26 sold at Martinmas, and 22 in murrain before lambing. 55 in tithe and not more because the skins of lambs before weaning are tithed separately; 1 in customary payment to the shepherd; 149 in murrain before weaning, 10 after weaning and before shearing, and 2 after shearing; 50 sold before shearing. Total, 267. 438 remain.
Boars (*Verr'*): 1 remains from the previous year; 1 addition. Total, 2. 1 in murrain; 1 remains.
Sows: 3 remain from the previous year. Total, 3. 3 remain.
Pigs: 55 remain from the previous year; 24 additions. Total, 79. 18 in murrain; 34 sold. Total, 52. 27 remain.
Hoggets: 30 remain from the previous year's piglets. 5 in murrain; 1 added to boars, 24 to pigs. Total, 30. None remain.
Piglets: 24 farrowed this year, 11 at the Purification (2 February), and 13 at Hockday (1 May). 5 in murrain; 2 in tithe. Total, 7. 17 remain.
Fleeces {yield of fleece 4¼*d*. plus 6*s*. 11¾*d*. in all}: 1396 from wethers, rams, ewes and hoggs produced at the shearing this year at East Knoyle; 287 received from Upton. Total, 1683. 168 in tithe; 2 in customary payment to the shepherd. Total, 170. 1513 sent to Wolvesey, which made 10 weys and 2 cloves.
Lamb's-wool {yield of fleece 1¼*d*. less 2*d*. in all}: 440 lambs' fleeces produced at the shearing this year; all sent to Wolvesey with the coarse wool, which made 25 cloves.
Wool locks: 1 wey 16 cloves, of which 2 cloves received from the reeve of Upton; all sold.
[Winter cheese]: nothing this year.
[Summer cheese] {yield of cow 3*s*. . . . sick and sheep . . . 3*s*. 9¾*d*. with . . . and provision of the harvest . . . }: 301 cheeses made in summer between Thursday before Palm Sunday (12 April) and Michaelmas, at 2 cheeses a day for the 131 days between Easter (22 April) and the decollation of the blessed John the Baptist (29 August), and 1 cheese for each of the other days within the said time. Total, 301. 30 in tithe; 1 in customary payment to the sheep-shearers; 1 in provision of the harvest.

Total, 32. 269 sold, which made 22 weys. Moreover, the dairymaid and milkmaid have milk on Sundays by ancient custom, which made 2 weys by estimation.
[Butter] { . . . and with milk . . . 2 weys}: 3½ weys, 1 clove, 4 lb from the issue of the dairy this year; all sold.
[Hides]: 4 from oxen, 4 from cows, 2 from steers, 10 from yearling calves, and 6 from calves, dead from murrain this year. Total, 26. All sold.
[Woolskins]: 53 from wethers, 2 from rams, 69 from ewes, and 75 from hoggs in murrain before shearing. Total, 199. All sold.
[Bare skins]: 16 from wethers, 1 from a ram, and 19 from ewes in murrain after shearing. Total, 36. And sold.
[Lambskins]: 149 from lambs in murrain before weaning, 10 after weaning and before shearing, and 2 after shearing. Total, 161. 16 in tithe; 145 sold.
[Hens]: 60 from boon-reaping according to custom; all sold.
[Cider]: 1 cask from this year's issue; 1 cask remains.
[Utensils]: 1 brass pot, 3 gallon vessels, 2 brass pots which contain 2 gallons, 1 brass posnet, 2 pans, 1 basin with a ewer, 3 tables with 3 pairs of trestles, 2 carts with iron tyres, 2 wagons with iron tyres, 2 axes, 2 barrels, 2 beams, 9 ploughs, 2 iron harrows, 3 locks, 8 sacks, 2 hemp ropes, 2 weights for weighing wool, and 3 empty casks remain from the previous year; all this remains.

m.6

Upton

Arrears
Theobald de Thygden', bailiff, and Robert atte Mersch', reeve, render account for £5 19*s*. 2¾*d*. of arrears from the previous year. Delivered to Sir *Geoffrey*, treasurer of Wolvesey, by 1 tally, £1 9*s*.

Rents of assize
The same render account for £1 3*s*. 2¾*d*. for all rents of assize from the manor of Upton for the year, that is, 7*s*. 4*d*. at the feast of St Andrew (30 November), 7*s*. 4*d*. at Palm Sunday (15 April), 7*s*. 4*d*. at Lammas (1 August), and 1*s*. 2¾*d*. at Michaelmas (29 September). Total, £1 3*s*. 2¾*d*.

Quittances
In quittance of 1 reeve for the year 2*s*.; 3 ploughmen for the year 6*s*., or 2*s*. each; 1 shepherd for the year 2*s*.; 2 workers for the year 4*s*. Total, 14*s*.

Defaults of rent
In default of 1 acre of land which John, formerly of le Wych', held drawn into demesne, 2¼*d*. for the year. Total, 2¼*d*.

Total of quittances and defaults of rent, 14*s*. 2¼*d*.

Total of rents remaining, 9*s*. ½*d*.

Issues of the manor
The same render account for £1 14*s*. 10½*d*. from 29 wethers sold at Martinmas (11 November), at 1*s*. 2½*d*. each; 14*s*. 10*d*. from 3 feeble and sick oxen sold, at 4*s*. 10*d*. for 1, and 5*s*. each for the others; 18*s*. 2*d*. from the hides sold of 7 oxen in murrain, at

2*s*. 4*d*. each for 3, and 2*s*. 9½*d*. each for 4; 3*s*. 3*d*. from the skins sold of 13 wethers in murrain before shearing; 10*d*. from the skins sold of 10 wethers after shearing; 3*s*. 8*d*. from 32 hens from churchscot and 12 from the vill for herbage, at 1*d*. each; nothing from cider because it remains in the casks; nothing from Luke Purhog, Walter Bithewod' and Richard Uppeh*u*ll' for release from labour service this year because they worked for the whole year. Total, £3 15*s*. 7½*d*.

Sale of corn
The same render account for £2 14*s*. 5½*d*. from 11 qrs 1 bus. of wheat sold, at 5*s*. a qr for 9 qrs 1 bus., and 4*s*. 5*d*. a qr for 2 qrs; 12*s*. from 6 qrs of curall sold, at 2*s*. a qr; £1 11*s*. 1½*d*. from 10 qrs 3 bus. of barley sold, at 3*s*. a qr; £1 13*s*. 3*d*. from 14 qrs 2 bus. of oats sold, at 2*s*. 4*d*. a qr; 9*s*. 6*d*. from 4 qrs 7 bus. of vetches sold, at 2*s*. a qr for 4½ qrs, and 2*d*. a bus. for 4 bus. Total, £7 4*d*.

Pleas and perquisites
The same render account for 16*s*. 4*d*. from the amercements of the court this year. Total, 16*s*. 4*d*.

Total of all receipts, £12 1*s*. 4*d*.

Cost of ploughs
In iron and steel bought for the ironwork of 2 ploughs for the year 4*s*. 9½*d*. In 1 ploughshare bought 9*d*. In 2 plough feet bought 6*d*. In 1 pair of wheels bought for ploughs 2*d*. In 2 yokes bought 2*d*. In stipend of the smith for the ironwork of 2 ploughs for the year 4*s*. In stipend of 1 oxherd for the year 5*s*. In making 2 ploughs from the lord's timber 5*d*. In 7 oxen bought for ploughs because of the loss of other oxen which died £2 12*s*. 10¾*d*., at 16*s*. 8*d*. for 2, and 7*s*. 3*d*. each for 5.[1] Total, £3 8*s*. 8¼*d*.

Cost of carts
In 4 tacks bought for the cart 3*d*. In 1 saddle-pad bought 9*d*. In grease bought 1*d*. In shoeing 2 plough-horses for the year 1*s*. 5*d*. In fitting the cart with axles 1½*d*. In stipend of 1 carter for the year 5*s*. Total, 7*s*. 7½*d*.

Sheepcote
In washing and shearing sheep 6*d*. In grease bought for greasing sheep 4*s*. Total, 4*s*. 6*d*.

Cost of buildings
In roofing and mending the hall and re-roofing the byre in places 7½*d*. In stipend of 1 man repairing and restoring the wall around the garden and ruined barn 2*s*. 1*d*. In mending the garden-gate 2*d*. In nails bought for the same 1½*d*. In 1 lock bought 1½*d*. In stipend of 1 man re-roofing the hay-barn and cart-house 1*s*. 4*d*. In 2 casks bought for cider 6*s*. 10*d*. Total, 11*s*. 3*d*.

Threshing of corn
In threshing 7½ qrs of wheat by piece-work 1*s*. 3*d*., at 2*d*. a qr. In winnowing the same 1½*d*. In threshing 10½ qrs of barley 1*s*. 3¾*d*., at 1½*d*. a qr of 10 bus. In winnowing the same 2*d*., at 1*d*. per 5 qrs. All the rest of the corn threshed by labour service this year. Total, 2*s*. 10¼*d*.

1 Figures add up to £2 12*s*. 11*d*.

Cost of the harvest
In weeding corn over and above that weeded by labour service 1*s*. 8*d*. In mowing and tossing the meadow of Pilemed' 4*d*. In cheese bought for the mowing and tossing of the meadow of Rech*am* by customary tenants 4*d*. In provision of the household at harvest-time 1*s*. 2*d*. In stipend of 1 reap-reeve who is overseer of the harvest 3*s*. In stipend of 1 stacker at harvest-time 1*s*. 8*d*. Total, 8*s*. 2*d*.

Total of all expenses, £5 3*s*. 1*d*.

And he owes, £6 18*s*. 3*d*.

None delivered. And he owes it all.

Issues of the grange
Wheat
{yield: 4½-fold less 1 bus.}
The same render account for 22 qrs 2 bus. from the whole issue of wheat by struck measure; 1 qr 3 bus. by estimation in sheaves given to the reapers at harvest-time because they received the seventeenth sheaf. Total, 23 qrs 1 bus.
Sown over 29½ acres in West Field, 11 qrs; that is, 3 bus. an acre. In customary payment for the mowing of the meadow, 1 bus. Given to the reapers by estimation in sheaves, 1 qr 3 bus. Sold, 11 qrs 1 bus.

Curall
The same render account for 6 qrs of curall from the whole issue. And sold.

Barley
{yield: two-and-a-half-fold plus 5½ bus.}
The same render account for 32 qrs from the whole issue of barley this year by struck measure; 2½ qrs by estimation in sheaves given to the reapers at harvest-time. Total, 34½ qrs.
Sown over 23½ acres which lie in West Field, 11 qrs 6 bus.; that is, ½ qr an acre. Delivered to 1 carter for the year, 5 qrs 1 bus., because he takes a quarter every 10 weeks. Delivered to 1 oxherd for the year, 4 qrs 6 bus., because he takes a quarter every 11 weeks. Given to the reapers by estimation in sheaves at harvest-time, 2½ qrs. Sold, 10 qrs 3 bus.

Oats
{yield: two-fold less 3 qrs}
The same render account for 29 qrs 2 bus. from the whole issue of oats by struck measure; 3½ qrs by estimation in sheaves given to the reapers at harvest-time. Total, 32 qrs 6 bus.
Sown over 40 acres which lie in West Field, 15 qrs; that is, 3 bus. an acre. Given to the reapers by estimation in sheaves, 3½ qrs. Sold, 14 qrs 2 bus.

Vetches
{yield: 3-fold plus 2 bus.}
The same render account for 6 qrs 6 bus. from the whole issue of vetches by struck measure; 1 qr by estimation in sheaves given to the reapers. Total, 7 qrs 6 bus.
Sown over 5 acres which lie in West Field, 1 qr 7 bus.; that is, 3 bus. an acre. Given to the reapers by estimation in sheaves at harvest-time, 1 qr. Sold, 4 qrs 7 bus.

Stock

Plough-horses: 2 remain from the previous year; they remain.
Oxen: 16 remain from the previous year; 7 bought this year. Total, 23. 3 sold; 7 in murrain. Total, 10. 13 remain.
Wethers: 313 remain from the previous year. 29 sold at Martinmas and afterwards; 13 in murrain before shearing, 10 after shearing. Total, 52. 261 remain.
Fleeces: 287 produced at the shearing this year, sent to East Knoyle and tithed there; 1 in customary payment to the shepherd; 286 delivered to the reeve of East Knoyle.
Wool locks {nothing here because enrolled under East Knoyle}: 2 stone; delivered to the reeve of East Knoyle with the coarse wool.
Woolskins: 13 from wethers in murrain before shearing, 10 after shearing. Total, 23. All sold.
Hens: 32 from churchscot; 12 from the vill for herbage. Total, 44. All sold.
Cider: 2 casks made this year; 2 casks remain.
Utensils: 1 cart with iron tyres, 5 ploughs, 3 harrows, 1 beam, 1 spade, 1 bucket for drawing water, 1 table with 3 trestles, and 3 sacks remain from the previous year; all this remains.

Bishops Fonthill

Arrears

Theobald de Thygden', bailiff, and William, reeve, render account for £11 7*s*. 9*d*. of arrears from the previous year. All delivered to Sir G*eoffrey*, treasurer of Wolvesey, by 1 tally. They are quit.

Rents of assize

The same render account for £5 3*d*. for all rents of assize from Bishops Fonthill for the year, that is, £1 5*s*. ¾*d*. at Christmas, £1 5*s*. ¾*d*. at Easter (22 April), £1 5*s*. ¾*d*. at the feast of St John the Baptist (24 June), and £1 5*s*. ¾*d*. at Michaelmas (29 September). Total, £5 3*d*.

Quittances

In quittance of 1 reeve for the year 2*s*.; 1 bartoner for the year 2*s*.; 1 smith for the year for the ironwork of 3 ploughs 2*s*.; 1 swineherd for the year who is overseer of the harvest 2*s*.; 2 shepherds, one of whom keeps the sheep in the pinfold (*potfold'*) for the year, 3*s*. 6*d*.; 5 ploughmen for the year 10*s*., or 2*s*. each. Total, £1 1*s*. 6*d*.

Total of rents remaining, £3 18*s*. 9*d*.

Annual recognizance

The same render account for 3*d*. from Thomas Tritur' for annual recognizance; 3*d*. from John le Charectyr for the same; 3*d*. from John, son of Matilda de Fontel, for the same. Total, 9*d*.

Issues of the manor

The same render account for 2*s*. 2*d*. from pannage of pigs at Martinmas (11 November), at 1*d*. a pig over a year old, and ½*d*. a younger pig; 1*s*. 11*d*. from the residue of Peter's pence; £2 18*s*. 7*d*. from 22 pigs sold at Martinmas, at 3*s*. a head for 10, and 2*s*. 4½*d*. a head for 12, plus 1*d*. in all; 16*s*. from 2 oxen sold, at 8*s*. each; £2

19*s*. 6*d*. from 51 wethers sold at Martinmas and afterwards, at 1*s*. 2*d*. a head; nothing from coarse wool because it is sent to Wolvesey; 2*s*. 3½*d*. from the skins sold of 11 wethers and 1 hogg in murrain before shearing, at 2½*d*. a skin; 9½*d*. from the skins sold of 9 wethers and 1 hogg after shearing, at 1*d*. a skin of wethers, ½*d*. of hoggs; 2*s*. 10*d*. from 34 hens from churchscot sold; 2*s*. 6*d*. from John, reeve, for release from labour service for the year, because it is commuted by order of the bishop; 2*s*. from the labour service and churchscot of the lands of William son of John, reeve, who has taken up land lying in le Hasard; 2*s*. from John atte Myln', Robert Faber and Thomas le Boys for release from their labour service at harvest-time; nothing from the pasturage on le Rygg' this year for the lord's livestock; nothing from underwood; 3*s*. 8*d*. from 2 stone of wool locks sold, at 1*s*. 10*d*. a stone; 10*d*. from the fleeces of 10 lambs sold. Total, £7 15*s*. 1*d*.

Sale of corn

The same render account for £14 16*s*. 10½*d*. from 59 qrs 3 bus. of wheat sold, at 5*s*. a qr; 2*s*. 3*d*. from 1 qr 1 bus. of curall sold, at 2*s*. a qr; £4 19*s*. 2*d*. from 29 qrs 6 bus. of barley sold, at 3*s*. 4*d*. a qr; £2 8*s*. 4*d*. from 25 qrs of oats sold, at 2*s*. a qr for 20 qrs, and 1*s*. 8*d*. a qr for 5 qrs; 6*s*. from 3 qrs of vetches sold, at 2*s*. a qr. Total, £22 12*s*. 7½*d*.

Entry and marriage fines

The same render account for 3*s*. from tithingpenny at the hundred-court of Martinmas; 3*s*. from the same tithing at the hundred-court of Hockday; 5*s*. from Alice Stevenes for marrying herself to a certain Thomas, son of Robert de Burton'. Total, 11*s*.

Pleas and perquisites

The same render account for £2 10*d*. from the pleas, perquisites and amercements of the court this year, as made clear in the court rolls. Total, £2 10*d*.

Total of all receipts, £36 19*s*. ½*d*.

Cost of ploughs

In iron and steel bought for the ironwork of 3 ploughs for the year, 10*s*. 6*d*. this year. In 3 pairs of wheels bought 1*s*. In 9 yokes bought 1*s*. In 3 plough feet bought 9*d*. In 2 ploughshares bought 1*s*. 8*d*. In stipend of 1 carpenter making 3 ploughs from the lord's timber 6*d*. Given to the smith in place of 2 trunks which he is accustomed to have for the year for the ironwork of ploughs, 2*s*. this year. In stipend of 1 oxherd for the year 3*s*. In 6 oxen bought for ploughs £2 12*s*., at 19*s*. 6*d*. for 2, 3*s*. each for 3, and 8*s*. 6*d*. for 1. Total, £3 12*s*. 5*d*.

Cost of carts

In clouts and nails bought for the cart 4*d*. In 2 axles bought for the cart 4*d*. In grease bought for the cart 2*d*. In stipend of 1 man making 2 collars from the lord's leather 3*d*. In 2 halters bought 2*d*. In shoeing 2 plough-horses for the year 3*s*. In 2 ropes bought for tethering plough-horses in the pasture 2*d*. In stipend of 1 carter for the year 3*s*. In 1 pair of traces bought 6*d*. In re-covering 1 saddle 1*d*. Total, 8*s*.

Cost of buildings

In stipend of 1 man re-roofing the hay-barn, byre and sheepcote in places 1*s*. In 1 cask bought and others repaired 3*s*. 4½*d*. In stipend of 1 man repairing the press with wood bought for the same 2*s*. In grease bought for the same 3*d*. In stipend of 1 man making anew 1 gate to the fields with boards sawn for the same and hooks and hinges and nails bought 2*s*. In 1 shovel bought 1½*d*. Total, 8*s*. 9*d*.

Sheepcote
In grease and verdigris bought at various times for greasing sheep 5*s*. In making anew 9 hurdles 3*d*. In 8 ells of canvas bought for packing wool 2*s*., at 3*d*. an ell. In packing the said wool 8*d*. Total, 7*s*. 11*d*.

Threshing
In threshing and winnowing 72 qrs 2 bus. of wheat, 1 qr 1 bus. of curall, and 7 qrs of bere by piece-work without heaped measure, 15*s*. ¾*d*., at 2¼*d*. a qr. In threshing and winnowing 58 qrs 7 bus. of barley, and 5 qrs 2 bus. of vetches by piece-work, 6*s*. 7¾*d*., at 1¼*d*. a qr. In threshing and winnowing 55 qrs 6 bus. of oats by piece-work, 2*s*. 9½*d*. In 1 sack bought 8*d*. Total, £1 5*s*. 2*d*.

Cost of the harvest
In weeding corn, that is, wheat, barley and oats, 2*s*. 8*d*. In customary payment to 1 overseer of the harvest who keeps the meadow of Stoketon' 4*d*. In mowing and tossing the said meadow 2*s*. In boon-works, nothing, because it was all reaped for sheaves. In stipend of 1 overseer of the harvest for the year 6*s*. 8*d*. Total, 11*s*. 8*d*.

Bailiff's expenses
In expenses of the bailiff for his visits 2*s*. 6*d*. Total, 2*s*. 6*d*.

Total of all expenses, £6 16*s*. 5*d*.

And thus he owes, £30 2*s*. 7½*d*.

Cash deliveries
Delivered to Sir G*eoffrey*, treasurer of Wolvesey, by 1 tally, £21 12*s*.

And thus he owes clear, £8 10*s*. 7½*d*.

Issues of the grange
Wheat
{yield: five-fold less 3 qrs 1 bus.}
The same render account for 72 qrs 2 bus. from the whole issue of wheat by struck measure; 5 qrs 2 bus. by estimation in sheaves given to the reapers at harvest-time because they received the same at East Knoyle; 6 bus. by estimation in 1 acre which the reeve has according to custom; 3 qrs 5 bus. from churchscot. Moreover, the rector ought to receive from the lord 4 bus. for 1 of his holdings and John, reeve, is appointed to pay this while he lives. Total, 81 qrs 7 bus.
Sown over 36 acres which lie in North Field, 13½ qrs; that is, 3 bus. an acre. Delivered to 1 overseer of the harvest for the year, 3 qrs, because he takes the rest in barley. Given to the reapers by estimation in sheaves at harvest-time, 5 qrs 2 bus. Delivered to the reeve by estimation in 1 acre which he has according to custom at his choice, besides folding and manure, 6 bus. Sold, 59 qrs 3 bus. It balances.

Curall
The same render account for 1 qr 1 bus. from the whole issue of curall by struck measure. And sold.

Bere
{yield: two-and-a-half-fold}
The same render account for 7 qrs from the whole issue of bere by struck measure; 1 qr by estimation in sheaves given to the reapers at harvest-time; 2 qrs by estimation in sheaves in 3 acres given to the overseer of the harvest, ploughmen and other workers according to custom, which they have because the overseer of the harvest, if he keeps the pigs, will have 1 acre, but if not, he will have ½, and all the ploughmen have 1 acre, and the workers of the lord's corn have the third acre. Total, 10 qrs.
Sown over 19 acres which lie in North Field, 7 qrs; that is, 3 bus. an acre. Given to the reapers by estimation in sheaves at harvest-time, 1 qr. Delivered to 1 overseer of the harvest, ploughmen and other workers, 3 acres in which there were 2 qrs by estimation. Total, 10 qrs.[1] None remains.

Barley
{yield: four-fold less 3 qrs}
The same render account for 1 qr of barley remaining from the previous year; 59 qrs from the whole issue of barley this year by struck measure; 4 qrs by estimation in sheaves given to the reapers at harvest-time. Total, 64 qrs.
Sown over 26 acres in South Field and North Field, 13 qrs; that is, 4 bus. an acre. Delivered to 1 overseer of the harvest, 3 qrs 2 bus., because he takes the rest in wheat, and takes a quarter every 8 weeks. Delivered to 1 carter and 1 oxherd for the year, 13 qrs, because they take a quarter every 8 weeks. In customary payment to 6 ploughmen, the hayward and smith for their food and drink at Christmas and Easter, 1 qr. Given to the reapers by estimation in sheaves at harvest-time, 4 qrs. Sold, 29 qrs 6 bus.

Oats
{yield: two-fold plus 3 qrs 6 bus.}
The same render account for 55 qrs 6 bus. from the whole issue of oats by struck measure; 4 qrs by estimation in sheaves given to the reapers at harvest-time. Total, 59 qrs 6 bus.
Sown over 53½ acres in North Field, 26 qrs 5 bus.; that is, 4 bus. an acre. In fodder of 2 plough-horses for the year, 4 qrs 1 bus. In fodder of oxen nothing this year because they had hay. Given to the reapers by estimation in sheaves at harvest-time, 4 qrs. Sold, 25 qrs. It balances.

Vetches
{yield: three-fold less 1 qr 2 bus.}
The same render account for 5 qrs 2 bus. from the whole issue of vetches by struck measure; 1 qr by estimation in sheaves given to the reapers at harvest-time. Total, 6 qrs 2 bus.
Sown over 5 acres which lie in North Field, 1 qr 7 bus.; that is, 3 bus. an acre. Given to the reapers by estimation in sheaves at harvest-time, 1 qr. In supporting pigs, 3 bus. Sold, 3 qrs. It balances.

m.6d

Stock

Plough-horses: 2 remain from the previous year; 2 females remain; no offspring because they were sterile.

1 MS omits 'qrs'.

Oxen: 24 remain from the previous year; 6 bought. Total, 30. 2 sold at Martinmas. Total, 2. 28 remain.
Wethers: 323 remain from the previous year; 34 additions. Total, 357. 11 in murrain before shearing, 10 after shearing; 31 sold at Martinmas, 20 afterwards. Total, 72. 285 remain.
Hoggs: 36 remain from the previous year's lambs. 1 in murrain before shearing, 1 after shearing; 34 added to wethers. Total, 36. None remain.
Lambs: 10 produced by 10 ewes which were bought to be among the wethers, for which 10 ewes were sent to East Knoyle in return for 10 wethers. Total, 10. 10 remain.
Pigs: 40 remain from the previous year, 1 of them a boar and 2 sows; 24[1] additions. Total, 64. 26 sold; 12 in murrain. Total, 38. 26 remain, 1 of them a boar and 2 sows.
Hoggets: 28 remain from the previous year's piglets. 4 in murrain; 24 added to pigs. Total, 28. None remain.
Piglets: 33 farrowed this year, 11 at All Saints (1 November), 12 at Easter (22 April), and 10 at Lammas (1 August); 3 in tithe; 17 in murrain; 13 remain.
Fleeces {yield of fleece 4*d*. plus 2*s*. 2*d*. in all}: 316 produced at the shearing this year; 34 in tithe; 1 in customary payment to the shepherd; 312 sent to Wolvesey, which made 2 weys 12 cloves.
Lamb's-wool {yield of fleece 1*d*.}: 10 lambs' fleeces produced at the shearing. And sold.
Wool locks: 2 stone. And sold.
Woolskins: 11 from wethers and 1 from a hogg in murrain before shearing; 10 from wethers and 1 from a hogg in murrain after shearing. Total, 23. And sold.
Cider: 2 casks made this year; 2 casks remain.
Hens: 48 from churchscot. 4 in quittance of 1 smith; 2 in default of Robert Snelgar; 4 in default of the land of Bagg' drawn into the liberty; 4 in default of the land of Godm' for the same reason. Total, 14. 34 sold.
Utensils: 1 cart with iron tyres and 3 ploughs with all equipment remain from the previous year; 1 cart bought; all this remains except 1 old cart which is worn out.

Downton

Arrears
Theobald de Thygd', bailiff, Robert, reeve, and Robert Saleman render account for £36 5*s*. ½*d*. of arrears from the previous year. All delivered to Sir G*eoffrey*, treasurer of Wolvesey, by 1 tally. They are quit.

Rents of assize
The same render account for £9 15*s*. 9½*d*. for all rents of assize from the said manor at Christmas; £10 15*s*. 3½*d*. at Easter (22 April); £9 15*s*. ½*d*. at the Nativity of the blessed John the Baptist (24 June); £27 13*s*. 10½*d*. at Michaelmas (29 September). Total, £58 9*d*.

Quittances
In quittance of 1 reeve for the year 5*s*.; 1 forester for the year 4*s*.; 2 haywards of Downton and Wick for the year 4*s*.; 1 hayward of Witherington who {is keeping} Privett for the year 1*s*. 8*d*.; 11 ploughmen for the year £1 2*s*., or 2*s*. each; 2

1 MS '34'.

ploughmen of Witherington 3*s*. 4*d*., or 1*s*. 8*d*. each; 2 oxherds for the year 4*s*.; 2 shepherds of Wick and Nunton for the year 4*s*.; 1 shepherd of Witherington for the year 1*s*. 8*d*.; 1 shepherd of Cokewyk' for the year 2*s*.; 1 keeper of lambs for ½ year 6*d*.; 1 cowherd for the year 2*s*.; 1 virgate of land for the repair of the bridge, as long as it pleases the lord, 5*s*.; 1 swineherd for the year 2*s*.; 1 park-keeper for the year 4*s*. 6*d*. Total, £3 5*s*. 8*d*.

Defaults of rent
In default of 2 ferlings of land drawn into burgage, 6*s*. for the year; 3 ferlings delivered to Fulk de Walton', 2*s*. for the year; 32½ acres which are called Coesetlelond' through Bishop John £1 7*s*. 1*d*., or 10*d*. an acre, which Simon de Stoppeh*a*m now holds, paying 18*s*. 11½*d*. each year, or 7*d*. an acre, which is included above with the rents; the fulling mill, 10*s*. for the year,[1] because nobody is willing to hold it at the old rent; the land which is called Hangres, which formerly belonged to Elias le Draper, which Roger de Stoppeh*a*m held, who neither wanted to hold it for longer nor found anybody to pass it on to, 10*s*. 6*d*. Total, £2 15*s*. 7*d*.

Total of quittances and defaults of rent, £6 1*s*. 3*d*.

Total of rents remaining, £51 19*s*. 6*d*.

Cumin
The same render account for 1 pair of gold spurs for the rent of Roger de Jardyn; 1 lb of cumin or 1*d*. from Simon de Stoppeh*a*m for holding at will the garden of Roger de Wyk'. Total, 1*d*.

Issues of the manor
The same render account for £2 3*s*. ¼*d*. from pannage of pigs at Martinmas (11 November), at 1*d*. a pig over a year old, and ½*d*. if it is under a year; nothing from foreign pannage this year because there was no mast; 11*s*. ½*d*. from pannage of oxen and sheep at Hockday (1 May) from the men of Nunton, at 4*d*. a fully-grown ox, and 1*d*. per 5 sheep; 6*s*. from the men of Witherington for the same at the said term; 6*s*. 1½*d*. from the men of Wick and Walton, at 1½*d*. a fully-grown ox, because nothing is given for the sheep except sheep; £1 from the pasturage of Suothemed'; 6*s*. 8*d*. from the pasturage of Nunton; nothing from the pasturage on the heath this year for the lord's livestock; 11*s*. 6*d*. from the turbary sold this year; 2*s*. from the pasturage of Edytheh*a*me sold this year; 4*s*. from the pasturage on Mauryg' sold; nothing from the pasturage in the park this year for the lord's livestock; 2*s*. from the pasturage next to the ditch of Roger Aleyn sold; nothing from the pasturage of Tynb*er*hull' because it was sown; £1 from the pasturage of Mywhull'; nothing from the pasturage in the fields this year for the lord's livestock; £1 16*s*. from hay sold this year; 4*s*. from the residue of Peter's pence; 1*s*. 1*d*. from the churchscot of Barford; nothing from murrained branches of Losh*a*ngr' this year; nothing from broom there and underwood in Privett this year; nothing from stubble this year; 9*s*. from 2 old and feeble plough-horses sold, at 5*s*. for 1, and 4*s*. for the other; 8*s*. from 1 old mare sold; 8*s*. 6*d*. from 1 horse from the heriot of Richard Mol*endinarius* sold; 5*s*. 6*d*. from 1 plough-horse from the heriot of Robert Wolgar sold; £3 14*s*. from 7 old oxen sold, at 8*s*. for 1, and 11*s*. each for the others; 9*s*. from 1 ox sold to the manor of Bishopstone; £1 14*s*. from 5 old cows sold, at 8*s*. each for 2, and 6*s*. each for 3; 8*s*. from 1 bull sold; 15*s*.

1 MS 'mol' {follerett'} p*er* ann*um* ⟨folent'⟩ x s.'.

4*d*. from 14 feeble and late-born calves sold; £2 from 40 kebb wethers sold at Martinmas, at 1*s*. each; 14*s*. 6*d*. from 15 ewes sold, at 6*d*. for 1, and 1*s*. each for the others; £1 2*s*. from 48 feeble lambs sold before shearing, at 5½*d*. each; £4 5*s*. from 30 pigs sold, at 2*s*. 10*d*. each; 16*s*. from 6 pigs sold afterwards, at 2*s*. 8*d*. each; nothing from coarse wool and lamb's-wool because it is sent to Wolvesey; 12*s*. 10*d*. from 14 cloves of wool locks sold, at 11*d*. a clove; £1 1*s*. 3*d*. from 2½ weys of winter cheese sold, at 8*s*. 6*d*. a wey; £8 11*s*. from 19 weys of summer cheese sold, at 9*s*. a wey; £1 1*s*. 7*d*. from 2 weys 12 cloves of butter sold, at 9*s*. a wey; 1*s*. 10*d*. from the hide sold of 1 heifer in murrain; 3*d*. from the hide sold of 1 bullock in murrain; 6*d*. from the hides sold of 4 calves in murrain; 3*d*. from the hides sold of 3 pigs in murrain; 18*s*. 10*d*. from the skins sold of 93 wethers, rams, ewes and hoggs in murrain before shearing, at 3*d*. a skin of wethers, 2½*d*. of rams and ewes, and 2*d*. of hoggs; 1*s*. 9*d*. from the skins sold wholesale of 10 wethers, 7 ewes and 2 hoggs in murrain after shearing; 6*s*. 9*d*. from the skins sold of 81 lambs before weaning, at 1*d*. a skin; 1½*d*. from the skins sold wholesale of 7 rotted sheep in murrain before and after shearing; 1*s*. from peacocks' feathers; £1 7*s*. 4*d*. from 324 hens from churchscot sold, at 1*d*. each; 12*s*. 2*d*. from 1 cask of cider sold apart from the vessel; 10*s*. from the bark sold of timber for making anew the mill's sluice; £1 from the whole hundred for refusing to stack (*tasso refutato*); 3*s*. 6½*d*. for release from ploughing 8½ acres in winter; £1 16*s*. for release from harvest labour service after reaping; 15*s*. from Walter Speye, Henry Goldwyr, William, son of Matilda Wych, and John Bolle for fishing. Total, £45 4*s*. 3¼*d*.

Annual recognizance

The same render account for 6*d*. from Roger Aylm' for annual recognizance; 6*d*. from Thomas de Bott*en*h' for the same; 6*d*. from John, son of William de Cruce, for the same; 6*d*. from Thomas le Sumetyr for the same; 3*d*. from John Turry for the same. Total, 2*s*. 3*d*.

Sale of corn

The same render account for £17 3*s*. 1½*d*. from 64 qrs 5 bus. of wheat sold, at 5*s*. 8*d*. a qr for 38 qrs, 5*s*. a qr for 18 qrs 5 bus., and 4*s*. 4*d*. a qr for 8 qrs; £6 10*s*. 5*d*. from 41 qrs 2 bus. of curall sold, at 3*s*. 4*d*. a qr for 20 qrs, and 3*s*. a qr for 21 qrs 2 bus.; £22 2*s*. 4*d*. from 116 qrs 2 bus. of barley sold, at 4*s*. a qr for 90½ qrs, 3*s*. 4*d*. a qr for 18 qrs, and 2*s*. 8*d*. a qr for 7 qrs 5 bus.; £3 11*s*. from 26 qrs 5 bus. of oats sold, at 2*s*. 8*d*. a qr; 2*s*. from ½ qr of beans sold; £3 3*s*. 9*d*. from 19 qrs 1 bus. of peas sold, at 3*s*. 4*d*. a qr; £1 from 7½ qrs of vetches sold, at 2*s*. 8*d*. a qr. Total, £53 12*s*. 7½*d*.

Mill

The same render account for £2 14*s*. 6½*d*. from 9 qrs 5 bus. of wheat sold, at 5*s*. 8*d*. a qr; £11 7*s*. from 56 qrs 6 bus. of barley sold, at 4*s*. a qr; £4 18*s*. 7½*d*. from 17 qrs 2 bus. of first-grade malt sold, at 6*s*. a qr for 9 qrs 1 bus., 5*s*. 8*d*. a qr for 1 qr 3 bus., 4*s*. 4*d*. a qr for 2 qrs 5 bus., and 5*s*. 4*d*. a qr for 4 qrs 5 bus.; £5 12*s*. 1½*d*. from 33 qrs 3 bus. of second-grade malt sold, at 3*s*. 8*d*. a qr for 6 qrs 2 bus., 3*s*. 4*d*. a qr for 23½ qrs, and 3*s*. a qr for 3 qrs 5 bus.; 1*s*. 5½*d*. from 2½ bus. of oatmeal sold, at 8½*d*. for 1 bus., and 9*d*. for 1½ bus.; 3*s*. 2½*d*. from 2 qrs 3 bus. of fine bran (*pulv'*) sold, at 1*s*. 4*d*. for 1 qr, 1*s*. 3*d*. for 6 bus., and 7½*d*. for 5 bus.; £2 5*s*. from fishing for eels sold. Total, £27 1*s*. 11½*d*.

Entry and marriage fines

The same render account for 5*s*. from tithingpenny from Bodenham at the hundred-court of Martinmas; 6*s*. 8*d*. from tithingpenny from Charlton; 2*s*. from the tithing of

Witherington for the same; 6*s*. 8*d*. from the tithing of la Church' for the same; 5*s*. from the tithing of Downton for the same; 5*s*. from the tithing of Wick for the same; £1 10*s*. 4*d*. from the same tithings at the hundred-court of Hockday for the same; £1 13*s*. 4*d*. from Thomas Ferneyr to have 1 messuage and 1 virgate of land by surrender of Robert Wolgar with Joan his daughter; £1 from Simon Fucher to have 1 messuage 2⌈½⌉ acres of land which belonged to John Foucher; £2 13*s*. 4*d*. from Robert Aylward to retain 1 messuage and 1 virgate of land which belonged to Alice Aylward his mother; 6*d*. from Nicholas le M*er*cer to retain 1 house which belonged to William his brother; 4*s*. from Hugh Alayn for marrying Alice his daughter within; 2*s*. from Stephen Scoundy to have Matilda, who was wife of Robert le Carecter, with ½ virgate of land; 1*s*. from Jordan le Norays for 1 messuage which belonged to Geoffrey le Prestes; 6*d*. from Nicholas le M*er*cer to retain 2½ acres of land and 1 strip by surrender of William his brother; 6*s*. 8*d*. from Emma, who was wife of Richard Molend*inarius*, to retain the holding of her husband; 2*s*. from Ralph Attesell' to retain 1 acre of land by surrender of William le Fayr'; 10*s*. from John Alwyn' to retain ½ virgate of land which belonged to Elias le Charecter; 10*s*. from Ralph Turel to retain ½ virgate of land which belonged to Alice his mother; 10*s*. from Christina, formerly wife of Richard Foucher, to retain 1 virgate of land which belonged to the said Richard her husband; 5*s*. from Ralph Luv*er*oun to retain 2 acres of land which belonged to Richard atte Hall' by surrender of Richard ad Aul*am*; 4*s*. from Robert Salema*n* for marrying Alice his daughter. Total, £11 3*s*.

Pleas and perquisites
The same render account for £7 4*s*. from the pleas and perquisites of the court this year; £1 from Thomas Trapyl for various transgressions made against the lord. Total, £8 4*s*.

Total of both, £19 7*s*.

Total of all receipts, £197 7*s*. 8¼*d*.

Cost of ploughs
In ironwork of 5 ox-ploughs and 2 horse-ploughs for the year, with ploughshares, coulters and other ironwork pertaining to the plough, and with the reward of the smith forging the same for the year, £1 13*s*. 6*d*., or 4*s*. 6*d*. a plough, plus 2*s*. in all. In ironwork of 1 plough ploughing for 3 terms of the year with the stipend of the smith 2*s*. 3*d*. In 9 pairs of wheels bought 1*s*. 10*d*. In shoeing the front feet of 12 plough-horses for the year by piece-work 5*s*. In shoeing the hind feet of the same in Lent 1*s*. 10*d*. In shoeing 2 plough-horses doing various works when not needed on the demesne and carrying dung at various times 1*s*. 3*d*. In 1 boon-work of 98 ploughmen in winter and 1 boon-work of as many ploughmen in Lent, each ploughman ploughing 1 acre measured by the perch, £1 13*s*. Moreover, they are bound to plough 81 acres at Charlton, 33 acres at Wick, 16 acres at Nunton, 4 acres at Downton, 8 acres at Barford, and 17[1] acres at Witherington according to the custom called 'landrych'. In 8 halters made from hair 1½*d*. In stipend of 1 stot-keeper (*stottehurd'*) for the year 3*s*. Total, £4 1*s*. 9½*d*.

Cost of carts
In 2 new pairs of wheels bought 5*s*. 2*d*. In 1 new binding with clamps and large nails and the stipend of 1 smith fitting 1 pair of the said wheels 8*s*. 8*d*. In renewing 1 old

1 MS 'xv⟨i⟩ij'.

binding and fitting it to the other pair of wheels with large and small nails and clamps and with the stipend of the smith 2*s*. 11*d*. In fitting the carts with axles 11*d*. In clouts, nails, tallow and grease bought for the carts 1*s*. 1*d*. In stipend of 1 carpenter trimming and making spokes for the aforesaid wheels from the lord's timber 3*d*. In 4 collars bought 1*s*. 11*d*. In 1 pair of traces bought 5*d*. In 1 cart-rope bought 11*d*. In shoeing 2 cart-horses and 2 mares for the year 4*s*. 6*d*. In stipend of 2 carters for the year 6*s*. Total, £1 12*s*. 9*d*.

m.7

Cost of buildings

In stipend of 1 carpenter mending the long stable and putting in place 1 new tie-beam by piece-work 3*s*. 4*d*. In 2,500 nails bought for laths for the same 2*s*. 3*d*. In tiles and ridge-tiles bought for the same 4*s*. 5*d*. In 3 qrs of lime bought for the same 1*s*. 3*d*. In stipend of 1 man roofing the same 4*s*. In plastering the walls of the said stable and mending the same in other places 1*s*. 1*d*. In stipend of 1 carpenter mending the cow-shed 1*s*. In stipend of 1 carpenter who repaired and restored the press 2*s*. In stipend of 1 man repairing and restoring the park-gate 6*d*. In 1 lock with a key bought for the same 5½*d*. In plastering and mending in places the walls of the byre 5*d*. In 2 locks bought to put on the garden-gates 4*d*. In 1 lock bought for the door of the dairy 2½*d*. In 1 tub bound with hoops bought for the same 8½*d*. In roofing the bullock-shed by piece-work 1*s*. 4*d*. In stipend of 1 carpenter making the west gate anew and mending the ox-stalls in the byre and other places by piece-work 2*s*. 11*d*. In large and small nails and iron bands bought for the same gate 1*s*. 4*d*. In boards sawn for the said gate and for a certain gate between the kitchen and the bailiff's house 6*d*. In 2 locks with keys bought for the same 2½*d*. In 1 tablecloth with a towel bought for the bailiff's use 2*s*. 1¼*d*. In castrating 13 pigs 4*d*. In enclosing 5 furlongs 16 perches around the park 6*s*., at 1*d*. per 3 perches. In enclosing 5 furlongs 24 perches around Tynb*er*hull' 5*s*., at 1*d*. per 3 perches. In enclosing 2 furlongs 30 perches around Mywh*u*ll' 3*s*., at 1*d*. per 3 perches. In mending 4 old cider-casks 1*s*. 9*d*. In stipend of 1 man covering the stacks of peas and vetches 2*s*. ½*d*. In spreading 2450 heaps of hay 3*s*. 6¾*d*. In planting beans in the garden 4*d*. Total, £2 12*s*. 4½*d*.

Cost of the dairy

In 2 qrs of salt bought for salting 23½ weys 12 cloves of winter and summer cheese and butter, 5*s*. 2*d*. this year. In a press bought 1*s*. In linen and woollen cloth bought 1*s*. 9¼*d*. In a tripod bought 10½*d*. In earthenware pots and pans bought 7*d*. In stipend of 1 dairymaid for the year 2*s*. 6*d*. In food and stipend of 1 keeper of lambs for the whole summer because they were being weaned in the park this year 3*s*. 6*d*. Total, 15*s*. 4¾*d*.

Sheepcote

In grease, vinegar and copperas bought for greasing sheep £2 6*s*. 8½*d*. In 26 ells of canvas bought for packing wool 6*s*. 7*d*., at 3*d*. an ell. In making sacks and packing the said wool 3½*d*. Total, £2 13*s*. 7*d*.

Threshing

In threshing 224 qrs 7 bus. of wheat, curall, beans, peas and vetches by piece-work, £1 17*s*. 5¾*d*., at 2*d*. a qr of 8 struck bushels. In winnowing the same 3*s*. 9¼*d*., at 1*d*. per 5 struck quarters. In stipend of 1 man and 1 woman cleaning, winnowing and gleaning 67 qrs 1 bus. of wheat for sowing, by piece-work for 9 weeks, 17*s*. 6*d*. In threshing 242 qrs of barley by piece-work £1 4*s*. 2½*d*., at 1½*d*. a qr of 10 struck bushels. In winnowing the same 2*s*. 8¼*d*., at 1*d*. per 7½ struck quarters. In threshing 110 qrs 1 bus. of oats by piece-work, 4*s*. 7*d*., at ½*d*. per 8 struck bushels. In winnowing the same 10¾*d*., at 1*d*. per 10 struck quarters. In 4 sacks bought 2*s*. Total, £4 13*s*. 1½*d*.

Mowing the meadow
In customary payment to the men mowing the meadow of Nunton 6*d*. In mowing and tossing a certain meadow of Witherington by piece-work this year, which the customary tenants of the manor are not bound to mow or toss, 11*d*. Total, 1*s*. 5*d*.

Cost of the harvest
In expenses of 3 boon-works of 470 men reaping 240 acres of corn £1 8*s*. 5*d*. Total, £1 8*s*. 5*d*.

Cost of the mill
In 1 millstone bought £2 8*s*. 5*d*. In 3 iron collars bought for the mill-spindles 2*s*. 10*d*. In timber bought for making cogs and rungs 7*s*. 5*d*. In grease, tallow and soap bought 3*s*. 2½*d*. In 13 iron bands bought for the inner wheels of both mills with large and small nails bought for the boards (*fisscherisbord'*) 3*s*. 7*d*. In stipend of 1 man re-roofing the said mill by piece-work and plastering and mending in places the walls of the mill 1*s*. 6*d*. In boards sawn to make the boards (*fisscherisbord*) for the mill-wheels 1*s*. 1*d*. In tithe of the mill for the year £1. In steeling and sharpening the mill bills with the stipend of the smith 4*s*. In stipend of the miller for the year 8*s*. In repairing the sluice at Car*ec*taresmed' £1 12*s*. 8½*d*. Total, £6 12*s*. 9*d*.

Cowyk'
In enclosing 4 furlongs 9 perches around Cowyke 4*s*. 8*d*., at 1*d*. per 3 perches. In weeding 23 acres of wheat and barley 1*s*. 11*d*. In 1 boon-work of 34 men reaping corn there 2*s*. 4*d*. In 1 boon-work of 10 carters carrying the said corn to Downton 1*s*. 9*d*. Total, 10*s*. 8*d*.

Steward's expenses
In expenses of the steward for his visits 6*s*. 8½*d*. Total, 6*s*. 8½*d*.

In expenses of Simon, clerk, going to and returning from Taunton on 2 occasions 7*s*. 9*d*. Total, 7*s*. 9*d*.

Bailiff's expenses
In expenses of the bailiff from Michaelmas until the arrival of Theobald, the next bailiff, £1 1*s*. 6*d*. In expenses of Theobald, the next bailiff, with expenses for holding the tourn by the same Theobald £2 16*s*. In fur bought for the summer livery of the same 3*s*. 4*d*. Total, £4 10*d*.

Building payments
In re-roofing in places the great hall, the bishop's chamber, the room below the east gate, the bishop's kitchen, and the rest of the buildings around the hall, 10*s*. by fixed agreement. In 2,000 nails bought for shingles and laths 1*s*. 9*d*. In 5 qrs of lime bought for the same 2*s*. 1½*d*. In 3,000 tiles bought for the same 5*s*. In hiring 1 carpenter for 14 days to mend and re-roof in places the bishop's chamber, and to lay and mend

1,500 shingles on the bishop's hall and the said chamber, by the carpenter at piece-work, 4*s*. Total, £1 2*s*. 10½*d*.

Total of all expenses, £31 5¼*d*.

And he owes, £166 7*s*. 3*d*.

Allowances

In allowance of Robert, reeve, for the expenses of the taxers who were assessing the fifteenth 5*s*. 10½*d*. In allowance of Robert Salema*n* for buying 3½ qrs of oats for the use of Sir Hugh le Despe*n*syr, by order of the steward, 10*s*. In allowance of the reeve for making a new sluice and 1 new mill-dam (*fisbedd'*) £4 12*s*. 11*d*. In allowance of the reeve for the provision of hens for the bishop's household at Farnham, now 3 years ago, £1. In allowance of the reeve for Robert, the bailiff's clerk, and for the stipend of a certain attendant staying at East Knoyle, under that this year, and concerned with the issue of the grange there £1 6*s*. 8*d*. Total, £7 15*s*. 5½*d*.

Cash deliveries

Delivered to Sir G*eoffrey*, treasurer of Wolvesey, by 1 tally, £121 12*s*.

Total of all allowances and cash deliveries, £129 7*s*. 5½*d*.

And thus he owes clear, £36 19*s*. 9½*d*.

Downton Borough

Rents of assize

Ralph le Mey, reeve, renders account for £3 1*d*. for all rents of assize at Easter; £3 3*s*. 6*d*. at Michaelmas. Total, £6 3*s*. 7*d*.

Quittances

In quittance of 1 reeve for the year 1*s*. Total, 1*s*.

Total of rents remaining, £6 2*s*. 7*d*.

Pleas and perquisites

The same render account for £1 18*s*. 7*d*. from the pleas and perquisites of the court and tourn this year as made clear in the court roll. Total, £1 18*s*. 7*d*.

Total of all receipts, £8 1*s*. 2*d*.

And he owes, £8 1*s*. 2*d*.

Cash deliveries

Delivered to Sir G*eoffrey*, treasurer of Wolvesey, by 1 tally, £8 1*s*. 2*d*. He is quit.

Issues of the grange

Wheat

{yield: two-and-a-half-fold plus 16 qrs 1 bus.}

The same render account for 139 qrs 2 bus. from the whole issue of wheat by struck measure.

Sown over 177½ acres in the field of Wick, 12 acres in the field of Nunton, 18½ acres in the field of Witherington, and 7 acres 1 perch in the field of Losha*n*gr', 67 qrs 1 bus.; that is, 2½ bus. an acre. In provision of the bailiff for the year, 7½ qrs. Sold, 64 qrs 5 bus. Total, 139 qrs 2 bus.

Curall

The same render account for 41 qrs 2 bus. from the whole issue of curall by struck measure. All sold.

Barley

{yield: three-and-a-half-fold less 16 qrs 6 bus.}

The same render account for 242 qrs from the whole issue of barley by struck measure; 6½ qrs by estimation in sheaves given to the workers, who are bound to reap all the barley according to custom for sheaves, and they reaped 126 acres of barley, for 2 sheaves an acre; 2½ qrs by estimation in sheaves given to cows, bullocks and calves. Total, 251 qrs.

Sown over 131 acres 1 perch in the field of Downton, 18 acres 1 perch in the field of Nunton, 10½ acres in the field of Witherington, and 9 acres 1 perch in the field of Losha*n*gr', 84 qrs 2 bus.; that is, ½ qr an acre. Delivered to 1 warrener, 2 carters and 1 stot-keeper for the year, 26 qrs, each taking a quarter every 8 weeks. Delivered to 1 dairymaid between the Annunciation (25 March) and Michaelmas, 3½ qrs. Delivered to 1 harrower at the time of both sowings, 1 qr. **{Henceforth the livery of the harrower is not allowed except a fixed tenth whilst the barley is sowed}** In clearing dung according to custom by customary tenants, 2 qrs. In customary payment to customary tenants for reaping 134 acres of barley, 6½ qrs by estimation in sheaves. In provision of cows, bullocks and calves, 2½ qrs by estimation in sheaves, for want of oats. In provision of the bailiff for the year, 2½ qrs. In 3 boon-works at Downton and Cowyk', 6½ qrs. Sold, 116 qrs 2 bus.

Oats

{yield: two-fold plus 9 qrs 3 bus.}

The same render account for 110 qrs 1 bus. from the whole issue of oats by struck measure; 19 qrs by estimation in sheaves given to oxen. Total, 129 ⌈qrs 1 bus.⌉

Sown over 7 acres in the field of Wick, 50½ acres in the field of Nunton, 13 acres 1 perch in the field of Witherington, 20 acres 1 perch in the field of Cowyk', and 34 acres in the field of Tymb*er*hull', 62½ qrs; that is, ½ qr an acre. In fodder of 2 cart-horses and 2 mares between Martinmas and the feast of St Gregory (12 March), 7 qrs 5 bus., taking ½ bus. a night and the rest in sheaves because of the scarcity of oats.[1] In fodder of the same and the plough-horses between the aforesaid feast and the feast of the Apostles Philip and James (1 May), 10½ qrs by estimation in sheaves. In fodder of oxen, 8½ qrs by estimation in sheaves. In fodder of the bailiff's horses for the year, 9 qrs 3 bus. Sent to the justices assigned to collect the fifteenth, 3 qrs. In provision of the steward and Simon de Pharh*a*m for their visits, 1 qr. Sold, 26 qrs 5 bus.

Beans

{yield: as sown}

The same render account for 1 qr 1 bus. from the whole issue of beans. Sown, 5 bus. Sold, ½ qr.

Peas

{yield: four-fold less 3 qrs}

The same render account for 34 qrs from the whole issue of peas by struck measure.

1 MS 'p*er* garb' ⟨*pro* p*ar*ciat'⟩ {*pro* p*ar*citate} aven*e*'.

Sown over 40 acres which lie in the field of Downton, 10 qrs; that is, 2 bus. an acre. In supporting pigs, 4 qrs 7 bus. Sold, 19 qrs 1 bus.

Vetches
{yield: four-fold less 1 qr}
The same render account for 9 qrs 2 bus. from the whole issue of vetches by struck measure; 2 qrs 2 bus. by estimation in husks. Total, 11½ qrs.
Sown over 5½ acres in the field of Downton, 1 qr 6 bus. In fodder of horses, 2 qrs 2 bus. by estimation in husks. Sold, 7½ qrs.

Issues of the mill

Wheat: 9 qrs 5 bus. from the whole issue of the mill; all sold.
Barley:[1] 63 qrs 2 bus. from the whole issue of the mill. Delivered to 1 miller for the year, 6½ qrs, taking a quarter every 8 weeks. Sold, 56 qrs 6 bus.
First-grade malt: 17 qrs 2 bus. from the whole issue of the same mill; sold.
Second-grade malt: 33 qrs 3 bus. from the whole issue of the same mill; sold.
Oatmeal: 6½ bus. from the whole issue of the same mill. In pottage, ½ qr. Sold, 2½ bus.
Fine bran: 2 qrs 3 bus. from the whole issue of the same mill; sold.

Stock
Cart-horses: 2 remain from the previous year; 2 remain.
Mares: 12 remain from the previous year; 2 additions; 2 strays. Total, 16. 1 sold; 15 remain.
Plough-horses: 8 remain from the previous year; 1 addition; 1 from the heriot of Richard Mol*endinarius*. Total, 10. 3 sold; 7 remain.
Colts: 3 aged two years and one term remain from the previous year; 2 added to mares, 1 to plough-horses; none remain.
Also colts: 2 aged 2 years remain from the previous year; they remain.
Also colts: 6 aged 1 year and 1 term remain from the previous year; 6 remain, 4 of them male.
Foals from this year's offspring: 2 from the offspring of the said mares because 10 were sterile. Total, 2. 2 remain.
Oxen: 54 remain from the previous year; 4 additions; 1 stray; 1 from the heriot of Alice le Hayward; 1 from the heriot of Richard Fouch'; 1 from the heriot of Alice Turel. Total, 62. 9 sold; 53 remain.
Bulls: 2 remain from the previous year; 1 addition. Total, 3. 1 sold; 2 remain.
Cows: 37 remain from the previous year; 8 additions. Total, 45. 1 in murrain before calving; 5 sold after calving about Lammas (1 August). Total, 6. 39 remain.
Steers: 10 remain from the previous year's bullocks; 1 stray. Total, 11. 5 added to oxen, 6 to cows. Total, 11. None remain.
Bullocks: 17 remain from the previous year's yearlings; 2 strays. Total, 19. 2 added to cows, 1 to bulls, because they were fully grown and overlooked among the bullocks the previous year. Total, 3. 16 remain.
Yearlings: 16 remain from the previous year's calves. Total, 16. 1 in murrain; 15 remain.
Calves: 36 from the offspring of the said cows this year because 8 sterile. 3 in tithe; 4 in murrain; 14 sold. Total, 21. 15 remain.
Wethers: 604 remain from the previous year; 140 additions; 44 from herbage at Hockday (1 May) before shearing, from Wick, Walton and Charlton, because each

1 MS 'ordeu*m* {molend'}'.

man of Wick who has 10 wethers will give 1, and if he has 20 he will give 2, at the lord's will, but if he has more he will not give more. And each man of Charlton who has 10 wethers or ewes will give 1 at the lord's will, and for the rest will give nothing. Total, 788. 40 sold at Martinmas; 28 in murrain before shearing, 10 after shearing; 1 in customary payment for the mowing of the meadow. Total, 79. 709 remain, which are in the keeping of Richard Bovedych', shepherd of Nunton, Ralph Bynschyf', shepherd of Witherington, and Adam Pyp*er*wyth', shepherd of Cowyk'.
Rams: 19 remain from the previous year; 3 additions. Total, 22. 2 in murrain before shearing. Total, 2. 20 remain.
Ewes: 622 remain from the previous year; 141 additions. Total, 763. 15 sold at Martinmas; 12 in murrain before lambing, 17 after lambing and before shearing, and 7 after shearing. Total, 51. 712 remain.
Hoggs: 330 remain from the previous year's lambs. 44 in murrain before shearing, 2 after shearing; 140 added to wethers, 3 to rams, and 141 to ewes. Total, 330. None remain.
Lambs: 547 from the offspring of the said ewes because 28 were sterile and 20 aborted. 89 in murrain before weaning; 7 in customary payment to the reeve, granary-keeper, smith, forester, hayward, shepherd, and 1 keeper of lambs; 44 in tithe; 48 sold before shearing; 5 in murrain after weaning and before shearing, 2 after shearing. Total, 195. 352 remain.
Boars: 2 remain from the previous year; 1 addition. Total, 3. 3 remain.
Sows: 3 remain from the previous year; 2 additions. Total, 5. 3 in murrain. Total, 3. 2 remain.
Pigs: 57 remain from the previous year; 36 additions. Total, 93. 4 in murrain; 36 sold. Total, 40. 53 remain.

m.7d
Hoggets: 45 remain from the previous year's piglets. 6 in murrain; 1 added to boars, 2 to sows, and 36 to pigs. Total, 45. None remain.
Piglets: 39 from the offspring of the said sows. 3 in tithe; 4 in customary payment to 1 reeve, granary-keeper, forester, and swineherd; 4 in murrain. Total, 11. 28 remain, and so few because the sows were sick and dying in the summer before farrowing.
Coarse wool {yield of fleece 4½*d*. plus 9*s*. 3*d*. in all}: 580 fleeces from wethers, 17 from rams, 578 from ewes, and 286 from hoggs produced at the shearing. Total, 1461. 146 in tithe; 2 in customary payment to 2 shepherds. Total, 148. 1313 sent to Wolvesey, which made 9 weys 6 cloves.
Lamb's-wool {yield of fleece 1½*d*.}: 354 lambs' fleeces produced at the shearing; all sent to Wolvesey with the coarse wool, which made 23 cloves.
Wool locks: 14 cloves; all sold.
Winter cheese:[1] 92 made; 9 in tithe; 2 in provision of the bailiff; 80 sold, which made 2½ weys.[2]
Summer cheese {yield of cow 3*s*. and sheep 2¾*d*., less 3*d*. in all this year, on account of selling cheese cheaply, with 13 cheeses for customary tenants and the provision of the harvest which are valued at 8*s*. 8*d*.}: 286 cheeses made between Thursday before Palm Sunday (12 April) and St Bartholomew's Day (24 August), at 2 cheeses a day during this time; 36 made between St Bartholomew's Day and Michaelmas, at 1 cheese a day. Total, 322. 32 in tithe; 6 in customary payment to 1 reeve, granary-keeper, forester, smith, shepherd, and hayward; 1 in customary

1 MS omits heading.

2 Figures add up to 91.

payment for the mowing of the meadow of Nunton; 3 in customary payment to the ploughmen; 3 in provision of the harvest. Total, 55.[1] 267 sold, which made 18 weys.
Butter:[2] 2 weys 12 cloves made this year; 2 weys 12 cloves sold.
Hides: 1 from a mare, 1 from a steer, and 6 from calves in murrain, and 3 from pigs; all sold.
Woolskins: 28 from wethers, 2 from rams, 29 from ewes, and 44 from hoggs in murrain before shearing. Total, 103. 10 in tithe; 93 sold.
Bare skins: 10 from wethers, 7 from ewes, and 2 from hoggs in murrain after shearing; all sold.
Lambskins: 80 from lambs in murrain before weaning; 8 in tithe; 72 sold.
Rotted skins: 6 from rotted sheep in murrain before shearing; all sold.
Peacocks: 11 remain from the previous year; 6 from this year's offspring. Total, 17. 4 in murrain; 13 remain.
Hens: 368 from churchscot. Total, 368. 16 in default of 3 ferlings of land drawn into burgage and 1 ferling of land delivered to Fulk de Waleton'; 4 in default of the land and mill of Standlynch; 24 from 12 widows, that is, the relict of Pochet, Joan Pyres, the relict of Ralph Tury, Alice Gilberd, the relict of Moyty*n*, Matilda Tryccheld', the relict of Bal, the relict of Scundy, of Walter de Venysch', of Nicholas Walkly*n*, the relict of Pal, of Rycher de Waleton', and Joan Athelard'.[3] Total, 44. 324 sold.
Cider: 4 casks this year. Total, 4. 1 sold; 3 remain.
Rabbits: nothing this year.
Utensils: 8 ploughs with ironwork for the same, 2 carts with iron tyres, 3 cart-ropes, 1 bushel measure in the granary, 2 baskets for carrying corn, 4 sacks for putting seeds in, 1 seed-basket, 6 locks for the doors of the barn and pig-sty, 1 lead vessel. In the kitchen, 2 brass pots, 3 pans, 2 tripods, 1 mortar, 1 axe, 5 casks, 2 tubs, 2 troughs of which 1 is in the bakehouse, 1 bucket, 4 cheese-baskets, 4 tables in the hall, 3 fixed tables in the same, 1 table in the small hall with trestles, 4 benches in the bishop's chamber, 4 benches in the bishop's chapel, 1 ewer with a basin, 1 table which was at Cowyk', 4 ladders bought this year, 1 cloth with a towel bought this year, 2 brass posnets remaining from the previous year. All this remains.

Bishopstone

Arrears

Theobald de Theygden', bailiff, and Thomas, reeve, render account for £10 18*s.* 8¼*d.* of arrears from the previous year. All delivered to Sir G*eoffrey*, treasurer of Wolvesey, by 1 tally. They are quit.

Rents of assize

The same render account for £3 1*s.* 8½*d.* for rents of assize at Christmas; £3 1*s.* 8½*d.* at Easter (22 April); £3 1*s.* 8½*d.* at the Nativity of the blessed John the Baptist (24 June); £3 4½*d.* at Michaelmas (29 September). Total, £12 5*s.* 6*d.*

Quittances

In quittance of 1 reeve for the year 4*s.*; 2 ploughmen for the year 5*s.*; 1 hayward for ½ year 1*s.* 3*d.*; 2 shepherds for the year 5*s.* Total, 15*s.* 3*d.*

1 Figures add up to 45. 19 weys sold according to the issues of the manor.

2 MS omits heading.

3 13 widows listed, but see below, p. 76.

Defaults of rent
In default of a certain plot which formerly belonged to John Vicar' of Bishopstone 6*d*. Total, 6*d*.

Total of quittances and defaults of rent, 15*s*. 9*d*.

Total of rents remaining, £11 9*s*. 9*d*.

Issues of the manor
The same render account for 3*s*. 11*d*. from pannage of pigs at Martinmas (11 November), at 1*d*. a pig over a year old, and ½*d*. if it is under a year; 10*s*. from pannage of oxen at the same feast, at 2½*d*. a fully-grown ox, 1¼*d*. a 2-year-old ox, and 1*d*. a 1-year-old bullock; 10*s*. 4*d*. from pannage of oxen at Hockday (1 May), as before for a fully-grown ox; 8½*d*. from pannage of sheep at Hockday, at 1*d*. per 4 sheep; nothing from pasturage this year for the lord's livestock; £1 4*s*. from hay sold this year; nothing from stubble and forage this year; 4*s*. 8*d*. from the residue of Peter's pence; 5*s*. 6*d*. from 1 feeble and sick ox sold; 7*s*. 9*d*. from 7 late-born calves sold; £2 14*s*. 1*d*. from 21 kebb wethers and 40 ewes sold, at 11*d*. each for wethers and ewes, but they have a gain (*vantag'*) of 2 sheep; 3*s*. 6*d*. from 6 old kebb wethers, at 7*d*. each; £1 2*s*. 5*d*. from 50 lambs sold after shearing, at 5½*d*. each; 1*s*. 10*d*. from the hide sold of 1 cow in murrain; 2*s*. 1*d*. from the hides sold of 2 bullocks in murrain, at 1*s*. 2*d*. for 1, and 11*d*. for the other; 5*s*. 3*d*. from the skins sold of 9 wethers, 11 ewes, and 6 hoggs in murrain before shearing, at 3*d*. a skin of wethers, 2½*d*. of ewes, and 2½*d*. of hoggs; 1*s*. 8*d*. from the bare skins sold of 20 wethers and ewes after shearing, at 1*d*. a skin; 9*d*. from the skins sold of 11 lambs in murrain before weaning; 1*d*. from the skins sold of 6 rotted sheep in murrain after shearing; nothing from coarse wool and lamb's-wool because it is sent to Wolvesey; 10*s*. 8*d*. from 7½ stone of wool locks sold, at 1*s*. 4*d*. a stone; 4*s*. 6*d*. from ½ wey of winter cheese sold; £3 12*s*. from 8 weys of summer cheese sold, at 9*s*. a wey; 9*s*. from 1 wey of butter sold; 5*s*. 4*d*. from 64 hens from churchscot; £1 from the whole hundred for refusing to stack; 5*s*. 3*d*. from the hall which was leased to John Vicar' of Bishopstone for the year, and which Andrew Vicar' is now holding at the lord's will; 4*s*. 5*d*. from dairy produce sold at the audit. Total, £14 9*s*. 8½*d*.

Annual recognizance
The same render account for 6*d*. from John Pavel for annual recognizance; 6*d*. from John Scherewy*nd* for the same; 6*d*. from Roger le Dregh' for the same, so that he may come to the steward's 2 tourns and pay suit for his tithing. Total, 1*s*. 6*d*.

Sale of corn
The same render account for £12 6*s*. 4½*d*. from 48 qrs 7 bus. of wheat sold, at 5*s*. 8*d*. a qr for 25 qrs, 4*s*. 6*d*. a qr for 13 qrs, and 4*s*. 3*d*. a qr for 10 qrs 7 bus.; 1*s*. 6*d*. from 3 bus. of wheat sold at the audit; £1 1*s*. 6¼*d*. from 7½ qrs 1 peck of curall sold, at 3*s*. a qr for 6 qrs ½ bus., 2*s*. 8*d*. for ½ qr, and 2*s*. for 1 qr; 4½*d*. from 1½ bus. sold at the audit; £15 1*d*. from 75 qrs 1½ bus. of barley sold, at 4*s*. a qr for 74 qrs 1½ bus., and 3*s*. 4*d*. for 1 qr; £4 13*s*. 4*d*. from 35 qrs of oats sold, at 2*s*. 8*d*. a qr; £2 5*s*. from 13½ qrs of peas sold, at 3*s*. 4*d*. a qr; 18*s*. 8*d*. from 7 qrs of vetches sold, at 2*s*. 8*d*. a qr. Total, £36 6*s*. 10¼*d*.

Entry and marriage fines
The same render account for 3*s*. from the tithing of Bishopstone for tithingpenny at the hundred-court of Martinmas; 3*s*. from the tithing of Flamston for the same; 2*s*.

from the tithing of Faulston for the same; 8*s.* from the aforesaid tithings at the hundred-court of Hockday for the same; 6*s.* 8*d.* from John Stacy to have 8 acres of land which belonged to Agnes Wudewal' for Agnes his daughter; 10*s.* from Joan, relict of Richard T*erry*, to retain 1 virgate of land which belonged to Richard her husband; 6*s.* 8*d.* from Thomas Ossbern for 8 acres of land which belonged to Agnes Ossebern; 1*s.* from Thomas Fab*er* for 1 messuage which belonged to Robert his father. Total, £2 4*d.*

Pleas and perquisites
The same render account for £2 3*s.* from the pleas and perquisites of the court this year; 2*s.* from Thomas, reeve, because he sowed the lord's land with bad seed; 1*s.* from John Perour for the same. Total, £2 6*s.*

Total of both, £4 6*s.* 4*d.*

Total of all receipts, £66 14*s.* 1¾*d.*

Cost of ploughs
In ironwork of 2 ploughs for the year with the stipend of the smith 12*s.* 6*d.* In 2 plough feet bought 6*d.* In 2 yokes bought 2*d.* In 4 wheels bought for ploughs 6*d.* In 1 boon-work of 16 ploughmen in winter and 14 in Lent 5*s.*, or 2*d.* a ploughman. And be it known that each ploughman will plough 1 acre as it lies. Moreover, they are bound to plough 78 acres in winter for 'landryght' without food and 14½ acres of fallow. In stipend of 2 ploughmen for the year 6*s.* In allowance of Thomas Mol*endinarius*, now reeve, for making a plough which he is bound to do according to custom when he is not reeve for the labour service of his land, and he takes nothing for that work, 1*s.* 6*d.*, because whilst he is reeve he ought to be quit of labour service. In 1 ox bought for the plough 9*s.* Total, £1 15*s.* 2*d.*

Cost of carts
In 4 clouts bought for the cart 3*d.* In 1 halter bought for the cart-horse 1*d.* In shoeing the cart-⌈horse⌉ 1*s.* 3*d.* In white leather bought 1½*d.* Total, 1*s.* 8½*d.*

Cost of buildings
In stipend of 1 man repairing the door of the byre 1*d.* In repairing and restoring the walls around the curia 5*d.* In stipend of 1 man covering the stack of vetches 5½*d.* In 1 sack bought 4½*d.* Total, 1*s.* 4*d.*

Cost of dairy
In 5 bus. of salt bought for salting 8 weys of cheese and butter 1*s.* 3*d.* In linen and woollen cloth bought for cheese 8½*d.* In earthenware pots and pans bought 2½*d.* In a press bought 6*d.* In stipend of 1 dairymaid for the year 2*s.* 6*d.* Total, 5*s.* 2*d.*

Sheepcote
In grease, vinegar and copperas bought for greasing sheep 16*s.* 8½*d.* In 1 stake bought which is called 'yppnigyre' 10*d.* In 27 hurdles bought 2*s.* 8*d.* In 16 ells of canvas bought for packing wool 4*s.* 4*d.*, at 3¼*d.* an ell. In packing the said wool and making sacks with thread bought for the same 8*d.* Total, £1 5*s.* 2½*d.*

Threshing {henceforth the threshing of peas and vetches is not allowed except as for barley}
In threshing 68 qrs 1 bus. of wheat, 7 qrs 7 bus. of curall, 21 qrs 7 bus. of peas, and 9½ qrs of vetches, 17*s.* 10¾*d.*, at 2½*d.* per 10 struck bushels. In winnowing the same

1*s*. 9½*d*. In threshing 120½ qrs of barley by piece-work, 12*s*. ½*d*., at 1½*d*. per 10 struck bushels. In winnowing the same 1*s*. 3*d*., at 1*d*. per 8 struck quarters. In threshing 60 qrs 1 bus. of oats by piece-work, 2*s*. 6¼*d*., at ½*d*. a qr. In winnowing the same 6*d*., at 1*d*. per 10 qrs. Total, £1 16*s*.

Expenses of the harvest
In weeding corn over and above that weeded by labour service 8*d*. In customary payment for the mowing of the meadow 8*d*. In 2 boon-works of 200 men who reaped and bound 104 acres of wheat, barley and oats, 9*s*. 6½*d*. In customary payment to 6 carters for carrying corn 1*s*. 4*d*. Total, 12*s*. 2½*d*.

Bailiff's expenses
In expenses of the bailiff for his visits with the expenses of the previous bailiff for holding the tourn and court and performing other business 9*s*. 6*d*. In wages of 1 overseer of the harvest from Michaelmas (29 September) until the Purification (2 February), for 18 weeks, 10*s*. 6*d*., because he takes a penny a day. In wages of 1 overseer of the harvest from Easter until Michaelmas, for 22 weeks 6 days, 13*s*. 4*d*., there not being an overseer of the harvest in between times. In stipend of the same overseer of the harvest 6*s*. 8*d*. Total, £2.

Total of all expenses, £7 16*s*. 9½*d*.

And he owes, £58 17*s*. 4¼*d*.

Cash deliveries
Delivered to Sir *Geoffrey*, treasurer of Wolvesey, by 1 tally, £47 8*s*.

And he owes clear, £11 9*s*. 4¼*d*.

Issues of the grange
Wheat
{yield: 4-fold less 3 qrs 6 bus.}
The same render account for 68 qrs 1 bus. from the whole issue of wheat by struck measure; 2 qrs 7 bus. by estimation in 5½ acres given to customary tenants at harvest-time, that is, 2 acres to the reeve and bartoner, ½ acre to the hayward, 1 acre to the men of Netton and Croucheston, and 2 acres to the men of Bishopstone, or ½ qr an acre by estimation as it lies. Total, 71 qrs.
Sown over 58 acres which lie in the field called Middelfeld, 18 qrs 1 bus.; that is, 2½ bus. an acre. In provision of the bailiff for his visits, ½ qr. Delivered to Roger Faber according to his fixed agreement this year, 2 bus. Given to customary tenants by estimation in 5½ acres according to custom, 2 qrs 7 bus. Sold, 48 qrs 7 bus. Sold at the audit, 3 bus.

Curall
The same render account for 7 qrs 6 bus. from the whole issue of curall by struck measure. And sold.

Barley
{yield: five-and-a-half-fold plus 2 qrs 7½ bus.}
The same render account for 120½ qrs from the whole issue of barley by struck measure. Total, 120½ qrs.

Sown over 61 acres in West Field, 22 qrs 6 bus.; that is, 3 bus. an acre. Delivered to 1 carter for 17 weeks, 2 qrs 1 bus., at 1 bus. a week. Delivered to 2 ploughmen for the year, who take a quarter every 10 weeks, 10 qrs 3 bus. Delivered to 1 hayward who sowed seed according to custom, 1 bus. Delivered to 1 dairymaid for ½ year, that is, for 25 weeks, 2½ qrs. Delivered to 1 harrower at the time of the summer sowing and for performing other business in the curia, 1 qr 1 bus. Delivered to 1 keeper of hoggs from Michaelmas (29 September) until Hockday (1 May), and thereafter keeping the lambs until Michaelmas, 3 qrs 2 bus. In provision of 2 boon-works at harvest-time, 2½ qrs. In provison of the bailiff for his visits, ½ qr. Sold, 75 qrs 1 bus. It balances.

Oats
{yield: two-and-a-half-fold less 1½ bus.}
The same render account for 60 qrs 1 bus. from the whole issue of oats by struck measure. Total, 60 qrs 1 bus.
Sown over 44 acres in ⌈Middle⌉ Field, 21 qrs 6 bus.; that is, ½ qr an acre. In fodder of the bailiff's horses for his visits, 3 bus. In fodder of 1 plough-horse of Downton staying there at the time of both sowings, and for carrying dung this year, 3 qrs. Sold, 35 qrs. It balances.

Peas
{yield: five-and-a-half-fold plus 6½ bus.}
The same render account for 21 qrs 7 bus. from the whole issue of peas by struck measure. Total, 21 qrs 7 bus.
Sown over 13 acres which lie in Middle Field, 3 qrs 2 bus.; that is, 2 bus. an acre. In pottage of the manorial servants, 2 bus. Sold, 13½ qrs. 4 qrs 7 bus. remain in the granary.

Vetches
{yield: four-fold less 2 qrs}
The same render account for 9 qrs 4 bus. from the whole issue of vetches by struck measure. Total, 9 qrs 4 bus.
Sown over 10 acres in Middle Field, 2 qrs 4 bus.; that is, 2 bus. an acre. Sold, 7 qrs. It balances.

m.8

Stock

Plough-horses: 1 remains from the previous year; 1 remains.
Oxen: 16 remain from the previous year; 1 addition; 1 received from bulls; 1 bought. Total, 19. 1 sold; 18 remain.
Bulls: 1 remains from the previous year; 1 addition. Total, 2. 1 added to oxen; 1 remains.
Cows: 11 remain from the previous year; 1 addition. Total, 12. 1 in murrain after calving; 11 remain.
Steers: 4 remain from the previous year's bullocks. 1 in murrain; 1 added to oxen, 1 to bulls, and 1 to cows. Total, 4. None remain.
Bullocks: 2 remain from the previous year's yearlings; 1 from the heriot of Richard Terry; 1 from the heriot of Agnes Osebern. Total, 4. 1 in murrain; 3 remain, 1 of them male.
Yearlings: 3 remain from the previous year's calves; 3 remain, 2 of them male.

Calves: 11 from the offspring of the said cows because 1 sterile. 1 in tithe; 1 in murrain; 7 sold. Total, 9. 2 remain, 1 of them male.
Wethers: 275 remain from the previous year; 81 additions. Total, 356. 27 sold at Martinmas; 9 in murrain before shearing, 17 after shearing; 2 in customary payment for the mowing of the meadow. Total, 55. 301 remain.
Rams: 4 remain from the previous year; 4 remain.
Ewes: 340 remain from the previous year; 71 additions. Total, 411. 40 sold at Martinmas; 6 in murrain before lambing, 5 after lambing and before shearing, and 3 after shearing. Total, 54. 357 remain.
Hoggs: 158 remain from the previous year's lambs. 6 in murrain before shearing; 81 added to wethers, 71 to ewes. Total, 158. None remain.
Lambs: 276 from the offspring of the said ewes because 18 were sterile; 7 from herbage at Hockday. Total, 283. 12 in murrain before weaning; 50 sold after shearing; 26 in tithe; 4 in customary payment to the reeve, bartoner, shepherd and smith; 4 in murrain after weaning and before shearing, 2 after shearing. Total, 98. 185 remain.
Fleeces {yield of fleece 4¼*d*. plus 2*s*. 6¼*d*. in all}: 684 produced at the shearing this year from wethers, rams, ewes and hoggs. 68 in tithe; 1 in customary payment to the shepherd. Total, 69. 615 sent to Wolvesey, which made 4 weys 5 cloves.
Lamb's-wool {yield of fleece 1¼*d*. less 3½*d*. in all}: 237 fleeces produced at the shearing this year; nothing from the agistment of lambs this year; 237 sent to Wolvesey, which made ½ wey.
Wool locks:[1] 7½ stone sold.
Winter cheese:[2] 24 sold, which made ½ wey.
Summer cheese {yield of cow 3*s*. and sheep 2¾*d*., and this on account of bad sales of cheese this year, with 3 in customary payment which are valued at 1*s*. 6*d*.}: 179 cheeses made between Thursday before Palm Sunday (12 April) and Michaelmas (29 September), both days included. 17 in tithe; 2 in customary payment for the mowing of the meadow; 1 in customary payment to 1 dairymaid and two maidservants. Total, 20. 159 sold, which made 8 weys.
Butter: 1 wey made this year; sold.
Hides: 1 from a cow and 2 from bullocks in murrain; sold.
Woolskins: 9 from wethers, 11 from ewes, and 6 from hoggs in murrain before shearing, with 17 from wethers and 3 from ewes in murrain after shearing. Total, 46. And sold.
Lambskins: 12 from lambs in murrain before weaning, with 6 from rotted sheep in murrain before and after shearing. Total, 18. 1 in tithe; 17 sold.
Churchscot: 88 hens from churchscot; 24 in default of 13 widows, that is, Avice, widow, Edith, the relict of Osebern, Edith, the relict of Carpen*ter*, Joan Maynard, Alice Newath,[3] the relict of le Dyker', of William Luce, the relict of Bulling', the relict of Fab*er*, the relict of Ryby, the relict of Tuvreweye, and the relict of Wodewale;[4] 64 sold.
Utensils: 2 ploughs with ironwork for the same, 1 cart with iron tyres, 1 rope for tying the cart, 1 bushel measure at the granary, 1 basket for carrying (*portand'*) corn, 2 sacks for carrying (*ducend'*) seed, 4 padlocks, 1 bucket, 2 cheese-baskets and other

1 MS omits heading.

2 MS omits heading.

3 MS '⟨Alic' Newathan⟩'.

4 12 widows listed, but see above, p. 71.

utensils pertaining to the dairy, 1 ewer with ⌈a basin⌉, and 1 pan remain from the previous year.

Merdon

Arrears

John de Herierd', bailiff, and John Wynt', reeve, render account for £40 7*s.* 4½*d.* of arrears from the previous year. All delivered to Sir G*eoffrey*, treasurer of Wolvesey, by 1 tally. They are quit.

Rents of assize

The same render account for £18 18*s.* 1¾*d.* for all rents of assize of the said manor at Easter (22 April); £19 19*s.* 4½*d.* at Michaelmas (29 September). Total, £38 17*s.* 6¼*d.*

Quittances

In quittance of 1 reeve and 1 beadle for the year 5*s.*; 1 hayward for the year 1*s.* 3*d.*; 1 swineherd for the year 2*s.* 6*d.*; 10 ploughmen for the year 12*s.* 6*d.*, or 1*s.* 3*d.* each; 12 workers for the year, working twice in 1 week and once in the other week, 15*s.*, or 1*s.* 3*d.* each; 1 keeper of wethers for the year 1*s.* 3*d.* Total, £1 17*s.* 6*d.*

Defaults of rent

In default of the land of William de Cruce, because the lord of Otterbourne does not permit that enclosure because it is within common land, 5*s.*; 1 plot in the vill of Hursley which William Fab*er* formerly encroached and built upon, pulled down because it was a nuisance to the neighbourhood, 6*d.* Total, 5*s.* 6*d.*

Total of quittances and defaults of rent, £2 3*s.*

Total of rents remaining, £36 14*s.* 6¼*d.*

Cumin

The same render account for 2 lb of cumin from the rent for 2 parcels of land in the vill of Hursley. Delivered to Sir G*eoffrey*, treasurer, and he is quit.

Issues of the manor

The same render account for £3 2*d.* from pannage of pigs of the whole manor at Martinmas (11 November) this year, as made clear in the details; nothing from pannage of pigs agisting in the wood this year because there were no pigs of strangers; 7*s.* from the whole hundred of Merdon to have heath at the lord's will without sale; 10*s.* 6*d.* from the pasturage next to Bouyat' sold for 36 yearlings, at 3½*d.* a yearling; 1*s.* 6*d.* from honey found in the wood sold this year; 14*s.* 10*d.* from the pasturage sold of 6 horses and mares, 11 oxen and cows, and 16 bullocks in the foreign park, at 8*d.* a horse or mare, 6*d.* an ox or cow, and 4*d.* a bullock; nothing from the pasturage on the hill this year, where wethers were accustomed to graze, for the lord's livestock; nothing from the pasturage sold to the men of Eastleigh this year because they did not come to pasture; 6*d.* from Adam le Bul' so that he may have dung from two cess-pits beside the road; nothing from timber and bark of timber felled for the use of the lord here because it was sold by Sir G*eoffrey*, treasurer of

Wolvesey; nothing from dead trees in the park this year; 3*s*. 3½*d*. for release of 26 labour services not done in winter this year, at 1½*d*. a labour service; £1 1*s*. for release of labour services not done at harvest-time this year; 8*s*. from 2 feeble plough-horses sold; £5 8*s*. 10*d*. from 12 old oxen sold, at 6*s*. each for 3, 6*s*. 8*d*. each for 3, and 11*s*. 4*d*. each for 6, plus 2*s*. 10*d*. in all; £2 5*s*. from 5 old cows sold before calving, at 7*s*. for 1, 9*s*. each for 2, and 10*s*. each for 2; 5*s*. from 5 feeble suckling calves sold; £1 7*s*. 6*d*. from 21 wethers and 1 ram sold before shearing, at 1*s*. 3*d*. each; £1 6*s*. from 2 rams and 24 ewes sold at the same feast; 17*s*. from 34 lambs sold after shearing to the reeve of Twyford, at 6*d*. each; £4 8*s*. 6*d*. from 29 pigs sold, at 3*s*. each for 20, and 3*s*. 2*d*. each for 9; nothing from coarse wool and lamb's-wool because it is sent to Wolvesey; 3*s*. from 2 cloves 4 lb of wool locks sold, at 2*d*. a lb; 1*s*. 7*d*. from 6 cloves of winter cheese sold, at 3½*d*. a clove; £3 8*s*. 9*d*. from 8 weys 7 cloves of summer cheese sold, at 8*s*. 4*d*. a wey; 9*s*. from 1 ox from the heriot of John Byssop; 4*s*. from 1½ cows from the heriot of Geoffrey le Glut; 4*s*. 5*d*. from 15 cloves 1 lb of butter sold, at 3½*d*. a clove; 6*s*. 4*d*. from the hides sold of 3 oxen in murrain; 2*d*. from the hides of 2 calves sold; 5*s*. 2*d*. from the skins sold of 7 wethers, 7 ewes and 3 hoggs in murrain before shearing, at 4*d*. a skin of wethers and ewes, and 2*d*. of hoggs; 6*d*. from the skins sold of 4 wethers and 1 ewe in murrain after shearing; 1*s*. 2*d*. from the skins sold of 4 lambs before weaning; 2*d*. from the skins sold of 4 lambs in murrain after shearing; 4*s*. from 48 hens from churchscot sold; 1*s*. from 400 eggs sold according to custom; 5*s*. 6*d*. from heath and broom sold in the foreign wood this year; £10 14*s*. 10*d*. from the sale of 27[1] oxen bought the previous year to agist in the park; 6*s*. 5*d*. from dairy produce sold at the audit; nothing from the pasturage in the park this year beacuse the pasture was a causeway (*calcata*) for the carriage of timber to the chapel by order of the lord and was pastured with the livestock of those who carried the same timber by order of the same. Total, £39 7½*d*.

Sale of corn

The same render account for £91 1*s*. 1*d*. from 308 qrs 3 bus. of wheat sold, at 5*s*. 4*d*. a qr for 25 qrs, 5*s*. 6*d*. a qr for 25 qrs, and 6*s*. a qr for 258 qrs 3 bus.; £3 6*s*. 6*d*. from 16 qrs 5 bus. of curall sold, at 4*s*. a qr; £1 8*s*. 9*d*. from 8 qrs 5 bus. of barley sold, at 3*s*. 4*d*. a qr; £4 12*s*. 5*d*. from 42 qrs of oats sold, at 1*s*. 8*d*. a qr for 8 qrs 3 bus., and 2*s*. 4*d*. a qr for 33 qrs 5 bus.; 1*s*. 4*d*. from 4 bus. of beans sold; £1 12*s*. 8*d*. from 12 qrs 2 bus. of peas sold, at 2*s*. 8*d*. a qr; £1 13*s*. 9*d*. from 16 qrs 7 bus. of vetches sold, at 2*s*. a qr; 4*s*. 2*d*. from 1 qr 2 bus. of barley sold at the audit. Total, £104 8*d*.

Annual recognizance

The same render account for 6*d*. from Adam Govayr' for annual recognizance; 6*d*. from William Wynter for the same; 6*d*. from Walter Cole for the same; 3*d*. from Ralph atte Wod' for the same; 3*d*. from Nicholas de Cantelsha*n*gr' for the same, for the first time this year; 3*d*. from John atte Floudstock' for the same, for the first time this year. Total, 2*s*. 3*d*.

Entry and marriage fines with tithingpenny

The same render account for 13*s*. 4*d*. from the tithing of Merdon for tithingpenny at Ma⌈r⌉tinmas; 1*s*. from the tithing of West Pitt for the same; 13*s*. 4*d*. from the tithing of Merdon for tithingpenny at the hundred-court of Hockday; 1*s*. from the tithing of West Pitt for the same; 13*s*. 4*d*. from Alice, relict of Nicholas Spayn', to retain ½ virgate of land which belonged to her husband; 13*s*. 4*d*. from Edith, who was wife of

1 MS 'x li. xiiij s. x d. de ⟨xxvij⟩ de xxvij bob*us*'.

John Bisshop, to retain 1 ferling of land which belonged to her husband; 13*s*. 4*d*. from Alice, relict of William Bullok, to retain 1 ferling of land and other purprestures which belonged to her husband; 1*s*. from Beatrice, relict of Geoffrey le Glut, to retain 1 cottage which belonged to her husband; 4*s*. from Juliana Davy for marrying Isabel her daughter outside; 13*s*. 4*d*. from John le Kynght to have Alice, relict of William Guty, and 1 ferling of her land; 6*s*. 8*d*. from Robert Crompe to have 1 ferling of land which belonged to William le Maresch*al*, father of Mabel his wife, having this by surrender of the aforesaid Robert and Mabel; 4*s*. from Joan atte Putte for marrying Edith her daughter outside; 3*s*. from Martin Shudde for marrying his daughter Beatrice; 13*s*. 4*d*. from Isabel Baldewyn' to have 1 messuage and 1 ferling of land which belonged to Juliana Baldewyn' her mother; 4*s*. from Joan, relict of John de Selksted', for marrying Alice her daughter outside; 1*s*. from William de Hyltingebury to have 1 house with a curtilage which belonged to John de Hiltyngebury; 2*s*. from Walter, son of Hugh de Bradenach', to have 1 garden by surrender of John P*arcarius*; 3*s*. from Walter, son of Hugh de Bradenach', to have Emma, daughter of Geoffrey atte Feld', with a certain house of hers; 13*s*. 4*d*. from Geoffrey Cleyhou to have 1 messuage 1 ferling of land by surrender of Henry Cleyhow his father; 2*s*. from Asketil, son of Robert Schal, to have ½ house by surrender of his father. Total, £6 19*s*. 4*d*.

Perquisites

The same render account for 13*s*. from Henry Cole, William Spayn', Clement Gyll', Roger Cod', Constantine Code, Robert le Glut, Thomas atte Sclade, William Roswyst, William le Lokar', Christina Dodd', the relict of le Vox, William le Vale*n*ce, John Wytlok and Thomas le Blak' because they declared against the payment of hens to the beadle which they and their ancestors were bound to pay; 3*s*. 4*d*. from the tithing of Merdon for concealment; 6*s*. 8*d*. from Adam le Freyr' because he did not do suit to the mill of Compton; 2*s*. from the relict of Charlemayn for the same; 2*s*. from Adam Calvesknave for trespass of wood in the park; 2*s*. from John le Sut*ere* for carrying off timber from the park; 2*s*. from Walter Saalebold' for the same; 2*s*. from the tithing of Merdon because it allowed ⌈Richard⌉ Phelyp to go, though it was ordered that he should be detained for a certain transgression done in the park; £4 15*s*. 10*d*. from various men for various transgressions. Total, £6 8*s*. 10*d*.

Total of both, £13 8*s*. 2*d*.

Total of all receipts, £193 6*s*. 2¾*d*.

Cost of ploughs

In iron and steel bought for the ironwork of 6 ploughs for the year £1 1*s*. 7*d*. In 3 ploughshares bought 2*s*. In 1 coulter mended with iron bought for the same 3*d*. In 10 plough feet bought 3*s*. 4*d*. In fitting ploughs with iron tyres 3*d*. In 4 pairs of wheels bought 1*s*. 4*d*. In 3 new harrows made 6*d*. In shoeing 12 plough-horses for the year 6*s*. In 8 halters made from hair 2*d*. In boon-works of 50 ploughmen who ploughed 225 acres as they lie, each ploughman ploughing 4½ acres, 16*s*. 8*d*., or 4*d*. a ploughman. In boon-works of 9 ploughmen of Slackstead who ploughed 18 acres of land as they lie 1*s*. 1½*d*., or 1½*d*. a ploughman. In boon-works of 2 free men ploughing 2 acres of land 3*d*. In stipend of 10 ploughmen for 211 Saturday ploughings this year, £2 2*s*. 11½*d*., or ¼*d*. each a day when they ploughed, which they were accustomed to have, because this year they were idle for 37 days. In stipend of the smith making the ironwork for as many days, 4*s*. 4¾*d*., just like 1 ploughman. In stipend of 2 ploughmen for the year 6*s*. In 2 plough-horses bought 15*s*. In 5 oxen bought £2 10*s*. 1¼*d*. In forage bought from the parson of Hursley £1. Total, £9 12*s*. 11*d*.

m.8d

Purchase of corn

In 29 qrs 1 bus. of wheat bought for sowing, £8 6*s*. 10¼*d*., at 5*s*. 4*d*. a qr for 4 qrs, 5*s*. 6*d*. a qr for 9 qrs 1 bus., 5*s*. 8*d*. a qr for 2 qrs, and 6*s*. a qr for 14 qrs. In 11 qrs of barley bought for sowing, £2 4*s*., at 4*s*. a qr. In 15 qrs of oats bought for sowing, £1 10*s*. Total, £12 10¼*d*.

Cost of carts

In a pair of wheels bought 3*s*. 1*d*. In 1 new binding bought and fitted to the said wheels with clamps and nails, and with all the equipment bought for the same, and with the stipend of the smith fitting the said wheels, 9*s*. 11*d*. In fitting the cart with axles and with axles bought for the same 10*d*. In clouts and nails and grease bought 2*s*. 6*d*., and so much this year for various carriages of the lord's victuals and for the carriage of timber and stone from Selborne for the use of the lord. In 1 collar bought and 1 pair of saddle-pads 1*s*. 2*d*. In 1 saddle bought for the cart 4*d*. In 1 cart-rope bought 1*s*. 4*d*. In 1 pair of traces bought 7*d*. In 1 pair of wheels bought for clearing dung 2*s*. In 4 wooden hoops bought 3*d*. In 1 cart-body made anew 6*d*. In mending harnesses of the cart at various times 4*d*. In white leather bought for harnesses 6*d*. In 8 ells of canvas bought for 6 sacks 2*s*., at 3*d*. an ell. In shoeing 4 cart-horses for the year 5*s*. 10*d*. In stipend of 2 carters for the year 6*s*. Total, £1 16*s*. 11*d*.

Cost of the dairy

In woollen and linen cloth bought for the dairy 8*d*. In a press bought 4½*d*. In earthenware pots and pans bought 5*d*. In mending the utensils of the dairy 6*d*., that is, tubs, buckets and tines. In plastering and mending the walls of the dairy 2*d*. In 5 bus. of salt bought 1*s*. 2½*d*. In grease, vinegar and copperas bought for greasing sheep 15*s*. 5½*d*. In 32 hurdles bought for the fold 3*s*. 4½*d*. In roofing the sheepcote with stubble collected for the same 6*s*. 2½*d*. In repairing and restoring in places the door and walls of the said sheepcote 7*d*. In 1 lath-work made anew 7*d*. In 3 buckets bought 1*s*. In 1 mould bought 10*d*. In 12 ells of canvas bought for packing wool 3*s*. 2*d*., at 3*d*. an ell, plus 2*d*. in all. In packing the said wool with thread bought for the same 6½*d*. In 1 brass pan bought 5*s*. In hooping the same with iron 1*s*. In stipend of 1 dairymaid for the year 2*s*. In stipend of 1 cowherd for the year 2*s*. In stipend of 1 keeper of ewes 3*s*. In stipend of 1 keeper of hoggs and lambs for the year 3*s*. In 27 yearlings bought the previous year for agisting in the park £7 4*s*. 4½*d*. In 3 cows bought £1 4*s*., 2 of them with calf and 1 after calving. Total, £10 19*s*. 5½*d*.

Cost of buildings {henceforth a day's allowance should be provided for a day's work if it be done by a day's work or by piece-work}

In re-roofing the wheat-barn, vetch-barn, hay-barn and byre in places 11*s*. 8*d*. In mending the crib of the stable and walls of the byre 1*s*. 1*d*. In mending 1 axe 3*d*. In digging 1 perch of ditch at Chakhull' 2*d*. In iron bought for the ironwork of forks and shovels 7*d*. In mending the palisade between the hall and chamber 4*d*. In 1 basket for corn bought 4*d*. In covering (*bywynd*) and mending the walls around the hay-barn 4*d*. In enclosing the great field with hedges 11*d*. In castrating piglets 4*d*. In 82 qrs 5 bus. of oats cast, cleaned and winnowed for sowing, 2*s*. 8*d*. Total, 18*s*. 8*d*.

Threshing

In threshing and winnowing 20 qrs of wheat by piece-work, 3*s*. 8*d*., at 2*d*. a qr threshed and 1*d*. per 5 qrs winnowed. In wages of William Kyrie carrying out the issue of the grange 11*s*. 1½*d*. In stipend of the same 2*s*., because he takes the rest at Crawley and did not stay at harvest-time. Total, 16*s*. 9½*d*.

Weeding {henceforth the acres weeded should be put down}

In weeding corn by piece-work over and above that weeded by labour service 10*s*., and so much this year on account of the multitude of thistles. In mowing 20 acres of meadow at Otterbourne according to custom 5*s*. 10*d*. In mowing 26 acres of meadow at Chast*er*lye according to custom 7*s*. 2*d*. Total, £1 3*s*.

Harvest-time

In bread bought for 4 boon-works of 756 men, nothing, because they had corn from the demesne's corn and reaped 284 acres. In meat bought for the great boon-work 8*s*. 8*d*. In herrings bought 6*s*. 10*d*. Total, 15*s*. 6*d*.

Provision of household servants at harvest-time {from now on the granger should not be at the lord's table at harvest-time nor at other times}

In provision of the reeve, hayward, beadle, granger, 1 keeper keeping the corn in the fields at night who by day helped to load the carts, and the bailiff's clerk, from Lammas (1 August) until the Nativity of the Blessed Mary (8 September), for 5 weeks, £1 13*s*. 11*d*., each taking 2*d*. a day, less 1*s*. 1*d*. in all, because they had nothing from stock. In stipend of 1 man keeping the corn in the fields at night who by day helped to load the carts 3*s*. Total, £1 16*s*. 11*d*.

Cost of the park

In mending the palisade of the park in places 2*s*. In enclosing 7 furlongs 36 perches in the park with hedges, with stakes made for the same, 19*s*. 9*d*., at ¾*d*. a perch. In splitting stakes for the same 1*s*. 2*d*., at 2*d*. a furlong. In enclosing 5 furlongs 16 perches in the foreign park with hedges 9*s*., at ½*d*. a perch. In wages of Richard, park-keeper, from Michaelmas (29 September) until Monday after the feast of St Matthew the Apostle (26 February), for 150 days, 12*s*. 6*d*., taking 1*d*. a day. In stipend of 1 attendant keeping the park in place of the said Richard 1*s*. 9*d*. Total, £2 6*s*. 2*d*.

Expenses of the steward

In expenses of the steward at the tourns of Martinmas and Hockday 7*s*. 1*d*. In expenses of N*icholas* Wodelok from Michaelmas (29 September) until All Saints (1 November) £1 3*s*. 7*d*. In expenses of John de Heryerd' for his visits £1 2*s*., because he took nothing from stock. In expenses of Simon returning from Taunton 5*d*. In expenses of the steward's attendant going to St Giles's Fair with 2 horses, in bread, ale and 1 bus. of oats, 5*d*. In expenses of Sir G*eoffrey*, treasurer of Wolvesey, for 1 visit to supervise the carpenter during the sale of bark 1*s*. 11*d*. Total, £2 15*s*. 5*d*.

Payments for building repairs

In 2,000 slates bought for re-roofing the new chamber in places 3*s*. In 3 qrs 5 bus. of lime bought for the same 2*s*. 4*d*. In stipend of 1 roofer and his mate (*garcionis*) roofing the aforesaid chamber 8*s*. 6*d*. In ridge-tiles bought for the same 2*d*. In 2,000 pegs bought for the same 2*d*. In mending the kitchen door, and the foundations of the sills and walls of the same kitchen, 1*s.* 8*d.* In a carpenter mending the sills and joists in the bishop's chamber 12*s.* In boards and planks sawn for the said chamber 7*s.* 6*d.* In large and small nails, that is, spike-nails and board-nails, bought for the same 1*s.* 8*d.* In stipend of 3 masons repairing and restoring the dairy and the said chamber, and building and mending the wall of the great kitchen, 12*s.* In making 1,600 shingles with 1 door to the granary made anew 4*s.* In hooks and hinges bought for the granary-door 8*d.* In timber felled and sawn crosswise for the bishop's chamber 1*s.* 9*d.* Total, £2 15*s.* 5*d.*

Total of all expenses, £47 18*s.* ¼*d.*

And he owes, £145 8*s.* 2½*d.*

Allowances
In allowance of the reeve 6*s.* 8*d.* In hay bought for the bishop 17*s.* 7*d.* In 80 qrs of charcoal made by order of the lord 10*s.*, at 1½*d.* a qr. Total, £1 14*s.* 3*d.*

Cash deliveries
Delivered to Sir G*eoffrey*, treasurer of Wolvesey, by 1 tally, £101 10*s.*

Total of all allowances and cash deliveries, £103 4*s.* 3*d.*

And thus he owes clear, £42 3*s.* 11½*d.*

Wheat
{yield: five-and-a-half-fold less 2½ qrs; henceforth an acre should be measured as it lies or by the perch on account of the sowing}
The same render account for 337½ qrs from the whole issue of wheat from the grange in the granary by struck measure; 1 qr of wheat in 3 acres by estimation delivered to customary tenants as made clear below; 29 qrs 1 bus. bought. Total, 367 qrs 5 bus.
Sown over 440 acres in the fields of Chasterly and la Lynches as they lie, 54½ qrs; that is, 1 bus. an acre as it lies, less ½ qr in all. In customary payment to 1 sower because he did not have his seed-lip as he is accustomed to have, although it is not found in the accounts before the time of Bishop William, 1 bus. In customary payment to 1 granger, 1 qr. In customary payment to 1 smith who is accustomed to have 1 little sheaf in the barn, 2 bus. Delivered to the reeve, beadle and hayward at their choice in 3 acres of wheat as they lie, without manure and double fallow, according to ancient custom, 1 qr. In bread made for the steward at the tourn of Martinmas, 1 bus. In provision of Nicholas Wodelok', bailiff from Michaelmas (29 September) until All Saints (1 November), 2 qrs 2 bus. Sold, 308 qrs 3 bus.

Curall
The same render account for 19 qrs 2 bus. from the whole issue of curall by struck measure. Mixed with barley for the liveries of the manorial servants, 2 qrs 5 bus. Sold, 16 qrs 5 bus.

Barley
{yield: three-and-a-half-fold plus 2 qrs 7 bus.}
The same render account for 57 qrs 1 bus. from the whole issue of barley by struck measure; 2 qrs 5 bus. of curall received for the liveries of the manorial servants; 7

bus. of peas and 3 bus. of vetches received for the same; 19 qrs 1 bus. bought. Total, 80 qrs 1 bus.
Sown over 37 acres 1 perch in the great field, 18 qrs 5 bus.; that is, ½ qr an acre measured by the perch. In customary payment to 1 sower, 1 bus. Delivered to 2 carters, ⌈2 ploughmen⌉ and 1 shepherd, who take a quarter every 8 weeks, 31½ qrs, because 1 carter was wanting for 8 weeks between the time of the wheat sowing and the time of the summer sowing. Delivered to 1 cowherd, who takes a quarter every 10 weeks, 5 qrs 2 bus. Delivered to 1 dairymaid between Michaelmas and Easter, 6 bus., and between Easter and Michaelmas, because she takes a quarter every 10 weeks, 2½ qrs. Delivered to 1 keeper of hoggs between Michaelmas (29 September) and the feast of St John the Baptist (24 June), and to the same keeping lambs between the said feast of St John and Michaelmas, taking a quarter every 16 weeks, 3 qrs 2 bus. In customary payment to 1 swineherd, ½ qr. In bread made for 4 harvest boon-works, 7 qrs 6 bus. Sold, 8 qrs 5 bus. Sold at the audit, 1 qr 2 bus.

Oats
{yield: two-fold less 10½ qrs}
The same render account for 164 qrs from the whole issue of oats by struck measure; 26 qrs by estimation in sheaves given to oxen; 15 qrs bought. Total, 205 qrs.
Sown over 195 acres 1 perch which lie in the great field, 97 qrs 5 bus.; that is, ½ qr an acre measured by the perch. In fodder of 4 cart-horses, 28 qrs. In fodder of 12 plough-horses between Christmas and Saturday before the feast of St George (21 April), 9 qrs 1 bus. In fodder of oxen by estimation in sheaves, 26 qrs. In fodder of the steward's horses for his visits, 2 bus. In fodder of the bailiff's horses for his visits, 2 qrs. Sold, 42 qrs.

Beans
{yield: 3-fold}
The same render account for 6 bus. from the whole issue of beans by struck measure.
Sown in the enclosure, 2 bus. Sold, 4 bus.

Peas
{yield: 3½-fold less 3 bus.}
The same render account for 2 qrs 1 bus. of peas remaining in the granary from the previous year; 16½ qrs from the whole issue of peas this year by struck measure. Total, 18 qrs 5 bus.
Sown in the great field, 3½ qrs. Mixed with barley for the liveries of the manorial servants, 7 bus. In supporting pigs in winter, 2 qrs. Sold, 12 qrs 2 bus.

Vetches
{yield: 4-fold plus 2 bus.}
The same render account for 22 qrs 2 bus. from the whole issue of vetches by struck measure.
Sown in the great field, 3 qrs. Mixed with barley for the liveries of the manorial servants, 3 bus. In supporting pigs, 2 qrs. Sold, 16 qrs 7 bus.

Stock
Cart-horses: 4 remain from the previous year; 4 remain.
Plough-horses: 11 remain from the previous year; 1 from the heriot of Nicholas Spayn'; 2 bought. Total, 14. 2 sold; 12 remain.

Foals: none because there were no mares there.
Oxen: 65 remain from the previous year; 3 additions; 1 from the heriot of John Bysspop; 1 from the heriot of William Bulluk; 5 bought. Total, 75. 3 in murrain in May; 13 sold, 1 of them a heriot. Total, 16. 59 remain.
Bulls: 1 remains from the previous year; 1 remains.
Cows: 23 remain from the previous year; 5 additions; 3 milch-cows bought, 2 of them with calf. Total, 31. 5 sold before calving; 26 remain.
Steers: 8 remain from the previous year's bullocks. 3 added to oxen, 5 to cows. Total, 8. None remain.
Bullocks: 9 remain from the previous year's yearlings; 9 remain, 7 of them male.
Yearlings: 9 remain from the previous year's calves; 9 remain, 6 of them male.
Calves: 17 from the offspring of the said cows because 6 were sterile; 2 bought. Total, 19. 2 in tithe for the arrears of the previous year; 2 in murrain; 5 sold. Total, 9. 10 remain, of which[1]
Wethers: 166 remain from the previous year; 37 added from stock. Total, 203. 21 sold at Martinmas; 7 in murrain before shearing, 4 after shearing. Total, 32. 171 remain.
Rams: 12 remain from the previous year; 5 additions. Total, 17. 3 sold at Martinmas; 14 remain.
Ewes: 238 remain from the previous year; 54 additions; 1 from the heriot of Robert Trewe before breeding. Total, 293. 24 sold at Martinmas; 6 in murrain before breeding, 1 after breeding and before shearing, and 1 after shearing. Total, 32. 261 remain.
Hoggs: 99 remain from the previous year's lambs; 3 in murrain before shearing; 37 added to wethers, 5 to rams, and 54 to ewes; none remain.
Lambs: 202 from the offspring of the said ewes because 7 sterile. 14 in murrain before weaning; 18 in tithe; 4 in customary payment to 1 reeve, 1 beadle, 1 hayward, and 1 shepherd; 3 sold after weaning and before shearing; 4 in murrain after shearing; 34 sold after shearing to the reeve of Twyford. Total, 77. 125 remain.
Boars: 1 remains from the previous year; 1 addition; 1 in murrain; 1 remains.
Pigs: 21 remain from the previous year; 22 added from stock; 1 stray. Total, 44. 29 sold; 15 remain.
Sows: 2 remain from the previous year; 1 addition. Total, 3. 1 in murrain before farrowing; 2 remain.
Hoggets: 28 remain from the previous year's piglets. Total, 28. 4 in murrain; 1 added to boars, 22 to pigs, and 1 to sows. Total, 28. None remain.
Piglets {from now on the age of the piglets should be distinguished}: 40 from the offspring of the said sows. 4 in tithe; 1 in customary payment to 1 swineherd. Total, 5. 35 remain.
Coarse [wool] {£5 a sack; yield of [fleece] thus . . . 4½*d*. plus 3*s*. ½*d*. in all}: 138 fleeces from wethers, 9 from rams, 208 from ewes and 96 from hoggs produced at the shearing. Total, 451. 45 in tithe; 1 in customary payment to 1 shepherd; 405 sent to Wolvesey, which made 3 weys 14 cloves with the lamb's-wool.
[Wool] locks: 2 cloves 4 lb; all sold.
Lamb's-wool {yield of fleece thus 1¾*d*. plus 1*s*. 2¾*d*. in all}: 163 fleeces from lambs produced at the shearing; all sent to Wolvesey with the coarse wool, which made 13 cloves.
Winter [cheese]: 18 made this year; all sold, which made 6 cloves.
Summer cheese {yield of cow 2*s*. 9*d*. and sheep 2*d*. this year on account of bad sales of cheese; customary payments valued at 1*s*. 11*d*. and milk and butter

1 MS omits final phrase.

consumed by the lord at 1*s*. 5*d*.}: 168 cheeses made between Sunday after the feast of SS Tiburtius and Valerian (15 April) and Michaelmas (29 September), both days included; 16 in tithe; 5 in customary payment to 1 reeve, 1 beadle, 1 smith, 1 hayward and 1 dairymaid; 157 sold, which made 8 weys 7 cloves.
[Butter]: 15 cloves 1 lb from the issue of the dairy; all sold.
[Hides]: 3 from oxen and 2 from calves dead from murrain; all sold.
[Woolskins]: 7 from wethers, 7 from ewes and 3 from hoggs dead from murrain before shearing; all sold.
[Bare skins]: 4 from wethers and 1 from a ewe in murrain after shearing; all sold.
Lambskins: 13 from lambs dead from murrain before weaning, 4 after shearing. Total, 16.[1] All sold; none remain.
[Eggs]: 400 from the beadle according to custom; all sold; none remain.
[Utensils]: 1 brass pot, 1 ewer, 1 basin and 2 pans remain from the previous year; 1 cloak bought; all this remains.
[Carts]: 2 with iron tyres remain from the previous year; 1 light cart (*jevonat'*); 1 worn out; 2 remain.

m.9

Crawley

Arrears

John de Herierd', bailiff, and David Martyn, reeve, render account for £7 8*s*. 8*d*. of arrears from the previous year. All delivered to Sir G*eoffrey*, treasurer of Wolvesey, by 1 tally. They are quit.

Rents of assize

The same render account for £3 1*s*. 4*d*. for all rents of assize at Christmas; £3 1*s*. 4*d*. at Easter (22 April); £3 1*s*. 4*d*. at the Nativity of the blessed John the Baptist (24 June); £4 17*s*. 7*d*. at Michaelmas (29 September). Total, £14 1*s*. 7*d*.

Quittances

In quittance of 1 reeve for the year 5*s*.; 6 ploughmen and 1 smith for the year 18*s*. 8*d*., or 2*s*. 8*d*. each; 2 shepherds for the year 5*s*. 4*d*.; 8 workers working 2 days a week from Michaelmas until Lammas (1 August) and every day at harvest-time £1 1*s*. 4*d*., or 2*s*. 4*d*. each; 1 swineherd and 1 cowherd for the year 5*s*. 4*d*., or 2*s*. 8*d*. each. Total, £2 15*s*. 8*d*.

Defaults of rent

In default of the land of le Stronge drawn into demesne 2*s*.; the land of William ad Cur' drawn into demesne, 2*s*. 8*d*. for the year; the land of Alebrok' which is now answered for at Merdon 5*s*.; the land of Robert Couch' drawn into demesne, 2*s*. 8*d*. for the year; the land of Robert Coye drawn into demesne, 2*s*. 8*d*. for the year; the land of Roger le Porkyr drawn into demesne, 2*s*. 8*d*. for the year; the land of Richard Vaccar' drawn into demesne, 2*s*. 8*d*. for the year. Total, £1 4*d*.

Total of quittances and defaults of rent, £3 16*s*.

Total of rents remaining, £10 5*s*. 7*d*.

1 Figures add up to 17.

Cumin

The same render account for 1 lb of cumin from the rent of Richard Fromund'. Delivered to Wolvesey.

Issues of the manor

The same render account for 6*s.* 2½*d.* from pannage of pigs at Martinmas (11 November); £2 5*s.* 4*d.* from pannage of 77 cows, 8 steers, 21 bullocks and 16 calves, at 6*d.* a cow, 3*d.* a steer, 2*d.* a yearling, and 1*d.* a calf; 2*s.* 8*d.* from 97 more of the men's sheep than the 25 maintained in the fold this year, at 1*d.* per 3 sheep; 11*d.* from the pasturage of 44 lambs sold at the Nativity of St John the Baptist (24 June) this year, at 1*d.* per 4 lambs; nothing from the pasturage in Puthull' this year for the lord's wethers; 8*s.* from the pasturage in Tre*n*dly sold; nothing from the pasturage in the wood this year for the lord's livestock; nothing from the pasturage in Drakenor' this year because it was sown; nothing from the pasturage in Cu*m*bfurla*ng*' this year for the lord's stock; nothing from the pasturage beside Northbury this year for the same reason; 1*s.* 6*d.* from the pasturage in Lokfurla*ng*' sold; 1*s.* 4*d.* from the pasturage in Shret sold; 5*s.* from 5 feeble and late-born calves sold; £2 14*s.* 10*d.* from 47 wethers sold at Martinmas, at 1*s.* 2*d.* each; £2 5*s.* 10*d.* from 55 ewes sold at the same feast, at 10*d.* each; £3 7*s.* 4*d.* from 26 pigs sold, at 2*s.* 7*d.* each, plus 2*d.* in all; 11*d.* from the hide sold of 1 plough-horse in murrain; 4*s.* 6½*d.* from the hides sold of 2 oxen dead from murrain; 2*s.* 8*d.* from the hide and flesh sold of 1 steer in murrain; 6*d.* from the hide sold of 1 bullock in murrain; 1½*d.* from the hide sold of 1 yearling in murrain; 1*d.* from the hide sold of 1 calf in murrain; 18*s.* 10*d.* from the skins sold of 21 wethers, 24 ewes and 23 hoggs in murrain before shearing, at 4*d.* a skin of wethers and ewes, and 2*d.* of hoggs; 4*s.* 6*d.* from the skins sold of 14 wethers and 13 ewes in murrain after shearing, at 2*d.* each; 5*s.* 2*d.* from the skins sold of 62 lambs in murrain before weaning, at 1*d.* each; 10*d.* from the skins sold of 20 rotted sheep in murrain before and after shearing; 1*s.* 6*d.* from 5 cloves 1 lb of winter cheese sold; £3 6*s.* 1*d.* from 7½ weys 12 cloves of summer cheese sold, at 8*s.* 4*d.* a wey; 4*s.* 8*d.* from 15 cloves 5 lb of butter sold; 7*s.* 11*d.* from 95 hens from churchscot sold; 2*s.* from Richard Cap*ellanus* for release from the labour service of 6 acres of land leased to him and his; 1*s.* from a certain curtilage which was hired to Roger le Porcher this year; 12*s.* from 23 acres of the lord's land hired this year which is now accounted for in defaults of rent above; 2*s.* from a certain curtilage which belongs to Robert Couch' this year; nothing from coarse wool and lamb's-wool because it is sent to Wolvesey; 4*s.* 4½*d.* from 5 cloves of wool locks sold, at 10½*d.* a clove; £1 3*d.* from dairy produce sold at the audit. Total, £19 19*s.*

Annual recognizance

The same render account for 6*d.* from Walter le Kynght for annual recognizance; 6*d.* from Robert le Pak' for the same; 6*d.* from Robert le Pott*ere* for the same; 3*d.* from John le Walsch' for the same. Total, 1*s.* 9*d.*

Wax

The same renders account for ½ lb of wax from John le Cart*ere* for annual recognizance, so that he has permission to dwell other than on the lord's land. He is bound to pay suit of court for his tithing at the 2 law-days, by pledge of Robert le Bu*nd*' and Robert Merywedyr. Delivered to Wolvesey.

Sale of corn

The same render account for £11 18*s.* 2*d.* from 40 qrs of wheat sold, at 5*s.* 4*d.* a qr for 2 qrs 6 bus., and 6*s.* a qr for 37 qrs 2 bus.; £2 5*s.* 6½*d.* from 12 qrs ½ bus. of curall sold, at 3*s*. 4*d*. a qr for 4 qrs ½ bus., and 4*s*. a qr for 8 qrs; £4 7*s*. 11*d*. from 21 qrs 6 bus. of barley sold, at 4*s*. a qr for 19 qrs, and 4*s*. 4*d*. a qr for 2 qrs 6 bus.; £4 7*s*. 8*d*. from 43 qrs of oats sold, at 2*s*. a qr for 38 qrs, and 2*s*. 4*d*. a qr for 5 qrs; 9*s*. 4½*d*. from 3 qrs 1 bus. of peas sold, at 3*s*. a qr; 9*s*. from 4½ qrs of vetches sold, at 2*s*. a qr; 2*s*. from 4 bus. of barley sold at the audit. Total, £23 19*s*. 8*d*.

Entry and marriage fines
The same render account for 6*s*. 8*d*. from the tithing for tithingpenny at the hundred-court of Martinmas; 6*s*. 8*d*. from the same tithing for the same at the hundred-court of Hockday; 2*s*. from Matilda Gode for marrying Emma her daughter outside; 2*s*. from Stephen Cl*ericus* for marrying Albreda his daughter outside. Total, 17*s*. 4*d*.

Perquisites
The same render account for 2*s*. from the tithing of Crawley for concealment; 2*s*. from the tithing of Crawley because it did not produce in court those (*quos*) it had bailed; 15*s*. 11*d*. from various men for various transgressions as made clear in the details of the various courts. Total, 19*s*. 11*d*.

Total of both, £1 17*s*. 3*d*.

Total of all receipts, £56 3*s*. 3*d*.

Cost of ploughs
In iron and steel bought for 4 ploughs for the year 9*s*. In 2 ploughshares bought and set up 1*s*. 8*d*. In 1 coulter mended 2*d*. In 2 plough feet bought 7½*d*. In 4 pairs of wheels bought 1*s*. 4*d*. In 2 ploughs made anew and other ploughs and harrows mended at various times 1*s*. 3*d*. In fitting ploughs with iron tyres 2½*d*. In shoeing 6 plough-horses 3*s*. 11*d*. In boon-works of 9 ploughmen ploughing 9 acres 9*d*. In 5 halters made from the horses' own hair (*de proprio pilo*) 1¼*d*. In stipend of 2 ploughmen for the year 6*s*. In 5 oxen bought £2 6*s*. Total, £3 11*s*. ¼*d*.

Purchase of corn
In 6 bus. of wheat bought for sowing 4*s*. 6*d*. In 3 qrs 6 bus. of barley bought for the liveries of the manorial servants 12*s*. 4*d*., at 3*s*. 4*d*. a qr for 3 qrs 2 bus., and 4½*d*. a bus. for 4 bus. Total, 16*s*. 10*d*.

Cost of carts
In 1 pair of wheels bought 3*s*. 4*d*. In 1 old binding renewed and fitted to the said wheels with clamps and large nails for the same 3*s*. In fitting the cart with axles with axles bought for the same 8*d*. In clouts, nails and grease bought for the same 1*s*. In 1 pair of traces bought 5½*d*. In 1 rope bought for tethering horses in the pasture 2*d*. In shoeing 2 cart-horses 2*s*. 6*d*. In white leather bought 4*d*. In mending old harnesses 2*d*. In 1 collar bought 7*d*. In stipend of 1 carter for the year 3*s*. In mending the cart at various times 2*d*. In 1 new cart-body bought 1*s*. Total, 16*s*. 4½*d*.

Dairy and sheepcote
In woollen and linen cloth bought 6*d*. In 6 bus. of salt bought 1*s*. 11*d*. In a press bought 4½*d*. In earthenware pots and pans bought 2½*d*. In mending the utensils of the dairy 1½*d*. In 1 mould bought 7½*d*. In 20 ells of canvas bought for packing wool 5*s*. 2*d*., at 3*d*. an ell, plus 2*d*. in all. In making the said sacks with thread bought for

the same 4*d*. In packing the said wool 8*d*. In grease bought for greasing sheep £2 9*d*. In re-roofing the ewe-house 2*s*. 6*d*. In collecting stubble for the same 1*s*. ½*d*. In 40 hurdles bought for the fold 5*s*., at 1½*d*. each. In hay bought for the sheep in Lent for a want of pasture 17*s*. 11*d*. In stipend of 1 dairymaid for the year 2*s*. In 1 tub bought for the dairy 4*d*. Total, £3 19*s*. 5½*d*.

Cost of buildings

In wattling and re-roofing the old barn in places with stubble collected for the same 2*s*. 9*d*. In plastering and mending the walls of various buildings in the curia and around the kitchen 10*d*. In re-covering the stack of vetches with stubble collected for the same 1*s*. 3*d*. In mending 1 cooking-pot and 1 pan 1¼*d*. In wattling and re-roofing the wheat-barn in places 9*d*. In 1 bushel measure bought 5*d*. In castrating piglets 4*d*. Total, 6*s*. 5¼*d*.

Threshing

In threshing and winnowing 40 qrs of wheat by piece-work 6*s*. 8*d*., at 2*d*. a qr. In threshing and winnowing 45 qrs of barley by piece-work 5*s*. 7½*d*., at 1½*d*. a qr. In threshing and winnowing 60 qrs of oats by piece-work 4*s*., at 1*d*. a qr of 10 bus. In wages of William Kyrye carrying out the issue of the grange 3*s*. 1½*d*. In stipend of the same 1*s*. Total, £1 5*d*.

Harvest-time

In weeding corn over and above that weeded by labour service 4*s*. 6*d*. In 1,000 herrings bought for 3 boon-works of 300 men with the officials of the curia and other keepers of corn 6*s*. 4*d*., who reaped and bound all the corn from 110 acres as they lie. Total, 10*s*. 10*d*.

Provision of household servants at harvest-time {from now on nobody should be at table, neither at harvest-time nor at other times}

In provision of 1 reeve, 1 hayward and 1 attendant of the hayward, and 1 keeper of the fields at night who by day helped to load the carts, from Lammas (1 August) until the Nativity of the Blessed Mary (8 September), for 5 weeks and 3 days, £1, because they had nothing from stock. In stipend of 1 man keeping the corn in the fields at night who by day helped to load the carts 3*s*. Total, £1 3*s*.

Expenses of the steward and bailiff

In expenses of Simon, clerk, at the tourn of Martinmas, 3*s*. 3*d*. by tally. In expenses of Simon, clerk, holding the tourn of Hockday, 1*s*. 6*d*. without tally. In expenses of the same for 1 visit 9¼*d*. In expenses of the bailiff for his visits 12*s*. 2*d*. Given by order of the steward and treasurer for the lord's business in the hundred of Buddlesgate 6*s*. 8*d*. Total, £1 4*s*. 4¼*d*.

Total of all expenses, £13 8*s*. ¾*d*.

And he owes, £42 14*s*. 6¼*d*.

Cash deliveries

Delivered to Sir *Geoffrey*, treasurer of Wolvesey, by 1 tally, £27 14*s*. 4*d*.

And thus he owes clear, £15 2¼*d*.

Wheat
{yield: 4-fold less 1½ bus.}
The same render account for 58 qrs 6 bus. from the whole issue of wheat by struck measure; 6 bus. bought. Total, 59½ qrs.
Sown over 89 acres which lie in the field of Drakenord' and in la Gerdelo*nd*' and Northbury, 16 qrs 5 bus.; that is, 1½ bus. an acre, less ½ bus. in all. Delivered to Hugh de Bradenach', sergeant, between Michaelmas (29 September) and Lammas (1 August) and between the Nativity of the Blessed Mary (8 September) and Michaelmas, because in between times he was at table, 2 qrs 7 bus., because he takes a quarter every 8 weeks and takes the rest in barley. Sold, 40 qrs.

Curall
The same render account for 12 qrs ½ bus. from the whole issue of curall by struck measure. All sold.

Bere
{yield: two-fold}
The same render account for 4 qrs 2 bus. from the whole issue of bere by struck measure. Mixed with oats for the fodder of horses.

Barley
{yield: two-and-a-half-fold less 4 qrs}
The same render account for 91 qrs 5 bus. from the whole issue of barley by struck measure; 3 qrs 6 bus. bought. Total, 95 qrs 3 bus.
Sown over 115½ acres as they lie in the fields of Shyppe*n*hufurla*n*g', Longelond, Shortelond and in Drakenore, 43 qrs 2 bus.; that is, 3 bus. an acre, less ½ bus. in all. Delivered to 1 carter and 2 drovers, who take a quarter every 8 weeks for the year, 19½ qrs. Delivered to 1 dairymaid between Michaelmas (29 September) and the Purification (2 February), ½ qr. Delivered to the same between the Purification and Michaelmas, 2 qrs 6½ bus., at 1 qr every 12 weeks. Delivered to 1 harrower at the time of both sowings, 6 bus. this year. In provision of 3 harvest boon-works, 3 qrs, and 100 loaves ought to be made from a quarter and each will have 1 loaf a day. Delivered to Hugh de Bradenach', sergeant, between Michaelmas and Lammas and between the Nativity of the Blessed Mary and Michaelmas, because in between times he was at table, 2 qrs 7 bus., because he takes a quarter every 8 weeks and takes the rest in wheat. In customary payment to 1 swineherd because he was with the lord's pigs outside the manor at the time of mast, ½ qr. Sold, 21 qrs 6 bus. Sold at the audit, ½ qr. Total, 95 qrs 3 bus. It balances.

Oats
{yield: two-fold less 12 qrs 6 bus.}
The same render account for 145 qrs 6 bus. from the whole issue of oats by struck measure; 20 qrs by estimation in sheaves; 4 qrs 2 bus. of bere received for the fodder of horses. Total, 170 qrs.
Sown over 222½ acres which lie by the east side of the wood, and la Hamme, Brech' and Brokkely, 83 qrs 3 bus.; that is, 3 bus. an acre, less ½ bus. In fodder of 6 plough-horses between Christmas and the Invention of the Cross (3 May), 6 qrs. In fodder of the same when they ploughed after dinner, 4 qrs. In fodder of 2 cart-horses for the year, 12 qrs 6 bus. In fodder of oxen, 20 qrs by estimation in sheaves. In fodder of the horses of Simon, clerk, at the tourn of Martinmas, 2 bus. In fodder of the bailiff's horses for his visits, 5 bus. Sold, 43 qrs. Total, 170 qrs. It balances.

Peas
{yield: two-fold plus 2 bus.}
The same render account for 6½ qrs from the whole issue of peas by struck measure. Sown in the field of Cu*m*befurla*ng*', 3 qrs. In supporting pigs, 3 bus. Sold, 3 qrs 1 bus. Total, 6½ qrs. It balances.

Vetches
{yield: two-fold less 4 bus.}
The same render account for 7 qrs 6 bus. from the whole issue of vetches by struck measure. Sown in the field of Buryfurla*ng*', 3 qrs 2 bus. Sold, 4½ qrs.

Stock
Cart-horses: 2 remain from the previous year; 2 remain.
Plough-horses: 5 remain from the previous year; 1 bought; 1 from the heriot of Hugh Bele. Total, 7. 1 in murrain; 6 remain.
Oxen: 30 remain from the previous year; 1 addition; 5 bought; 1 stray. Total, 37. 2 in murrain in May; 35 remain.
Bulls: 1 remains from the previous year; 1 remains.
Cows: 17 remain from the previous year; 2 added from stock. Total, 19. 19 remain.
Steers: 4 remain from the previous year's bullocks. 1 in murrain; 1 added to oxen, 2 to cows. Total, 4. None remain here.
Bullocks: 5 remain from the previous year's yearlings; 1 in murrain; 4 remain, 2 of them male.
Yearlings: 6 remain from the previous year's calves; 1 in murrain; 5 remain, 2 of them male.
Calves: 13 from the offspring of the said cows because 6 sterile. 1 in tithe; 1 in murrain; 5 sold. Total, 7. 6 remain, 2 of them male.
Wethers: 383 remain from the previous year; 132 additions. Total, 515. 47 sold at Martinmas; 21 in murrain before shearing, 14 after shearing. Total, 82. 433 remain.
Ewes: 536 remain from the previous year; 131 additions. Total, 667. 55 sold at Martinmas; 14 in murrain before breeding, 10 after breeding and before shearing, and 13 after shearing. Total, 92. 575 remain.
Hoggs: 286 remain from the previous year's lambs. 23 in murrain before shearing; 132 added to wethers, 131 to ewes. Total, 286. None remain.
Lambs: 392 from the offspring of the ewes because 72 were sterile and 3 aborted. 32 in tithe; 68 in murrain before weaning; 4 in customary payment to 1 reeve, 2 shepherds and 1 smith; 5 in murrain after weaning and before shearing, 15 after shearing. Total, 124. 268 remain.
Coarse wool {yield of fleece 4¼*d.* plus 6*s.* 1¼*d.* in all}: 1035 fleeces produced at the shearing this year. 103 in tithe; 3 in customary payment to 2 shepherds and 1 dairymaid. Total, 106. 929 sent to Wolvesey, which made 6½ weys 3 cloves.
Lamb's-wool {yield of fleece 1¼*d.* less 7¾*d.* in all}: 283 fleeces produced at the shearing; all sent to Wolvesey, which made 15 cloves.
Wool locks: 5 cloves; all sold.
Boars: 1 remains from the previous year; 1 remains.
Pigs: 27 remain from the previous year; 29 additions. Total, 56. 26 sold; 30 remain.

m.9d
Sows: 2 remain from the previous year; 2 remain.
Hoggets: 29 remain from the previous year's piglets. 29 added to pigs. Total, 29. None remain.

Piglets: 32 from the offspring of the said sows; 2 strays. Total, 34. 3 in tithe; 8 in murrain; 23 remain.
Winter cheese: 5 cloves 1 lb; all sold. {**Note that all the writing about all the coarse wool and lamb's-wool should be together**}
Summer cheese {yield of cow thus 2*s*. 6*d*. and sheep 2*d*. this year on account of bad sales of cheese}: 168 cheeses made between the seventeenth calends of May (15 April) and Michaelmas (29 September), both days included. 16 in tithe; 4 in customary payment to 1 reeve, 1 shepherd, 1 smith and 1 dairymaid. Total, 20. 148 sold, which made 7½ weys 12 cloves.
Butter: 15 cloves 5 lb made this year; all sold.
Hens: 125 from churchscot. 4 in default of the land of le Stro*ng*' drawn into demesne; 4 in default of the land of William de Cruce drawn into demesne; 4 in default of the land of Robert Couch' drawn into demesne; 4 in default of the land of le Swoun; 4 in default of the land of Richard Vaccar'; 4 in default of the land of Richard Canane; 2 in default through the death of John Marti*n*; 2 in default of the land of the relict of Thewolf; 2 in default through the death of the wife of William le Whyte. Total, 30. 95 sold.
Hides: 1 from a plough-horse, 2 from oxen, 1 from a steer, 1 from a bullock, 1 from a yearling and 1 from a calf dead from murrain; all sold.
Woolskins: 21 from wethers, 24 from ewes and 23 from hoggs dead from murrain before shearing; all sold.
Bare skins: 14 from wethers and 13 from ewes dead from murrain after shearing; all sold.
Lambskins: 68 from lambs dead from murrain before weaning; 5 from rotted sheep in murrain after weaning and before shearing; 15 from lambs in murrain after shearing. Total, 88. 6 in tithe; 82 sold.
Utensils: 1 cauldron, 1 brass pot, 1 pan, 1 basin and 1 ewer remain from the previous year; all this remains.
Tron: 1 remains from the previous year; 1 remains.
Cart: 1 with iron tyres remains from the previous year; 1 renewed; 1 worn out; 1 remains.

Overton

Arrears
Henry la Wayte and John Lunt, reeve, render account for £17 4*s*. 3½*d*. of arrears from the previous year. All delivered to Sir G*eoffrey*, treasurer of Wolvesey, by one tally. They are quit.

Rents
The same render account for £6 6*s*. for all rents of assize at Christmas; £6 11*s*. 4*d*. at Easter (22 April); £6 3*s*. 4*d*. at the Nativity of St John (24 June); £11 19*s*. 2¼*d*. at Michaelmas (29 September). Total, £30 19*s*. 10¼*d*.

Quittances
In quittance of 1 reeve for the year 5*s*.; 1 bartoner for the year 3*s*.; 2 haywards for the year 6*s*.; 3 ploughmen for the year 9*s*.; 1 ploughman for ½ year 1*s*. 6*d*.; 1 smith for the year 3*s*.; 2 shepherds for the year 6*s*.; 1 keeper of hoggs for 1 term 6*d*.; 1 cowherd for the year 3*s*. Total, £1 17*s*.

Defaults of rent

In default of the mill of Lynch' drawn into demesne, £1 for the year; the land of Bascon drawn into demesne, 3*s.* for the year; the land of Strockyng drawn into burgage, 3*s.* for the year; that of Gilbert drawn into burgage, 3*s.* for the year; the land of Agnes drawn into demesne, 1*s.* for the year; the land of Buvyth' drawn into demesne, 1*s.* 6*d.* for the year; the land of Springlon drawn into demesne, 1*s.* 6*d.* for the year; the land of le Cran drawn into demesne, 2*s.* for the year; that of Ivo drawn into demesne 2*s.*; the land of William drawn into burgage, 1*s.* 6*d.* for the year; the land of Jordan drawn into demesne, 2*s.* for the year; the land of Codeboye drawn into demesne 2*s.*; that of Joye drawn into demesne, 2*s.* for the year; the land of le Bol' drawn into demesne, 1*s.* 10*d.* for the year; that of Nicholas drawn into burgage, 1*s.* for the year; the land of the same drawn into demesne, 2*s.* for the year; the land of Byssop drawn into burgage, 1*s.* for the year; the land of Thurbun drawn into burgage, 1*s.* 6*d.* for the year; the land of Bovette drawn into burgage, 2*s.* for the year; the land of Scatehorn Joye drawn into burgage, 3*s.* for the year; the land of the smith drawn into burgage, 6*d.* for the year; the land of Waghetayl drawn into burgage, 1*s.* for the year; the land of John de Wynton' drawn into burgage, 2*s.* for the year; the land of Pavy drawn into burgage, 3*s.* 6*d.* for the year; the land of le Ber' drawn into burgage, 3*s.* for the year; the land of Peter Mol*endinarius* drawn into burgage, 6*s.* for the year; the mill of the same drawn into demesne, 12*s.* for the year; the rent of Tadley 4*s.* 5*d.*; the mill which belonged to Ralph Othyn drawn into demesne, £1 for the year. Total, £5 12*s.* 3*d.*

Total of quittances and defaults of rent, £7 9*s.* 3*d.*

Total of all rents remaining, £23 10*s.* 7¼*d.*

Issues of the manor

The same render account for £2 15*s.* 9*d.* for release from winter-ploughing, that is, from 90 ploughs of Hurstbourne Tarrant and Whitchurch, 4 ploughs of Ybbeworch', ½ plough of Matilda de Lavynton', 13 ploughs of Wocton', and 4 ploughs of Freefolk, at 6*d.* a plough; £1 1*s.* 5*d.* from pannage of pigs within at Overton, that is, from 50 pigs over a year old, 60 pigs of 3 terms, 40 pigs of ½ year, and 54 weaned piglets, at 2*d.* a pig over a year old, 1½*d.* a pig of 3 terms, 1*d.* a pig of ½ year, and ½*d.* a weaned piglet; nothing from foreign pannage for a want of mast; 1*s.* 2½*d.* from 9 pigs and 11 piglets at Tadley, at 1*d.* a pig and ½*d.* a piglet; 15*s.* 9*d.* from foreign pannage at Tadley this year; 6*s.* from 1 old, feeble and blind cart-horse sold; 19*s.* 6*d.* from 2 oxen sold at Martinmas (11 November); 10*s.* from 1 bull sold; 16*s.* from 2 cows sold at Martinmas; 7*s.* from 1 female steer sold; 9*s.* 10*d.* from 11 calves sold, at 10*d.* each for 3, and 11*d.* each for 8; £1 9*s.* 3*d.* from 29 ewes sold at Martinmas, at 9*d.* each; £1 12*s.* 8*d.* from 24 wethers sold at the same feast, at 9*d.* each for 2, and 1*s.* 5*d.* each for 22; 6*s.* from 12 hoggs sold at the same feast because feeble, at 6*d.* each; 7*s.* 7*d.* from 2 pigs sold; 9*s.* 4*d.* from 16 cloves of wool locks sold, at 7*d.* a clove; nothing from coarse wool or lamb's-wool here because it was sent to Wolvesey; 1*s.* 8*d.* from the hide sold of 1 cow in murrain; 10*d.* from the hide sold of 1 yearling in murrain; 3*d.* from the hides sold of 3 calves in murrain; 6*s.* 4*d.* from the skins sold of 19 ewes, 6 wethers and 9 hoggs in murrain before shearing, at 2½*d.* a skin of ewes and wethers, and 1½*d.* of hoggs; 1*s.* 6*d.* from the skins sold wholesale of 12 ewes, 4 wethers and 2 hoggs in murrain after shearing; 5*s.* 1*d.* from the skins of 61 lambs in murrain before weaning, at 1*d.* a skin; 4½*d.* from the skins sold wholesale of 14 lambs in murrain after shearing; 7*s*. 3*d*. from the herbage of the cottars, that is, for 23 cows and 12 steers, at 3*d*. a cow and 1½*d*. a steer; 3*s*. from winter pasturage in la Estmed sold; 2*s*. from winter pasturage in la Suthmed'; 3*s*. 6*d*. from winter pasturage in the meadow of Chini sold; 6*s*. from summer pasturage sold in various places; 2*s*. from heath at Tadley this year; nothing from honey this year; 10*s*. 4*d*. from 1 wey 4 cloves of winter cheese sold, at 9*s*. a wey; £4 10*s*. from 10 weys of summer cheese sold, at 9*s*. a wey; 9*s*. from 1 wey of butter sold; 6*s*. from 72 hens from churchscot sold; 3*s*. 4*d*. from 10 dozen pigeons sold, at 4*d*. a dozen; 10*d*. from the feathers and tails of 4 peacocks sold; nothing from loppings and bark this year; £2 6*s*. 8*d*. from customary tenants for release from harrowing this year; 7*s*. from dairy produce sold at the audit. Total, £23 3*d*.

Sale of corn
The same render account for £14 16*s*. 4*d*. from 50½ qrs of wheat sold, at 5*s*. 6*d*. a qr for 2 qrs, 5*s*. 4*d*. a qr for 8½ qrs, and 6*s*. a qr for 40 qrs; 9*s*. from 2 qrs 2 bus. of curall sold, at 4*s*. a qr; £7 4*s*. 9*d*. from 48 qrs 2 bus. of bere sold, at 3*s*. a qr; £14 9*s*. from 75 qrs 5 bus. of barley sold, at 3*s*. a qr for 13½ qrs, and 4*s*. a qr for 62 qrs 1 bus.; £4 3*s*. from 37 qrs of oats sold, at 2*s*. a qr for 19 qrs, and 2*s*. 6*d*. a qr for 18 qrs; 3*s*. from 1 qr 1 bus. of peas sold; 4*s*. 4½*d*. from 4 qrs 3 bus. of vetches sold, at 1*s*. a qr. Total, £41 9*s*. 5½*d*.

Town mill
The same render account for 16*s*. from 3 qrs of wheat from the issue of the town mill sold, at 5*s*. 4*d*. a qr; 2*s*. 6*d*. from 5 bus. of maslin sold, at 6*d*. a bus.; £1 15*s*. 3*d*. from 5 qrs 7 bus. of coarse-ground corn (*gruti*) sold, at 6*s*. a qr; £2 16*s*. 3½*d*. from 24 qrs 1 bus. of malt sold, at 2*s*. 4*d*. a qr. Total, £5 10*s*. ½*d*.

Mills of Lynch' and S*u*bhurn'
The same render account for £6 from the mills of Othini and Lynch' let at farm this year. Total, £6.

Total of all mills, £11 10*s*. ½*d*.

Entry fines
The same render account for 2*s*. from the tithing of Bradley for tithingpenny at the 2 hundred-courts for the year; 6*s*. from the tithing of Tadley for the same; 4*s*. from the tithing of Deane for the same; 4*s*. from the tithing of Ashe for the same; 6*s*. from the tithing of Polhampton for the same; 4*s*. from the tithing of Quidhampton for the same; 4*s*. from the tithing of Laverstoke for the same; 10*s*. from the tithing of Overton for the same; 10*s*. from Nicholas Nyweman to have Joan de Woussy*n*gton' with 1 virgate of her land; £1 from William Ywhurst to have Agnes Coys with 1½ virgates of her land; £1 from Margery, daughter of Gilbert, to have 3 houses and purprestures which came into the lord's hands as his escheat on the death of Gilbert Cl*ericus* because he died without heir; 1*s*. from Wymark atte Wat*er*e for marrying Alice her daughter within; 5*s*. from Roger Car*eter* and Matilda his wife to have 1 cotland which they recovered from Cecilia Tug of the inheritance of the said Matilda. Total, £4 16*s*.

Perquisites
The same render account for £2 18*s*. from Geoffrey Knyȝt, Nicholas Fab*er* and more of their fellows for various transgressions; 4*s*. from Roger Mastr' for having suckling

ewes in the pasture with the lord's sheep; £1 3*s*. 3*d*. from John Colebro*n*d, Nicholas Forst and their fellows for trespass of wood, corn and pasture, breaking the assize, and other transgressions; 2*s*. from John M*e*rd' for trespass of pasture; 10*s*. from Ralph Bond', Henry Edward and their fellows for more trespasses of wood, corn, meadow, pasture, and other transgressions; 2*s*. from William Pyris, bartoner, for not doing his office well and for trespass of pasture. Total, £4 19*s*. 3*d*.

Total of both, £9 15*s*. 3*d*.

Total of all receipts, £109 5*s*. 7¾*d*.

Cost of ploughs
In iron and steel bought for the ironwork of 2 ox-ploughs and 1 horse-plough for the whole year and 1 horse-plough for nearly ½ year 10*s*. 6*d*. In 2 ploughshares bought 1*s*. 8*d*. In 7 plough feet bought 1*s*. 9*d*. In 2 ploughs made anew 6*d*. In fitting the same and others with iron tyres 6½*d*. In 7 pairs of wheels made from the lord's timber 7*d*. In old ploughs fitted with share-beams, covered with boards, and mended, 6*d*. In 14 halters made from the horses' own hair 3½*d*. In shoeing 9 plough-horses for the year 9*s*. In shoeing horses aiding the harrowing at Lent 11*d*. In ale and relish (*com-panagio*) bought for 2 boon-works of 18 ploughmen in winter and as many in Lent, 6*s*. 8*d*., each ploughing, sowing with the lord's seed and harrowing 4 acres in winter and 2 in Lent. In stipend of 3 oxherds for the year 9*s*. In 2 oxen bought £1 2*s*. 8*d*. In 1 qr 2 bus. of wheat bought 6*s*. 3*d*. In 12 qrs 2 bus. of bere bought for sowing £1 4*s*. 8½*d*., at 2*s*. 10*d*. a qr. In 7 qrs 1 bus. of barley bought for sowing £1 6*s*. 1½*d*., at 3*s*. 8*d*. a qr. In 4 bus. of peas bought for sowing 1*s*. 8*d*. In 1 qr 1 bus. of vetches bought for sowing 1*s*. 10½*d*. Total, £6 5*s*. 2½*d*.

Cost of carts
In 1 pair of wheels bought for the cart 2*s*. 4*d*. In fitting an old binding to the said wheels, with clamps and large and small nails bought for the same, and with the stipend of the smith, 3*s*. 4*d*. In hooping (*frectand'*) the felloes (*intel'*) of the cart 3*d*. In clouts, nails, grease and white leather bought for the year 1*s*. ½*d*. In fitting the cart with axles for the year 6*d*. In mending the old cart many times during the year 9*d*. In 1 pair of traces bought 4*d*. In 1 collar and 1 pair of tie-beams (*lac'*) bought 1*s*. In 1 halter bought ½*d*. In 1 pair of wheels made for dung 9*d*. In shoeing 2 cart-horses for the year 2*s*. 6*d*. In 1 cart-horse bought £1. In stipend of 1 carter for the year 3*s*. Total, £1 15*s*. 10*d*.

Cost of buildings
In laying 1,200 new shingles and other old shingles on the hall with nails bought for the same 4*s*. 9½*d*. In re-roofing the wheat and oats barn unroofed by the wind 3*s*. 9*d*. In roofing and mending 1 bakehouse 1*s*. 6*d*. In collecting 35 acres of stubble for the same 5*s*. 10*d*. In re-roofing the dovecote and kitchen which had been unroofed, and covering the wall between the hall and dairy with sand collected for the same, 1*s*. 5*d*. In 4,000 tiles bought for the same 4*s*. 4*d*. In enclosing 76 perches around the curia and garden with hedges 1*s*. 7*d*., at 1*d*. per 4 perches. In forage bought 7*s*. 8*d*. In 1 wheel for the wheelbarrow 2*d*. In 2 pigs bought 4*s*. 6*d*. In 2 pots and 2 brass pans bought 13*s*. 6*d*. In 2 cider casks made 4*d*. Total, £2 9*s*. 4½*d*.

Weeding
In weeding corn this year 3*s*. 6*d*. In mowing 10 acres of meadow at Overton 3*s*. 6*d*. In mowing the meadow which belonged to Matilda Sc*e*rveys' 6*d*. In mowing the meadow which belonged to Orthini 7*d*. Total, 8*s*. 1*d*.

Expenses for wool

In 24 ells of canvas bought for putting the wool of Overton and North Waltham in 7*s*., at 3*d*. an ell. In making sacks with thread bought for the same and packing the said wool 1*s*. Total, 8*s*.

Harvest-time

In ale and relish bought for 2 harvest boon-works of 191 men, who eat twice a day and have 2 loaves each, who reaped and bound 139 acres as they lie, 13*s*. 4*d*., because 2 mills which were accustomed to give 16 sesters of ale, of 17 gallons a sester, are now in the lord's hands. In reaping 33½ acres of bere and barley and 25 acres of oats by piece-work, 11*s*. 1¾*d*., at 2½*d*. an acre of bere and barley, and 2*d*. an acre of oats. Total, £1 4*s*. 5¾*d*.

Threshing

In threshing and winnowing 67 qrs 1 bus. of wheat and curall by piece-work, 8*s*. 11½*d*., at 2*d*. per 10 struck bushels. In threshing and winnowing 83 qrs 3 bus. of bere and 4 qrs 2 bus. of peas and vetches, 8*s*. 9*d*., at 1½*d*. per 10 struck bushels. In threshing and winnowing 81½ qrs of barley, 6*s*. 9½*d*., at 1¼*d*. per 10 struck bushels. In threshing and winnowing 128 qrs 3½ bus. of oats, 5*s*. 4*d*., at 1¼*d*. per 20 struck bushels. In 1 basket bought 4*d*. Total, £1 10*s*. 2*d*.

Dairy

In 1½ qrs of salt bought for salting 11 weys of cheese and 1 wey of butter 3*s*. 6*d*., at 2*s*. 4*d*. a qr. In linen and woollen cloth bought 8*d*. In pots and pans 6*d*. In a press bought 6*d*. In mending buckets and other utensils of the dairy 4*d*. In stipend of the dairymaid for the year 2*s*. In stipend of 1 keeper of hoggs and lambs for 3 terms 2*s*. 3*d*. In 2 sacks bought 1*s*. 5*d*. Total, 11*s*. 2*d*.

Sheepfold and sheepcote

In re-roofing the unroofed sheepcotes of Suthlye and Wyllardesly 2*s*. 6*d*. In a carpenter mending the sheepcote of la Conyng' 6*d*. In roofing 1 part of the said sheepcote 3*s*. 2*d*. In 73 hurdles made from the lord's withies 2*s*., at 1*d*. per 3 hurdles. In wattling 66 hurdles 1*s*. 10*d*. In grease, copperas, vinegar and tar bought for greasing sheep £1 16*s*. 9*d*. In 39 ewes bought after lambing and before shearing £1 19*s*., at 1*s*. each. In 1 ram bought 1*s*. In a carpenter knocking down and rebuilding anew 1 sheepcote at Garnhor' £1 6*d*. In roofing the same 5*s*. 2*d*. In 4,000 nails bought for laths 3*s*., at 9*d*. a 1,000. In hooks and hinges bought for 3 timbers (*boscia*) of the same sheepcote 1*s*. 8*d*. In 1 piece of iron bought for the door of the said sheepcote and 1 for the door of the sheepcote at Cony*ng*' 5*d*. In plastering the walls of the sheepcote of Garnhor' and propping up the sills 5*s*. In collecting ⌈15⌉½ acres of stubble for roofing the said sheepcote 2*s*. 7*d*., at 2*d*. an acre. In hay bought 12*s*. Total, £6 17*s*. 1*d*.

Keeper of the mill of Lynch'

In roofing the buildings of the mill of Lynch' 6*d*. In repairing broken spindles with iron bought for the same 4*d*. In sharpening and steeling bills 3½*d*. In stopping up and drawing the water in order to renew the sluice of the mill 10*d*. In timber sawn for the new sluice 3*s*. Total, 4*s*. 11½*d*.

Town mill

In roofing the buildings of the town mill 1*s*. 4*d*. In hooping the driving-shaft and wheels of the same mill with iron bands, made with iron bought for the same, 1*s*. 3*d*.

In steeling and sharpening bills for the year 6*d*. In stipend of 1 miller for the year 3*s*. Total, 6*s*. 1*d*.

Nothing from the mill of Othin this year.

Total of all the mills, 11*s*. ½*d*.

Wages of the warrener
In wages of the warrener from Michaelmas (29 September) until Sunday after the Assumption (19 August), the last day included, that is, for 324 days at 1*d*. a day, £1 7*s*. In stipend of the same 6*s*. 8*d*., and this because there is not there a bailiff who keeps the manor separately. Total, £1 13*s*. 8*d*.

Expenses of the steward
In expenses of the steward at the tourn of Martinmas by 1 tally 7*s*. In expenses of the steward for 1 visit on Thursday after the feast of St Barnabas (14 June) by tally 1*s*. 5*d*. In expenses of Master Richard de Aby*nd*' for 1 visit 6*s*. Total, 14*s*. 5*d*.

Expenses of the bailiff
In expenses of the bailiff for his visits, as in meat, fish and ale, £1 10*s*. Total, £1 10*s*.

Total of all expenses, £25 18*s*. 6¼*d*.

And he owes, £83 7*s*. 1½*d*.

Allowances
In allowance of the same for 67 ewes bought, 54 of them after shearing, to better the manor's stock than it was before, £3 14*s*., at 1*s*. 1*d*. each, plus 1*s*. 5*d*. in all. Total, £3 14*s*.

[Cash deliveries]
Delivered to Sir G*eoffrey*, treasurer of Wolvesey, by 1 tally, £36 15*s*.

Total of all allowances and cash deliveries, £40 9*s*.

And he owes clear, £42 18*s*. 1½*d*.

m.10

Issues of wheat and the grange

Wheat
{yield: 5-fold plus 2 qrs 1 bus.}
The same render account for 64 qrs 7 bus. from the whole issue of wheat by struck measure; 1 qr 2 bus. bought. Total, 66 qrs 1 bus.
Sown over 63 acres as they lie in the fields of Lovegarston', Bytwewod', and beside la Conyng', 11 qrs 2 bus.; that is, 1½ bus. an acre, less 4 bus. in all. In provision of the steward for his visit at Martinmas, 3 bus. In provision of the bailiff for his visits, 4 qrs. Sold, 50½ qrs.

Curall
The same render account for 2 qrs 2 bus. from the whole issue of curall from the same wheat by struck measure; all sold.

Bere
{yield: 5½-fold less 2 qrs 3 bus.}
The same render account for 13½ qrs remaining in the granary from the previous year; 83 qrs 3 bus. from the whole issue of bere by struck measure; 2 qrs by estimation in 4 acres delivered to 2 haywards, 1 bartoner and 1 shepherd according to custom; 1 qr by estimation in 2 acres delivered to customary tenants at Ryptowel according to custom; 2 qrs by estimation in 88 sheaves delivered for the reaping of 44 acres by labour service, at 2 sheaves an acre; 12 qrs 2 bus. bought. Total, 114 qrs 1 bus.
Sown over 53 acres as they lie in the fields of Luvegarston', Bytwenewod', and at He*n*path', 20 qrs, plus 1 bus. in all. Delivered to 1 carter and 3 oxherds for the year, because they take a quarter every 8 weeks, 26 qrs. Delivered to 1 keeper of hoggs and lambs for three terms, who takes a quarter every 8 weeks, 4 qrs 7 bus., because for the fourth term he is served by customary tenants. Delivered to 1 dairymaid for the year on account of the cows, 4 qrs. Delivered to 1 harrower in Lent, 1 qr, because of the release of the villeins from harrowing this year as made clear in the issues of the manor. In boon-work ploughings in winter and Lent, 1½ qrs. In bread made for 2 harvest boon-works, 3 qrs. In customary payment to those who give churchscot, 4 bus. In customary payment to 2 haywards, 1 bartoner and 1 shepherd by estimation in 4 acres, 2 qrs. In customary payment to customary tenants at Ryptowel by estimation in 2 acres, 1 qr. Delivered to the reapers by estimation in 88 sheaves, 2 qrs. Sold, 48 qrs 2 bus.

Barley
{yield: 4½-fold less 2 qrs 7 bus.}
The same render account for 81½ qrs from the whole issue of barley by struck measure; 7 qrs 1 bus. bought. Total, 88 qrs 5 bus.
Sown over 70 acres as they lie in the fields of Basseburg' and Bytwenewod', 13 qrs; that is, 1½ bus. an acre, less 7 bus. in all. Sold, 75 qrs 5 bus.

Oats
{yield: two-fold less 19½ qrs ½ bus.}
The same render account for 134 qrs 3½ bus. from the whole issue of oats by struck measure; 10 qrs by estimation in sheaves given to oxen. Total, 144 qrs 3½ bus.
Sown over 127 acres as they lie in the fields of Grunnesli*n*ch' and Kove*n*hull' on the south side of Suthlye, 65 qrs; that is, 4 bus. an acre, plus 1½ qrs in all. In fodder of 2 cart-horses for the year, 15 qrs. In fodder of 9 plough-horses from the Purification (2 February) until Hockday (1 May), for 98 nights at 1 bus. a night, 12 qrs 2 bus. In supporting oxen by estimation in sheaves, 10 qrs. In fodder of the steward's horses for his visits, 1 qr 1½ bus. In fodder of the bailiff's horses for his visits, 4 qrs. Sold, 37 qrs.

Peas
{yield: 2 bus. more than sown}
The same render account for 2 bus. of peas remaining in the granary from the previous year; 7 bus. from the whole issue by struck measure; ½ qr bought. Total, 1 qr 5 bus.
Sown over 4 acres as they lie in Lovegarston', 4 bus. Sold, 1 qr 1 bus.

Vetches
{yield: 3-fold}
The same render account for 1 qr of vetches remaining in the granary from the previous year; 3 qrs 3 bus. from the issue; 1 qr 1 bus. bought. Total, 5½ qrs.

Sown over 6 acres as they lie opposite the gate, 1 qr 1 bus. Sold, 4 qrs 3 bus.

Town mill

The same render account for 3 qrs from the whole issue of wheat from the town mill, and all sold; 4 qrs 5 bus. from the whole issue of maslin from the same mill, of which 4 qrs delivered to 1 miller for the year, and 5 bus. sold; 5 qrs 7 bus. from the whole issue of coarse-ground corn from the same mill, and all sold; 24 qrs 1 bus. from the whole issue of malt from the same mill, and all sold.

Nothing from the issue of the mills of Ly*n*ch' and Othini here because they are let at farm this year.

Stock

Cart-horses: 2 remain from the previous year; 1 bought. Total, 3. 1 sold; 2 remain.
Plough-horses: 9 remain from the previous year; 1 stray. Total, 10. 10 remain.
Oxen: 20 remain from the previous year; 2 bought. Total, 22. 2 sold at Martinmas; 20 remain.
Bulls: 1 remains from the previous year; 1 addition. Total, 2. 1 sold; 1 remains.
Cows: 25 remain from the previous year; 3 additions; 1 stray. Total, 29. 2 sold at Martinmas; 1 in murrain before calving. Total, 3. 26 remain.
Steers: 5 remain from the previous year's bullocks; 1 sold at Martinmas; 1 added to bulls, 3 to cows; none remain.
Bullocks: 9 remain from the previous year's yearlings; they remain.
Yearlings: 10 remain from the previous year's calves; 1 in murrain; 9 remain.
Calves: 25 from the offspring of the said cows because 1 was sterile; 2 in tithe; 3 in murrain; 11 sold; 9 remain.
Ewes: 495 remain from the previous year; 102 added from hoggs; 106 bought after lambing, 54 of them after shearing. Total, 703. 39 sold at Martinmas; 7 in murrain before lambing, 14 after lambing and before shearing, and 12 after shearing. Total, 72. 631 remain.
Rams: 20 remain from the previous year; 7 additions; 1 bought sheared. Total, 28. 11 castrated and added to wethers; 17 remain.
Wethers: 323 remain from the previous year; 101 added from hoggs, 11 from rams. Total, 435. 24 sold at Martinmas; 6 in murrain before shearing, 4 after shearing. Total, 34. 401 remain.[1]
Hoggs: 234 remain from the previous year's lambs; 12 sold at Martinmas; 10 in murrain before shearing, 2 after shearing; 102 added to ewes, 7 to rams, 101 to wethers; none remain.
Lambs: 401 from the offspring of the said ewes this year because 16 were sterile and 6 aborted. 61 in murrain before weaning; 34 in tithe; {2 in customary payment to 1 hayward and 1 shepherd}; 12 in murrain after weaning and before shearing, 14 after shearing. Total, 121. 280 remain.[2]
Pigs: 2 bought; 2 sold; none remain.
Coarse fleeces: 487 from ewes, 21 from rams, 293 from wethers, 212 from hoggs produced at the shearing this year. Total, 1013. 101 in tithe; 2 in customary payment to 2 shepherds; 910 sent to Wolvesey, which made[3]
Lamb's-wool: 294 fleeces from lambs produced at the shearing this year; all sent to Wolvesey, which made[4]

1 MS illustration in margin; see above, p. x.

2 Unidentifiable drawing in text, probably to mark the interlineation above.

3 MS omits weight.

4 MS omits weight.

Woolskins: 21 from ewes, 6 from wethers and 10 from hoggs in murrain before shearing. Total, 37. 3 in tithe; 34 sold.
Bare skins: 12 from ewes and 4 from wethers in murrain after shearing. Total, 16. All sold.
Lambskins: 61 from lambs ⌈in murrain⌉ before weaning. 6 in tithe; 55 sold. 13 in murrain after weaning and before shearing, 14 after shearing. Total, 27.[1] All sold.
Winter cheese: 1 wey 4 cloves made this year; all sold.
Summer cheese {yield of cow thus 3*s*. and sheep 2¾*d*., less 3½*d*. in all}: 173 cheeses made between Sunday after the feast of SS Tiburtius and Valerian (15 April) and Michaelmas (29 September), both days included. 17 in tithe; 3 in customary payment to the hayward, shepherd and dairymaid. Total, 20. 153 sold, which made 10 weys.
Butter: 1 wey from the issue of the dairy; all sold.
Peacocks: 10 remain from the previous year; 2 offspring. Total, 12. 1 in murrain; 11 remain.
Hens: 60 from churchscot. 72 in default of land drawn into burgage; 2 in default of Alice atte Hurnn' because she did not have a husband; 12 in default of Edith Cleyr', Isabel Quelloxe, Wymark Yve, Ermegard Crokker', Alice Yve, Agnes P*ra*ns because they did not have husbands; 2 in default of Adam Long' because he did not have a wife. Total, 88. 72 sold.
Utensils: 1 old brass pot without feet which is exchanged inside; 2 pots bought; 1 old pan and old gallon vessel, one other gallon vessel, and 1 ewer remain; 2 pans bought; 1 cloth, 1 towel, and 1 posnet remain; 2 casks remain. They remain, besides 1 old basin.
Carts: 2 remain from the previous year; 1 made anew this year. Total, 3. 1 used in the curia; 2 others fitted with iron tyres remain.
Sacks: 6 remain from the previous year; 2 bought. Total, 8. 2 used in the curia; 6 remain.
Cider: 2 casks made this year from the issue of the garden with apples from North Waltham; 2 casks remain.

Overton Borough

Arrears
Henry la Wayte, bailiff, and Roger Lu*n*t, reeve, render account for £2 1*s*. 2½*d*. of arrears from the previous year. All delivered to Sir G*eoffrey*, treasurer of Wolvesey, by 1 tally. They are quit.

Rents
The same render account for £8 4*s*. 3½*d*. for all rents of assize in the borough of Overton for the year and all paid at Michaelmas (29 September). Total, £8 4*s*. 3½*d*.

Quittances
In quittance of 1 reeve for the year 2*s*. Total, 2*s*.

Defaults of rent
In default of the house of Gilbert le Pynk', pulled down by statute, 6*d*. Total, 6*d*.

Total of both, 2*s*. 6*d*.

1 MS omits '27'.

Total of rents remaining, £8 1*s*. 9½*d*.

Annual recognizance
The same render account for 6*d*. from Richard Hayward' for annual recognizance. Total, 6*d*.

Selds and stalls
The same render account for 10*s*. 8*d*. from 16 selds hired in the borough this year, at 8*d*. a seld; 5*s*. 4*d*. from 32[1] stalls in the borough this year, at 2*d*. a stall. Total, 16*s*.

Perquisites[2]
The same render account for 8*s*. 9*d*. from William Sueyn and other of his fellows for many and various transgressions; 2*s*. from John Wylly for release from his suit of court until Michaelmas; 7*s*. 6*d*. from John Cap*ellanus* of Basing and Henry Pellip' for transgression and false measure; 4*s*. 6*d*. from John Blakeman and his fellows for various transgressions; £2 2*s*. 6*d*. from those who brewed ale for breaking the assize. Total, £3 5*s*. 3*d*.

Farm of Freefolk
The same render account for 10*s*. for the farm of Freefolk at Michaelmas. Total, 10*s*.

Total of all receipts, £12 13*s*. 6*d*.

Expenses
In roofing, pointing and mending selds in places 1*s*. 8*d*. In collecting sand for the same and mending the walls with nails bought for the same 5*d*. In making 1 tumbrel anew and mending the pillory 3*s*. 1*d*. Total, 5*s*. 2*d*.

And he owes, £12 8*s*. 4½*d*.

Delivered to Sir G*eoffrey*, treasurer of Wolvesey, by 1 tally, £7.

And he owes clear, £5 8*s*. 4½*d*.

{nothing for the expenses of Richard Norton', steward of the whole bishopric}[3]

North Waltham

Arrears
Henry la Wayte, bailiff, and Thomas, reeve, render account for £8 1*s*. 5¼*d*. of arrears from the previous year. All delivered to Sir G*eoffrey*, treasurer of Wolvesey, by 1 tally. They are quit.

Rents
The same render account for £3 9*s*. 8*d*. for all rents of assize at Christmas; £2 7*s*. 9*d*. at Easter (22 April); £2 7*s*. 9*d*. at the Nativity of St John the Baptist (24 June); £2 7*s*. 9*d*. at Michaelmas (29 September). Total, £[10] 12*s*. 11*d*.

1 MS 'xxxj{j}'.

2 Unidentifiable drawing in margin, almost certainly to mark the later additions (see notes 1 and 3).

3 Written on a separate piece of paper, in a sixteenth-century hand, tied to MS through the word 'perquisites' to act as a marker.

Quittances
In quittance of 1 reeve for the year 5*s*.; 3 ploughmen for the year 9*s*.; 1 shepherd for the year 3*s*. Total, 17*s*.

Total of rents remaining, £9 15*s*. 11*d*.

Issues of the manor
The same render account for 13*s*. 1*d*. from pannage of pigs at Martinmas (11 November), that is, from 42 pigs over a year old, 21 pigs of three terms, 26 pigs of ½ year, and 31 weaned piglets, at 2*d*. a pig over a year old, 1½*d*. a pig of 3 terms, 1*d*. a pig of ½ year, and ½*d*. a weaned piglet; 2*s*. 3*d*. from winter pasturage sold; 2*s*. 9*d*. from summer pasturage sold; 1*s*. from 1 smith hired this year; 4*s*. 6*d*. from 54 hens from churchscot sold; 3*s*. from 1 feeble plough-horse sold; £1 5*s*. 8*d*. from 22 wethers sold at Martinmas, at 1*s*. 2*d*. each; 8*s*. from 1 feeble ox sold; 1*s*. 10*d*. from the hides sold of 2 plough-horses in murrain; 2*d*. from the skins sold of 2 wethers in murrain; 5¼*d*. from the skins sold of 7 lambs in murrain before shearing; 3*d*. from the skins sold wholesale of 10 lambs in murrain after shearing; 8*s*. 8*d*. from 3 pigs sold; nothing from coarse wool or lamb's-wool here because it was sent to Wolvesey; nothing from suckling ewes in the lord's fold this year; £2 from customary tenants for release from harrowing in Lent this year; nothing from wool locks this year. Total, £5 11*s*. 7¼*d*.

Sale of corn
The same render account for £13 8*s*. 3*d*. from 44 qrs of wheat sold, at 5*s*. 6*d*. a qr for 3½ qrs, and 6*s*. a qr for 41½ qrs; £1 3*s*. 4*d*. from 10 qrs of bere sold, at 2*s*. 4*d*. a qr; £3 7*s*. 6*d*. from 16 qrs 7 bus of barley sold, at 4*s*. a qr; £10 11½*d*. from 88 qrs 1 bus. of oats sold, at 2*s*. a qr for 14 qrs, and 2*s*. 4*d*. a qr for 74 qrs 1 bus.; 2*s*. 6*d*. from 5 bus. of peas sold, at 6*d*. a bus. Total, £28 2*s*. 6½*d*.

Entry fines
The same render account for 6*s*. from tithingpenny at the two hundred-courts for the year; 6*s*. 8*d*. from Henry Frye to have 1 virgate of land which belonged to Juliana la Frye his mother who surrendered the said land into the lord's hands through poverty; 2*s*. from Robert B*ercarius* to have 1 cotland which belonged to John Stub, which came into the lord's hands as his escheat for a felony which the same John committed; 1*s*. from Richard atte Putte to have 1 cotland for which he was chosen by the whole tithing. Total, 15*s*. 8*d*.

Perquisites
The same render account for 4*s*. 9*d*. from William atte Flod', Gilbert Em*ery* and their fellows for trespass of wood and pasture and other transgressions; 2*s*. from Thomas, reeve, for laying waste the land of Juliana Frye; 2*s*. from William Laggy for trespass of pasture and other transgressions; 5*s*. 3*d*. from William atte Feld', Robert Joye, William Longo for trespass of corn, wood and pasture and various other transgressions. Total, 14*s*.

Total of both, £1 9*s*. 8*d*.

Total of all receipts, £44 19*s*. 8¾*d*.

Cost of ploughs
In shoeing 14 plough-horses for the year 14*s*. In ironwork of 1 ox-plough and 2 horse-ploughs for the year 9*s*. 4½*d*. In stipend of the smith repairing and restoring the

ironwork of the said ploughs for the year 6*s*. 6*d*. In 4 ploughs made anew and others mended many times in the year 1*s*. 1*d*. In trimming and treating timber for ploughs and harrows 3*d*. In fitting ploughs with iron tyres 4½*d*. In 1 ploughshare bought 10*d*. In 3 pairs of wheels bought 9*d*. In 3 plough feet bought 1*s*. In 14 halters and 1 rope made from the horses' own hair 4*d*. In customary payment to 3 ploughmen and 1 shepherd in place of 3 ewes which they are accustomed to have at Martinmas 1*s*. In shoeing oxen 9*d*. In ploughing boon-works of 7 ploughmen, each ploughing, sowing with the lord's seed and harrowing 4 acres in winter and 2 acres in Lent, 3*s*. 6*d*., or 6*d*. a ploughman. In stipend of 3 drovers for the year 9*s*. In ⌈2⌉ plough-horses bought 9*s*. 8*d*. In 1 ox bought 11*s*. 4*d*. In 7½ qrs of bere bought for sowing £1 2*s*. 6*d*., at 3*s*. a qr. Total, £4 12*s*. 3*d*.

Carts
In 1 pair of wheels bought for the cart 2*s*. 6*d*. In fitting 1 old binding to the said wheels with clamps and large and small nails bought for the same 3*s*. 10*d*. In hooping the felloes of the cart 4*d*. In fitting the cart with axles for the year with nails and clouts bought for the same for the year 1*s*. In clamping and mending the old cart 6*d*. In shoeing 2 cart-horses for the year 2*s*. In stipend of 1 carter for the year 3*s*. Total, 13*s*. 2*d*.

Cost of buildings
In re-roofing and mending the hall, byre, and other buildings within the curia, and the sheepcote in places, 2*s*. 7½*d*. In collecting 10 acres of stubble for the same 1*s*. 8*d*. In iron bought 5*s*. In 3 pigs bought 4*s*. 6*d*. Total, 13*s*. 9½*d*.

Sheepcote
In 7 hurdles bought for the fold 7*d*. In wattling 15 hurdles 5*d*., at 1*d*. per 3 hurdles. In grease bought for greasing sheep 7*s*. 3½*d*. In 24 wethers bought after shearing £1 4*s*. In stipend of 1 keeper of lambs for ½ year 2*s*. 6*d*. Total, £1 14*s*. 9½*d*.

Weeding
In weeding corn this year 1*s*. 1*d*. In mowing, tossing and gathering in a certain small meadow 1*s*. Total, 2*s*. 1*d*.

Threshing
In threshing and winnowing 45 qrs of wheat by piece-work 7*s*. 6*d*., at 2*d*. a qr. In threshing and winnowing 41 qrs 4 bus. of bere and 4½ qrs 2 bus. of peas and vetches by piece-work 5*s*. 9¼*d*., at 1½*d*. a qr. In threshing and winnowing 17½ qrs of barley by piece-work 1*s*. 9¾*d*., at 1¼*d*. a qr. In threshing and winnowing 128 qrs 4 bus. of oats 6*s*. 8¼*d*., at 1¼*d*. per 2 qrs. In 2 sacks bought 11*d*. Total, £1 2*s*. 8¼*d*.

Harvest-time
In ale and relish bought for 3 harvest boon-works of 77[1] men who reaped and bound 22 acres of wheat and 106 acres of oats 8*s*. In reaping and binding 6 acres of wheat, 16 acres of barley, 48 acres of oats by piece-work, 12*s*. 10*d*., at 3*d*. an acre of wheat, 2½*d*. an acre of barley, and 2*d*. an acre of oats. Moreover, each virgater is bound to reap and bind 1½ acres of wheat and 1 acre of oats for reaping service (*nidrepp'*) and to cart at their own expense. Total, £1 10*d*.

Stipend of the hayward
In stipend of 1 hayward keeping the strips of ploughland, pasture, wood and other things, who is not otherwise hayward there, nor does he have the acre which the hayward is accustomed to have, 6*s*. 8*d*. Total, 6*s*. 8*d*.

1 MS '⟨C⟩Lxxvij'.

Total of all expenses, £10 6*s*. 3¼*d*.

And he owes, £34 13*s*. 5½*d*.

Allowances
In allowance of the same for 15 wethers bought after shearing 15*s*. In allowance of the same for 165 lambs bought before shearing £3 14*s*. 2*d*., at 5*d*. each for 100, and 6*d*. each for 65. Total, £4 9*s*. 2*d*.

Cash deliveries
Delivered to Sir G*eoffrey*, treasurer of Wolvesey, by 1 tally, £23 10*s*.

Total of all allowances and cash deliveries, £27 19*s*. 2*d*.

And he owes clear, £6 14*s*. 3½*d*.

m.10d

Issues of the grange

Wheat
{yield: 6½-fold plus 1 qr}
The same render account for 56 qrs 2 bus. from the whole issue of wheat by struck measure.
Sown over 68 acres as they lie in la Middelfeld', 12 qrs 2 bus.; that is, 1½ bus. an acre, less 4 bus. in all. Sold, 44 qrs.

Bere
{yield: 3½-fold plus 2 qrs 6 bus.}
The same render account for 51 qrs 6 bus. from the whole issue of bere by struck measure; 7½ qrs bought; 4 qrs 6 bus. of peas and vetches mixed for the liveries of the manorial servants. Total, 64 qrs.
Sown over 72 acres as they lie in la Middelfeld', 18 qrs; that is, 2 bus. an acre. Delivered to 1 hayward for the year, 6½ qrs, because he takes a quarter every 8 weeks. Delivered to 1 carter, 1 oxherd and 2 drovers for the year, 26 qrs. In making bread for 3 harvest boon-works, 3 qrs. Delivered to 1 harrower in Lent, ½ qr, because of the release of the villeins from harrowing this year as made clear in the issues of the manor. Sold, 10 qrs.

Barley
{yield: two-and-a-half-fold plus 1½ qrs}
The same render account for 21 qrs 7 bus. from the whole issue of barley by struck measure.
Sown over 22 acres as they lie, 5 qrs; that is, 2 bus. an acre, less ½ qr in all. Sold, 16 qrs 7 bus.

Oats
{yield: 3½-fold less 10 qrs 7 bus.}
The same render account for 160 qrs 4 bus. from the whole issue of oats by struck measure; 4½ qrs by estimation in sheaves given to oxen. Total, 165 qrs.
Sown over 180 acres as they lie in la Northfeld', 51 qrs 3 bus.; that is, 2½ bus. an acre, less 4 qrs 7 bus. in all. In fodder of 2 cart-horses and 14 plough-horses, 21 qrs. In supporting oxen by estimation in sheaves, 4½ qrs. Sold, 88 qrs 1 bus.

Peas
{yield: 6½-fold}
The same render account for 4 qrs 7 bus. from the whole issue of peas by struck measure.
Sown over 4 acres as they lie in Northfeld', 4 bus. Mixed with bere for the liveries of the manorial servants, 3 qrs 6 bus. Sold, 5 bus.

Vetches
{yield: as sown}
The same render account for 1 qr of vetches remaining in the granary from the previous year; 1 qr from the issue because the rest was consumed in husks by various of the lord's livestock. Total, 2 qrs.
Sown, 1 qr. Mixed with bere for the liveries of the manorial servants, 1 qr.

Stock
Horses: 2 cart-horses remain from the previous year; 2 remain.
Plough-horses: 16 remain from the previous year; 2 bought. Total, 18. 2 in murrain; 1 sold; 15 remain, 6 of them male.
Foals:[1] none this year because the mare did not foal.
Oxen: 9 remain from the previous year; 1 bought. Total, 10. 1 sold; 9 remain.
Wethers: 152 remain from the previous year; 39 bought after shearing. Total, 191. 22 sold at Martinmas; 2 in murrain after shearing. Total, 24. 167 remain.
Lambs: 165 bought before shearing. 7 in murrain before shearing, 10 after shearing. Total, 17. 148 remain.
Pigs: 3 bought; 3 sold; none remain.
Coarse fleeces: 152 from wethers produced at the shearing this year. 15 in tithe; 1 in customary payment to 1 shepherd. Total, 16. 136 sent to Wolvesey.
Lambs' fleeces: 158 produced at the shearing this year; all sent to Wolvesey.
Hides: 2 from plough-horses in murrain; 2 sold.
Woolskins: 2 from wethers in murrain after shearing; 2 sold.
Lambskins: 7 from lambs in murrain before shearing, 10 after shearing; all sold.
Hens: 62 from churchscot; 8 in default of Alice Wytegr*o*m, William Wagetayl, Alice Wodewe and John Broun because they are widowed; 54 sold.
Carts: 2 remain from the previous year; 2 remain, 1 with iron tyres and 1 of wood.
Sacks: 2 remain from the previous year; 2 bought; 2 worn out; 2 remain.

Highclere

Arrears
Henry la Wayte, bailiff, and Thomas Swon, reeve, render account for £1 8*s*. of arrears from the previous year. All delivered to the lord treasurer of Wolvesey, by 1 tally. They are quit.

Rents of assize
The same render account for £1 14*s*. for all rents of assize at Christmas; £3 6*s*. at Easter (22 April); £2 at the Nativity of St John the Baptist (24 June); £15 8*s*. {1½*d*.} at Michaelmas (29 September). Total, £22 8*s*. 1½*d*.

1 MS omits heading.

Quittances

In quittance of 1 reeve for the year 4*s*.; 1 hayward for the year 2*s*.; 1 woodward of Holehurst for the year 2*s*. 4*d*.; 3 ploughmen for the year 6*s*.; 1 ploughman for 2½ terms 1*s*. 3*d*.; 1 smith making the ironwork of the ploughs for the year 2*s*.; 1 keeper of ewes for 2½ terms 1*s*. 3*d*.; 1 cowherd for the year 2*s*. Total, £1 10*d*.

Defaults of rent

In default of 24 acres of land drawn into demesne, 10*d*. for the year; 10 virgates of land drawn into the park, 13*s*. 4*d*. for the year; the land of the skinner (*pellip'*) drawn into demesne, 1*s*. for the year; the land which belonged to Benedict Cl*ericus* drawn into demesne, 4*s*. 6*d*. for the year; the land which belonged to Alexander le Rych' drawn into demesne, 17*s*. 9*d*. for the year; the rent of Hawkley, 3*s*. for the year; the house which belonged to Nicholas atte Zele, pulled down by statute, 4*d*. for the year. Total, £2 9*d*.

Total of quittances and defaults of rent, £3 1*s*. 7*d*.

Total of rents remaining, £19 6*s*. 6½*d*.

Issues of the manor

The same render account for 5*s*. 4½*d*. from pannage of pigs within, that is, from 58 pigs and 13 piglets, at 1*d*.[1] a pig and ½*d*. a piglet; £1 5*s*. 7*d*. from foreign pannage in la Wasch', that is, from 212 pigs and 6 piglets, at 1*d*. a pig, apart from 92 which paid 2*d*. each, and ½*d*. a piglet; 17*s*. from pannage sold wholesale in the park; 1*s*. 6*d*. from the men of Hawkley according to custom for not mowing the meadow of Wolvesey and paid at Michaelmas; 2*s*. from the pinfold at Michaelmas according to custom, the number of oxen or sheep not being put down because they give the same whatever the number; nothing from the pasturage in Groforost this year on account of the lord's stock; nothing from the herbage of the meadow of Grostrof this year because the meadow was mowed; nothing from the pasturage in the foreign enclosure in winter or summer on account of the lord's stock; nothing from the pasturage in the park on account of the lord's cows; 1*s*. 7*d*. from loppings sold of timber felled for the repair of houses in Brightwell and Harwell; £4 8*s*. from 8 old oxen sold, at 11*s*. each; £2 6*s*. from 6 cows sold at Martinmas, at 7*s*. 8*d*. each; 5*s*. from 1 feeble cow sold; 8*s*. from 1 steer from a heriot sold; £1 from 17 calves sold, at 1*s*. each for 11, and 1*s*. 6*d*. each for 6; £1 9*s*. 3*d*. from 39 ewes sold at Martinmas, at 9*d*. each; 2*s*. 2*d*. from the hide sold of 1 ox in murrain; 1*s*. 7*d*. from the hide sold of 1 cow in murrain; 1*s*. 7*d*. from the hides sold of 1 steer and 2 yearlings in murrain; 2*d*. from the hides of 2 calves in murrain; 2*s*. 3*d*. from the skins sold of 9 ewes and rams in murrain before shearing, at 3*d*. a skin; 2*d*. from the skins sold of 2 ewes in murrain after shearing; 2*s*. 10*d*. from the skins sold of 34 lambs in murrain before weaning, at 1*d*. each; 11*s*. from 1 wey 6 cloves of winter cheese sold, at 9*s*. a wey; £6 19*s*. 6*d*. from 8 weys of cows' cheese and 7½ weys of ewes' cheese made in summer sold, at 9*s*. a wey; £2 11*s*. 1*d*. from 5½ weys 5 cloves of Burghclere cheese made in summer sold, at 9*s*. a wey; 15*s*. 9*d*. from 1½ weys 7 cloves of butter sold, at 9*s*. a wey; 5*d*. from the feathers and tails of peacocks sold; 2*s*. from honey found in the wood sold; 2*s*. 7½*d*. from 9 dozen pigeons sold, at 3½*d*. a dozen; nothing from coarse wool this year because it was sent to Wolvesey; 17*s*. 2*d*. from 39 cloves 2 lb of wool locks sold, at 7*d*. a clove; 5*s*. 4*d*. from 64 hens from churchscot sold; 2*s*. 11*d*. from 1,005 eggs sold

1 MS omits '*d*.'

according to custom; 11*s*. from 3 pigs sold wholesale; 5*s*. 3*d*. from the dairy produce of cows sold at the audit; 5*s*. 5½*d*. from the dairy produce of Burghclere ewes sold at the audit. Total, £26 9*s*. 6½*d*.

Annual recognizance
The same render account for 1*s*. from Elias Snow for annual recognizance. Total, 1*s*.

Sale of corn
The same render account for £7 11*s*. 6*d*. from 25 qrs 2 bus. of wheat sold, at 6*s*. a qr; £1 13*s*. from 8 qrs 2 bus. of barley sold, at 4*s*. a qr; 12*s*. 2¼*d*. from 4 qrs 7 bus. of oats sold, at 2*s*. 6*d*. a qr. Total, £9 16*s*. 8¼*d*.

Entry and marriage fines
The same render account for 4*s*. from the tithing for tithingpenny at the 2 hundred-courts for the year; 6*s*. 8*d*. from William Yong' to have 1 virgate of land which belonged to Agnes his mother; 10*s*. from Alveva Snow to have 1 cotland which belonged to Dyon' her sister; 1*s*. from Matilda atte Den' for marrying Isabel her daughter outside; 1*s*. from Juliana Elys for marrying Matilda her daughter outside; 6*d*. from Thomas le Pott*ere* for marrying Agnes, daughter of Nicholas atte Zele, within; 6*s*. 8*d*. from Richard Duk to have 1 virgate of land which belonged to Christina his mother; 2*s*. from John atte Cruch' to have 1*s*. of purpresture beside la Wasslo*n*d' which belonged to Simon Drywod' and John Thorm*ere*; 2*s*. from John atte Zele for marrying Alice his daughter outside. Total, £1 13*s*. 10*d*.

Perquisites
The same render account for 1*s*. from the whole tithing because it did not produce in court those it had bailed; 6*d*. from Robert Ely because he is convicted; 6*d*. from John atte Zele for keeping the cows badly; 3*d*. from John Gouh*a*m for transgression; 6*d*. from the tithing because it did not produce in court; 3*s*. from John Snow, John Swon,[1] Juliana la Sone, Michael B*ercarius* and their fellows for trespass of pasture; 9*d*. from Geoffrey Crorou' and his fellows for contempt; 3*d*. from Felicia Sewal' for breaking an agreement; 2*s*. 3*d*. from Adam de Whyteweye for trespass of wood and other transgressions; 1*s*. 6*d*. from the reeve and bartoner for trespass of their horses in the curia; 9*d*. from Sarah Conestabil' and fellows for breaking the assize; 6*d*. from the tithing because it did not produce in court; 3*d*. from Richard Duk for default; 6*d*. from a ploughman for bad ploughing; 2*s*. from Nicholas le Fox to have an inquest; 1*s*. from Maurice Lynt for the recovery and custody (*ward' et forfeng'*) of 1 cow; 2*s*. from 3 ploughmen because they came late to their ploughs and for bad ploughing; 1*s*. 6*d*. from John Swon, John atte Zele and their fellows for trespass of wood and pasture; 1*s*. 9*d*. from Robert Ken', William Edgar and their fellows for breaking the assize of ale; 6*d*. from Adam le Ryd' for raising the hue; 1*s*. from Richard K*am*be for the recovery and custody of 1 cow; 6*d*. from John atte Zele because he is not proceeding against Gervase Gill'. Total, £1 2*s*. 9*d*.

Total of both, £3 6*s*. 7*d*.

Total of all receipts, £58 10*s*. 4¼*d*.

Cost of ploughs
In the ironwork of 2 ploughs for the year {2*s*.} 10*d*. In 2 plough-irons bought 7*d*. In 1 ploughshare bought 10*d*. In frequently mending and fitting the ploughs with share-

1 MS omits 'John', but recorded below.

beams for the year 4½*d*. In fitting 1 plough with iron tyres 2½*d*. In 2 pairs of wheels bought 8*d*. In trimming and treating timber for ploughs and harrows 2*s*. 1½*d*. In ploughing boon-works of 15 ploughmen in winter and as many in Lent who ploughed as many acres as they lie 5*s*., or 2*d*. a ploughman a day. Moreover, each ploughman will plough 1 acre in summer for fallow without food according to custom. In reward of 3 ploughmen for the year and 1 ploughman for 2½ terms for their Saturday ploughings 16*s*. 10½*d*., or 4*s*. 6*d*. each for the year, and this through Bishop John, because before they had nothing except 3*s*. a year. In stipend of 1 oxherd for 1½ terms 9*d*. In 9 oxen bought for ploughs £5 1*s*. 3*d*., at 11*s*. 3*d*. each. In 6 qrs 7 bus. of wheat bought £1 14*s*. 4½*d*., at 5*s*. a qr. In 10 qrs 6 bus. of bere bought for sowing and for the liveries of the manorial servants £1 10*s*. 8½*d*., at 2*s*. a qr for 4 qrs, 3*s*. 1*d*. a qr for 2½ qrs, and 3*s*. 4*d*. a qr for 4 qrs 2 bus. Total, £9 16*s*. 7*d*.

Cost of carts

In clouts, nails, grease and white leather bought, and in fitting 3 carts with axles many times during the year, 1*s*. 10*d*. In 1 bought 6½*d*.[1] In 1 pair of tie-beams 6*d*. In 1 cart-saddle bought 4*d*. In 1 pair of traces 6½*d*. In 1 cart-rope 1*s*. 2*d*. In 1 cart-body made anew 6*d*. In mending the ironwork of the old dung-cart 3*d*. In 2 halters bought 4*d*. In shoeing 2 cart-horses for the year 2*s*. 2*d*. In stipend of 1 carter for the year 3*s*. Total, 11*s*. 2*d*.

Cost of the dairy

In linen and woollen cloth bought for the dairy 1*s*. 2*d*. In 1 new bucket 10½*d*. In earthenware pots and pans bought 8*d*. In a press 6*d*. In 3 qrs of salt bought 7*s*., at 2*s*. 4*d*. a qr. In stipend of 1 dairymaid for the year 2*s*. 4*d*. Total, 12*s*. 6½*d*.

Cost of buildings

In re-roofing the unroofed barn 2*s*. 6*d*. In collecting 12 acres of stubble for the same 2*s*., at 2*d*. an acre. In roofing the kitchen, dairy and larder in places 1*s*. 3*d*. In mending the walls of the small barn 1*s*. In hooks and hinges bought for the gate to the part of the park beside the granary and for the garden-gate 1*s*. ½*d*. In a carpenter rebuilding a certain part of the long chamber which had collapsed 3*s*. 4*d*. In laying 4,000 tiles on the same 2*s*. In pegs bought for the same 4*d*. In 1,500 nails bought for laths 1*s*. ¾*d*. In 100 large nails bought for the said chamber 3*d*. In a carpenter making 1 new leaf for the outside gate and mending the same gate within 3*s*. In hooks, hinges, large and small nails bought for the same 2*s*. In 1 new lock bought for the gate to the cemetery and 1 bought for the wicket gate within and in mending the lock on the great gate with 1 key bought for the same 1*s*. In repairing and restoring 2 broken glass windows in the lord's chapel 1*s*. 6*d*. In ironwork bought for the same 6*d*. In stipend of 1 carpenter rebuilding and mending the gutter between the hall and lord's chamber with boards sawn for the same 2*s*. 6*d*. In nails bought 4*d*. In 8½ feet 6 lb of lead bought £1 1*s*. 6*d*. In stipend of the plumber smelting the said lead and laying it on the aforesaid gutter 2*s*. 6*d*. In 1,500 slates bought for roofing the oriel of the chapel 2*s*. 2*d*. In pegs bought for the same 3*d*. In laths made 4*d*. In 2,000 nails bought for laths 1*s*. 8*d*. In roofing the said oriel 1*s*. 10*d*. In roofing and mending the hall, lord's chamber and chapel in places 3*s*. 8*d*. In making 7,000 tiles and 8 qrs of lime 8*s*. 7*d*., at 1*s*. 1*d*. per 1,000 tiles, and 1½*d*. per quarter of lime. In making 100 ridge-tiles 1*s*. 1*d*. In 1 rope bought for the well 8*s*. 4*d*. In hay and forage bought £1 5*s*. 2*d*. In 1 lock bought for the door to the forage-shed and in mending various others in the curia 8*d*.

1 No object recorded in MS.

In 3 pigs bought 7*s*. 4*d*. In 2 casks bought 6*s*. In hooping and mending the casks 1*s*. 6*d*. Total, £5 19*s*. 2¼*d*.

Sheepfold and sheepcote
In roofing the sheepcote of Suthdon' 2*s*. In collecting 6 acres of stubble for the same 1*s*. In grease bought for greasing sheep 12*s*. In stipend of 1 shepherd for 1½ terms 9*d*. In wattling the sheepfold 5*d*. In 59 ewes bought after shearing £2 18*s*., at 1*s*. each, less 1*s*. in all because there was a gain of 1. In 36 ells of canvas bought for putting the coarse wool and lamb's-wool in, 9*s*. 9*d*., at 3¼*d*. an ell. In sacks made and stitched together with thread bought for the same 6*d*. In packing and treating the wool 1*s*. 4*d*. Total, £4 5*s*. 9*d*.

Threshing and winnowing
In threshing and winnowing 22 qrs 2 bus. of wheat by piece-work 3*s*. 8½*d*., at 2*d*. a qr. In threshing and winnowing 13 qrs 6 bus. of bere by piece-work 1*s*. 11¾*d*., at ¾*d*. a qr. In threshing and winnowing 11 qrs 6 bus. of barley 1*s*. 2½*d*., at 1¼*d*. a qr. In threshing 27 qrs of oats by piece-work 1*s*. 1½*d*., at ½*d*. a qr. In winnowing the same 3½*d*., at 1*d*. per 8 qrs. Total, 8*s*. 3¾*d*.

Harvest-time
In 210 acres of wheat, bere, barley and oats weeded by piece-work 5*s*. 10*d*., at 1*d*. per 3 acres. In 1 boon-work of 66 men with the officials of the curia who reaped and gathered 42 acres of wheat as they lie 6*s*. 10½*d*., as in bread, ale and relish. In the bartoner mowing, tossing and gathering in the sheepcote of Suthdon' 10*d*. Total, 13*s*. 6½*d*.

Cost of the park
In enclosing 1½ furlongs 19 perches with hedges in the park 5*s*. 11*d*., at 3*s*. a furlong. Total, 5*s*. 11*d*.

Expenses of the steward
In expenses of the steward for 1 visit at the tourn of Martinmas 3*s*. 1*d*. Total, 3*s*. 1*d*.

Expenses of the bailiff
In expenses of the bailiff and his household for the year £5. In 1 fur for the summer livery of the same 3*s*. Total, £5 3*s*.

Total of all expenses, £27 19*s*. 1*d*.

And thus he owes, £30 11*s*. 3¼*d*.

Cash deliveries
Delivered to Sir G*eoffrey*, treasurer of Wolvesey, by 1 tally, £19 12*s*.

And thus he owes clear, £10 19*s*. 3¼*d*.

m.11
Wheat
{yield: 3½-fold plus 5 bus.}
The same render account for 27 qrs 6 bus. from the whole issue of wheat by struck measure; 1 qr by estimation in 2 acres delivered to the reeve and hayward according to custom; 6½ qrs 3 bus. bought. Total, 35 qrs 5 bus.

Sown over 58 acres as they lie in Hauethfeld, 8 qrs 3 bus.; that is, 2½ bus. per 2 acres, less 4 bus. in all. Mixed with bere for sowing, 5 bus. In customary payment to the hayward, 1 bus. In customary payment to 1 reeve and 1 hayward by estimation in 2 acres, 1 qr. In provision of the steward for his visits, 2 bus. Sold, 25 qrs 2 bus.

Bere
{yield: two-fold less 3½ qrs}
The same render account for 17 qrs 1 bus. from the whole issue of bere by struck measure; 4 bus. by estimation in 67 sheaves delivered for the reaping of 33½ acres by labour service, at 2 sheaves an acre; 10 qrs 6 bus. bought; 5 bus. of wheat mixed for sowing. Total, 29 qrs.
Sown over 81 acres as they lie in Hathfeld, 15 qrs 1 bus.; that is, 1 bus. an acre, less ½ bus. in all. Delivered to 1 carter, who takes a quarter every 10 weeks for the year, 5 qrs 1½ bus. Delivered to 1 oxherd from Michaelmas (29 September) until Sunday after the feast of St Matthew the Apostle (25 February), for 21 weeks 3 days, 2 qrs 1 bus. Delivered to 1 shepherd from Michaelmas until the Purification (2 February), for 18 weeks, 1 qr 6 bus. Delivered to 1 dairymaid for the year, who takes a quarter every 12 weeks, 4 qrs 2½ bus. Delivered to the reapers by estimation in 67 sheaves, 4 bus.

Barley
{yield: two-and-a-half-fold less 5 bus.}
The same render account for 14 qrs 6 bus. from the whole issue of barley by struck measure; 2 bus. by estimation in 24 sheaves delivered for the reaping of 12 acres by labour service, at 2 sheaves an acre. Total, 15 qrs.
Sown over 26 acres as they lie in le Westfeld', 6½ qrs; that is, 2 bus. an acre. Delivered to the reapers by estimation in 24 sheaves, 2 bus. Sold, 8 qrs 2 bus.

Oats
{yield: two-fold less 5½ qrs}
The same render account for 33 qrs 6 bus. from the whole issue of oats by struck measure; 8 qrs by estimation in sheaves given to oxen; 2 bus. by estimation in 1½ acres delivered to the hayward according to custom; 1½ qrs by estimation in 108 sheaves delivered to the reapers for reaping 54 acres by labour service, at 2 sheaves an acre. Total, 43½ qrs.
Sown over 25 acres as they lie in the fields of Westfeld and Cre*m*pesh*a*m, 21 qrs 1 bus.; that is, 2 bus. an acre, less 1 bus. in all. In customary payment to 1 hayward, 1 bus. In fodder of 2 cart-horses for the year, 7 qrs. In supporting 18 oxen by estimation in sheaves, 8 qrs. In fodder of the steward's horses for his visits, 5 bus. In customary payment to the hayward by estimation in ½ acre, 2 bus. Delivered to the reapers by estimation in 108 sheaves, 1½ qrs. Sold, 4 qrs 7 bus.

Peas
Nothing from the issue of peas this year because none were sown; ½ qr bought. Sown, 2 bus. In provision of the bailiff, 2 bus.

Nothing from the issue of vetches this year for the same reason.

Stock
Horses: 2 cart-horses remain from the previous year; 2 remain.

Oxen: 21 remain from the previous year; 9 bought. Total, 30. 1 in murrain; 3 delivered to the reeve of Ecchinswell; 8 sold. Total, 12. 18 remain.
Bulls: 1 remains from the previous year; 1 added from steers. Total, 2. 2 remain.
Cows: 50 remain from the previous year; 1 addition. Total, 51. 1 in murrain; 7 sold at Martinmas (11 November). Total, 8. 43 remain.
Steers: 4 remain from the previous year's bullocks; 1 from the heriot of Agnes atte Assch'. Total, 5. 1 in murrain; 1 added to bulls, 1 to cows; 1 delivered to the reeve of Ecchinswell; 1 sold; none remain.
Bullocks: 15 remain from the previous year's yearlings; 4 delivered to the reeve of Ecchinswell; 11 remain, 7 of them male.
Yearlings: 18 remain from the previous year's calves; 2 in murrain; 16 remain, 2 of them male.
Calves: 36 from the offspring of the cows this year because 6 sterile, 1 in murrain, 7 sold at Martinmas, and 1 aborted. 2 in murrain; 3 in tithe; 17 sold. Total, 22. 14 remain.
Ewes: 383 remain from the previous year; 48[1] added from the hoggs of Ecchinswell after shearing; 59 bought after shearing. Total, 500. 39 sold at Martinmas; 6 in murrain before lambing, 3 after lambing and before shearing, and 2 after shearing; 1 sent to Ashmansworth after shearing. Total, 51. 449 remain.
Rams: 15 remain from the previous year. 1 in murrain; 4 castrated and added to the wethers of Ecchinswell before shearing. Total, 5. 10 remain.
Lambs: 324 from the offspring of the ewes because 14 sterile, 6 in murrain, and 39 sold at Martinmas; 37 in murrain before weaning; 28 in tithe; 4 in customary payment to 1 reeve, 1 hayward, 1 shepherd and 1 smith; 255 sent to Ecchinswell; none remain.
Pigs: 3 bought; 3 sold; none remain.
Coarse wool: 335 fleeces from ewes and 10 from rams produced at the shearing this year; 237 from wethers received from the reeve of Ashmansworth; 570 from wethers and hoggs received from the reeve of Ecchinswell; 320 from rams and ewes received from the reeve of Burghclere. Total, 1472. 34 in tithe for the wool of Highclere; 1 in customary payment to the shepherd. Total, 35. 1437 sent to Wolvesey, which made 10 weys.
Lamb's-wool: 243 fleeces received from the reeve of Ecchinswell; 249 received from the reeve of Ashmansworth. Total, 492. All sent to Wolvesey, which made 1½ weys 5 cloves.
Hides: 1 from an ox, 1 from a cow, 1 from a steer, 2 from yearlings and 2 from calves in murrain; all sold.
Woolskins: 9 from ewes and 1 from a ram in murrain before shearing. Total, 10. 1 in tithe; 9 sold.
Bare skins: 2 from ewes in murrain after shearing; 2 sold.
Lambskins: 37 from lambs in murrain before weaning; 3 in tithe; 34 sold.
Winter cheese: 1 wey 6 cloves made; all sold with the tithe deducted therefrom.
Summer cheese {yield of cow 3*s*. 6*d*. because customary payments estimated at ½ wey and 1 wey of butter; yield of sheep thus 2½*d*. this year}: 162 cheeses made this year from the said cows between the tenth calends of May (22 April) and Michaelmas (29 September), both days included, at 1 cheese a day. 16 in tithe; 1 in customary payment to the reeve of Highclere; 3 in customary payment to 1 outside smith of Holehurst and 1 dairymaid; 1 in customary payment for the mowing of the meadow of Ecchinswell. Total, 21. 141 sold, which made 8 weys. 162 cheeses made from the aforesaid ewes this year; 16 in tithe; 146 sold, which made 7½ weys.

1 '58' according to the Ecchinswell account, the correct figure.

Burghclere cheese {yield of sheep thus 2½*d.* because customary payments estimated at 9 cloves and butter at ½ wey}: 169 cheeses made this year from the ewes of Burghclere between the seventeenth calends of May (15 April) and Michaelmas, both days included. 17 in tithe; 3 in customary payment to 1 reeve, 1 hayward and 1 dairymaid; 1 in customary payment for the mowing of the meadow of Burghclere. Total, 21. 148 sold, which made 5½ weys 5 cloves.
Butter: 1⌈½⌉ weys 7 cloves; all sold.
Peacocks: 15 peacocks and peahens remain from the previous year; no offspring this year. 2 in murrain; 6 delivered to the bishop when the count of Savoy and earl of Lincoln were attending at Wolvesey. Total, 8. 7 remain, 2 of them peacocks.
Hens: 20 from the forester of Holehurst; 60 from churchscot. Total, 80. 8 in quittance of the smith; 2 in default of Cecilia Swon because a widow; 2 in default of Felicia Sewal' for the same; 2 in default of Alice, relict of the reeve, for the same; 2 in default of Alice Bolt for the same. Total, 16. 64 sold.
Eggs: 1,005 received according to custom at Easter; all sold.
Cider: 2 casks made this year; they remain.
Carts: 2 remain from the previous year; 1 used in the curia; 1 with iron tyres remains.
Utensils: 2 brass pots, 1 posnet, 2 brass pans, 1 tripod, 1 ewer with a basin, and 3 casks remain; 2 casks bought; 4 barrels, 4 bowls and 4 tubs remain from the previous year; 1 lead vessel remains from the previous year; all this remains.

Newtown

Rents
Henry la Wayte, bailiff, and William atte Wat*ere*, reeve, render account for £7 10*s.* 4*d.* for all rents of assize of Newtown; all paid at Michaelmas (29 September). Total, £7 10*s.* 4*d.*

Increment
The same render account for ½*d.* from William Boveyt for 1 increment of rent for 1 small plot beside his gate. Total, the same.

Total of rents with increment, £7 10*s.* 4½*d.*

Quittances
In quittance of 1 reeve for the year 1*s.* In default of the land of le Nywema*n*, 1*s.* for the year. In default of 1 small plot which Alice Basely held, pulled down by statute, 2*d.* Total of quittances and defaults of rent, 2*s.* 2*d.*

Total of rents remaining, £7 8*s.* 2½*d.*

Entry fines
The same render account for 2*s.* from tithingpenny at the two hundred-courts for the year; 6*d.* from William Boveyt to have entry to a certain small plot beside his gate which he previously encroached upon without licence. Total, 2*s.* 6*d.*

Perquisites
The same render account for 3*d.* from Hugh Tineker' for default; 3*d.* from Thomas Paste for false presentment; 3*d.* from Thomas Gudd' for unjustly withholding; 6*d.*

from Henry Jacob for the hue; 4*s.* 6*d.* from Peter Basely, Philip Chartayn, Felicia Greyte, Christina Car*eter*, John Noel, Nicholas Mol*endinarius*, Hugh atte Thorn', William Hayward, John Gill', Ralph Mol*endinarius*, John Cute, Walter Nywe, John atte Mol*endinum*, Edith Waltr' and Robert Fillot for breaking the assize; 6*d.* from the whole community for concealment; 3*d.* from Philip Diud; 3*d.* from Henry B*ercarius* for unjustly withholding. Total, 6*s.* 9*d.*

Total of both, 9*s.* 3*d.*

Total of all receipts, £7 17*s.* 5½*d.*

And he owes it all.

Cash deliveries
Delivered to Sir G*eoffrey*, treasurer of Wolvesey, by 1 tally, £7 17*s.* 5½*d.*

He is quit.

Burghclere

Arrears
Henry la Wayte, bailiff, and John le Sone, reeve, render account for £37 19*s.* 10½*d.* of arrears from the previous year. All delivered to Sir G*eoffrey*, treasurer of Wolvesey, by 1 tally. They are quit.

Rents
The same render account for £2 7*s.* for all rents of assize at Christmas; £2 7*s.* at Easter (22 April); £2 7*s.* at the Nativity of St John the Baptist (24 June); £16 4*s.* 6*d.* at Michaelmas (29 September). Total, £23 5*s.* 6*d.*

Increment
The same render account for 1*d.* from John Scissor' for increment of rent to have entry to 1 plot, 36 feet long and 24 feet wide, beside the forge of la Wydegate. Total, 1*d.*

Total of rents with increment, £23 ⌈5*s.* 7*d.*⌉

Quittances
In quittance of 1 reeve for the year 4*s.* 8*d.*; 1 hayward for the year 3*s.*; 7 ploughmen for the year £1 1*s.*; 2 ploughmen for 1 term 1*s.*; 1 shepherd for 2½ terms 1*s.* 3*d.* Total, £1 10*s.* 11*d.*

Defaults of rent
In default of 335 acres of land drawn into demesne, £1 17*s.* for the year; the land of Alwyn' drawn into demesne, 3*s.* for the year; 10 acres of land of Roger Mainpetyt drawn into demesne, 1*s.* 8*d.* for the year; 10 acres of land of Osmund' drawn into demesne, 2*s.* 6*d.* for the year; 10 acres of land of Simon Cl*ericus* drawn into demesne, 1*s.* 8*d.* for the year; the land of Alwyn drawn into demesne, 1*s.* for the year; the land of Osmund Dustr' drawn into demesne, 1*s.* for the year. Total, £2 7*s.* 10*d.*

Total of quittances and defaults of rent, £3 18*s.* 9*d.*

Total of rents remaining, £19 6*s.* 10*d.*

Release from labour service
The same render account for 7*s.* from Richard le Eyr for release from his labour service for 1 virgate of land for the year. Total, 7*s.*

Issues of the manor
The same render account for £1 1*s.* 9½*d.* from pannage of pigs within, that is, from 253 pigs and 13 piglets, at 1*d.* a pig and ½*d.* a piglet; nothing from foreign pannage this year for a want of mast; £1 from the pasturage of Oldehull' at Michaelmas; 5*s.*[1] from the men of Earlstone according to custom at the Nativity of St John the Baptist for herbage; 5*s.* for the farm of the quarry at Michaelmas; 3*s.* from the men of Addebury for not making charcoal at Christmas; 3*s.* from the free men of Earlstone for release from ploughing at Michaelmas because the villeins plough for the winter sowing and fallow; 2*s.* from honey according to custom at Michaelmas for land which Thomas Gerard holds; 7*s.* from the pasturage of la G*ar*sto*n* sold at Michaelmas; nothing from winter pasturage on account of the lord's stock; nothing from summer pasturage for the same reason; 4*s.* from 1 plough-horse from a heriot sold; £6 7*s.* from 14 oxen sold at Michaelmas, at 9*s.* each for 13, and 10*s.* for 1; 11*s.* from 2 half-dead oxen sold soon after Easter; £1 6*s.* 8*d.* from 1 ram and 29 ewes sold at Martinmas, at 8*d.* each; 16*s.* 4*d.* from the hides sold of 7 oxen in murrain, at 2*s.* 6*d.* each for 3, 2*s.* 4*d.* each for 2, 2*s.* 2*d.* for 1, and 2*s.* for 1; 2*s.* 4*d.* from the flesh sold of 2 oxen in murrain; 6*s.* from the skins of 2 rams and 22 ewes in murrain before shearing, at 3*d.* a skin; 7*d.* from the skins sold of 7 ewes in murrain after shearing; 4*s.* 4*d.* from the skins sold of 52 lambs in murrain before shearing, at 1*d.* a skin; 12*s.* 1*d.* from 145 hens from churchscot sold; 3*s.* 2½*d.* from 1,100 eggs sold, received according to custom at Easter, at 3½*d.* a hundred; 8*s.* 8*d.* from 3 pigs sold; 6*s.* 8*d.* from the heriot of Edith Cuteles who withdrew from the manor and surrendered her lands and tenements into the lord's hands. Total, £14 15*s.* 8*d.*

Annual recognizance
Nothing from Roger Maresch*al* because he is dead; 3*d.* from Richard atte Heth' for annual recognizance; nothing from John Lunt because he is dead. Total, 3*d.*

Sale of corn
The same render account for £30 3*s.* 4*d.* from 90½ qrs of wheat sold, at 6*s.* 8*d.* a qr; £5 7*s.* 6*d.* from 26 qrs 7 bus. of bere sold, at 4*s.* a qr; 18*s.* 6*d.* from 4 qrs 5 bus. of barley sold, at 4*s.* a qr; £4 12*s.* 10½*d.* from 39 qrs 6 bus. of oats sold, at 2*s.* a qr for 13 qrs, and 2*s.* 6*d.* a qr for 26 qrs 6 bus. Total of all corn sold, £41 2*s.* 2½*d.*

Sale of the mill's corn
The same render account for 1*s.* 6*d.* from 2 bus. of wheat from the issue of the mill sold, at 9*d.* a bus.; £2 8*s.* 9*d.* from 14 qrs 5 bus. of maslin sold, at 3*s.* 4*d.* a qr; 10*s.* from 4 qrs of malt sold, at 2*s.* 6*d.* a qr. Total, £3 3*d.*

Entry and marriage fines
The same render account for £1 6*s.* 8*d.* from tithingpenny at the two hundred-courts for the year; 13*s.* 4*d.* from Cecilia Marescall' to retain ½ virgate of land which belonged to her husband; 1*s.* from John le Sone for marrying Agnes his daughter

1 MS omits '*s.*'

outside; 5*s*. from Roger atte Garst*on* to have 1 messuage 6½ acres of purpresture which belonged to Robert atte Garston' his uncle; 2*s*. from Walter le Son' for marrying Isabel his daughter outside; 1*s*. from John le Tayllor to have entry to a certain small plot, 36 feet long and 24 feet wide, beside the forge of la Wydeg*ate*; 1*s*. from Edith (*Aldich'*) Cuteles for marrying herself outside the manor; 5*s*. from John Cutel of Whitway to have land which belonged to Adam Kutel his father by resignation of Edith Cutel his stepmother. Total, £2 15*s*.

Perquisites

The same render account for 2*s*. from Juliana Sone, John atte Park' and their fellows for trespass of pasture; 2*d*. from William Tokelyn because he is convicted;[1] 6*d*. from William Fre*n*sch' and his fellows for concealment; 1*s*. 3*d*. from Richard Kuppe and his fellows for trespass of pasture; 1*s*. 3*d*. from John Lu*nt*, Stephen Rotelo*nd* and Robert Lot for bad ploughing; 2*s*. 3*d*. from John Cutel, Robert Lot and their fellows for trespass of pasture; 6*d*. from Nicholas T*ri*tur' and Stephen B*ercarius* for transgression; 3*s*. from Ralph le Koc for carrying off 1 oak; 3*d*. from William Bykem*ere* and Richard le Sone for transgression; 3*d*. from Stephen de Aul' for unjustly withholding; 3*s*. from John Burch' and his fellows for breaking the assize; 2*s*. from John Druery for bloodshed; 1*s*. from the reeve because his horse spent the night in the curia; 3*d*. from William Freynsch' for false presentment; 1*s*. from William Edgar and his fellows for ploughing; 1*s*. 9*d*. from John atte Tunesh*end*' and his fellows for trespass in the corn; 9*d*. from Richard le Sone and his fellows for trespass of pasture; 1*s*. from the whole tithing because it did not produce in court; 3*d*. from Robert Tastard because he came late; 3*d*. from John Elys for transgression; 1*s*. from Edith Godd' to have an enrolment; 2*s*. from Richard atte Well' and his fellows because convicted by inquest against Edith Gudd'; 6*d*. from William Bykem*ere* for unjustly withholding; 2*s*. from Richard atte Well' because his horse spent the night in the curia; 3*d*. from William Edgar for trespass of ploughing; 6*d*. from William Fre*n*ssh' for false presentment; 1*s*. from Richard H*er*berd, Roger Cuppi*ng* for trespass of wood and corn; 2*s*. 3*d*. from Roger Cuppi*ng*, Nicholas Burch', John atte Tonesh*end*' and their fellows for trespass of pasture; 4*s*. 6*d*. from Roger Cuppy*ng*, Robert Gal', Hugh Servi*ent*', Roger Cuppy*ng* and their fellows for trespass of corn; 1*s*. 6*d*. from 3 oxherds for contempt; 6*s*. 3*d*. from 7 ploughmen, John Cutel and their fellows for bad ploughing; 6*d*. from John de P*arco* and fellows because they did not come to the shearing; 4*s*. from Geoffrey atte Den' and other of his fellows for breaking the assize; 6*d*. from William Rod' for the hue; 3*d*. from Roger Cuppy*ng* for trespass of the enclosure; 3*d*. from Cecilia Maresschall' for suit of mill; 1*s*. from Walter Malot and his fellows for trespass of pasture; 1*s*. from Adam atte Ford' for the recovery and custody of his livestock. Total, £2 13*s*. 3*d*.

Total of both, £5 8*s*. 3*d*.

Total of all receipts, £84 5½*d*.

m.11d

Cost of ploughs

In the ironwork of 5 ploughs for the year and 1 plough for 1 term 6*s*. 3*d*. In stipend of 1 smith, nothing, because he takes 1 acre of wheat for his stipend. In 6 plough-irons bought 1*s*. 6*d*. In 1 coulter bought 10*d*. In 4 ploughshares 3*s*. 4*d*. In 3 ploughs made

1 Small space left in MS.

anew and others mended, fitted with share-beams, and covered with boards for the year, 1*s*. 4*d*. In yokes and wooden halters made 6*d*. In 4 pairs of wheels bought 1*s*. In boon-works of 40 ploughmen in winter and as many in Lent who ploughed as many acres as they lie 13*s*. 4*d*., or 2*d*. a ploughman a day. Moreover, each ploughman will plough 1 acre in summer for fallow without food according to custom. In reward of 8 ploughmen for the year and 2 for 1 term for their Saturday ploughings 19*s*. 3*d*., each taking 2*s*. less than they are accustomed, because more than accustomed was delivered to one sergeant who is there, and besides this they should each remove 1 horse which they are accustomed to have in the lord's pasture. In healing (*medicinand'*) oxen 4*d*. In 24 oxen bought for ploughs £13 19*s*. 5*d*., at 10*s*. 3*d*. each for 2, 11*s*. 2*d*. each for 15, and 13*s*. each for 7, plus 5*d*. in all. In stipend of 3 oxherds for the year 9*s*. In 10 qrs 6 bus. of maslin bought for the liveries of the manorial servants £1 15*s*. 10*d*., at 3*s*. 4*d*. a qr. In 3 qrs of barley bought for sowing 12*s*., at 4*s*. a qr. Total, £19 3*s*. 11*d*.

Cost of carts

In clouts, nails, grease and white leather bought for the carts for the year, and fitting 3 carts with axles at various times, 2*s*. In 2 collars bought 1*s*. 1*d*. In 1 pair of tie-beams 6*d*. In 2 pairs of traces bought 1*s*. 1*d*. In 2 halters bought 5*d*. In 1 saddle-base bought 4*d*. In 1 cart-rope 1*s*. 2*d*. In shoeing 3 cart-horses for the year and 1 for 1 term 3*s*. 6*d*. In stipend of 1 carter for the year 3*s*. Total, 13*s*. 1*d*.

Cost of buildings

In roofing the wheat-barn in places 1*s*. 6*d*. In roofing and mending the byre and sheepcote beside the church in places 3*s*. In roofing the sheepcote of Landecu*m*be 1*s*. 3*d*. In constructing 2 perches of palisade between the curia and the cemetery 1*s*. 6*d*. In pulling down the old byre 1*s*. In cleaning the grips in the field 4*s*. In marling the land sown with barley 1*s*. 6*d*. In forage bought 13*s*. 10*d*. In 3 pigs bought 5*s*. Total, £1 8*s*. 11*d*.

Sheepcote and sheepfold

In grease bought for greasing sheep 12*s*. 4*d*. In stipend of 1 shepherd for ½ year 1*s*. In wattling the fold 5*d*. In mending hurdles bought 2*d*. Total, 13*s*. 11*d*.

Threshing and winnowing

In threshing and winnowing 104 qrs of wheat by piece-work 17*s*. 4*d*., at 2*d*. a qr. In threshing 39 qrs 1 bus. of bere by piece-work 5*s*. 8½*d*., at 1¾*d*. a qr. In threshing and winnowing 8 qrs 2 bus. of barley by piece-work 10¼*d*., at 1¼*d*. a qr. In threshing 123½ qrs of oats by piece-work 5*s*. 1¾*d*., at ½*d*. a qr. In winnowing the same 1*s*. 3½*d*., at 1*d*. per 8 qrs. In 4 sacks bought 1*s*. 9¾*d*. In 1 basket bought 3*d*. Total, £1 12*s*. 4¾*d*.

Weeding

In weeding corn this year 3*s*. 4*d*. Total, 3*s*. 4*d*.

Harvest-time

In mowing 10 acres of meadow according to custom 6*d*. In 2 boon-works of 167 men with the officials of the curia who reaped 65 acres of wheat and 66 acres of oats as they lie 13*s*. 4*d*. In 1 boon-work of 81 free men of Enebur*n* and Earlstone who reaped 33 acres of wheat as they lie 6*s*. 9*d*., as in bread, ale and relish. In 36 acres of oats reaped by piece-work 6*s*., at 2*d*. an acre. Total, £1 6*s*. 7*d*.

Cost of the mill
In roofing the mill-building 4*d*. In steeling and mending bills 4*d*. In 1 gudgeon for the driving-shaft of the mill 3*d*. In 1 large mill-iron made under the driving-shaft of the mill with iron bought for the same 2*s*. 1½*d*. In 40 ells of canvas bought for the mill's sails 10*s*. 2*d*., at 3¼*d*. an ell. In grease bought 6*d*. In stipend of 1 miller for the year 6*s*. Total, £1 4½*d*.

Total of all expenses, £26 2*s*. 6¼*d*.

And he owes, £57 17*s*. 11¼*d*.

Cash deliveries
Delivered to Sir *Geoffrey*, treasurer of Wolvesey, by 1 tally, £30 13*s*. 4*d*.

And he owes clear, £27 4*s*. 7¼*d*.

Issues of the grange

Wheat
{yield: five-fold plus 4 qrs 3 bus.}
The same render account for 130 qrs from the whole issue of wheat by struck measure; 1½ qrs by estimation in 3 acres delivered to 1 reeve, 1 hayward and 1 smith according to custom; 4 qrs 1 bus. by estimation in 412 sheaves delivered to the reapers of 206 acres, at 2 sheaves an acre. Total, 135 qrs 5 bus.
Sown over 252 acres as they lie in the fields of Stok' and Suthlond', 31 qrs 1 bus.; that is, 1 bus. an acre, less 3 bus. in all. In customary payment to the hayward, 1 bus. In customary payment for the mowing of the meadows, 6 bus. In customary payment to 1 reeve, 1 hayward, 1 smith by estimation in 3 acres according to custom, 1½ qrs. Delivered to the reapers by estimation in 412 sheaves, 4 qrs 1 bus. In the bailiff's bread, 7½ qrs, because he takes the rest at Ecchinswell. Sold, 90½ qrs.

Bere
{yield: two-fold plus 1 bus.}
The same render account for 48 qrs 7 bus. from the whole issue of bere by struck measure; 10 qrs 6 bus. bought; 1 qr 2 bus. by estimation in 128 sheaves delivered to the reapers of 64 acres, at 2 sheaves an acre. Total, 60 qrs 7 bus.
Sown over 25 acres as they lie in the field of Stok', 4 qrs 5 bus.; that is, 1½ bus. an acre, less ½ bus. in all. Delivered to 1 carter, 3 oxherds for the year, 20 qrs 6 bus., each taking a quarter every 10 weeks. Delivered to 1 keeper of ewes from Michaelmas (29 September) until the Annunciation (25 March), that is, for 25 weeks, 2½ qrs. Delivered to 1 harrower at the time of the summer sowing, 4 bus. Delivered to 1 rook-scarer (*rochurd'*), 3 bus. Delivered to the reapers by estimation in 128 sheaves, 1 qr 2 bus. In provision of the bailiff for the year, 4 qrs. Sold, 26 qrs 7 bus.

Barley
{yield: two-fold less 2 bus.}
The same render account for 10 qrs 2 bus. from the whole issue of barley by struck measure; 4 bus. by estimation in 44 sheaves delivered to the reapers of 32 acres, at 2 sheaves an acre; 3 qrs bought. Total, 13 qrs 6 bus.
Sown over 35 acres as they lie in the field of Legh', 8½ qrs 1 bus.; that is, 2 bus. an acre, less 1 bus. in all. Delivered to the reapers by estimation in 44 sheaves, 4 bus. Sold, 4 qrs 5 bus.

Oats
{yield: two-fold plus 17 qrs 1 bus.}
The same render account for 154 qrs 3 bus. from the whole issue of oats by struck measure; 24 qrs by estimation in sheaves given to oxen; 2 bus. by estimation in 1½ acres delivered to the hayward according to custom; 2½ qrs by estimation in 366 sheaves delivered to the reapers of 183 acres, at 2 sheaves an acre. Total, 181 qrs 1 bus.
Sown over 364 acres as they lie in the fields of Ligh', Hareberd and la Nywelond', 90 qrs 7 bus.; that is, 2 bus. an acre, less 1 bus. in all. In customary payment to the hayward, 1 bus. In fodder of 2 cart-horses at sowing-time, 6½ qrs. In fodder of horses harrowing at both sowings, 4 qrs 5 bus. In supporting oxen by estimation in sheaves, 24 qrs. In fodder of the bailiff's horses, 12½ qrs, because he took the rest at Ecchinswell. In customary payment to the hayward in 1½ acres, 2 bus. Delivered to the reapers by estimation in 366 sheaves, 2½ qrs. Sold, 39 qrs 6 bus.

Mill
Wheat:[1] 2 bus. from the whole issue of the mill this year; all sold.
Maslin:[2] 19 qrs 6 bus. from the whole issue of the mill this year; 5 qrs 1 bus. delivered to 1 miller; 14 qrs 5 bus. sold.
Malt:[3] 4 qrs from the whole issue of the same mill; all sold.

Stock

Horses: 4 cart-horses remain from the previous year; 4 remain.
Mares: 1 from the heriot of John Maressch*al*; 1 sold; none remain.
Oxen: 56 remain from the previous year; 24 bought. Total, 80. 14 sold at Martinmas; 7 in murrain; 2 sold soon after Easter because feeble. Total, 23. 57 remain.
Rams: 16 remain from the previous year; 4 received from the hoggs of Ecchinswell. Total, 20. 1 sold at Martinmas; 2 in murrain before shearing; 3 castrated and added to the wethers of Ecchinswell. Total, 6. 14 remain.
Ewes: 409 remain from the previous year; 138 added from the hoggs of Ecchinswell. Total, 547. 39 sold at Martinmas; 7 in murrain before giving birth, 18 after giving birth and before shearing, and 7 after shearing. Total, 71. 476 remain.
Lambs: 345 from the offspring of the said ewes this year because 18 sterile, 7 in murrain before giving birth, and 39 sold at Martinmas; 57 in murrain before weaning; 28 in tithe; 3 in customary payment to 1 reeve, 1 hayward and 1 shepherd; 257 sent to Ashmansworth; none remain.
Pigs: 3 bought; 3 sold; none remain.
Fleeces: 10 from rams, 345 from ewes produced at the shearing this year. Total, 355. 35 in tithe; 320 delivered to the reeve of Highclere.
Woolskins: 2 from rams, 25 from ewes in murrain before shearing. Total, 27. 3 in tithe; 24 sold.
Bare skins: 7 from ewes in murrain after shearing; all sold.
Lambskins: 57 from lambs in murrain before weaning; 5 in tithe; 52 sold.
Hens: 172 from churchscot. 12 in default of the land in Spoltlond drawn into demesne for the year; 2 in default of Roger Elys because he has no wife; 2 in default of Alice le Webb' because she has no husband; 2 in default of Alveva la Prute for the same; 2 in default of Christina Byke for the same; 2 in default of Alice Druery for the

1 MS omits heading.

2 MS omits heading.

3 MS omits heading.

same; 2 in default of Matilda atte Holme for the same; 2 in default of Edith Cuteles for the same; 1 in default of Henry atte Pund' because he has no wife. Total, 27. 145 sold.
Eggs: 1,100 received according to custom at Easter; all sold.
Carts: 3 remain from the previous year; 1 of wood worn out; 2 remain.
Wagons: 2 remain from the previous year; 2 remain, 1 with iron tyres and 1 of wood.

Ecchinswell

Arrears
Henry la Wayte, bailiff, and Richard le Yo*ng*', reeve, render account for £16 13*s.* 2¾*d.* of arrears from the previous year. All delivered to Sir G*eoffrey*, treasurer of Wolvesey, by 1 tally. They are quit.

Rents
The same render account for £1 17*s.* 3½*d.* for all rents of assize at Christmas; £1 17*s.* 3½*d.* at Easter (22 April); £1 17*s.* 3½*d.* at the Nativity of St John the Baptist (24 June); £6 7*s.* 3½*d.* at Michaelmas (29 September). Total, £11 19*s.* 2*d.*

Quittances
In quittance of 1 reeve for the year 3*s.* 6*d.*; 1 hayward for the year 2*s.*; 3 ploughmen for the year 6*s.*; 1 ploughman for 2½ terms 1*s.* 3*d.*; 2 ploughmen for ½ year 2*s.*; 1 keeper of wethers for the year 2*s.*; 1 keeper of hoggs for 2½ terms 1*s.* 3*d.* Total, 18*s.*

Defaults of rent
In default of the land of Greg' drawn into demesne, 4*d.* for the year. Total, 4*d.*

Total of quittances and defaults of rent, 18*s.* 4*d.*

Total of rents remaining, £11 10*d.*

Release from labour service
The same render account for 7*s.* 1*d.* from Richard de Brochurst for release from his labour service for 1 virgate of land which belonged to Walter le Maresch*al* for the year; 3*s.* 6*d.* from William Fab*er* for release from his labour service for 1 virgate of land for the year. Total, 10*s.* 7*d.*

Issues of the manor
The same render account for 15*s.* 5½*d.* from pannage of pigs at Martinmas, that is, from 180 pigs, 11 piglets, at 1*d.* a pig and ½*d.* a piglet; nothing from foreign pannage this year for a want of mast; 6*s.* 2½*d.* from 32 oxen and 13 bullocks within, and 15 foreign oxen and 6 foreign bullocks, agisted in the pasture of Asselye in summer, at 1*d.* an ox and ½*d.* a bullock within, and 2*d.* a foreign ox and 1*d.* a foreign bullock; nothing from the pasturage in Stapeleost and Privet on account of the lord's stock; nothing from the pasturage in la Lynde for the same reason; nothing from the herbage of the meadow of Sydmonton because the meadow was mowed this year; 3*s.* from the pasturage sold in the same meadow after mowing; 8½*d.* from the pinfold this year, at 1*d.* for 10 sheep; 16*s.* from 1 mare sold; 7*s.* from 1 ox from a heriot sold; £1 11*s.* 6*d.* from 27 wethers sold at Martinmas, at 1*s.* 2*d.* each; 10*s.* 1*d.* from 22 feeble

lambs sold at Martinmas, at 5½*d*. each; 1*s*. from the skins sold of 4 wethers in murrain before shearing, at 3*d*. a skin; 3*s*. 10½*d*. from the skins sold of 31 hoggs in murrain before shearing, at 1½*d*. a skin; 3*d*. from the skins sold wholesale of 2 wethers and 2 hoggs in murrain after shearing; 6*d*. from the skins sold wholesale of 4 lambs in murrain before shearing and 4 after shearing; 9*s*. 9*d*. from 117 hens from churchscot sold; 2*s*. from 800 eggs sold, received according to custom at Easter, at 3*d*. a hundred; 10*s*. from 2 pigs sold. Total, £5 17*s*. 4*d*.

Annual recognizance

The same render account for 3*d*. from William atte Flod' for annual recognizance; 3*d*. from William le Yong' for the same; 6*d*. from John Cumy*n* for the same; 6*d*. from Richard Pollard for the same. Total, 1*s*. 6*d*.

Sale of corn

The same render account for £17 11*s*. 5*d*. from 53 qrs of wheat sold, at 6*s*. a qr for 2 qrs 7 bus., 6*s*. 8*d*. a qr for 50 qrs 1 bus.; 4*s*. from 1 qr of curall sold; £1 10*s*. 3*d*. from 7 qrs 4½ bus. of bere sold, at 4*s*. a qr; £2 13*s*. 6*d*. from 13 qrs 3 bus. of barley sold, at 4*s*. a qr; £3 5*s*. from 26 qrs of oats sold, at 2*s*. 6*d*. a qr; 6*d*. from 4 bus. of vetches sold. Total, £25 4*s*. 8*d*.

Entry and marriage fines

The same render account for 13*s*. 4*d*. from tithingpenny at the two hundred-courts for the year; £2 from Thomas atte Norhmull' to have 1 messuage, 1 mill and 1 cotland which belonged to Juliana his mother; 1*s*. from Edith Legat for marrying Agnes her daughter within; 4*s*. from Hugh atte Place for marrying Edith his daughter outside; 10*s*. from John Legat to have Alice Laȝ with her land; £1 from Christina de Brochurst to retain 1 virgate of land which belonged to her husband and to have 1 virgate of land which belonged to Walter Mareschall'. Total, £4 8*s*. 4*d*.

Perquisites

The same render account for 9*d*. from Edith Rolf for keeping the meadow badly; 6*d*. from the tithing of Ecchinswell because it did not produce in court; 6*d*. from Henry le Whyte for concealment; 9*d*. from Edith Rolf and her fellows for concealment; 6*d*. from Alice Laȝ for concealment of pannage; 1*s*. from G. le Knyt for levying a debt; 6*d*. from the whole tithing because it did not produce in court; 1*s*. 6*d*. from John Den', John Tylye, John Porch' for not doing their offices well; 6*d*. from Hugh atte Place for unjustly withholding; 6*d*. from Stephen atte Brigg' for bad threshing; 2*s*. 9*d*. from John atte Suthmull', John Duce and their fellows for trespass of pasture and wood; 1*s*. 6*d*. from Scholastica (*Scolast'*), Alice le Tav*er*ner' and their fellows for breaking the assize; 4*s*. from the whole tithing for no longer guaranteeing the default of John and John Raynold until they have returned; 2*s*. from Richard Ram, William Wale and their fellows for trespass of wood and pasture; 6*d*. from the whole tithing because it did not produce in court those it had bailed; 3*d*. from John atte Hurn' for default; 6*d*. from Adam Lunt and William Fab*er* for trespass of pasture; 4*s*. from 4 ploughmen for keeping the oxen badly and bad ploughing; 6*d*. from Richard Mokel for default; 3*s*. 6*d*. from Henry Lanceleveye and his fellows for trespass of corn and pasture; 6*d*. from John Wolfrich and Matilda Den' because they came late to the lord's labour service; 3*d*. from John Bukel for trespass of wood. Total, £1 7*s*. 3*d*.

Total of both, £5 15*s*. 7*d*.

Total of all receipts, £48 10*s*. 6*d*.

m.12

Cost of ploughs

In iron and steel bought for the ironwork of 2 ploughs for the year and 1 plough for nearly ½ year for fallowing 4*s*. 6*d*. In stipend of the smith, nothing, because he takes 1 acre of wheat for repairing the said ironwork for the year. In 3 plough-irons bought 9*d*. In 2 ploughshares 1*s*. 8*d*. In 3 ploughs made anew and others mended 1*s*. In fitting the same with iron tyres 6*d*. In 6 yokes bought 6*d*. In 6 wheels bought 1*s*. In boon-works of 25 ploughmen in winter and 23 in Lent who ploughed as many acres as they lie 8*s*., at 2*d*. each a day. Moreover, each ploughman will plough 1 acre in summer for fallow without food according to custom. In reward of 3 ploughmen for their Saturday ploughings for the year, 1 for 2½ terms, and 2 for ½ year, except for those Saturdays which were feast days or on which it was raining, £1 9½*d*., or 4*s*. 6*d*. each for the year, and this through Bishop John because before they had nothing except 3*s*. a year. In 1 seed-basket bought 1*d*. In stipend of 1 oxherd for 1½ terms 9*d*. In 3 oxen bought £1 14*s*., at 11*s*. 4*d*. each. In 6 bus. of wheat bought 3*s*. 9*d*., at 7½*d*. a bus. In 2 qrs 7 bus. of bere bought for sowing and for the liveries of the manorial servants 9*s*. 7*d*., at 3*s*. 4*d*. a qr. Total, £4 6*s*. 10½*d*.

Cost of carts

In 1 pair of wooden wheels made from the lord's timber 8*d*. In clouts, nails and grease bought for the cart for fitting the same with axles for the year 1*s*. 5½*d*. In white leather bought for mending harnesses 3*d*. In 1 pair of saddle-pads 6*d*. In 1 saddle 2½*d*. In 2 collars bought 1*s*. 1*d*. In 1 pair of traces bought 7*d*. In 1 cart-rope bought 1*s*. 2*d*. In shoeing 2 cart-horses for the year 2*s*. 2*d*. In stipend of 1 carter for the year 3*s*. Total, 11*s*. 1*d*.

Cost of buildings

In re-roofing and mending the unroofed wheat-barn in places 1*s*. 6*d*. In roofing the hall and byre all over and mending the small barn in places 9*s*. In collecting 34 acres of stubble for the same 5*s*. 8*d*., at 2*d*. an acre. In fitting 2 shovels with iron 3*d*. In 1 lock bought for the door of the wheat-barn 3*d*. In stipend of 1 hayward keeping the curia and pastures of Burghclere and Ecchinswell for the year 6*s*. 8*d*. In 2 pigs bought 6*s*. 8*d*. In forage bought 3*s*. Total, £1 13*s*.

Sheepcote and sheepfold

In re-roofing and mending the hogg-house unroofed by the wind 1*s*. 3*d*. In grease bought for greasing sheep and hoggs £1 15*s*. 10*d*. In 15 hurdles bought for the fold 1*s*. 3*d*. In 2 new cribs made and others mended 3*s*. In wattling the fold whilst the sheepcote has no ewes 5*d*. In stipend of 1 keeper of hoggs for ½ term 3*d*. In stipend of 1 attendant from the time of weaning until Michaelmas 2*s*. Total, £2 4*s*.

Threshing and winnowing

In threshing and winnowing 57 qrs of wheat and curall 9*s*. 6*d*., at 2*d*. a qr. In threshing and winnowing 24 qrs 1 bus. of bere 3*s*. 6*d*., at 1¾*d*. a qr. In threshing and winnowing 15 qrs 2 bus. of barley 1*s*. 7*d*., at 1¼*d*. a qr. In threshing 56 qrs of oats 2*s*. 4*d*., at ½*d*. a qr. In winnowing the same 7*d*., at 1*d*. per 8 qrs. In 1 basket bought 3*d*. Total, 17*s*. 9*d*.

Harvest-time

In 6 sesters of ale bought for the mowing of 45 acres in the great meadow of Ecchinswell according to custom 7*s*. In 1 boon-work of 86 men who reaped 36 acres of wheat 9*s*., as in bread, ale and relish. Total, 16*s*.

Total of all expenses, £10 8*s*. 8½*d*.

And he owes, £38 1*s*. 9½*d*.

Cash deliveries {on the day after All Souls (3 November)}
Delivered to Sir G*eoffrey*, treasurer, by 1 tally, £24.

And he owes clear, £14 1*s*. 9½*d*.

Issues of the grange

Wheat
{yield: five-fold plus 3 qrs 3 bus.}
The same render account for 70 qrs 2½ bus. from the whole issue of wheat by struck measure; 1½ qrs by estimation in 3 acres delivered to the reeve, hayward and 1 smith according to custom; 5 qrs 1 bus. from churchscot; 6 bus. bought. Total, 77 qrs 5½ ⌈bus.⌉
Sown over 107½ acres as they lie in the field below the wood, 15½ qrs; that is, 1½ bus. an acre over 33 acres, and 1 bus. an acre over 74½ acres. In default of 1 virgate of land which is called Frihlo*n*d, 1½ bus. for churchscot. In default of 1 virgate of land of Richard de Britheurst, 3 bus. In customary payment to the hayward, 1 bus. In customary payment for the mowing of the meadow of Ecchinswell, 1½ qrs. In customary payment to the reeve, hayward and smith by estimation in 3 acres, 1½ qrs. In provision of the bailiff, 5½ qrs. Sold, 53 qrs.

Curall
The same render account for 1 qr of curall from the whole issue; all sold.

Bere
{yield: five-fold plus 5 bus.}
The same render account for 30 qrs 1 bus. from the whole issue of bere by struck measure; 4 bus. by estimation in 48 sheaves delivered for the reaping of 24 acres by labour service, at 2 sheaves an acre; 2 qrs 7 bus. bought. Total, 33½ qrs.
Sown over 35 acres as they lie below the wood, 8 qrs 6 bus.; that is, 2 bus. an acre. Delivered to 1 hayward keeping the strips of ploughland and pastures of Burghclere and Ecchinswell for the year, 6½ qrs, because he takes a quarter every 8 weeks. Delivered to 1 carter for the year, 5 qrs 1½ bus., because he takes a quarter every 10 weeks. Delivered to 1 oxherd from Michaelmas (29 September) until the feast of St Gregory (12 March), for 23 weeks 3 days, 2 qrs 2 bus. Delivered to 1 shepherd for 5 weeks, ½ qr. Delivered to 1 keeper of lambs from Easter until Michaelmas, for 23 weeks, 2 qrs 2 bus. Delivered to the reapers by estimation in sheaves, 4 bus. Sold, 7 qrs 4½ bus.

Barley
{yield: four-fold plus 1½ qrs}
The same render account for 19 qrs from the whole issue of barley by struck measure; 4 bus. by estimation in 36 sheaves delivered for the reaping of 18 acres by labour service, at 2 sheaves an acre.
Sown over 23 acres as they lie in the field of Estlye, 5 qrs 5 bus.; that is, 2 bus. an acre, less 1 bus. in all. Delivered to the reapers by estimation in 36 sheaves, 4 bus. Sold, 13 qrs 3 bus.

Oats
{yield: two-fold plus 8 qrs 5 bus.}
The same render account for 69 qrs 7 bus. from the whole issue of oats by struck measure; 8 qrs by estimation in sheaves given to oxen; 2 bus. by estimation in 1½ acres delivered to the hayward according to custom; 1½ qrs by estimation in 192 sheaves delivered for the reaping of 96 acres by labour service, at 2 sheaves an acre. Total, 79 qrs 5 bus.
Sown over 126 acres as they lie in la Estlye, 28 qrs 6 bus.; that is, 2 bus. an acre, less 2 bus. in all. In fodder of 2 cart-horses at sowing-time, 6½ qrs. In supporting 19 oxen in winter by estimation in sheaves, 8 qrs. In customary payment to the hayward, 1 bus. In customary payment to the same by estimation in 1½ acres, 2 bus. Delivered to the reapers by estimation in 192 sheaves, 1½ qrs. In fodder of the bailiff's horses, 8½ qrs., who takes the rest at Burghclere. Sold, 26 qrs.

Vetches
The same render account for 6 bus. from the issue of vetches by struck measure. Sown, 2 bus. Sold, ½ qr.

Stock

Horses: 2 cart-horses remain from the previous year; 2 remain.
Mares: 1 from the heriot of Richard de Brochurst; 1 sold; none remain.
Oxen: 19 remain from the previous year; 8 received from Highclere; 1 from the heriot of Juliana de la Nortmull'; 6 bought. Total, 31.[1] 1 sold; 30 remain.
Wethers: 275 remain from the previous year; 4 from the reeve of Highclere before shearing, 3 from the reeve of Burghclere before shearing; 180 added from hoggs. Total, 362.[2] 27 sold at Martinmas; 4 in murrain before shearing, 2 after shearing; 2 in customary payment for the mowing of the meadow of Ecchinswell; 1 in customary payment for the mowing of the meadow of Sydmonton; 1 in customary payment for the mowing of the meadow of Burghclere. Total, 37. 425 remain.
Hoggs: 435 remain from the previous year's lambs; 22 sold at Martinmas; 31 in murrain before shearing, 2 after shearing; 180 added to the wethers of Ecchinswell, 138 to the ewes of Burghclere, 4 to the rams of Burghclere, 58 to the ewes of Highclere; none remain.
Lambs: 255 from the reeve of Highclere; 2 from the gift of Gert'. Total, 257. 4 in murrain before shearing, 4 after shearing; 249 remain.
Pigs: 2 bought; 2 sold; none remain.
Coarse fleeces: 251 from wethers and 382 from hoggs produced at the shearing this year. Total, 533.[3] 63 in tithe; 1 in customary payment to the shepherd of wethers; 570 sent to Highclere.[4]
Lambs' fleeces: 243 fleeces produced at the shearing this year because 6 not sheared because late-born; all sent to Highclere.
Woolskins: 4 from wethers and 31 from hoggs in murrain before shearing. Total, 35. 3 in tithe; 32 sold.
Bare skins: 2 from wethers and 2 from hoggs in murrain after shearing; all sold.
Lambskins: 4 from lambs in murrain after shearing, and 4 before; all sold.

1 Figures add up to 34.

2 Figures add up to 462.

3 Figures add up to 633.

4 Figures add up to 634.

Hens: 140 from churchscot. 2 in quittance of 1 hayward; 2 in default of Juliana atte Nortmull' because she has no husband; 2 in default of Edith atte Folod' for the same; 2 in default of Ascelote Goude for the same; 2 in default of William Mokel because he has no wife; 1 in default of Agnes Geffray for the same; 2 in default of Alice Palm*ere* because she has no husband; 2 in default of Robert Stul for the same; 2 in default of Alice Amyg' for the same; 2 in default of Juliana Wauncy for the same; 4 in default of Edith Legat for the same. Total, 23. 117 sold.
Eggs: 800 received according to custom at Easter; all sold.
Carts: 2 remain from the previous year; 1 of wood made this year; 1 worn out; 2 remain, 1 with iron tyres, the other of wood.

Woodhay

Arrears
Henry la Wayte, bailiff, and John Wyxy, reeve, render account for £16 6*s*. 5½*d*. of arrears from the previous year. All delivered to Sir G*eoffrey*, treasurer of Wolvesey, by 1 tally. They are quit.

Rents
The same render account for £1 17*s*. 6*d*. for all rents of assize at Christmas; £12 14*s*. at Easter (22 April); £1 19*s*. at the Nativity of St John the Baptist (24 June); £21 18*s*. 4¾*d*. at Michaelmas (29 September). Total, £38 8*s*. 10¾*d*.

Quittances
In quittance of 1 reeve for the year 2*s*. 4*d*.; 1 hayward for the year 2*s*.; 1 forester in la Wayssch' for the year 2*s*. 4*d*.; 5 ploughmen for the year 10*s*.; 1 ploughman for 2½ terms 1*s*. 3*d*. Total, 17*s*. 11*d*.

Defaults of rent
In default of 1 purpresture which John Fab*er* held at Holwynto*n*, who was elected by the constable to keep the peace by order of the king, 1*d*. Total, 1*d*.

Total of quittances and defaults of rent, 18*s*.

Total of rents remaining, £37 10*s*. 10¾*d*.

Rents of pepper
The same render account for 2 lb of pepper for the rent of assize of John de Insula and Henry de Staweye at Michaelmas; all delivered to Wolvesey.

Sparrow-hawk
The same render account for 2*s*. from 1 sparrow-hawk from the tenement of Freefolk. Total, 2*s*.

Issues of the manor
The same render account for 19*s*. 4*d*. from pannage of pigs within this year, that is, from 225 pigs and 14 piglets, at 1*d*. a pig over a year old, and ½*d*. a piglet; 9*s*. 9*d*. from foreign pannage in la Wayssch'; £1 from pannage in the park sold wholesale this year; 2*s*. 6*d*. from the pinfold at Michaelmas according to custom, for 12 cattle

(*av'*) and 180 sheep, at 1*d.* a bovine and 1*d.* per 10 sheep; 10*s.* from the whole vill for not doing suit at the windmill, that is, 5*s.* at Easter and 5*s.* at Michaelmas; 7*s.* from 1 mare from a heriot sold; 3*s.* from 1 old cow from a heriot sold; 8*s.* 6*d.* from 2 bullocks from heriots sold, at 4*s.* for 1, and 4*s.* 6*d.* for 1; £2 12*s.* 6*d.* from 42 wethers sold at Martinmas, at 1*s.* 3*d.* each; 2*s.* from winter pasturage in the fields sold; 1*s.* from the pasturage in the fallow sold this year; 1*s.* from winter pasturage in Cossingemor' sold this year; nothing from the pasturage in the meadow of Stoford' this year on account of the lord's stock; 7*s.* from 84 hens from churchscot sold; 3*s.* 2½*d.* from 1,100 eggs sold according to custom; 9*s.* from 3 pigs sold. Total, £7 15*s.* 9½*d.*

Annual recognizance

The same render account for 4*d.* from John Macy for annual recognizance; 4*d.* from Stephen le Nywema*n* for the same; 3*d.* from William Fab*er* for the same; 3*d.* from John atte Hetth' for the same; 6*d.* from John Copinor for the same; 6*d.* from William le Gome, so that he has licence to dwell outside the bishop's lands, although he remains the lord's villein in the tithing and in all suits of tithing; 1*s.* from William le Nywe, so that he has licence just like William le Gome. Total, 3*s.* 2*d.*

Sale of corn

The same render account for £20 4*s.* 10*d.* from 70 qrs 5 bus. of wheat sold, at 5*s.* a qr for 9 qrs, 5*s.* 4*d.* a qr for 19 qrs, 5*s.* 6*d.* a qr for 22 qrs, and 6*s.* 8*d.* a qr for 20 qrs 5 bus.; 12*s.* 1*d.* from 3 qrs 5 bus. of bere sold, at 3*s.* 4*d.* a qr; £3 4*s.* 6*d.* from 16 qrs 1 bus. of barley sold, at 4*s.* a qr; £4 2*s.* 2¼*d.* from 32 qrs 7 bus. of oats sold, at 2*s.* 6*d.* a qr. Total, £28 3*s.* 7¼*d.*

Entry and marriage fines

The same render account for £1 from tithingpenny at the 2 hundred-courts for the year; 13*s.* 4*d.* from Emma Miles to retain 1 cotland and 6 acres of purpresture which belonged to her husband; 10*s.* from Christina atte Zele to retain 1 cotland and 9 acres of purpresture which belonged to Nicholas atte Zele her husband; 13*s.* 4*d.* from Matilda Purchel, wife of William de H*a*mpton', to have 1 cotland which belonged to Alice Purch*el* her sister; 1*s.* from Agnes Persones to have 1 house, 2 acres of land which Henry Brun her husband held, for each of which Agnes has fined before; 1*s.* from Matilda, relict of William Moune, to retain 1 house with a curtilage which belonged to her husband; 1*s.* from Nicholas Sexy to have the said Matilda for her said lands; 2*s.* from Nicholas Knappely to have 1 house and 3 pennyworths of purpresture which belonged to William Cnappely his uncle; 1*s.* from William atte Hurne for marrying Agnes his daughter within; 1*s.* from William Wyky*ng* for marrying Agnes, daughter of[1] William de H*a*mpto*n*, within the manor; 2*s.* from John Wyxy for marrying Agnes his daughter within. Total, £3 5*s.* 8*d.*

Perquisites

The same render account for 1*s.* 9*d.* from John atte Pund', John atte Barr', William de H*a*mpto*n* and their fellows for trespass of pasture; 6*d.* from Robert Fra*n*kelayn for default of court; 3*d.* from William atte Hurn' for bad threshing; 3*d.* from 5 carters for trespass in the curia; 2*s.* from William de Anglo*n* and his fellows for trespass of pasture; 1*s.* from Thomas le Gome for transgression against a neighbour; 6*d.* from Isabel Hayward for selling timber from a certain house which was pulled down; 9*d.* from Nicholas Knappely and his fellows for trespass of hedges and wood; 3*d.* from

1 MS 'fil*ia* ⟨sua⟩'.

Nicholas Fox for rights of common by inquest; 2*s.* from Robert Cusyn for laying waste land in widowhood; 3*s.* from the whole tithing because it concealed that Henry Bru*n* holds land in villeinage within the demesne without having made fine; 3*s.* 6*d.* from Robert Cusyn, Nicholas atte Bernn' and their fellows for breaking the assize; 6*d.* from John Mich' for pledging them; 6*s.* 8*d.* from the reeve of Woodhay for maintaining his horse in the curia at night; 1*s.* from the reeve and hayward for bad harrowing; 6*d.* from the ploughmen because they came late; 3*d.* from Alice Suveneys for default of enclosure; 6*d.* from the whole tithing because it did not produce in court; 1*s.* from Geoffrey Osegod and G. le Kyng and their fellows for trespass of wood and pasture; 1*s.* 3*d.* from Matilda Purcheyl and her fellows for default of ploughing and harrowing; 9*d.* from William and W. Nywe for default; 1*s.* from Nicholas atte Bern' for trespass of wood and pasture; 2*s.* from William atte Ford' and his fellows for trespass of wood and pasture; 6*d.* from Matilda Wyxi for the recovery (*forfeng'*) of 1 bullock; 6*d.* from Thomas de Sto*n*hll' because of remarks against Matilda Cole; 1*s.* 6*d.* from John Crowe and his fellows for default at the shearing; 3*s.* 6*d.* from Agnes P*er*sones and her fellows for breaking the assize; 9*d.* from John atte Pu*n*d' for trespass of wood and pasture; 3*d.* from Henry Maresch*a*l for false complaint; 6*d.* from Sarah atte Heth' for waste. Total, £1 18*s.* 10*d.*

Total of both, £5 4*s.* 4*d.*

Total of all receipts, £78 19*s.* 9½*d.*

m.12d

Cost of ploughs

In the ironwork of 3 ploughs for the year with the stipend of the smith 7*s.* 6*d.* In 3 plough feet 9*d.* In 1 ploughshare bought 10*d.* In 2 new ploughs made and others mended 1*s.* 1*d.* In 2 harrows made 4*d.* In 3 pairs of wheels bought 9*d.* In ploughing boon-works of 32 ploughmen in winter and as many in Lent who ploughed as many acres as they lie 10*s.* 8*d.*, or 2*d.* a ploughman a day. Moreover, each ploughman will plough 1 acre in summer for fallow without food according to custom. In reward of 5 ploughmen for their Saturday ploughings for the year £1 2*s.* 6*d.*, and this through Bishop John because before they had nothing except 3*s.* a year. In reward of 1 ploughman for 2½ terms for the same 2*s.* 10¾*d.* In shoeing 6 plough-horses hauling ploughs for the year 2*s.* 2*d.* In shoeing oxen 1*s.* 9*d.* In 2 oxen bought £1 4*s.* 2*d.*, at 12*s.* 1*d.* each. In stipend of 1 oxherd for 1 term 6*d.* In stipend of 1 harrower in Lent 6*d.* In 7½ qrs of wheat bought £1 17*s.* 6*d.*, at 5*s.* a qr. In 4 qrs of bere bought 10*s.* 8*d.*, at 2*s.* 8*d.* a qr. In 5 bus. of vetches bought 7½*d.* Total, £6 5*s.* 2¼*d.*

Carts

In 1 pair of wheels bought 1*s.* 6*d.* In clouts, nails, grease and white leather bought for the cart for the year and in fitting the cart with axles at various times 1*s.* In 1 pair of saddle-pads 6*d.* In 1 collar bought 6*d.* In mending the old cart many times and making 1 new cart-rail 1*s.* In shoeing 2 cart-horses for the year 2*s.* 2*d.* In stipend of 1 carter for the year 3*s.* Total, 9*s.* 8*d.*

Cost of buildings

In roofing and mending the room of the overseer of the harvest and the granary 3*s.* In collecting 10 acres of stubble for the same 1*s.* 8*d.*, at 2*d.* an acre. In mending the porch of the barn 6*d.* In cleaning and mending the park ditch, and hedging (*sepib*us *fac'*), 2*s*. In stipend of the hayward keeping the strips of ploughland and pastures of Woodhay and Ashmansworth for the year 6*s*. 8*d*. In forage bought 4*s*. 6*d*. In 3 pigs bought 4*s*. 9*d*. In mending the park 6*d*. Total, £1 3*s*. 7*d*.

Nothing for the sheepfold and sheepcote this year because none of the lord's sheep were there.

Threshing
In threshing and winnowing 62½ qrs 1 bus. of wheat by piece-work 10*s*. 5¼*d*., at 2*d*. a qr. In threshing and winnowing 21 qrs 2 bus. of bere by piece-work 3*s*. 1*d*., at 1¾*d*. a qr. In threshing and winnowing 25½ qrs 2 bus. of barley by piece-work 2*s*. 8*d*., at 1¼*d*. a qr. In threshing 66½ qrs 2½ bus. of oats by piece-work 2*s*. 9¼*d*. In winnowing the same 8¼*d*., at 1*d*. per 8 qrs. Total, 19*s*. 7¾*d*.

Harvest-time
In mowing the meadow of Cossyngemor 1*s*. 6*d*. In mowing 4 acres 1 perch of meadow in the park according to custom 6*d*. In 1 boon-work of 114 men with the officials of the curia who reaped 90 acres of wheat as they lie 10*s*. 7*d*., as in bread, ale and relish. Total, 12*s*. 7*d*.

Total of all expenses, £9 10*s*. 8*d*.

And he owes, £69 9*s*. 1½*d*.

Cash deliveries
Delivered to Sir G*eoffrey*, treasurer of Wolvesey, by 1 tally, £45.

And he owes clear, £24 9*s*. 1½*d*.

Wheat
{yield: four-fold plus 3 qrs 6 bus.}
The same render account for 78 qrs 2 bus. from the whole issue of wheat by struck measure; 1 qr by estimation in 2 acres delivered to the reeve and hayward according to custom; 4 bus. by estimation in 1½ acres delivered to the Prior of Sandleford according to custom; 2 qrs by estimation in 144 sheaves delivered to the reapers of 72 acres, at 2 sheaves an acre; 5 qrs 1½ bus. received from churchscot; 7½ qrs bought. Total, 94 qrs 3½ bus.
Sown over 104½ acres as they lie in Middelfeld', 20 qrs 1½ bus.; that is, 1½ bus. an acre, plus 4½ bus. in all. Delivered to 1 reeve and 1 hayward by estimation in 2 acres, 1 qr. Delivered to the Prior of Sandleford by estimation in 1½ acres according to custom, 4 bus. In customary payment to the hayward, 1 bus. Delivered to the reapers by estimation in 144 sheaves, 2 qrs. Sold, 70 qrs 5 bus.

Bere
{yield: four-fold less 1 qr}
The same render account for 26 qrs 4 bus. from the whole issue of bere by struck measure; 4 bus. by estimation in 56 sheaves delivered to the reapers for the reaping of 28 acres by labour service, at 2 sheaves an acre; 4 qrs bought; 9 qrs mixed with barley for liveries. Total, 40 qrs.
Sown over 98 acres as they lie in the field of Middelfeld', 18 qrs 2 bus.; that is, 1½ bus. an acre, less 1 bus. in all. Delivered to 1 hayward keeping the strips of

ploughland and pastures of Woodhay and Ashmansworth for the year, 6½ qrs, who takes a quarter every 8 weeks. Delivered to 1 carter for the year, who takes a quarter every 10 weeks, 5 qrs 1½ bus. Delivered to 1 drover from Michaelmas (29 September) until the Purification (2 February), that is, for 18 weeks, 1 qr 6 bus. Delivered to 1 shepherd for the year, 4 qrs 1½ bus., who takes the rest from the men whose sheep he keeps. Delivered to the reapers by estimation in 56 sheaves, ½ qr. Sold, 3 qrs 5 bus.

Barley
{yield: three-and-a-half-fold plus 2 qrs}
The same render account for 32 qrs 1 bus. from the whole issue of barley by struck measure; 1 qr by estimation in 72 sheaves delivered for the reaping of 36 acres by labour service, at 2 sheaves an acre. Total, 33 qrs 1 bus.
Sown over 35 acres as they lie in the field of Westfeld', 7 qrs; that is, 1½ bus. an acre, plus 3½ bus. in all. Delivered to the reapers by estimation in 72 sheaves, 1 qr. Mixed with bere for the liveries of the manorial servants, 9 qrs. Sold, 16 qrs 1 bus.

Oats
{yield: two-and-a-half-fold less 3 qrs 6 bus.}
The same render account for 83 qrs 4 bus. from the whole issue of oats by struck measure; 7 qrs by estimation in sheaves given to oxen; 1½ qrs by estimation in 154 sheaves delivered for the reaping of 77 acres by labour service, at 2 sheaves an acre; 4 bus. by estimation in one acre delivered to the Prior of Sandleford according to custom. Total, 92½ qrs.
Sown over 200 acres which lie in the field of Westfeld', 37½ qrs; that is, 1½ bus. an acre, less 1 bus. in all. In customary payment to the hayward, 1 bus. Delivered to the Prior of Sandleford by estimation in an acre, ½ qr. In fodder of 2 cart-horses at sowing-time, 6½ qrs. In fodder of 6 plough-horses hauling ploughs at sowing-time, 6½ qrs. In supporting 21 oxen by estimation in sheaves, 7 qrs. Delivered to the reapers by estimation in 77[1] sheaves, 1½ qrs. Sold, 32 qrs 7 bus.

Vetches
The same render account for 5 bus. of vetches bought. Sown over 6 acres, 5 bus.

Stock
Horses: 2 remain from the previous year; 2 cart-horses remain.
Plough-horses: 6 remain from the previous year; 1 from the heriot of Nicholas atte Zele; 1 sold; 6 remain, 5 of them male.
Foals: 1 from the offspring of 1 mare this year; 1 male remains.
Oxen: 23 remain from the previous year; 1 from the heriot of Alice Purchel; 2 bought. Total, 26. All remain.
Cows: 1 from the heriot of Henry Broun; 1 sold; none remain.
Bullocks: 2 from the heriots of John Miles and William Moun'; 2 sold; none remain.
Wethers: 142 remain from the previous year. 42 sold at Martinmas; 100 delivered to the reeve of Ashmansworth. Total, 142. None remain.
Hens: 98 from churchscot. 2 in quittance of 1 hayward; 2 in default of Isabel le Car' because she has no husband; 2 in default of Juliana le Cart*ere* for the same; 2 in default of Matilda Fryman because she has no husband; 2 in default of Sarah atte Hetth' for the same; 2 in default of Emma Miles for the same; 2 in default of Geoffrey Chaffyng because he has no wife. Total, 14. 84 sold.

1 '154 sheaves' in the charge.

Pigs: 3 bought; 3 sold; none remain.
Eggs:[1] 1,100 received according to custom at Easter; all sold.
Carts: 2 remain from the previous year; 1 made anew this year. Total, 3. 1 of wood worn out; 2 remain, 1 with iron tyres and the other of wood.

Ashmansworth

Arrears

Henry la Wayte, bailiff, and William, reeve, render account for £7 9*s*. 7½*d*. of arrears from the previous year. All delivered to Sir G*eoffrey*, treasurer of Wolvesey, by 1 tally. They are quit.

Rents of assize

The same render account for £1 9*s*. 9¾*d*. for all rents of assize at Christmas; £1 11*s*. 2*d*. at Easter (22 April); £1 10*s*. 3¾*d*. at the Nativity of the blessed John the Baptist (24 June); £2 2*s*. 7½*d*. at Michaelmas (29 September). Total, £6 17*s*. 11*d*.

Quittances

In quittance of 1 reeve for the year 4*s*. 8*d*.; 1 hayward for the year 2*s*.; 3 ploughmen for the year 6*s*.; 1 ploughman for 2½ terms 1*s*. 3*d*.; 1 keeper of wethers for the same time 1*s*. 3*d*. Total, 15*s*. 2*d*.

Total of rents remaining, £5 18*s*. 9*d*.

Issues of the manor

The same render account for 5*s*. 2*d*. from pannage of pigs within at Martinmas (11 November), that is, from 59 pigs and 7 piglets, at 1*d*.[2] a pig and ½*d*. a piglet; nothing from foreign pannage this year; 10*d*. from winter pasturage in Privet sold for 10 oxen, at 1*d*. an ox; 15*s*. 10½*d*. from summer pasturage in Privet sold for 8 horses, 40 oxen and 21 bullocks, at 3*d*. a horse or ox, and 1½*d*. a bullock; nothing from the pasturage in la Worth' this year because it was sown; nothing from summer pasturage in various places for[3] the lord's stock; 5*s*. from 1 feeble plough-horse sold; £1 10*s*. from 3 oxen sold at Martinmas; £3 10*s*. 10*d*. from 50 wethers sold at the same feast, at 1*s*. 5*d*. each; 2*s*. 6*d*. from the skins sold of 10 wethers in murrain before shearing, at 3*d*. a skin; 1*s*. from the skins sold of 6 wethers in murrain after shearing; 8*d*. from the skins sold of 8 lambs in murrain after weaning and before shearing; 1*d*. from the skins sold of 3 lambs in murrain after shearing; 3*s*. 8*d*. from 44 hens from churchscot sold; 10*d*. from 300 eggs sold, received according to custom at Easter; 4*s*. 7*d*. from the whole vill for not doing suit at the windmill; nothing from profit of the parks this year because there were no pigs there for scarcity of corn. Total, £7 1*s*. ½*d*.

Sale of corn

The same render account for £3 18*s*. 9*d*. from 13 qrs 1 bus. of wheat sold, at 6*s*. a qr; 17*s*. 4*d*. from 6½ qrs of bere sold, at 2*s*. 8*d*. a qr; 2*s*. 7½*d*. from 7 bus. of barley sold, at 4½*d*. a bus.; 11*s*. 3*d*. from 5 qrs 5 bus. of oats sold, at 2*s*. a qr. Total, £5 9*s*. 11½*d*.

Entry and marriage fines

The same render account for 4*s*. from tithingpenny at the 2 hundred-courts for the year; 2*s*. from Matilda Swyft to have 1 cotland which belonged to Matilda her

1 MS omits heading.

2 MS omits '*d*.'

3 MS 'pro ⟨pastur*a*⟩ instaur''.

mother; 1*s*. from John Ywolf for marrying Edith (*Ydich'*) his daughter within. Total, 7*s*.

Perquisites

The same render account for 9*d*. from Simon Mess', Edith le Beyr, William atte Groyn' and Emma atte Hurn' for trespass of pasture; 3*d*. from Matilda Frankelay*n* because she is convicted; 9*d*. from Stephen Sop*ere* and his fellows for trespass of pasture; 1*s*. from William Stub for levying a debt; 6*s*. from G. Symo*n*, Nicholas Copinor, Stephen le Sop*er*e, Edith Beyr, John Sema*n*, John B*er*car*ius*, Henry Beyr, Isabel Fab*e*r, W. Wyky*ng*, John Walkelyn, Roger S*t*eph*en*, W. Ywolf, J*ohn* Ywolf, Andrew atte Hurn', Olympias (*Olympo*), John Bruny*ng*, Simon H*er*berd' and their fellows for trespass of pasture; 6*d*. from John B*er*car*ius* for keeping the sheep badly; 6*d*. from W*illiam* Stub for an inquest; 3*d*. from Olympias for unjustly withholding; 6*d*. from Robert atte More because he was not licensed to have a fold; 3*d*. from Richard Ude for bad ploughing; 2*s*. from Hugh Joye and his fellows for breaking the assize; 1*s*. 3*d*. from the reeve because his horse spent the night in the curia; 9*d*. from John Car*eter*, Emma atte Hurn' for trespass of ploughing; 3*d*. from John Kyng for bad harrowing; 6*d*. from Henry Beyr and John Car*eter* because they are penalised alternately; 9*d*. from ploughmen for bad ploughing; 3*d*. from the carter for trespass; 6*d*. from Nicholas atte Bern' and Matilda Buky for trespass of wood; 10*s*. from the reeve for keeping the corn badly in the barn and at harvest-time. Total, £1 7*s*.

Total of both, £1 14*s*.

Total of all receipts, £20 3*s*. 9*d*.

Cost of ploughs

In ironwork of 2 ploughs for the year 4*s*. In 2 plough-irons bought 6*d*. In 2 ploughshares bought 1*s*. 8*d*. In 1 new coulter made 4*d*. In stipend of the smith forging and repairing the ironwork of the said ploughs for the year 3*s*. In 2 new ploughs made 7*d*. In 2 new harrows made 6*d*. In trimming timber for ploughs and harrows 6*d*. In 2 pairs of wheels bought for ploughs 4*d*. In shoeing 4 plough-horses for the year 1*s*. 8*d*. In 4 halters made from the horses' own hair 1*d*. In boon-works of 8 ploughmen in winter and as many in Lent who ploughed and harrowed as many acres as they lie 2*s*. 8*d*.,[1] or 2*d*. a ploughman a day. Furthermore each ploughman will plough 1 acre for fallow in summer at his own expense according to custom. In reward of 3 ploughmen for their Saturday ploughings for the year, and 1 for 2½ terms, except for those Saturdays which were feast days and on which it was raining, 16*s*. 3¾*d*., or 4*s*. 6*d*. each for the year, and this through Bishop John because before they had nothing except 3*s*. a year. In 5 oxen bought £2 18*s*. 8*d*., at 12*s*. each for 2, 12*s*. 4*d*. each for 2, and 10*s*. for 1. In 1 plough-horse bought 7*s*. In stipend of 1 oxherd for 1½ terms 9*d*. In stipend of 1 harrower at various times in Lent 4½*d*. In 4½ qrs of wheat bought for sowing £1 2*s*. 6*d*., at 5*s*. a qr. In 7 qrs of bere bought for the same 16*s*. 4*d*., at 2*s*. 4*d*. a qr. In forage bought for oxen 8*s*. Total, £7 5*s*. 5¼*d*.

Carts

In 1 pair of wheels made for the cart 1*s*. In 1 new binding bought for the same and fitted to the said wheels 9*s*. In clouts, nails and grease bought for the cart and fitting the cart with axles for the year 10*d*. In mending the old cart at various times 1½*d*. In 1

1 MS omits '*d*.'

new cart-body made 6*d*. In 1 tumbrel made for dung 2*d*. In shoeing 2 horses for the year 2*s*. In stipend of the carter for the year 3*s*. Total, 16*s*. 7½*d*.

Cost of buildings
In roofing the barn in places 1*s*. In collecting 6 acres of stubble 1*s*., at 2*d*. an acre. In making a certain partition in the barn between the corn and seed with nails bought for the same 3*s*. In mending the granary 6*d*. In mending 1 lock on the barn-door and others 3½*d*. In rebuilding the sills of the forage-shed and the ruined studs and making traces for the sheep on every side 6*s*. 8*d*. In plastering and treating the walls of the same building 3*s*. 6*d*. Total, 16*s*. 2½*d*.

m.13
Sheepcote
In grease bought for greasing sheep 10*s*. 6*d*. In stipend of the shepherd for 1½ terms 9*d*. In wattling the fold this year 5*d*. In 50 wethers bought after shearing £3 3*s*. 10*d*., at 1*s*. 4*d*. each for 16, and 1*s*. 3*d*. each for 34. In stipend of 1 keeper of lambs for ½ year 2*s*. Total, £3 17*s*. 6*d*.

Harvest-time
In 2 boon-works of 84 men with the officials of the curia who reaped, bound and gathered in 38 acres of wheat and 38 acres of oats 7*s*. 1½*d*., as in bread, ale and relish. Total, 7*s*. 1½*d*.

Threshing
In threshing and winnowing 12 qrs 6 bus. of wheat 10½*d*., at 2*d*. per 10 struck bushels. In threshing and winnowing 33 qrs 3 bus. of bere 3*s*. 4*d*., at 1¾*d*. per 10 struck bushels. In threshing and winnowing 9 qrs 7 bus. of barley 11¼*d*., at 1¼*d*. per 10 struck bushels. In threshing 42 qrs 6 bus. of oats 1*s*. 5*d*., at ½*d*. a struck quarter. In winnowing the same 4¼*d*., at 1*d*. per 8 qrs. Total, 6*s*. 11*d*.

Total of all expenses, £13 9*s*. 9¾*d*.

And he owes, £6 13*s*. 11¼*d*.

Cash deliveries
Delivered to Sir *Geoffrey*, treasurer of Wolvesey, by 1 tally, £6 1*s*. 3*d*.

And he owes clear, 12*s*. 8¼*d*.

Issues of the grange

Wheat
{yield: three-fold plus 1½ bus.}
The same render account for 12 qrs 7 bus. from the whole issue of wheat by struck measure; 1 qr by estimation in 2 acres delivered to the reeve and hayward according to custom; 2 qrs 5½ bus. received from churchscot; 4½ qrs bought. Total, 21 qrs ½ bus.
Sown over 48 acres as they lie in the field of la Worth', 6½ qrs 2½ bus.; that is, 1 bus. an acre, plus 5½ bus. in all. Delivered to 1 reeve and 1 hayward by estimation in 2 acres according to custom, 1 qr. In customary payment to the hayward, 1 bus. Sold, 13 qrs 1 bus.

Bere
{yield: two-fold plus 1 qr 7 bus.}
The same render account for 33 qrs 3 bus. from the whole issue of bere by struck measure; 4 bus. by estimation in 82 sheaves[1] for the reaping of 42 acres by labour service, at 2 sheaves an acre; 7 qrs 3 bus. bought. Total, 41 qrs 2 bus.
Sown over 126 acres as they lie in the fields of Sum*erdon* and Worth', 22 qrs 7 bus.; that is, 1½ bus. an acre, less 6 bus. in all. Delivered to 1 carter for the year, 5 qrs 1½ bus., because he takes a quarter every 10 weeks. Delivered to 1 oxherd from Michaelmas (29 September) until Friday after St Valentine's day (16 February), for 20 weeks, 2 qrs. Delivered to 1 shepherd for the same time, 2 qrs, because thereafter he keeps both oxen and sheep for customary tenants. Delivered to 1 keeper of lambs from Easter Day until Michaelmas, that is, for 23 weeks, 2 qrs 1½ bus. Delivered to the reapers of 42 acres by estimation in 82 sheaves, ½ qr. Sold, 6½ qrs.

Barley
{yield: two-fold plus 5 bus.}
The same render account for 9 qrs 7 bus. from the whole issue of barley by struck measure.
Sown over 34 acres of Donhangr', 9 qrs; that is, 2 bus. an acre, plus 4 bus. in all. Sold, 7 bus.

Oats
{yield: 2-fold less 6 qrs 2 bus.}
The same render account for 42 qrs 6 bus. from the whole issue of oats by struck measure; 4 qrs 6 bus. by estimation in sheaves given to oxen; 2 bus. by estimation in one-and-a-half acres delivered to the hayward according to custom; 4 qrs remaining in the granary from the previous year. Total, 51 qrs 6 bus.
Sown over 134 acres as they lie in the fields of Donhangre and Som*er*do*n*, 30 qrs 2 bus.; that is, 2 bus. an acre, less 3 qrs 2 bus. in all. In fodder of the cart-horses at sowing-time, 6½ qrs. In fodder of the plough-horses hauling ploughs for the year, 4 qrs 3 bus. In supporting 13 oxen this year, 4 qrs 6 bus. In customary payment to the hayward by estimation in 1½ acres, 2 bus. Sold, 5 qrs 5 bus.

Stock

Cart-horses: 2 remain from the previous year; 2 remain.
Plough-horses: 4 remain from the previous year; 1 bought. Total, 5. 1 sold; 4 remain.
Oxen: 14 remain from the previous year; 5 bought. Total, 19. 3 sold at Martinmas. Total, 3. 16 remain.
Wethers: 235 remain from the previous year; 100 received from Woodhay before shearing; 1 received from Highclere after shearing; 50 bought. Total, 386. 50 sold at Martinmas; 11 in murrain before shearing, 6 after shearing. Total, 67. 319 remain.
Lambs: 257 received from Burghclere after weaning and before shearing. 8 in murrain before shearing, 3 after shearing. Total, 11. 246 remain.
Fleeces: 264 from wethers produced at the shearing this year; 26 in tithe; 1 in customary payment to the shepherd; 237 delivered to the reeve of Highclere.
Lamb's-wool: 249 fleeces produced at the shearing this year; all delivered to the reeve of Highclere.
Woolskins: 11 from wethers in murrain before shearing; 1 in tithe; 10 sold; none remain.

1 MS omits '82 sheaves', but recorded in the discharge.

Bare skins: 6 from wethers in murrain after shearing; all sold; none remain.
Hens: 50 from churchscot. 2 in default of Thomas H*ar*vest because he has no wife; 2 in default of Robert de Cruce for the same; 2 in default of Matilda Swyft because she has no husband. Total, 6. 44 sold.
Eggs: 300 received according to custom at Easter; all sold.
Carts: 2 remain from the previous year; 1 bought anew this year. Total, 3. 1 of wood worn out; 2 with iron tyres remain, of which 1 is feeble.

Witney

Arrears

Roginald de Lynh*a*m, bailiff, and Roger atte Hetth', reeve, render account for £34 2*s*. 3½*d*. of arrears from the last account, which account was delivered to Sir G*eoffrey*, treasurer of Wolvesey, by 1 tally. Nothing remains.

Rents

The same render account for £15 13*s*. 11*d*. for all rents of assize at Christmas; £16 5*s*. at Easter (22 April); £15 12*s*. 10½*d*. at the Nativity of the blessed John (24 June); £17 7*s*. 2½*d*. at Michaelmas (29 September). Total, £64 19*s*.

Quittances[1]

In quittance of 1 reeve for the year 5*s*.; 1 shepherd keeping wethers for the year 5*s*.; 1 keeper of ewes for the year 5*s*.; 14 ploughmen holding the lord's ploughs for the year £3 10*s*., or 5*s*. each, of whom 7 hold for 1 week and 7 for the other; 8 virgaters harrowing with their horses on alternate days from Michaelmas until Easter, that is, from morning until evening, £1, or 2*s*. 6*d*. each; 44 virgaters working on alternate days from the Nativity of the blessed John the Baptist until Michaelmas £2 15*s*., or 1*s*. 3*d*. each. And be it known that they themselves should weed[2] the corn, mow and toss the hay, reap corn, carry hay and corn, collect and spread dung, and do other works known to be necessary on the manor. Total of quittances, £8.

Defaults of rent

In default of the rent of Eustacia (*Cristach'*) de Hale 12*s*., because the vill held it at the time of the war and paid £1 for it, but William, son of the same Eustacia (*Eustoch'*), now holds it as heir for 8*s*. a year; the land which belonged to Roger de Carswoll' 13*s*. 4*d*., for the same reason as before; the land of William B*ercarius* drawn into demesne 2*s*.; the land of Roger le Knyhȝt drawn into demesne 2*s*.; 2 hides of land which the men of the borough used to hold drawn into demesne £2 8*s*.; the rent which the Prior of Cogges used to pay for the mill-pond of Cogges, which pond the prior exchanged with Bishop Peter for 1 meadow called Grimesmod' 5*s*.; the land of Costewey £2 10*s*. 6*d*., which was paid before in Upelond' and now is paid in the borough; 2 acres of land and 1 acre of meadow which Roger de Abb*er*bury formerly held drawn into demesne 2*s*.; the rent for 6 acres of land which John de Ramesdon' formerly held drawn into demesne 3*s*., because he did not wish to hold it of the demesne; the rent for 2 acres of land which Roger le Crocker' held drawn into demesne 1*s*. Total, £6 18*s*. 10*d*.

Total of quittances and defaults of rent, £14 18*s*. 10*d*.

1 MS omits heading.

2 MS 'blad' ⟨scl⟩ sarcl*antur*'.

Total of rents remaining, £50 2*d*.

Annual recognizance

The same render account for 3*d*. from Henry de Lewe for annual recognizance; 6*d*. from Geoffrey le Bor for the same; 2*d*. from Walter, son of Geoffrey Cherdesle, for the same; 2*d*. from Roger, son of the said Geoffrey, for the same; 4*d*. from Simon de Hole*n*den' for the same, whilst he pays to remain within the lord's liberty, for the first time this year. Total, 1*s*. 5*d*.

Farms

The same render account for £1 5*s*. from the moiety of 1 fulling mill which Lovekyn' Full' and William le Noble hold at farm; £1 from the other moiety of the said mill let at farm to Adam, son of the said Love*kyn*; £2 from 1 corn mill which Margery, who was wife of William Galewey, holds; 10*s*. from the moiety of 1 fulling mill let at farm to Walter P*ro*phete at Wodeford*e*mull' which before pertained to the farm of the mill; 13*s*. 4*d*. for a certain fishery let at farm to William Hogeman of Witney. Total, £5 8*s*. 4*d*.

Issues of the manor

The same render account for 14*s*. 5*d*. from the pasturage behind the curia sold in winter to various men for the agistment of livestock, sold by the head; 16*s*. 7*d*. from pannage of pigs at Martinmas (11 November); 8*s*. 8*d*. from the herbage of the moor sold for agistment, that is, for 7 horses, 71 oxen and cows, and 38 bullocks, at 2*d*. a horse, 1*d*. an ox, and ½*d*. a bullock, and know that sheep should not be agisted on that pasture; 4*s*. 10½*d*. from the herbage of Swenheye for agistment by the head, that is, for 470 sheep, at 1*d*. per 8 sheep, and there are no oxen there this year for a want of pasture, because the larger part of it was cultivated by Bishop William and therefore there is less to give than there used to be; 9*s*. 6*d*. from the pasturage in the marsh (*marisco*) behind the curia sold in parcels to John de Husto*n*, John de Fayreford' and John de Bureford'; 10*s*. from the pasturage in Asschemor sold to Walter Gibbes of Witney; 2*s*. from the pasturage of the road to Waylesmll' sold to Matilda Hara*n*g; nothing from the pasturage of livestock on the pasture with the lord's oxen this year because it was not permitted; nothing from the pasturage in the park because it was to maintain the wild beasts of the chase (*feris bestiis*); nothing from the pasturage of Rugfeld this year because that land is leased for a fixed rent; nothing from the pasturage in the garden this year because there is not enough for the lord's animals; £1 from refusals to stack; 2*s*. 6*d*. from tolls on inns; 2*s*. from pigeons sold, which came as squabs and which have reached maturity; 6*d*. from 3 capons from the recognizances of John de Boxor' and John B*ercarius* sold; 3*s*. 4*d*. from the residue of Peter's pence; 3*d*. from Walter Gylemy*n* for 1 plot to build 1 potter's kiln; 4*s*. 6*d*. from 36 rowen cheeses (*cas' de reluc*ro) sold; £3 6*s*. from 6 weys of cheese made in summer sold, at 11*s*. a wey; 8*s*. 11½*d*. from 30 cloves 5 lb of butter sold, at 3½*d*. a clove; 2*s*. 11*d*. from 1 qr 2 bus. of nuts sold from the previous year, at 2*s*. 4*d*. a qr; nothing from coarse wool here because it is sent to Wolvesey; 1*s*. 6*d*. from wool locks (*lobes lane*) sold to John de Fayreford'; nothing from lamb's-wool this year because none were sheared; 3*s*. from 3 calves sold to John de Fayreford'; 5*s*. 5*d*. from 5 calves sold to the same; 1*s*. 2*d*. from 1 calf sold to the same; 11*d*. from 1 calf sold to Roger de Stanlak'; 4*s*. 4*d*. from 52 hens from churchscot sold at Martinmas; 2*d*. from 2 peacocks' tails sold; 1*s*. 3*d*. from 5 carcasses of wethers sold, dead from murrain since (*cit*ra) the feast of St Nicholas (6 December); 2*s*. 11*d*. from the hide of a certain ox dead from murrain since Hockday (1 May), sold to John de Fayreford' because it was rotting; 2*s*. from the hide of a certain cow dead from murrain sold to Thomas Sau*n*dres; 2*s*. from the carcass of a certain cow sold to the same; 6*d*. from the hide of 1 bullock dead from murrain in Lent sold to Richard Car*eter*; 9*d*. from 12 gallons of milk from the manor sold for the lambs; 3*s*. 7½*d*. from the skins of 8 wethers and 8 hoggs dead from murrain before shearing sold to Henry Stacy about (*circa*) the feast of the blessed Thomas the Apostle (21 December), at 2¾*d*. a skin, less ½*d*. in all; 5*s*. 5*d*. from the skins of 9 wethers, 4 ewes, 3 of them before lambing, dead from murrain, sold to Henry Stacy since the Annunciation (25 March), at 5*d*. a skin, plus 1*d*. in all; 2*s*. 4*d*. from the skins of 1 ram, 6 ewes dead from murrain before shearing sold to Henry Stacy about Hockday, at 4*d*. a skin; 4*s*. 11½*d*. from the skins of 4 wethers, 4 ewes and 6 hoggs dead from murrain about the feast of St Dunstan (19 May), sold to Simon le Ber', at 4¼*d*. a skin, plus 1*d*.; 4*d*. from 4 bare skins sold; 1*s*. 9½*d*. from the skins of 32 lambs dead from murrain before weaning sold to Henry Stacy, at ¾*d*. a skin, less 2½*d*.; 5*d*. from the skins sold of 5 lambs dead from murrain after weaning; 6*s*. 9*d*. from 10 qrs 1 bus. of apples from the issue of the garden sold, at 8*d*. a qr; 8*s*. 5*d*. from dairy produce sold at the audit. Total, £11 16*s*. 11½*d*.

Sale of hay

The same render account for £1 11*s*. from hay sold to Thomas Mu*n*fort; £1 4*s*. from hay sold to William Raulyn; £2 10*s*. from hay sold to Hugh de Stanlak'; 14*s*. from hay sold to Walter de Roccot'; 11*s*. from hay sold to Simon le Ber'; 13*s*. from hay sold to Adam Lospic'; 3*s*. from hay sold in le Swonh*a*m to Roger Simo*n*d of Hailey. Total, £7 6*s*.

Sale of stock

The same render account for £3 8*d*. from 26 pigs over a year old sold to Walter Gibbes and John de Fayreford, at 2*s*. 4*d*. a head; £1 11*s*. 8*d*. from 40 kebb wethers sold at Martinmas to the same, at 9½*d*. a head; 3*s*. 4*d*. from 4 kebb wethers sold to the same, at 10*d*. a head; 17*s*. 5*d*. from 22 kebb ewes sold at Martinmas to the same, at 9½*d*. a head; 11*s*. 2*d*. from 11 kebb ewes sold at the same feast to the same, at 10*d*. a head; 1*s*. 7*d*. from 2 rams sold after shearing. Total, £6 3*s*. 10*d*.

Sale of the manor's corn

The same render account for £27 7*s*. 10¾*d*. from 126 qrs 3½ bus. of wheat sold, at 4*s*. 4*d*. a qr; 6*d*. from 1 bus. of wheat sold at the audit; 4*s*. 8*d*. from 2 qrs of curall sold, at 2*s*. 4*d*. a qr; £1 18*s*. from 12 qrs of barley sold, at 3*s*. 2*d*. a qr; 2¼*d*. from ½ bus. of barley sold at the audit; £5 3*s*. 6½*d*. from 44 qrs 3 bus. of dredge sold, at 2*s*. 4*d*. a qr; £3 18*s*. 3*d*. from 39 qrs 1 bus. of oats sold, at 2*s*. a qr; 1*s*. from 1 qr of vetches from casting the oats for sowing. Total, £38 14*s*. ½*d*.

Sale of the mill's corn[1]

The same render account for £2 6*s*. ½*d*. from 10 qrs 5 bus. of wheat from the issue of the mill sold, at 4*s*. 4*d*. a qr; 2*s*. 3½*d*. from ½ qr 1 peck of wheat sold at the audit; £6 7*s*. 4*d*. from 50 qrs 7½ bus. of second-grade malt from the issue of the said mill sold, at 2*s*. 6*d*. a qr; ¾*d*. from 1 peck of maslin sold at the audit; 4*s*. from 6 bus. of meal from the same issue sold. Total, £8 19*s*. 8¾*d*.

1 MS omits heading.

Fixed payments (*Certus visus*)
The same render account for £1 6*s*. 8*d*. from 11 tithings for fixed tithingpenny at the hundred-court of Martinmas; £1 6*s*. 8*d*. from the same tithings for fixed tithingpenny at the hundred-court of Hockday. Total, £2 13*s*. 4*d*.[1]

Entry and marriage fines
The same render account for 4*s*. from Richard Dorm' to have 2 acres of assarted land by surrender of Walter Rauly*n*; 2*s*. from Roger de Ministr' to have 1 acre of assart by surrender of the said Walter; 1*s*. relief from Robert Pirck' and Edith his wife to have 1½ acres of assart by surrender of the said Walter; 1*s*. from Simon le Ber' to have 1½ acres of assart by surrender of John Joppes and Isabel his mother; 4*s*. from Walter le Cachepol to have 2 acres of assart by surrender of Richard Saundres; 1*s*. relief from Richard Dorm' to have 1½ acres of assart by surrender of Walter Raulyn; 3*s*. 3*d*. relief from Hugh de Stanlak' to have 1 acre of assart in le Longebrech' and 1½ acres ½ rood of assart upon Swanewull*e*rugg' by surrender of the said Walter; 10*s*. relief from John de Husto*n* to have 3 acres of assart at Pottokesdich' and 2 acres of assart in the old assart of Witney which is called Doudeac*res* by surrender of the said Walter; 2*s*. from William, son of William Rauly*n*, to have 1 acre of assart by surrender of the said Walter; 3*s*. from Henry, son of Thomas le Mu*n*fort, to have 1½ acres of assart by surrender of the said Walter; 2*s*. relief from Godesdeu to have 1 acre of assart by surrender of the said Walter; 5*s*. 6*d*. relief from Robert le Trewe to have 2½ acres 1 rood of assart by surrender of the said Walter; 2*s*. from Roger Symo*nd* to have 1 acre of assart by surrender of Thomas le Wyte; 4*s*. relief from Geoffrey Hard*e*kyl to have 2 acres of assart by surrender of Walter Hardekyl; 1*s*. from Peter Maynborn to have ½ acre of assart by surrender of William Legos; 6*d*. relief from Roger, son and heir of Walter Wade, to have 1 acre of assart by succession to the said Walter his father; 6*d*. from Robert Pyrck' to have 1 rood of assart by surrender of William Pyrck'; 2*d*. relief from Robert Smalprou*t* to have 1 halfpennyworth of assarted land at Doddesh*u*ll' by surrender of Isabel Rauly*n*; 1*s*. relief from John Pyrch*e*k' to have 1½ acres of assart by surrender of Richard le Reve; 2*s*. from Roger de Ministr' to have 1 acre of assart by surrender of Walter Rauly*n*; 10*s*. from Richard le Reve for marrying Isabel his daughter outside; 3*d*. from Thomas, son of William Petyt, to have 1½ acres of assart by succession to Juliana Petyt; 1*s*. from Richard Powele to have 1½ acres of assart by surrender of Nicholas de Taunton'. (*m.13d*) And for 2*s*. from Henry, son of Henry de Denlye, to have 1 acre of assart by surrender of Alan de Denlye; 1*s*. from Henry Edon to have 1½ acres of assart by surrender of John le Car*eter*; 2*s*. from Robert Pyrk' to have 1 acre of assart by surrender of Walter Rauly*n*; 1*d*. from William, son of William Rauly*n*, to have 1 furlong of assart by surrender of Thomas de Sclouȝtr'; 1*d*. relief from the same William to have 1 furlong of assart by surrender of Walter Rauly*n*; 1*s*. relief from the same William to have 1½ acres of assart by surrender of Thomas Smalprout; 4*s*. from Simon Hery*n*g to have 2 acres of assart by surrender of Robert Mol*endinarius* in the old assart; 1*s*. from John le Cachepol to have 1½ acres of assart in the new assart by surrender of William Bosci; 1*s*. relief from Agnes le Cachepol to have 1½ acres of assart by surrender of the said John; 1*s*. relief from John de Husto*n* to have 1½ acres of assart at Totelye by surrender of William Bosci; 4*s*. from Walter de Bampto*n* to have entry to the third part of 1 acre of assart at Suellesly; 2*s*. from John Wyld' to have entry to 1 acre of assart at le Blakerod'; 1*s*. relief from John de Fonte to have 1 acre of assart by surrender of Richard Will'; 2*s*. 6*d*. from Richard, son of Richard Pyres, to have 1 acre 1 rood of assart by surrender

1 MS omits total.

of Simon le Ber'; 4*s.* from Walter le Val to have 2 acres of assart by surrender of Agnes le Val; 1*s.* from John de Stocle to have 1½ acres of assart by surrender of Richard Wycherod' of Hailey; 1*s.* from Richard Godesdeu to have 1½ acres of assart by surrender of Henry Lambard'; 4*s.* from Matilda, daughter of William Mol*en-dinarius*, to have 2 acres of assart by surrender of Simon Petyt; 13*s.* 4*d.* from Richard Gareford' for entry to 1 cotland which Cecilia la Couhurdes formerly held and surrendered into the lord's hands for the use of the same; 4*s.* 6*d.* from Matilda, daughter of Richard le Pocyr, to have 2 acres 1 rood of assart by surrender of the said Richard; 6*s.* from Juliana, daughter of Matilda de Font', to have 2 acres of assart by surrender of the said Matilda at Ronfeld'; 1*s.* from Martin le Bond' to have 1½ acres of assart by surrender of Richard Bald'; 6*d.* from the same Martin to have 1 rood of assart by surrender of John Wych'; 8*s.* from John de Husto*n* and Agnes his wife to have 4 acres of assart by surrender of Walter de Foresta; 6¼*d.* from William Bemgh' to have 1 acre and 1 furlong of assart by succession to John his brother; £5 from Robert le Butelyr to have entry for himself and his heirs to 14 acres 1 rood of assart which came into the bishop's hands as his escheat through the death of Richard le Butelyr who died without heirs, and Margery, relict of the said Richard, surrendered in full court into the bishop's hands the dower which formed part of the aforesaid 14 acres 1 rood of land for the use of the said Robert and his heirs; 2*s.* from Richard Goudesdeu to have 1 acre of assart by surrender of Walter de Foresta; 2*s.* from John de Huston' to have 1 acre of assart by surrender of Clarice, relict of Robert La*m*bard; 2*s.* from Matilda, daughter of John Bu*n*ty*n*g, to have 1 acre of assart by surrender of Roger her brother; 1*s.* from the same Matilda to have 1½ acres of assart at Panchewll' by surrender of the said John Bu*n*ting her father; 2*s.* from Clarice, daughter of John Bu*n*ty*n*g, to have 1 acre of assart at le Hatth' by surrender of the said John her father; 1*s.* from the same Clarice to have 1½ acres of assart by surrender of Roger Bu*n*ty*n*g her brother; 4*s.* from Joan, daughter of John Bu*n*ty*n*g, to have 2 acres of assart by surrender of John Bu*n*ty*n*g her father; 1*s.* from the same Joan to have 1½ acres of assart in Swyheye by surrender of Roger Bu*n*ty*n*g her brother; 1*s.* from Geoffrey le Bor to have 1½ acres of assart by surrender of Richard le Reve; 5½*d.* from Margery, daughter of Richard le Port', to have ½ acre, 1 rood, and 1 pennyworth of assarted land by succession to the said Richard her father; 5½*d.* from Agnes, daughter of Richard le Port', to have 1½ acres, 1 rood, and 1 pennyworth of assarted land by succession to the said Richard; 5½*d.* from Clarice, daughter of Richard le Port', to have 1½ acres, 1 rood, and 1 pennyworth of assarted land by succession to the said Richard; 3*s.* from John de Husto*n* to have 1½ acres of assarted land by surrender of Thomas de W*o*rth'; 10*s.* from John le G*ra*nt for marrying Agnes his daughter outside; 11*s.* 6*d.* from John de Husto*n* to have 5½ acres 1 rood of assarted land by surrender of Walter Rauly*n*. Total, £16 2*s.* 10¾*d.*

Perquisites
The same render account for 11*s.* from the small amercements of the hundred-court held at Martinmas; £2 16*s.* 1*d.* from the small amercements of the hundred-court of Hockday; £1 7*s.* from the small amercements of the manorial court (*curia*). Total, £4 14*s.* 1*d.*

Total of both, £20 16*s.* 11¾*d.*

Total of all receipts, £149 7*s.* 5½*d.*

Cost of ploughs
In 6 ploughs made anew from demesne timber by piece-work 1*s.* In 10 plough-beams (*bemis*) fitted with iron by piece-work for 1 day by 2 men 3*d.* In fitting the said

ploughs and other old ploughs with share-beams at various times 1*s*. 5*d*. In mending 3 harrows, that is, fitting 3 bindings, 1½*d*. In stipend of the smith forging the iron for the iron apparel of 7 ploughs[1] for the year, 8*s*. according to custom, because James de C*ra*ule, forester, provides iron and steel for a certain assart which he holds of the lord. In expenses of 86 men with 43 ploughs who ploughed 43 acres of land at 1 winter boon-work 7*s*. 2*d*., or 2*d*. each according to custom. In expenses of 90 men with 45 ploughs who ploughed 45 acres of land at 1 Lenten boon-work 7*s*. 6*d*., or 2*d*. each according to custom. Moreover there were 2 boon-works at their own cost. In stipend of 1 overseer of the harvest and 7 ploughmen for ½ year 8*s*. Total, £1 13*s*. 5½*d*.

Cost of carts and ironwork

In 2 new pairs of wheels bought for the carts fitted with tyres 9*s*. 1*d*. In 1 piece of iron for the same 5*s*. 6*d*. In 5½ pieces of iron bought for making large nails for the same 2*s*. 2*d*. In stipend of the smith forging the said nails out of the said iron 2*s*. 2*d*. In 10 clamps made from the iron of the demesne for the same 5*d*. In small nails made for the said clamps 2*d*. In 2 strakes (*stak'*) lengthened for the second cart ½*d*. In fitting tyres to the said wheels with the said iron by piece-work 10*d*. In 3 pairs of traces bought for carts 1*s*. 2½*d*. In white leather for mending the harnesses of carts 11½*d*. In 1 new horse-collar bought 6*d*. In 3 felloes bought and fitted to the old dung-cart 10*d*. In 4 stakes lengthened for the same cart 1½*d*. In 24 large nails and 5 clamps made from the iron of the demesne for the same cart 4½*d*. In stipend of the smith fitting part of the said wheel with a binding by piece-work 1½*d*. In 10 metal plates (*clupell'*) and 4 dowels bought for the old cart at various times 1*s*. 2*d*. In 1 cart-saddle without saddle-pads bought 3*d*. In 13 lb of grease bought for the carts for the year at various times 1*s*. 1*d*. In 24 clouts with nails bought for the carts 1*s*. 5*d*., at ¾*d*. each, less ¼*d*. in all. In fitting the carts with axles at various times 7*d*. In stipend of 2 carters for ½ year 2*s*., because both take 1 acre of wheat for ½ year in summer. In shoeing 4 horses with all necessaries pertaining to the provision of the same together with their removal and fastening 5*s*. Total, £1 16*s*.

Small expenses

In all the forage from 1 stacking of the Lenten corn bought for supporting oxen in winter from William, proctor of Witney, £1 4*s*. In forage from 1 stacking and the straw (*palea*) from 2 stackings bought from and for the same £1 6*s*. 8*d*. In forage from 2 stackings bought for the same from John de Husto*n* £1 6*s*. 8*d*. In forage bought for supporting oxen from Richard de Du*n*stapl*e* 1*s*. 8*d*. In forage bought for the same in parcels from the proctor of Witney 2*s*. 8½*d*. In hiring a certain man for 3 days to make a certain new hearth for the oven and to mend the kiln 6*d*. In mending 1 wheelbarrow 1*d*. In fitting with iron 1 shovel bought from William Fab*e*r 4*d*. In 1 tripod bought for making the pottage of the manorial servants on in the park 1*s*. In 1 earthenware pot bought for the same 1*d*. In 1 piece of iron bought for a certain shovel 2*d*. In 5 ells of canvas bought for making sacks therefrom 1*s*. 5¼*d*. In 1 wooden bucket bought for the water well and in hooping the same 4*d*. In 1 lock bought for the door to the hay-house, and in 1 lock on the door to the great stable, 1 lock on the door to the clerk's chamber, 1 lock on the garden-gate, and 1 lock on the door to the dovecote removed, mended and replaced again, together with a certain new key bought for the door to the dovecote and 1 new key bought for the door to the hay-house, 5*d*. In 1 new rope bought for the louver in the bailiff's chamber 1¼*d*. In

1 MS omits 'ploughs', which appears on other rolls.

making 3 hoops and 2 iron dowels for the gate to the field 1½*d*. In making well 6 sows 2*d*. In hiring a certain man with his mate for 3 days to rebuild a certain wall 1 perch long beside the byre to the park 9*d*. In hiring the same for 2 days to rebuild a certain piece of wall which had collapsed beside the byre, cow-shed and pinfold 6*d*. In hiring the same for 1 day to rebuild a certain piece of wall which had collapsed upon le Wote 3*d*. In hiring the same for 5 days to rebuild a certain piece of wall outside the bishop's chamber which had collapsed 1*s*. 3*d*. In 3 bus. of salt bought for the pease pottage (*legum'*) of the manorial servants for the year 1*s*. In stipend of 1 swineherd for the year 2*s*. 8*d*. Total, £4 12*s*. 10½*d*.

Threshing

In threshing 112 qrs 4½ bus. of wheat by struck measure and 2 qrs of curall 19*s*. 1*d*., at 2*d*. a qr. In threshing 55 qrs of barley 4*s*. 7*d*., at 1*d*. a qr. In threshing 28 qrs of dredge 2*s*. 4*d*., at 1*d*. a qr. In threshing 72½ qrs of oats 4*s*. 6*d*., at ¾*d*. a qr. In afterwards winnowing all the corn, that is, 268 qrs ½ bus., 4*s*. 6*d*., at 1*d*. per 5 qrs, because the rest of the corn was winnowed by labour service and the dairymaid. In a riddle sieve bought 1¾*d*. In wages of John Touresmer' overseeing the threshing and winnowing of the corn at various times 16*s*. 4½*d*., taking 1½*d*. a day. In stipend of the same 4*s*., because he takes the rest, up to 10*s*., elsewhere. Total, £2 15*s*. 6¼*d*.

Cost of buildings

In 2,200 slates bought for the said roofing[1] 2*s*. In 11 qrs of lime for pointing the bishop's barn and stable 2*s*. 9*d*., at 3*d*. a qr. In hiring a certain tiler with his mate to point the barn for 9½ days 3*s*. 2*d*., taking 4*d*. a day. In moss collected for the same by 4 women hired for the same for 2 days 8*d*. In hiring the same tiler with his mate to point the byre in the park for 4 days 1*s*. 1½*d*. In hiring 1 roofer to roof the barn for 3 days by piece-work 7½*d*., at 2½*d*. a day. In hiring the same to roof the cow-shed for 7½ days 1*s*. 6¾*d*., taking for a day as above. In 2 women assisting him for ½ day because customary tenants do not work on Saturdays 1*d*. In hiring the same about Hockday (1 May) for 6½ days to roof the barn because the roof was ruined on account of the wind 1*s*. 7½*d*., taking 3*d*. a day. In 2 women assisting him for the same time 1*s*. 1*d*., or 1*d*. each a day. In a certain tiler to point the great stable for 15½ days 5*s*. 2*d*., at 4*d*. a day for himself and his mate. Total, 19*s*. 10¼*d*.

Cost of sheep (*bidenc'*)

In 11 stone and 4 lb of grease bought for greasing sheep 12*s*. 10*d*., at 1*s*. 2*d*. a stone, plus 4 lb in all. In 4½ lb and 1 qr of verdigris for the same 3*s*. 2*d*., at 8*d*. a lb. In 4½ lb of vinegar for the same 2*s*. 11*d*., at 10*d*. a lb. In 12 gallons of milk bought from the manor for the lambs 9*d*. In 57 gallons of milk bought for the same from various places at the aforesaid price 3*s*. 6¾*d*. Total, £1 3*s*. 2¾*d*.

Cost of the dairy

In 2 strainers for cleaning milk 1*d*. In 4 earthenware pans bought 2½*d*. In linen cloth bought to make cheese cloth therefrom at the dairy 3½*d*. In mending and hooping anew 4 buckets 4*d*. In 4 bus. of salt bought for the dairy 1*s*. 4½*d*. In stipend of 1 cowherd for ½ year 1*s*. In stipend of the dairymaid for the same time 6*d*. Total, 3*s*. 9½*d*.

Cost of the mill

In 1 millstone bought for the mill of Modeford*e*mull' £3 5*d*. In carrying the same from Wallingford to Witney 1*s*. 6*d*. In 1 piece of iron to lengthen and strengthen the

1 MS omits object.

mill-spindle at Wodeford*e*mull' 4*d*. In stipend of the smith forging the said iron 4*d*. In 1 piece of iron to make other necessaries at the said mill 5*d*. In stipend of the smith making anew 4 iron hoops to hoop 2 trestles (*tresel'*) at both ends to fix them to the large iron hoop holding the millstone lying around the spindle and the base of the said spindle 5*d*. In smelting a certain pole made anew together with 2 lb of brass bought for the same 5*d*. In cogs and rungs bought at Wodeford*e*mll' by view of R*oginald* the bailiff 1*s*. 8½*d*. In 1 piece of iron to mend the spindle of the malt mill 5*d*. In stipend of the smith making the said spindle with the said iron 5*d*. In 1 piece of steel bought for the bills of the mill of Wodeford' 7*d*. In stipend of the smith repairing and restoring the said bills with the said steel 5*d*. In 1 basket bought for the mill to carry corn to the grain-chest (*bynna'*) 1½*d*. In small nails bought for the outer wheel of the mill of Wodeford' 1½*d*. In 2 women assisting a certain roofer roofing the mill of Waleys for 4 days 6*d*., or ¾*d*. each a day. In 1 piece of steel bought to mend the bills of the mill of Waleys 7*d*. In stipend of the smith repairing and restoring the said bills with the said steel 5*d*. In 3 boards bought for the mills of Wodeford' and Waleys 10*d*. In stipend of 1 miller of Wodeford*e*mll' for the year 10*s*., because the same miller repaired all the carpentry necessary for the mills and ploughs. Total, £3 19*s*. 11½*d*.

Cost of meadows

In mowing the meadows according to custom, 2*s*. for the meat owed to them. Moreover they have 3 bus. of wheat and 1 cheese from stock. Total, 2*s*.

Cost of the harvest

In bread, ale, fish, meat and cheese bought for 9 harvest boon-works of 1,188 men, as if for 1 day, of whom 22 men were from 1 boon-work of free men and 25 from 1 boon-work of Ducklington, £5 2*s*. 4*d*., who reaped all the corn. Total, £5 2*s*. 4*d*.

Expenses of the steward and bailiff with certain other items

In expenses of the steward and Simon for their visits on 3 occasions £1 12*s*. 4½*d*. In expenses of William de Letch', bailiff from Michaelmas (29 September) until the feast of St Lucia the Virgin (13 December), 17*s*. 4*d*. In fee of Roginald de Lynh*a*m from the feast of St Lucia until Michaelmas, in parts to £10 for the year, £3, because he takes the rest at Brightwell and Harwell. In fur for the summer livery of the bailiff 3*s*. In expenses of a certain attendant bearing a certain writ to Winchester 4*d*. In 10 ells of canvas bought for putting wool in 2*s*. 11*d*., at 3½*d*. an ell. In packing the said wool and stitching together the sacks with thread bought for the same 7*d*. In carrying the said wool to Wolvesey on the manor's carts, that is, by 2 men and 3 horses, 1*s*. 1½*d*., at 1*d*. a man a day and ½*d*. for hay for each horse at night. In expenses of a certain attendant keeping 1 of the steward's horses at Witney for 3 weeks 2*s*. 7½*d*. Total, £6 3½*d*.

Total of all expenses, £28 9*s*. 3¾*d*.

And he owes, £120 18*s*. 1¾*d*.

Allowances[1]

In allowance of the reeve building anew 1 chimney which fell down in the room above the new gate, £1 for all costs. Also for the expenses of Sir Thomas de Gard' and Sir William de Scalebrok', knights, for 1 day, 6*s*. 5*d*. Also in allowance of the

1 MS omits heading.

same 13*s*. 4*d*., who was being paid by Walter Raulyn by fixed agreement, for the first time this year, to mend selds which he holds from the bishop in the borough of Witney. Total of all allowances, £1 19*s*. 9*d*.

Cash deliveries
Delivered to Sir G*eoffrey*, treasurer of Wolvesey, by 1 tally, £88.

Total of all allowances and cash deliveries, £89 19*s*. 9*d*.

And thus he owes clear, £30 18*s*. 4¾*d*.

Issues of the grange

Wheat
{yield: three-fold plus 11 qrs 6½ bus.}
The same render account for 73 qrs 6 bus. of wheat from the whole issue of the grange from the time of William le Letch', bailiff, by 2 tallies of struck measure, of which 58 qrs 1 bus. threshed (*talliat'*) by labour service, 15 qrs 1 bus. according to custom; 125 qrs ½ bus. from the same issue by 2 tallies of John Touresm*ere* and William le Peck', grangers, of which 112 qrs 4½ bus. by piece-work, 12½ qrs by labour service; 9 qrs 6 bus. by estimation in 13 acres given to the manorial servants for their stipends in summer. Total, 208 qrs 4½ bus.
Sown over 180 acres as they lie in the fields[1] towards Crodebrigg' and Hauekeslewe, 68½ qrs by 2 tallies; that is, 3 bus. an acre, plus 1 qr in all. In provision of Sir Robert, steward, holding the hundred-courts of Martinmas and Hockday, 7 bus. by tally, with provision of the same. In customary payment for the crossing of Babbelak', 1 qr. In customary payment for the mowers' sheep (*medsscepe*), 3 bus. Given to 1 reeve, 1 overseer of the harvest, 2 carters, 7 ploughmen, 1 cowherd and 1 dairymaid for ½ year in summer, 9 qrs 6 bus. by estimation in 13 acres of wheat as they lie in the fields, or 6 bus. each. In provision of William le Letch', bailiff after Michaelmas, 1½ qrs by 1 tally. Sold as noted above, 126 qrs 3½ bus. Sold at the audit, 1 bus. Total, 208 qrs 4½ bus. None remains.

Curall
The same render account for 2 qrs of wheat curall from the issue of the grange, threshed by piece-work and by struck measure, by 1 tally as mentioned above. Total, 2 qrs. Sold within. None remains.

Barley
{yield: four-fold plus 4 qrs 1 bus.}
The same render account for 68 qrs 1 bus. of barley from the whole issue of the grange by 2 tallies of struck measure, of which 55 qrs threshed by piece-work, 13 qrs 1 bus. by labour service. Total, 68 qrs 1 bus.
Sown over 34 acres of demesne as they lie in the field, 16½ qrs by 1 tally, and over mill land, ½ qr by the same tally; that is, 3 bus. an acre. Delivered to 1 overseer of the harvest for the year, 5 qrs 1½ bus., taking a quarter every 10 weeks. Mixed for the liveries of the other manorial servants, 33 qrs 7 bus. Sold, 12 qrs. Sold at the audit, ½ bus. Total, 68 qrs 1 bus. None remains.

1 MS 'camp' ⟨de⟩'.

m.14

Dredge

{yield: three-fold plus 3 qrs 6 bus.}

The same render account for 65 qrs 2 bus. of dredge from the whole issue of the grange by 3 tallies of struck measure, of which 28 qrs by piece-work, 37 qrs 2 bus. by labour service. Total, 65 qrs 2 bus.

Sown over 32 acres as they lie in the field, 19½ qrs; that is, 5 bus. an acre, less ½ qr in all. In casting dredge to clean the seed, 1 qr 3 bus. Sold, 44 qrs 3 bus. Total, 65 qrs 2 bus. None remains.

Oats

{yield: two-fold less 1 qr 2 bus.}

The same render account for 176 qrs 2 bus. of oats frrom the issue of the grange by 4 tallies of struck measure, of which 72½ qrs threshed by piece-work, 55 qrs 6 bus. according to custom, and 51½ qrs by labour service. Total, 176 qrs 2 bus.

Sown over 128½ acres of demesne as they lie in the field which is called[1] Lynlond', Assceforlong and below le Oldefeld, 96 qrs 3 bus.; that is, 6 bus. an acre by 1 tally. And over 8½ acres of mill land, 6 qrs 1 bus. by the same tally; that is, over an acre as before, less 2 bus. In fodder of the horses of Sir Robert, steward, and Simon, clerk, for their visits, 4½ qrs by 3 tallies, with provision of the same. In fodder of the horses of William le Letch', bailiff, 2 qrs by 1 tally. In fodder of 1 horse of Sir Robert, steward, sojourning at Witney from Friday the eve of Epiphany (5 January) until Friday after the conversion of St Paul (26 January), both days included, 1 qr 3½ bus. by 1 tally, with the wages of Ralph de Hok*e*nortton'. In fodder of the horses of Sir Thomas de Gard' and Sir William de Scalebrok', collectors of the fifteenth, for 1 day and night, 5 bus. In oatmeal for the pottage of the manorial servants, 2 qrs. In fodder of 4 cart-horses from Michaelmas (29 September) until Lammas (1 August), which harrowed at the time of the winter and Lenten sowings, carried forage for the oxen from the curia to the park, and brought dung to the fields, 18 qrs 3 bus., at ½ bus. a night, less 5 bus. In casting oats to clean the seed, the aforesaid 5 qrs 5½ bus. Sold, 39 qrs 1 bus. Total, 176 qrs 2 bus. None remains.

Vetches[2]

The same render account for 7 qrs ½ bus. of vetches from casting dredge and oats as made clear above. Total, 7 qrs ½ bus.

In supporting pigs in winter and summer when it was necessary, 6 qrs ½ bus. Sold, 1 qr. Total, 7½ qrs. None remains.

Issues of the mill

Wheat

The same render account for 15 qrs 7½ bus. of wheat from the whole issue of the 2 mills of Wodeford and Walays by 4 tallies. Total, 15[3] qrs 7½ bus.

Delivered to 1 miller at Wodeford*e*mll' for the year, 2½ qrs 3 pecks, because he takes the rest in maslin. In tithe, 1 qr 4½ bus. In stipend and allowance of food of the second miller at Walaysmll', that is, for 5 qrs 7 bus. of wheat from the issue of the said mill, 5 bus., because he will have the ninth bushel. Sold, 10 qrs 5 bus. Sold at the audit, ½ qr 1 peck. Total, 15 qrs 7½ bus. None remains.

1 MS '⟨Huȝelond⟩'.

2 MS omits heading.

3 MS omits '15'.

Maslin

The same render account for 35 qrs 5 bus. of maslin from the issue of the said 2 mills by the said 4 tallies. Total, 35 qrs 5 bus.

In tithe, 3 qrs 4 bus. Delivered to 1 miller of Wodeford*e*mll' for the year, 2½ qrs 3 pecks, because he takes the rest in wheat. In stipend and allowance of food of 1 miller of Waleysmll', that is, for 11 qrs 2½ bus., who takes the ninth bushel from the issue of the said mill, 1 qr 2 bus. Mixed for the liveries of the manorial servants, 28 qrs. Sold at the audit, 1 peck. Total, 35 qrs 3 bus. 2 bus. remain.

Malt

The same render account for 57 qrs ½ bus. of second-grade malt from the issue of the said 2 mills by 3 tallies. Total, 57 qrs ½ bus.

In tithe, 5 qrs 5½ bus. In stipend and allowance of food of 1 miller of Walaysmull', for 4 qrs 1 bus. from the issue of the said mill, 3½ bus., because he will have the ninth bushel. Sold, 50 qrs 7½ bus. Total, 57 qrs ½ bus. None remains.

Meal (*farin*a)

The same render account for 6½ bus. of oatmeal (*farine aven'*) from the issue of the mill of Wodeford'. Total, 6½ bus.

In tithe, ½ bus. Sold, 6 bus. Total, 6½ bus. None remains.

Liveries of the manorial servants

The same render account for 33 qrs 7 bus. of barley and 28 qrs of maslin received above to mix for the manorial servants. Total, 61 qrs 7 bus.

Delivered to 2 carters, 7 ploughmen and one cowherd for the year, 51 qrs 7 bus., or 5 qrs 1½ bus. each, taking a quarter every 10 weeks. Delivered to 1 dairymaid for the year, 4 qrs 2½ bus. Delivered to 1 swineherd for the year, 3 qrs 6 bus. of maslin, taking a quarter every 14 weeks, for the first time this year. Delivered to 1 keeper of lambs from Thursday the feast of the Invention of the Cross (3 May) until Michaelmas (29 September), for 22 weeks, 1 qr 2½ bus., taking a quarter every 16 weeks. Total, 61 qrs 7 bus. None remains.

Stock

Cart-horses: 3 remain. Total, 3. 3 remain.

Oxen: 58 remain; 1 added from steers. Total, 59. 1 in murrain, the hide of which was sold within. Total, 1. 58 remain.

Bulls: 1 remains; 1 added from steers. Total, 2. 2 remain.

Cows: 20 remain; 6 added from steers. Total, 26. 1 in murrain in Lent before calving, the hide of which was sold within. Total, 1. 25 remain.

Steers: 8 remain, of which 2 males were bullocks at the last account. Total, 8. 1 added to oxen, 1 to bulls, 6 to cows. Total, 8. None remain.

Bullocks: 7 remain, of which 5 males were yearlings at the last account; 1 female from the heriot of Elias Gareford'. Total, 8. 8 remain, 5 of them male.

Yearlings: 10 remain, of which 3 males were calves at the last account. Total, 10. 1 young heifer (*bovicul' fem'*) in murrain in Lent, the hide of which was sold within. Total, 1. 9 remain, 3 of them male.

Calves: 21 from the offspring of the said cows this year, and not more because 1 died before calving and 4 were sterile. Total, 21. 2 in tithe; 10 sold as made clear within. Total, 12. 9 remain, 5 of them male.

Wethers: 223 remain; 34 added from hoggs. Total, 257. 23 in murrain before shearing, 3 after shearing; 44 sold at Martinmas (11 November), 2 of them after shearing. Total, 70. 187 remain.

Rams: 8 remain. Total, 8. 1 in murrain before shearing; 2 sold for the provision of the harvest. Total, 3. 5 remain.
Ewes: 183 remain; 38 added from hoggs; 2 black ewes after shearing, the penalty for the fornication of Margaret le Hode and Agnes, daughter of John Bele. Total, 222. 3 in murrain before lambing, 13 after lambing and before shearing, and 1 after shearing; 33 kebbs sold at Martinmas. Total, 50. 172 remain.
Hoggs: 86 remain, which were lambs at the last account. Total, 86. 15 in murrain before shearing; 34 added to wethers, 37 to ewes. Total, 86. None remain.
Lambs: 143 from the offspring of the said ewes this year, and not more because 3 died before lambing and 4 were sterile. Total, 143. 11 in tithe; 1 in customary payment to the shepherd; 35 in murrain before weaning, 5 after weaning. Total, 52. 91 remain.
Pigs: 26 gelded pigs (*porc' mas*) and 1 boar (*apro*) remain; 31 added from the piglets of the last account; 1 sow from the heriot of Richard le Porter about the Nativity of St John the Baptist. Total, 59. 1 in murrain; 26 sold at Martinmas. Total, 27. 32 remain over a year old, 4 of them sows.
Piglets: 26 from the offspring of the said sows; 6 from the heriot of Richard le Porter, with the aforesaid sow. Total, 32. 2 in tithe. Total, 2. 30 remain, 8 of them aged ½ year, 13 aged 1 quarter, and 9 aged 6 weeks.
Fleeces {yield 4¾*d*. plus 2*s*. 9*d*. in all}: 370 from the shearing of the above-mentioned sheep. Total, 370. 37 in tithe; 1 in customary payment to the shepherd keeping wethers; 332 sent to Wolvesey, which made 2 weys 17 cloves. Total, 370. None remain.
Woolskins: 23 from wethers, 1 from a ram, 16 from ewes and 15 from hoggs from the murrain of the above-mentioned sheep. Total, 55. 5 in tithe; 50 sold as made clear within. Total, 55. None remain.[1]
Bare skins: 3 from wethers and 1 from a ewe from the above-mentioned murrain after shearing. Total, 8.[2] All sold within; none remains.
Lambskins:[3] 35 from lambs dead from murrain before weaning, 5 before weaning.[4] Total, 40. 3 in tithe; 37 sold as made clear within. Total, 40. None remain.
Hides: 1 from an ox, 1 from a cow, and 1 from a yearling from the above-mentioned murrain; sold within.
Winter cheese: 36 winter rowen cheeses. Total, 36. Sold within; none remain.
Summer cheese {yield of cow 3*s*. 6*d*. and sheep 1½*d*. this year with 2 cheeses given in customary payment which are valued at 1*s*.}: 149 cheeses made between Friday the morrow of the Invention of the Cross (4 May) and Michaelmas (29 September), both days included, at 1 cheese a day. Total, 149. 15 in tithe; 1 in customary payment to the dairymaid; 1 in customary payment for the mowers' sheep (*medschip'*); 132 sold, which made 6 weys. It balances.
Butter: 30 cloves 5 lb from the issue of the dairy; sold within; none remain.
Peacocks: 6 remain, 3 of them male; 3 offspring this year. Total, 9. 9 remain, 3 of them male.
Capons: 2 from the rent of John de Boxor' for annual recognizance; 1 from the rent of John Berch' whilst he pays to remain within ⌈the lord's liberty.⌉ Total, 3. Sold within; none remain.

1 MS repeats 'Id*em* r*eddunt* comp*otum* de xxiij'.

2 Figures add up to 4.

3 MS omits heading.

4 'after weaning' according to lambs above.

Cocks and hens: 52 from churchscot at Martinmas; sold within; none remain.
Utensils: 2 carts with iron tyres remain and 2 bought, of which 2 are worn out; 2 carts and 2 wagons with iron tyres remain. 2 cart-ropes remain. 2 ropes of bast remain, which are used and none remain. 1 pot and 1 pan remain. 2 tripods remain and 1 bought, of which 1 is used and 2 remain. A lead oven, 1 axe, 1 mortar, 1 ewer, 1 basin, 2 iron forks remain. 2 sacks remain and 2 bought, of which 2 are used and 2 remain. 1 basket remains. 3 tubs, 1 tine, 1 barrel containing 60 gallons, 2 three-pronged iron dung-forks, and 2 ladders remain.

Witney Borough

Rents

Roginald de Lynh*a*m, bailiff, and Simon le Ber' and Robert Pyrk', reeves of the borough, render account for £2 6*s*. 10¾*d*. for all rents of assize at Christmas; £2 6*s*. 10¾*d*. at Hockday (1 May); £2 6*s*. 10¾*d*. at the Nativity of the blessed John the Baptist (24 June); £2 6*s*. 11¼*d*. at Michaelmas (29 September). Total, £9 7*s*. 7½*d*.

Quittances

In quittance of 2 reeves of the borough for the year 3*s*. Total, 3*s*.

Total of rents remaining, £9 4*s*. 7½*d*.

Tolls, stalls and selds

The same render account for 12*s*. 9*d*. from the tolls of 2 fairs, and so little because the merchants were discouraged by the prises taken for the queen who was lying in childbed at Woodstock; 13*s*. 6*d*. from selds, of which 10*s*. was from the farm of Walter Raulyn for ½ year, and in the following year he will give £1 because the same Walter took the said selds at annual fee-farm and for this he has bound himself and his heirs and his lands and tenements by his written bond which is in the treasury; 10*s*. 5*d*. from stalls. Total, £1 16*s*. 8*d*.

Perquisites

The same render account for 6*d*. from Isabel de Cruc' for release from suit of 2 views; 3*d*. from Gilbert Marti*n* for harbouring Robert de Pyngh*a*m against the assize; 3*d*. from John le Gu*n*t' for stopping up a certain watercourse; 6*d*. from Henry Stacy for transgression done to Richard Godesdeu; 6*d*. from Matilda Lambeky*n* for removing a certain leaden vessel from the tenement of John le Cart*er*e; 6*d*. from Walter de Irmo*n*gare to have a certain seld; 3*d*. from Thomas Warock for stopping up a certain watercourse; 3*d*. from Thomas Rog' for breaking the assize of bread; 6*d*. from Thomas Aylward for the same; 3*d*. from Walter le Val for the same; 6*d*. from Walter Gibbes for the same; 6*d*. from Juliana la Daye to have freedom; 3*d*. from Adam le Fuller for unjustly withholding a debt from John Locte; 3*d*. from John de Ministr', clerk, for transgression done to Richard le Keyne; 1*s*. from John Stoyl for breaking the assize of bread; 3*d*. from Ralph le Hutheward for transgression done to John le Gu*n*t'; 3*d*. from Thomas Rog' for breaking the assize of bread; 3*d*. from John de Bureford for default; 2*s*. from Henry le Ledbeter' and Alice his wife to have freedom; 1*s*. from Robert de Den' because he is not proceeding against the Abbot of Eynsham; 4*d*. from Nicholas Pauly*n* for default; 3*d*. from Walter le Gr*a*nt for brewing ale against the liberties of the vill; 3*d*. from Roger Broket for the same; 4*d*.

from William Buk' for transgression done to Nicholas Paul*yn*; 1*s*. from John de Ministr' for default of his law-worthiness regarding the surety of John de Bureford'; 3*d*. from Geoffrey le Ber' for assault done to Matilda le Ber'; 6*d*. from Richard de Du*n*staple because he did not produce in court Robert de Den' whom he had pledged; 3*d*. from the same Richard for false countersigns made to free 7*s*. 6*d*. from the chattels of Robert de Den'; 6*d*. from Richard Sandr' because he did not produce in court Robert de Den' whom he had pledged; 1*s*. from Roger de Ministr' because he defaulted in his law-worthiness regarding the surety of the bailiff; 3*d*. from the same Roger for licence to agree with Matilda Bu*n*ting; 6*d*. from Nicholas de Cog' for false complaint against the men of the Abbot of Eynsham; 3*d*. from Ralph le Crocker' for licence to agree with Robert Lacy; 3*d*. from Robert[1] de Cog' because he bought and sold merchandise within the liberty of the vill without licence of the bailiffs; 6*d*. from Henry Bolay to have licence to agree with Isabel Ben*er*eth'; 3*d*. from Andrew Ov*er*lether for licence to agree with Richard le Sclater'; 6*d*. from Walter le Baker' for breaking the assize of bread; 6*d*. from John Stoyl for the same; 3*d*. from Thomas Cre*n* the younger because he did not proceed against John atte Hull'; 4*d*. from Richard Pyres for transgression done to Gilbert Jordain; 3*d*. from Thomas Cre*n* the younger for licence to agree with Isabel atte Hull; 3*d*. from Thomas Rog' because he bought and sold against the liberties of the vill; 3*d*. from John le Gogger' for harbouring a certain stranger against the assize; 3*d*. from Gilbert M*a*rti*n* for transgression done to Thomas Sandr'; 6*d*. from John Colly to have judgement (*cons'*) of the court; 3*d*. from Richard Gu*n*tyr because he is unwilling to keep the peace; 3*d*. from Matilda Gu*n*tir for transgression done against the lord and bailiffs; 4*d*. from Matilda de Hayle for brewing and selling ale against the liberties of the vill; 6*d*. from Richard Perys for unjustly raising the hue on John Cally; 6*d*. from Walkelin Mondelgom' and his ward for a certain concealment; 6*d*. from John le Pechar' and his ward for false presentment; 3*d*. from Andrew Ov*er*lether for false complaint against John P*ri*vite; 6*d*. from John le Pechar' and his ward for concealment; 3*d*. from Matilda la Daye for selling ale within the liberty of the vill without licence; 6*d*. from Robert de Cog' for unjustly raising the hue on the king's highway; 6*d*. from Walkelin Mondelg*om* for selling ale with the measures not sealed; 3*d*. from the same Walkelin for selling ale against the liberty of the assize; 3*d*. from John Lucie for an encroachment made on Robert Mol*endinarius*; 6*d*. from William Tinctor' for unjustly withholding a debt from Thomas Aylward'; 6*d*. from John Pruду*m*me for unjustly raising the hue on Adam le Spic*er*; 3*d*. from Geoffrey Wytherod' for assault done to Adam St*rag*on; 3*d*. from the same Adam for the same done to Geoffrey Wytherod'; 3*d*. from Geoffrey Wytherod' for licence to prosecute Thomas St*ra*gon; 3*d*. from William de Bu*r*to*n* for licence to agree with Ralph Bro*n*; 3*d*. from Alice Danays for licence to agree with Henry le Ledbet*ere*; 6*d*. from Robert Dobb' for enrolling a certain agreement; 3*d*. from Nicholas Wynet' for transgression done to William Produ*m*me; 1*s*. from Christina le Ber' for breaking the assize of ale; 1*s*. from Alice Padenhal' for the same; 1*s*. from Dionysia (*Dyon'*) le Maystr' for the same; 6*d*. from Joan le White for the same; 6*d*. from Agnes le Cachepol for the same; 1*s*. from Agnes Stacy for the same; 1*s*. from Joan, wife of Thomas Fab*er*, for the same; 6*d*. from Dionysia Curveys for the same; 6*d*. from Alice le Cup*ere* for the same; 6*d*. from Alice de C*ra*ule for the same; 1*s*. from Juliana le Salt*ere* for the same; 1*s*. from Margery Bre*n*ton' for the same; 6*d*. from Agnes le Smethes for the same; 6*d*. from Joan Dorm' for the same; 1*s*. from Agnes Dychele; 9*d*. from Matilda Petyt for the same; 1*s*. from Matilda Rauly*n* for the same. Total, £2 1*s*. 4*d*.

1 MS 'Rob' ⟨Lacy⟩ de Cog''.

Total of all receipts, £13 2*s.* 7½*d.*

Expenses
In a certain scaffold (*schulfinstayl*) made anew together with boards sawn for the same by piece-work 3*s.* 7*d.*

Total of all expenses, 3*s.* 7*d.*

And he owes, £12 19*s.* ½*d.*

Cash deliveries
Delivered to Sir G*eoffrey*, treasurer of Wolvesey, by 1 tally, £7 9*s.* ½*d.*

And thus he owes clear, £5 10*s.*

m.14d

Adderbury

Arrears
William, reeve of Adderbury, renders account for £18 11*s.* 6¾*d.* of arrears of John, reeve at the previous year's account.

Rents of assize
The same renders account for £6 8*s.* 9½*d.* for rents of assize at the feast of St Thomas the Apostle (21 December); £6 8*s.* 9½*d.* at Easter (22 April); £6 8*s.* 9½*d.* at St John the Baptist (24 June); £6 8*s.* 10*d.* at Michaelmas (29 September). Total of all rents for the year, £25 15*s.* 2½*d.*

Quittances
In quittance of 1 reeve for the year 5*s.*; 1 smith forging iron for 4 ploughs for the year 4*s.*; 1 hayward who is beadle for the year 4*s.*; 1 cowherd for the year 3*s.* 6*d.*; 1 shepherd for the year 4*s.*; 4 ploughmen who provided all necessaries for 4 ploughs, apart from iron, with 8 oxen for the year, £1 1*s.*, or 5*s.* 3*d.* each; 37 virgaters working every other day each week between the Nativity of St John the Baptist and Michaelmas £1 7*s.* 9*d.*, or 9*d.* a virgater; 5 cottars working for the same time 2*s.* 6*d.*, or 6*d.* each, and know that these workers are bound to weed[1] all the corn, mow all the meadows, toss and carry the hay, and make haycocks therefrom, clean all the lord's buildings within the curia and outside, ditch around the fields, collect dung within the curia and outside and around the sheepcote, reap and bind all the corn, together with 1 boon-work of 166 men, and carry and stack the corn, and collect stubble. Total of quittances, £3 11*s.* 9*d.*

Defaults of rent
In default of the meadow which John de Briddeshorn' held for his life, drawn into demesne because of John's death, 10*s.* Total of defaults of rent, 10*s.*

Total of quittances and defaults of rent, £4 1*s.* 9*d.*

Total of rents remaining, £21 13*s.* 5½*d.*

1 MS omits 'weed', which is used in the rolls dated 1300-1 and 1302-3.

Issues of the manor

The same renders account for 6*s*. 2*d*. from pannage of pigs; 6*s*. from the pasturage of Mihelh*am* sold; 3*s*. from the pasturage of Swetenye sold; 3*s*. from the pasturage of Wlput sold; 2*s*. from Haliwll*e*sterto sold; 6*d*. from Stoplek sold; 3*s*. from Buriholi sold; nothing from the pasturage of oxen on the pastures of Bodicote, Goldewll*e*broc, Asschewll*e*lak' and other parcels of pasture because it was needed for the lord's livestock; 2*s*. 1*d*. from 20 hens from churchscot; 1*s*. from 6 capons from the rent of Richard Mol*endinarius* sold; 4*d*. from 2 capons from the recognizance of Richard Strod' sold; 1*s*. 6*d*. from tolls on inns sold; 15*s*. 6*d*. from 2 cows sold before calving; 7*s*. from 7 calves owed before weaning; £2 9*s*. from 29 wethers, 20 ewes sold from the old of the flock (*recroyn*) before shearing, at 1*s*. a sheep; £3 2*s*. 8*d*. from 21 pigs sold, at 3*s*. each for 20, and 2*s*. 8*d*. for 1; 2*s*. from the hide sold of 1 ox in murrain, the carcass of which was worth nothing; 7*d*. from the hide sold of 1 yearling in murrain; 8*d*. from the carcass of the same yearling sold; 16*s*. 6½*d*. from the skins sold of 17 wethers, 12 ewes and 24 hoggs in murrain before shearing; 1*s*. 7*d*. from the skins sold of 19 sheep[1] in murrain after shearing; 1*s*. 5*d*. from the skins sold of 17 lambs in murrain before weaning; 7½*d*. from the skins sold of 5 lambs in murrain after weaning; 3*s*. from 18 winter rowen cheeses sold after Michaelmas; £2 6*s*. 8*d*. from 116 cheeses sold, which made 4 weys, at 11*s*. 8*d*. a wey; 4*s*. 1*d*. from 16 cheeses sold, weighing ½ wey; 10*s*. from 20 gallons of butter sold, at 6*d*. a gallon; £2 16*s*. 8*d*. from hay sold; £1 from refusals to stack; 15*s*. from the labour services of 3 virgaters sold this year; 8*s*. 9*d*. from dairy produce sold at the audit. Total, £17 10*s*. 4*d*.

Annual recognizance

The same renders account for 3*d*. from Richard Toly so that he may be outside the tithing; 3*d*. from Richard T*ritur*at' so that he may remain within the lord's liberty; 4*d*. from W. Grottew*o*rth' for the same; 4*d*. from John de Ippewll' for the same. Total, 1*s*. 2*d*.

Wheat, rye, dredge, peas and oats sold

The same renders account for £3 5*s*. from 19 qrs of wheat sold, at 3*s*. 4*d*. a qr; £14 19*s*. 7*d*. from 111 qrs of rye sold, at 3*s*. a qr for 62½ qrs, 2*s*. 4*d*. a qr for 42 qrs, and 2*s*. 2*d*. a qr for 6½ qrs; £11 14*s*. 7*d*. from 85 qrs of dredge sold, at 3*s*. a qr for 60½ qrs, and 2*s*. 2*d*. a qr for 24½ qrs; 8*s*. 10*d*. from 6 qrs 5 bus. of peas sold, at 1*s*. 4*d*. a qr; £5 6*s*. from 53 qrs of oats sold, at 2*s*. a qr; 1*s*. 10½*d*. from 5 bus. of rye sold at the audit. Total, £35 15*s*. 10½*d*.

Entry and marriage fines

The same renders account for £1 from six tithings for tithingpenny at the hundred-court of Martinmas; £1 from the same for the same at the hundred-court of Hockday; £1 from W*illiam*, reeve, for marrying his daughter Joan outside. Total £3.

Perquisites

The same renders account for 4*s*. 9*d*. from the perquisites of the court held on Monday after the feast of St Edmund King and Martyr (27 November); 5*s*. 3*d*. from the small amercements of the hundred-court of Martinmas held on Sunday the morrow of the Conception (10 December); 11*s*. from the small amercements of the hundred-court of Hockday held on the eve of the Apostles Peter and Paul (28 June); 11*s*. 9*d*. from the amercements of the court held on Saturday before the Exaltation of the Cross (8 September). Total, £1 12*s*. 9*d*.

1 MS omits 'sheep'.

Total of both, £4 12*s*. 9*d*.

Total of all receipts, £79 13*s*. 7*d*.

Expenses of ploughs
In customary payment to 4 ploughmen who provided all necessaries for the lord's ploughs apart from iron and steel 2*s*. Moreover, they have 1 acre of corn, not manured, at their choice. In iron and steel bought for 4 ploughs for the year 2*s*. 4½*d*. In 2 new ploughshares bought for ploughs 1*s*. 8½*d*. In payment to 4 ploughmen which they are accustomed to have for Saturday ploughings £1 4*s*., because they have the ploughs for 2 Saturdays and the lord for the third Saturday. In payment to the shepherd for the same 3*s*. In 1 ox bought for the plough 10*s*. 6*d*. In 2 oxen bought for the same £1 7*s*. Total, £3 10*s*. 7*d*.

Carts
In 1 new cart bought fitted with iron tyres 11*s*. In 18 clouts with nails bought for the same 1*s*. 1½*d*. In 1 saddle with 1 pair of saddle-pads and 2 collars bought new 1*s*. 8*d*. In other saddle-pads and 2 collars mended 4*d*. In putting 1 felloe on the broken cart with large nails bought for the same and in lengthening the strakes 6*d*. In staffs bought for the cart 2*d*. In fitting 1 cart with axles at various times and in frets bought for the same 8½*d*. In white leather bought for the cart 1*s*. In 2 harnesses bought 4*d*. In stipend of 1 carter for the year 5*s*., because he does not take an acre of corn like the other manorial servants. In shoeing 2 cart-horses for the year which bring dung to the fields 2*s*., for the first time this year. Total, £1 3*s*. 10*d*.

Necessary expenses
In stipend of 1 sawyer of boards for gates, 2*s*. 8*d*. by piece-work. In 1 piece of iron bought for making gudgeons and hoops for the said gates 4*d*. In stipend of the smith working the same 4*d*. In 100 large nails bought for the said gates 1*s*. In hiring 2 carpenters to make and repair the said gates for 8 days 4*s*. In a key bought for the gate of the barton 3½*d*. In washing and shearing 322 sheep 1*s*. 4*d*., at 1*d*. per 20 sheep. In stipend of 1 carpenter making the gate to the hay barton 6*d*. In 2 masons building 2 pieces of wall on both sides of the gate of the barton for 12 days 5*s*., at 2½*d*. each a day. In fattening 22 pigs in the park of Woodstock 3*s*. 8*d*., at 2*d*. a pig. Total, 19*s*. 1½*d*.

Cost of buildings
In 1,000 slates bought for pointing buildings 1*s*. 3*d*. In 60 laths bought for mending the barn 3½*d*. In 90 shaped tiles (*vanelis*) bought for the gutter of the barn 4*s*. In 4½ qrs of lime bought for the same 2*s*. 6*d*. In pointing and mending by piece-work all the defects on the barn and hall with the said slates, laths and lime 4*s*. In hiring 1 roofer to roof the other buildings with straw for 8 days 1*s*. 4*d*. In stipend of 2 women assisting him for the same time 1*s*. In 1 roofer roofing the sheepcote anew for 10 days 2*s*. 6*d*., at 3*d*. a day. In stipend of 2 women assisting him for the same time 1*s*. 8*d*. Total, 18*s*. 6½*d*.

Cost of sheep (*ovium*)
In 8½ stone of grease and 11 gallons of fat bought for sheep 13*s*. 1*d*., at 1*s*. a stone and 5*d*. a gallon. In 3 lb of verdigris bought for the same 1*s*. 8*d*., at 7*d*. a lb, less 1*d*. in all. In 2 lb of vinegar bought for the same 1*s*. 6½*d*. In 4 stalls bought for sheep 6*d*. In

31 hurdles bought for the fold 3*s*. 2½*d*. In 72 gallons of milk bought for the lambs 6*s*., at 1*d*. a gallon. Total, £1 6*s*.

Dairy
In 3 bus. of salt bought for the dairy 1*s*. In 1 cheese-basket bought 7*d*. In canvas bought 6½*d*. In earthenware pans bought 3½*d*. In buckets mended and a press bought 4½*d*. Total, 2*s*. 9½*d*.

Threshing
In threshing 38 qrs 3 bus. of wheat and 149 qrs 1 bus. of rye, old and new grain, by piece-work £1 11*s*. 3*d*., at 2*d*. a qr. In winnowing the same quarters of corn by piece-work 3*s*. 1½*d*., at 1*d*. per 5 struck quarters. In threshing 116 qrs 3 bus. of dredge and 81 qrs 7 bus. of oats by piece-work 16*s*. 6¼*d*., at 1*d*. a qr. In winnowing the same with 12 qrs of oats threshed by manorial servants 2*s*. 11*d*. In 2 sieves bought and others mended 3*d*. In wages of John de Turesmer' carrying out the threshing, 6*s*. 9*d*. by 1 tally. In stipend of the same in part payment of 10*s*., because he takes the rest at Harwell, Witney and Brightwell, 2*s*. Total, £3 2*s*. 9¾*d*.

Barley
In 7 qrs 3 bus. of barley bought to mix with dredge for sowing £1 2*s*. 1½*d*., at 3*s*. a qr. Total, £1 2*s*. 1½*d*.

Harvest-time[1]
In expenses of 1 boon-work of 199 men reaping 140 acres of corn at harvest-time, in bread, ale, meat and cheese bought, 16*s*. 7*d*., or 1*d*. of food (*mensa*) each a day. Moreover customary tenants do 2 boon-works at their own cost, of 8 men for each hide of land; if a third boon-work was done at the lord's cost, each hide would provide 1 man at their own cost; and for a fourth boon-work if it was needed. Total, 16*s*. 7*d*.

Expenses of the steward and bailiff, and other particulars
In expenses of Simon, clerk, for 2 visits for the tourns at Martinmas and Hockday, 6*s*. 8½*d*. by 2 tallies. In 7½ ells of canvas bought for packing wool 1*s*. 10½*d*., at 3*d*. an ell. In packing the said wool 6*d*. In carrying the said wool to Wolvesey 1*s*. 10*d*., with hay and oats bought for the horses and with the hire of 1 boat on the Thames. In expenses of the bailiff for ale, meat, fish, herrings, sheep and other small things bought £1 19*s*. 6*d*. Total, £2 10*s*. 5*d*.

Total of all expenses, £15 12*s*. 9¾*d*.

And he owes, £64 9¼*d*.

Allowances
In allowance of the reeve for mending the bishop's chamber and wardrobe at Adderbury, £1 15*s*. 5*d*. for all costs. Total of allowances, £1 15*s*. 5*d*.

Cash deliveries
Delivered to Sir G*eoffrey*, treasurer of Wolvesey, by 1 tally, £46.

Total of all allowances and cash deliveries, £47 15*s*. 5*d*.

1 MS omits heading.

And he owes clear, £16 5*s.* 4¼*d.*

Issues of the grange

Wheat

{yield: 3-fold plus 1 qr 5 bus.}

The same renders account for 38 qrs 3 bus. of wheat from the issue of the grange, threshed by piece-work, by 2 tallies of struck measure. Total, 38 qrs 3 bus.

Sown over 58 acres, 14½ qrs; that is, 2 bus. an acre. In provision of the bailiff for the year in bread, 4 qrs. In bread for Simon, clerk, 3 bus. by 2 tallies. Sold as noted above, 19½ qrs. Total, 38 qrs 3 bus. None remains.

Rye

{yield: five-fold less 4 qrs 2 bus.}

The same renders account for 150 qrs of rye from the issue of the grange by 3 tallies of struck measure, of which 34 qrs 7 bus. was old grain from the previous year; all threshed by piece-work, apart from 7 bus. by manorial servants. Total, 150 qrs.

Sown over 105 acres, 26 qrs 2 bus.; that is, 2 bus. an acre. Delivered to 1 carter for the year, 4 qrs 2½ bus., taking a quarter every 12 weeks. Delivered to the other carter for the year apart from 7 weeks, 3 qrs 6 bus., taking the same livery this year for the great mixing of dung. Delivered to 1 dairymaid from the Annunciation (25 March) until Michaelmas (29 September), 2 qrs 2 bus., taking the same livery and this year taking it all in rye because rye did not sell as dearly as dredge. Delivered to 1 keeper of lambs for 6 weeks, 2 bus. Delivered to 1 shepherd, ½ qr. In provision of the bailiff's attendant for the year, 1 qr. Sold as noted above, 111 qrs. Sold at the audit, 5 bus. Total, 150 qrs. None remains.

Dredge

{yield: four-fold less 1 qr 5 bus.}

The same renders account for 116 qrs 3 bus. of dredge from the issue of the grange, by 2 tallies of struck measure; 7 qrs 3 bus. of barley bought as noted above. Total, 123 qrs 6 bus.

Sown over 102 acres, 38 qrs 2 bus.; that is, 3 bus. an acre. Delivered to 1 shepherd, ½ qr. Sold as noted above, 85 qrs. Total, 123 qrs 6 bus. None remains.

Peas

The same renders account for 11 qrs 1 bus. of peas from the issue of the grange, threshed by labour service. Total, 11 qrs 1 bus.

Sown, 3 qrs 5 bus. In supporting pigs, 7 bus. Sold as noted above, 6 qrs 5 bus. Total, 11 qrs 1 bus. None remains.

Oats

{yield: 3½-fold plus 5 qrs 7½ bus.}

The same renders account for 93 qrs 7 bus. of oats from the issue of the grange by struck measure, of which 81 qrs 7 bus. threshed by piece-work and 12 qrs threshed by manorial servants. Total, 93 qrs 7 bus.

Sown over 80 acres, 30 qrs; that is, 3 bus. an acre. In fodder of the horses of Simon, clerk, for 2 visits, 5 bus. by 2 tallies. In fodder of the lord's cart-horses for the year, 9 qrs 2 bus., because they have 2 horses on loan (*prest'*). In making meal, 1 qr. Sold as noted above, 53 qrs. Total, 93 qrs 7 bus. None remains.

Stock

Cart-horses: 2 remain. Total, 2. 2 remain.

Oxen: 24 remain; 1 addition; 3 bought. Total, 28. 1 in murrain, the carcass of which was worth nothing. Total, 1. 27 remain.
Bulls: 1 remains. Total, 1. 1 remains.
Cows: 14 remain; 3 additions. Total, 17. 2 sold before calving at Martinmas (11 November) as noted above. Total, 2. 15 remain.
Steers: 4 remain, which were bullocks and heifers at the last account. 1 added to oxen, and 3 to cows. Total, 4. None remain.
Bullocks: 4 remain, 2 of them male, which were yearlings at the last account. Total, 4. They remain, 2 of them male.
Yearlings: 7 remain, 5 of them male, which were calves at the last account; 1 from strays. Total, 8. 1 in murrain, the hide and carcass of which was sold as noted above. Total, 1. 7 remain, 4 of them male.
Calves: 15 from the offspring of the aforesaid cows, because 2 sold before calving at Martinmas. Total, 15. 1 in tithe; 7 sold as noted above. Total, 8. 7 remain, 2 of them male.
Wethers: 145 remain; 49 added from stock. Total, 194. 29 sold before shearing at Martinmas as noted above; 18 in murrain before shearing, 4 after shearing; 1 in customary payment for the mowing after shearing. Total, 52. 142 remain, 7 of them rams.
Ewes: 140 remain; 58 additions. Total, 198. 20 sold at Martinmas before breeding and shearing; 6 in murrain before breeding and shearing, 7 after breeding and before shearing, 5 after shearing. Total, 38. 160 remain.
Hoggs: 144 from lambs. Total, 144. 27 in murrain before shearing, 10 after shearing; 49 added to wethers, and 58 to ewes. Total, 144. None remain.
[Lambs]: 93 from the offspring of the said ewes, and not more because 20 sold before breeding and shearing, 6 in murrain before breeding, and 21 sterile. Total, 93. 19 in murrain before weaning; 7 in tithe; 1 in customary payment to the shepherd; 5 in murrain after weaning. Total, 32. 61 remain of both sexes.
Pigs: 23 remain over a year old; 15 additions as made clear below. Total, 38. 3 in murrain; 21 sold as noted above; 3 in the larder. Total, 27. 11 remain, 1 of them a boar (*verr'*).
Sows: 2 remain. Total, 2. 2 remain.
Hoggets: 15 from piglets. Total, 15. 15 added to pigs above.
Piglets: 25 from the offspring of the said sows. Total, 25. 2 in tithe; 1 in customary payment to 1 reeve. Total, 3. 22 remain, 13 of them aged three quarters of a year, 3 aged one quarter of a year, and 6 suckling.

m.15
Cheese {yield of cow 4*s*. and sheep 2*d*. with 2 cheeses valued at 1*s*.}: 18 rowen cheeses received after Michaelmas. Total, 18. All sold as noted above. 149 cheeses from the issue of the dairy between Friday the morrow of the Invention of the Cross (4 May) and Michaelmas (29 September), at 1 cheese a day, both days included. Total, 149. 15 in tithe; 1 in customary payment to the dairymaid; 1 in customary payment for the mowers' sheep (*machsipp'*); 132 sold as noted above, which made 4½ weys. Total, 149. None remain.
Fleeces {yield 5¾*d*. less ¾*d*. in all}: 322 from the shearing of the said sheep. Total, 322. 32 in tithe; 1 in customary payment to the shepherd; 289 sent to Wolvesey. Total, 322. None remain.
Skins before shearing: 58 from 18 wethers, 13 ewes and 27 hoggs in murrain before shearing. Total, 58. 5 in tithe; 53 sold as noted above. Total, 58. None remain.

Bare skins after shearing: 19 from sheep[1] in murrain after shearing. Total, 19. All sold as noted above.
Lambskins: 19 from lambs in murrain before weaning, 5 after weaning. Total, 24. 22 sold as noted above; 2 in tithe. Total 24. None remain.
Peacocks: 7 peacocks and peahens remain; 3 offspring. Total, 10. All remain, 3 of them male.
Capons: 10 from rents and recognizances. Total, 10. All sold as noted above.
Hens: 20 from churchscot. Total, 20. All sold as noted above.
Larder: ⌈6⌉ hams received for the larder as noted above. Total, 6. 3 in provision of the bailiff. Total, 3. 3 remain.
Butter: 20 gallons from the issue of the dairy. Total, 20. All sold as noted above.
Utensils: 4 ploughs with equipment remain. 1 cart with iron tyres and 1 of wood remain; 1 cart with iron tyres bought. Total, 3. 1 broken wooden cart used. Total, 1. 2 carts with iron tyres remain. 1 iron fork, 1 pick-axe, 2 tables in the hall, 1 spade, 1 shovel, 1 ½-bushel measure, 2 ladders, 1 lead oven, 4 large tubs, 4 kimnels, 3 tines, 3 buckets, 1 hemp rope, 1 ewer with a basin, a brass pot with 1 pitcher, 1 mortar, 2 sacks, 1 cloth for winnowing, 1 cooking-pot, 1 brass pan remain.

Ivinghoe

Arrears

William, bailiff, and William, reeve, render account for £2 5*s*. 1*d*. of arrears from the previous year. Delivered to Sir G*eoffrey*, treasurer of Wolvesey, £2 5*s*. 1*d*. by 1 tally. They are quit.

Rents of assize

The same render account for £6 9*s*. 10½*d*. for all rents of assize at Christmas; £6 9*s*. 10½*d*. at the Annunciation (25 March); £6 9*s*. 10½*d*. at the Nativity of the blessed John the Baptist (24 June); £6 9*s*. 10¾*d*. at Michaelmas (29 September). Total of all rents for the year, £25 19*s*. 6¼*d*.

Quittances

In quittance of 1 reeve for the year 5*s*.; 1 beadle who is hayward and sowed corn for the year 2*s*.; 1 forester who kept Cherlewod' and Cu*mbe* for the year 2*s*. 2*d*.; 1 swineherd for the year 2*s*.; 5 of the lord's ploughmen for the year 15*s*., or 3*s*. each; 4 workers working every day apart from Saturday from Michaelmas until Christmas who, together with the cart-horses of the curia, harrowed lands for wheat and drained water from the same, 3*s*. 10*d*., of whom 1 was quit of 1*s*. 3*d*., 1 of 1*s*., 1 of 10*d*., and 1 of 9*d*.; 4 workers working the same between Christmas and the Annunciation who, together with the cart-horses of the curia, harrowed lands for oats, 3*s*. 10*d*., of whom 3 were each quit of 1*s*., and 1 of 10*d*.; 2 workers working the same between the Annunciation and the Nativity of the blessed John the Baptist who harrowed lands for barley and enclosed with hedges, 1*s*. 10½*d*., of whom 1 was quit of 1*s*., and 1 of 10½*d*.; 10 workers working the same between the feast of St John the Baptist and Michaelmas who weeded corn, mowed and gathered hay, and carried corn, 10*s*. 3*d*., of whom 1 was quit of 1*s*. 3*d*., and 9 of 1*s*. each. Total of quittances, £2 5*s*. 11½*d*.

Defaults of rent

In default of the land of the earl of Salisbury at Gaddesden 18*s*. Total of defaults of rent, 18*s*.

1 MS omits 'sheep'.

Total of quittances and defaults of rent, £3 3*s*. 11½*d*.

Total remaining, £22 15*s*. 6¾*d*.

Issues of the manor
The same render account for 9*s*. 8*d*. from pannage of pigs of the whole vill; nothing from foreign pannage because there was no mast; £1 from dead wood blown down by the wind in Cherlewod'; 10*s*. from winter ploughing this year, that is, 6*d*. a ploughman from 20 ploughmen; nothing from Lenten ploughing because it was ploughed; 5*s*. from 10 ploughmen for release from summer ploughing, at 6*d*. a ploughman; £1 10*s*. 3*d*. from 60½ virgates of land for release from transport-service this year, at 6*d*. a virgate, because no transport-service was done to London or elsewhere; 12*s*. from the agistment of 6 old beasts (*av'*) and 18 bullocks in the pasture of the grove for the summer, at 6*d*. an old beast and 4*d*. a bullock; nothing from coarse wool this year because it is sent to Wolvesey; nothing from lambs' fleeces this year because the lambs were not sheared; 1*s*. 3*d*. from wool locks this year; 3*s*. 1*d*. from winter cheese sold; £2 17*s*. 6*d*. from 5¾ weys of summer cheese sold, at 10*s*. a wey; 7*s*. 1*d*. from 17 gallons of butter sold, at 5*d*. a gallon; 5½*d*. from honey and wax sold from stock; 3*s*. 8*d*. from stubble sold; 9*s*. from old hay sold; 17*s*. from old hay sold for the queen's use; £1 from hay sold this year; 1*s*. 4*d*. from taverns; 1*s*. 4*d*. from 2 qrs of apples sold; 10*s*. from 40 geese sold, received from the beadle at Michaelmas according to custom, at 3*d*. a goose; 3*s*. 4*d*. from 80 chickens sold, received from the same beadle at the same Michaelmas according to custom; 1*s*. from 303 eggs sold, received from the same beadle at Easter according to custom; 8*s*. from the men of Netley for release from their labour service at harvest-time this year; 2½*d*. from the tail and feathers of 1 peacock sold; nothing from weaning lambs this year because the corn was thin; 2*s*. 2*d*. from 1 tunic from the heriot of Richard Sutoris sold; 4*d*. from 1 axe from the heriot of William Peck' sold; 19*s*. 8*d*. from dairy produce sold at the audit. Total, £12 13*s*. 4*d*.

Issues of stock
The same render account for £1 3*s*. from 6 old and feeble plough-horses sold, at 5*s*. each for 2, 3*s*. 6*d*. each for 2, and 3*s*. each for 2; £3 19*s*. 2*d*. from 8 oxen sold, at 11*s*. each for 4, 10*s*. each for 3, and 5*s*. 2*d*. for 1 killed for fear of murrain; 11*s*. from 1 bull sold; £1 8*s*. 6*d*. from 4 cows sold, 3 of them at Martinmas, at 8*s*. 6*d*. each for 2, 7*s*. 6*d*. for 1, and 4*s*. for 1 sick cow before calving; 4*s*. from 1 steer sold; 10*s*. from 11 calves sold, at 1*s*. each for 4, 11*d*. each for 2, and 10*d*. each for 5; 2*s*. 4*d*. from the hide sold of 1 ox in murrain; 1*s*. from the hides sold of 2 yearlings in murrain; £1 15*s*. from 26 wethers and 4 ewes sold at Martinmas, at 1*s*. 2*d*. each; £1 4*s*. 6*d*. from the skins sold of 40 wethers, 31 ewes and 26 hoggs in murrain before shearing, at 4*d*. a wether, 3*d*. a ewe, and 2½*d*. a hogg; 1*s*. 2½*d*. from the skins sold of 1 wether, 5 ewes, in murrain after shearing, and 5 lambs, at 2*d*. a wether, 1½*d*. a ewe, and 1*d*. a lamb; 3*s*. 4*d*. from 3 peacocks sold, 1 of them a male; £3 15*s*. from 30 gelded pigs sold, at 3*s*. each for 10, 2*s*. 6*d*. each for 10, and 2*s*. each for 10; 2*s*. from 2 calves sold at the audit; £1 16*s*. from 54 wethers sold at Martinmas because sick, at 8*d*. each. Total, £16 15*s*. 11½*d*.

Annual recognizance
The same render account for 6*d*. from Gilbert son of Richard for annual recognizance; 3*d*. from Gilbert Lylye for the same; 6*d*. from Richard son of Gilbert for the same; nothing from Richard Sutor' this year because he is dead, that is, 6*d*. from

Martin Fab*er* of Netley for the same; 3*d*. from Hugh Reygnild' for the same; nothing from Gervase de Asschewoll' this year because he is dead, that is, 3*d*. from Thomas le Bolt*ere* for the same; 6*d*. from John le Nywebond' for the same; 3*d*. from Guy Car*eter* for the same; 3*d*. from Peter son of Michael for the same. Total, 3*s*. 3*d*.

Corn and malt mill[1]

The same render account for £2 19*s*. 11*d*. from 23 qrs 5 bus. of corn from the whole issue of the mill sold, at 3*s*. a qr for 8 qrs, 2*s*. 8*d*. a qr for 7 qrs, and 2*s*. a qr for 8 qrs 5 bus.; 10*s*. 4*d*. from 3 qrs 5 bus. of malt sold, at 3*s*. a qr for 2 qrs, and 2*s*. 8*d*. a qr for 1 qr 5 bus. Total, £3 10*s*. 3*d*.

Wheat, barley, oats and beans sold

The same render account for £41 14*s*. from 168 qrs of wheat sold, at 5*s*. a qr for 162 qrs, and 4*s*. a qr for 6 qrs; £2 2*s*. 3*d*. from 9 qrs 6 bus. of wheat sold for the queen's use, at 4*s*. 4*d*. a qr; £1 13*s*. 4*d*. from 10 qrs of barley sold, at 3*s*. 4*d*. a qr; £5 1*s*. from 60½ qrs of oats from the demesne sold, at 2*s*. a qr for 20½ qrs, and 1*s*. 6*d*. a qr for 40 qrs; £3 18*s*. 9*d*. from 39 qrs 3 bus. of oats from the vill sold according to custom, at 2*s*. a qr; 12*s*. 3*d*. from 6 qrs 1 bus. of beans sold, at 2*s*. a qr; 1*s*. 5½*d*. from 3½ bus. of barley sold at the audit, at 5*d*. a bus. Total of all corn sold, £55 3*s*. ½*d*.

Entry and marriage fines

The same render account for 2*s*. from Geoffrey atte Slade for marrying Matilda his daughter outside; 1*s*. from Agnes atte Slad' for marrying herself within; 2*s*. from Matilda la Dreyestr' for marrying Alice her daughter outside; 2*s*. from Muriel, who was wife of William Peck', to retain 1 house and ½ acre of asserted land which belonged to the said William her husband; 13*s*. 4*d*. from Walter Mol*endinarius* to have Alice atte Pu*nd*' with her land; 2*s*. from Juliana, who was wife of Richard Sutoris, to have entry to 1 house which Richard Sutor formerly held; £1 6*s*. 8*d*. from John, son of John Jacob, for entry to two virgates of land which the said John his father held; 4*s*. from Richard le Wych' for marrying Leticia his daughter within; 6*s*. 8*d*. from Walter Bast for marrying Matilda his daughter outside; 3*s*. 4*d*. from John Bucok' to have entry to 1 butt of land by concession and surrender of John Hod, and he will relieve the said John Hod of 4*d*. annual rent; 3*s*. 6*d*. from William le Car*eter* to have entry to 1½ acres of assart by concession and surrender of Robert de Chyssend'; £4 from William, son of Herbert Reygnild, to have entry to 1 messuage with 1 virgate of customary land which he has held of his father because his elder brother John said in full court that he was unwilling to fine for the said land, that is, he quitclaimed wholly his right to the use of the said William; 18*s*. 8*d*. from 10 tithings for tithingpenny at the hundred-court of Martinmas; 18*s*. 8*d*. from the same tithings for tithingpenny at the hundred-court of Hockday. Total, £9 3*s*. 10*d*.

Pleas and perquisites

The same render account for £3 10*s*. 11*d*. from the pleas and perquisites of all the courts this year; £2 from the reeve for many transgressions of which he was convicted at the audit. Total, £5 10*s*. 11*d*.

Total of entry fines with perquisites, £14 14*s*. 9*d*.

Total of all receipts, £125 16*s*. 1¾*d*.

1 Scribe misspelt 'bladum' as 'doladum' and 'braes*ium*' as 'doraes*ium*'.

Expenses for ploughs

In ironwork of 5 ploughs for the year 7*s*. 10*d*. In 2 ploughshares bought 1*s*. 6*d*. Moreover they have 1 ploughshare as made clear above. Nothing accounted for forging the said ironwork because the smith takes 2 acres of wheat as they lie in the field for forging the same when the ploughmen are ploughing for the whole year. In 4 iron spurs bought 8*d*. In stipend of 1 carpenter making new ploughs, repairing old ploughs, and making harrows and yokes from the lord's timber 3*s*. 2*d*., because the manorial servant who by custom made these is dead. In 15 oxen bought £8 18*s*. 2*d*., at 13*s*. 5*d*. each for 2, 12*s*. 6*d*. each for 4, 12*s*. each for 3, 11*s*. 5*d*. each for 3, 10*s*. 6½*d*. each for 2, and 10*s*. for 1. In 12 qrs 2 bus. of wheat bought for sowing £2 4*s*. 11*d*., at 3*s*. 8*d*. a qr. In 34 qrs of maslin bought for the liveries of the manorial servants £4 4*s*., at 3*s*. a qr for 8 qrs, 2*s*. 8*d*. a qr for 12 qrs, and 2*s*. a qr for 14 qrs. In 4½ qrs of oats bought for fodder of horses 6*s*. 9*d*., at 1*s*. 6*d*. a qr. In hay bought £1, because hay was taken for the queen's use. In forage bought for stock £1 16*s*. 1*d*. In stipend of 5 oxherds for ½ year in winter 6*s*. 8*d*., or 1*s*. 4*d*. each, because each manorial servant takes corn at harvest-time for the other ½ year in summer, that is, ½ acre of wheat and ½ acre of oats as they lie in the field. Total, £19 8*s*. 3*d*.

Expenses for carts and wagons

In clouts and nails for the cart for the year 1*s*. 2*d*. In white leather for mending harnesses of the cart 1*s*. 1*d*. In grease bought for the year 4*d*. In 5 halters for plough-horses made from their own hair 1*d*. In mending saddle-pads 1½*d*. In 1 collar bought 6*d*. In a wooden base for 1 cart-saddle 1½*d*. In repairing old collars 1*d*. In 1 pair of traces bought 7*d*. In making 2 pairs of wheels from the lord's timber for the cart with iron tyres and for clearing dung. In new large nails and clamps and frets with the stipend of the smith fitting 1 pair of wheels with old iron tyres 6*s*. 2*d*. In fitting the cart with axles for the year 4*d*. In shoeing 2 cart-horses for the year by piece-work 2*s*. In stipend of 1 carter for ½ year in winter 1*s*. 4*d*., because for the other ½ year he takes corn in the field like the rest of the manorial servants. In clouts and nails bought for wagons 6*d*. In grease and tallow bought for the same 2*d*. Total, 15*s*. 5*d*.

Dairy

In linen cloth for the dairy 3*d*. In earthenware pots and pans bought 3½*d*. In a press 3*d*. In ½ qr of salt bought 1*s*. 10*d*., at 7*d*. for 1 bus., and 5*d*. each for 3 bus. In 1 colander bought 1½*d*. In vinegar and pigs' fat for greasing sick sheep 5*s*. 3*d*. In hurdles for the fold, nothing this year. In 5 ells of canvas for packing wool 1*s*. 1½*d*., at 2½*d*. an ell. In stipend of 1 shepherd and 1 cowherd in winter 2*s*., because for the other ½ year they take corn in the field like the rest of the manorial servants. In stipend of 1 dairymaid this year 2*s*. 6*d*., because for 13 weeks there was no dairymaid. In carrying wool to Wolvesey 4*d*. Total, 13*s*. 11½*d*.

Expenses of buildings and small necessaries

In propping up the wardrobe of the bishop's chamber 2*d*. In re-roofing in places the larger barn, unroofed by the wind, where it was necessary 1*s*. 8*d*. In re-roofing the small barn in places 8*d*. In roofing one part of the long stable throughout 10*d*. In 1 lock with a key bought for the garden-gate 1½*d*. In ⌈planting⌉ and watering beans 10*d*. In gelding (*masculand'*) 26 piglets 5½*d*. Total, 4*s*. 9*d*.

Mowing of the meadow

In customary payment for the mowing of the meadow 1*s*. Total, 1*s*.

Purchase of stock
In 28 wethers bought before shearing £2 8*s*. 7*d*., at 1*s*. 9*d*. each for 18, and 1*s*. 8½*d*. each for 10. Total, £2 8*s*. 7*d*.

Threshing and winnowing
In mending 1 new sieve and other old ones 3½*d*. In 1 new sack bought 9¼*d*. In remaking (*refic'*) old broken baskets 2*d*. In threshing 169½ qrs of wheat with curall £1 8*s*. 3*d*., at 2*d*. a qr. In winnowing, nothing, because it was winnowed by labour service. In threshing barley and beans, nothing this year, because it was threshed by the lord's manorial servants. In winnowing, nothing, for the above[1] reason. In threshing 134 qrs of oats 8*s*. 4½*d*., at ¾*d*. a qr, and winnowed by labour service as above. Total, £1 17*s*. 10¼*d*.

Cost of the mill
In 20 ells of canvas bought for the sails of the mill 5*s*., at 3½*d*. each for 10, and 3*d*. each for 10. In steeling and sharpening bills for the year 3*d*. In tallow and grease bought for the same for the year 6*d*. In white leather for the clapper of the mill 2*d*. In stipend of 1 miller for ½ year in winter 1*s*., because for the other ½ year he takes corn at harvest-time. Total, 6*s*. 11*d*.

Expenses of the steward
In expenses of the steward at the hundred-court of Martinmas 8*s*. In expenses of the steward for his 1 visit about the Purification (2 February) 5*s*. 9¼*d*. In expenses of Simon de Farham holding the tourn of Hockday (1 May) 10*s*. 1*d*. Total, £1 3*s*. 10½*d*.

Expenses of the bailiff
In expenses of the bailiff until the feast of St Thomas the Apostle (21 December) 7*s*. 11*d*. In wages of the same bailiff from the feast of St Thomas the Apostle until Michaelmas £3 15*s*. In fur for the winter livery of the same 2*s*. Total, £4 4*s*. 11*d*.

Expenses of the sheriff
In expenses of the sheriff of Buckinghamshire for his 1 visit about the feast of St Vincent (22 January) 5*s*. 9*d*. In expenses of the assessors of the fifteenth to have their favour in the assessment 1*s*. 7*d*. Total, 7*s*. 4*d*.

Total of all expenses, £31 12*s*. 10*d*.

And he owes, £94 3*s*. 3¾*d*.

Cash deliveries
Delivered to Sir *Geoffrey*, treasurer of Wolvesey, by 1 tally, £80.

And thus he owes clear, £14 3*s*. 3¾*d*.

Issues of the mill
The same render account for 23 qrs 5 bus. from the whole issue of the corn mill, and all sold as noted above; 3 qrs 5 bus. from the whole issue of the malt mill, and all sold as noted above.

1 MS '⟨p*r*ius⟩'.

Issues of the grange

Wheat

{yield: 5-fold less . . . qrs[1] 2 bus.}

The same render account for 201 qrs[2] 5 bus. of wheat from the whole issue of the grange in the granary by struck measure; 6½ qrs by estimation given to the manorial servants in acres as they lie in the field; 12 qrs 2 bus. bought. Total, 220 qrs 3 bus. Sown over 84 acres measured by the perch which lie in the middle field, 32 qrs 2 bus.; that is, 3 bus. an acre, plus 6 bus. in all, because the sowing season was showery and miry; and know that two roods were sown by workers with their own seed. In customary payment for the mowing of the meadows, 6 bus. In provision of the steward at the hundred-court of Martinmas, 3 bus. In provision of the same at the hundred-court of Hockday in bread, 3 bus. In provision of the bailiff from Michaelmas until the feast of St Thomas the Apostle (21 December) in bread, 1½ qrs, because he took the rest at West Wycombe. Given to the manorial servants for their stipend by estimation in acres as they lie in the field, 6½ qrs; that is, 2 qrs to 1 smith for the year, 4½ qrs to 1 carter, 5 ploughmen, 1 miller, 1 cowherd and 1 shepherd for ½ year in summer. **{Henceforth the manorial servants should be hired for money just like the [other] workers in the manor and the corn be reserved for the use of the lord}**[3] In provision of the sheriff for his 1 visit about the feast of St Vincent (22 January) in bread, 3 bus. Given to a certain marshal purveying for the Lord Edward, son of the king, in preparation for the tournament at Dunstable, to have his favour, ½ qr of oats and hay. Sold as noted above, 177 qrs 6 bus.

Curall

The same render account for 10 qrs 3 bus. from the whole issue of curall, of the same wheat, from the grange in the granary by struck measure; all mixed below with barley for the liveries of the manorial servants.

Mancorn

Nothing from mancorn this year because the white field (*alb*us *ca*m*p'*) is not sown.

m.15d

Barley

{yield: 4-fold plus 1 qr 6 bus.}

The same render account for 19 qrs 6 bus. from the whole issue of barley from the grange in the granary by struck measure; 10 qrs 3 bus. of curall received above and mixed with that for the liveries of the manorial servants; 9 qrs 7 bus. of beans received below and mixed with barley for the same; 34 qrs of maslin bought above and mixed with that for the same. Total, 74 qrs.

Sown over 8½ acres and 1 rood measured by the perch which lie above Benam, 4 qrs 3 bus.; that is, ½ qr an acre. Delivered to 1 carter, 5 ploughmen, who each take a quarter every 8 weeks for the year, 39 qrs. Delivered to 1 miller, 1 shepherd, 1 cowherd and 1 dairymaid, who each take a quarter every 10 weeks for the year, except the dairymaid who takes one every 12 weeks, 18 qrs 6½ bus., because there was no dairymaid for 13 weeks for a want of milking. Delivered to 1 keeper of lambs for the time of their weaning, that is, from Wednesday the feast of St Mark the

1 MS '. . .ij qrs'.

2 MS '⟨j qr⟩'.

3 MS '. . . co loc*entur* fam' pro denar' sic' . . . i op*er*arii i*n* pat*ria* & reserve*tur* blad' . . . opus d*om*ini'.

Evangelist (25 April) until Wedenesday before the feast of St Barnabas the Apostle (6 June), for 6 weeks, 3 bus. In supporting pigs and piglets in winter, 1 qr. Sold as noted above, 10 qrs. Sold at the audit, 3½ bus.

Oats from the demesne
{yield: two-fold less 7 qrs 5 bus.}
The same render account for 167 qrs 7 bus. from the whole issue of oats from the demense from the grange in the granary by struck measure; 4½ qrs by estimation in acres as they lie in the field given to the manorial servants for their stipends in summer; 39 qrs 3 bus. of oats from the vill according to custom; 4½ qrs bought. Total, 216 qrs 2 bus.
Sown over 145 acres measured by the perch which lie above Benam, 90 qrs 5 bus.; that is, 5 bus. an acre. In fodder of 2 cart-horses for the year, 15 qrs. In fodder of the steward's horses at the hundred-court of Martinmas, 7 bus. In fodder of the steward's horses for his 1 visit about the Purification, ½ qr. In fodder of the horses of Simon de Farh*am* holding the tourn of Hockday, ½ qr. In fodder of the bailiff's horse from Michaelmas until the feast of St Thomas the Apostle, 1 qr 2 bus., because he took the rest at West Wycombe. Given to 9 manorial servants for their stipends for ½ year in summer by estimation in acres as they lie in the field, 4½ qrs; that is, ½ qr each by estimation in an acre as it lies. In fodder of the sheriff's horses for his 1 visit about the feast of St Vincent, ½ qr. Given to the marshal purveying for the Lord Edward, son of the king, in preparation for the tournament at Dunstable, to have his favour, 2 qrs of oats and hay. In fodder of the horses of the bishop's squires coming for the tournament at Dunstable, 5 bus. Sold as noted above, 99 qrs 7 bus.

Beans
{yield: six-fold plus 1 bus.}
The same render account for 20 qrs 1 bus. from the whole issue of beans from the grange in the granary by struck measure.
Sown, 4 qrs 1 bus. Mixed above with barley for the liveries of the manorial servants, 9 qrs 7 bus. Sold as noted above, 6 qrs 1 bus.

Stock

Cart-horses: 2 remain from the previous year; 2 remain.
Plough-horses: 10 remain from the previous year; 6 sold; 4 remain.
Foals: none this year because the female plough-horses were feeble and sold.
Oxen: 32 remain from the previous year; 2 added from steers; 1 from the heriot of Alice Reygnild; 1 from the heriot of John Jacob; 15 bought. Total, 51. 1[1] in murrain about the Annunciation (25 March), the hide of which is answered for and the flesh worth nothing; 1 sold about Hockday (1 May) because sick and was killed for fear of murrain; 7 sold at Martinmas (11 November). Total, 9. 42 remain.
Bulls: 2 remain from the previous year; 1 sold; 1 remains.
Cows: 22 remain from the previous year; 5 added from steers; 1 from the heriot of Henry de Wytewey, which was sterile. Total, 28. 1 sold before calving for fear of murrain; 3 sold at Martinmas. Total, 4. 24 remain.
Steers: 8 remain from the previous year's bullocks; 1 sold; 2 added to oxen, 5 to cows; none remain.
Bullocks: 3 remain from the previous year's yearlings; 3 remain, all of them male.
Yearlings: 5 remain from the previous year's calves; 2 in murrain; 3 remain, 2 of them male.

1 MS omits '1'.

Calves: 21 from the offspring of the cows from stock this year, because 4 sold before calving and 3 sterile; 2 in tithe; 11 sold; 2 sold at the audit; 6 remain, 1 of them male.
Wethers: 175 remain from the previous year; 16 added from hoggs; 28 bought before shearing. Total, 219. 40 in murrain before shearing, 1 after shearing; 54 sold at Martinmas; 1 in customary payment for the mowing of the meadows after shearing; 26 sold at Martinmas. Total, 122. 97 remain, 3 of them rams.
Ewes: 85 remain from the previous year; 11 added from hoggs. Total, 96. 33 in murrain before giving birth and shearing, 5 afterwards; 4 sold at Martinmas. Total, 42. 54 remain.
Hoggs: 56 remain from the previous year's lambs; 29 in murrain before shearing; 16 added to wethers, 11 to ewes; none remain.
Lambs: 34 from the offspring of the ewes from stock this year, because 4 sold at Martinmas, 33 in murrain before giving birth, and 14 sterile; 3 in tithe; 5 in murrain; 26 remain.
Boars: 1 remains from the previous year; 1 remains.
Gelded pigs: 36 remain from the previous year; 24 added from hoggets. Total, 60. 30 sold; 30 remain.
Sows: 2 remain from the previous year; 2 remain.
Hoggets: 25 remain from the previous year's piglets; 1 in murrain; 24 added to gelded pigs; none remain.
Piglets: 18 from the offspring of 2 sows about the feast of St Thomas the Apostle (21 December); 13 from the offspring of the same sows about the Nativity of St John the Baptist (24 June). Total, 31. 3 in tithe; 1 in customary payment to the swineherd. Total, 4. 27 remain, 16 of them of 3 terms, and 11 of 1 term, and all of them male and gelded.
Coarse fleeces {yield of fleece 4½*d.* plus 1*s.* 1*d.* in all}: 158 produced at the shearing; 13 in tithe, because the wool of 28 wethers not tithed; 1 in customary payment to the shepherd; 144 sent to Wolvesey, which made 1 wey and 2 cloves. A wey is of 26 cloves and a clove of 7 lb.
Lambs' fleeces: none this year because the lambs not sheared.
Skins before shearing: 94 from wethers, 34 from ewes, 29 from hoggs in murrain before shearing. Total, 157. 11 in tithe, because 47 in murrain before the Purification (2 February) which ought not to be tithed; 146 sold; none remain.
Skins after shearing: 1 from a wether, 5 from ewes in murrain after shearing, and 5 from lambs after weaning. Total, 11. All sold.
Winter cheese: 41 made, because 16 gallons of milk consumed by the lord's lambs. All sold as noted above.
Summer cheese {yield of cow 4*s.* and sheep 2*d.* with 16 gallons of milk and 1 cheese for customary payment which are valued at 1*s.* 8*d.*}: 158 cheeses made between Wednesday the feast of St Mark the Evangelist (25 April) and Michaelmas, both days included; 15 in tithe; 1 in customary payment for the mowing of the meadows; 142 sold as noted above, which made 5¾ weys.
Butter: 17 gallons from the issue of the dairy; all sold as noted above.
Peacocks: 8 remain from the previous year; no offspring from them; 3 sold; 2 sent to the bishop at Southwark; 3 remain.
Geese: 40 from the beadle at Michaelmas according to custom; all sold as noted above.
Chickens: 80 from the same beadle at Michaelmas according to custom; all sold as noted above.
Eggs: 303 from the same beadle at Easter according to custom; all sold as noted above.

Wood:[1] 1 swarm of bees produced from waifs (*vago*) this year; 1 swarm produced from the offspring of that. Total, 2. 2 remain, which yield honey and wax.
Cider: 1 full cask made this year; 1 remains.
Ploughshares: 1 from Roger de Clav*er*lye for the tenement which William Sewale held for annual recognizance; used for ploughs; none remain.
Utensils: 1 cart with iron tyres with its equipment remains from the previous year. 2 wagons remain from the previous year. 4 hemp ropes remain from the previous year; 2 bought. Total, 6. 2 used in the manor; 4 remain. 2 sacks remain from the previous year; 1 bought. Total, 3. 2 used in the manor; 1 remains. 1 basket remains from the previous year. 1 brass pan remains from the previous year. 1 ewer and 1 basin remain from the previous year. 1 cask remains from the previous year. 1 tine remains from the previous year. 1 mattock remains from the previous year.

West Wycombe

Arrears

William, bailiff, and Robert, reeve, render account for £14 7*s*. 1¾*d*. of arrears from the previous year. Delivered to Sir G*eoffrey*, treasurer of Wolvesey, £14 7*s*. 1¾*d*. by 1 tally. They are quit.

Rents of assize

The same render account for £10 5*s*. 4½*d*. for all rents of assize at Christmas; £10 12*s*. ¾*d*. at the Annunciation (25 March); £10 5*s*. 4¼*d*. at the Nativity of the blessed John the Baptist (24 June); £10 16*s*. 5½*d*. at Michaelmas (29 September). Total of all rents for the year, £41 19*s*. 3*d*.

Increment

The same render account for 1*d*. from Hugh Fab*er* for the increment of rent for 1 small plot to enlarge his house. Total of rents with increment, £41 19*s*. 4*d*.

Quittances

In quittance of 1 reeve for the year 5*s*.; 2 workers holding 2 virgates of land working every day apart from Saturday between Michaelmas and Christmas, 2 workers working the same between Christmas and the Annunciation, 2 workers working the same between the Annunciation and the Nativity of the blessed John the Baptist, and 4 workers working the same between the Nativity of St John the Baptist and Michaelmas, 12*s*. 6*d*., each having 1*s*. 3*d*. a term in quittance of his rent when he works. Total of quittances, 17*s*. 6*d*.

Defaults of rent

In default of the curtilage of Swetyng' drawn into demesne, 6*d*. for the year; the land of Girard' drawn into demesne, 5*s*. for the year; the land of Geoffrey de Marisco drawn into demesne, 6*s*. for the year; the land of Derewyn' drawn into demesne, 3*s*. for the year; the land of Ralph Kake drawn into demesne, 9*d*. for the year; the land of Erneburgh' drawn into demesne, 1*s*. for the year; the land of Chestesheye which Matilda, relict of the estate (*territi*), held in dower, 13*s*. 4*d*. for the year, and although in some other original roll it is stated that the land which Matilda held in dower should revert after her death into the lord's hands, however, by an inquest made by

1 Scribe misspelt 'busch*ia*' as 'dusch*ia*'.

special command of the lord A*ymer*, bishop elect, it passed in fact after her death to her heirs; the land of Humphrey de Cu*m*ba which Bishop P*eter* bought from the same drawn into demesne, £1 1*s*. 4½*d*. for the year, and this rent is included in defaults because Bishop P*eter* gave that land with the tenement to Michael Pync*er*ne, and before that the said bishop held the said tenement in his hands and entered the said rent in chief. Total of defaults of rent, £2 10*s*. 11½*d*.

Total of quittances and defaults of rent, £3 8*s*. 5½*d*.

Total remaining, £38 10*s*. 10½*d*.

Annual recognizance
The same render account for 6*d*. from Richard Agmotesh*am* for annual recognizance; 4*d*. from John Carpe*nter* for the same; 4*d*. from Henry de North*e*ne for the same; 6*d*. from Gervase de Chalvelye for the same; 6*d*. from Andrew Ernald for the same; 4*d*. from Walter, son of Mariote de la Vyninge, for the same; 3*d*. from John son of Richard for the same; 4*d*. from Richard Coplaund for the same; 3*d*. from Richard Ken' for the same; 6*d*. from Richard, son of Juliana de Hav*er*ingdon', for the same; 4*d*. from Henry Carpent*er* for the same; 3*d*. from Richard, son of John de la Vyninge, for the same; 3*d*. from John Carp*enter* for the same; 3*d*. from Robert de Hav*er*inged' for the same, for the first time this year. Total, 4*s*. 11*d*.

Issues of the manor
The same render account for 10*s*. from pannage of pigs of the whole vill; nothing from foreign pannage because there was no mast there; nothing from figs (*figul'*) because they are dead; 4*s*. 2*d*. from the pasturage in la Bronemed' sold after mowing; 1*s*. from the pasturage sold in Yrildefeld'; 1*s*. from the pasturage sold in Senghet; nothing from the pasturage in the castle this year because it was pastured with sheep for a want of pasture; 2*s*. from the agistment of bullocks in the pasturage of the park of Wydyndon'; 11½*d*. from cablish sold and dead wood blown down by the wind; nothing from coarse wool and lamb's-wool this year because it was sent to Wolvesey; 1*s*. 4*d*. from wool locks sold; 5*s*. 10*d*. from winter cheese sold; £3 10*s*. from 7 weys of summer cheese sold, at 10*s*. a wey; 9*s*. 3*d*. from 18½ gallons of butter sold, at 6*d*. a gallon; 3*s*. 5*d*. for release from threshing (*bat*erie) according to custom; 2*s*. 3*d*. from the residue of Peter's pence; £1 11*s*. 6*d*. for release from transport-service this year because no transport-service was done to London or elsewhere; 7*d*. from taverns; nothing from the retting of flax because no flax was put in water; 6*d*. from 3 capons from the recognizances of Richard Carpe*nter*, William Rolues and Richard le Theccher'; 1*s*. 8*d*. from hens from churchscot; 3*s*. 4*d*. from squabs from the issue of the dovecote; nothing from apples because cider made therefrom; nothing from hay sold this year on account of the great drought of the summer; 3*d*. from the old fence of the park sold; 2*s*. 6*d*. from ½ bullock from the heriot of Henry le Murie sold; £1 2*s*. 2*d*. from dairy produce sold at the audit. Total, £8 13*s*. 8½*d*.

Stock
The same render account for 5*s*. from 2 old and feeble plough-horses sold, at 3*s*. for 1 which was from a heriot, and 2*s*. for 1; £1 3*s*. from 3 old cows sold at Martinmas, at 8*s*. for 1, and 7*s*. 6*d*. each for 2; 4*s*. 2*d*. from 1 bullock sold; 10*s*. from 10 calves, at 1*s*. each; 6*d*. from the hide sold of 1 yearling in murrain; 2*d*. from the hide sold of 1 calf in murrain; £2 15*s*. from 22 ewes, 1 ram, 16 wethers and 24 hoggs sold before

shearing, at 1*s*. each for the ewes, ram and wethers, and 8*d*. each for the hoggs; 16*s*. from the skins sold of 5 ewes, 1 ram, 9 wethers, 3 hoggs and 18 lambs before shearing, at 3*d*. a skin of ewes, ram, wethers, and hoggs, and 1*d*. a lambskin; 4*d*. from the skins sold of 2 ewes, 1 wether, 1 hogg and 1 lamb after shearing, at 1*d*. a skin of ewes and wether, ¾*d*. a hogg, and ¼*d*. a lambskin; £3 7*s*. 6*d*. from 27 gelded pigs sold, at 2*s*. 6*d*. each; 2*s*. from 2 calves sold at the audit. Total, £8 13*s*. 8*d*.

Corn and malt mill
The same render account for £2 4*s*. 6*d*. from 22 qrs 2 bus. from the whole issue of corn from the mill sold, at 2*s*. a qr; 6*s*. 9*d*. from 3 qrs 1 bus. of malt from the mill sold, at 2*s*. 4*d*. a qr for 1½ qrs, and 2*s*. a qr for 1 qr 5 bus. Total, £2 11*s*. 3*d*.

Wheat and barley
The same render account for £13 5*s*. 7½*d*. from 53 qrs 1 bus. of wheat sold, at 5*s*. a qr; 10*s*. 5*d*. from 3 qrs 1 bus. of poor (*debil'*) barley sold, at 3*s*. 4*d*. a qr; 4*s*. 10¾*d*. from 1 qr 3½ bus. and 1 peck of barley sold at the audit; 4*s*. from 2 qrs of oats sold at the audit, at 2*s*. a qr. Total of all corn, £14 4*s*. 11¼*d*.

m.16
Entry and marriage fines
The same render account for 6*s*. 8*d*. from Agnes, who was wife of John atte Lych', to have 1 messuage and ½ virgate of land which belonged to the said John her husband; 13*s*. 4*d*. from Isabel, who was wife of John de Lurteburn', to have entry to 1 messuage and 1 virgate of land which belonged to the said John her husband; 10*s*. from William de Hav*er*ingd' to have entry to 1½ virgates and 1 ferling of land which Agnes de Hav*er*ingd' held; £1 from Henry atte Putmull' to have entry to 1½ virgates of land and the moiety of 1 mill which Richard atte Putmull' held; 4*s*. from Gunilda, who was wife of Henry le Murie, to have entry to 1 messuage with ½ virgate of land which belonged to the said Henry her husband; 1*s*. from Joan, who was wife of Thomas de la Den', to have entry to 1 messuage and the moiety of 1 acre of land which the aforesaid Thomas held; £1 10*s*. from William atte Zilbech' to have entry to 1 messuage with ½ virgate of land for the use of Isabel his daughter which Juliana atte Zilbech held; 6*s*. 8*d*. from William, son of Ralph Thurthayn, to have entry to 1 messuage with ½ virgate of land which belonged to the said Ralph his father; £1 from Hugeman and Gunilda his wife to have ½ virgate of land which belonged to Agnes, mother of Jordan atte Vyninge, which land the same Jordan was about to have worked himself, that is, because he held other land and the lord bishop does not permit that one man should hold 2 villein lands,[1] therefore, the same Jordan was given the choice to fine for that ½ virgate of land and let go the land which he held, or to retain the land which he held before and let go the ½ virgate, and he preferred to retain the land which he held before, by reason of which the said Gunilda, who was consanguineous with the said Jordan, fined for the said land; £1 6*s*. 8*d*. from 13 tithings for tithingpenny at the hundred-court of Martinmas; £1 6*s*. 8*d*. from the same tithings for tithingpenny at the hundred-court of Hockday; 1*s*. from Hugh Fab*er* to have entry to one plot 3 feet long to enlarge his house. Total, £8 6*s*.

Perquisites
The same render account for £1 14*s*. 1*d*. from the small perquisites of the court this year. Total, £1 14*s*. 1*d*.

1 MS 'ij ⌈terr'⌉ ⟨ten'⟩ *ser*vil''.

Total of both, £10 1*d*.

Total of all receipts, £82 19*s*. 5¼*d*.

Expenses for ploughs
In ironwork of 3 ploughs for the year, that is, in iron, steel and iron shoes (*calconibus ferr'*) bought for the ironwork of ploughs, £1, and so much this year on account of especially expensive iron. In 3 ploughshares bought 2*s*. In stipend of the smith making the ironwork of 3 ploughs for the year 6*s*. In shoeing 12 plough-horses hauling ploughs and harrows for the year 19*s*. In 12 halters for plough-horses made from their own hair 2*d*. In 1 plough-horse bought 10*s*. In 2 bus. of wheat bought 1*s*. 3*d*. In 41 qrs 7 bus. 1 peck of maslin bought for sowing and the liveries of the manorial servants £4 7*d*., at 2*s*. a qr for 32 qrs 2 bus., and 1*s*. 8*d*. a qr for 9 qrs 5 bus. 1 peck. In 3 qrs of barley bought for sowing 10*s*., at 3*s*. 4*d*. a qr. In 11 qrs 3½ bus. of oats bought for the fodder of horses £1 1*s*. ¾*d*., at 2*s*. a qr for 6 qrs, and 1*s*. 8*d*. a qr for 5 qrs 3½ bus. In stipend of 3 ploughmen and 3 drovers (*tynctorum*) from Michaelmas until the Annunciation, holding and driving the lord's ploughs for the year, 12*s*., and for the rest of their stipend each takes at harvest-time 61 sheaves of wheat which contain by estimation 1 qr, and 61 sheaves of oats which contain 1 qr 2 bus. In forage bought for stock 8*s*. Total, £9 10*s*. ¾*d*.

Expenses for carts
In 5 pairs of wheels made from the lord's timber for carrying corn and clearing dung 3*s*. 4*d*. In 2 pairs of cart-shafts made from the lord's timber 8*d*. In fitting carts with axles 2*d*. In clouts, nails and grease for the cart with iron tyres and three others without (*plan'*) for the year 1*s*. In 1 halter bought 3*d*. In 1 new collar bought 7*d*. In putting right (*dirig'*) the old saddle-pads and collars 7*d*. In 1 pair of traces bought 4*d*. In 1 hemp rope bought for the carts 8*d*. In white leather for mending harnesses of the carts, 6*d*. this year. In shoeing 2 cart-horses for the year 4*s*. In stipend of 1 carter for ½ year in winter 2*s*., and for the other ½ year he takes for his stipend sheaves at harvest-time like the rest of the manorial servants. Total, 14*s*. 1*d*.

Dairy
In 5 bus. of salt bought for the dairy 2*s*. 1*d*., at 5*d*. each. In woollen cloth 3*d*. In a press bought 2*d*. In 1 new bucket bought and other old ones put right 3*d*. In earthenware pots and pans bought 2*d*. In stipend of 1 dairymaid for ½ year in winter 1*s*. In stipend of 1 cowherd for the same time 1*s*. In stipend of 1 shepherd for the same time 2*s*. And for the rest of their stipend each takes sheaves at harvest-time like the rest of the manorial servants. In vinegar, copperas and pigs' fat bought for greasing sick sheep 8*s*. 2¾*d*. In 8 hurdles bought for the sheepfold 8*d*. In 7 ells of canvas for packing wool 1*s*. 9*d*., at 3*d*. an ell. In carrying the said wool to Wolvesey 4*d*., because it was carried with the wool of Ivinghoe. Total, 17*s*. 10¾*d*.

Expenses of the meadow
In customary payment for the mowing of the meadows 1*s*. Total, 1*s*.

Expenses of buildings and small necessaries
In tiles bought for the hall 1*s*. 1*d*. In tiling the same hall in places where it was necessary 9*d*. In 1 new lock with a key bought for the barn-door because the old lock was broken by the earl of Lincoln's marshal 3*d*. In repairing another lock on the other

barn, broken by the same, 1*d*. In stipend of a carpenter rebuilding the new sheepcote with the lord's own timber, because the old sheepcote collapsed through rotten timber, 6*s*. 2*d*. In roofing the same sheepcote 4*s*. In walling bought for the same sheepcote 6*d*. In roofing the old sheepcote in places 6*d*. In roofing 2 barns in places 1*s*. 4*d*. In roofing the byres for oxen and cows in places 1*s*. In a new park-gate made from the lord's timber 6*d*. In roofing the small stable and dairy in places 6*d*. In gelding piglets 4*d*. In stipend of 1 swineheard for ½ year in winter 1*s*., and ⌈for⌉ the rest of his stipend he takes sheaves at harvest-time like the rest of the manorial servants. Total, 18*s*.

Threshing and winnowing
In threshing and winnowing 78 qrs 5 bus. of wheat with curall and 29 qrs 6 bus. of mancorn 19*s*. 2¼*d*., at 2¼*d*. a qr. In threshing and winnowing 12 qrs 6 bus. of barley 1*s*. 2*d*., at 1*d*. a qr threshed, and 1*d*. per 6 qrs winnowed. In threshing and winnowing 82 qrs 2 bus. of oats 5*s*. 7½*d*., at ¾*d*. a qr threshed, and 1*d*. per 6 qrs winnowed, because half winnowed by the dairymaid. In new sieves bought and other old ones remade 3*d*. In 1 new sack bought 8*d*. Total, £1 6*s*. 10¾*d*.

Cost of the mill
In boards sawn for the walls of the water-mill 1*s*. 4*d*. In new sills[1] for the mill laid and shaped 4*s*. In hooping the mill spindle with iron bands 1*s*. In hooping the cog-wheel with iron bands 6*d*. In sharpening and steeling mill bills 1*s*. 1½*d*. In nails bought for fastening boards 1*d*. In tallow and grease bought for the same 4½*d*. Total, 8*s*. 5*d*.

Expenses of the steward
In expenses of the steward at the hundred-court of Martinmas 7*s*. 5*d*. In expenses of Simon de Farh*am* holding the hundred-court of Hockday 8*s*. Handed over to certain attendants going to London by order of Simon de Farh*am* 4*d*. In expenses of the attendants of Simon remaining there with one horse 6*d*. Total, 16*s*. 3*d*.

Expenses of the bailiff
In expenses of the bailiff from Michaelmas (29 September) until the feast St Thomas the Apostle (21 December) 5*s*. 2½*d*. In fur for the summer livery of the same 2*s*. Total, 7*s*. 2½*d*.

Wages
In wages delivered to Gilbert de Escher' who kept the corn at harvest-time and the meadows and pasture after the harvest 3*s*. 10*d*., that is, for two weeks and two days at 1½*d*. a day, and for 22 days at 1*d*. a day. Total, 3*s*. 10*d*.

Foreign expenses
In expenses of the assessors of the fifteenth to have their favour in the assessment 2*s*. Total, 2*s*.

Total of all expenses, £15 5*s*. 7¾*d*.

And he owes, £67 13*s*. 9½*d*.

Cash deliveries[2]
Delivered to Sir G*eoffrey*, treasurer of Wolvesey, by 1 tally, £63 10*s*.

1 MS 'nov' ⌈sullivis⌉ ⟨collivis⟩ mol''.

2 MS omits heading.

And thus he owes clear, £4 3*s*. 9½*d*.

Issues of the mill

The same render account for 22 qrs 2 bus. from the whole issue of corn from the mill of Wytedych, and all sold as noted above; 3 qrs 1 bus. of malt from the whole issue of the same mill, and all sold as noted above.

Issues of the grange

Wheat

{yield: three-fold less 2 qrs 2 bus.}

The same render account for 97 qrs 3 bus. from the whole issue of wheat from the grange in the granary by struck measure; 11 qrs by estimation in sheaves given to the manorial servants; 2 bus. bought for the provision of Simon Farh*a*m holding the tourn of Hockday. Total, 108 qrs 5 bus.

Sown over 111 acres measured by the perch which lie in the fields of Chetenore, Foxore and below Hav*er*yngdon', 41 qrs 1 bus.; that is, 3 bus. an acre, less 1 bus. in all. In customary payment for the mowing of the meadows, 6 bus. In provision of the steward at the hundred-court of Martinmas, 2 bus. In provision of Simon de Farh*a*m holding the tourn of Hockday, 2 bus. In provision of the bailiff from Michaelmas (29 September) until the feast of St Thomas the Apostle (21 December), 1 qr 1 bus., because he took the rest at Ivinghoe. Given to 11 manorial servants, that is, 1 carter, 6 ploughmen, 1 shepherd, 1 cowherd, 1 dairymaid and 1 swineherd, for their stipends for ½ year in summer by estimation in sheaves, 11 qrs, or 1 qr each. Taken for the use of King Edward by John, bailiff of the hundred of Desborough, 1 qr. Sold as noted above, 53 qrs 1 bus.

Curall

The same render account for 1 qr 7 bus. of curall from the whole issue of the said wheat from the grange in the granary by struck measure; all mixed below with barley for the liveries of the manorial servants.

Mancorn

{yield: two-fold less 7 qrs 5 bus.}

The same render account for 37 qrs 1 bus. from the whole issue of mancorn from the grange in the granary by struck measure; 41 qrs 7 bus. 1 peck bought. Total, 79 qrs 1 peck.

Sown over 51 acres measured by the perch which lie in the fields of Chettenor', Foxor' and below Hav*er*ygdon', 19 qrs 1 bus.; that is, 3 bus. an acre. Mixed below with barley for the liveries of the manorial servants, 59 qrs 7 bus. 1 peck.

Barley

{yield: two-fold plus 7 bus.}

The same render account for 15 qrs 7 bus. from the whole issue of barley from the grange in the granary by struck measure; 3 qrs bought; 1 qr 7 bus. of curall received above and mixed with that for the liveries of the manorial servants; 59 qrs 7 bus. 1 peck of mancorn received above and mixed with that for the same; 2 bus. of peas received below and mixed with that for the same; 6 bus. of vetches received below and mixed with that for the same. Total, 81 qrs 5 bus. 1 peck.

Sown over 19½ acres measured by the perch which lie in the fields of East and West Tourugg', Yrildefeld', and Senghet, 9 qrs 6 bus.; that is, ½ qr an acre. Delivered to 1 carter, 3 ploughmen, 3 drovers and 1 shepherd, who each take a quarter every 8 weeks for the year, 52 qrs. Delivered to 1 cowherd, 1 dairymaid and 1 swineherd, of whom the cowherd takes a quarter every 10 weeks, the swineherd every 12 weeks, and the dairymaid for ½ year every 16 weeks and for the other ½ year every 12 weeks, 13 qrs 2½ bus. this year, on account of the cheapness of corn. Delivered to 1 keeper of lambs from their weaning for 16 weeks, because after weaning they are kept separately in the pasture, 1 qr. In supporting pigs and piglets in winter, 1 qr. Sold as noted above, 3 qrs 1 bus. Sold at the audit, 1 qr 3½ bus. 1 peck.

Oats

{yield: two-fold less 21½ qrs}

The same render account for 104 qrs 6 bus. from the whole issue of oats from the grange in the granary by struck measure; 4 qrs by estimation in sheaves given to oxen; 13 qrs 6 bus. by estimation in sheaves given to the manorial servants; 11 qrs 3½ bus. bought. Total, 133 qrs 7½ bus.

Sown over 96½ acres measured by the perch which lie in the fields of East and West Tourigge, Yrildefeld, and Senghet, 72 qrs 3 bus.; that is, 6 bus. an acre. In fodder of 2 cart-horses for the year, 15 qrs 6 bus. In fodder of 12 plough-horses hauling ploughs and harrows from All Saints (1 November) until the Invention of the Cross (3 May), for 26 weeks, 22 qrs 6 bus., at 1 bus. each night. In supporting 8 oxen the following winter by estimation in sheaves, 4 qrs. Given to 11 manorial servants, that is, to 1 carter, 6 ploughmen, 1 shepherd, 1 cowherd and 1 swineherd, for their stipends for ½ year in summer by estimation in sheaves, 13 qrs 6 bus., or 1 qr 2 bus. each. In fodder of the steward's horses for his two visits, at his tourn of Martinmas and the tourn of Hockday, 1 qr 6 bus. In fodder of the horse of Simon de Farham sojourning for 9 nights, 4½ bus. In fodder of the bailiff's horse from Michaelmas until the feast of St Thomas the Apostle, 1 qr. Sold at the audit, 2 qrs.

Peas

{yield: two-fold plus 1 bus.}

The same render account for 5 bus. from the whole issue of peas from the grange in the granary by struck measure.

Sown, 3 bus. Mixed above with barley for the liveries of the manorial servants, 2 bus.

Vetches

{yield: three-fold less 1 bus.}

The same render account for 11 bus. from the whole issue of vetches from the grange in the granary by struck measure.

Sown, 5 bus. Mixed above with barley for the liveries of the manorial servants, 6 bus.

Stock

Cart-horses: 2 remain from the previous year; 2 remain.

Plough-horses: 12 remain from the previous year; 1 from the heriot of Agnes atte Finyng'; 1 bought. Total, 14. 2 sold; 12 remain, all of them male.

Oxen: 14 remain from the previous year; 1 added from steers. Total, 15. 15 remain.

Bulls: 1 remains from the previous year; 2 added from steers. Total, 3. 3 remain.

Cows: 23 remain from the previous year; 4 added from steers. Total, 27. 3 sold at Martinmas (11 November); 24 remain.

Steers: 7 remain from the previous year's bullocks; 1 added to oxen, 2 to bulls, and 4 to cows; none remain.

Bullocks: 7 remain from the previous year's yearlings; 1 from the heriot of John de Lurteburn. Total, 8. 1 sold; 7 remain, 3 of them male.
Yearlings: 7 remain from the previous year's calves; 1 from the heriot of Ralph Thurstayn. Total, 8. 1 in murrain by[1] snake-bite, the hide of which is answered for; 7 remain, 3 of them male.
[Calves]: 22 from the offspring of the cows from stock, because 3 sold at Martinmas and 2 sterile; 2 in tithe; 1 in murrain, the hide of which is answered for; 10 sold; 7 remain, 6 of them male; 2 sold at the audit.
Ewes: 169 remain from the previous year; 49 added from hoggs; 1 from the heriot of Richard Putmull' before lambing. Total, 219. 22 sold at Martinmas; 5 in murrain before lambing and shearing, 2 after shearing. Total, 29. 190 remain.
[Rams]: 11 remain from the previous year; 1 added from hoggs. Total, 12. 1 in murrain before shearing; 1 sold before shearing. Total, 2. 10 remain.
[Wethers]: 119 remain from the previous year; 30 added from hoggs; 1 from the heriot of Thomas atte Den' before shearing. Total, 150. 9 in murrain before shearing, 1 after shearing; 16 sold at Martinmas; 2 in customary payment for the mowing of the meadows after shearing. Total, 28. 122 remain.
Hoggs: 109 remain from the previous year's lambs; 4 in murrain before shearing, 1 after shearing; 49 added to ewes, 1 to rams, 30 to wethers; 24 sold before shearing; none remain.
Lambs: 135 from the offspring of the ewes, because 22 sold before giving birth, 5 in murrain before giving birth, 8 sterile. 12 in tithe; 19 in murrain before shearing, 1 after shearing. Total, 32. 103 remain.
Gelded pigs: 31 remain from the previous year; 30 added from hoggets; 1 from the heriot of John atte Lyche. Total, 62. 27 sold; 35 remain.
Boars: 1 remains from the previous year; 1 remains.
Sows: 2 remain from the previous year; 2 remain.

m.16d
Hoggets: 32 remain from the previous year's piglets; 2 in murrain; 20[2] added to gelded pigs; none remain.
Piglets: 14 from the offspring of 2 sows about Christmas; 17 from the offspring of the same about Lammas. Total, 31. 3 in tithe, 2 in murrain. Total, 5. 26 remain, 13 of them of 3 terms and 12 of ½ term; all are male and gelded.
Coarse fleeces {yield of fleece 4*d*. less 3*s*. 5*d*. in all}: 330 produced at the shearing; 33 in tithe; 297 sent to Wolvesey, which made 1½ weys 10 cloves, and a wey is 26 cloves, a clove 7 lb.
Lambs' fleeces {yield of fleece 1¼*d*. less 5¼*d*. in all}: 97 produced at the shearing, because 7 not sheared on account of feebleness, 12 in tithe before shearing, and 19 in murrain before shearing; 97 sent to Wolvesey, which made 5 cloves.
Skins before shearing: 5 from ewes, 1 from a ram, 9 from wethers, 4 from hoggs and 19 from lambs in murrain before shearing. Total, 38. 2 in tithe; 36 sold.
Skins after shearing: 2 from ewes, 1 from a wether, 1 from a hogg and 1 from a lamb in murrain after shearing. Total, 5. All sold.
Winter cheese: 62 made, because 31 gallons of milk consumed by the lord's lambs; all sold as noted above.
Summer cheese {yield of cow 4*s*. and ewe 2*d*. with 2 cheeses in customary payment valued at 8*d*. this year}: 171 cheeses made between Thursday after the

1 MS 'In mor' j per mors' ⟨sep'⟩ serpent''.

2 Figures add up to 30.

feast of St Ambrose (5 April) and Michaelmas (29 September), both days included; 17 in tithe; 2 in customary payment for the mowing of the meadows; 152 sold as noted above, which made 7 weys, and a wey is 28 cloves, a clove 7 lb.
Butter: 18½ gallons; all sold as noted above.
Swans: 3 remain from the previous year; 3 remain, 1 nesting (*err'*).
Peacocks: 9 remain from the previous year and no offspring from them; 3 in murrain; 6 sent to the bishop at Southwark; none remain.
Capons: 3 from recognizances of Richard Carpent*er*, William Rolues and Richard le Theccher'; all sold as noted above.
Hens: 64 from churchscot. 4 in default of the land of Giles because the holding is vacant; 4 in default of the land of Robert de Ra*m*mesm*ere* because the holding is vacant for doing the ancient service; 4 in default of the land of Matilda, widow, for the same; 4 in default of the land of Geoffrey de A*n*gulo for the same; 4 in default of the land of Geoffrey de Throp for the same; 4 in default of the land of Henry le Son' for the same; ⌈4 in default of the land of Godelote Fork'⌉; 2 in default of Margaret atte Crofte because she has no husband; 2 in default of Robert de Ra*m*mesm*ere* for the same; 4 in default of the land of Ralph le Bolt*ere* because the holding is vacant for doing the ancient service; 2 in default of the land of Ralph le Kachier' because he has no wife; 4 in default of the land of Alice, relict of the smith, because she has no husband; 2 in default of the land of Margery Derewyn' for the same; 2 in default of the land of Adam le Couh*er*d' because he has no wife. Total, 44. 20 sold as noted above; none remain.
Cider: 1 cask made this year; it remains.
Utensils: 2 carts with iron tyres remain from the previous year; 1 used; 1 remains. 3 hemp ropes remain from the previous year; 1 bought; 4 remain. 2 sacks remain from the previous year; 1 bought. Total, 3. 1 used in the manor; 2 remain. 2 baskets remain from the previous year; 1 used in the manor; 1 remains. 7 casks remain from the previous year; 7 remain. 1 brass pan remains from the previous year; 1 remains. 1 ewer and 1 basin remain from the previous year; both remain.

Morton

Arrears
William, bailiff, and Richard, reeve, render account for £3 10*s*. 3*d*. of arrears from the previous year. Delivered to Sir G*eoffrey*, treasurer of Wolvesey, by 1 tally, £3 10*s*. 3*d*. They are quit.

Rents
The same render account for £1 3*s*. 3¼*d*. for all rents of assize at Christmas; £1 3*s*. 3¼*d*. at the Annunciation (25 March); £1 3*s*. 3¼*d*. at the Nativity of St John the Baptist (24 June); £1 3*s*. 3¼*d*. at Michaelmas (29 September). Total of all rents for the year, £4 13*s*. 1*d*.

Quittances
In quittance of 1 reeve for the year 2*s*.; 6 men holding 6 virgates of land, 3 of whom hold the lord's ploughs for 1 week and the other three for the other week, 12*s*. for the year. Total of quittances, 14*s*.

Defaults of rent
In default of 1 virgate of land which belonged to William de Bury drawn into demesne, 4*s*. for the year; 1½ virgates and 1 ferling of land which belonged to Roger

drawn into demesne, 3*s.* for the year; 1½ virgates and a farthing of land which belonged to William Alfrith drawn into demesne, 1*s.* 8*d.* for the year; 1 ferling of land which belonged to William le Nywman drawn into demesne, 9*d.* for the year; 1 ferling and a farthing of land which belonged to Alice drawn into demesne, 1*s.* 3*d.* for the year; a curtilage which belonged to Roger Pound' drawn into demesne, 7½*d.* for the year. Total of defaults of rent, 11*s.* 3½*d.*

Total of quittances and defaults of rent, £1 5*s.* 3½*d.*

Total remaining, £3 7*s.* 9½*d.*

Annual recognizance
Nothing from annual recognizance.

Issues of the manor
The same render account for 9½*d.* from common pannage of the whole vill; 1*s.* 6*d.* from stubble sold; 2*s.* from mast in the grove sold; 3*s.* from winter cheese sold; £1 15*s.* from 3½ weys of summer cheese sold, at 10*s.* a wey; 4*s.* 3*d.* from 8½ gallons of butter sold, at 6*d.* a gallon; nothing from hay sold this year; 8*d.* from apples from the issue of the garden sold this year; nothing from the agistment of bullocks in the pasture this year because there were sheep; 1*s.* 9*d.* from dairy produce sold at the audit. Total, £2 8*s.* 11½*d.*

Issues of stock
The same render account for £1 4*d.* from 4 plough-horses sold, at 6*s.* for 1, 5*s.* 6*d.* each for 2, and 3*s.* 4*d.* for 1; £1 9*s.* from 3 oxen sold because old, at 10*s.* each for 2, and 9*s.* for 1; 8*s.* 6*d.* from 1 cow sold because sterile; 4*s.* 4*d.* from 1 feeble young heifer sold; 6*s.* from 6 calves sold, at 1*s.* each; 8*d.* from the hide sold of 1 plough-horse in murrain; 2*s.* 1*d.* from the hide sold of 1 ox in murrain; 8*d.* from the flesh of the same ox sold; 2*d.* from the hide sold of 1 calf in murrain. Total, £3 11*s.* 9*d.*

Sale of corn
The same render account for £10 16*s.* 9½*d.* from 48 qrs 6 bus. of wheat sold, at 5*s.* a qr for 25 qrs 1 bus.,[1] 4*s.* a qr for 18½ qrs 1 bus., and 3*s.* 4*d.* a qr for 5 qrs; £5 8*s.* 9*d.* from 32½ qrs 1 bus. of barley sold, at 3*s.* 4*d.* a qr; 2*s.* from 1 qr of beans sold; £1 6*s.* 8*d.* from a certain part of the stack of beans sold wholesale. Total, £17 14*s.* 2½*d.*

Entry and marriage fines
The same render account for 5*s.* from John atte Wat*er*e for marrying Claricia his daughter outside; 8*s.* from 2 tithings for tithingpenny at the hundred-court of Martinmas; 8*s.* from the same tithings for tithingpenny at the hundred-court of Hockday. Total, £1 1*s.*

Pleas and perquisites
The same render account for 2*s.* 6*d.* from the pleas and perquisites of all the courts for the whole year. Total, 2*s.* 6*d.*

Total of both, £1 3*s.* 6*d.*

Total of all expenses, £28 6*s.* 2½*d.*

1 MS omits 'bus.'.

Expenses for ploughs

In ironwork of 3 ploughs for the year 3*s.* 1*d.* In 2 plough-shoes (*calconib*us) bought 4*d.* In 2 ploughshares bought 1*s.* 4*d.* In stipend of the smith making the ironwork of 3 ploughs for the year 2*s.* ½*d.* In 4 new ploughs made from the lord's timber 8*d.* In repairing the same 2*d.* In ox-bows, withies and draught-chains (*hart'*) for the ploughs 11*d.* In 1 harrow made from the lord's timber 1½*d.* In blood-letting of oxen 2*d.* In 6 halters made from their own hair 1½*d.* In stipend of 3 oxherds driving the lord's ploughs from Michaelmas until the Annunciation 6*s.*, and for the rest of their stipends each takes at harvest-time 72 sheaves of wheat which contain by estimation 1 qr 2 bus., and 72 sheaves of oats which contain by estimation 1 qr. In stipend of 3 ploughmen for working 36 Saturdays 4*s.* 6*d.*, or ½*d.* each, because they are not obliged to work on Saturdays. In 10 oxen bought £6 11*s.* 1*d.*, at 14*s.* 1*d.* each for 3, 13*s.* 6*d.* each for 3, and 12*s.* 1*d.* each for 4. In 20 qrs 1 bus. of wheat bought for sowing and the provision of the harvest boon-works £3 13*s.* 1½*d.*, at 3*s.* 8*d.* a qr for 18 qrs 1 bus., and 3*s.* 4*d.* a qr for 2 qrs. In 2½ qrs of oats bought for sowing and the fodder of plough-horses 4*s.* 2*d.*, at 1*s.* 8*d.* a qr. In expenses of the boon-work of 39 ploughmen fallowing the lord's land 6*s.* 6*d.*, at 2*d.* a ploughman. In forage bought for stock £1 3*s.* 6½*d.* Total, £12 17*s.* 10½*d.*

Expenses for carts

In 2 pairs of wheels made from the lord's timber for clearing dung 1*s.* 4*d.* In fitting the cart with axles, with clouts, nails and grease for the same for the year, 1*s.* In white leather for mending harnesses of the cart 4*d.* In 1 pair of traces bought 4½*d.* In 2 hemp ropes bought 1*s.* 1*d.* In 2 collars bought 1*s.* 2*d.* In shoeing 2 plough-horses hauling the cart for the year 2*s.* In stipend of 1 carter from Michaelmas until the Annunciation 2*s.*, and for the rest of his stipend he takes sheaves at harvest-time like the rest of the manorial servants. Total, 9*s.* 3½*d.*

Dairy

In 5 qrs 1 bus. of beans planted and watered 2*s.* 6*d.* In 2 ⌈bus.⌉ of salt bought for the dairy 9*d.*, at 4½*d.* a bus. In a press bought 2*d.* In linen cloth bought 4*d.* In putting right a bucket 1*d.* In earthenware pots and pans bought 1½*d.* In 36 hurdles bought for the fold on account of the sheep of a certain stranger manuring the lord's land for want of the lord's sheep 2*s.* 11*d.*, at 1*d.* a hurdle. In 1 colander repaired ½*d.* In stipend of 1 cowherd for ½ year in winter 1*s.* In stipend of 1 shepherd for ½ year 1*s.*, and for the rest of his stipend he takes sheaves at harvest-time like the rest of the manorial servants. Total, 8*s.* 11*d.*

Cost of buildings and small necessaries

In rebuilding below the roof of the barn which had collapsed through rotten timber, that is, in carpentry, 3*s.* 6*d.* In making 500 laths for the same from the lord's own timber 1*s.* In 1500 lath-nails (*lathenayl*) bought for the same 11½*d.* In roofing the same barn 1*s.* Total, 6*s.* 5½*d.*

Threshing and winnowing

In threshing and winnowing 54 qrs 2 bus. of wheat with curall 10*s.* 1¼*d.*, at 2¼*d.* a qr. In threshing and winnowing 51 qrs 6 bus. of barley 5*s.* 4*d.*, at 1¼*d.* a qr. Nothing from threshing beans this year because they were threshed by the manorial servants. In 8 qrs 1 bus. winnowed 2*d.* In 1 sack bought 8*d.* In remaking old sieves 2*d.* In making 1 winnowing-fan from the lord's own timber 8*d.* Total, 17*s.* 1¾*d.*

Harvest-time
In 1 sickle bought 1*s*. In sharpening 3 sickles 2*d*. In spreading and tossing the meadow 3*s*. 6*d*. In weeding corn 1*s*. 6*d*. In relish and ale bought for 96 men with 8 free men who were overseeing the reapers at 2 harvest boon-works as if for 1 day and having bread from the grange 8*s*. They reaped almost all the corn together with the other 2 boon-works which are without food, each thus taking 1½*d*. a day. Total, 14*s*. 2*d*.

Wages
In wages of Ralph, sergeant, from Sunday before the feast of St Vincent (21 January) until Michaelmas (29 September), for 36 weeks, £1 11*s*. 6*d*., that is, 10½*d*. every week.[1] In stipend of the same sergeant for the year 6*s*. 8*d*. Total, £1 18*s*. 2*d*.

Total of all expenses, £17 12*s*. ¼*d*.

And he owes, £10 14*s*. 2¼*d*.

[Cash deliveries]
Delivered to Sir G*eoffrey*, treasurer of Wolvesey, by 1 tally, £2 10*s*.

And he owes clear, £8 4*s*. 2¼*d*.

Issues of the grange

Wheat
{yield: three-fold less 4 qrs 2 bus.}
{Henceforth no corn should be withheld for the stipends of the manorial servants; that is, money should be withheld for them, the best price that is able to be had, so that all the lord's corn reaches the grange}
The same render account for 64 qrs 6 bus. from the whole issue of wheat from the grange in the granary by struck measure; 7½ qrs by estimation in sheaves given to the manorial servants; 20 qrs 1 bus. bought. Total, 92 qrs 3 bus.
Sown over 94 acres measured by the perch which lie in the fields of Buryfurlo*n*g, Rodelond, Cheldebreth', Langilond', Stocky*n*g', Berhgforlo*n*g, Sevenacr', and Annaysbuttes, 35 qrs 1 bus.; that is, 3 bus. an acre, less 1 bus. in all. In bread for 2 harvest boon-works, 1 qr. Given to 6 manorial servants this year, that is, 1 carter, 3 oxherds, 1 cowherd, 1 shepherd, for their stipends in summer by estimation in sheaves, 7½ qrs, or 1 qr 2 bus. each. Sold as noted above, 48 qrs 6 bus.

Curall
The same render account for 13½ qrs from the whole issue of curall of the same wheat from the grange in the granary by struck measure; mixed below with beans for the liveries of the manorial servants, 13½ qrs.

Barley
{yield: 4½-fold plus 5½ bus.}
The same render account for 65 qrs 3 bus. from the whole issue of barley and dredge from the grange in the granary by struck measure.
Sown over 48½ acres measured by the perch which lie in Eldefeld', Gores and Buttes, 24 qrs 1 bus.; that is, ½ qr an acre. Mixed below with beans for the liveries of the manorial servants, 8 qrs 5 bus. Sold as noted above, 32½ qrs 1 bus.

1 MS 'p*er* ⟨viij⟩ sep*timanas* x d. ob.'.

Oats
{yield: three-fold less 7 bus.}
The same render account for 2 qrs 7 bus. from the whole issue of oats from the grange in the granary by struck measure; 6 qrs of oats by estimation in sheaves given to the manorial servants; 2½ qrs bought. Total, 11 qrs 3 bus.
Sown over 3 acres measured by the perch which lie below Bereth', 2 qrs 2 bus.; that is, 6 bus. an acre. Given to 6 manorial servants, that is, 1 carter, 3 oxherds, 1 cowherd and 1 shepherd, for their stipends for ½ year in summer by estimation in sheaves, 6 qrs, or 1 qr each. In fodder of 2 plough-horses hauling ploughs and harrows for the year, 3 qrs 1 bus.

Beans
{yield: four-fold less 1½ qrs 3 bus.}
The same render account for 11 qrs 5 bus. remaining from the previous year; 10 qrs 1 bus. from the whole issue from the grange in the granary by struck measure, because a certain part of 1 stack of beans was sold wholesale; 13½ qrs of curall received above and mixed with that for the liveries of the manorial servants; 8 qrs 5 bus. of barley received above and mixed with that for same. Total, 43 qrs 7 bus.
Sown over 13½ acres measured by the perch which lie above Bereth' and Wykmedforlondg', 5 qrs 1 bus.; that is, 3 bus. an acre, plus ½ bus. in all. Delivered to 1 carter, 3 drovers, who each take a quarter every 8 weeks for the year, 26 qrs. Delivered to 1 cowherd for the year, taking a quarter every 12 weeks, 4 qrs 2½ bus. Delivered to 1 shepherd who keeps 200 sheep by agreement with his own sheep, who takes a quarter every 10 weeks for the year, 5 qrs 1½ bus. Delivered to 1 dairymaid, who takes a quarter every 12 weeks from the feast of St Mary in March (25 March) until Michaelmas (29 September), for 26 weeks and 6 days, 2 qrs 2 bus. Sold as noted above, 1 qr.

m.17

Stock

Plough-horses: 9 remain from the previous year; 1 in murrain, the hide of which is answered for; 4 sold; 4 remain, 2 of them male. They are cart-horses.
Foals: none this year because the mares did not foal.
Oxen: 19 remain from the previous year; 4 added from steers; 10 bought. Total, 33. 1 in murrain about the Annunciation, the hide and flesh of which are answered for; 3 sold. Total, 4. 29 remain.
Cows {henceforth there should be up to 20 cows there}: 12 remain from the previous year; 1 sterile cow sold; 11 remain.
Bulls: 1 remains from the previous year; 1 remains.
Steers: 5 remain from the previous year's bullocks; 1 female sold; 4 added to oxen; none remain.
Bullocks: 3 remain from the previous year's yearlings; 3 remain, 2 of them male.
Yearlings: 5 remain from the previous year's calves; 5 remain, 2 of them male.
Calves: 11 from the offspring of the cows from stock, because 1 sterile cow sold; 1 in murrain; 1 in tithe; 6 sold; 3 remain, 1 of them male.
Geese: 2 from the pasturage of Crouchweye; 4 from the right to drive beasts (*av'*) through the droveway (*Drofwey*); they remain.
Chickens: 12 from the trespasses of outsiders in the lord's pasture; they remain.
Coarse wool: nothing because the lord's sheep are not there.

Winter cheese: 39 made; all sold as noted above.
Summer cheese {yield of cow 4*s*.}: 171 cheeses made between Thursday after the feast of St Ambrose (5 April) and Michaelmas (29 September), both days included; 17 in tithe; 154 sold as noted above, which made 3½ weys.
Butter: 8½ gallons sold; all sold as noted above.
Utensils: 1 cart with iron tyres remains from the previous year. 3 hemp ropes remain from the previous year; 2 bought. Total, 5. 2 used in the manor; 3 remain. 2 sacks remain from the previous year; 1 bought this year. Total, 3. 1 used in the manor; 2 remain. 2 baskets remain from the previous year; 1 bought. Total, 3. 1 used in the manor; 2 remain. 4 sickles remain from the previous year; 1 bought. Total, 5. 1 used in the manor; 4 remain. 1 tripod remains from the previous year. 1 brass pan remains from the previous year. 1 brass pot remains from the previous year.

Wargrave

Arrears

James de Northon', bailiff, and William de Wurdly, reeve, render account for £86 9*s*. 1½*d*. of arrears from the previous year. All delivered to Sir G*eoffrey*, treasurer of Wolvesey. They are quit.

Rents of assize

The same render account for £13 13*s*. ¼*d*. for all rents of assize at Easter (22 April); £13 14*s*. 3¼*d*. at Michaelmas (29 September). Total, £27 7*s*. 3½*d*.

Quittances

In quittance of 1 reeve for the year 1*s*. 6*d*.; 1 forester at la Northber' for the year 2*s*.; 4 ploughmen for the year 2*s*.; 1 hayward who is hayward and cowherd for the year 6*d*.; 1 shepherd for the year 6*d*.; 1 swineherd for the year 6*d*. Total, 7*s*.

Defaults of rent

In default of the land of Robert Palm*er*e drawn into demesne 2*s*.; the land of William H*er*berd' drawn into demesne 3*s*., because before it used to be in rents of assize for release from labour service, because the labour service is worth more now it is worked; the land of Agatha for the same reason 1*s*.; 3 acres of land of William Fab*er* drawn into demesne 2*s*. 2*d*.; the mill which is in the lord's hands, £2 for the year; the land of Robert, son of William le Keu, drawn into demesne because it was sold by charter and was held by villein tenure 1*s*. 6*d*.; the land of William le Keu drawn into demesne 6*d*.; the land of Robert, son of Adam le Keu, for the same reason 1*s*. 6*d*.; 3 acres of land of Hamo 'infr*a* po*n*te*m*' drawn into demesne 2*s*. 3*d*.; 2 acres of land of Little (*petyt*) Ivo drawn into demesne, 1*s*. 1½*d*. for the year. Total, £2 15*s*. ½*d*.

Total of quittances and defaults of rent, £3 2*s*. ½*d*.

Total of rents remaining, £24 5*s*. 3*d*.

Annual gifts

The same render account for £2 7*s*. 1*d*. from annual gifts at Easter; £2 7*s*. 1*d*. at Michaelmas. Total, £4 14*s*. 2*d*.

Farm of the weir

Nothing from the farm of the weir this year because the fishery is in the lord's hands.

Issues of the manor

The same render account for 18*s*. 3*d*. from common pannage of pigs at Martinmas (11 November), from 150 pigs over a year old and 142 piglets, at 1*d*. a pig over a year old, and ½*d*. a piglet; nothing from foreign pannage this year; 4*s*. from 1 old plough-horse sold; £1 10*s*. from 3 feeble oxen sold, at 10*s*. each; £1 15*s*. from 5 cows sold before calving, at 7*s*. 1*d*. each for 4, and 6*s*. 8*d*. for 1; 3*s*. 6*d*. from ½ steer from the heriot of Richard le Blake sold; 11*s*. 11*d*. from 10 calves sold; £1 6*s*. from 8 wethers, at 1*s*. each, 15 ewes, at 8*d*. each, sold together; £5 3*s*. 10*d*. from 1 sow and 30 pigs sold at Martinmas, at 3*s*. 4*d*. each, plus 6*d*. in all; 2*s*. 6*d*. from the hide sold of 1 ox in murrain; 3*s*. 6*d*. from the hides sold of 2 cows in murrain, at 1*s*. 6*d*. for 1 and 2*s*. for the other; 6*d*. from the hide sold of 1 bullock in murrain; 3*d*. from the hide sold of 1 yearling in murrain; 2¼*d*. from the skins sold of 2 hoggs in murrain before shearing; 3*d*. from the skins sold of 3 wethers in murrain after shearing; 4*d*. from the skins sold of 6 lambs in murrain before weaning; £3 7*s*. 6*d*. for release from labour service; nothing from coarse wool and lamb's-wool because it is sent to Wolvesey; 5*s*. 6*d*. from ½ wey 3 cloves of winter cheese sold; £4 15*s*. 7*d*. from 9 weys and 1 stone of summer cheese sold, at 10*s*. 4*d*. a wey; 10*s*. from 20 cloves of butter sold; 3*s*. 6*d*. from 42 hens sold **{henceforth cocks should be sold for 1*d*. and hens for 1½*d*.}**; £2 4*s*. 1*d*. from the fishery of la Bulehuch' sold apart from the tithe; 2*s*. from John atte Wygate for release from his labour service; 10*d*. from the herbage sold in the garden; 9*s*. 6*d*. from gavel (*gabillonib*us) sold; 1*s*. from bark sold from timber felled above the crest of the ditch for repairing the stable; 4½*d*. from 3 lb of wool locks, at 1½*d*. a lb; 6*s*. 8*d*. from 2 swans sold at the audit; 5*s*. from 1 pipe of cider sold; 4*s*. from the flesh of 1 ox, 2 cows and 1 steer dead from murrain sold at the audit; 10*s*. 7*d*. from the profit on livestock bought the previous year for the agistment of pasture and sold. Total, £24 19*s*. 7¾*d*.

Sale of corn

The same render account for £14 10*s*. from 54 qrs 3 bus. of wheat sold, at 5*s*. 4*d*. a qr; £4 9*s*. 8*d*. from 33½ qrs 1 bus. of mancorn sold, at 2*s*. 8*d*. a qr; £2 5*s*. 10*d*. from 13½ qrs 2 bus. of barley sold, at 3*s*. 4*d*. a qr; 11*s*. 5½*d*. from 3 qrs 3½ bus. sold at the audit; 6*s*. 10½*d*. from 2 qrs 6 bus. of dredge sold, at 2*s*. 6*d*. a qr; £2 14*s*. 6*d*. from 27 qrs 2 bus. of oats sold, at 2*s*. a qr; 1*s*. 4*d*. from 2 bus. of peas sold. Total, £24 19*s*. 8*d*.

Corn mill

The same render account for 10*s*. 7½*d*. from 4 qrs 2 bus. of mancorn from the issue of the mill sold, at 2*s*. 6*d*. a qr; 11*s*. 6¾*d*. from 4½ qrs 1 bus. of malt from the issue of the mill sold, at 2*s*. 6*d*. a qr. Total, £1 2*s*. 2¼*d*.

Entry and marriage fines

The same render account for 6*s*. 7*d*. from 8 tithings for tithingpenny at the hundred-court of Martinmas; 6*s*. 7*d*. at the hundred-court of Hockday for tithingpenny; 6*s*. 8*d*. from Alice, daughter of Richard le Blak', to have 1 messuage 9½ acres of land which belonged to the aforesaid R*ichard* her father; 10*s*. from John Godwyn' to have the said Alice with her land; 2*s*. 6*d*. from John Wudewyk' to have 1 pennyworth of land by surrender of Walter le Hare; 10*s*. from John atte Ford' for marrying Matilda his daughter outside the demesne; 5*s*. from Adam Orplyth' to have 1 messuage and 1 acre of land which belonged to Thomas Orplyth' his father; £1 from Nicholas Cha*m*b*er*layn to have 1 messuage 2 virgates of land which belonged to John his father; 10*s*. from Walter Folcry to have 1 messuage and ½ virgate of land which belonged to John his father; 4*s*. from Thomas Larg' to have 1 messuage 3 halfpennyworths of land which escheated into the lord's hands by the death of Cecil Larg'; 2*s*. from John Pistor' to have 1 messuage 1 butt by surrender of Thomas Cl*ericus*. Total, £4 3*s*. 4*d*.

Perquisites

The same render account for 6*d*. from Agatha Acruma*n* for assize; 3*d*. from H*enry* Pistor' for the same; 6*d*. from Hamo Nig*er* for the same; 6*d*. from Gilbert, son of G. ate Lak', for trespass (*trans*gressione); 3*d*. from John Giffard' for trespass; 3*d*. from Nicholas Serle for trespass; 3*d*. from Robert Algar for the same; 3*d*. from John Hamu*nd* for the same; 9*d*. from John Pistor' for the same; 3*d*. from Hamo Nig*er* for the same; 2*s*. 6*d*. from Ralph Mylys, Hamo Nig*er*, Thomas Brone, Robert Wayte, Matilda Sule, the relict of William Fab*er*, and William Fab*er* for assize; 3*d*. from John Pyk' for trespass; 6*d*. from William, son of W. de Wurdy, for false complaint; 2*s*. 6*d*. from Thomas Brun', William Smarty*n*, Hamo '*i*n*fra* po*n*te*m*', the relict of Holfort', Robert atte Lak', William Cusyn, Cecilia M*are*chal for assize; 6*d*. from Nicholas de Erly for trespass; 5*s*. from John ate Den' to have an agreement; 3*d*. from the son of Roginald Hurd' for trespass; 6*d*. from Christina But' to fix a boundary; 1*s*. from William Thurad' for trespass; 3*d*. from Thomas Brun' for trespass; 3*d*. from Hamo Nigr' for the same; 6*d*. from John Sadelare and Hugh Fab*er* for assize; 1*s*. from John Blak' for not doing his suit of court; 3*s*. from Hugh Fab*er*, John Sadeler', William Porc', Henry Pistor', Ralph ate Lak', Robert Wayte, Hamo Nig*er*, and Matilda Acruman, Ralph Milys, Agatha Acruma*n*, Robert Cl*ericus*, William Smart', John Nig*er* for assize; 6*d*. from G. ate Lake for false complaint; 1*s*. from Roginald Wygod' for the same; 3*d*. from Ralph H*er*berd' for trespass; 3*d*. from William de Holuuey for the same; 3*d*. from John Pist' for the same; 2*s*. from the tithing of Wargrave because it did not further challenge the default of William Milys; 6*d*. from the tithing at Cruchened' because it did not further challenge the default of Giles Boldro; 6*d*. from Thomas de Seleb' to have licence to sow 2 acres of land of R. de Rygges and 2 acres of land of John Pyk'; 6*d*. from the tithing at Wudereuue because it did not produce in court John Sadelar'; 3*d*. from the relict of Robert Cl*ericus* for assize of 2 acres of W. Lord', 3 acres of purpresture of J. de Mayneston, 3 acres of Walter Hare, 1 acre of J. Keu, for the term of 4 years; 3*d*. from Matilda Acruman for[1] assize; 3*d*. from Hamo Byhynebrigg' for the same; 3*d*. from Henry Pistor' for the same; 2*d*. from William Wyte for trespass; 3*d*. from William de Holeweye for trespass. Total, £1 8*s*. 11*d*.

Total of both, £5 12*s*. 3*d*.

Foreign receipts

Nothing from entry to purprestures this year. Nothing from green wax this year. The same render account for £17 1*s*. 10*d*. from Culham; £39 3*s*. from the reeve of Waltham St Lawrence; £37 4*s*. 7¾*d*. from Warfield; £6 1*s*. 5*d*. from Billingbear. Total, £99 10*s*. 10¾*d*.

Total of all receipts, £185 4*s*. ¾*d*.

Expenses for ploughs

In steel bought for 2 ploughs for the year 12*s*. In stipend of the smith for the year 3*s*. 8*d*. In shoeing 4 plough-horses for the year 2*s*. 10¼*d*. In 2 ploughshares bought 1*s*.

1 MS '⟨si*mi*li⟩'.

7*d*. In fodder bought 15*s*. 3*d*. In 1 pair of wheels bought 3*d*. In 1 sack bought 9*d*. In 3 oxen bought £1 18*s*. 1½*d*., at 15*s*. ¼*d*. for 1, and 12*s*. for another, and 11*s*. 1¼*d*. for 1. In 1 plough-horse bought 7*s*. Total, £4 1*s*. 5¾*d*.

Purchase of corn
In 2 qrs of oats bought for the fodder of cart-horses 3*s*. 8*d*. Total, 3*s*. 8*d*.

Carts
In shoeing cart-horses for the year 3*s*. 9*d*. In 1 pair of wheels bought 1*s*. 4*d*. In clouts with nails 2*s*. 10*d*. In grease bought for 2 carts 1*s*. 9½*d*. In 1 pair of saddle-pads and 3 collars bought 1*s*. 9*d*. In 1 saddle bought for the cart 2*d*. In 2 pairs of traces 10*d*. In 1 cart-rope 10*d*. In white leather bought 1*s*. 8*d*. In fitting the cart with axles 4*d*. In stipend of the smith mending the old cart with iron bought for the same 4½*d*. In 2 swingletrees bought 4½*d*. In 2 swingletrees bought 2*d*. In stipend of 1 carter for the year 3*s*. Total, 18*s*. 10*d*.

Cost of buildings
In roofing the great barn, byre and sheepcote in places 3*s*. 5½*d*. In mending the door to the stable 5*d*. In stipend of 1 man covering all the walls around the curia and the lord's arbour (*erbar'*) with stubble collected for the same 6*s*. 11½*d*. In a pig-ring bought to stop the pigs grubbing in the pasture 1½*d*. In mending the gate to the pinfold 1½*d*. In 1 stall for idle animals 2½*d*. In mending the room (*dom*us) above the gate 6*d*., with a key bought for the same. In mending the key bought for the great gate 1½*d*. Total, 11*s*. 11*d*.

Dairy
In 6 bus. of salt bought 2*s*. 4*d*., at 4*d*. a bus. In linen and woollen cloth bought 6*d*. In earthenware pots and pans bought 4*d*. In 1 brass pan bought 5*s*. ¼*d*. In new buckets bought 4*d*. In a press bought 7*d*. In 18 hurdles bought for the fold 1*s*. 6*d*. In grease, verdigris and vinegar bought 8*s*. In canvas bought for packing wool 1*s*. 9½*d*. In packing the wool 3*d*. In 1 cow bought with calf 8*s*. 8*d*. In stipend of 1 dairymaid for the year 3*s*. In roofing the house of the dairymaid by piece-work 1*s*. 2*d*. Total, £1 13*s*. 5¾*d*.

Threshing and winnowing
In threshing and winnowing 20 qrs 2 bus. of wheat, 35 qrs 2 bus. of mancorn by piece-work, which is over and above that threshed by labour service, 10*s*. 5*d*., at 2¼*d*. a qr. Total, 10*s*. 5*d*.

Cost of the meadows
In tossing the meadows of Rughedych' and la Morer' 5*d*., because they were tossed on a Saturday when no labour service was owed. In mowing, nothing, because they were mown by labour service. In expenses for mowing the portion of the meadows held by Jakeman which the lord gave by his charter for certain services, and for tossing and carrying the hay and stacking it in the barn, 1*s*. 3*d*. In expenses for stacking the corn from the same land 1*s*. In mowing, spreading and tossing the meadow of Keu' 2*s*. 2*d*., because the customary tenants were unwilling to enter it. Total, 4*s*. 10*d*.

Harvest-time
In weeding corn, nothing, on account of labour service. In expenses of 8 riders at 3 harvest boon-works 5*s*. In reaping corn which remains over and above that reaped by

customary tenants 5*s*. 1*d*. In stipend of 1 hayward who takes care of the grange and ploughing because there is no bailiff who stays there 5*s*. Total, 15*s*. 1*d*.

Expenses of the mill
In stipend of 1 carpenter mending the mill-building for 4 days by piece-work 1*s*. In mending the inner wheel and making 2 trundle-wheels anew by piece-work 3*s*. In cleaning the ditch of Muledych' for 3 days 8*d*. In steel bought for the small bills (*bekett'*) of the mill 4*d*. In lengthening the spindle, with the stipend of the smith, and iron bought for the same, 10*d*. In steeling the small bills 2*d*. Total, 6*s*.

Expenses of the steward
In expenses of the steward for the tourn of Martinmas 11*s*. 10*d*. In expenses of the steward for the tourn of Hockday £1 3*s*. 11½*d*. by tally. Total, £1 15*s*. 9½*d*.

Expenses of the bailiff
In expenses of the bailiff for his visits £7 1*s*. 9½*d*. In fur for his winter and summer livery 6*s*. Total, £7 7*s*. 9½*d*.

Expenses for the fishery
In expenses made mending and reinforcing the weir by bringing piles and marl thither 1*s*. 11*d*. In stipend of 1 fisherman for the year 3*s*. Total, 4*s*. 11*d*.

Total of all expenses, £18 14*s*. 2½*d*.

And he owes, £166 9*s*. 10¼*d*.

Foreign expenses
In expenses of Nicholas de Wodema*n*kot' and others who came with him on 1 occasion 3*s*. 2*d*. In gifts to the same 6*s*. 8*d*. In 1,000 pieces of talwood made by piece-work and carried to London by order of the bishop 4*s*. 2*d*., at 5*d*. a 100. In 30 qrs of charcoal made by piece-work 3*s*. 9*d*., at 1½*d*. a qr. In 1 boat hired to take the said 900 pieces of talwood and 20 qrs of charcoal to London £1. In 1 man looking after the said talwood and charcoal as far as Southwark 1*s*. In a man hired to load the said boat 1*s*. 2*d*. In a writ of the steward sent to Simon at Winchester for the law-day held on Hockday at Farnham 4*d*. In stipend of 1 carpenter propping up the old stable 1*s*. 5*d*. In re-roofing the room above the gate with 6,000 old tiles by piece-work 3*s*. 9*d*. In stipend of 1 man helping the said tiler 1*s*. 2*d*. In building a wall between the road and the stable 5*d*. In making ½ cask of cider with 2 qrs of apples bought for the same 1*s*. 6*d*. Total, £2 8*s*. 9*d*.

m.17d
New Building
In 8 men keeping watch on the first night that the stable burned down (*combussit circa igne'*) 1*s*. 4*d*. In men hired to collect the old timber and see what was not burned in the same 2*s*. In ale bought for the men putting out the fire 1*s*. 5*d*. In men hired to clear the underpinning and stalls 2*s*. 10½*d*. In 8 carpenters hired to drag away the old timber and carry that not approved to the garden 9*s*. 4*d*. In men hired to gather and separate tiles, stone and mortar 7*s*. 3*d*. In clearing dung from the old stable, cleaning the plot, 2*s*. 8*d*. In 1 new cart bought with all equipment to carry timber to the stable 12*s*. 5*d*. In 1 horse bought for the same £1 1*s*. 9¼*d*. In stipend of 1 man bringing the

said cart, for stipend and livery for ½ year, 11*s.* 10*d.* In expenses of the men coming with 7 carts to carry timber from Farnham to Wargrave for a boon-work 1*s.* 4*d.* In 1 qr of oats bought for fodder for their horses for 1 night 2*s.* In timber bought at Waltham St Lawrence 19*s.* In timber carried from Farnham to Wargrave 5*s.* 1*d.* In timber carried from Billingbear and Waltham St Lawrence 1*s.* 9*d.* In 1 windlass bought for raising timbers 1*s.* In 5 long ladders made 2*s.* 5*d.* In agreement of the carpenters for piece-work £7 14*s.* In expenses of the same and their fellows when raising the stable for 4 days 10*s.* In 1 rope bought for the timber 1*s.* In expenses of the men helping to raise the timbers of the said stable for the aforesaid 4 days 6*s.* 10½*d.* In 7,000 laths bought £1 15*s.*, at 5*s.* a 1,000. In 29,700 lath-nails bought 17*s.* 4½*d.*, at 7½*d.* a 1,000. In large nails, that is, plank-nails, 2*s.* 2*d.* In 37,500 tiles and 25 ridge-tiles with lime and tile-pins, with the stipend of the roofer laying the said tiles, £5 12*s.* 3*d.*, at 3*s.* a 1,000. In stipend of 1 man cleaning the foundations for the walls of the stable 1½*d.* In 3 carters hired to collect stones and quarry chalk (*alb*am *terr*a*m*) and cart it to the stable 10½*d.* In agreement with the masons to build the wall on the east side of the stable and the foundations below the sills by piece-work £1 19*s.* 7½*d.* In 2 men hired for 6 weeks to provide for the said masons 7*s.* 4*d.* In plastering the walls of the said stable on the west side and the southern end 6*s.* 2*d.* In making hip-tile nails 6*d.* In 1 cask to bring lime put right with iron bought for the same 8*d.* In boards sawn and sheds and mangers made 2*s.* In mangers, stalls and fodder-racks made and put right 1*s.* 9*d.* In 'mora' pins which were used to make mangers 2*d.*[1] In hooks, hinges and nails bought for the stable door 7*s.* In 1 lock bought 5*d.* In 16 qrs of lime bought for roofing the stable walls and the room above the gate and other buildings in places 6*s.* 8*d.*, at 5*d.* a qr. Total, £25 17*s.* 5¼*d.*

Total of all allowances, £28 6*s.* 2¼*d.*

Cash deliveries
Delivered to Sir G*eoffrey*, treasurer of Wolvesey, by 1 tally, £58 6*s.*

Total of all allowances and cash deliveries, £86 12*s.* 2¼*d.*

And thus he owes clear, £79 17*s.* 8*d.*

Issues of the grange

Wheat
{yield: 5½-fold less 2 qrs 3 bus.}
The same render account for 64 qrs 2 bus. from the whole issue of wheat from the grange with the increment of the granary.
Sown over 22 acres measured by the perch which lie in the field of la Den', 8 qrs 2 bus.; that is, 3 bus. an acre, plus 1 bus. in all. Mixed with mancorn, 1½ qrs. Sold, 54 qrs 3 bus.

Mancorn
{yield: 3-fold less 6 bus.}
The same render account for 58½ qrs 3 bus. from the whole issue of mancorn from the grange with the increment of the granary; 1½ qrs mixed from wheat. Total, 60 qrs 3 bus.
Sown over 40 acres measured by the perch which lie in the field of Den', 17 qrs 2 bus.; that is, 3½ bus. an acre, less 2 bus. in all. In customary payment for the mowing

1 MS 'In mora pynne ij d. q*uo*d' manger' f*act*i fuer' ij d.'.

of the meadow, 1 qr. Delivered to 1 warrener who takes care of the grange and ploughing for the year, 6½ qrs, because he takes a quarter every 8 weeks. Delivered to 1 man who helped with the fishery in the Thames when it was necessary, 1 qr. In supporting pigs in winter, 1 qr. Sold, 33½ qrs 1 bus.

Barley
{yield: 3½-fold less 1 qr 2½ bus.; he should have a term for the livery of the dairymaid}
The same render account for 42 qrs 2 bus. from the whole issue of barley from the grange with the increment of the granary.
Sown over 31 acres measured by the perch as they lie in the field within the ditch, 15 qrs 2 bus.; that is, 4 bus. an acre. Delivered to 1 carter for the year, 5 qrs 2½ bus., because he takes a quarter[1] every 10 weeks. Delivered to 1 dairymaid, 4 qrs 2 bus., because she takes a quarter every 16 weeks in winter. In supporting weaned piglets and peacocks, 4 bus. Sold, 13½ qrs 2 bus. Sold at the audit, 3 qrs 3½ bus.

Dredge
The same render account for 5 qrs 2 bus. from the whole issue of dredge from the grange with the increment of the granary.
Sown over 5 acres which lie in the field within the ditch, 2½ qrs; that is, 4 bus. an acre. Sold, 2 qrs 6 bus.

Oats
{yield: two-fold less 11 qrs 2 bus.}
The same render account for 78½ qrs 2 bus. from the whole issue of oats from the grange with the increment of the granary; 2 qrs bought. Total, 80½ qrs 2 bus.
Sown over 50 acres which lie in the field within the ditch, 31 qrs 3 bus.; that is, 5 bus. an acre, plus 1 bus. in all. In fodder of the cart-horses for the year and 2 cart-horses for ½ year, 18½ qrs 2 bus., and this for labour at the stable. In fodder of the steward's horses at the tourn of Martinmas, 1 qr by tally. In supporting 31 pigs after mast until they were sold, 2 qrs 3 bus. Sold, 27 qrs 2 bus.

Peas
{yield: two-fold}
The same render account for 3 bus. of peas from the whole issue of the grange with the increment of the granary. Sown, 1 bus. Sold, 2 bus.

Mill
Mancorn: 4 qrs 2 bus. from the whole issue of the mill; all sold.
Malt: 4½ qrs 1 bus. from the issue of the malt mill; all sold.

Stock

Cart-horses: 2 remain from the previous year; 1 bought. Total, 3. 3 remain.
Plough-horses: 4 females remain from the previous year; 1 added from colts; 1 bought. Total, 6. 1 sold; 5 females remain.
Colts: 1 remains from the previous year's young colts; added above to plough-horses; none remain.
Young colts: 1 remains from the previous year's foals; 1 two-year old female remains.

1 MS omits 'a quarter'.

Foals: 1 from this year's offspring; 1 male remains.
Oxen: 17 remain from the previous year; 2 added from stock; 3 bought. Total, 22. 3 sold; 1 in murrain. Total, 4. 18 remain.
Bulls: 1 added from steers; 1 remains.
Cows: 26 remain from the previous year; 8 added from stock; 1 bought with calf; 1 from the heriot of John Folcr' after calving at the feast of St James (25 July). Total, 36. 2 in murrain before calving; 5 sold before calving. Total, 7. 29 remain.
Steers: 11 remain from the previous year's bullocks; ½ from the heriot of Richard le Blak'. 2 added to oxen, 1 to bulls, 8 to cows; ½ sold. Total, 11½. None remain.
Bullocks: 9 remain from the previous year's yearlings; 1 in murrain; 8 remain, 3 of them male.
Yearlings: 9 remain from the previous year's calves; 1 in murrain; 8 remain.
Calves: 20 from this year's offspring, and 1 accounted with cows, because 7 sterile; 2 in tithe; 11 sold; 8 remain.
Wethers: 79 remain from the previous year; 17 hoggs added from stock. Total, 96. 8 sold at Martinmas; 1 in customary payment for the mowing of the meadows; 3 in murrain after shearing. Total, 12. 84 remain.
Ewes: 61 remain from the previous year; 12 added from hoggs; 1 from the heriot of Thomas Orplyth' before lambing. Total, 74. 15 sold at Martinmas; 59 remain.
Hoggs: 31 remain from the previous year's lambs. 2 in murrain before shearing; 17 added to wethers, 12 to ewes. Total, 31. None remain.
Lambs: 39 produced by the ewes this year because 8 were sterile. 6 in murrain before weaning; 3 in tithe; 1 in customary payment to the shepherd. Total, 10. 29 remain.
Sows: 4 remain from the previous year; 1 sold at Martinmas; 3 remain.
Pigs: 41 remain from the previous year; 18 added from stock. Total, 59. 30 sold at Martinmas; 29 remain.
Hoggets: 22 remain from the previous year's piglets. 4 in murrain; 18 added to pigs. Total, 22. None remain.
Piglets: 36 from the offspring of the said sows. 3 in tithe; 1 in customary payment to the swineherd. Total, 4. 32 remain.
Fleeces {yield of fleece 4½*d.* plus 1*s.* 7½*d.* in all}: 147 produced at the shearing this year; 79 produced at Culham. Total, 226. 14 in tithe for the wool of Wargrave; 212 sent to Wolvesey, which made 1½ weys 3 cloves.
Lamb's-wool {yield of fleece 1½*d.* plus 2½*d.* in all}: 29 produced at the shearing this year; all sent to Wolvesey, which made 16 lb.
Winter cheese: 40 made this year; 4 in tithe; 38 sold, which made ½ wey 3 cloves.
Summer cheese {yield of cow 5*s.* and sheep 3*d.*, less 3*s.* 3*d.* in all this year with 1 cheese in customary payment valued at 6*d.*}: 161 cheeses made between Monday the morrow of Easter (23 April) and Michaelmas (29 September), both days included; 16 in tithe; 1 in customary payment for the mowing of the meadows; 144 sold, which made 9 weys and 1 quarter.
Butter: 20½ cloves sold from the issue of the dairy this year; all sold.
Swans: 3 remain from the previous year; 2 sold; 1 remains.
Peacocks: 5 remain from the previous year; 1 from this year's offspring. Total, 6. 1 in murrain; 5 remain.
Hens: 48 from churchscot. 6 in default of William Bost', Juliana Hamu*n*d, Edith Holfout', Agatha Acruma*n*, Matilda Sule; 42 sold. Total, 48. None remain.
Carts: 1 cart with iron tyres and 1 of wood remain from the previous year; 1 new cart with iron tyres and 1 of wood bought this year. Total, 4. 1 wooden cart used in the manor; 2 carts with iron tyres, 1 of wood remain.

[Sacks]: 1 remains from the previous year; 1 bought. Total, 2. 1 used in the manor; 1 remains.
Rakes and sickles: 1 rake and 1 sickle remain from the previous year; they remain.
[Cider]: ½ cask remains from the previous year; 7 casks from the issue of the garden this year. Total, 7½ casks. 1 pipe sold; 7 casks remain.
Hides: 1 from an ox, 2 from cows, 1 from a bullock, 1 from a yearling in murrain. Total, 5. All sold.
[Skins]: 2 woolskins from hoggs in murrain before shearing and 3 skins from wethers after shearing. Total, 5. All sold.
[Lambskins]: 6 from lambs in murrain before weaning; 6 sold; none remain.
Utensils: 1 brass pan of 3 gallons bought; it remains.

Culham

[Rents of assize]
James de North', bailiff, and William Kepe, reeve, render account for £2 1*s*. ½*d*. for all rents of assize at Easter (22 April); £2 1*s*. ½*d*. at Michaelmas (29 September). Total, £4 2*s*. 1*d*.

[Increment]
Nothing this year from increment of rent.

[Quittances]
In quittance of 1 reeve for the year 1*s*.; 1 carter for the year 6*d*.; 1 shepherd for the year 6*d*.; 1 hayward for the year 6*d*. Total, 2*s*. 6*d*.

Total of rents remaining, £3 19*s*. 7*d*.

[Annual gifts]
The same render account for 9*s*. ½*d*. from annual gifts at Easter; 9*s*. ½*d*. at Michaelmas. Total, 18*s*. 1*d*.

[Annual recognizance]
The same render account for 6*d*. from the annual recognizance of William Piscator' of Culham so that he may remain outside the manor and pay suit to the tithing. Total, 6*d*.

Issues of the manor
The same render account for 3*s*. ½*d*. from common pannage of pigs, that is, from 27 pigs, 19 piglets, at 1*d*. a pig over a year old, and ½*d*. a piglet; 9*s*. 6*d*. from pannage of Kylh*a*mfryth', from 42 pigs and 30 piglets agisted in the wood of Kylh*am*fryth', at 2*d*. a pig, 1*d*. a piglet; £1 8*d*. from 3 oxen sold, at 7*s*. each for 2, and 6*s*. 8*d*. for 1; 16*s*. from 2 cows sold together; 16*s*. 8*d*. from 14 calves sold together; £1 6*d*. from 20 old kebb wethers sold at Martinmas; 1*s*. 7*d*. from the hide sold of 1 cow in murrain; 2*s*. 3*d*. from the hides sold of 3 bullocks and 3 yearlings in murrain; 1*d*. from the hide sold of 1 calf in murrain; 1*s*. 5½*d*. from the skins of 5 wethers in murrain before shearing; 9*d*. from the skins sold of 6 wethers in murrain after shearing; 3*s*. 11*d*. from 12 cloves of winter cheese sold; £3 3*s*. from 7 weys of summer cheese sold, at 9*s*. a wey; 10*s*. from 20 cloves of butter sold; 1*s*. 4*d*. from 16 hens from churchscot sold;

7*s*. 6*d*. for release from labour service; 2*s*. 8*d*. from the pasturage upon la Hethe sold; 2*s*. from the heriot of Walter ate Mull'; 6*d*. from the heriot of N*icholas* Nel because he did not have one animal; 1*s*. 4*d*. from the pasturage of Westgarsto*n* sold; £1 12*s*. 3*d*. from the dairy produce of cows sold at the audit. Total, £10 17*s*.

Sale of corn
The same render account for £1 7*s*. 7½*d*. from 6 qrs 3 bus. of wheat sold, at 4*s*. 4*d*. a qr; £3 10*s*. 11¼*d*. from 28 qrs 3 bus. of mancorn sold, at 2*s*. 6*d*. a qr; 3¾*d*. from 1 bus. sold at the audit; £1 18*s*. 9*d*. from 11½ qrs 1 bus. of barley sold, at 3*s*. 4*d*. a qr. Total, £6 17*s*. 7½*d*.

Entry and marriage fines
The same render account for 3*s*. ½*d*. for tithingpenny at the hundred-court of Martinmas; 3*s*. ½*d*. at the hundred-court of Hockday; 13*s*. 4*d*. from William, son of Walter Mol*endinarius*, to have 4½ acres of land which belonged to Walter his father; 2*s*. from Alice, who was wife of N*icholas* Nel, to have 1 messuage ½ virgate of land which belonged to Nicholas her husband; 3*s*. from John, son of John Boul', to have 1 acre of purpresture by surrender of the said John his father; 2*s*. from William le Walays for marrying Matilda his daughter outside the demesne. Total, £1 6*s*. 5*d*.

Perquisites
The same render account for 1*s*. from Alice Croyll', Walter Ryd', John Gay, Agnes ate Strod' for breaking the assize of ale; 3*d*. from Thomas Buthory for trespass; 3*d*. from Thomas ate Wod' for trespass; 3*d*. from Justina Juveni for the same; 3*d*. from John Crys for the same; 6*d*. from William Wallno*n* for trespass; 3*d*. from the same for trespass; 1*s*. from William Kepe for trespass; 1*s*. from John Baldewyn' for trespass; 3*d*. from John Crys for trespass; 9*d*. from John Baldeweyn', Cecilia Boul', Christina P*ro*final for assize; 6*d*. from William Wallyno for trespass; 3*d*. from the same because he married his daughter without licence; 1*s*. from Agnes ate Strod', Christina P*ro*final, John Baldewyn' for assize; 3*d*. from Agnes atte Strod' for assize; 6*s*. 8*d*. from John P*arson*a of Remenham for trespass made in the lord's wood of Culh*a*mfryth'; 1*s*. from the same for unjustly taking the chattels of Amice Heryng'; 1*s*. from William Ke for trespass; 6*d*. from Walter ate Fryth' for the same; 1*s*. from Adam Coc*us* for the same; 6*d*. from Geoffrey Coleby; 3*d*. from John Baldewyn' for the same; 6*d*. from G. de Cruce that he may be removed from his office; 3*d*. from John Crys for trespass; 2*d*. from Richard Gosemayn for trespass; 2*d*. from G. de Cruce for trespass. Total, 19*s*. 9*d*.

Total of both, £2 6*s*. 2*d*.

Entry to purprestures
Nothing this year from entry to purprestures.

Total of all receipts, £24 18*s*. 11½*d*.

Expenses for ploughs
In steel for ploughs 7*s*. 5*d*. In stipend of the smith repairing ironwork 3*s*. In shoeing 7 horses for the year 9*s*. 8*d*. In 2 ploughshares bought 1*s*. 5*d*. In 4 plough-irons bought 1*s*. In 2 pairs of wheels bought 6*d*. In 7 halters and 1 rope made from hair 2½*d*. In stipend of 1 drover for the year 4*s*. 6*d*. In 1 sack bought 9*d*. Total, £1 8*s*. 5½*d*.

Expenses for sowing and liveries

In 1 qr of wheat bought 4*s*. 4*d*. In 19 qrs of mancorn bought for sowing £2 13*s*., at 2*s*. 6*d*. a qr for 8 qrs, and 3*s*. a qr for 11 qrs. Total, £2 17*s*. 4*d*.

Carts

In 1 pair of wheels bought for the cart 2*s*. 2*d*. In clouts with nails bought 10½*d*., and so much because it was at Farnham in order to collect timber and talwood at the water (*quesivit talu*erud*' ad aq'*). In grease for the cart 5*d*. In fitting the cart with axles 3*d*. In 1 pair of cart-shafts made from their own timber 4½*d*. In 1 pair of saddle-pads bought 6*d*. Total, 4*s*. 7*d*.

m.18

Cost of buildings

In roofing the byre at various times 1*s*. 4*d*. In roofing the barn in places 7*d*. In mending the walls of the byre at various times 9½*d*. In mending 1 barrow 2*d*. In 1 shovel bought 1*d*. Total, 2*s*. 11½*d*.

Dairy

In small cloths bought for the dairy 4*d*. In 5 bus. of salt bought 1*s*. 8*d*. In earthenware pots and pans bought 4*d*. In a press bought 1*s*. 4*d*. In 2 buckets bought 4*d*. In grease, copperas and verdigris bought 6*s*. ½*d*. In forage bought to support the livestock and cows 4*s*. 4*d*. In 2 cows bought before calving £1 2½*d*., at 9*s*. 1½*d*. for 1. In a cow bought after calving 9*s*. In stipend of 1 dairymaid for the year 3*s*. Total, £2 6*s*. 7*d*.

Threshing and winnowing

In threshing and winnowing 8½ qrs 2 bus. of wheat by piece-work, with 20 qrs of mancorn and 10 qrs of oats, 5*s*. 5½*d*., at 2*d*. a qr of wheat and mancorn threshed and 1*d*. per 5 qrs winnowed, and ¾*d*. a qr of oats threshed and 1*d*. per 8 qrs winnowed. Total, 5*s*. 5½*d*.

Expenses for dung {henceforth dung should be carried by the lord's plough-horses}

In clearing dung in winter from the curia to the fields 1*s*. 6*d*. Total, 1*s*. 6*d*.

Harvest-time

In corn reaped and bound by piece-work 6*s*. 4½*d*. In expenses of 1 boon-work for reaping corn 3*s*. 10½*d*. Total, 10*s*. 3*d*.

Total of all expenses, £7 17*s*. 1½*d*.

In William de Wordly, reeve of Wargrave, £17 1*s*. 10*d*.

Issues of the grange[1]

Wheat

{yield: two-fold less 6 bus.}

The same render account for 8½ qrs 2 bus. from the whole issue of wheat from the grange with the increment of the granary; 1 qr bought. Total, 9½ qrs 2 bus.
Sown over 9 acres measured by the perch which lie in the field upon the heath, 3 qrs[2] 3 bus. Sold as noted above, 6 qrs 3 bus.

1 MS omits heading.

2 MS '⟨ij bus.⟩'.

Mancorn
{yield: two-and-a-half-fold plus 2 qrs}
The same render account for 39½ qrs from the whole issue of mancorn from the grange with the increment of the granary; 19 qrs bought. Total, 58½ qrs.
Sown over 51 acres measured by the perch as they lie[1] in the field upon the heath, 19 qrs; that is, 3 bus. an acre, less 1 bus. in all. Delivered to 1 drover and 1 dairymaid for the year, 10 qrs 3 bus., because they take a quarter every 10 weeks. In customary payment for the mowing of the meadows, 5 bus. Sold, 28 qrs 3 bus. Sold at the audit, 1 bus.

Barley
{yield: three-fold less 1 bus.}
The same render account for 19 qrs from the whole issue of the grange with the increment of the granary.
Sown over 15 acres which lie in the field of la Doun', 7 qrs 3 bus.; that is, 4 bus. an acre, less 1 bus. in all. Sold, 11½ qrs 1 bus.

Oats
{yield: 2 bus. more than sown}
The same render account for 20 qrs from the whole issue of oats from the grange with the increment of the granary.
Sown over 26 acres measured by the perch as they lie in the fields of la Doun' and Stanlych', 15½ qrs 3 bus.; that is, 5 bus. an acre, plus 2 bus. in all. In fodder of 7 plough-horses, 4 qrs 1 bus.

Stock

Plough-horses: 7 males remain from the previous year; they remain.
Oxen: 3 remain from the previous year; 2 added from stock. Total, 5. 3 sold; 2 remain.
Bulls: 1 remains from the previous year; it remains.
Cows: 23 remain from the previous year; 2 added from stock; 3 bought, 1 after calving. Total, 28. 1 in murrain before calving; 2 sold at Martinmas. Total, 3. 25 remain.
Steers: 4 remain from the previous year's bullocks. 2 added to oxen, 2 to cows. Total, 4. None remain.
Bullocks: 9 remain from the previous year's yearlings; 3 in murrain; 6 remain, of which[2]
Yearlings: 6 remain from the previous year's calves; 3 in murrain; 3 remain.
Calves: 22 from this year's offspring because 2 cows sterile. 2 in tithe; 14 sold; 1 in murrain after weaning. Total, 15.[3] 5 remain.
Wethers: 112 remain from the previous year. 5 in murrain before shearing, 6 after shearing; 1 in customary payment for the mowing of the meadows; 20 sold. Total, 32. 80 remain.
Fleeces: 87 produced at the shearing this year; 8 in tithe; 79 sent to Wargrave.
Winter cheese: 37 made; 3 in tithe; 34 sold, which made 12 cloves.
Summer cheese {yield of cow 5*s*. with 1 cheese in customary payment valued at 10*d*. this year and not more on account of the cleaning of the temses}: 159

1 MS repeats 'iace*nt*'.

2 MS omits final phrase.

3 Figures add up to 17. '5 remain' written again in MS between calves sold and in murrain.

cheeses made between the eve of St Mark the Evangelist (24 April) and Michaelmas (29 September), both days included; 15 in tithe; 1 in customary payment for the mowing of the meadows; 143 sold, which made 7 weys.
Butter: 20 cloves from the issue of the dairy this year; all sold.
Hens: 20 from churchscot this year; 4 in default through the death of husbands; 16 sold; none remain.
Utensils: 1 wooden cart remains from the previous year; 1 bought. Total, 2. 1 used in the manor; 1 remains. 1 cart-rope, 1 pair of traces, 1 collar, 1 cart-saddle with saddle-pads, 3 old swingletrees for the horses; all remain.
Sacks: 1 remains from the previous year; 1 bought. Total, 2. 1 used in the manor; 1 remains.
Pans: 1 remains from the previous year; 1 remains.

Waltham St Lawrence

Rents of assize
James de North', bailiff, and Alexander de Ponte, reeve, render account for £6 1*s.* 8½*d.* for all rents of assize at Easter (22 April); £6 1*s.* 8¾*d.* at Michaelmas (29 September). Total, £12 3*s.* 5¼*d.*

Quittances
In quittance of 1 reeve for the year 2*s.*; 1 forester for the year 2*s.*; 1 hayward for the year 6*d.*; 4 ploughmen for the year 2*s.* Total, 6*s.* 6*d.*

Total of rents remaining, £11 16*s.* 11¼*d.*

Annual gifts
The same render account for £1 7*s.* 7½*d.* from annual gifts at Easter; £1 7*s.* 7½*d.* at Michaelmas. Total, £2 15*s.* 3*d.*

Issues of the manor
The same render account for 17*s.* 2½*d.* from common pannage of pigs, that is, from 150 pigs over a year old and 113 piglets, at 1*d.* a pig and ½*d.* a piglet; 8*d.* from the pasturage in Brodmed' sold after mowing; 6*d.* from the pasturage of Selemed' sold; 1*s.* 6*d.* from the pasturage of the field of Muldelye sold in winter; 3*s.* 2½*d.* from loppings sold; 1*s.* 6*d.* from 2 ploughshares sold; £2 3*s.* 6*d.* for release from labour services; 2*s.* from 24 hens from churchscot sold {**henceforth the reeve should take the hens and not the money**}; 2*s.* 6*d.* from fish sold; 18*s.* from 2 oxen sold at Martinmas (11 November). Total, £4 10*s.* 7*d.*

Sale of corn
The same render account for £6 8*d.* from 22½ qrs 1 bus. of wheat sold, at 5*s.* 4*d.* a qr; £6 11*s.* from 56 qrs 1 bus. of mancorn sold, at 2*s.* 4*d.* a qr; £1 15*s.* 3*d.* from 11½ qrs 2 bus. of barley sold, at 3*s.* a qr; 2*s.* 9¾*d.* from 1 qr 1 bus. of dredge sold, at 2*s.* 6*d.* a qr; £3 3*s.* 3*d.* from 31½ qrs 1 bus. of oats sold, at 2*s.* a qr; 13*s.* 4*d.* from 5 qrs of peas sold, at 2*s.* 8*d.* a qr. Total, £18 6*s.* 4¼*d.*

Entry and marriage fines
The same render account for 8*s.* 7*d.* from 4 tithings for tithingpenny at the hundred-court of Martinmas; 8*s.* 7*d.* from 4 tithings for tithingpenny at the hundred-court of

Hockday; 2*s.* from Joan, who was wife of Alexander ate Hocch', to retain a halfpennyworth of land which belonged to the said Alexander her husband; £1 from Walter, son of Hamo Blak', to have 1 messuage, ½ virgate and 2 pennyworths of land and 1 ferling of purpresture which belonged to his said father. Total, £1 19*s.* 2*d.*

Perquisites

The same render account for 1*s.* 6*d.* from Joan Fullar', Seva*rus*, William Hony, William Ferin, Alexander Fab*er*, Eva Doget' and John Grimme for assize; 1*s.* from Hamo Joldewyn' to confirm an agreement; 3*d.* from John de Mayd' for trespass; 3*d.* from Robert de Gard' for trespass; 3*d.* from the relict of Yve for the same; 3*d.* from Nicholas Tony for the same; 3*d.* from Thomas le Webbe for the same; 3*d.* from William de Piro for the same; 6*d.* from William Nu*n*co*n* for trespass; 3*s.* 3*d.* from N. de Gard', William ate Westend', Stephen Luffryth', Robert Palm*ere*, Roger Abraa*m*, Hamo Strong', Eva Doget', the relict of Tony, Cecilia Smewyn', Robert Godwy*n*, William de Fonte and John de Cruce for assize; 3*d.* from Thomas le Webb*e* for trespass; 3*d.* from Alice Webb' for an agreement; 3*d.* from Alexander Lyp for trespass; 1*s.* 3*d.* from William Wyky*ng*, Alexander Fab*er*, Robert Fullar', William Hony, W*illiam* Feur for assize; 1*s.* from Agnes Wyȝ because she withdrew from court without licence; 6*d.* from Robert de Holebrok' so that he may be removed (*am*mo*veat*ur); 6*d.* from John Pychou and John de Cruce for an agreement; 6*d.* from Hamo, son of Jordan Sygar, for unjustly withholding; 3*d.* from N. ate Heth' because he did not produce in court; 6*s.* 8*d.* from Walter Wyte because he did not wish to be elected reeve; 3*d.* from Hamo St*ro*nge for assize; 2*s.* from William ate Heth' for trespass; 3*d.* from Thomas Aynolf for the same; 3*d.* from John Fab*er* for the same; 1*s.* from Robert Palm*ere*, William Wyky*ng*', Christina Pech', Alexander Fab*er* for assize; 6*d.* from Thomas Webb' for trespass; 6*d.* from the same for the same; 3*d.* from John de Cruce because he did not produce in court; 1*s.* from Alexander Lyp because he sold marl without licence; 1*s.* from John de Cruce for the same; 1*s.* 9*d.* from William Hony, John ate Thute, William Ferur, Robert Palm*ere*, Christina Sut*ere*, Robert Fullar', John Sutar' for assize; 6*d.* from Simon ate Selebrig' because he did not make presentment; 3*d.* from Margery Tony because she sold marl; 1*s.* 6*d.* from the tithing of Waltham according to custom; 1*s.* from the tithing at Hall' because it did not challenge the default of N. Fullar'; 6*d.* from Richard Wyteb' for the hue; 6*d.* from the tithing of South Lake because it did not attach Agnes ate Barr'; 6*d.* from William Hony and William Ferin for assize; 2*s.* from Robert Fullar', W*illiam* Hony, W*illiam* Ferin, John ate Thite, Alexander Fab*er*, Richard Smewyn', the relict of Frewyn', John Wyky*ng* for assize; 3*d.* from John Sutor' for trespass; 3*d.* from William Wyky*ng* for the same. Total, £1 15*s.* 2*d.*

Total of both, £3 14*s.* 4*d.*

Nothing from entry to purprestures and green wax this year.

Total of all receipts, £41 3*s.* 5½*d.*

Cost of ploughs

In steel bought for 2 ploughs for the year 6*s.* 9*d.* In stipend of the smith repairing the ploughs for the year 4*s.* In shoeing 6 plough-horses for the year 1*s.* 9½*d.* In 2 pairs of wheels bought for the year 8*d.* In 1 sack bought 9*d.* Total, 13*s.* 11½*d.*

Cost of buildings

In roofing the great barn 6*s.* 2*d.* In mending 2 locks for the doors to the barn and the bailiff's chamber 2½*d.* In making the gate of Rug*ro*ve and the gate to Holbrok' 7½*d.* Total, 7*s.*

Threshing and winnowing
In threshing corn for the forage of oxen and other livestock 1*s*. Total, 1*s*.

Expenses for clearing dung
In clearing dung to the field which is called la Lygh' 5*s*. Total, 5*s*.

Expenses for weeding
In weeding the corn remaining over and above that able to be weeded by labour service, 1*s*. this year, on account of the large number of thistles. Total, 1*s*.

Expenses for the meadows
In 1 wether bought after shearing according to custom for the mowing of the meadows 1*s*. In cheese bought for the same 8*d*. Total, 1*s*. 8*d*.

Harvest-time
In reaping and binding the remainder of the corn not reaped by labour service 10*s*. 10*d*. Total, 10*s*. 10*d*.

Total of all expenses, £2 5½*d*.

Cash deliveries
Delivered to William de Wurdly, reeve of Wargrave, £39 3*s*.

Issues of the grange

Wheat
{yield: 8-fold plus 1 bus.}
The same render account for 27 qrs 1 bus. from the whole issue of wheat from the grange with the increment of the granary.
Sown over 15 acres measured by the perch which lie in the field of Muldelych', 4½ qrs; that is, 2½ bus. an acre, less 1 bus. in all. Sold, 22½ qrs 1 bus.

Mancorn
{yield: four-and-a-half-fold plus 1½ qrs}
The same render account for 75½ qrs from the whole issue of mancorn from the grange with the increment of the granary.
Sown over 49 acres measured by the perch which lie in the fields of Muldelygh' and la Den', 18½ qrs 1 bus.; that is, 3 bus. an acre, less 3 bus. in all. In customary payment for the mowing of the meadows, 6 bus. Sold, 56 qrs 1 bus.

Barley
{yield: 4-fold less 3 bus.}
The same render account for 16 qrs 1 bus. from the whole issue of barley from the grange with the increment of the granary.
Sown over 9 acres measured by the perch which lie in the field of Greyte, 4 qrs 3 bus.; that is, 4 bus. an acre, less 1 bus. in all. Sold, 11½ qrs 2 bus.

Dredge
{yield: 4½-fold}
The same render account for 4½ qrs from the whole issue of dredge from the grange with the increment of the granary.

Sown over 7 acres measured by the perch which lie in the field of Greyt', 3 qrs 3 bus.; that is, 4 bus. an acre, less 1 bus. in all. Sold, 1 qr 1 bus.

Oats
{yield: two-fold less 2 qrs 1 bus.}
The same render account for 54½ qrs 3 bus. from the whole issue of oats from the grange with the increment of the granary.
Sown over 38 acres measured by the perch which lie in the field of Greyte, 23 qrs 2 bus.; that is, 5 bus. an acre, plus 4 bus. in all. Sold, 31½ qrs 1 bus.

Peas
{yield: six-fold less ½ qr}
The same render account for 6 qrs 2 bus. from the whole issue of peas from the grange with the increment of the granary. Sown, 1 qr 2 bus. Sold, 5 qrs.

Stock

Plough-horses: 5 females remain from the previous year; 1 from the heriot of Hamo Blast'; 2 added from colts. Total, 8.[1] 8 remain, 1 of them male.
Colts: 2 remain from the previous year's young colts; 2 added to plough-horses; none remain.
Young colts: 1 remains from the previous year's foals; 1 female remains.
Foals: no offspring this year.
Oxen: 14 remain from the previous year; 2 sold at Martinmas; 12 remain.
Wethers: 1 bought after shearing; 1 in provision for the mowing of the meadows; none remain.
Cheese: 1 bought; 1 in customary payment for the mowing of the meadows; none remain.
Hens: 28 from churchscot. 2 in default of the land of William[2] le Messag' because he held by charter; 2 in default through the death of Gilbert Joldewyn' and Alexander Bron; 24 sold; none remain.
Ploughshares: 4 from rents of assize, that is, 1 from William de Cruce, 1 from John de Mayd' who holds the land of William Milys, 1 from Asselota, widow of Aylward Flyrt', 1 from Alexander de Ponte. 2 used for ploughs; 2 sold. Total, 4. None remain.
Sacks: 1 remains from the previous year; 1 bought; 1 used in the manor; 1 remains.

Billingbear

Issues of the manor

James de North', bailiff, and Robert Godwyn', reeve, render account for £3 6*s*. 8*d*. from pasturage sold in summer; 3*s*. from winter pasturage sold in the fields of Midelfeld' and Westfeld'; nothing from the pasturage of Werles because the horses carrying marl were pastured on it; 12*s*. 11*d*. from pannage of Billingbear, that is, from 66 pigs and 24 piglets, at 2*d*. a pig, 1*d*. a piglet; 9*s*. from 1 ox sold; £1 9*s*. from 3 cows sold, at 10*s*. each for 2, and 9*s*. for 1; 18*s*. 2*d*. from 19 calves sold before weaning; 1*s*. 4*d*. from the hide sold of 1 plough-horse in murrain; 3*s*. 10*d*. from the hides sold of 2 cows in murrain, at 1*s*. 8*d*. for 1, and 2*s*. 2*d*. for the other; 1*s*. 2*d*. from the hide sold of 1 steer in murrain; 7*d*. from the hide sold of 1 bullock in murrain;

1 MS omits '8'.

2 MS 'te*rr*e gill'⟨⟩i le messag''.

1½*d*. from the hide sold of 1 yearling in murrain; 2*s*. from 6 cloves of winter cheese sold; £1 3*s*. 10*d*. from 2 weys, 1 quarter, 4 cloves of summer cheese sold, at 10*s*. a wey; 5*s*. 3*d*. from 10½ cloves of butter sold; 6*s*. 6*d*. from loppings sold; £1 11*s*. 5*d*. from dairy produce sold at the audit. Total, £10 14*s*. 9½*d*.

Sale of corn
The same render account for 15*s*. from 5½ qrs 1 bus. of mancorn sold, at 2*s*. 8*d*. a qr; 8*d*. from 2 bus. sold at the audit; £2 17*s*. 6*d*. from 28½ qrs 2 bus. of coarse oats sold, at 2*s*. a qr; 6*s*. 4¾*d*. from 5 qrs 1 bus. of small oats, at 1*s*. 3*d*. a qr. Total, £3 18*s*. 10¾*d*.

Total of all receipts, £14 14*s*. 4¼*d*.

Ploughs
In steel bought for 1 plough with the stipend of the smith 3*s*. In 2 plough-irons bought 5*d*. In 1 pair of wheels bought 3*d*. In shoeing 2 plough-horses for the year 1*s*. 4*d*., at the term for marling. In 1 ploughshare bought 8½*d*. In 1 man hired to dig the marl-pit 5*s*. 1*d*. In stipend of 1 harrower at both sowings 6*d*. In 5 halters made from the horses' own hair (*de proprio pilo*) 1¼*d*. In forage 1*s*. 6*d*. In stipend of 1 ploughman and drover for the year 9*s*. Total, £1 1*s*. 10¾*d*.

m.18d
Nothing for purchase of seed this year.

Carts and wagons
In 1 pair of wheels bought for the cart 2*s*. 9*d*. In large and small nails with clamps bought for the same 4*s*. In stipend of the smith fitting the said wheels with old iron tyres and lengthening the strakes 10*d*. In clouts with nails bought for the cart and wagon 10*d*. In bands of withies for hooping the hubs of wheels 2*d*. In fitting the cart and wagon with axles at various times 4*d*. In grease bought for the cart and wagon 1*s*. 1*d*. In shoeing cart-horses 2*s*. 8*d*. In stipend of 1 carter for ½ year 3*s*. 6*d*. Total, 16*s*. 2*d*.

Cost of buildings
In roofing the byre in places 1*s*. 1*d*. In enclosing 172 perches around the wood and fields 3*s*. 7*d*., at ¼*d*. a perch. In cleaning the horse-pond (*waeriis*) where the livestock are bound to water 7*s*. Total, 11*s*. 8*d*.

Dairy
In 2 bus. of salt 8*d*. In earthenware pots and pans bought 6*d*. In a press bought 4*d*. In buckets mended 3*d*. In linen and woollen cloth bought 6*d*. In 65 hurdles bought for the fold of oxen and sheep 5*s*. In stipend of 1 cowherd for the year 3*s*. 6*d*. In stipend of 1 dairymaid for the year 2*s*. 6*d*. In 6 cows with calf bought £2 14*s*. 7½*d*., at 9*s*. each for 5, and 9*s*. 7½*d*. for 1. In stipend of 1 shepherd for ½ year 2*s*. 6*d*. Total, £3 10*s*. 4½*d*.

Threshing and winnowing {henceforth 10 bus. of oats should be threshed for ¾*d*. and 8 qrs winnowed for 1*d*.}
In threshing and winnowing 40 qrs 2 bus. of mancorn by piece-work 7*s*. 6½*d*., at 2¼*d*. a qr. In threshing and winnowing 38½ qrs 1 bus. of coarse oats and 17½ qrs 1 bus. of small oats by piece-work 4*s*. 8¼*d*., at 1*d*. a qr. In winnowing the said oats 9¼*d*., at 1*d*. per 6 qrs. Total, 13*s*.

Harvest-time
In weeding corn 1*s*. In reaping and binding all the corn by piece-work £1 13*s*. 10*d*. Total, £1 14*s*. 10*d*.

Expenses for keeping the woods {henceforth the reeve should have nothing except 2*s*.}
In stipend of 1 keeper of the woods, grange and pasture 5*s*. Total, 5*s*.

Total of all expenses, £8 12*s*. 11¼*d*.

Cash deliveries
Delivered to William Wordly, reeve of Wargrave, £6 1*s*. 5*d*.

Issues of the grange

Mancorn
{yield: four-fold less 1 qr 1 bus.}
The same render account for 40 qrs 2½ bus. from the whole issue of mancorn from the grange with the increment of the granary.
Sown over 27½ acres in the field of Estfeld', 10 qrs 2 bus.; that is, 3 bus. an acre, less 1½ bus. in all. Delivered to 1 ploughman and 1 drover for the year, 10 qrs 3 bus., because they took a quarter every 10 weeks. Delivered to 1 carter for ½ year, 2½ qrs 1 bus. Delivered to 1 cowherd for the year, 5 qrs 1½ bus. Delivered to 1 dairymaid for ½ year, 2½ qrs 1 bus., because the cowherd filled the office of dairymaid for ½ year. Delivered to 1 harrower at both sowings, 6 bus. Delivered to 1 shepherd for ½ year, 2½ qrs 1 bus. Sold, 5½ qrs 1 bus. Sold at the audit, 2 bus.

Coarse oats
{yield: three-fold less 6 bus.}
The same render account for 38½ qrs 1 bus. from the whole issue of the grange with the increment of the granary.
Sown over 13 acres measured by the perch which lie in the field of Midelfeld', 9½ qrs 3 bus.; that is, 6 bus. an acre, plus 1 bus. in all. Sold, 28½ qrs 2 bus.

Small oats
{yield: two-fold plus 1 qr 3 bus.}
The same render account for 17½ qrs 1 bus. from the whole issue of small oats with the increment of the granary.
Sown over 14½ acres measured by the perch which lie in the field of Midelfeld, 11 qrs; that is, 6 bus. an acre, plus 1 bus. in all. In fodder of the plough-horses harrowing, 1½ qrs, and so much because they carried timber from Farnham and la Ber' for the stable of Wargrave. Sold, 5 qrs 1 bus.

Stock

Plough-horses: 5 remain from the previous year; 1 in murrain; 4 remain, 2 of them male.
Foals: no offspring this year.
Oxen: 14 remain from the previous year; 2 added from stock. Total, 16. 1 sold; 15 remain.
Bulls: 1 remains from the previous year; 1 remains.
Cows: 20 remain from the previous year; 8 added from stock; 6 bought with calf. Total, 34. 2 in murrain before calving; 3 sold before calving. Total, 5.[1] 29 remain.

1 MS omits '5'.

Steers: 11 remain from the previous year's bullocks. 1 in murrain in winter; 2 added to oxen, 8 to cows. Total, 11. None remain.
Bullocks: 5 remain from the previous year's yearlings; 1 in murrain; 4 remain, 1 of them male.
Yearlings: 5 remain from the previous year's calves; 1 in murrain; 4 remain, 3 of them male.
Calves: 19 from this year's offspring, because 4 cows sterile; 6 bought with cows. Total, 25. 2 in tithe; 19 sold. Total, 21. 4 remain, 3 of them male.
Winter cheese: 39 made; 4 in tithe; 35 sold, which made 6 cloves.
Summer cheese {yield of cow 2*s*. 6*d*. this year}: 134 cheeses made between St Dunstan's day (19 May) and Michaelmas (29 September), both days included; 13 in tithe; 121 sold, which made 2 weys, 1 quarter, 4 cloves.
Butter: 10½ cloves from the issue of the dairy; all sold.
Utensils: 1 cart with iron tyres remains from the previous year; 1 wagon remains from the previous year; 2 collars, 2 pairs of traces, 1 pick-axe, 3 iron shovels, 1 brass pan remain from the previous year; all this remains.

Warfield

Rents of assize
James de North', bailiff, and William de Stanrig', reeve, render account for £12 19*s*. ½*d*. for all rents of assize at Easter (22 April); £12 19*s*. ¼*d*. at Michaelmas (29 September). Total, £25 18*s*. ¾*d*.

Quittances
In quittance of 1 reeve for the year 2*s*. Total, 2*s*.

Total of rents remaining, £25 16*s*. ¾*d*.

Annual gifts
The same render account for 16*s*. 3*d*. from annual gifts at Easter; 16*s*. 3*d*. at Michaelmas. Total, £1 12*s*. 6*d*.

Issues of the manor
The same render account for 5*s*. 5*d*. from pannage of 41 pigs, 48 piglets at Martinmas (11 November), at 1*d*. a pig over a year old, and ½*d*. a piglet; 2*s*. from pannage of Yuwod'; 1*s*. from 1 ploughshare sold from the rent of Renfred (*Renerii*) de Bracke*n*hal'; 1*s*. 1*d*. from the heriot of G*ilbert* Aleman because he did not have 1 animal; 12*s*. from 1 ox sold from the heriot of Henry Botte. Total, £1 1*s*. 6*d*.

Entry and marriage fines
The same render account for 9*s*. 5½*d*. from 4 tithings for tithingpenny at the hundred-court of Martinmas; 9*s*. 5½*d*. from 4 tithings for tithingpenny at the hundred-court of Hockday; £3 from William Botte to have 1 messuage 3 virgates of land, 12 acres 1 rood of purpresture which belonged to H*enry* his father; 6*s*. 8*d*. from Robert Alema*n* to retain 2 acres 1 pennyworth of land which belonged to Gilbert his father; 6*d*. from Agnes, who was wife of Robert ate Westend', to retain 1 messuage, 3 pennyworths of land which belonged to Robert her husband; £3 6*s*. 8*d*. from Maurice atte Westend' to have 1 messuage which escheated into the lord's hands through the death of Richard Momfort' by hanging. Total, £7 12*s*. 9*d*.

Perquisites
The same render account for 1*s*. from John Pulm*ent*, Agnes Striman and William ate Fryth' for assize; 3*d*. from William Fryse for unjustly withholding; 6*d*. from William Aylwyn' for trespass; 1*s*. from John Doyvyl', John Fab*er*, John Polme*nt*' for assize and John Fab*er*; 6*d*. from Stephen de Upton' for trespass; 1*s*. from Stephen Thirgar for trespass; 1*s*. from Gillemyn Fryse, John Fab*er*, Agnes Stryman and John Polme*nt*' for assize; 3*d*. from Nicholas Cupe for trespass; 6*d*. from Gillemyn Fryze, John Fab*er* for assize; 1*s*. 9*d*. from Gillemyn Fryze, John Fab*er*, Joan ate Rygweye, John ate Den', Robert Alema*n*, Isabel Walt*er*, Ralph Robelot' for assize; 9*d*. from John Polme*nt*, Christina ate Westend' and Gillemyn Frys*e* for breaking the assize of ale. Total, 8*s*. 6*d*.

Total of both, £8 1*s*. 3*d*.

Nothing from green wax and entry to purprestures this year.

Chattels of felons
The same render account for 13*s*. 4*d*. from the chattels of Richard Monfort', hanged. Total, 13*s*. 4*d*.

Total of all receipts, £37 4*s*. 7¾*d*.

Cash deliveries
Delivered to William de Wordly, reeve of Wargrave, £37 4*s*. 7¾*d*.

The same render account for 1 ox from the heriot of Henry Botte; 1 sold; none remain.

Brightwell

Arrears
Roginald de Lynh*a*m, bailiff, and Richard Elyȝ, reeve, render account for £25 11*s*. 11*d*. of arrears from the last account. All delivered to Sir *Geoffrey*, treasurer of Wolvesey, and they are quit.

Rents
The same render account for £3 2*d*. for all rents of assize at Christmas; £3 2*d*. at Easter (22 April); £3 2*d*. at the Nativity of the blessed John (24 June); £5 8*s*. 4½*d*. at Michaelmas (29 September). Total, £14 8*s*. 10½*d*.

Quittances
In quittance of 1 reeve for the year 5*s*.; 1 smith working the iron of 3 ploughs for the year 2*s*. 6*d*.; 1 overseer of the harvest sowing the land, and keeping the meadow, pasture and corn for the year 2*s*. 2*d*.; 1 swineherd for the year 2*s*. 2*d*.; 7 ploughmen for the year 15*s*. 2*d*., or 2*s*. 2*d*. each; 8 virgaters in Brightwell working every other day each week, apart from Saturdays and celebrated feasts, from Michaelmas until the feast of the Apostles Peter and Paul (29 June), that is, for 3 terms, 15*s*., or 1*s*. 10½*d*. each; the same working every day except Saturdays from the said feast of the Apostles Peter and Paul until Michaelmas 2*s*. 4*d*., or 3½*d*. each, and know that there are appointed here 8 half-virgaters where before there were appointed 10, because 2 half-virgates of land were made into 1 whole virgate of land which John H*er*be*r*d

holds by fine made in the steward's court which he answers for from now on and works with the other virgaters of land and is the fifth virgater of land in Brightwell; 13 virgaters of land in Sotwell working every other day each week, except feast-days and Saturdays, for the aforesaid time, 14*s.* 1*d.*, or 1*s.* 1*d.* each; 7 virgaters in Mackney working every day apart from Saturdays for the aforesaid time 9*s.* 4*d.*, or 1*s.* 4*d.* each; 5 virgaters in Brightwell, to whom the fifth should be added here, working in the same way for the same time 5*s.* 5*d.*, or 1*s.* 1*d.* each; 1 tenant working 2 days a week, that is, Monday and Friday, for the same time, 5½*d.* Total, £3 13*s.* 7½*d.*

Defaults of rent

In default of the land of Andrew de Walingeford' from the old land to the castle ditch 3¾*d.* Total, 3¾*d.*

Total of both, £3 13*s.* 11¼*d.*

Total of rents remaining, £10 14*s.* 11¼*d.*

Annual recognizance

The same render account for 4*d.* from Thomas Cl*ericus* for annual recognizance whilst he wishes to reside within the lord's liberty; 6*d.* from John Bordel' for the same; nothing from John Long*us* because he is sold outside the tithing by William de Mackeney his lord. Total, 10*d.*

Issues of the manor

The same render account for 13*s.* 4*d.* from the pasturage in the east field sold; 7*s.* 1½*d.* from pannage of pigs at Martinmas (11 November); 2*s.* from the pasturage in the croft sold, which formerly belonged to William le Fisscher', because it is in the lord's hands through the death of Thomas de Mack' who held that tenement of the lord after the decease of the said William; 2*s.* 6½*d.* from 29 rowen (*relucro*) cheeses sold by warrant (*per man'*); 3*s.* ½*d.* from 36½ gallons of milk sold for the lambs, at the price made clear; £1 18*s.* 9*d.* from 117 cheeses, weighing 3½ weys 4 lb, sold at 11*s.* a wey; 5*s.* 4*d.* from 16 cloves of butter sold, at 4*d.* a clove; 4*d.* from 2 capons from the rent of William le Fisscher' sold; 8*s.* 7*d.* from 103 cocks and hens from churchscot at Martinmas sold; 1*s.* 2*d.* from 350 eggs sold, received according to custom at Easter; 1*s.* 2*d.* from the hide sold of 1 mare from the mill dead from murrain; 4*s.* 10*d.* from the carcass of 1 cow dead from murrain about the feast of St Nicholas (6 December) sold together with the hide; 1*d.* from the hide sold of 1 calf of the same cow; 1*s.* 3*d.* from the heriot of Thomas de Mack' for the tenement of William le Fisscher'; 1*s.* 10*d.* from 2 calves sold to the butcher of Shillingford; 2*s.* from 2 calves sold to Richard Beneyt of Wallingford; 1*s.* 2*d.* from 1 calf sold to Richard Spriwel of Shillingford; 13*s.* 4*d.* from 1 bull sold; 8*s.* from 1 cask of cider sold to Henry Mess' apart from the vessel; 3*s.* 4*d.* from 10 acres of stubble sold; 1*s.* 1*d.* from dairy produce sold at the audit. Total, £6 4½*d.*

Sale of plough-horses

The same render account for 9*s.* from 2 mares sold to Henry Horlok by warrant; 6*s.* from 1 mare sold to William le Frensch' by warrant; 4*s.* 6*d.* from 1 mare sold to William ad Aq*ua* by warrant; 6*s.* from 1 mare sold to Thomas de Mack' by loan (*per acommod'*); 4*s.* 6*d.* from 1 mare sold to William atte Lan' by loan; 3*s.* 6*d.* from 1 mare sold to Richard Cullebol' by loan; 8*s.* from 1 mare to Stephen Godefr*ay* by loan; 3*s.* from 1 mare sold to Thomas le Venour by loan; 5*s.* from 1 mare sold to Robert le Mere by loan; 6*s.* 8*d.* from 1 mare sold to Henry Deme de Hakeb*orn*e. Total, £2 16*s.* 2*d.*

Sale of pigs

The same render account for £1 3*s.* 4*d.* from 8 pigs over a year old sold to Jordan le Carpe*nter*, at 4*s.* 2*d.* each; 16*s.* from 4 pigs over a year old sold to Richard Beye and John H*er*berd, at the price made clear; 8*s.* from 2 pigs over a year old sold to Walter le Gol; 7*s.* from 2 pigs over a year old sold to Robert Sangar; 7*s.* from 2 pigs over a year old sold to Robert atte Nywerewe; 3*s.* 6*d.* from 1 pig over a year old sold to Thomas de Fonte; 3*s.* 8*d.* from 1 pig over a year old sold to Thomas Kepe; 7*s.* 4*d.* from 2 pigs over a year old sold to William Beye; 3*s.* from 1 pig over a year old sold to Simon Fab*er*; 10*s.* from 3 pigs over a year old sold to Richard Beneyt of Wallingford; 5*d.* from 1 sick hogget sold. Total, £4 19*s.* 3*d.*

Sale of corn

The same render account for £29 16*s.* 9¼*d.* from 105 qrs 2½ bus. of wheat sold, at 5*s.* 8*d.* a qr; £4 9*s.* 10¼*d.* from 28 qrs 3 bus. of rye sold, at 3*s.* 2*d.* a qr; £20 16*s.* ¾*d.* from 118 qrs of barley sold, at 3*s.* 6*d.* a qr; £2 8*s.* 9*d.* from 16 qrs 2 bus. of dredge sold, at 3*s.* a qr; 2*s.* 4½*d.* from 6 bus. of rye sold at the audit; 1*s.* 9*d.* from ½ qr of barley sold at the audit; 8*d.* from ½ qr of vetches sold at the audit. Total, £57 16*s.* 2¾*d.*

Sale of the mill's corn

The same render account for £2 17*s.* 4*d.* from 13 qrs ½ bus. of wheat from the mill sold, at 4*s.* a qr for 4 qrs, 4*s.* 4*d.* a qr for 3 qrs, and 4*s.* 8*d.* a qr for 6 qrs ½ bus.; £2 2*s.* 11*d.* from 17½ qrs of maslin sold, at 2*s.* a qr for 5 qrs 5 bus., and 2*s.* 8*d.* a qr for 11 qrs 7 bus.; £1 3*s.* 2*d.* from 5 qrs 2 bus. of coarse-ground corn from the mill sold, at 4*s.* a qr for 2 qrs, and 4*s.* 8*d.* a qr for 3 qrs 2 bus.; £3 9*s.* 3*d.* from 22½ qrs of second-grade malt sold, at 3*s.* a qr for 12 qrs, and 3*s.* 2*d.* a qr for 10½ qrs; 5*s.* 4*d.* from eels sold at various times. Note that there was no more from the issue of the mill this year because for 4 weeks after Christmas and for 2 weeks in Lent it was idle due to torrents. And for 3*d.* from 1 bus. of maslin sold at the audit. Total, £9 18*s.* 3*d.*

m.19

Fixed payments, entry and marriage fines

The same render account for £1 6*s.* 8*d.* from fixed payments at the 2 hundred-courts for tithingpenny; £2 13*s.* 4*d.* from the fine of Roger ate Grove to have Agnes, relict of Henry Wys, with ½ virgate of customary land; 13*s.* 4*d.* from the fine of John Giffard to recover a certain cottage which he sold to John Coc*us* without licence. Total, £4 13*s.* 4*d.*

Perquisites

The same render account for 1*s.* from Geoffrey de Brighwalto*n* for release from his suit at 2 views; 1*s.* from Osbert de Nutle for the same; 6*d.* from Emma ate Strem' for trespass of pasture; 6*d.* from John ate Strem' for trespass in the curia; 6*d.* from William le Kingȝ for trespass with his sheep in the pasture; 3*d.* from Juliana de Wodek' for the assize of ale; 3*d.* from Christina le Cart*er*e for the same; 3*d.* from the relict of Thomas Amys for the same; 3*d.* from Alice Poukeput for the same; 3*d.* from Richard the reeve for the same; 3*d.* from Agnes Nich' for the same; 6*d.* from Thomas Hugh' because he is not proceeding against the officer of the tithing; 1*s.* from

Thomas Wys, carter, because he sent inadequate service to the lord's carts; 2*s*. from William le Frensch' for the same; 6*d*. from John Giffard because he is convicted of forgery in the steward's court; 6*d*. from the same John because he sold 1 cottage from his holding to William Coc*us* without licence of the bailiffs; 3*d*. from Robert Raubrin for unjustly raising the hue against W*illiam* Piscat'; 3*d*. from the same William for transgression against Sir Robert; 3*d*. from William ate Slad' for default; 6*d*. from the tithing because it did not produce in court Thomas Flexma*n* whom it had bailed; 3*d*. from John Amys for default; 6*d*. from the tithing because it did not produce in court John Lo*ngus* whom it had bailed; 6*d*. from William le Tayllor because he did not produce in court Robert Rauly*n* whom he had pledged; 3*d*. from Thomas Hugh', tithingman, because he did his office inadequately; 3*d*. from Alice, relict of the smith, for the assize of ale; 3*d*. from Matilda Edm*und*' for the same; 6*d*. from Robert Rauly*n* for unjustly raising the hue against Stephen, the lord's overseer of the harvest; 3*d*. from John Giffard for trespass of pasture; 3*d*. from William Cristemass' for trespass in the lord's corn; 3*d*. from William le Frensch' for the same; 3*d*. from Robert Rauly*n* for the assize of ale; 3*d*. from Duce Norays for regrating bread; 6*d*. from Robert Rauly*n* for making an encroachment against Adam de Mack'; 6*s*. 8*d*. from Stephen, the lord's overseer of the harvest, for trespass; 1*s*. from Geoffrey de Brighw*a*lto*n* for default at the view; 6*d*. from Walter Beye for the same; 1*s*. from the tithing because it did not produce in court John Fox and Thomas le Fox; 3*d*. from William Cissor' for default; 3*d*. from Thomas Smerebat for the same; 6*d*. from Robert Rauly*n* because he is not proceeding against the tithing; 3*d*. from Thomas le Venur for the assize of ale; 3*d*. from Agnes ate Wat*ere* for the same; 6*d*. from William Cissor for licence to agree with Robert Boilloun; 1*s*. from John Giffard for having his sheep in the meadow and his horse in the pasture in Wardesto*n*; 3*d*. from William ad Aq*ua* for the assize of ale; 3*d*. from Emily (*Amel'*), relict of G. le Tayllor, for the same; 6*d*. from Thomas Flexma*n* for the same; 1*s*. from Alice ate Hall' for unjustly raising the hue. Total, £1 9*s*. 2*d*.

Total of both, £6 2*s*. 6*d*.

Green wax

The same render account for £1 from the vill of Brightwell for murder-fine from the amercements of the court held before Solomon de Roff' and his fellows in the year 12 Edward I (1284); 6*s*. 8*d*. from the vill of Mackney for the same from the amercements of the same court. Total, £1 6*s*. 8*d*.

Total of all receipts, £99 15*s*. 2½*d*.

Cost of ploughs

In 3 pieces of iron bought for the ploughs 1*s*. 2*d*. In 6 pieces of steel bought for the same 4*s*. 10*d*. In 2 new ploughshares bought for the ploughs with the repair of the same 1*s*. 6*d*. In 9 wheels bought for ploughs 1*s*. 9*d*. In withies bought for the draught-chains (*hart'*) of the ploughs 10½*d*. In stipend of the smith working the iron of 2 ploughs for the year 4*s*., because 1 acre of wheat was removed from his stipend, and he quits ½ virgate of land through the iron for 2 ploughs. In 1 new wheelbarrow bought 8*d*. Total, 14*s*. 9½*d*.

Carts and ironwork

In 2 new horse-collars bought 1*s*. 4*d*. In 1 hemp rope bought for tethering the cart at Reading 1*s*. 4*d*. In 1 pair of traces bought there 5*d*. In fitting 1 cart with axles, with axles, white leather, clouts and nails bought for the year, 1*s*. 8¾*d*. In frets bought for the cart 2*d*. In 1 metal plate bought for the cart 1*d*. In 1 leather halter bought for 1 cart-horse 3*d*. In shoeing 2 cart-horses for the year, for all necessaries which pertain to their provision, together with their removal and fastening, 3*s*. Total, 8*s*. 3¾*d*.

Small necessaries

In 12 dishes, 8 pans, 12 saucers.[1] In 12 cart-loads of wood felled in the wood of Wargrave 1*s*. In 2½ bus. of salt bought for the pease pottage of the manorial servants 11*d*. In 4 new sacks bought for corn 2*s*. 6½*d*. In 1 basket (*sporta*) bought 4*d*. In castrating 12 male and spaying 9 female piglets 7*d*. In 1½ bus. of oatmeal bought for pease pottage for the year, 1*s*. 1½*d*. this year. In withies bought for penning oxen in the byre in winter 2½*d*. In 1 piece of iron made for a certain shovel out of the demesne iron 1*d*. In hiring a certain man to clean the inside of 2 tuns for putting cider in and moreover hooping them anew and hooping anew 5 tubs by piece-work for 10 days 2*s*. 6*d*. In hiring a certain roofer for 2½ days to roof over the enclosure between the bishop's chamber and chapel 7½*d*. In small nails for fastening laths to the walls of the byre 1*d*. Total, 11*s*.

Threshing and winnowing

In threshing 26 qrs of barley 3*s*. 2*d*., at 1½*d*. a qr. In winnowing the said corn 5*d*., at 1*d*. per 5 qrs. In wages of John Touresm*ere* overseeing the threshing and winnowing of corn at various times 7*s*. 5½*d*., taking 1½*d*. a day. In stipend of the same here 2*s*., because he takes the rest elsewhere up to 10*s*. Total, 13*s*. 1½*d*.

Purchase of corn

In 7 qrs 6 bus. of wheat bought for sowing £1 15*s*. 1*d*., at 4*s*. 8*d*. a qr for 4½ qrs, and 4*s*. 4*d*. a qr for 3 qrs 2 bus. In 10 qrs 5 bus. of oats bought for fodder for the year 17*s*. 8½*d*., at 1*s*. 8*d*. a qr. In 5 bus. of beans bought for pigs 1*s*. ½*d*. Total, £2 13*s*. 10*d*.

Purchase of stock

In 1 ox bought for the ploughs at Warb*e*wey 14*s*. In 1 ox bought for the same at Abingdon 14*s*. 6*d*. In 1 ox bought there for the same 16*s*. In 1 ox bought there for the same 12*s*. 6*d*. In 2 oxen bought there for the same £1 4*s*. ½*d*. In 1 ox bought there for the same 15*s*. In 1 ox bought there for the same 14*s*. 6*d*. In 1 ox bought there for the same 15*s*. In 1 ox bought there for the same 11*s*. 6*d*. In 1 ox bought there for the same 12*s*. In 1 ox bought there for the same 15*s*. 6*d*. Total, £8 4*s*. 6½*d*.

Cost of the dairy

In 4 bus. of salt bought for the dairy 1*s*. 4*d*. In 2 buckets bought for the dairy 6*d*. In 2 ells of canvas bought for making cheese cloth therefrom 6*d*. In earthenware pans bought for the same 2*d*. In 1 cheese mould bought 2*d*. Total, 2*s*. 8*d*.

Cost of the mill

In 1 mare bought for the mill 16*s*. ¼*d*. In 1 millstone lying at the said mill bought £2 13*s*. 9*d*. In customary payment to the vill of Wallingford for buying the said stone within the vill 8*d*. In 7 oaks felled at la Wassch' for the bridge of the mill of Wallingford 7*d*. In sawing the said oaks crosswise for carrying (*ducend'*) 6½*d*. In sawing the timber for the bridge of Wallingford lengthwise 2*s*. 6*d*. In 100 nails bought for the bays of the mill 10*d*. In hiring 1 water-axe (*wat*er*ax*) to level the

1 MS omits price.

foundations of the bridge where the timber was being placed 2*d*. In ironwork of 1 pier to enlarge the holes in the foundations where the other piers were being placed 4*d*. In carpentry done for the said bridge by piece-work by fixed agreement £1 6*s*. 8*d*., and ½ qr of wheat from the granary. In 8 cart-loads of stones bought for the bays of the said bridge and for the bays of the lake (*la Lak'*) 1*s*. 4*d*. In piers bought for the said bridge and other necessaries of the said mill 3*s*. Total, £5 6*s*. 4¾*d*.

Customary payments

In customary payments to 1 reeve, 1 overseer of the harvest, 1 smith, 1 swineherd and 7 ploughmen for their corrodies (*corred'*) at Christmas 1*s*. 10*d*., or 2*d*. each. In customary payment to 28 men mowing the northern meadow and 3 men spreading hay in the same, 4*s*. 4*d*. and 1 summer cheese. In customary payment for the mowing of the meadows in place of 2 wethers owed to them 2*s*. Total, 8*s*. 2*d*.

Cost of the harvest

In expenses of 5 harvest boon-works of 375 men reaping as if for 1 day £1 17*s*. 4*d*., because they have a meal twice a day. Total, £1 17*s*. 4*d*.

Expenses of the steward

In expenses of Sir Robert, steward, and Simon, clerk, for their visits for the year to hold the hundred-courts, £1 3*s*. 11½*d*. by 3 tallies. In expenses of Walter de Poulton', bailiff from Michaelmas (29 September) until the feast of St Lucy the Virgin (13 December), 9*s*. 3*d*. by 1 tally, paid to Roginald de Lynh*am*, bailiff, as part of his wages of £3 by 1 tally. In a certain robe with fur bought for the said Roginald at Christmas £1 4*s*. In expenses of a certain attendant pleading for the steward and Simon, clerk, for the aforesaid distraint taken against the lord bishop 4*d*. Total, £5 17*s*. 6½*d*.

Total of all expenses, £26 17*s*. 8½*d*.

And he owes, £72 17*s*. 6*d*.

Allowances

In allowance of the reeve for contributions made to certain amercements by the vill of Wallingford to the court of the lord king's marshal, because the bishop has a mill in the vill which was taken into the hands of the lord king by the lord king's marshal, £1. Given to a certain man for release from a certain distraint taken against the lord bishop 1*s*. Total of all allowances, £1 1*s*.

Cash deliveries

Delivered to Sir G*eoffrey*, treasurer of Wolvesey, by tally, £53 3*s*. 1*d*.

Total of all allowances and cash deliveries, £54 4*s*. 1*d*.

And he owes clear, £18 13*s*. 5*d*.

Issues of the grange

Wheat

{yield: 4½-fold less 1 qr[1] 6½ bus. in all}

The same render account for 139 qrs 7½ bus. of wheat from the whole issue of the grange, threshed by labour service by 2 tallies of struck measure; 6 qrs 6 bus. of

1 'bus.' in MS.

wheat by estimation in 5½ acres given to the manorial servants for their stipends in summer; 7 qrs 6 bus. of wheat bought as noted above. Total, 154 qrs 3½ bus.
Sown over 103 acres of land as they lie in the field, 38 qrs 3 bus. by 1 tally; that is, 3 bus. an acre, less 2 bus. in all. In provision of Sir Robert, steward, and Simon, clerk, for their visits, that is, in bread baked for their use, 1 qr 1 bus. by 3 tallies with their expenses. In provision of Walter de Polton' after Michaelmas, 1 qr, that is, in bread by 1 tally with his expenses. Given to the steward and constable of Wallingford Castle, 1 qr. In agreement with Jordan (*Joriad'*) le Carpe*n*ter for making the bridge of the mill, ½ qr. Given to Sibyl de Morton', 2 bus. In customary payment to the overseer of the harvest for his fee, 1 bus., because it is found to be the custom. In stipend of 1 reeve, 1 overseer of the harvest, 1 carter and 3 ploughmen for their stipends in summer, 6 qrs 6 bus., that is, in 5½ acres of wheat delivered to them. Sold, 105 qrs 2½ bus. Total, 154 qrs 3½ bus. None remains.

Rye
{yield: 3½-fold plus 4 qrs 6 bus.}
The same render account for 73 qrs from the issue of the grange, threshed by labour service by 2 tallies of struck measure. Total, 73 qrs.
Sown over 52 acres of land as they lie in the field, 16 qrs 3 bus. by 1 tally; that is, 2½ bus. an acre, plus 1 bus. in all. Delivered to 1 carter and 3 ploughmen for the year, 20 qrs 6 bus., or 5 qrs 1½ bus. each, taking a quarter every 10 weeks. Delivered to 1 cowherd for the year, 3 qrs of rye, taking a quarter every 14 weeks and not more because he takes the rest from the men whose cows have rights of common with the lord's cows. Delivered to 1 dairymaid for the year, 3 qrs 6 bus., taking a quarter every 14 weeks. Sold, 28 qrs 3 bus. Sold at the audit, 6 bus. Total, 73 qrs. None remains.

Barley
{yield: 5½-fold less 4 qrs 7 bus.}
The same render account for 150½ qrs of barley from the whole issue of the grange by 1 tally of struck measure, 26 qrs by piece-work, and 124 qrs by labour service. Total, 150½ qrs.[1]
Sown over 65 acres of land as they lie in the field, 31 qrs by 1 tally; that is, 3½ bus. 1 peck an acre, plus ½ qr 1 peck. In customary payment to 1 overseer of the harvest for sowing (*sedcod*), 1 bus., because it is found to be the custom and always received. Sold, 118 qrs 7 bus. Sold at the audit, ½ qr. Total, 150 qrs.[2] None remains.

Dredge
{yield: three-fold plus 1 bus.}
The same render account for 33 qrs 1 bus. of dredge from the whole issue of the grange, threshed by labour service by 1 tally of struck measure. Total, 33 qrs 1 bus.
Sown over 55 acres of land as they lie in the field, 15½ qrs by 1 tally. In supporting pigs for the year, 1 qr 3 bus. Sold, 16 qrs 2 bus. Total, 33 qrs 1 bus. None remains.

Oats
{yield: 6 bus. less than sown}
The same render account for 8 qrs 7 bus. of oats from the whole issue of the grange, threshed by labour service by 2 tallies of struck measure; 10 qrs 5 bus. of oats bought. Total, 19½ qrs.
Sown over 23 acres of land as they lie in the field, 8 qrs 1 bus. by 1 tally; that is, 2 bus. 3 pecks an acre, [plus] 1 bus. 3 pecks. In fodder of the horses of the steward and

1 Figures add up to 150 qrs.

2 Figures add up to 150½ qrs.

Simon for their visits for the year, 2 qrs by 2 tallies with their expenses. In fodder of the horse of Walter de Poulton', bailiff from Michaelmas until the feast of St Lucy the Virgin, 2 qrs by 1 tally with his expenses. In fodder of 2 cart-horses for the year, 7 qrs 2 bus., sometimes more, sometimes less, as they laboured. In customary payment to the overseer of the harvest for sowing (*sedcod*), 1 bus., because it is found to be the custom and always had. Total, 19½ qrs. None remains.

Beans, peas, vetches {henceforth each kind of corn should have its own title}
The same render account for 5½ qrs of peas **{yield: five-and-a-half-fold}**; 5 qrs 1 bus. of vetches from the issue of the grange, threshed by labour service by 2 tallies of struck measure **{yield: 5-fold less ½ qr}**; 5 bus. of beans bought. Total, 11[1] qrs 2 bus. Sown over 8 acres of land, 1½ qrs of peas; over 2 acres of land, 3 bus. of vetches by 1 tally. In fattening pigs for sale, 3 qrs 4½ bus. of peas. In pease pottage for the manorial servants for the year, 3½ bus. of peas. In supporting pigs in the manor in winter and summer when it was necessary, 4 qrs 2 bus. of vetches and 5 bus. of beans. Sold at the audit, ½ qr of vetches. Total, 10 qrs 6 bus.[2] None remains.

Issues of the mill
Wheat: 14 qrs ½ bus. from the whole issue of the mill, of which 1 qr 7 bus. from the time of Walter de Poulton', bailiff. Total, 14 qrs ½ bus. In tithe, 1 qr. Sold, 13 qrs ½ bus. None remains.
Maslin: 18½ qrs 1 bus. from the whole issue of the mill, of which 3 qrs 1 bus. from the time of Walter de Poulton', bailiff. Total, 18½ qrs. In tithe, 1 qr. Sold, 17½ qrs. Sold at the audit, 1 bus. Total, 18½ qrs 1 bus. None remains.
Coarse-ground corn: 5 qrs 2 bus. from the whole issue of the mill; all sold; none remains.
Second-grade malt: 22½ qrs from the whole issue of the malt mill, of which 3½ qrs from the time of W*alter* de Poulton', bailiff. Total, 22½ qrs. All sold; none remains.

Stock

Cart-horses: 2 remain from the previous year; 1 addition. Total, 3. 3 remain.
Mares of the mill: 1 remains; 1 bought. Total, 2. 1 in murrain, of which the hide is sold within; 1 remains.
Plough-horses: 11 females remain. Total, 11. All sold within; none remain.
Colts: 1 remains from the previous year aged 2½ years; added to cart-horses; none remain.
Young colts: 2 remain from the previous year aged 1½ years, one of them a male; 1 remains from the previous year's foals. Total, 3. 3 remain, 2 of them aged 2½ years, 1 of them a male, and 1 male aged 1½ years.
Oxen: 31 remain; 2 added from steers; 12 bought as noted above. Total, 45. 45 remain.
Bulls: 1 remains; sold within; none remain.
Cows: 13 remain; 4 additions. Total, 17. 1 in murrain before calving, of which the hide and carcass are sold within. Total, 1. 16 remain.
Steers: 6 remain, of which 2 males were bullocks at the last account. Total, 6. 2 added to oxen,[3] 4 to cows; none remain.
Bullocks: 6 remain which were yearlings at the last account; 6 remain, 3 of them male.

1 MS omits '11'.

2 Figures add up to 11 qrs 2 bus.

3 MS omits 'oxen'.

Yearlings: 6 remain which were calves at the last account; 6 remain, 3 of them male.
Calves: 13 from the offspring of the aforesaid cows this year, and no more because 1 died before calving and 3 were sterile. Total, 13. 1 in tithe; 5 sold. Total, 6. 7 remain, 1 of them male.
Sows: 3 remain.
Pigs: 36 remain; 33 additions. Total, 69. 26 sold. Total, 26. 43 remain over a year old.
Hoggets: 34 remain from piglets. Total, 34. 33 added to pigs; 1 sold. Total, 34. None remain.

m.19d
Piglets: 43 offspring this year. Total, 43. 4 in tithe; 1 in customary payment to the swineherd. Total, 5. 38 remain.
Winter cheese: 29 made; all sold within; none remain.
Summer cheese {yield of cow 4*s*. with 2 cheeses in customary payment and 2 consumed by the steward which are valued at 1*s*. 2*d*.}: 133 cheeses made between Sunday after the feast of St Dunstan (20 May) and Michaelmas (29 September), both days included. Total, 133. 13 in tithe; 2 consumed by the steward and Simon, clerk, at the tourn of Hockday by tally with their expenses; 2 in customary payment for the mowing of the meadows; 116 sold, which made 3½ weys 4 lb. Total, 133. None remain.
Butter: 16 cloves from the issue of the dairy this year; all sold.
Swans: 2 remain; 7 offspring this year. Total, 9. 1 in murrain. Total, 1. 8 remain, 3 of them old.
Peacocks: 3 remain; 4 offspring this year. Total, 7. 2 in murrain. Total, 2. 5 remain, 3 of them old.
Capons: 2 from the rent of William le Fisscher'; sold within; none remain.
Hens {henceforth they should have the hens and answer for the offspring}: 138 cocks and hens from churchscot at Martinmas. Total, 138. 2 in default of the land of Henry M*ercat*o*r* and Walter de Mongewell'; 8 in default of Richard le King, Christina Alex', Agnes Smerebat and Christina le Frith because dead; 4 in default of the pasture of Richard son of Emma drawn into demesne; 2 in default of Henry le Blund because he is not able to build; 2 through the death of William Bunte; 2 through the death of the wife of Richard Beye; 8 in default of 2½ virgates of land drawn into 1 virgate of land which John He*r*berd holds; 2 through the death of Stephen Bordel; 2 through the death of the wife of Henry Norays; 1 through the death of William le Chapman; 2 through the death of Henry Wys. 103 sold.
Hides: 1 from a mare and 1 from a cow dead from murrain; 2 sold; none remain.
Eggs: 350 received at Easter according to custom; sold within.
Cider: 1 cask remains; 2 from this year's issue. Total, 3. 1 cask sold. Total, 1. 2 casks remain.
Carts: 2 remain, 1 of them wooden and the other with iron tyres. Total, 2. 1 wooden cart used. Total, 1. 1 cart with iron tyres remains.[1]
Utensils: 2 brass pots, 2 posnets, 2 brass pans, 1 ewer with a basin, and 1 gridiron remain.

Harwell

Arrears

Roginald de Lynh*am*, bailiff, and John Leyrmonger', reeve, render account for £27 3*s*. 6*d*. of arrears from the last account. Delivered to Sir G*eoffrey*, treasurer of Wolvesey, £27 3*s*. 6*d*. by 1 tally. They are quit.

1 MS omits 'remains'.

Rents of assize
The same render account for £16 ⌈12*s*.⌉ 6*d*. for rents of assize for the whole year at Michaelmas (29 September). Total, £16 12*s*. 6*d*.

Quittances
In quittance of 1 reeve for the year 5*s*.; 4 ploughmen for the year 12*s*., or 3*s*. each. Total, 17*s*.

Defaults of rent
In default of the rent of 1 croft which Roger Gunth' held drawn into demesne 3*s*. Total, 3*s*.

Total of quittances and defaults of rent, £1.

Total of rents remaining, £15 12*s*. 6*d*.[1]

Annual recognizance
The same render account for 6*d*. from Walter, son of Walter Edward, for annual recognizance; 6*d*. from Thomas in Angl*e* so that he may remain where he pleases, and nonetheless pay suit for his tithing and pay tithingpenny. Total, 1*s*.

Issues of the manor
The same render account for 7*s*. 4*d*. from pannage of pigs at Martinmas (11 November); 5*s*. 5*d*. from tolls on inns; 5*s*. from winter pasturage sold; 5*s*. 6*d*. from 66 cocks and hens from churchscot at Martinmas; 1*s*. 3*d*. from the heriot of John Miles for 1½ virgates of land which he held of the lord, and note that noone will give more for ½ virgate for a heriot even if he has 1 beast; 4*s*. from the herbage in the garden sold; 8*s*. from 1 feeble cart-horse sold; £1 17*s*. from 1 cart-horse sold; £1 7*s*. 6*d*. from 2 horses from the heriot of John Miles for 2 virgates of land which he held of the bishop sold to the relict of the same John; 8*s*. from 1 ox sold to Richard Tockesmal because rotten; 7*s*. from 1 sterile cow from the heriot of Walter Roed sold; 6*s*. from 2 pigs sold; 1*s*. 6*d*. from stubble sold; 1*d*. from the tail of 1 peacock sold. Total, £6 3*s*. 7*d*.

Farm
The same render account for 13*s*. 4*d*. for the farm of the mill of Blaer' let at farm to Laurence de Styventon'. Total, 13*s*. 4*d*.

Sale of corn
The same render account for £19 7*s*. 7½*d*. from 68 qrs 7 bus. of wheat sold, at 5*s*. a qr for 4 qrs, and 5*s*. 8*d*. a qr for 64 qrs 7 bus.; £2 10*s*. 3¾*d*. from 14 qrs 3 bus. of barley sold, at 3*s*. 6*d*. a qr; £4 12*s*. 3*d*. from 30 qrs 6 bus. of dredge sold, at 3*s*. a qr; 7½*d*. from 5 bus. of vetches sold, at 1½*d*. a bus.; 7½*d*. from 1½ bus. of wheat sold at the audit; 2*s*. 4¾*d*. from 5½ bus. of barley sold at the audit; 10*s*. 6*d*. from 3½ qrs of dredge sold at the audit, at 3*s*. a qr. Total, £27 4*s*. 4*d*.

Entry and marriage fines[2]
The same render account for £1 6*s*. 8*d*. from all the tithings for tithingpenny at the 2 hundred-courts for the year; 2*s*. from Christina le Rop for marrying Matilda her

1 MS omits '*d*.'

2 MS 'Fines t*errarum* et maritag*ia*' as opposed to the usual 'Fines et maritag*ia*'.

daughter outside; £3 from John Bartelot to have Matilda, relict of Richard le Kyng, with ½ virgate of her land; 6*s*. 8*d*. from Richard Huscarl so that he may till the holding of Matilda de Hyb' until the arrival of the said Matilda in England if she should live; 6*s*. 8*d*. from Roger le Ber' for marrying Matilda his daughter outside, because thus far he has not shown his feoffment. Total, £5 2*s*.

Perquisites

The same render account for 4*s*. 9*d*. from the small amercements of the court held on the Saturday of Martinmas (11 November); 11*s*. 2*d*. from the small amercements of the hundred-court of Martinmas held on Thursday the morrow of St Lucy the Virgin (14 December); 5*s*. 9*d*. from the perquisites of the court held on Thursday after Epiphany (11 January); 3*s*. 6*d*. from the perquisites of the court on Tuesday before the feast of St Peter's Chair (20 February); 9*s*. 2*d*. from the perquisites of the court held on Tuesday before the feast of St Dunstan (15 May); 17*s*. 10*d*. from the small amercements of the hundred-court of Hockday held on the eve of the Nativity of the blessed John (23 June); 9*s*. 9*d*. from the perquisites of the court held on Sunday before the Assumption (12 August); 13*s*. from the perquisites of the court held on Sunday before Michaelmas (23 September). Total, £3 14*s*. 11*d*.

Cost of ploughs

In 4 pieces of steel bought for 3 ploughs for the year 3*s*. 7½*d*. In stipend of the smith forging the said steel for the said ploughs 3*s*. 2*d*. In stipend of the smith repairing the said ploughs with the demesne's iron 6*d*. In 5 ploughs made anew, 3 of them for winter, and other old ploughs mended 2*s*. In hooping 3 ploughs around the holes for the coulters with the demesne's iron 6*d*. In 1 ploughshare and 2 coulters bought new for the ploughs with repairs to the same 2*s*. 10*d*. In 4 ox-yokes bought 9*d*. In 15 ox-bows bought for the same 11*d*. In 2 plough feet bought for ploughs 4*d*. In 2 wheels bought for the same 4*d*. In oak withies bought for ploughs, for making the draught-chains (*hart'*) therefrom, 1*s*. 1*d*. In 1 wheelbarrow bought 5*d*. In fitting 1 plough with a share-beam together with buying the share-beam 2*d*. In customary payment to 1 reeve and 4 ploughmen for their corrodies at Christmas and Easter 10*d*. Paid to 2 ploughmen and 1 carter for their pease pottage for the year 6*s*. 6*d*., or ½*d*. each a week. In 1 ox bought for ploughs 14*s*. Total, £1 17*s*. 11½*d*.

Cost of carts, wains and ironwork

In 1 cart-horse bought £1 4*s*. In 1 cart-horse bought at Abingdon £1 6*s*. In 1 pair of new wheels bought for clearing dung 2*s*. 5¼*d*. In 1 new cart saddle with 1 pair of new saddle-pads bought 10¾*d*. In 2 new horse-collars bought 1*s*. 4*d*. In clouts, nails, grease, and fitting the cart with axles at various times, 10*d*. In white leather bought for harnesses 3*d*. In 1 hame bought 2*d*. In 1 tumbrel for dung bought 8*d*. In 1 leather halter bought 3*d*. In shoeing 2 cart-horses for the year 1*s*. 7*d*. Total, £2 18*s*. 5*d*.

Cost of wagons

In 2 pairs of wheels bought for wagons 7*s*. 11*d*. In clouts, nails, grease bought for wagons 11*d*. In fitting the said 2 wagons with axles 6*d*. In hiring 1 carpenter to repair the bodies of wagons and to make 8 new frets for the abovesaid wheels for 5 days 1*s*. Total, 10*s*. 4*d*.

Small necessaries

In 2 sacks bought for carrying corn 1*s*. 4*d*. In 1 linen sheet for winnowing (*bintheamine ventator'*) bought 2*s*. 8*d*. In improving the vines 3*d*. In castrating 8 piglets 2*d*. In felling 15 cart-loads of wood in the wood of Wargrave and repairing to bring it 1*s*. 3*d*. In expenses of 2 horses for 1 night in search of the said wood 2*d*. In hiring 1 carpenter for 4 days to build the head of the fishpond at the mill for keeping fish and in sawing boards for the same 1*s*. In 1 tripod bought for making the pottage of the manorial servants on 4½*d*. In hiring 5 women to clear forage from the barn and to make a stack of forage therefrom for 1 day 5*d*. In forage bought from Matilda Semes for oxen 3*s*. 6*d*. In 3 hoggets bought 5¼*d*. In 1 padlock bought for the barn-door 1*d*. In mending 1 bushel measure 1*d*. In 1 basket (*sporta*) bought 4½*d*. In expenses of 2 of the lord's horses hidden for 2 days and 2 nights at Garsington so that they should not be taken for the king's use 5½*d*. Total, 17*s*. 1¾*d*.

Threshing and winnowing

In threshing 57 qrs 2 bus. of wheat by piece-work 9*s*. 6*d*., at 2*d*. a qr. In threshing 49 qrs 6 bus. of barley 6*s*. 1½*d*., at 1½*d*. a qr. In threshing 43 qrs 1 bus. of dredge by piece-work 4*s*. 5¾*d*., at 1¼*d*. a qr. In threshing 1 qr 3 bus. of vetches by piece-work 2¼*d*. In winnowing all the abovesaid corn, that is, 151 qrs 4 bus. of whatever kind of corn, 2*s*. 6*d*., at 1*d*. per 5 qrs of whatever kind of corn by struck measure. In wages of John Touresm*ere* overseeing the threshing and winnowing of corn by the day, 4*s*. 3*d*. for 1 term, taking 1½*d*. a day. In stipend of the same 2*s*., because he takes the rest up to 10*s*. elsewhere. Total, £1 9*s*. ½*d*.

Purchase of corn

In 3 qrs of beans bought for sowing 5*s*., at 1*s*. 8*d*. a qr. In 1 qr of beans bought for the same and for fodder 1*s*. 8*d*. In 1 qr of beans bought for fodder 1*s*. 4½*d*. In 2 bus. of beans bought for the same 4½*d*. Total, 8*s*. 5*d*.

[Cost] of buildings

In felling and sawing timber together with repairing the said timber to bring it from the wood of la Wassch' 1*s*. 6*d*. In 1,000 lath-nails bought for the walls of the barn 10*d*., that is, for fastening the laths. In hiring 1 carpenter to repair the said barn with the said timber by piece-work 9*s*. 6*d*. In hiring 1 roofer to roof over 2 barns for 22½ days 5*s*. 7½*d*., taking 3*d*. a day. In 3 women assisting him for the same time 5*s*. 7½*d*., or 1*d*. each a day. In hiring a certain roofer to roof over the said barn for 1 day in winter 2*d*. In 2 women assisting him for the same time 2*d*. In making 1 hinge for the gate and mending 2 latches for the hall door 1½*d*. Total, £1 3*s*. 6½*d*.

[Customary payments]

In food and drink for 41 men mowing 18 acres of meadow according to custom 6*s*. 10*d*. Total, 6*s*. 10*d*.

[Cost of the harvest]

In expenses of 5 harvest boon-works of 302 men reaping for a whole day, who reaped 228 acres of whatever kind of corn and had a meal twice a day, £1 17*s*. 9*d*., and thus each took 1½*d*. a day for 2 meals. In hiring 1 man to follow the cart in search of corn at harvest-time for 6 days 1*s*., because the ploughmen were at the ploughs for the whole day. Total, £1 18*s*. 9*d*.

[Expenses of the bailiff and] other [expenses]

Paid to Roginald de Lynh*am*, bailiff, for part of his wages, £2 for 1 term. Given to the clerk of the justices assessing the fifteenth for a certain distraint against the lord bishop, taken for the fifteenth, 6*s*. 8*d*. Given to the king's marshal for not taking the lord's hay 2*s*. 1*d*. In stipend of 1 overseer of the harvest for the year 6*s*. 8*d*. Total, £2 15*s*. 5*d*.

Total of all expenses, £14 5*s*. 10¼*d*.

And he owes, £44 5*s*. 9¾*d*.

[Cash deliveries]
Delivered to Sir G*eoffrey*, treasurer of Wolvesey, by 1 tally, £33 10*s*.

And thus he owes clear, £10 15*s*. 9¾*d*.

Issues of the grange

[Wheat]
{yield: . . . less . . .}
The same render account for 81 qrs 7 bus. of wheat from the whole issue of the grange by 3 tallies of struck measure, of which 57 qrs threshed by piece-work and 24 qrs 5 bus. by labour service; 14 qrs from churchscot at Martinmas. Total, 95 qrs 7 bus.
Sown over 133 acres of land as they lie in the field, 23 qrs 5 bus. by 1 tally; that is, 1½ bus. an acre, less 1 qr 2 bus. in all. Delivered to 1 overseer of the harvest for the year, 3 qrs 2 bus., because he takes the rest in barley, taking a quarter every 8 weeks. Sold, 68 qrs 7 bus. Sold at the audit, 1 bus. Total, 95 qrs 7 bus. None remains.

Barley
{yield: 4-fold plus 3 qrs 6 bus.}
The same render account for 49 qrs 6 bus. of barley from the whole issue of the grange, threshed by piece-work by 1 tally of struck measure. Total, 49 qrs 6 bus. Sown over 26 acres of land as they lie in the field, 12 qrs 7 bus. by 1 tally; that is, ½ qr an acre, less 1 bus. in all. Delivered to 1 overseer of the harvest for the year, 3 qrs 2 bus., because he takes the rest in wheat, taking a quarter every 8 weeks. Delivered to 1 carter and 2 drovers for the year, 15 qrs 3½ bus., or 5 qrs 2 bus. each, taking a quarter every 10 weeks. Mixed with dredge for sowing as made clear below, 3 qrs. Sold, 14 qrs 3 bus. Sold at the audit, 5½ bus. Total, 49 qrs 6 bus. None remains.

Dredge
{yield: three-fold less 3 qrs 7 bus.}
The same render account for 51 qrs 5 bus. of dredge from the whole issue of the grange by 2 tallies of struck measure, of which 43 qrs 1 bus. threshed by piece-work and 4 qrs 2 bus. by labour service; 3 qrs of barley received to mix with dredge for sowing. Total, 54 qrs 5 bus.
Sown over 63 acres of land as they lie in the field, 20 qrs 3 bus.; that is, 3 bus. an acre, plus 1 bus. in all. Sold, 20 qrs 6 bus. Sold at the audit, 3½ qrs. Total, 54 qrs 5 bus. None remains.

Vetches
{yield: 4-fold, less 1 bus.}
The same render account for 1 qr 3 bus. of vetches from the issue of the grange, threshed by piece-work by struck measure; 3 qrs from the same issue by estimation in sheaves for oxen. Total, 4 qrs 3 bus.

Sown, 6 bus. In fodder of oxen by estimation in sheaves, 3 qrs. Sold, 5 bus. Total, 4 qrs 3 bus. None remains.

Beans[1]

The same render account for 5 qrs 2 bus. of beans bought as noted above. Total, 5 qrs 2 bus.

Sown over 7 acres of land, 3 qrs. In fodder of 2 cart-horses, 2 qrs 2 bus. Total, 5 qrs 2 bus. None remains.

Stock[2]

Cart-horses: 2 remain; 2 from the heriot of John Miles for 2 tenements which he held of the bishop; 2 bought as noted above. Total, 6. 4 sold. Total, 4. 2 remain.

Oxen: 24 remain from the previous year; 1 bought as noted above. Total, 25. 1 sold because rotten. Total, 1. 24 remain.

Cows: 1 from the heriot of Walter Roed'; sold within; none remain.

Pigs: 3 hoggets bought, 2 of them male. Total, 3. 2 sold. Total, 2. 1 female pig remains.

Piglets: 8 from the offspring of the aforesaid young sow (*succule*). Total, 8. 8 remain aged 1 quarter.

Peacocks: 3 remain. Total, 3. 1 in murrain. Total, 1. 2 remain, 1 of them male.

Cocks and hens: 76 hens from churchscot at Martinmas. Total, 76. 4 in default of the land of Ydelote because she withheld (*angebat*) her rent; 2 in default of the land of Walter Gromes through his death; 2 in default of the land of Stephen le Rop for the same; 2 in default of the land of Robert atte Brok' for the same; 66 sold. Total, 76. None remain.

Carts: 2 remain, 1 of them wooden; 1 wooden cart bought. Total, 3. 1 wooden cart used. Total, 1. 2 remain, 1 of them wooden.

Wagons: 2 wagons and 1 body of a wagon remain. 1 ewer, 1 basin remain. 2 sacks and 1 horse-collar bought; they remain.

m.20

Farnham

Arrears

James de Norton', constable, and John le Fader, reeve, render account for £88 3*s.* 9¾*d.* of arrears from the previous year. All delivered to Sir G*eoffrey*, treasurer of Wolvesey, and they are quit by tally.

Rents of assize

The same render account for 19*s.* 4*d.* for all rents of assize at Christmas; £64 11*s.* 5¼*d.* at Easter (22 April); 19*s.*[3] 4*d.* at St John the Baptist (24 June); £67 19*s.* 9¾*d.* at Michaelmas (29 September). Total, £134 9*s.* 11*d.*

Increment of rent

The same render account for ½*d.* of increment of rent from Roger de Durh*am* for 1 small plot in Elston' leased to him this year; 1*s.* from John, son of John de Hale, for 2½ acres of waste of Hale leased to him this year. Total, 1*s.* ½*d.*

1 MS omits heading.

2 MS omits heading.

3 MS omits '*s.*'

Total of rents with increment, £134 10*s*. 11½*d*.

Quittances
In quittance of 1 reeve at Farnham 5*s*., and nothing should be provided for the reeve of Seale because the land is let at farm and there is no reeve there; 1 beadle for the year 3*s*., because he is bound to be overseer of the harvest over the land under cultivation (*wannag'*) and to make summonses; 1 park-keeper for the year 2*s*., and he will give 80 hens for keeping the park and he will have no greenery from the park, neither dried greenery nor any other customary payment; 1 smith for the year 10*d*., because there is nothing there except 1 plough; 1 cowherd for the year 2*s*.; 1 swineherd for the year 2*s*.; 1 ploughman for the year at Farnham 2*s*., because the lord has no ploughs at Seale; 1 shepherd at Farnham 2*s*.; 1 beadle at Seale, nothing, because the land is let at farm. Total, 18*s*. 10*d*.

Defaults of rent
In default of the land of James le Bel which was taken into the lord's hands and leased (*ass'*) for rent and afterwards restored without the rent of £6 5*s*. 10*d*. for the year being paid; the land of Peter de Sneyleslych' for a similar reason 12*s*. 3*d*.; the land of Seale drawn into demesne and not leased because it would be more detrimental than profitable 4*s*. 2*d*.; a certain weir which Henry de Elested' now holds because the same weir was set up in place of a weir elsewhere by Bishop William in water which William de Byke*n*hollt' now holds 1*s*. 6*d*.; a certain plot of Katharine, widow, overrun by the quarry 2*d*.; a certain plot of Margaret G*ri*ffyn overrun by the quarry 1*d*.; a certain plot of Alexander le P*ar*me*n*tyr overrun by the quarry 2*d*.; a curtilage of the same Alexander drawn into demesne 6*d*.; two parts of the mill of la Burn' and the adjoining meadows which were in the lord's hands £2 13*s*. 6*d*., because Juliana, who was wife of Richard ate Burn', has in dower the third part of the said mill and meadows and pays £1 6*s*. 9*d*., which payments are running in default; the mill of la Medmll' for the same reason £1, because the said Juliana has in dower the third part of the said mill and pays 10*s*., which payments are running in default; the land of la Medmll' drawn into demesne 1*s*. Total, £10 19*s*. 2*d*.

Total of quittances and defaults of rent, £11 18*s*.

Total of rents remaining, £122 12*s*. 11½*d*.

Release from labour service
The same render account for £14 12*s*. 3*d*. for release from labour service at Easter; £14 12*s*. 3*d*. for release from labour service at Michaelmas for 146 virgates of land, of which £9 1*s*. 8*d*. are for release from transport-service. And know that all those who hold the said virgates of land are bound to be quit for the said £29 4*s*. 6*d*. of the labour service which by custom they do for the lord, except that at each visit of the lord king and lord bishop to Farnham they are bound to fell and carry sufficient firewood to the castle, and to mow the meadows, spread, toss and carry the hay, by fixed agreement with the lord, just as they were by custom, together with help from the cottars. And there are 12 cottars whose services are not commuted, that is, they are reserved because each are bound to be ploughmen, cowherds, shepherds or swineherds at the will of the lord, and they are bound to spread, toss and stack the hay, and the lord's corn, and wash and shear the sheep. Moreover, there are at the same place 6 small cottars whose services are not commuted, that is, they are

reserved because small, but they are held to drive the animals to the manor, where they are bound to be slaughtered or to be in mast, and to carry hens and eggs to Wolvesey and to clean the castle buildings in preparation for each visit of the lord. Total, £29 4*s*. 6*d*.

Quittance of labour service

In quittance of 1 reeve who does not do labour service whilst he is in such an office, for 2 virgates of land for the year, 8*s*. 1*d*. Nothing should be provided for the reeve of Seale because the land is let at farm and there is no reeve there. In quittance of 1 beadle for ½ virgate of land, 2*s*. ¼*d*. for a similar reason; 1 hayward of Cockner for ½ virgate of land, 2*s*. ½*d*. for a similar reason; 2 woodwards at Churt for 1 virgate of land for the year, 3*s*. 4*d*. for a similar reason. Total of quittances of labour service, 15*s*. 5¾*d*.

Total of labour services remaining, £28 9*s*. ¼*d*.

Farm of the borough

The same render account for £12 for the farm of the borough paid in equal portions at Hockday and Martinmas in the following year because of such respite conceded to them by charter from of old. Total, £12.

Nothing from annual recognizance here because it is at Bentley.

Issues of the manor

The same render account for £2 8*s*. 4*d*. from common pannage of pigs at Martinmas (11 November), from 406 pigs and 348 piglets, at 1*d*. a pig over a year old, and ½*d*. a piglet; nothing from pannage of Ot*er*yngwod' this year because there was no mast there; 16*s*. from pannage in the park, from 48 pigs over a year old, at 4*d*. a pig; 8*s*. 5*d*. from pannage of Cockner, from 32 pigs over a year old and 37 piglets, at 2*d*. a pig and 1*d*. a piglet; 3*s*. from the pasturage of Tyghebbed' sold this year; 4*s*. from the pasturage of Nortmed' sold, and so little on account of the livestock of the lord king and Sir W. de Hameld' which was pastured in the same meadow; nothing from the pasturage of Wyssimeremed' and Risschemed' on account of the lord's stock; £1 from livestock agisted in the park; 6*s*. 3*d*. from wool locks; 6*d*. from 2 fleeces sold at the audit; 1*s*. from 2 lambs sold; 8*s*. from 8 wethers sold; 15*s*. from 6 pigs sold; 9*s*. 5*d*. from dairy produce sold at the audit; 5*s*. from 1 brass pot sold at the audit; £1 10*s*. from profit on animals bought the previous year for agisting in the pasture sold; 15*s*. from 104 hens received from the park-keeper and three woodwards according to custom, because the reeve, beadle and hayward do not collect hens in the hundred on account of the land leased and labour services commuted and for this reason they neither collect nor give; 3*s*. 4*d*. from 1,000 eggs received from three woodwards according to custom, and they do not[1] answer as they did before the release of the labour services of Rykestresch' and of ploughing became customary, because they are included above in the labour services commuted; 2*s*. 6*d*. from potters' clay (*t' figulato*rum) sold; 10*d*. from the pasturage of the rabbit-warren on la Hull' sold; 17*s*. 4*d*. from 2 oxen sold, at 9*s*. for 1, and 8*s*. 4*d*. for the other; 14*s*. from 2 cows sold; 7*s*. from 7 calves sold, at 1*s*. a head; 3*s*. 2*d*. from the hides sold of 2 horses in murrain, at 2*s*. for 1, and 1*s*. 2*d*. for the other; 1*s*. 10*d*. from the hide sold of 1 ox in murrain; 6*s*.

1 MS omits 'do not', but given in other rolls. The previous obligation was 3,000 eggs, for which see E. Robo, *Medieval Farnham* (Farnham, 1935), p. 15.

8*d.* from 1 horse sold at the audit; 1*s.* 2*d.* from 4 woolskins similarly sold, that is, from 2 ewes, 1 wether and 1 hogg in murrain, sold before shearing; 4*d.* from the skins sold of 1 ewe, 1 wether and 2 hoggs in murrain after shearing; 5*d.* from the skins sold of 5 lambs in murrain before weaning; nothing from coarse wool and lamb's-wool because it is sent to Wolvesey; 1*s.* from 18 winter cheeses sold; 15*s.* 3*d.* from 1½ weys 6 cloves of summer cheese sold, at 9*s.* a wey; 2*s.* 6*d.* from 40 lb of butter sold, at ¾*d.* a lb; nothing from hay this year; nothing from honey this year; £4 13*s.* 4*d.* from William de Homly for the land of Seale which is let to him at farm; 6*d.* from the same for the service of 1 smith at Farnham, whose service he was bound to retain for the ironwork of 1 plough and the shoeing of 1 plough-horse; 6*d.* from the same for the mowing of 2 acres of the meadow of Renemed', for tossing and carrying the hay, and for the customary tenants of the manor, and for tossing and carrying the hay of the meadow of Elstead, just as with Renemed', as it used to be done whilst it was in the lord's hands; 6*d.* from the same for the service of the cottars stacking corn and washing and shearing sheep; 6*s.* from the fisheries on the river-banks at Farnham and Frensham sold; 10*s.* from loppings in the park sold from timber felled there for making boards therefrom for the chapel of St Elizabeth; 10*s.* from bark in the park sold. Total, £19 8*s.* 1*d.*

Sale of corn

The same render account for £5 6*s.* 10½*d.* from 21 qrs 3 bus. of wheat sold, at 5*s.* a qr; 13*s.* 9*d.* from 3½ qrs 2 bus. of winter barley sold, at 3*s.* 8*d.* a qr; £1 3*s.* 5¾*d.* from 10 qrs ½ bus. of oats sold, at 2*s.* 4*d.* a qr. Total, £7 4*s.* 1¼*d.*

Mill of la Medmll'

The same render account for 8*s.* 9*d.* from 1½ qrs 2 bus. of wheat sold, at 5*s.* a qr; 16*s.* 6*d.* from 4½ qrs of multure (*tolcorn*) sold, at 3*s.* 8*d.* a qr; 12*s.* 6*d.* from 2½ qrs of coarse-ground corn sold, at 5*s.* a qr; 12*s.* 4*d.* from 4½ qrs 1 bus. of malt sold, at 2*s.* 8*d.* a qr. Total, £2 10*s.* 1*d.*

Mill of la Burn'

The same render account for £1 3*s.* 9*d.* from 4 qrs 6 bus. of wheat sold, at 5*s.* a qr; £2 11*s.* 4*d.* from 14 qrs of multure sold, at 3*s.* 8*d.* a qr; £1 from 4 qrs of coarse-ground corn sold, at 5*s.* a qr; 18*s.* from 6 qrs 6 bus. of malt sold, at 2*s.* 8*d.* a qr. Total, £5 13*s.* 1*d.*

Entry and marriage fines

The same render account for £2 9*s.* 10*d.* from the 15 inner tithings for tithingpenny at the hundred-court of Martinmas; 4*s.* from the 4 tithings of Crondall for the same; £2 9*s.* 10*d.* from the 15 tithings for tithingpenny at the hundred-court of Hockday; 4*s.* from the 4 tithings of Crondall for the same; £1 1*s.* from Richard de Wuly to have 1 messuage, 1 mill, and the hire of 1 mill, and 3 acres of purpresture, by surrender of Cecilia his mother; 13*s.* 4*d.* from Juliana, relict of Thomas Dunseked', to retain 1 messuage, 1 virgate of land and 1 acre of purpresture which belonged to Thomas her husband; 10*s.* from Agnes, who was the daughter of Richard Boylet', to have 1 messuage, ½ virgate of land which belonged to Christina her mother; £1 from Hugh ate Holte for 1 messuage, ½ virgate of land which he recovered from Richard Prat' and Juliana his wife; 4*s.* from Richard Crul to have ½ acre of land by surrender of John de Hale and ½ acre of purpresture by surrender of John, son of John de Hale; 1*s.* from Agnes, who was wife of John le Vyn', to retain 1 house and 4 half-acres of land which belonged to John her husband; 6*s*. 8*d*. from William Chatur to have 3 acres and 1 rood of land and 1 acre of purpresture which belonged to John de Farnh*am* his brother; 1*s*. 6*d*. from Adam de Pyp*er*hargh' to have 1 house and 1 small plot of land by surrender of Gilbert Chupp*man*; 6*s*. 8*d*. from Stephen Dorinal to have 1 messuage and 1 virgate of land which belonged to William his father; 1*s*. from Agnes, relict of Seuuale, for marrying Matilda her daughter within the demesne; 3*s*. from William de Ford' for marrying Cecilia his daughter; 4*s*. from Emma, relict of Osmund, for marrying Margery her daughter within; 2*s*. from G*ilbert* le Chupma*n* to have 1 house and 1 plot of land by surrender of Henry Fullar'; 13*s*. 4*d*. from Thomas le Stybber' to have 1 messuage, ½ virgate of land by surrender of John Fyssere; 4*s*. from Richard, son of Robert de Homly, to have 3 acres of purpresture by surrender of Thomas de Oxeneford'; 5*s*. from William Vel to have 1 messuage, 6 acres of purpresture which belonged to Adam Vel by surrender of Matilda his mother; 4*s*. from William Cule and Matilda his wife, daughter of William Virly, to have 1 messuage, 3 acres of land which belonged to her father; 4*s*. from Jordan, son of Ivo de Ecc*lesi*a de Thursly, to have 2 acres of purpresture which belonged to his father; 2*s*. from William ate Sond' to have 1 acre of purpresture which belonged to Sibyl his aunt; 2*s*. from John Hendybody to have 1 messuage and 1 acre of purpresture which belonged to William his father; 13*s*. 4*d*. from Stephen ate M*er*e to have Agnes, relict of William Thurbyn, with ½ virgate of land and 4 acres of purpresture; 2*s*. from Thomas Duk' for marrying Emma his daughter within the demesne; £2 from John Hyned' to have 1 messuage, ½ virgate and 1 ferling of land and 8 acres of purpresture which belonged to Juliana his mother and 1 acre which he recovered from William de Hale; 2*s*. from Roginald de Westbrok*e* to have 2 acres of purpresture by surrender of Henry de Mol*endino*; 10*s*. from Thomas de Halyb' to have Isabel la Vixne with 1 messuage and 8 acres of land; 3*s*. from Richard Synnard to have 8 acres of purpresture which belonged to Agnes his mother; 8*s*. from John, son of John ate Hale, for 2½ acres and 1 rood of purpresture leased to him this year; 6*d*. from Roger de Durh*am* for 1 small plot leased to him this year. Total, £15 15*s*.

Perquisites
The same render account for 3*d*. from John Gres for trespass (*tr'*); 3*d*. from Henry the new cook (*nov' coco*) for false complaint; 2*s*. from Peter le Hu*n*te for trespass; 3*d*. from Andrew Vynetyr for trespass; 6*d*. from T*ra*pes for the same; 3*d*. from Richard Gayt' for the same; 3*d*. from Emma Byssop for false complaint; 3*d*. from William Trig' for trespass; 3*d*. from Henry Fab*er* for the same; 3*d*. from William Fab*er* of Waverley for trespass; 3*d*. from Peter Wareremar' for trespass; 3*d*. from John de Stokto*n* for breaking an agreement; 6*d*. from Henry Wyllot' for false complaint; 3*d*. from Agatha Wannastr' for trespass; 3*d*. from William Freir' for false complaint; 3*d*. from John de Heghe for trespass; 3*d*. from John Cok' for default; 1*s*. 1*d*. from William Portyr and Robert Portyr for trespass; 3*d*. from Walter Rand' for trespass; 3*d*. from John G*ro*s for trespass; 3*d*. from Robert Cop*ere* because he did not produce in court; 3*d*. from Henry le Gol' for trespass; 3*d*. from William de Churt' for trespass; 3*d*. from Godfrey de Humweye for trespass; 3*d*. from Adam Forst' for the same; 3*d*. from John Du*mmere* for trespass; 3*d*. from Richard Chik' because he did not produce in court; 3*d*. from John Capell*anus* of Frensham for trespass; 6*d*. from Godfrey de Hu*m*weye because he did not produce in court; 3*d*. from William de Churt' for breaking an agreement; 3*d*. from William de C*ru*ce for trespass; 3*d*. from Richard P*rat*' for trespass; 2*s*. from the lady of Colrych' for suit of court; 3*d*. from Henry de Bath' for trespass; 3*d*. from William Ta*n*nat' for trespass; 6*d*. from John de

Hal' for confirming an agreement; 3*d.* from Agnes de Stakelford' for trespass; 6*d.* from William de Schakelford' for unjustly withholding; 4*s.* from Henry le Butelir for his suit of court; 2*s.* from the lady of Fonte for the same; 6*d.* from William de Humwey because he did not come; 1*s.* from Agnes Thurbern' and William Webb' for assize; 2*s.* from the tithing of Badshot because it did not produce in court; 6*d.* from Joan Fullar'; 6*d.* from Godfrey W*u*lfrich for assize; 6*d.* from Walter Rand' for the hue; 3*d.* from Christina Lanewynch' for the same; 6*d.* from Colin de Compto*n* for the same; 3*d.* from John Wyk' for the same; 6*s.* 8*d.* from Luke le Gol and Andrew Pell' because they did not produce in court Fre*nus* Elya*s*; 6*d.* from John le Mul' and G. Fisser' because they did not produce in court; 1*s.* from Peter P*ra*t and J*ohn* Cok' for assize; 2*s.* from the tithing of Runwick because it did not produce in court; 3*d.* from Richard P*ra*t' for the hue; 6*d.* from Joan Bagge for assize; 3*s.* 9*d.* from Isabel ate Stonhull', William de Cateford', Jordan Hatt*ere*, Adam son of Juliana, Richard ate Lane, G*ilbert* le Chupma*n*, John, son of John Eddel' de Po*n*te, G. de Fughelesbrock' and Agnes de Byke*n*holt' for assize; 3*d.* from the wife of William de Schakeford' for the hue; 2*s.* from Robert Sclut', Richard Carpe*n*tir, G. ate Rye and John Cisscir' for assize; 4*s.* from the tithing of Cove for[1] concelament; 1*s.* from Adam ate Lye for assize; 1*s.* 6*d.* from Roger Jermay*n*, Robert Fynche*n*t' and John G*er*may for assize; 1*s.* from Hugh Carp' for assize; 6*d.* from Nicholas ate Bur' for release from suit of court; 6*d.* from Richard Sema*n* for trespass; 6*d.* from John de Po*n*te for the same; 6*d.* from William Abbod for the hue; 6*d.* from John Chalenir for the same; 6*d.* from John Du*mm*er*e* for the same; 6*d.* from William Abbod' for the same; 6*d.* from William Bregh' for the same; 6*d.* from Peter Burel for the same; 6*d.* from Robert de Assch' for trespass; and from Richard Durvassal for the same; 3*d.* from Juliana ate Burn' for trespass; 3*d.* from G. Porc' for trespass; 3*d.* from John de Stokton' for trespass; 3*d.* from Adam Forst' for trespass; 3*d.* from Agnes Forst' for false complaint; 6*d.* from the tithing of James le Bel because it did not produce in court; 2*s.* from the tithing of Badshot because it did not challenge the default of W*illiam* de Hu*m*weye; 6*d.* from the tithing of Compton because it did not produce in court John Smart'; 6*d.* from Roger de Fr*a*xino for default; 1*s.* from the tithing of Itchel because it did not produce in court; 3*d.* from Richard de Fo*n*te for unjustly withholding; 3*d.* from Henry Gol for trespass; 6*d.* from the same for the same; 6*d.* from Matilda, wife of W. Wuduuard', for confirming an agreement; 6*d.* from Adam Forst' for the same; 3*d.* from Joan Aylnat' for assize; 1*s.* from the tithing of Tilford for concealment ⌈and⌉ 6*d.* from John Mol*endinarius* for assize; 6*d.* from William Wayt' for the same; 3*d.* from Emma Fre*n*ch' for the same; 3*d.* from Robert Draper for the same; 6*d.* from Joan Fullar' for the same; 1*s.* from Roger B*ercarius* for the hue; 1*s.* from the tithing of Bogflod' for concealment; 6*d.* from Henry Gol for the hue; 6*d.* from Richard de Uschate for assize; 3*d.* from John Somere for the same; 6*d.* from William de Stakelford' for the same; 2*s.* from Robert Hub*er*d for false complaint; 6*d.* from John Cissore for assize; 6*d.* from William Ra*m*pel for the same; 6*d.* from Alexander Rog' for the same; 6*d.* from Roger Sclut' for the same; 6*d.* from Richard Carpe*nter* for the same; 3*d.* from Henry Douns for the same; 3*d.* from Emma Kutel for the same; 3*d.* from Stephen Rand' for the same; 3*d.* from Roger G*er*may for the same; 1*s.* from William Est' and John ate Lye for the same; 6*d.* from Stephen ate Rok' for the same; 1*s.* from William de Hal' for unjustly withholding; 2*s.* from the tithing of Runwick for concealment; 3*d.* from William Hub*er*d for assize; 3*d.* from Richard de Ronewyk' for the same; 6*d.* from Robert Hub*er*d for trespass; 3*d.* from N. Mu*n*dely for the same; 3*d.* from Nicholas Byssop for trespass; 6*d.* from Robert Hub*er*d to have

1 MS 'pro ⟨ass'⟩ consel".

an inquest; 3*d.* from William Bastg' for trespass; 3*d.* from Robert Hub*er*d for trespass; 6*d.* from Adam Fluyr for default; 3*d.* from Luke le Gol because he is not proceeding; 6*d.* from the tithing of Itchel for concealment; 3*d.* from William Cutel for default; 3*d.* from Robert Hub*er*d because he did not make amends; 3*d.* from John Pag' for trespass; 3*d.* from Agnes Costar' for the same; 3*d.* from Thomas de Glome for trespass; 3*d.* from John Uggelwyn' for trespass; 3*d.* from William ate So*n*d'; 3*d.* from Schakelford' for trespass; 6*d.* from Adam Dunrych' for false complaint; 2*d.* from William Flodma*n*; 2*d.* from Richard Cop*ere* for trespass; 1*s.* from Richard Tyngor' and others for trespass; 6*d.* from William de Dupe*n*hale for trespass; 6*d.* from John Boltar' for trespass; 3*d.* from William de Hal' for false complaint; 3*d.* from Hawis Gol for trespass; 3*d.* from Thomas de North' for trespass; 3*d.* from William de Brodeford' for trespass; 3*d.* from Andrew Vynetyr for the same; 6*d.* from W*illiam* ate So*n*d' for trespass; 3*d.* from Henry Gol for trespass; 3*d.* from Walter Webb' for trespass because he did not produce in court Juliana ate B*er*n'; 3*d.* from W. Crokfonte; 3*d.* from Matilda M*a*rti*n*; 3*d.* from Dyonisia Weylo*n*d' for trespass; 3*d.* from Margaret (*Mogge*) Buck' for trespass; 3*d.* from William ate Sond' for trespass; 3*d.* from Agatha Famastr' for trespass; 1*s.* from Richard Caym and Richard Cornmo*n*gar' to have an inquest; 6*d.* from Richard Athelard' for false complaint; 3*d.* from John de Sneleslynch' for trespass; 6*d.* from Alice Large for confirming an agreement. Total, £4 15*s.* 10*d.*

Total of both, £20 10*s.* 10*d.*

m.20d
Nothing from chattels of felons this year; nothing from reliefs this year; nothing from green wax this year.

Total of all receipts, £218 8*s.* 2*d.*

Cost of ploughs
In ironwork of 1 plough for the year 6*s.* 8*d.* In shoeing 2 plough-horses for the year 1*s.* 8*d.* In 1 ploughshare bought and the same rebuilt (*relev'*) 10*d.* In 1 pair of wheels bought 3*d.* In quittance of 22 Saturday ploughings by the cowherd, shepherd and swineherd from Michaelmas until Easter, because 6 were free on account of feast-days and 1 on account of frost and snow, 3*s.* 8*d.*, at 2*d.* a ploughing-day. In quittance of 21 Saturday ploughings by the aforesaid cowherd, shepherd and swineherd from Easter until Michaelmas, because 2 Saturdays were free on account of feast-days, 1*s.* 9*d.*, at 1*d.* a ploughing-day.[1] In forage for supporting oxen this year, and for the sojourn of the bishop's horses, 5s. In shoeing 2 oxen 2*s.* 1*d.* In stipend of 1 drover for the year 2*s.* 6*d.* Total, £1 4*s.* 5*d.*

Purchase of seed
In 12 qrs 2 bus. of barley bought for the liveries of the manorial servants £2 4*s.* 11*d.*, at 3*s.* 8*d.* a qr; 16½ qrs 1 bus. of oats bought £1 8*s.* 8¼*d.*, at 1*s.* 6*d.* a qr for 9 qrs 1 bus., and 2*s.* a qr for 7½ qrs. Total, £3 13*s.* 7¼*d.*

Carts
In 1 pair of wheels bought to fit with iron 3*s.* 1*d.* In clamps with nails bought 3*s.* 4*d.* In stipend of the smith fitting the said wheels with old tyres 10½*d.* In 1 pair of wheels

1 MS '⟨In stip' j garco*n*is⟩'.

bought for clearing dung 1*s*. 6*d*. In fitting the carts with axles 4*d*., and so much on account of the prises of the lord king and other visitors. In mending the carts at various times 3½*d*. In 1 halter bought 1*d*. In grease bought 6*d*. In clouts with nails bought 1*s*. 5*d*. In 1 collar bought 5*d*. In 1 pair of traces 4*d*. In 1 saddle-pad bought 4 ½*d*. In 1 cart-rope 1*s*. 3*d*. In white leather bought for mending harnesses 5*d*. In shoeing 2 cart-horses for the year 2*s*. 4*d*. In 1 cart-horse bought 19*s*. 3*d*. In stipend of the carter for the year 3*s*. Total, £1 18*s*. 9½*d*.

Stipends
In stipend of 1 door-keeper for the year 6*s*. 8*d*. In stipend of 1 watchman, nothing this year, because there was none. In expenses of 24 customary tenants for 3 days according to custom at Christmas, the beginning of Lent, and Easter, 9*s*., or 1½*d*. each a day, because the reeve and 3 manorial servants of Seale no longer have food as they were accustomed to have because the land is let at farm, and they were accustomed to take for their bread 7½*d*. Total, 15*s*. 8*d*.

Dairy
In linen and woollen cloth 4*d*. In earthenware pots and pans bought 4½*d*. In salt bought 7*d*. In a press bought 3*d*. In verdigris and vinegar 10½*d*. In 44 lb of grease for sick sheep 5*s*. 5½*d*., at 1½*d*. a lb. In 3 lb of grease bought for greasing the said sheep 4*d*., at 1¼*d*. a lb this year, on account of the number infected with scab. In 14 hurdles bought for the fold 1*s*. 2*d*. In 4 ells of canvas bought for packing wool 1*s*. In packing the said wool with thread bought for the same 3*d*. In 1 cow bought after calving 6*s*. 9*d*. In 1 bull bought 7*s*. Total, £1 4*s*. 4½*d*.

Small expenses
In collecting stubble for 4 days by piece-work 6*d*. In roofing the byre with the said stubble by piece-work 1*s*. In mending the walls around the byre 3½*d*. In 1 wheel bought for the wheelbarrow 1½*d*. In pruning the vines 3½*d*. In drawing the water-bucket from the well on 10 occasions 6*d*. In mending a breach around la Rude 11*d*. In 1 bucket bought 2½*d*. In hooping old casks with hoops bought for the same 1*s*. 3*d*. In mending the pinfold 7½*d*. Total, 5*s*. 8½*d*.

Threshing and winnowing
In threshing and winnowing 29 qrs of wheat by piece-work 5*s*. 5¾*d*., at 2¼*d*. a qr. In threshing and winnowing 3½ qrs 2 bus. of winter barley by piece-work 6¼*d*., at 1¾*d*. a qr. In threshing and winnowing 14 qrs 1 bus. of barley by piece-work 2*s*. ½*d*., at 1¾*d*. a qr. In threshing and winnowing 29 qrs of oats by piece-work 1*s*. 9¼*d*., at ¾*d*. a qr. Total, 9*s*. 9¾*d*.

Cost of 2 parts of Medmull'
{henceforth there should only be 1 horse there and no cart if that seems to be right}
In steel bought to mend the small bills 6*d*. In 2 pairs of wheels bought for the mill cart 2*s*. 4½*d*. In 1 collar and new saddle-pads bought 8*d*. In clouts with nails bought 8*d*. In shoeing the mill-horse for the year 1*s*. 4*d*. In 1 hair rope bought for pasturing the said horse 3½*d*. In 1 halter of hair bought ½*d*. In mending the roof of the cart 3¼*d*. In fitting the cart with axles 1½*d*. Total, 6*s*. 3¼*d*.

Cost of 2 parts of la Burn'
In steel bought for the small bills of the mill of la Burn' 7*d*. In steel for lengthening the spindle and mending and renewing the mill-rind 10*d*. In stipend of the smith

repairing the said spindle and mill-rind 8*d*. In 2 pairs of wheels bought for the cart 2*s*. 7*d*. In clouts with nails bought 5½*d*. In 1 collar and new saddle-pads bought 9*d*. In 1 new cart-saddle bought 1½*d*. In fitting the cart with axles on 2 occasions 3*d*. In shoeing the mill-horse for the year 1*s*. 4*d*. In a hair rope with a halter bought for pasturing the horse 3½*d*. In an iron band for hooping the inner wheel 4*d*. In 1 mill-horse bought 11*s*. 4*d*. Total, 19*s*. 6½*d*.

Cost of the meadows and weeding

In weeding corn 5*s*. In mowing and spreading 54 acres of meadow which the hundred is bound to mow according to custom 15*s*. 9*d*., at 3½*d*. an acre. In spreading the meadow which is called Wulmed' 6*d*. In mowing, spreading and tossing 2 roods in the meadow which is called Suthmed' 2*d*. In mowing 2 roods of meadow in the land of la Medm*u*ll' 2*d*. Total, £1 1*s*. 7*d*.

Harvest-time

In reaping, turning and binding all the corn by piece-work £1 17*s*. 4*d*., at 7*d*. an acre this year, because of the dearness of the reapers. In stipend of 1 man found to carry the corn 4*d*. Total, £1 17*s*. 8*d*.

Expenses of the steward with the fee of the constable

In expenses of the steward at the tourn of Martinmas by 1 tally 9*s*. In expenses of the steward at the tourn of Hockday £1 9*s*. 7½*d*. by 1 tally. Also by another tally 5*s*. 9*d*. In wages of the constable for the year £10. Total, £12 4*s*. 4½*d*.

Total of all expenses, £26 1*s*. 9¾*d*.

And he owes, £192 6*s*. 4¼*d*.

Allowances

In 1 letter of the treasurer sent to Wargrave 3*d*. In a letter of Master John de Esto*n* sent to Esher 4*d*. In a letter of the treasurer sent to Esher 4*d*. In a letter of the steward sent to the constable at Wargrave 3*d*.[1] In a letter of the steward to Newark Priory about the account 3*d*. In a letter to the constable staying overnight at Wargrave 4*d*. In a letter of the bishop sent to Wargrave about the fifteenth 3*d*. In a letter of the constable sent to Simon about the stable at Wargrave 4*d*. In a letter of the constable sent to Wolvesey about the fifteenth 4*d*. In a letter of Simon and the treasurer sent to the constable at Wargrave on the eve of Philip and James (30 April) about the business of the bishop 3*d*. In a letter of the treasurer sent to Esher on Monday after the feast of St John the Baptist (25 June) 4*d*. In a letter of the treasurer sent to Wargrave about the rent of St John the Baptist 3*d*. In a letter of the treasurer sent to the constable at Wargrave 3*d*. In a letter of the treasurer sent to Wargrave on Monday after Michaelmas (1 October) about the rent and arrears of the last account 3*d*. In 3 letters of the treasurer borne to Wargrave at various times 9*d*. Total, 4*s*. 9*d*.

Cost of the castle buildings

In mending the walls around the buildings of the bakehouse and dairy 7*d*. In stipend of 1 carpenter making the door of the dairy 4*d*. In hooks and hinges bought for the same 3*d*. In 1 lock with a key bought for the same 2*d*. In stones bought for laying the foundations under the bridge before the tower 2*s*. 5*d*. In hiring 2 men to help load the

1 MS 'co*n*st*abularius* de ⌈ap*u*d⌉ Wergr*a*ve'.

said timber 1*s*. 2*d*. In hiring 3 men to get rid of the old timber of the said bridge and clean the site under the bridge 1*s*. 2*d*. In hiring a carter to carry lime, sand and stones to the said foundations 2*s*. In 16 qrs of lime bought for the said foundations 5*s*. 4*d*., at 4*d*. a qr. In stipend of the mason laying the said foundations 3*s*. 8*d*. In iron bought for making hoops and nails for the bridge of the said tower with the stipend of the smith 1*s*. 3*d*. In 300 board-nails bought to fasten the lead to the chamber beyond the hall door 7*d*. In tin and lead bought to solder together for want of old lead 3*s*. In stipend of the plumber roofing and mending the said chamber with the said tin and lead 2*s*. In stipend of the carpenter making supports in the said chamber 11*d*. In hiring 1 man to mend the table in the hall for 2 days 7*d*. In mending the gutter between the archdeacon's chamber and the privy 3*d*. In hiring 1 man to prop up the joists in the neck of the tower for 2 days by piece-work 7*d*. In mending the walls beyond the door of the tower 6*d*. In felling, trimming and sawing timber to mend the bridge outside the gate and the houses beyond the water well by piece-work 7*s*. 3*d*. In 100 large nails to fasten the said boards 4*d*. In pulling down the corner tower facing the vill by order of the bishop and separately collecting the large stones by piece-work 8*s*. 2*d*. In throwing out and disposing of the old masonry by means of hurdles 4*s*. 2*d*. In examining and cleaning the foundations of the said tower 2*s*. 6*d*. In agreed payment of the masons for building the said tower by piece-work £6. In hauling the free stones and digging in the quarry of the pinfold £1 16*s*. In carrying the said stones from the pinfold to the castle £6 16*s*. 2*d*. In 142 qrs of lime bought for the said tower £2 7*s*. 4*d*., at 4*d*. a qr. In hiring a cart to carry the said lime from the tile-kiln to the castle whilst the castle cart was at Newark Priory and Winchester on the bishop's business 1*s*. 3*d*. In water drawn from the well at various times to make mortar 6*s*. 5*d*. In troughs and other utensils for masonry and stones carried to the mason 1*s*. 1*d*. In 25 rafters of alder bought 1*s*. 6*d*. In felling and trimming the said rafters 6*d*. In 10 hurdles bought for scaffolding 10*d*. In 200 tiles and 1 qr of hip-tiles bought for mending the kitchen 1*s*. 7½*d*. In 2 qrs of lime bought for the same 8*d*. In hiring 2 men for 2 days to roof the said kitchen 1*s*. Total, £20 6½*d*.

Expenses for arms
In hiring 1 man to set up and dry the arms for 6 days 1*s*. 6*d*. Total, 1*s*. 6*d*.

Cost of the park and fishponds
In renewing again the palisade of the park because the lord is bound to enclose at the various places which were blown down by stormy winds 4*s*. 3*d*. In wholly renewing the head of the small fishpond £29 6*s*. 8*d*. In hiring 2 men to collect fish which had escaped from the great fishpond and replacing the same again 2*s*. In cleaning the small ditch at the great fishpond 4*d*. Total, £29 13*s*. 4*d*.

Allowances
In wages of the warrener for the year £1 10*s*. 5*d*., or 1*d*. a day. In stipend of the same 6*s*. 8*d*. Total, £1 17*s*. 1*d*.

Foreign expenses
In 18 qrs of charcoal made by piece-work 2*s*. 3*d*., at 1½*d*. a qr. In re-hooping 2 casks of wine at various times 6*d*. In hiring men to haul 1 cask of wine from the cellar to the cart and to load it onto the cart 3*d*. In 1 man remaining at Cove for 3 weeks for the death of the lord bishop of Worcester 2*s*. 7½*d*. In expenses of 1 man remaining at Itchel for the same time 2*s*. 7½*d*. In expenses of 8 men going to Cove and remaining

there for 2 days to maintain the lord bishop's state 4*s*. 6*d*. In expenses of Sir John Randolf for 1 visit 7*s*. 11*d*. Delivered to Robert Dunek*an* going to Winchester on Thursday after the feast of the Apostles Philip and James (3 May) by order of Simon 4*d*. In expenses of the knights assessing the fifteenth in Surrey 10*s*. 5½*d*. In expenses of the knights coming to Farnham to take corn, oats and meat for the use of the king 14*s*. 2*d*. In expenses of the cart-horses going to Selborne and bringing stones to Wolvesey 2*d*. In expenses of the same bringing victuals to the bishop at Wolvesey 2*d*. In ale bought for the men hauling casks of wine from the carts to the cellar 4*d*. In 23 pigs bought for the bishop's larder, £3 6*s*. by writ. In expenses of John de Westcot' remaining in London on the bishop's business about the Annunciation (25 March) for 6 days 19*s*. In expenses of Robert Dunekan in London on the bishop's business 1*s*. 4*d*. In hay bought for the lord's horses sojourning at Farnham £1 2*s*. 3*d*. Given to Dunek*an* going to York and bearing there 1 letter on the bishop's business 6*s*. Total, £8 10½*d*.

Total of all allowances, £60 1*s*. 1*d*.

[Cash deliveries]
Delivered to Sir G*eoffrey*, treasurer of Wolvesey, by 1 tally, £72 15*s*.

Total of all allowances and cash deliveries, £132 16*s*. 1*d*.

And thus he owes clear, £59 10*s*. 3¼*d*.

Issues of the grange

[Wheat]
{yield: two-fold plus . . .}
The same render account for 29 qrs 2 bus. from the whole issue of the grange with the increment of the granary. Total, the same.
Sown over 22 acres measured by the perch which lie in the field of Langenh*am*, 6½ qrs 3 bus.; that is, 2½ bus. an acre. In provision of the steward at the tourns of Martinmas and Hockday, 1 qr. Sold, 21 qrs 3 bus. Total, 29 qrs 2 bus. It balances.

[Winter barley]
{yield: two-and-a-half-fold plus . . .}
The same render account for 3½ qrs 2 bus. from the whole issue of winter barley from the grange with the increment of the granary. Sold, 3½ qrs 2 bus.

[Barley]
{yield: . . . drover . . . 10 weeks}
The same render account for 14 qrs 1 bus. from the issue of barley from the grange, again with the increment of the granary; 12 qrs 2 bus. bought. Total, 26 qrs 3 bus. Sown over 10 acres measured by the perch which lie in the field of Westspend', 5 qrs 3 bus.; that is, 4½ bus. an acre, less 2 bus. in all. Delivered to 1 door-keeper, 1 carter, 1 drover for the year, 19½ qrs. Delivered to 1 dairymaid for the time when the cheese is made, 1 qr 2 bus. In supporting pigs and weaning piglets, 2 bus. Total, 26 qrs 3 bus. And none remains.

Oats
{yield: 23 qrs 1 bus. more than sown}
The same render account for 30 qrs 3 bus. from the whole issue of oats from the grange with the increment of the granary; 6 qrs by estimation in sheaves given to

oxen, and so much this year because they have no hay; 16½ qrs 1 bus. bought. Total, 53 qrs.
Sown over 32½ acres measured by the perch as they lie in the field of Westssend', 18 qrs 2 bus.; that is, 4½ bus. an acre, plus ½ bus. in all. In fodder of the steward's horses at the tourn of Martinmas, 6 bus. In fodder of the steward's horses at the tourn of Hockday, 3 qrs ½ bus. by tally. In fodder of 2 cart-horses for the year, 12 qrs, and so much this year for carrying stone, sand and lime to the tower. In fodder of 2 plough-horses for the year, 2½ qrs 3 bus. In supporting oxen by estimation in sheaves, 6 qrs. Sold, 10 qrs ½ bus. Total, 53 qrs. It balances.

Issue of the mill of la Medmull'
The same render account for 1½ qrs 2 bus. from the whole issue of wheat from 2 parts of la Medmull', because Juliana, who was wife of Richard de la Burn', has the third part for her dower, and all sold; 4½ qrs from the whole issue of multure from la Medm*u*ll' this year, and so small for the aforesaid reason, and all sold; 2½ qrs from the whole issue of coarse-ground corn from la Medm*u*ll', and so small for the aforesaid reason, and all sold; 4½ qrs 1 bus. from the whole issue of malt from la Medmull', and so small for the aforesaid reason, and all sold.

Issue of the mill of la Burn'
The same render account for 4 qrs 6 bus. from the whole issue of wheat from the mill of la Burn', and so small for the aforesaid reason, and all sold; 14 qrs of multure from the whole issue of la Burn', and so small for the aforesaid reason, and all sold; 4 qrs from the whole issue of coarse-ground corn from the mill of la Born', and so small for the aforesaid reason, and all sold; 6 qrs 6 bus. from the issue of malt from the mill of la Burn', and so small for the aforesaid reason, and all sold.

Stock

Cart-horses: 2 remain from the previous year; 1 bought. Total, 3. 1 in murrain; 2 remain.
Plough-horses: 2 females remain from the previous year; 1 female from the heriot of Peter ate Nywe. Total, 3. 3 females remain.
Colts: 1 remains from the previous year's foals; 1 colt remains now aged 1½ years.
Foals: 1 from this year's offspring; 1 in murrain; none remain.
Horses of the mill of la Burn': 2 remain from the previous year; 1 bought. Total, 3. 1 in murrain; 1 sold; 1 remains.
Horses of the mill of Medm*u*ll': 1 remains from the previous year; 1 remains.
Oxen: 8 remain from the previous year; 1 from the heriot of Thomas de Wolygh'; 1 from the heriot of Thomas Dousekod'. Total, 10. 2 sold; 1 in murrain. Total, 3. 7 remain.
Bulls: 1 bought; 1 remains.
Cows: 8 remain from the previous year; 1 from the heriot of Juliana Hyned' after calving; 1 bought after calving; 1 added from steers. Total, 11. 2 sold before calving; 9 remain.
[Steers]: 1 female from the heriot of Walter Hendybody; 1 added above to cows; none remain.
Bullocks: 2 remain from the previous year's yearlings; 2 remain, 1 of them male.
Yearlings:[1]
Calves: 7 from the said cows this year because 1 cow was sterile; all sold; none remain.

1 MS omits entry.

Rams: 2 remain from the previous year; 2 remain.
Ewes: 53 remain from the previous year; 19 added from hoggs. Total, 72. 2 in murrain before giving birth, and 1 after shearing. Total, 3. 69 remain.
Wethers: 46 remain from the previous year; ⌈1⌉ from the heriot of Sibyl ate Sonde after shearing; 16 added from hoggs. Total, 63. 8 sold at Martinmas; 1 in murrain before shearing and 1 after shearing. Total, 10. 53 remain.
Hoggs: 38 remain from the previous year's lambs. 1 in murrain before shearing and 2 after shearing; 19 added above to ewes and 16 to wethers. Total, 38. None remain.
Lambs: 50 produced by the ewes this year because 1 was sterile. 3 in murrain before weaning; 2 in murrain by castration; 4 in tithe; 3 in customary payment to the reeve, beadle and shepherd; 2 sold before shearing. Total, 14. 36 remain.
Fleeces {yield of fleece 3*d*. this year}: 127 fleeces of coarse wool produced at the shearing this year; 12 in tithe; 1 in customary payment to the shepherd; 112 sent to Wolvesey, which made ½ wey; 2 sold at the audit. Total, 127. None remain.
Lamb's-wool {yield 1¼*d*. plus 1*d*. in all}: 36 fleeces of lamb's-wool produced at the shearing this year; all sent to Wolvesey, which made 2 cloves; none remains.

m.21
Woolskins: 2 from ewes, 1 from a wether, 1 from a hogg in murrain before shearing. Total, 4. All sold; none remain.
Bare skins: 1 from a ewe, 1 from a wether, 2 from hoggs. Total, 4. 4 sold; none remain.
Lambskins: 5 from lambs in murrain before weaning; all sold; none remain.
Pigs: 8 remain from the previous year; 6 added from stock; 2 from pannage according to custom. Total, 16. 2 in murrain; 6 sold. Total, 8. 8 remain, 1 of them a sow.
Hoggets: 7 remain from the previous year's piglets; 1 from the heriot of John Wyn'. Total, 8. 2 in murrain; 6 added to pigs. Total, 8. None remain.
Piglets {henceforth they should have 2 sows so that they have a full keeping of pigs}: 11 from this year's offspring; 1 in tithe; 3 in customary payment to the reeve, beadle and swineherd. Total, 4. 7 remain.
Winter cheese: 18 made; all sold.
Summer cheese {yield of cow 3*s*. and sheep 2*d*. with 5 cheeses given in customary payment valued at 1*s*. this year}: 166 cheeses made between Monday after the feast of St John before the Latin Gate (7 May) and Michaelmas (29 September), both days included, at the rate of 1 everyday; 14 in tithe; 5 in customary payment to the reeve, beadle, smith, shepherd and dairymaid; 127 sold, which made 1½ weys 6 cloves.
Butter: 40 lb from the issue of the dairy this year; all sold.
Hens: 380 received from the park-keeper and 3 woodwards according to custom; 200 in default of the reeve of Seale, the beadle and hayward on account of the land being leased and the labour services commuted; 180 sold.
Eggs: 3,000 received from 3 woodwards according to custom; 2,000 in default of the reeve of Seale, the beadle and hayward; 1,000 sold.
Chapel: 1 gradual, 1 missal, 1 temporal, 1 antiphoner, 2 bound texts remain from the previous year; all remain here.
Kitchen: 1 lead vessel and 3 brass pots, of which 1 is sold, 1 axe and 1 brass pan remain from the previous year; they remain.
Utensils: 1 cart with iron tyres and 1 of wood, 1 shovel, 1 spade and 1 iron fork remain from the previous year; 1 pair of wheels fitted with iron tyres and 1 of wood bought; 1 pair of wheels for the wooden cart used in the manor; all the other utensils remain.

Arms: 10 shields, 12 crossbows, 1 of them with a winch and 1 with 2 feet, 10 iron helmets, 10 padded tunics, 40 iron-tipped lances, 52 large crossbow bolts, 200 small crossbow bolts, 3 sets of trappers, 3 sets of plate armour, 3 iron basnets[1] remain from stock of the previous year; 2 saddles for arms, 2 sets of plate armour with arm-guards, 4 gorgets of plate, 5 pairs of plate gloves, 2 iron basnets, 5 pairs of greaves with armour for knees and cuisses of plate, 1 set of trappers, 4 padded tunics, 2 saddles for arms, 4 harnesses for arms, 4 hatchets remain from the previous year; all remain.

Bentley

Arrears

James de Northon', bailiff, and William le Stynt', reeve, render account for £9 18*s*. 9½*d*. of arrears from the previous year. All delivered to Sir G*eoffrey*, treasurer of Wolvesey, and they are quit.

Rents of assize

The same render account for £8 16*s*. 10¼*d*. for all rents of assize at Easter (22 April); £8 16*s*. 10¾*d*. at Michaelmas (29 September). Total, £17 13*s*. 9*d*.

Quittances

In quittance of 1 reeve for the year 5*s*.; 1 shepherd for the year 3*s*.; 3 ploughmen for the year 6*s*.; 1 smith for the year 2*s*. Total, 16*s*.

Defaults of rent

In default of 2 acres of Sampson drawn into demesne 1*s*. 3*d*.; 2½ acres in Costouue 4*s*. 9*d*.; certain land of Gundevyl' drawn into demesne 6*d*.; 1½ acres and 1 perch which belonged to John Edward drawn into demesne 10*d*.; 2 acres of land of Thomas de Cam*er*a drawn into demesne 2*s*.; 1 house of Joan de la Forde which was pulled down on account of the king's highway 1*d*. Total of defaults of rent, 9*s*. 5*d*.

Total of quittances and defaults of rent, £1 5*s*. 5*d*.

Total of rents remaining, £16 8*s*. 4*d*.

Annual recognizance

The same render account for 6*d*. from the annual recognizance of the relict of Thomas de Badely, for the term of 13 years which John le Cornmongare granted her to hold the land of Richard Vassal. She thus pays 6*d*. yearly, and this will be the second year. Total, 6*d*.

Issues of the manor

The same render account for 14*s*. 1*d*. from common pannage of 114 pigs and 106 piglets, at 1*d*. a pig over a year old, ½*d*. a piglet; 6*s*. from pannage of Luxegr*o*ve and Woodgarston, of 36 pigs of Robert Archyr, Richard atte Ford', William Duk' and other men of Bentley, at 2*d*. a pig; 1*s*. 6*d*. from the pasturage of la Rygg' sold to the men of Crondall; 1*s*. from the pasturage of Woodgarston sold; 2*s*. from the pasturage of Coleford'; 1*s*. from the pasturage of la Brodemed' sold; 4*s*. from the pasturage of Midelfeld' sold; nothing from the pasturage of la Den' and Westssend' because it

1 MS 'iij ⟨lanc'⟩ bacinis'.

was reserved for the lord's oxen; nothing from the pasturage of Luxeg*ro*ve this year for the lord's oxen; £1 10*s*. from 3 oxen sold, at 10*s*. each; 4*s*. 6*d*. from an old feeble ox sold; 6*s*. from 1 cow from the heriot of John ate Pull' sold; 4*s*. from 1 bullock sold; 2*s*. 3*d*. from the hide sold of 1 ox in murrain; 8*d*. from 1 piglet from a heriot sold; 1*s*. 3*d*. from 10 hens from churchscot sold; 3*s*. 10¼*d*. from 19 qrs of wheat from Rikestreth'; 6*s*. 9*d*. from customary tenants for release from harrowing which is called 'Dustsegynge'; £1 6*s*. 8*d*. from 2 casks of cider remaining from the previous year sold without the wood; 5*s*. from ½ cask of cider sold. Total, £6 6¼*d*.

Sale of corn
The same render account for £25 4*s*. from 84 qrs of wheat sold, at 6*s*. a qr; 8*s*. 1½*d*. from 3 qrs 3 bus. of curall sold, at 2*s*. 4*d*. a qr; 3*s*. from 1 qr of barley sold at the audit; £1 8*s*. from 12 qrs of oats sold, at 2*s*. 4*d*. a qr. Total, £27 3*s*. 1½*d*.

Entry and marriage fines
The same render account for 2*s*. from Peter Burel for 5 acres of purpresture which he recovered from Joan de Mar*i*sco; £1 6*s*. 8*d*. from Richard, son of Richard le Hyne, and Margaret his wife, daughter of John ate Pull', for 1 messuage and ½ virgate of land which belonged to John ate Pull' by quitclaim of Hugh ate Slade and Richard le Hyne; 13*s*. 4*d*. from William ate Hole to have 1 messuage and 1 ferling of land which belonged to Robert ate Hole his father; £1 13*s*. 4*d*. from John Knygt' to have 1 messuage 8 acres of land which he recovered from Robert de Tymb*e*den' by inquest taken in the absence of the said Robert for his many defaults; 13*s*. 4*d*. from Robert Babbe and Emma his wife to have 1 messuage and 1 curtilage and 4 acres of land which belonged to Blyssot', relict of Sampson. Total, £4 8*s*. 8*d*.

Perquisites
The same render account for 6*d*. from the reeve of Bentley because he put himself on an inquest; 2*s*. from Robert de Tettemoll' for false complaint; 2*s*. from the tithing of Bentley because it did not produce in court Richard Babb' and William Archyr; 3*d*. from Richard Vassal for default; 6*d*. from Peter Sweyn for the hue; 1*s*. from John de Wuly for the same; 6*d*. from Blyssiot', daughter of Gylemyn, for breaking the assize; 1*s*. from Robert Stel for the same; 3*d*. from Robert ate Hacch' for the same; 3*d*. from the relict of Laurence for the same; 1*s*. from Joan de Marisco for false complaint; 6*d*. from the tithing of Bentley because it did not produce in court Richard Babb'; 3*d*. from Aunor', servant of Joan de Marisco, for default; 3*d*. from William Hayward' for trespass; 6*d*. from John Burnyf' to have a view; 3*d*. from John Certayn for trespass; 6*d*. from John ate Pleystouue for trespass; 1*s*. from Avice de Wuly because she sowed the land of the vill; 3*d*. from Matilda ate Slad' for trespass; 3*d*. from the same for the same; 2*d*. from John de Tymb*e*d' for the same; 6*d*. from William Hayward' for unjustly withholding; 3*d*. from Robert Pyletayl for trespass; 3*d*. from John le Car*eter* for the same; 3*d*. from Richard le Hyn' for trespass; 3*d*. from Richard Harold because he leased his land; 3*d*. from Robert de C*ru*ce for trespass; 6*d*. from Hugh ate Slade for confirming an agreement; 3*d*. from John Ust*ra*d for trespass; 3*d*. from John le Car*eter* for trespass; 3*d*. from Richard Hyn' for trespass; 6*d*. from John Slad' for the same; 6*d*. from John Gu*n*dewyle for trespass; 3*d*. from Nicholas de Ysenhurst for trespass; 6*d*. from William Ydwyn' for trespass; 3*d*. from Richard ate Ford' for trespass. Total, 18*s*. 2*d*.

Total of both, £5 6*s*. 10*d*.

Total of all receipts, £54 19*s*. 3¾*d*.

Expenses of ploughs

In steel bought for 3 ploughs for the year 11*s*. 5*d*. In 3 ploughshares bought 2*s*. 6*d*. In 3 pairs of wheels bought 1*s*. In 2 ploughs made anew 6*d*. In 3 ploughs fitted with iron tyres 7½*d*. In 8 oxen bought £4 5*s*. 11*d*., at 11*s*. 5*d*. each for 3, 10*s*. 7*d*. each for 2, 10*s*. 6*d*. for 1, and 10*s*. each for 2. In stipend of 3 drovers for the year 9*s*. In forage bought for oxen 8*s*. Total, £5 18*s*. 11½*d*.

Purchase of seed and liveries

In 20½ qrs of barley bought for the liveries of the manorial servants £2 16*s*. 4*d*., at 3*s*. 4*d*. a qr for 7 qrs, 2*s*. 8*d*. a qr for 4½ qrs, and 2*s*. 4*d*. a qr for 9 qrs. Total, £2 16*s*. 4*d*.

Carts

In 1 pair of wheels bought 2*s*. ½*d*. In clouts with nails bought 8*d*. In grease bought 3½*d*. In 2 new collars 8¼*d*. In 1 pair of saddle-pads bought 4½*d*. In 1 pair of traces bought 3*d*. In girths and cruppers bought 1½*d*. In white leather bought for mending harnesses 2*d*. In a cart made anew and another mended for dung 6*d*. In fitting the said carts with axles 2*d*. In shoeing 2 cart-horses for the year 2*s*. 6*d*. In stipend of 1 carter for the year 3*s*. Total, 10*s*. 9¼*d*.

Cost of buildings

In roofing the great barn and hay-barn in places 2*s*. 4*d*. In mending the granary with tiles and lime bought for the same 1*s*. 8½*d*. In 1 barrow bought 4½*d*. In making 1 gate for the enclosure between the king's highway and the lord's field 4½*d*. In sawing boards 10½*d*. Total, 5*s*. 8*d*.

Threshing and winnowing

{henceforth 1¾*d*. should always be owed for threshing and winnowing 10 struck bus. of barley and the same for vetches and ¾*d*. for threshing 10 bus. of oats, 1*d*. for winnowing 8 qrs}

In threshing and winnowing 118 qrs 2 bus. of wheat by piece-work £1 1*s*. 8¼*d*., at 2*d*. a qr threshed and 1*d*. per 5 qrs winnowed. In threshing and winnowing 7½ qrs 2 bus. of winter barley and 4 qrs 2 bus. of barley by piece-work 1*s*. 9¾*d*., at 1¾*d*. a qr. In threshing and winnowing 61½ qrs 1 bus. of oats by piece-work 3*s*. 2½*d*., at ¾*d*. a qr threshed and 1*d*. per 8 qrs winnowed. In threshing and winnowing 2 qrs 2 bus. of vetches by piece-work 3¾*d*., at 1¾*d*. a qr. Total, £1 7*s*. ¼*d*.

Weeding and customary payments

In cheese bought for the weeders 5*d*. In mowing 14 acres and 1 perch of meadow 3*s*. 6¾*d*. In spreading the same 3*d*. In mowing and tossing the meadow of Auedem*ere* by piece-work 6*d*. Total, 4*s*. 8¼*d*.

Harvest-time

In 350 herrings bought for 138 men with 9 officials of the curia 2*s*. 4*d*., at 8*d*. a 100, because they ought not to have other relish, and 2 men are owed 5 herrings a day according to custom. In meat bought for 2 boon-works 6*s*. In ale bought for 4 boon-works 9*s*. 10*d*. In cheese bought for 37 carters carrying the lord's corn 1*s*. 3*d*. In salt bought 3*d*. In reaping corn and oats which remained beyond the boon-works £1 11*s*. 10*d*. In stipend of 1 overseer of the harvest for the year 5*s*. In expenses of 1 reap-reeve, who oversaw the reapers and who kept the corn at night until the end of the harvest, 3*s*. In stipend of the same 3*s*. Total, £3 2*s*. 6*d*.

Expenses for cider
In expenses of 1 man who helped make 4 casks of cider and who oversaw the collection of apples 1*s*. 4*d*. In repairing and re-hooping 2 casks with hoops and boards bought for the same, with the stipend of the cooper, 2*s*. 4*d*. In grease bought for the cider-press 2*d*. Given by order of the lord 2*s*. Total, 5*s*. 10*d*.

Total of all expenses, £14 11*s*. 9¼*d*.

And he owes, £40 7*s*. 6½*d*.

Cash deliveries[1]
Delivered to Sir G*eoffrey*, treasurer of Wolvesey, by 1 tally, £23 10*s*.

And thus he owes clear, £16 17*s*. 6½*d*.

Issues of the grange

Wheat
{yield: 4½-fold plus 3½ qrs}
The same render account for 118 qrs 2 bus. from the whole issue of wheat and curall from the grange with the increment of the granary.
Sown over 75 acres measured by the perch which lie in the fields of Quidacr' and la Estdon', 23½ qrs 1 bus.; that is, 2½ bus. an acre, plus 7 bus. in all. Delivered to 1 sergeant for the year, 4 qrs 2 bus., because he takes the rest in barley. In bread made for the weeders and carriers of hay, 1 qr. In provision of 4 harvest boon-works, 3 qrs. Sold, 87 qrs 3 bus., of which 3 qrs 3 bus. are curall.

Winter barley
{yield: 4-fold plus 2 bus.}
The same render account for 7½ qrs 2 bus. from the whole issue of winter barley from the grange with the increment of the granary.
Sown over 4 acres measured by the perch which lie in the field of . . . , 1 qr 2 bus. Mixed below with barley for the liveries of the manorial servants, 6½ qrs.

Barley
{yield: three-fold plus 2 bus.}
The same render account for 4½ qrs 2 bus. from the whole issue of barley from the grange with the increment of the granary; 6½ qrs received above from winter barley; 1½ qrs [received] below from vetches; 20½ qrs bought as noted above. Total, 33 qrs 2 bus.
Sown over 6 acres measured by the perch which lie in the field of Westssend', 3 qrs; that is, 4 bus. an acre. Delivered to 1 sergeant for the year, 3 qrs 2 bus., because he takes the rest in wheat. Delivered to 1 carter and 3 drovers for the year, 26 qrs. Sold at the audit, 1 qr.

Oats
{yield: 26 qrs more than sown}
The same render account for 61½ qrs 1 bus. from the whole issue of oats from the grange with the increment of the granary; 13 qrs by estimation in sheaves given to oxen. Total, 74½ qrs 1 bus.

1 MS omits heading.

Sown over 78 acres measured by the perch which lie in the field of Westfeld', 40½ qrs 2 bus.; that is, 4 bus. an acre, plus 1½ qrs 2 bus. in all. In fodder of 2 cart-horses for the year, 7½ qrs. In fodder of 1 plough-horse harrowing at the Lenten sowing, 1 qr 3 bus. this year, because the harrowing for 'dustlond' was sold, as mentioned inside (*interi*or). In supporting oxen by estimation in sheaves, 13 qrs. Sold, 12 qrs.

Vetches
{yield: two-fold}
The same render account for 2 qrs 2 bus. of vetches from the whole issue of the grange with the increment of the granary.
Sown, 6 bus. Mixed above with barley, 1½ qrs.

Stock

Cart-horses: 2 remain from the previous year; 2 remain.
Oxen: 34 remain from the previous year; 8 bought. Total, 42. 3 sold at Martinmas; 1 enfeebled; 1 in murrain. Total, 5. 37 remain.
Cows: 1 from the heriot of John ate Pull' after calving; sold; none remain.
Bullocks: 1 remains from the previous year; 1 sold; none remain.
Piglets:[1] 1 from the heriot of Alice, who was wife of Robert ate Hole; 1 sold; none remain.
Hens: 10 from churchscot; all sold; none remain.
Cider: 2½ casks remain from the previous year; 4 casks and 2 tuns from the issue of the garden this year; 2½ casks sold; 4 casks and 2 tuns remain.
Utensils: 1 wooden cart remains from the previous year; 1 bought; 1 used in the manor; 1 remains. 7 casks, 4 tubs, 2 tuns, 1 axe, 2 pruning-knives, 1 shovel, 2 iron forks, 1 hoe. 2 iron forks used in the manor; all other utensils remain. 6 boards, 8 feet long and 2 feet wide, sawn this year from a poplar.

Fareham

Arrears
Robert de Froyle, bailiff, and Thomas Bovel, reeve, render account for £36 6¼*d*. of arrears from the previous year. All delivered to the lord treasurer of Wolvesey by 1 tally.

Rents of assize
The same render account for £6 2*s*. 8¼*d*. for all rents of assize at Christmas; £6 8*s*. 10¼*d*. at Easter (22 April); £6 2*s*. 8¼*d*. at the Nativity of St John the Baptist (24 June); £10 19*s*. 7¼*d*. at Michaelmas (29 September). Total, £29 13*s*. 10*d*.

Increment of rent
The same render account for 5*s*. 7½*d*. for the increment of rent of Simon le Cup*ere* for 11 acres and 1 rood of land in 3 crofts at Alnetu*m*; 5*s*. 7½*d*. for the increment of rent of Peter le Url for 11 acres and 1 rood of land there. Total, 11*s*. 3*d*.

Total of all rents with increment, £30 5*s*. 1*d*.

m.21d
Quittances
In quittance of 1 reeve for the year 5*s*.; 1 bartoner for ½ year 1*s*.; 1 shepherd of wethers this year, nothing, because he receives an allowance, for which allowance

1 MS omits heading.

the men of the hundred, who are accustomed to keep the wethers, give 3 qrs of barley for the keeping of the wethers and this because they were kept badly; 1 shepherd of ewes, nothing this year, because there are no ewes there; 6 cottars doing 138 labour services threshing corn, as made clear in the details outside the roll (*ext*eri*o*r), 4*s*. 11*d*., at 1*s*. per 28 labour services, because the rest of the corn was threshed by piece-work; 1 smith for the year 3*s*. 6*d*.; 1 swineherd, nothing this year, because he receives an allowance; 1 cowherd for the year 2*s*. Total, 16*s*. 5*d*.

Defaults of rent

In default of the land of the falconer drawn into demesne, 3*s*. for the year; the land of Anketyl drawn into demesne, 2*s*. 6*d*. for the year; the land of Ingolf drawn into demesne, 1*s*. for the year; the land of Hawise drawn into demesne, 1*s*. for the year; the land of Meteol drawn into demesne which Thomas de la Corn*er*e held by gift of Bishop John Gervais, 10*s*. 1*d*. for the year; the land of Wynter drawn into the park, 3*s*. for the year; a certain plot in the marsh of Wallington which John Fort held inundated by the sea 6*d*.; a certain plot which Geoffrey Spyring' held inundated by the sea 6*d*.; a certain plot there which the relict of Germayn held inundated by the sea 1*s*. Total, £1 2*s*. 7*d*.

Total of quittances and defaults of rent, £1 19*s*.

Total of rents remaining, £28 6*s*. 1*d*.

Cumin

The same render account for nothing from cumin because the heir of Simon Stak' is in the custody of the lord.

Issues of the manor

The same render account for £1 10*s*. 6*d*. from pannage of pigs this year; 2*s*. from the hundred of Fareham for the mowing of the meadow of Wolvesey; nothing from foreign pannage this year; 2*s*. from 4 qrs of apples sold this year, at 8*d*. a qr; 18*s*. 10*d*. from 3 old plough-horses sold, at 5*s*. 6*d*. for 1, and 6*s*. 8*d*. each for 2; 6*s*. from 1 ox from the heriot of the relict of Ude; £1 8*s*. from 3 oxen sold, at 9*s*. for 1, and 9*s*. 6*d*. each for 2; 4*s*. from 4 calves sold, at 1*s*. each; 16*s*. 10*d*. from 23 wethers sold at Martinmas (11 November), at 1*s*. 2*d*. each; £3 11*s*. 4*d*. from 27 pigs sold, at 2*s*. 6*d*. each for 16, 2*s*. 8*d*. each for 5, and 3*s*. each for 6; nothing from coarse wool here because it was sent to Wolvesey; 6*d*. from 4 lb of wool locks sold; 2*s*. 2*d*. from 6½ cloves of rowen cheese sold; £1 9*s*. 9*d*. from 3½ weys of summer cheese sold, at 8*s*. 6*d*. a wey; 2*s*. 8*d*. from 8 cloves of butter, at 4*d*. a clove; 3*s*. 1*d*. from the hide sold of 1 ox in murrain; 6*d*. from the hide sold of 1 yearling in murrain; 2*s*. from the skins sold of 8 wethers in murrain before shearing, at 3*d*. a skin; 5*d*. from the skins sold of 4 wethers after shearing; 2*s*. from clay (*argill'*) sold; 2*s*. from heath sold according to custom; 12*s*. from Hawise, who was wife of Geoffrey Hamelyn, for release from the labour service of the land of Bro*m*man; nothing from wood sold this year; nothing from the pasturage on the downs (*dona'*) at Alnetu*m* and Purifeld'; nothing this year from bark and stubble; £1 from seldage this year; 6*s*. 8*d*. from stallage this year; £1 3*s*. 7*d*. from agisting livestock on the pasturage in the park this year; 1*s*. from 1 ewe from the heriot of Henry ate Bere sold; 6*d*. from the heriot of William le Jol because he did not have 1 beast; 6*d*. from Alice Bysngchebrigg' for the same; 6*d*. from Richard Mol*endinarius* for the same; 3*s*. from 1 pig from the heriot of Luke

G*er*mayn; 1*s.* 9*d.* from Isabel, daughter of Richard Moyse*n*t, for release from the labour service of the land of Stygan this year; 2*s.* from the aforesaid Isabel for release from the labour service of the land of Sweyn this year; £8 17*s.* 2*d.* from 24 animals bought the previous year and agisted in the park sold; 4*s.* 5*d.* from dairy produce sold at the audit. Total, £23 17*s.* 8*d.*

Annual recognizance

The same render account for 6*d.* from Walter le Tayllor for annual recognizance; 6*d.* from William Arnold' for the same; 6*d.* from Peter, son of Hugh Mol*endinarius*, for the same; 3*d.* from Robert Gilb*er*d for the same; 6*d.* from David ate Stygle for annual recognizance whilst he wishes to remain on the land of Drecon; 3*d.* from Thomas le P*ar*men*t*yr for annual recognizance; nothing from Simon Sutor' because he withdrew; 3*d.* from William Turnays for annual recognizance. Total, 2*s.* 9*d.*

Sale of corn

The same render account for £14 13*s.* 5¼*d.* from 53 qrs 1 bus. and a third of 1 bus. of wheat[1] sold, at 4*s.* 6*d.* a qr for 7 qrs and a third of 1 bus., 5*s.* a qr for 15 qrs, and 6*s.* a qr for 31 qrs 1 bus.; £1 7*s.* 10*d.* from 6 qrs 2 bus. and a third of 1 bus. {of rye} sold, at 4*s.* a qr for 4 qrs 2 bus. and a third of 1 bus., and 5*s.* 4*d.* a qr for 2 qrs; £2 19*s.* 9*d.* from 14 qrs 7½ bus. of barley sold, at 4*s.* a qr; 6*s.* 6¾*d.* from 2 qrs ⌈2⌉½ bus. of oats sold, at 2*s.* 4*d.* a qr; 7*s.* 1*d.* from 2 qrs 1 bus. of beans sold, at 3*s.* 4*d.* a qr; £1 5½*d.* from 9½ qrs ½ bus. of peas sold, at 2*s.* a qr for 7½ qrs ½ bus., and 2*s.* 8*d.* a qr for 2 qrs; 18*s.* 3¼*d.* from 11 qrs 6½ bus. of vetches sold, at 1*s.* 8*d.* a qr for 3½ qrs ½ bus., 2*s.* a qr for 2 qrs, and 1*s.* 4*d.* a qr for 6 qrs 2 bus.; 2*s.* from 5 bus. 2 pecks of curall sold at the audit, at 4½*d.* a bus.; 5*s.* 8*d.* from 2 qrs 1 bus. of bere sold at the audit. Total, £22 1*s.* ¾*d.*

Sea-mill

The same render account for 11*s.* 7½*d.* from 2 qrs 1 bus. of wheat from the issue of the mill sold, at 5*s.* a qr for 1 qr 1 bus., and 6*s.* for 1 qr; £2 7*s.* 2*d.* from 13 qrs 1 bus. of maslin from the issue of the same mill sold, at 3*s.* a qr for 2 qrs, 3*s.* 4*d.* a qr for 5 qrs, and 4*s.* a qr for 6 qrs 1 bus.; £1 17*s.* 8*d.* from 7 qrs of course-ground corn sold, at 5*s.* a qr for 3 qrs, 5*s.* 4*d.* a qr for 2 qrs, and 6*s.* a qr for 2 qrs; £1 9*s.* 4*d.* from 12 qrs 2 bus. of malt from the issue of the same mill, at 2*s.* a qr for 3 qrs, 2*s.* 4*d.* a qr for 4 qrs, and 2*s.* 8*d.* a qr for 5 qrs 2 bus. Total, £6 5*s.* 9½*d.*

Mill of Hok'

The same render account for 5*s.* 7½*d.* from 1 qr 1 bus. of wheat from the same mill sold, at 5*s.* a qr; 10*s.* ½*d.* from 3 qrs 1 bus. of maslin from the same mill sold, at 3*s.* a qr for 1 qr 1 bus., and 3*s.* 4*d.* a qr for 2 qrs; 7*s.* 9*d.* from 1 qr 3 bus. of coarse-ground corn from the same mill sold, at 7½*d.* a bus. for 4 bus., and 9*d.* a bus. for 7 bus.; 6*s.* from 2 qrs 3 bus. of malt from the same mill sold, at 2*s.* 4*d.* for 1 qr, and 2*s.* 8*d.* a qr for 1 qr 3 bus. Total, £1 9*s.* 5*d.*

Wallington

The same render account for 5*s.* from 7 bus. of wheat from the issue of the same mill sold, at 8*d.* a bus. for 3 bus., and 9*d.* a bus. for 4 bus.; 16*s.* 6*d.* from 4½ qrs 3 bus. of maslin from the same mill sold, at 3*s.* a qr for 3 qrs, and 4*s.* a qr for 1½ qrs 3 bus.; 16*s.* 3*d.* from 2½ qrs 3 bus. of coarse-ground corn from the same mill sold, at 5*s.* for 1 qr,

1 MS omits 'of wheat'.

and 6*s*. a qr for 1½ qrs 3 bus.; 11*s*. from 4 qrs 5 bus. of malt from the issue of the same mill sold, at 2*s*. for 1 qr, 2*s*. 4*d*. a qr for 2 qrs, and 2*s*. 8*d*. a qr for 1 qr 5 bus. Total, £2 8*s*. 9*d*.

Total of all corn sold from all the mills, £10 3*s*. 11½*d*.

Entry and marriage fines
The same render account for £1 from the 5 inner tithings at the hundred-court of Martinmas for tithingpenny; £1 from the same tithings at the hundred-court of Hockday for the same; 4*s*. from the tithing of Oysel at the two hundred-courts for the same; 4*s*. from the tithing of Roche at the two hundred-courts for the same; 4*s*.[1] from the tithing of Brownwich at the two hundred-courts for the same; 1*s*. from the tithing of Bedenham at the two hundred-courts for the same; 2*s*. 6*d*. from William le Kayte for relief for 8 acres of land which belonged to John his brother whose heir he is; 1*s*. from John le Cup*ere* to have 2 acres of land by surrender of William le Cayt, and relieving the said William of 9*d*. annual rent; 2*s*. from Richard ate Bere to have 4 acres of land of Forepelond' which belonged to Henry his brother whose heir he is; 4*s*. from Alice, relict of William Jacob, to retain 1 house and 1 acre of land which belonged to her husband; 13*s*. 4*d*. from Alice ate Alre to have 1 messuage and 1 ferling of land by surrender of William le Il; 2*s*. from Walter Blakebroc for ½ virgate which belonged to Thomas le Gur, father of Juliana his wife, whose heir she is; 3*s*. from Walter de Suthebrigg' to have 1 house and 4 acres of land which belonged to Alice his mother; 13*s*. 4*d*. from William Hereberd to have 1 messuage and ½ virgate of land which belonged to Herbert Ude his father whose heir he is; 1*s*. from Peter But*er*weg for marrying Christina his daughter within; 1*s*. from John Isat for marrying Joan his sister within; 1*s*. from Roger Russel for marrying Alice his daughter outside; 1*s*. from William Vinter for marrying Margery his daughter within; £1 from Stephen Spule for 1 messuage and 1 ferling of land which belonged by right to Alice his mother which he recovered from Henry ate Styele; £2 from Agnes, relict of Matthew le Bunekede, to retain 1 messuage and ½ virgate of land which belonged to her husband for her widowhood; 3*s*. from Isabel, daughter of Richard Moysent, to have ½ virgate which is called Sweneslond and 1 ferling of land which is called Stygandeslond' and 4 acres of land which is called Forteslond' which belonged to her aforesaid father, concerning which Isabel afterwards came and in full court leased, granted and demised to Geoffrey Spyring all the aforesaid lands, to hold for the term of his life, doing therefor all services pertaining to the said lands; 6*s*. 8*d*. from John Mol*endinarius* for 1 messuage and 4 acres of land from ½ ferling of land which his father held because this same John fined for the other part whilst his father was living; 13*s*. 4*d*. from John le Pouke to have 1 ferling of land which was taken away from Richard le Crok' because he held two holdings; £1 from Christina, relict of Richard le Meyr', to retain 1 virgate of land which belonged to her husband; 1*s*. from John Frogomor' to have 1 house situated on the king's highway which belonged to William Ace; 6*d*. from Henry Piscat' for relief to have ½ burgage by the legacy of Matthew le Bunekede; 8*d*. from Petronilla Hamelyn for relief to have ½ burgage and a quarter of one burgage by the legacy of the said Matthew; 1*s*. from Agnes, relict of Matthew le Bunek*ede*, for relief to have 1 burgage by the legacy of the said Matthew le Bunek*ede*; 6*d*. from Lancelm*a*, relict of William Ace, and Joan, daughter of William Ace, for relief to have ½ burgage by the legacy of the said William; 4*d*. from Margery, daughter of William Coc*us*, for relief to have a third of 1 burgage by surrender of Euphemia, daughter of John le Fisschar'. Total, £10 5*s*. 2*d*.

1 MS omits '*s*.'

Perquisites

The same render account for 2*s*. from Richard le Crok' because he absented himself from court; £3 6*s*. 8*d*. from the executors of Matthew le Bunekede for waste and destruction which the same Matthew made in formerly holding Wytheyr; £2 13*s*. 1*d*. from various men for various transgressions; 6*s*. 8*d*. from Thomas the reeve for keeping the forage badly; 2*s*. from William Robbustr' for the assize of bread; £2 6*d*. from various men for various transgressions. Total, £8 10*s*. 11*d*.

Total of both, £18 16*s*. 1*d*.

Total of all receipts, £103 7*s*. 7¼*d*.

Cost of ploughs

In iron and steel bought for 2 ploughs for the year and 1 plough for ½ year 6*s*. In 2 ploughshares bought 1*s*. 6*d*. In 3 plough feet bought 1*s*. 6*d*. In 2 pairs of wheels bought 8*d*. In 3 ploughs made anew and others mended frequently 1*s*. In fitting the same with iron tyres 4*d*. In 6 yokes bought 3*d*. In 1 harrow bought 4*d*. In 2 plough-horses bought £1. In shoeing 4 plough-horses hauling before the oxen 3*s*. In shoeing 27 oxen 2*s*. 3*d*. In 5 halters made from their own hair 1¼*d*. In boon-works of 13 ploughmen for the winter sowing 3*s*. 3*d*., each ploughman ploughing 1 acre, and know that there are 28 virgaters of land who work there who will plough 56 acres for 'landrich' whether they have a plough or not, unless they are in the office of reeve or another office of the curia, at 2 acres a virgater. Moreover, each having a plough will plough 2 acres at their own cost and another two acres for the lord's food, apart from the ploughmen of Cartefeld' who do not plough except for 2 acres each for the lord's food. In cleaning the corn for sowing 2*s*. 6*d*. In stipend of 4 ploughmen for the year 12*s*., or 3*s*. each. In stipend of 2 ploughmen for ½ year 3*s*. In forage bought for supporting oxen and livestock (*av'*) £1 11*s*. 8*d*. Total, £4 9*s*. 4¼*d*.

[Carts]

In 1 pair of wheels 2*s*. 9*d*. In fitting old tyres to the said wheels with large and small nails and clamps bought for the same and with the stipend of the smith 4*s*. In mending another cart 11*d*. In fitting the carts with axles at various times with axles bought for the same 6*d*. In 1 pair of traces bought 5*d*. In 1 cart-body made anew 6*d*. In white leather bought 5*d*. In 1 collar and 1 pair of saddle-pads bought 1*s*. 2*d*. In clouts, nails and grease bought 1*s*. 4*d*. In 1 halter bought 1½*d*. In shoeing 2 cart-horses for the year 2*s*. 6½*d*. In stipend of 1 carter for the year 3*s*. In stubble mixed with mown grass for the horses 1*s*. 4*d*. Total, 19*s*.

[Harvest-time]

In 1½ weys of cheese bought for 3½ harvest boon-works of 680 men who reaped 416 acres as they lay, 12*s*. 9*d*., and this on account of the dearness of herrings. In 2 acres of barley from the new garden reaped and bound by piece-work 1*s*. 2*d*. Total, 13*s*. 11*d*.

[Cost of the sea-mill]

In mending the spindle of the same mill with iron and steel bought 10*d*. In sharpening the bills of the same mill with steel for the same 6*d*. In spike-nails bought for fastening planks underneath the water-wheel 6¾*d*. In small nails bought for mending the outer wheels 1½*d*. In 1 rope bought for raising the sluice 2*d*. In 1 lock bought for the chest of the same mill 1½*d*. Total, 2*s*. 3¾*d*.

[Cost of the mill of Hok']

In sharpening the bills of the same mill with iron and steel bought for the same 5*d*. In 1 basket for carrying corn 1½*d*. In mending the sluice of the same mill 1*s*. Total, 1*s*. 6½*d*.

[Cost of the mill of Wallington]

In 1 outer wheel made anew with timber boards sawn for the same and nails bought for the same 5*s*. 3*d*. In 3 bands of iron for hooping the inner wheel 10*d*. In sharpening the bills with iron and steel bought for the same 5*d*. In mending the sluice of the same mill with nails bought for the same 1*s*. 1*d*. In mending the walls of the same mill with boards sawn for the same 2*s*. Total, 9*s*. 7*d*.

[Threshing and winnowing]

In threshing and winnowing 52½ qrs of wheat, 3 qrs 3 bus. of curall, 2½ qrs 3 bus. of rye, 16 qrs 3 bus. of bere, 2 qrs 2 bus. of beans, and 5½ qrs 2 bus. of vetches by piece-work, 19*s*. 2½*d*., at 2¾*d*. a heaped quarter. In threshing and winnowing 2½ qrs of barley by piece-work 4¼*d*., at 1¾*d*. a heaped quarter. In threshing and winnowing 34 qrs of oats by heaped measure 2*s*. 5¾*d*., at ¾*d*. a heaped quarter threshed, ¼*d*. per 2 qrs winnowed. In mending 1 basket 1*d*. Total, £1 1*s*. 9¼*d*.

Cost of buildings

In repairing the great barn of the village (*casa*) and re-roofing it anew throughout by the hundred on behalf of the lord 6*s*. In 50 large nails bought to fasten the rafters 6*d*. In covering the same barn throughout with laths 2*s*. 6*d*. In making laths for the same 1*s*. 6*d*. In 10,000 nails bought for laths 6*s*. 8*d*. In re-roofing the other barn in places by the hundred on behalf of the lord 6*d*. In repairing the great gate and the other gates in the curia 9*d*. In nails bought for the same 4*d*. In re-roofing the hall, lord's chamber, chapel, kitchen and great stable in places 4*s*. In 3,000 slates bought for the same 4*s*. In 1 qr of lime bought for the same 6*d*. In pegs bought for the same 3*d*. In 1 lock bought for the great barn and other locks of the barn mended 7½*d*. In mangers for the stable with nails for the same 2*d*. In 3 shovels made with iron bought 5*d*. In castrating piglets 2½*d*. In 1 lock bought for the park-gate 3*d*. In 1 lock bought for the wood of Westhok' 3*d*. In offertory-boxes made anew 8*d*. In 1 tripod made anew 1*s*. 6*d*. In mowing, spreading and tossing the meadow which belonged to Bartholomew Etemet' 3*d*. In the meadow of Wolvesey as far as (*pro*) the land of Rechergate 3¾*d*. In the meadow of Chaelpuk, nothing this year, because it was sown. In mowing the meadow as far as the land of Bru*n*ma*n* and Stiga*nt* 5*d*. In mending the palisade of the park by the sewer (*cloca*) 1*s*. In enclosing 96 perches in the park with hedges 5*s*., at 1¼*d*. per 2 perches. Total, £1 18*s*. 6¾*d*.

Cost of the dairy

In 4½ bus. of salt bought 11¼*d*. In a press bought 4*d*. In woollen and linen cloth 3*d*. In earthenware pots and pans bought 2½*d*. In 1 bucket bought for the dairy and others mended 4½*d*. In soap bought for greasing the cows for worms 6¼*d*. In grease bought for greasing sheep 4*s*. 1*d*. In 1 mould bought and in hooping the same with iron 2½*d*. In 22 hurdles made from their own withies 11*d*. In re-roofing in places the shepherd's house with stubble collected for the same 10*d*. In stipend of 1 shepherd for the year 3*s*. In stipend of 1 dairymaid for the year 2*s*. In 1 cow bought 8*s*. ¼*d*. In stipend of 1 attendant keeping the pigs for the year 2*s*. In 7 ells of canvas bought for putting the wool in 2*s*. ½*d*., at 3½*d*. an ell. Total, £1 5*s*. 8¾*d*.

Expenses of the steward
In expenses of the steward for two tourns by 2 tallies 13*s.* 6*d.* In expenses of the bailiff for his visits £1 8*s.* Total, £2 1*s.* 6*d.*

Purchase of stock
In 24 animals bought the previous year at various prices and agisted in the park £8. Total, £8.

In expenses of the reeve and beadle at harvest-time 3*s.*, because the bailiff did not stay there. In expenses of the assessors of the fifteenth 3*s.* Total, 6*s.*

Total of all expenses, £21 9*s.* 3¼*d.*

And he owes, £81 18*s.* 4*d.*

Cash deliveries
Delivered to Sir G*eoffrey*, treasurer of Wolvesey, by 1 tally, £49 14*s.*

And thus he owes clear, £32 4*s.* 4*d.*

m.22

Issues of the grange

Wheat
{yield: three-fold less 2 qrs 3 bus.}
The same render account for 7 qrs of wheat remaining in the granary from the previous year; 92 qrs from the whole issue of wheat this year by struck measure; 1 qr 3 bus. by estimation in 132 sheaves delivered to the men of the manor according to custom, for carrying-service which is called 'weyncheves'. Total, 100 qrs 3 bus.
Sown over 204 acres as they lie on la Nortchdon', Brocforlong', Schippelond', Westebury, the land of Bartholomew and Etemete, and at Alnetu*m*, 31½ qrs 3 bus.; that is, 1 bus. and 1 peck an acre. In provision of the steward for 2 visits by 2 tallies, 7 bus. Delivered to the threshers for 28 labour services, 28 pecks, which made 4½ bus. 1 peck, and know that 6 pecks make a struck bushel, and they have 1 peck for threshing 6 heaped bushels. In provision of the bailiff for his visits, 5½ qrs. In customary payment to the men of the manor at harvest-time by estimation in sheaves, 1 qr 3 bus. Mixed below with barley for the liveries of the manorial servants, 7 qrs remaining from the previous year because it is poor. Sold, 53 qrs 1 bus. and a third of 1 bus.

Curall
The same render account for 8 qrs of curall remaining in the granary from the previous year; 4½ qrs 3 bus. from the whole issue this year. Total, 12½ qrs 2 bus.
Mixed below with barley for the liveries of the manorial servants, 12 qrs 1 bus. Delivered to the threshers for 4 labour services, 4 pecks, which made ½ bus. 1 peck. Sold, ½ qr 1 bus. and 2 pecks, which made a third of a bushel.

Rye
{yield: two-fold plus 1 qr 1 bus.}
The same render account for 7 qrs 3 bus. from the whole issue of rye by struck measure; 2 qrs from churchscot. Total, 9 qrs 3 bus.

Sown over 16 acres as they lie in Westebury, 3 qrs; that is, 1½ bus. an acre. Delivered to the threshers for 4 labour services, 4 pecks, which made ½ bus. 1 peck. Sold, 6 qrs 2 bus. and a third of 1 bus.

Bere
{yield: two-fold plus 1 qr 3 bus.}
The same render account for 22½ qrs from the whole issue of bere by struck measure.
Sown over 69 acres as they lie on la Norsdoun', Ymppyehegg' and in la Blakelond', 12½ qrs 3 bus.; that is, 1½ bus. an acre, less ½ bus. in all. Mixed below with barley for the liveries of the manorial servants, 7½ qrs. It balances. Sold at the audit, 2 qrs 1 bus.

Barley
{yield: two-and-a-half-fold less 3 qrs ½ bus.}
The same render account for 5 qrs remaining from the previous year; 51½ qrs 1 bus. from the whole issue of barley this year; 7 qrs received above from wheat; 12 qrs 1 bus. received above from curall; 7½ qrs received above from bere, and mixed for the liveries of the manorial servants; 6 bus. received below from beans and mixed for the same; 1½ qrs received below from peas; 3½ qrs 3 bus. received below from vetches; 3 qrs received from the hundred for the livery of 1 keeper of wethers. Total, 92 qrs 3 bus.
Sown over 60 acres as they lie at Ymppyhegg', beside Marler' and in Horgarston', 18½ qrs 1 bus.; that is, 2½ bus. an acre, less 1 bus. in all. Delivered to 1 carter for the year, 6½ qrs, taking a quarter every 8 weeks. Delivered to 4 ploughmen for the year, 26 qrs, taking a quarter every 8 weeks. Delivered to 2 ploughmen from Michaelmas until Easter, for 29 weeks, 7 qrs 2 bus., who take the same as before. Delivered to 1 shepherd of wethers for the year, 4 qrs 2 bus., taking a quarter every 12 weeks. Delivered to 1 dairymaid for the year, 3 qrs 2 bus., taking a quarter every 16 weeks. In bread made for 3½ harvest boon-works, 8½ qrs. In provision of 1 keeper of pigs for the year, 2 qrs. Delivered to the threshers for 51 labour services, 51 pecks, which made 1 qr ½ bus. Sold, 14 qrs 7½ bus.

Dredge
{yield: 1 qr 6 bus. less than sown}
The same render account for 3½ qrs 3 bus. from the whole issue of dredge by struck measure.
Sown over 6 acres as they lie in Horgarsto*n*, 1 qr; that is, 3 bus. an acre. Mixed with oats, 2 qrs 2 bus. and a third of 1 bus. Delivered to the threshers for 4 labour services, 4 pecks, which made ½ bus. 1 peck. It balances.

Beans
{yield: three-fold plus 2 bus.}
The same render account for 2½ qrs 3 bus. from the whole issue of beans. Mixed above with barley, 6 bus. Sold, 2 qrs 1 bus.

Peas
{yield: 4 qrs 7 bus. more than sown}
The same render account for 1 qr of peas remaining in the granary from the previous year; 14½ qrs 3 bus. from the whole issue of peas this year. Total, 15½ qrs 3 bus.

Sown over 18 acres as they lie in la Suthdon' and Ymppyhegg', 4½ qrs; that is, 2 bus. an acre. Delivered to the threshers for 15 labour services, 15 pecks, which made 2½ bus. Mixed above with barley, 1½ qrs. Sold, 9½ qrs ½ bus.

Oats
{yield: 17 qrs 6 bus. more than sown}
The same render account for 64½ qrs 2 bus. from the whole issue of oats by struck measure; 17 qrs by estimation in sheaves given to oxen; 1 qr 3 bus. in 132 sheaves delivered to the men of the manor according to custom for carrying-service at harvest-time; 2 qrs 3 bus. received from dredge. Total, 85½ qrs.
Sown over 161 acres as they lie at Swelden', Wyldegateschorn' and in Horgarston', 45 qrs 2 bus.; that is, 2 bus. 1 peck an acre, less 1 peck in all. In fodder of cart-horses for the year, 13 qrs. Given to oxen by estimation in sheaves, 17 qrs. In fodder of the steward's horses for his visits by 2 tallies, 1½ qrs 3 bus. In provision of the bailiff and clerk for their visits, 4 qrs. In customary payment to the men of the manor for carrying-service at harvest-time by estimation, 1 qr 3 bus. Delivered to the threshers for 11 labour services, 11 pecks, which made 2 bus., less 1 peck. Sold, 2½ qrs 2½ bus.

Vetches
{yield: two-fold}
The same render account for 3 qrs of vetches remaining from the previous year; 27 qrs[1] of vetches from the whole issue this year. Total, 30 qrs.
Sown over 40 acres as they lie in Purifeld', at Ymppygg' and in Horgarston', 6 qrs 2 bus.; that is, 1 bus. 1 peck an acre. Delivered to the threshers for 21 labour services, 21 pecks, which made 3½ bus. In fattening 25 pigs, 6 qrs 2 bus. In supporting pigs and piglets in winter, 1 qr 3 bus. Mixed above with barley for the liveries of the manorial servants, 3½ qrs 3 bus. Sold, 11 qrs 6½ bus.

Issues of the mills
Sea-mill
Wheat: 2 qrs 1 bus. from the whole issue of the mill; all sold.
Maslin: 13 qrs 1 bus. from the same mill; all sold.
Coarse-ground corn: 7 qrs from the whole issue of the same mill; sold.
Malt:[2] 12 qrs from the whole issue of the same mill; sold.

Hok'
Wheat: 1 qr 1 bus. from the whole issue of the mill; all sold.
Maslin: 3 qrs 1 bus. from the whole issue of the same mill.
Coarse-ground corn: 1 qr 3 bus. from the whole issue of the same mill; sold.
Malt: 2 qrs 3 bus. from the issue of the same mill; sold.

Wallington
Wheat: 7 bus. from the whole issue of the mill; sold.
Maslin: 4 qrs 7 bus. from the issue of the same mill; sold.
Coarse-ground corn: 2½ qrs 3 bus. from the issue of the same mill; sold.
Malt: 4 qrs 5 bus. from the issue of the same mill; sold.

Stock

Cart-horses: 2 remain from the previous year; 2 remain.

1 MS omits 'qrs'.

2 MS omits heading.

Plough-horses: 5 remain from the previous year; 2 bought. Total, 7. 3 sold; 4 remain.
Oxen: 28 remain from the previous year; 1 from the heriot of Alice, relict of Herbert Ude; 1 from the heriot of Matthew le Bunek*e*d*e*; 1 from the heriot of Richard le Meir'; 1 added from steers. Total, 32. 1 in murrain in March; 4 sold. Total, 5. 27 remain.
Bulls: 1 remains from the previous year; 1 remains.
Cows: 13 remain from the previous year; 2 added from steers; 1 from the heriot of William Jacob before calving; 1 bought after calving. Total, 17. 17 remain.
Steers: 3 remain from the previous year's bullocks; 2 added to cows, 1 to oxen; none remain.
Bullocks: 3 remain from the previous year's yearlings; 3 remain, 2 of them male.
Yearlings: 4 remain from the previous year's calves; 1 in murrain since Christmas; 3 remain, 2 of them male.
Calves: 12 produced by the said cows this year because 4 were sterile; 1 in tithe; 4 late-born sold; 7 remain, of which[1]
Wethers: 205 remain from the previous year; 26 bought, 2 of them before shearing; 9 from strays. Total, 240. 23 sold at Martinmas; 8 in murrain before shearing, 4 after shearing. Total, 35. 205 remain, 2 of them rams.
Pigs: 30 remain from the previous year; 35 additions. Total, 65. 27 sold at Martinmas; 38 remain.
Sows: 4 remain from the previous year; 1 in murrain; 3 remain.
Hoggets: 40 remain from the previous year's piglets; 5 in murrain; 35 added to pigs; none remain.
Piglets: 39 from the offspring of the said sows this year. 4 in murrain; 3 in tithe. Total, 7. 32 remain.
Coarse wool {yield of fleece 3¾*d*. plus 7½*d*. in all}: 185 fleeces produced at the shearing this year; 18 in tithe; 167 sent to Wolvesey, which made, with the wool of Cams, 2 weys 3 cloves.
Wool locks: 4 lb; sold.
Rowen cheese: 30 made in winter; all sold, which made 6½ cloves.
Summer cheese {yield of cow 3*s*. Henceforth they should have 20 cows under pain of £2}: 166 cheeses made between Thursday before the feast of St George (19 April) and Michaelmas (29 September), both days included. 16 in tithe; 150 sold, which made 3½ weys.
Butter: 8 cloves made this year; all sold.
Hides: 1 from an ox, 1 from a yearling, dead from murrain; all sold.
Woolskins and bare skins: 8 woolskins, 4 bare skins from wethers in murrain; all sold.
Utensils: 2 carts with iron tyres and 5 ploughs remain from the previous year; they remain.
Vessels: 1 cask, 4 tubs, 1 small tub, 1 tine, 2 troughs, 1 bucket hooped with iron, 4 trestles, 2 great tables, 1 small brass pan, and 1 great table-top with 2 trestles remain from the previous year; all this remains.

Alverstoke

Arrears

John de Forton', bailiff, renders account for £2 2*s*. 7*d*. of arrears from the previous year. All delivered to G*eoffrey*, treasurer of Wolvesey, by 1 tally, and he is quit.

1 MS omits final phrase.

Rents

The same renders account for £13 for rents of assize at All Saints (1 November); £13 at the Purification (2 February); £13 at the Invention of the Cross (3 May); £14 7½*d*. at Michaelmas (29 September); 10*s*. from the rent of Robert de Chark at the same feast; 8*d*. from John Aze and Alexander Cred' for 1 marsh and 2 water-channels at the same feast. Total, £53 11*s*. 3½*d*.

Farm of the mill

The same renders account for £2 10*s*. for the farm of the mill of Forton'. Total, £2 10*s*.

The same renders account for 1*d*. for the annual recognizance of Adam Guldebrigg'. Total, 1*d*.

Reliefs

The same renders account for 13*s*. 3*d*. from John le Pope for relief for the lands and tenements which belonged to William Pope his father; 1*s*. from Joan le Pope for relief for the lands which belonged to Joan her mother; 13*s*. 6*d*. from Bartholomew Hendel for relief for the lands and tenements which belonged to William He*n*del his father; 8*d*. from William Mol*endinarius* for relief for the lands and tenements which belonged to John Mol*endinarius* his brother; 2*d*. from William Arnold for relief for 1 half-acre (*aulve*) of land by surrender of John le Bege; ⌈2*d*.⌉ from Richard Arnold for relief for 1 half-acre of land by surrender of Thomas Bild'; 1*d*. from Richard Piris for relief for the land which belonged to Peter Randoldf his father; 4*d*. from Agnes and Alice Bild' for relief for the land which belonged to Adam Bild' their father. Total, £1 9*s*. 2*d*.

Perquisites

The same renders account for 6*d*. from Sarah de Forton' for breaking the assize of ale; 6*d*. from William Page for the same; 3*d*. from John Sp*ar*k' for the same; 6*d*. from John Aubr' for the same; 3*d*. from Robert Cl*ericus* for the same; 3*d*. from John Walt' for the same; 6*d*. from the relict of Edward for the same; 6*d*. from John Fontay*n* for the same; 6*d*. from Henry Bissop for the same; 1*s*. from William Lote for the same; 6*d*. from William Unwyn' for the same; 6*d*. from John Bege for the same; 6*d*. from Roger Alward for the same; 1*s*. from Robert Ricard for the same; 6*d*. from Richard de Alnet' for the same; 6*d*. from the relict of Pope for the same; 6*d*. from Matilda Pope for the same; 1*s*. from Walter Lo*n*t' for the same; 3*d*. from Henry Arnold' for the same; 3*d*. from Peter Avice for the same; 3*d*. from Peter Speg for the same; 1*s*. from Thomas Pell' for the same; 3*d*. from Henry Sou*n* for the same; 6*d*. from William Esto*n* for the same; 6*d*. from William Be*n*del for the same; 6*d*. from William Westo*n* for the same; 3*d*. from John Barth*olomew* for the same; 1*s*. from William de Bury for the same; 6*d*. from John Wytlot for the same; 3*d*. from Richard de Bury for the same; 3*d*. from Alexander de Po*n*te for shedding the blood of Richard Sto*n*ma*n*; 3*d*. from John Mansir for the same; 3*d*. from John Halygod for transgression against John Coc; 6*d*. from Richard Age for raising the hue against William Sou*n*; 3*d*. from John Rolf for licence to agree with Richard Barbir; 3*d*. from Robert Ricard for transgression against John de Forto*n*; 3*d*. from Richard Brok for transgression against the same; 3*d*. from John de Po*n*te for transgression against Richard Sto*n*ma*n*; 3*d*. from Alexander de Po*n*te for the same; 3*d*. from John Rolf for licence to agree with Amice Rolf; 3*d*. from Robert de Burga because he is not proceeding against

Robert de Burg'; 1*s*. from John Aubroy for breaking the assize of ale; 3*d*. from Matilda de la Don' for the same; 9*d*. from John Walt' for the same; 1*s*. from Matilda Edward for the same; 3*d*. from John Fontay*n* for the same; 3*d*. from Henry Bissop for the same; 6*d*. from Roger le Suther' for the same; 1*s*. from William Lote for the same; 6*d*. from William Unwyn' for the same; 6*d*. from William de C*am*po for the same; 1*s*. from Robert Ricard' for the same; 1*s*. from Isabel le Pope for the same; 1*s*. from Matilda le Pope for the same; 1*s*. from Walter Lonte for the same; 1*s*. from William Mol*endinarius* for the same; 1*s*. from Henry Sou*n* for the same; 1*s*. from Thomas Pell*e*par' for the same; 1*s*. from William Esto*n* for the same; 1*s*. from Maurice Dura*n*t for the same; 1*s*. from William de Bury for the same; 6*d*. from John Wytlot for the same; 6*d*. from Alice H*er*vy for the same; 3*d*. from John Som' for transgression against John Bege; 6*d*. from John Rolg for transgression against Alan Randolf; 3*d*. from Bartholomew He*n*del for transgression against Alexander de Po*n*te; 6*d*. from Alexander Cred' for transgression against John P*re*vet; 2*d*. from Alexander and Laura his wife for transgression against Richard le Deken'; 3*d*. from Henry de Burga for transgression against John Kewen; 4*d*. from Richard le Child for licence to agree with Ella Gill'; 3*d*. from John Rolf for licence to agree; 3*d*. from the same John for licence to agree; 6*d*. from John Som' for transgression against Richard Barbur; 3*d*. from John Bege for transgression against the same Richard; 3*d*. from William de Bury for transgression against John le Tayllor; 3*d*. from Robert Cissor ⌈for⌉ licence to agree; 3*d*. from Alice Arnold for licence to agree; 6*d*. from Simon Fab*er* for licence to agree with John Lokyar'; 3*d*. from Henry de Burga for licence to agree with Walter Aylward'; 6*d*. from William Unwyn' because he is proceeding against Thomas Aze; 6*d*. from other small perquisites. Total, £2 2*s*. 6*d*.

Total of both, £3 11*s*. 8*d*.

Total of all receipts, £59 13*s*. ½*d*.

Expenses
In expenses of the steward for the tourns of Martinmas and Hockday by 2 tallies, 9*s*. 7¼*d*.

And he owes, £59 3*s*. 5¼*d*.

Delivered to Sir G*eoffrey*, treasurer of Wolvesey, by 1 tally, £52 15*s*.

And thus he owes clear, £6 8*s*. 5¼*d*.

Gosport

Rents
John Pulayn renders account for £6 10*s*. 8½*d*. for all rents of assize for the year. Total, £6 10*s*. 8½*d*.

Defaults of rent
In default of 1½ plots which belonged to Amice, relict of the cobbler, inundated by the sea 9*d*.; 1 plot of land which belonged to Henry Curtays inundated by the sea 6*d*.; 1 plot of land which belonged to Thomas Poyn inundated by the sea 6*d*.; ½ plot of land which belonged to John Davel inundated by the sea 3*d*.; 1 plot of land which

belonged to Agnes Mulet inundated by the sea 6*d*.; 1½ plots of land which belonged to Henry Fossadam' inundated by the sea 9*d*.; 2 plots which belonged to Bartholomew Bonekar' inundated by the sea 1*s*.; 1 plot of land which belonged to John He*n*del inundated by the sea 6*d*.; 1 plot of land which belonged to Sibyl Lablake inundated by the sea 6*d*.; 1 plot of land which belonged to Rose Swole inundated by the sea 6*d*.; 1 plot of land which belonged to Richard Trut inundated by the sea 6*d*.; ½ plot of land which belonged to Thomas Edward' inundated by the sea 3*d*.; 1 plot of land which belonged to Henry de la Putte inundated by the sea 6*d*.; ½ plot of land which belonged to William Godefr*a*y inundated by the sea 3*d*.; 1 plot of land which belonged to Laurence le Blak' inundated by the sea 6*d*.; ½ plot of land which belonged to Matilda de Schale inundated by the sea 3*d*. Total, 8*s*.

Total of rents remaining, £6 2*s*. 8½*d*.

Reliefs
The same render account for 4*d*. from Robert de Forto*n* for relief for 1 acre of land by the legacy of John his brother; 4*s*. 1*d*. from Bartholomew He*n*del for relief for 12 acres and 1 perch of land and tenements which belonged to William Hendel his father; 1*s*. from William He*n*del for relief for 3 acres of land by the legacy of William Hendel his father; 10*d*. from John, Richard, John, Henry, Alice, Matilda and Emma Hendel for relief for 2½ acres which belonged to William le Hendel their father by legacy; 8*d*. from Alice and Agnes, daughters of Adam Bild', for relief for 2 acres of land and tenements which belonged to Adam Bild' their father. Total, 6*s*. 11*d*.

Perquisites
The same render account for 3*d*. from William le Kyngt for transgression against Alice, relict of William le Kynge; 3*d*. from Thomas Dura*n*t for transgression against John de la Frith'; 3*d*. from John Reynold' for breaking the assize of ale; 3*d*. from John F*ra*nceys for the same; 3*d*. from Henry Walt*er* for the same; 3*d*. from Alice le Tug for the same; 3*d*. from John Aze for the same; 3*d*. from Alice Schynnyld for the same; 3*d*. from Thomas Edward for the same; 3*d*. from John Prevet for the same; 3*d*. from Alice He*n*del for the same; 3*d*. from Alexander le Mey for transgression against Alice Edward; 3*d*. from Richard Goyr for transgression against Dyser', wife of William Pa*n*te; 3*d*. from Thomas Dura*n*t for transgression against John le Frith'; 3*d*. from Joan Edward' for transgression against Alice, wife of John Prest, at the tourn of Hockday; 6*d*. from Richard Schutel for transgression against William Bond'; 6*d*. from John P*re*st for breaking the assize of ale; 6*d*. from John Fr*a*nceys for the same; 6*d*. from Alice Schymnyld for the same; 6*d*. from Thomas Edward' for the same; 6*d*. from John Prevet for the same; 6*d*. from Matilda Bild' for the same; 6*d*. from Alice He*n*del for the same; 6*d*. from Alexander Cred' for the same. Total, 8*s*. 3*d*.

Total of both, 15*s*. 2*d*.

Total of all receipts, £6 17*s*. 10½*d*. And he owes it all.

Delivered to Sir G*eoffrey*, treasurer of Wolvesey, by 1 tally, £5.

And thus he owes clear, £1 17*s*. 10½*d*.

Havant

Arrears
John David, sergeant, renders his account for £18 13*s*. 2¾*d*. of arrears from the previous year. All delivered and paid to Sir G*eoffrey*, treasurer of Wolvesey, by 1 tally, and he is quit.

Rents of assize

The same renders account for 2*s*. 2*d*. for rents of assize at the feast of St Faith (6 October); £7 16*s*. 9¼*d*. at Martinmas (11 November); £3 12*s*. 7*d*. at the feast of St Thomas the Apostle (21 December); £1 6*s*. 8*d*. at the Purification (2 February); £2 5*s*. on the first Sunday in Lent (11 March); £3 10*s*. 4*d*. in the middle of Lent (30 March); 1*d*. at Easter (22 April); 8*d*. at St Mark the Evangelist (25 April); £2 9*s*. 8*d*. at Hockday (1 May); £1 6*s*. 11½*d*. at the feast of St James the Apostle (25 July); £4 4*s*. 6*d*. at Lammas (1 August); £3 3*s*. 8*d*. at Michaelmas (29 September). Total, £29 19*s*. ¾*d*.

m.22d

Defaults of rent

In default of the land and mill of Petronilla de Broch*a*mt' drawn into demesne, £1 4*s*. 9½*d*. for the year; the land ⌈and⌉ mill formerly of William de Aschewll' drawn into demesne, £1 1*s*. 10½*d*. for the year; the land formerly of Walter Chaf, 4*s*. 7½*d*. for the year; the land of la Stok', 9*d*. for the year; 1 plot leased to Henry Parys on the eastern side of the cemetery of Havant 6*d*.; 1 plot leased to Richard le Tayllor there, 6*d*. for the year; a certain purpresture of 4 acres and 1 rood which Ralph de Warh*a*m formerly rented from the demesne because it is now in the demesne 4*s*. 7*d*.; the land of Hugh de Bynlygh' 3½*d*., because Philip de Hors*ham* paid 5*s*. 5*d*. Total, £2 17*s*. 11*d*.

Total of rents remaining, £27 1*s*. 1¾*d*.

Also rents

The same renders account for 6*s*. 8*d*. from 1 messuage with a garden leased to Geoffrey Harewest at the lord's will; 2*s*. 4*d*. from Peter de la Sale or two silver cockle-shells at the lord's will. Total, 9*s*.

Issues of the manor

The same renders account for £2 10*s*. 3*d*. from pannage of pigs this year; 2*s*. from the forester of the wood for ½ qr of nuts according to custom; 2*s*. 7½*d*. from 21 harvest labour services sold, at 1½*d*. a labour service; 6*s*. from 1 feeble cart-horse sold; 5*s*. from 1 feeble plough-horse from the heriot of William Trockem*ere* sold; 9*s*. from 1 ox from the heriot of William Hamu*n*d' sold; 7*s*. from 1 ox from the heriot of Henry Parys sold; 8*s*. from 1 sterile cow from the heriot of William le Scut sold; 1*s*. from 1 calf from the heriot of William de Bynlygh' sold; 1*s*. 10*d*. from the hide sold of 1 ox dead from murrain; 12*s*. from the pasturage of Bynlygh' sold, because at the tourn of Martinmas it was sold to Philip de Horsh*a*m; £2 2*s*. from 3 casks of cider sold, at 14*s*. each, apart from the vessels; £1 from the loppings of timber felled for the mill sold by warrant of the reeve of Hambledon. Total, £8 6*s*. 8½*d*.

Annual recognizance

The same renders account for 6*d*. from William le[1] Cop*ere* for annual recognizance; 6*d*. from Robert Fab*er* for the same; 6*d*. from Anketil Cl*ericus* for the same; 6*d*. from Stephen de Drayto*n* for the same; 6*d*. from Richard de Bosh*a*m for the same; 3*d*. from Richard Coop*ertor* for the same; 6*d*. from Adam Capon for the same; 6*d*. from Walter de Clanefeld' for the same; 6*d*. from John Clib for the same; 6*d*. from John le Ray for the same; 3*d*. from Nicholas de Halvenaked' for the same; 3*d*. from Stephen

1 MS 'Willo' ⟨d⟩ le'.

de Oll*e*; 3*d*. from Adam Poppe for the same; 3*d*. from Richard le Fox for the same. Total, 5*s*. 9*d*.

Sale of corn

The same renders account for £7 2*s*. 6*d*. from 23 qrs 6 bus. of wheat sold, at 6*s*. a qr; 5*s*. 3*d*. from 1 qr 6 bus. of curall sold, at 3*s*. a qr; £3 8*s*. 6*d*. from 17 qrs 1 bus. of barley sold, at 4*s*. a qr; 6*d*. from 1 bus. of barley sold at the audit; £1 6*s*. 3*d*. from 11 qrs 2 bus. of oats sold, at 2*s*. 4*d*. a qr; £3 17*s*. 9*d*. from 38 qrs 7 bus. of vetches sold, at 2*s*. a qr. Total of all corn sold, £16 9*d*.

Mill of Brockhampton

The same renders account for £1 6*s*. from 5 qrs of wheat from the whole issue of the mill sold, at 6*s*. a qr for 3 qrs, and 4*s*. a qr for 2 qrs; £1 6*s*. 8*d*. from 8 qrs of barley sold, at 3*s*. 4*d*. a qr; £3 10*s*. from 12½ qrs of coarse-ground corn sold, at 6*s*. a qr for 7½ qrs, and 5*s*. a qr for 5 qrs; £2 5*s*. ½*d*. from 20 qrs 3 bus. of malt sold, at 2*s*. 4*d*. a qr for 12 qrs 7 bus., and 2*s*. a qr for 7½ qrs. Total, £8 7*s*. 8½*d*.

Mill of Aschewell'

The same renders account for £1 16*s*. 9*d*. from 7 qrs of wheat from the whole issue of the mill sold, at 6*s*. a qr for 4 qrs 3 bus., and 4*s*. a qr for 2 qrs 5 bus.; £1 9*s*. 7*d*. from 8 qrs 7 bus. of barley sold, at 3*s*. 4*d*. a qr. Total, £3 6*s*. 4*d*.

Total of all the mills, £11 14*s*. ½*d*.

Entry and marriage fines

The same renders account for 2*s*. from Walter Ysmo*n*gar' to have enrolled the quitclaim of the house in which he dwells of Henry ate Seylde who came and in full court quitclaimed to the same Walter and his heirs the said tenement; 2*s*. from the same Walter to have 1 half-acre (*helva*) of land by surrender of William Trockem*ere*; £1 from Isabel, relict of John Sewatte, to retain 1 messuage ½ virgate of land which belonged to John her husband; £1 13*s*. 4*d*. from William Haymo*nd*' to have 1 messuage ½ virgate of land which belonged to William his father; 1*s*. from Henry de Harting' to have 1 plot of land by surrender of Adam Silvestr'; 4*s*. from William Drappar' to have 1 messuage by surrender of Segar ate Asche; 1*s*. from Henry Ponfald to have 1 plot of land by surrender of Cecilia Savel and John her son; 1*s*. from Richard Cauntelou the younger to have 1 house by surrender of Richard his father; 2*s*. from Thomas Canon to have 1 seld by surrender of Cecilia la Wytemsche; 5*s*. from Philip Bucher to have 1 house by surrender of Robert de Wichet; 1*s*. from William Mayll' to have 1 plot by surrender of Henry Cauntelou; 1*s*. from Godfrey de M*er*don' to have 1 plot of land by surrender of Richard de M*er*do*n*; 2*s*. from Richard Morvyll' to have 1 half-acre of land by surrender of Lucy Curtays; 13*s*. 4*d*. from Luke Kynel to have 1 messuage ½ virgate of land which belonged to Roger his father; 1*s*. from Petronilla ate More for marrying Petronilla her daughter within; 1*s*. from Luke de Broch*am*pton' for marrying Rose his daughter within; 6*d*. from Alice Hikely*ng* for marrying Alice her daughter within; £1 6*s*. 8*d*. from Joan, who was wife of William Trockem*ere*, to retain 1 messuage 1 virgate of land which belonged to William her husband; 3*s*. 4*d*. from Robert Cardewell' to have 1 plot of land, 40 feet long and 30 feet wide, by surrender of William ate Ywe for the term of his life and that of Matilda his wife, so that he may build upon the said plot; 2*s*. from John Schirwold' to have 1 house built upon 1 half-acre of land which belonged to Walter his father; 10*s*. from Stephen de Olle to have 2 messuages and 2 curtilages which contain 1 acre of land by surrender of Richard de Bosh*am*; 6*d*. from Margery, relict of Roger Gossebird, to retain the moiety of 1 shop (*schappe*) which belonged to Roger her husband; 6*d*. from the same Margery to retain the seld which belonged to Roger her husband; 1*s*. from Mabel, daughter of Sewate, to have 1 house and a quarter of 1 half-acre of land by surrender of Lucy her sister; £3 6*s*. 8*d*. from Isabel de Bynlygh' to have ½ virgate of land which belonged to William her father, although she or whosoever holds that land will provide Hugh de Bynlygh', who held the said land undividedly and who was thrown off it for laying waste his own aforesaid land, will give for the life of the aforesaid Hugh each year 2½ qrs of wheat; £6 13*s*. 4*d*. from Philip de Horsam to have the aforesaid messuage and ½ virgate of land by surrender of the aforesaid Isabel de Bynlygh'. Total, £16 15*s*. 2*d*.

Perquisites

The same renders account for 4*d*. from William Schirwold' for unjustly withholding a debt from Isabel Heri*n*gand; 3*d*. from John Cau*n*telou for transgression against John de Raketo*n*; 6*d*. from Robert le Wock' for transgression done to John de Harmed'; 3*d*. from John Ca*n*tel*ou* for transgression against John Potard'; 3*d*. from Adam Smalstec for false complaint against Martin Pastor; 3*d*. from John Potard for transgression done to Robert le Lul; 6*d*. from Stephen de Oll*e* for unjustly withholding a debt from Richard Collem'; 3*d*. from Richard Cantelou for unjustly withholding a debt from William Body; 3*d*. from Robert ate Po*n*fold' for unjustly withholding a debt from Richard Hayward'; 6*d*. from Adam le Ra*m* because he broke the lord's hedge; 3*d*. from William Mulsop for transgression done to Cecilia la Pichuste; 3*d*. from Robert Cardewill' for unjustly withholding a debt from William Drapp'; 3*d*. from John Schirwold for unjustly withholding a debt from William Drapp'; 6*d*. from John Tosto*n* for trespass in la Thichette; 1*s*. from Thomas le Frensch' for the same; 3*d*. from Geoffrey Harliost for transgression against William de Hirti*ng*'; 6*d*. from William Mulcsop for false complaint against Cecilia Pitusch'; 3*d*. from Richard Cler' for false bread; 3*d*. from Walter le Tanor for the same; 3*d*. from William Heresin for the same; 3*d*. from William Fulagh' for the same; 3*d*. from William Robost for the same; 3*d*. from William le Fox for the same; 6*d*. from John Fab*er* because he did not produce in court Roger Comalond whom he had bailed; 3*d*. from John Ca*n*telou for transgression done to John de Raketo*n*; 6*d*. from Richard Grigg' because he did not produce in court Stephen Russel whom he had bailed; 6*d*. from Richard de Bosh*am* because he did not produce in court Roger his son whom he had bailed; 6*d*. from Adam Poppe because he brewed against the assize; 6*d*. from Walter de Wynt' for the same; 6*d*. from Walter Ysmo*n*gar' for the same; 6*d*. from Nicholas Sut*or* for the same; 3*d*. from Matilda Chochil for the same; 3*d*. from John Cauntel*ou* for the same; 6*d*. from Cecilia Bedell' for the same; 6*d*. from William Heri*n*gand for the same; 6*d*. from William Mayll' for the same; 6*d*. from Henry Ca*n*telou for the same; 6*d*. from Richard Collem' for the same; 6*d*. from John Plu*m*b' for the same; 6*d*. from Walter Rollebag' for the same; 6*d*. from Henry Rotyr for the same; 6*d*. from John Coket for the same; 6*d*. from Philip Bucher for the same; 6*d*. from William Fulaʒg' for the same; 6*d*. from John Ray for the same; 3*d*. from Godfrey Tippe for the same; 3*d*. from John de Harmeden' for the same; 3*d*. from Matilda Bro*n* for the same; 6*d*. from William Robost; 3*d*. from John Stuar' for the same; 3*d*. from Roger Gossebird' for the same; 3*d*. from Adam Capo*n* for the same; 6*d*. from Richard Morwill' for the same; 3*d*. from William Cochel for the same; 6*d*. from Ro*n*pay*n* for the same; 3*d*. from William Schussebird for the same; 3*d*. from

Har⌈me⌉den' for the same; 3*d*. from William Jouedy for the same; 6*d*. from Godfrey ate Thorn' for false complaint against William Drapp'; 6*d*. from Robert le Bogh' because he did not produce in court Thomas le Hosche whom he had bailed; 3*d*. from Matilda Lande because she sold ale against the assize; 6*d*. from William ate Hull' to have an inquest against William Her*in*gand; 2*s*. from William ate Hull' for false complaint against William Her*in*gand; 3*d*. from Cecilia la Ysma*n*gastr' because she sold ale against the assize; 3*d*. from Robert le Fuȝeglar' for the same; 3*d*. from William Heresin for the same; 3*d*. from Richard Burg' for the same; 3*d*. from Robert le Wowk' for the same; 3*d*. from Robert Sussa*nn*' for the same; 6*d*. from Simon Sut*or* for the same; 6*d*. from William ate Yve for the same; 3*d*. from Thomas le Wyte for the same; 6*d*. from William Semard' for the same; 3*d*. from Robert Landma*n* for the same; 6*d*. from William Schirwold for the same; 6*d*. from William Cardewill' for the same; 6*d*. from Robert Benayt for the same; 3*d*. from Richard Crul for the same; 3*d*. from Thomas M*er*don' for transgression against Henry de Hirt*in*g'; 6*d*. from Walter Suple for transgression done to Alice Wery; 6*d*. from John Clib for transgression against William Her*in*gand'; 3*d*. from John Wynchastr' for transgression done to John Cantel*ou*; 1*s*. from Peter Theggar for false complaint against Peter de Aul'; 3*d*. from Henry Rotyr because he did not produce in court Richard, the said bailiff, whom he had bailed; 6*s*. 8*d*. from whole tithing of Hayling because it did not produce in court William le Cup*er*e whom it had bailed on arrest; 6*d*. from William de Drapp' because he brewed against the assize; 6*d*. from William Stiuard' for the same; 6*d*. from Robert Benayt for the same; 6*d*. from Robert Cocce for the same; 6*d*. from Richard Coop*ertor* because he encroached upon the king's highway; 3*d*. from Cecilia, daughter of Ysmo*n*g*ar*, because she brewed against the assize; 3*d*. from Robert atte Brigg' for the same; 3*d*. from Richard Burgar' for the same; 3*d*. from Robert le Wok' for the same; 3*d*. from Henry ate Po*n*fold' for the same; 2*s*. from Henry Rotyr and John Tral' because they did not produce in court Geoffrey Rollebag' whom they had bailed; 3*d*. from John Potard' for the hue; 3*d*. from John Cau*n*tel*ou* for the same; 6*d*. from Adam Poppe because he brewed against the assize; 6*d*. from Euala Bedell' for the same; 6*d*. from Petronilla Ma*nn*y*n*g for the same; 1*s*. from William de Wynt' for the same; 6*d*. from Nicholas Sut*or* for the same; 3*d*. from John Ca*n*telou for the same; 3*d*. from William Mulcsop for the same; 3*d*. from William Heringand for the same; 3*d*. from Richard Collem' for the same; 3*d*. from Richard Ca*n*telou for the same; 6*d*. from Walter Rollebagg' for the same; 1*s*. from Henry Rotyr for the same; 1*s*. from John Coket for the same; 6*d*. from Philip Buchir for the same; 6*d*. from William Fulagh' for the same; 1*s*. from John Ray for the same; 6*d*. from Matilda Bro*n* for the same; 3*d*. from William Robost for the same; 3*d*. from John Stuar for the same; 3*d*. from the relict of Roger Gossebird for the same; 3*d*. from William de Hirt*in*g' for the same; 3*d*. from Isabel Heresin for the same; 3*d*. from Richard Morwill' for the same; 3*d*. from William Cutel for the same; 6*d*. from Henry Danyel for the same; 3*d*. from William Jouedy for the same; 6*d*. from William Hamely*n* for the same; 6*d*. from Thomas Noun for the same; 6*d*. from William le None for the same; 6*d*. from the same for forestalling fish; 6*d*. from William Bartely*n* for the same; 6*d*. from Henry Pist' for the same; 6*d*. from Robert Snouto*n* for the same; 4*d*. from Richard Ca*n*tel*ou* for the same; 1*s*. from Cecilia de Haniwell' for false complaint against Richard de Bosh*am*; 3*d*. from Godfrey Tipp' because he did not produce in court Thomas M*er*do*n* whom he had bailed; 6*d*. from John Potard for transgression done to William Aylm'; 2*s*. from the tithing of Havant because it did not produce in court Robert Gosseden' whom it had bailed; 4*s*. from the tithing of Hayling because it did not produce in court William Cop*er*e whom it had bailed; 6*d*.

from Roger Fox for false bread; 6*d.* from John de Harmden' for the same; 6*d.* from Richard Cler' for the same; 6*d.* from Richard Morwill' for the same; 6*d.* from William Fuȝlagh' for the same; 6*d.* from William Robust for the same; 6*d.* from William Hor*e*fen for the same. Total, £3 13*s.* 11*d.*

Total of both, £20 9*s.* 1*d.*

Total of all receipts, £84 6*s.* 5¾*d.*

[Cost of ploughs]
In iron and steel bought for the ironwork of 1 plough for the year 4*s.* 2*d.* In stipend of the smith repairing the ironwork for the same time 2*s.* 2*d.* In repairing 1 ploughshare 4*d.* In 1 new plough bought 8*d.* In 1 plough foot bought 6*d.* In 1 plough-iron made 2*d.* In shoeing 4 oxen in winter 2*d.* In stipend of 1 ploughman and 1 drover for the year 9*s.* In stipend of 1 harrower at both sowings 1*s.* In 1 ox bought for ploughing 10*s.* Total, £1 8*s.* 2*d.*

[Purchase of seed and liveries]
In 16 qrs of barley bought from the mill for the liveries of the manorial servants £2 13*s.* 4*d.*, at 3*s.* 4*d.* a qr. Total, £2 13*s.* 4*d.*

[Carts]
In 1 pair of wheels bought with hoops fitted 2*s.* 8*d.* In old tyres fitted to the said wheels with large nails, small nails, clamps and linch-pins bought, with the stipend of the smith, 3*s.* 8*d.* In shoeing 2 cart-horses for the year 4*s.* 8*d.* In clouts, nails and grease 2*s.* 6*d.* In 2 collars mended 3*d.* In fitting the cart with axles with axles bought for the same 10*d.* In 1 rope bought for the same 1*s.* In 1 pair of traces bought 5*d.* In whitening 2 hides for harnesses 7*d.* Total, 16*s.* 7*d.*

[Cost of buildings]
In re-roofing the great barn and small barn in places 1*s.* 9*d.* In furrowing the garden and planting beans in the same 1*s.* 10*d.* In straw bought for forage for oxen 6*s.* 6*d.* In roofing the byre, 2*s.* 6*d.* by piece-work. Total, 12*s.* 7*d.*

[Sheepcote]
In 11 hurdles bought for the sheepfold 1*s.* 3*d.* In stipend of 1 shepherd for the year 3*s.* In 2 casks mended 6*d.* In watercress grown 1*s.* 1*d.* In collecting stubble 2*s.* Total, 7*s.* 10*d.*

[Threshing and winnowing]
In threshing and winnowing 30½ qrs of wheat and curall by piece-work 7*s.*, at 2¾*d.* a heaped quarter. In threshing and winnowing 20 qrs 2 bus. of barley by piece-work 3*s.* 2½*d.*, at 1¾*d.* a heaped quarter. In threshing and winnowing 21 qrs 2 bus. of oats by piece-work 1*s.* 2¼*d.*, at ¾*d.* a heaped quarter. In threshing and winnowing 32 qrs 2 bus. of vetches by piece-work 4*s.* 9*d.*, at 1¾*d.* a heaped quarter. Total, 16*s.* 1¾*d.*

[Weeding and mowing]
In weeding corn 3*s.* 10*d.* In mowing 5 acres of meadow in Hugelo*nd*' by piece-work 2*s.* 6*d.*, at 6*d.* an acre. In spreading and tossing the said meadow 1*s.* 3*d.* In mowing, spreading and tossing 1 acre on Boylo*nd*' 8*d.* In mowing, spreading and tossing 2

acres in la Smalmed*e*plask', Binortheto*n* beside Colverpik', and the moor, 1*s*. 4*d*. In mowing, spreading and tossing 2 acres of Aschewellmor' 1*s*. 4*d*. Total, 10*s*. 11*d*.

Harvest-time
In reaping 42 acres of wheat as they lie in various fields £1 1*s*., at 6*d*. an acre. In reaping 16 acres of barley as they lie in various fields 8*s*., at 6*d*. an acre. In reaping 22 acres of oats as they lie in various fields 9*s*. 2*d*., at 5*d*. an acre. In reaping 26 acres of vetches as they lie in various fields 13*s*., at 6*d*. an acre. Total, £2 11*s*. 2*d*.

Mill of Brockhampton
In iron and steel bought for the bills of the said mill with the stipend of the smith repairing the said bills 3*s*. 10*d*. In shoeing 4 plough-horses with the stipend of the smith for the year 4*s*. 10*d*. In 1 basket bought 1*d*. In 1 wooden hoop bought for the said mill 1*s*. 1½*d*. Total, 9*s*. 10½*d*. These expenses were made before the renovation of the mill this year.

Mill of Aschewll'
In iron and steel bought for the bills of the said mill with the stipend of the smith repairing the said bills 1*s*. 5*d*. In shoeing 1 plough-horse for the year 1*s*. 1*d*. In 1 basket bought 1*d*. In hiring a carpenter for 1 week to mend the sluice of the mill 1*s*. 3*d*. In making 1 mill-iron 6*d*. In mending 1 hoop of the said mill 6*d*. Total, 4*s*. 10*d*.

Expenses of the steward
In expenses of the steward and Simon, clerk, at the tourns of Martinmas and Hockday by 1 tally 15*s*. 10*d*. In wages of John, sergeant, for the year £2 5*s*. 7½*d*., or 1½*d*. a day. In 1 stoup made from the manor's own timber (*proprio merem'*) 6*d*. Total, £3 1*s*. 11½*d*.

Total of all expenses, £13 13*s*. 4¾*d*.

And he owes, £70 13*s*. 1*d*.

Allowances
In allowance of the bailiff for building anew the mill of Brockhampton, for all costs, with 1 millstone bought, and with 8*s*. 8*d*. given to the marshal of the king, £12 5*s*. 2*d*.

Cash deliveries
Delivered to Sir G*eoffrey*, treasurer of Wolvesey, by 1 tally, £50.

Total of allowances and cash deliveries, £62 5*s*. 2*d*.

And he owes clear, £8 7*s*. 11*d*.

Issues of the grange

Wheat
{yield: 4-fold plus 2 qrs}
The same renders account for 36 qrs 2 bus. from the whole issue of wheat from the grange in the granary without heaped measure.
Sown over 42 acres as they lie, 12½ qrs. Sold, 23 qrs 6 bus.

Curall
The same renders account for 1 qr 6 bus. from the whole issue of curall from the grange in the granary without heaped measure. All sold.

Barley
{yield: three-and-a-half-fold less 6½ bus.}
The same renders account for 27 qrs 5 bus. from the whole issue of barley from the grange in the granary without heaped measure; 16 qrs bought for the liveries of the manorial servants. Total, 43 qrs 5 bus.
Sown over 16 acres as they lie in various fields, 10½ qrs. Delivered to 1 ploughman and 1 drover for the year, 10 qrs 3 bus., because they take a quarter every 10 weeks. Delivered to 1 shepherd for the year, 3½ qrs, because he takes a quarter every 14 weeks. Delivered to 1 harrower in winter at the time of the sowing of the summer corn, for 24 weeks, 2 qrs. Sold, 17 qrs 1 bus. Sold at the audit, 1 bus.

Oats
{yield: 3-fold less 1 qr 7 bus.}
The same renders account for 26 qrs 5 bus. from the whole issue of oats from the grange in the granary without heaped measure; 6 qrs by estimation in sheaves given to oxen. Total, 32 qrs 5 bus.
Sown over 22 acres as they lie in various fields, 11 qrs. In fodder of the horses of the lord's steward for his visits, 3 bus. In fodder of 2 cart-horses for the year, 4 qrs. In fodder of oxen by estimation in sheaves, 6 qrs. Sold, 11 qrs 2 bus.

Beans
{yield: 3-fold}
The same renders account for 6 bus. from the whole issue of beans from the grange in the granary without heaped measure. All sown.

Vetches
{yield: two-and-a-half-fold plus 1 qr 7 bus.}
The same renders account for 8 qrs of vetches remaining in the granary from the previous year; 10 qrs by estimation in sheaves remaining in the granary from the previous year; 29 qrs 3 bus. from the issue this year. Total, 47 qrs 3 bus.
Sown over 26 acres as they lie in various fields, 8½ qrs. Sold, 38 qrs 7 bus.

Mill of Brockhampton
Wheat: 5 qrs from the issue of the mill.
Barley: 8 qrs from the whole issue of the mill; all sold.
Coarse-ground corn: 12½ qrs from the whole issue of the mill; all sold.
Malt: 20 qrs 3 bus. from the whole issue of the mill; all sold.

Mill of Aschewll'
Wheat: 7 qrs from the whole issue of the mill; all sold.
Barley: 8 qrs 7 bus. from the whole issue of the mill; all sold.

m.23

Stock

Cart-horses: 3 remain from the previous year; 1 sold; 2 remain.
Plough-horses: 1 from the heriot of William T*ro*ckem*er*e; 1 sold; none remain.
Asses: 5 remain from the previous year; 1 in murrain; 4 remain, 1 of them female.
Young asses: 1 remains from the previous year aged 1½ years, now 2½ years; 1 male remains.

Also young asses: 1 female remains from the previous year; 1 in murrain; none remain here.
Oxen: 8 remain from the previous year; 1 bullock from the heriot of William Haymo*nd*; 1 steer from the heriot of John Sewatte; 1 bullock from the heriot of Henry Parys; 1 bought. Total, 12. 1 in murrain; 2 sold; 9 remain.
Cows: 1 from the heriot of William Scut; 1 sold; none remain here.
Hides: 1 from an ass and 1 from an ox in murrain used for harnesses and the mill; 1 from a young ass sold.
Cider: 3 casks remain from the previous year; 2 casks made this year; 3 sold; 2 full casks remain.
Utensils: 2 ploughs with ironwork and equipment; 1 cart with iron tyres; 2 brass pots, 1 of them small; 1 posnet; 1 ewer with a basin; 1 pan; 1 tripod; 2 shovels for dung.

Bitterne

Arrears
William de Worsted', sergeant, and Walter le Parker, reeve, render account for £7 14*s*. 4½*d*. of arrears from the previous year. All delivered to Sir G*eoffrey*, treasurer of Wolvesey.

Rents of assize
The same render account for £2 3*d*. for all rents of assize at Christmas; £2 3*d*. at Easter (22 April); £2 3*d*. at the Nativity of St John the Baptist (24 June); £3 2*s*. 11½*d*. at Michaelmas (29 September). Total, £9 3*s*. 8½*d*.

Quittances
In quittance of 1 reeve for the year 4*s*.; 2 ploughmen for the year 3*s*.; 1 park-keeper for the year 4*s*. Total, 11*s*.

Defaults of rent
In default of the land of Vyel drawn into demesne, 2*s*. 1*d*. for the year. Total, 2*s*. 1*d*.

Total of quittances and defaults of rent, 13*s*. 1*d*.

Total of rents remaining, £8 10*s*. 7½*d*.

Annual recognizance
The same render account for 6*d*. from Roger le Salt*er*e for annual recognizance; 3*d*. from Richard Seuar' for the same; 6*d*. from William Austy*n* for the same; 6*d*. from Robert Cl*ericus* of Fawley for the same. Total, 1*s*. 9*d*.

Issues of the manor
The same render account for 10*s*. from pannage of pigs this year; 9*s*. 4*d*. from the agistment of pigs in the park; 17*s*. 6*d*. from the agistment of livestock in the park in summer; nothing from winter pasturage on account of the lord's stock; 1*s*. from the pasturage in P*r*estemed' sold after mowing; nothing from winter pasturage for the lord's stock; nothing from the pasturage on the land of Bathard and in Pistok' this year because it was sown; 6*d*. from the pasturage in various places sold this year; 15*s*.

from 2 cart-horses sold, at 3*s*. for 1 because feeble, and 12*s*. for 1; 8*s*. from 1 old mare sold; 6*s*. from 6 late-born calves sold, at 1*s*. each; 17*s*. from 17 wethers sold at Martinmas (11 November), at 1*s*. each; 11*s*. from 4 pigs sold, at 2*s*. 9*d*. each; 12*s*. 11*d*. from 151 hens from churchscot sold; nothing from nuts collected in the park this year; nothing from rushes in the park this year; 2*s*. from heath sold this year; 3*s*. 1½*d*. from rowen cheese sold; £1 14*s*. from 4 weys 7 cloves of summer cheese sold, at 8*s*. a wey; 2*s*. 3*d*. from 6 cloves of butter sold, at 4½*d*. a clove; 5*s*. from hay sold this year; nothing from heath in the quagmire (*q*ua*bbemer'*) this year because none was obtained to sell; nothing from underwood in the park this year for the same reason; 10*d*. from the hide sold of 1 cart-horse in murrain; 8*d*. from the hide sold of 1 plough-horse in murrain; 4*s*. from the hide and flesh sold of 1 bullock dead from murrain; 8*d*. from the hides sold of 2 yearlings in murrain; 1½*d*. from the hide sold of 1 calf in murrain; 10*d*. from the skins sold of 4 wethers in murrain before shearing; 1*s*. 6*d*. from the skins sold wholesale of 17 wethers in murrain after shearing; nothing from cider this year; nothing from small labour services this year because of the cider-making; nothing from coarse wool here because it is sent to Wolvesey; 3½*d*. from 3 lb of wool locks sold; 1*s*. from Adam ate Hall' and William de Worstede to have licence to dig up marl in the marsh; 2*s*. 7½*d*. from dairy produce sold at the audit. Total, £8 7*s*. 3*d*.

Fishery

The same render account for £7 4*s*. from 53 salmon sold, at 4*s*. each for 19, and 2*s*. each for 34. Total, £7 4*s*.

Sale of corn

The same render account for £2 12*s*. 6*d*. from 8 qrs 6 bus. of wheat sold, at 6*s*. a qr; 5*s*. 5*d*. from 1 qr 2 bus. of curall sold, at 4*s*. 4*d*. a qr; £1 6*s*. 5*d*. from 11 qrs 3 bus. of dredge sold, at 2*s*. a qr for 3 qrs 7 bus., 2*s*. 4*d*. a qr for 4 qrs, and 2*s*. 8*d*. a qr for 3½ qrs; 1*s*. from ½ qr of dredge sold at the audit; 2*s*. from 4 bus. of peas sold, at 6*d*. a bus.; 2*s*. from 6 bus. of peas sold at the audit. Total, £4 9*s*. 4*d*.

Sale of the mill's corn

The same render account for 10*s*. 3*d*. from 1 qr 7 bus. of wheat sold, at 7½*d*. a bus. for 2 bus., 5*s*. 4*d*. a qr for 1 qr 1 bus., and 9*d*. a bus. for 4 bus.; £1 15*s*. 10*d*. from 11 qrs 6 bus. of barley sold, at 2*s*. 8*d*. a qr for 3 qrs, 3*s*. a qr for 4 qrs, and 3*s*. 4*d*. a qr for 4 qrs 6 bus.; 11*s*. from 2 qrs 1 bus. of coarse-ground corn sold, at 5*s*. for 1 qr, and 5*s*. 4*d*. a qr for 1 qr 1 bus.; 10*s*. 9*d*. from 4 qrs 7 bus. of malt sold, at 2*s*. a qr for 1 qr 7 bus., and 2*s*. 4*d*. a qr for 3 qrs; 8*d*. from 1 bus. of oatmeal sold. Total, £3 8*s*. 6*d*.

Entry and marriage fines

The same render account for 6*s*. 8*d*. from the tithing of Bitterne at the hundred-court of Martinmas for tithingpenny; 6*s*. 8*d*. from the tithing of Fawley at the said hundred-court for the same; 13*s*. 4*d*. from the same at the hundred-court of Hockday for the same; 1*s*. from John le Car*eter* for marrying Joan his stepdaughter outside; 3*s*. from Hawise, daughter of Austin Mich', to have 1 house and 2 acres of land which belonged to Edith her mother; 6*s*. 8*d*. from Matilda, daughter of Mabel Ace, to have 1 messuage and 1 ferling of land by surrender of Mabel her mother, so that the said Mabel be supported by holding the same land equally with her; 6*s*. 8*d*. from Nicholas le Pyn to have the said Matilda with her land; 6*s*. 8*d*. from Walter le Schepphurd' to have the land which belonged to his mother; 13*s*. 4*d*. from Roger ate Clive to have the land which belonged to Gunilda Gardenir; 3*s*. 4*d*. from Roger Westsyd' to have 1 house and 1 curtilage by surrender of Walter le Schiphurd', and he will relieve the said Walter of 6*d*. annual rent; 1*s*. from Joan Alayn for marrying herself; 1*s*. from Margery, daughter of Walter le Schiphurd', for marrying herself; 1*s*. from Alice Baron for 1 messuage 1 acre of land by surrender of Robert ate Slade and Alice his wife. Total, £3 10*s*. 4*d*.

Perquisites
The same render account for 2*s*. from the tithing of Fawley because it did not present the default of John Baro*n* at the tourn of Martinmas; 2*s*. from the same tithing because it did not produce in court the individual whom it had bailed; £2 10*s*. 4*d*. from small amercements from various men for various transgressions. Total, £2 14*s*. 4*d*.

Total of both, £6 4*s*. 8*d*.

Total of all receipts, £38 6*s*. 1½*d*.

Cost of ploughs
In iron and steel bought for 2 ploughs for the year 3*s*. 1*d*. In 1 plough foot bought 5*d*. In 3 wheels bought for ploughs 4½*d*. In making a new plough and mending others and harrows 9½*d*. In 1 ploughshare bought 9*d*. In stipend of the smith making the ironwork of the ploughs 2*s*. 4*d*. In fitting the wain with axles 3*d*. In clouts, nails and grease bought for the same 1*s*. 5½*d*., and so much because it went to the marling for the whole summer. In cleaning iron tyres 1½*d*. In 1 rope, 6 halters and 1 pair of traces made from their own canvas 5*d*. In 1 ox bought 10*s*. In stipend of 2 ploughmen for the year 6*s*. In 4 bus. of beans bought for sowing 1*s*. 4*d*. In forage bought for supporting oxen 12*s*. 8*d*. Total, £2.

Cost of carts
In fitting the cart with axles at various times with axles bought for the same 5½*d*. In clouts, nails, grease bought for the same 6½*d*. In 1 collar bought 8*d*. In white leather bought for mending harnesses 6*d*. In a broad-axe bought for mending the cart 7*d*. In hooping the hubs of wheels with bands of wood 3*d*. In shoeing 2 cart-horses for the year 2*s*. 6*d*. In shoeing 2 plough-horses going to harrow at both sowings 8*d*. In stipend of 1 carter for the year 3*s*. In 4 qrs 2 bus. of oats bought for the fodder of horses 8*s*. 8*d*. Total, 17*s*. 8*d*.

Cost of the dairy
In woollen and linen cloth bought for the dairy 5*d*. In 5 bus. of salt bought 1*s*. ½*d*. In earthenware pots and pans bought for the same 2*d*. In 1 new bucket bought and another mended 5*d*. In a press bought for the same 3*d*. In 6 ells of canvas bought for putting the wool in 1*s*. 7½*d*., at 3¼*d*. an ell. In packing the wool 2*d*. In grease bought for greasing sheep 3*s*. In 1 mould bought for making cheese 4*d*. In stipend of 1 dairymaid for the year 1*s*. 6*d*. In stipend of 1 shepherd for the year 3*s*. In 7 cows bought for the lord's stock £2 19*s*. 1*d*., at 7*s*. 9½*d*. each for 2, 8*s*. 6*d*. each for 3, and 9*s*. each for 2. In 1 wether bought before shearing 1*s*. 6*d*. Total, £3 12*s*. 6*d*.

Threshing
In threshing 30 qrs of wheat, curall and rye by piece-work 5*s*., at 2½*d*. per 10 struck bushels. In threshing 64 qrs 1 bus. of barley, dredge, peas and vetches by piece-work

6*s*. 4½*d*., at 1½*d*. per 10 struck bushels. In threshing 20 qrs 3 bus. of oats by piece-work 1*s*., at 1½*d*. per 20 struck bushels. In winnowing all the corn beyond that winnowed by the dairymaid 9*d*. Total, 13*s*. 1½*d*.

Cost of buildings
In 6 lb of tin and 2 fotmals of lead bought for mending the lord's tower and various gutters in the curia 6*s*. 11*d*. In 1 plumber with 1 mate cutting the said tin and lead and mending the tower and various gutters in the curia for 3 days 1*s*. 6*d*., at 6*d*. a day.[1] In nails for the same 2*d*. In re-roofing in places the hall and lord's chamber, the archdeacon's chamber, knights' chamber, bailiff's room and granary, which had been partly unroofed, 13*s*. 6*d*. In 3 qrs of lime bought for the same 2*s*., at 8*d*. a qr. In 200 nails bought for fastening the laths 2*d*. In re-roofing in places the great barn, byre, cow-shed and building of the press which had been unroofed 2*s*. 6*d*. In re-roofing the sheepcote in places 6*d*. In 2 locks bought for the building of the press and the[2] door to the chamber of the chapel 7*d*. In 1 band of iron for hooping the beam of the press 10*d*. In 1 iron shovel bought 3½*d*. Total, £1 8*s*. 11½*d*.

Cost of the park
In mending the palisade of the park in places 3*s*. In enclosing 54 perches in the said park 4*s*. 5*d*., at 1*d*. a perch. In mending the old fences of the said park in places 11*d*. Total, 8*s*. 4*d*.

Cost of the harvest
In mowing the meadow of Botley and Hove which contains 6 acres measured by the perch by piece-work 2*s*. In mowing le Longemor' 2*s*. In mowing Bathardesmed' 2*s*. In mowing the meadow which belonged to the Abbot of Netley 7½*d*. In tossing and tedding all the hay 1*s*. 3*d*. In 864 herrings bought for 1½ boon-works of 108 men who reaped and bound 68 acres of wheat, 12 acres of rye and 40 acres of barley 5*s*. 9*d*.; and know that each of them has 5 herrings a day, 3 at lunch and 2 at supper; and know that the rest of the corn is reaped by labour service. In 6 casks bought for cider 16*s*., at 2*s*. 8*d*. a cask. In hooping and binding the same 2*s*. 4*d*. In hooping and mending 3 tubs, 1 small tub and 1 tine 1*s*. Total, £1 12*s*. 11½*d*.

Cost of the mill
In lengthening 2 spindles with iron bought and with the stipend of the smith 2*s*. 10*d*. In mending 1 mill-rind with iron for the same and with the stipend of the smith for the same 1*s*. 4*d*. In steeling, mending and sharpening bills for the year 2*s*. In 1 millstone bought for the said mill £1 18*s*. In carrying the same from Southampton to the mill 1*s*. In 2 iron bands made with iron bought for the same for hooping the head of the beam 8*d*. In casting 1 pole with brass bought for the same 4*s*. 7*d*. In 2 iron bands made with iron bought for the same and with the stipend of the smith for hooping the inner wheel 1*s*. 5*d*. Total, £2 11*s*. 10*d*.

Fish-trap (*hiltr*a)
In 1 lock bought for the same 10*d*. In 3 salmon caught by nets in the sea 1*s*. 8*d*. Total, 2*s*. 4*d*.

Water-pipe (*wymond'*)
In 5 lb of tin bought 1*s*. 1½*d*. In pitch, canvas and grease bought for the same 2*s*. 2*d*. In stipend of 1 man for 7 days mending the said water-pipe 2*s*. 4*d*., or 4*d*. a day. Total, 5*s*. 7½*d*.

1 MS 'per diet' vj d.' placed after the entry for nails.

2 MS 'ad ⟨hock'⟩ host''.

Expenses of the steward and wages of the bailiff
In expenses of the steward for his visits at 2 tourns by 2 tallies 5*s.* 7*d.* In wages of William, sergeant, for the year £3 10*d.* In 1 lb of wax bought for making candles for the chapel 5½*d.*, and this by order of Sir G*eoffrey*, treasurer of Wolvesey. In expenses of Roger Cosyn, bailiff of Bishops Waltham, for his visits 5*s.* Total, £3 11*s.* 10½*d.*

Total of all expenses, £17 5*s.* 2½*d.*

And he owes, £21 11*d.*

Allowances
In allowance of the reeve for building the arbour and the enclosure around the arbour at Bitterne by writ £6 6*s.* 3*d.* In allowance of the same for mending the kitchen which was ruinous, for all costs, £2 11*s.* 8*d.* Total of all allowances, £8 17*s.* 11*d.*

And thus he owes clear, £12 3*s.*

Issues of the grange

Wheat
{yield: two-fold plus 1 qr 4 bus.}
The same render account for 18½ qrs from the whole issue of wheat by struck measure.
Sown over 68 acres as they lie in Gildewyneslo*nd*', 9½ qrs 1 bus.; that is, 1 bus. an acre, plus 1 qr 1 bus. in all. In provision of the steward for his visits, 1 bus. Sold, 8 qrs 6 bus.

Curall
The same render account for 8 qrs ½ bus. from the whole issue of curall from the same wheat by struck measure.
Mixed with barley for the liveries of the manorial servants, 3 qrs 1 bus. In supporting pigs, 1 qr 1 bus. Sold, 1 qr 2 bus. Total, 5½ qrs. And 2½ qrs ½ bus. remain in the granary.

Rye
{yield: two-and-a-half-fold plus ½[1]}
The same render account for 3½ qrs from the whole issue of rye by struck measure.
Sown over 12 acres as they lie in Westbynne, 1 qr 6 bus.; that is, 1 bus. an acre, plus 2 bus. in all. Mixed with barley for the liveries of the manorial servants, 1 qr 6 bus. It balances.

Barley
{yield: two-and-a-half-fold plus 2 qrs}
The same render account for 39 qrs 1 bus. from the whole issue of barley by struck measure; 3 qrs 1 bus. received from curall and mixed with barley for the liveries of the manorial servants; 1 qr 6 bus. received from rye; 4 qrs 2 bus. received from peas; 1 qr 1 bus. received from vetches and mixed for the same. Total, 49 qrs 3 bus.
Sown over 75 acres as they lie in Bathardefeld', 14 qrs 2 bus.; that is, 1½ bus. an acre, less 1½ bus. in all. Delivered to 1 carter and 2 drovers for the year, 19½ qrs, taking a quarter every 8 weeks. Delivered to 1 cowherd for the year, 4 qrs 2 bus., taking a

1 MS omits measure.

quarter every 12 weeks. Delivered to 1 dairymaid for the year, 3 qrs 1 bus., taking a quarter every 16 weeks. Delivered to 1 shepherd for the year, 6½ qrs, taking a quarter every 8 weeks. In customary payment to 1 park-keeper, 1 qr. Delivered to 1 harrower at various times at both sowings, 6 bus. It balances.

Dredge
{yield: four-fold less ½ qr}
The same render account for 14½ qrs from the whole issue of dredge by struck measure.
Sown over 18 acres as they lie in Westbune, 2 qrs 5 bus.; that is, 1 bus. an acre, plus 3 bus. in all. Sold, 11 qrs 7 bus.

Oats
{yield: two-fold less 3 qrs 5 bus.}
The same render account for 20 qrs 3 bus. from the whole issue of oats by struck measure; 4 qrs 2 bus. bought. Total, 24 qrs 5 bus.
Sown over 57 acres as they lie in Pustukes and Bathardeslo*n*d', 14 qrs 2 bus.; that is, 2 bus. an acre. In provision of the steward for his visits, 4½ bus. In fodder of the clerk's horse for his visits, 1½ bus. In fodder of 2 cart-horses for the year, 7 qrs this year. In fodder of 2 plough-horses going to harrow at both sowings, 2 qrs 5 bus. this year, and this because the carts carried wood for fencing (*claustr'*) from the park to the curia for the enclosure by order of the lord. It balances.

Beans
The same render account for 4 bus. of beans bought. All sown in the garden.

Peas
{yield: six-fold}
The same render account for 7½ qrs from the whole issue of peas by struck measure.
Sown over 16 acres as they lie in Chapelecrofte, 2 qrs. Mixed with barley for the liveries of the manorial servants, 4 qrs 2 bus. Sold, 1 qr 2 bus.

Vetches
{yield: two-fold plus ½ qr}
The same render account for 3 qrs from the whole issue of vetches by struck measure.
Sown over 15 acres as they lie in Chare⌈l⌉scroft and Pollescroft, 1 qr 7 bus.; that is, 1 bus. an acre. Mixed with barley for the liveries of the manorial servants, 1 qr 1 bus.

Mill
Wheat: 1 qr 7 bus. from the whole issue of the mill; all sold.
Barley: 19½ qrs 2 bus. from the issue of the mill. Delivered to 1 miller, 6½ qrs. Delivered to 1 carter, nothing, because there was no carter there. In provision of the harvest, 1½ qrs. Sold, 11½ qrs 2 bus.
Coarse-ground corn: 2 qrs 1 bus. from the whole issue of the mill; all sold.
Malt: 4½ qrs 3 bus. from the whole issue of the mill; all sold.
Oatmeal: 1 bus. from the issue of the mill; all sold.

Stock

Cart-horses: 5 remain from the previous year; 1 in murrain; 2 sold; 2 remain.

Mares: 3 remain from the previous year; 1 sold; 2 remain.
Plough-horses: 1 remains from the previous year; 1 in murrain; none remain.
Colts: 1 aged 1½ years remains from the previous year; 1 male now aged 2½ years remains.
Foals: 1 aged ½ year remains from the previous year; 1 now 1½ years remains.
Also foals: 2 from the offspring of the mares this year; 2 now ½ year remain.
Oxen: 22 remain from the previous year; 1 bought. Total, 23. 1 in murrain; 22 remain.
Bulls: 1 remains from the previous year; 1 remains.
Cows: 10 remain from the previous year; 1 added from steers; 7 bought, 5 of them before calving. Total, 18. All remain.
Steers: 1 remains from the previous year's bullocks; 1 added to cows; none remain.
Bullocks: 5 remain from the previous year's yearlings; all remain, all of them male.
Yearlings: 5 remain from the previous year's calves; 2 in murrain; 3 males remain.
Calves: 15 from the offspring of the said cows this year because 1 was sterile. 1 in tithe; 1 in murrain; 6 sold. Total, 8. 7 remain, 5 of them male.

m.23d
Wethers: 277 remain from the previous year; 1 bought before shearing. Total, 278. 17 sold at Martinmas; 4 in murrain before shearing, 17 after shearing. Total, 38. 240 remain.
Sows: 1 remains from the previous year; 1 remains.
Pigs: 6 remain from the previous year; 4 sold; 2 remain, 1 of them a boar.
Hoggets: 1 remains from the previous year's piglets; 1 in murrain; none remain.
Piglets: 8 from the offspring of the said sow this year; 8 remain.
Hens: 195 from churchscot this year. 4 in quittance of 1 reeve; 4 in default of the land of Vyel; 2 in default of the land of Gunilda le Gardenir because a widow; 2 in default of the land of Agnes Hevedma*n* because a widow; 2 in default of the land of Lucy le Whyte because a widow; 2 in default of the land of Herbert Hevedma*n* because he has no wife; 2 in default of the land of le Prute because a widower; 2 in default of the land of Augustine Seman because a widower; 2 in default of the land of Walter Schiphurd' because a widower; 2 in default of the land of Walter le Havekar' because a widower; 2 in default of Roger Westsyd' because a widower; 2 in default of the land of Michael le Crokker' because he has no wife; 2 in default of the land of Cukk' because a widower; 2 in default of the land of Wysdon because a widower; 2 in default of the land of John Ace because he has no wife; 2 in default of the land of William le Prute because he has no wife; 2 in default of the land of Richard Edrad because a widower; 2 in default of the land of Roger ate Clyve because a widower. Total, 40. 155 sold.
Coarse wool {yield of fleece 3½*d*. less 1*s*. 8*d*. in all}: 257 fleeces produced at the shearing of wethers this year; 26 in tithe; 231 sent to Wolvesey, which made 1 wey 8 cloves.
Hides: 1 from a cart-horse, 1 from a plough-horse, 1 from an ox, 2 from yearlings; all sold.
Woolskins: 4 from wethers in murrain before shearing; all sold.
Bare skins: 17 from wethers in murrain after shearing; all sold.
Winter cheese: 33 made; all sold.
Summer cheese {yield of cow 3*s*., because 7 cows bought at the feast of St Barnabas (11 June) were accounted as 4}: 137 cheeses made between Monday before the feast of St Dunstan (14 May) and Michaelmas (29 September), both days included; 13 in tithe; 124 sold, which made 4 weys 7 cloves.

Butter: 6 cloves made this year; all sold.
Salmon: 55 from the fish-trap (*hiltra'*) this year; 2 sent to the queen when she was in Winchester about the Invention of the Cross (3 May); 53 sold, 19 of them before Easter.
Utensils: 2 brass pots with 1 posnet, 2 ewers with 2 basins, 2 pans, 2 tubs and 1 tine remain from the previous year; all this remains.
Carts: 2 carts with iron tyres and one wain with equipment remain from the previous year; they remain, of which 1 cart is worn out.
Pavymor': 5*s*. from Pavymor; all delivered to Sir G*eoffrey*, treasurer of Wolvesey, by 1 tally, and he is quit.
Slates: 17,000 remain from the previous year; all used.
Cider: 6 casks made this year; they remain.

Bishops Waltham

Arrears
Robert de Froyl*e*, bailiff, and Robert Stretthe, reeve, render account for £71 18*s*. 3½*d*. of arrears from the previous year. All delivered to Sir G*eoffrey*, treasurer of Wolvesey, by 1 tally, and they are quit.

Rents
The same render account for £14 10*s*. 10¾*d*. for all rents of assize at Christmas; £23 8¾*d*. at Easter (22 April); £14 10*s*. 10½*d*. at the Nativity of St John the Baptist (24 June); £23 19*s*. 3½*d*. at Michaelmas (29 September). Total, £76 1*s*. 9½*d*.

Quittances
In quittance of 1 reeve for the year 5*s*.; 1 beadle for the year 5*s*.; 1 swineherd, 1 smith, 1 hayward who kept the lord's corn and pasture and sowed the wheat and barley, 1 shepherd of wethers, and 1 keeper of ewes, 10*s*., or 2*s*. each; 4 ploughmen for the year, and 1 ploughman for 1 term, 8*s*. 6*d*.; 9 workers, each of whom are bound to reap everyday at harvest-time 1 acre as it lies and after the harvest are bound to work twice a week, 18*s*., or 2*s*. each; 3 cottars for the year, each of whom are bound to reap everyday ½ acre as it lies and after the harvest are bound to work once a week, 3*s*.; 2 workers who are bound to reap everyday at harvest-time 1 acre as it lies and after the harvest are bound to work twice a week with their carts, working at the lord's pleasure, besides carrying dung, 6*s*. for the year; 1 granary-keeper for the year 2*s*. Total, £2 17*s*. 6*d*.

Defaults of rent
In default of the land between the barton and garden drawn into demesne, £1 2*s*. 8*d*. for the year; the land of Osbert de Langely, 8*d*. for the year; the land of Richard Baton, 6*d*. for the year; the land of Hugh son of Agnes, 6*d*. for the year; the land of Richard Swanem*ere*, 3*d*. for the year; the land of the mill drawn into the park, 6*s*. 5*d*. for the year; the rent of Peter Cl*ericus*, 1*s*. 6*d*. for the year. Total, £1 12*s*. 6*d*.

Total of quittances and defaults of rent, £4 10*s*.

Total of rents remaining, £71 11*s*. 9½*d*.

Farm of the mills
The same render account for 12*s*. for the farm of the mill of Caldekot' for the year; 10*s*. for the farm of the mill of Mattokeford'; 8*s*. for the farm of the mill of Frogg' for the year; £1 for the farm of the fulling mill for the year. Total, £2 10*s*.

Cumin

The same render account for 1 lb of cumin from Peter Cl*ericus* for a certain messuage; 1 lb from John Sunebur*n* and Thomas Canon for the same; 1 lb from Robert Fab*er* to have 1 plot beside the fishpond; 1 lb from William Burg' for the same; 1 lb from Robert Ude for the same; 1 lb from Richard Doggecherl for the same. Total, 6 lbs. All delivered to Wolvesey.

Pepper

The same render account for ½ lb of pepper from Roger Ev*er*ard for certain land which his father bought from Henry Philipp'. All delivered to Wolvesey.

Annual recognizance

The same render account for 6*d*. from Adam de M*ar*well' for annual recognizance; 6*d*. from Geoffrey le Ware*r*nyr for the same; 6*d*. from Richard de Derly, clerk,[1] whilst he wishes to remain outside the manor; 6*d*. from John Pyk for annual recognizance; 6*d*. from Geoffrey de Eccl*esia* for the same; 6*d*. from Henry Wldred' for not being in a tithing; 3*d*. from John, son of Robert Marescal, for annual recognizance; 3*d*. from John Gyles for no longer being prosecuted by the tithing; 3*d*. from John Smermongar' for the same; 6*d*. from William de Bottely for no longer being prosecuted for tithingpenny, but he will come to court for the two law-days only, and this during the lord's pleasure; 3*d*. from Henry Burd*en* for annual recognizance. Total, 4*s*. 6*d*.

Issues of the manor

The same render account for £2 12*s*. 7*d*. from pannage of pigs within this year; nothing from foreign pannage of pigs this year; £5 3*s*. 2*d*. from pannage of pigs in the park this year; £5 15*s*. 6*d*. from the agistment of livestock in the park, as made clear in the details; 8*s*. from 1 old plough-horse sold; 3*s*. 4*d*. from 1 feeble plough-horse from the heriot of John Schore sold; £2 16*s*. from 6 old oxen sold, at 8*s*. for 1, 9*s*. each for 2, and 10*s*. each for 3; £1 16*s*. from 6 feeble cows sold, at 6*s*. each; 6*s*. from 6 late-born calves sold, at 1*s*. each; 7*s*. from 7 old wethers sold at Martinmas; 5*s*. 10*d*. from 7 old ewes sold at the same feast; 13*s*. from 26 hoggs sold, at 6*d*. each; 4*s*. from 12 feeble lambs sold, at 4*d*. each; 1*s*. from the flesh sold of 1 boar which suddenly died; 12*s*. 6*d*. from 5 pigs sold, at 2*s*. 6*d*. each; 6*d*. from the heriot of William Edmu*nd* because he did not have 1 beast; 6*d*. from the heriot of William Fab*er* of Bursledon for the same; 6*d*. from the heriot of Juliana Brond' for the same; 6*d*. from the heriot of John ate Fryrth' for the same; 1*s*. from the heriot of Walter Oxenh*erd*' for the same; 4*s*. from the hide and flesh sold of 1 ox dead from murrain in March; 2*s*. 8*d*. from the hide sold of 1 ox dead from murrain in April; 1*s*. 9*d*. from the hide of 1 cow dead from murrain in the same month; 8*d*. from the hides of 2 steers dead from murrain; 9*d*. from the hides of 3 bullocks in murrain; 10*d*. from the hides sold of 4 yearlings dead from murrain; 2*d*. from the hide sold of 1 calf in murrain; 10*s*. 1*d*. from the skins sold of 18 wethers, 31 ewes and 5 hoggs in murrain before shearing, at 3*d*. a skin of wethers, 2*d*. a skin of ewes, and 1*d*. a skin of hoggs; 1*s*. 2*d*. from the skins sold of 11 wethers and 3 ewes in murrain after shearing, at 1*d*. each; 1*s*. 4*d*. from the skins sold of 16 lambs in murrain before weaning, at 1*d*. a skin; 1½*d*. from the skins sold of 3 rotted sheep; nothing from coarse wool here because it is sent to Wolvesey; 5*s*. 3*d*. from 6 cloves of wool locks sold, at 10½*d*. a clove; 4*s*. 3*d*. from ½ wey of winter cheese sold; £4 13*s*. 6*d*. from 11 weys of cheese made in summer sold,

1 MS 'Ric*ardo* de ⌈d⌉ ⟨b*er*ly cl*er*ico⟩ Derly cl*er*ico'.

at 8*s*. 6*d*. a wey; 6*s*. 10½*d*. from 22 cloves of butter sold, at 3¾*d*. a clove; £1 18*s*. from the men of Bursledon for 76 sesters of salt sold, at 6*d*. a sester; £1 16*s*. 6*d*. from 73 sesters of salt from rents sold this year; £7 6*s*. 3*d*. from 292½ sesters of salt from the arrears of the last account; 12*s*. 10*d*. from 154 hens from churchscot sold; 9*s*. from the hundred for the mowing of Cribelescrofte; 6*s*. 4*d*. from the pasturage sold in various places, that is, 5*s*. from la Worth' and 1*s*. 4*d*. from various remnants around Orkelestret; 1*s*. 6*d*. from the hundred for the mowing of the meadow of Bitterne; 6*s*. 8*d*. from heath in the park sold this year; nothing from nuts collected in the park this year; 10*s*. 6*d*. from the loppings of oaks felled to mend the palisade; 5*s*. from cablish in the park sold this year; 2*s*. 2*d*. from 2 dead trees sold felled in le Hordareswod' for the bees; nothing from dead trees in the wood of P*ar*khurst this year; nothing from wood in Holemor' this year; 1*s*. 3*d*. from honey sold this year; 3*s*. from plough-services sold this year; nothing from the bee-hives (*meller'*) this year; 1*s*. 8*d*. from Richard Ywon for release from his labour service for a third of 1 virgate of land this year; 4*s*. from Adam de Yulley and Robert de Yulley for the same; nothing from Robert de Wodecote because he worked; 3*s*. 4*d*. from Robert de la Bech for the same; 2*s*. 8*d*. from John son of Azonis for the same; 1*s*. 8*d*. from John, son of Robert Cl*ericus* of Upham, for the land of Bance; 2*s*. from Walter Bues for release from the labour service for the land of Suuenel'; 1*s*. from Mark de Yully for the same for the land of Godderehele; 1*s*. from Guy ate Ford' for the same for the land of Godderehele; 1*s*. from Thomas Sauser for the same; 3*s*. from Peter le P*ar*ker for the same for the land which formerly belonged to Adam Prest; 2*s*. from John ate Broke for the same for the land which belonged to William ate Wll'; 9*s*. from John Bance for the labour service of the land which belonged to Richard Bance; nothing from Thomas Cangeler and William le Byke this year because they worked; 13*s*. from Margery Moysaut, Robert Fab*er*, William Chubb', Adam Thoremond, William Pyk, Richard Ev*er*ard', William Bos, William Cantoy, Richard Boll', William Asser, John de Anne, Robert le Cup*ere* and Richard Mol*endinarius* for the same, at 1*s*. each; 1*s*. 6*d*. from Hugh Balhorn for the same; 4*s*. from William Hudayn for the same; nothing from Walter Bues for the land which belonged to Danyl because he worked; 5*s*. from Alice Ram for the same; 1*s*. from Richard Ywon for release from the labour service for the land of le Capon this year; 2*s*. from John Waremo*nd* for the same; 2*s*. from Henry le Whyte for the land which belonged to Wrench'; 3*s*. from Henry de Porcestr' for the same for the land of Dulch; 2*s*. 6*d*. from John Rygou and Gilbert Frogg' for the same; 2*s*. from Henry de Porcestr' for the same; 1*s*. 8*d*. from John Chop' for the same; 4*s*. from Richard Jacob for the same for the land at la Pund'; 4*s*. from Henry Lypse for the same; 6*s*. 8*d*. from Matilda ate Forde for release from her labour service at harvest-time; 3*s*. from Thomas ate Ford' for the same; £4 11*s*. from the labour services of 7 carters sold this year, at 13*s*. 4*d*. a carter; nothing from small labour services before and during harvest-time this year because they were worked; £4 16*s*. 10½*d*. from the hundred for release from the labour service for the demesne lands leased for rent, because so many more were accustomed to work, and because 3*s*. 2½*d*. are subtracted for the lands which Richard Wodeloc and John Ev*er*ard hold who are now affirmed free by charter of the lord, that is, for the land of la Fryth' which John Ev*er*ard holds and the land of Cotehull' which Richard Wodoloc holds; £1 5*s*. from oaks felled in the park for killing foxes; 16*s*. 8*d*. from 50 acres of land on Almesholte let at farm this year, at 4*d*. an acre; 5*d*. from the tails and feathers of 2 peacocks; 3*s*. 5½*d*. from dairy produce sold at the audit; £19 7*s*. 7*d*. from 50 yearlings bought and agisted in the park the previous year and afterwards sold. Total, £77 8*s*. 1*d*.

Sale of corn

The same render account for £22 15*s*. 8½*d*. from 73½ qrs of wheat sold, at 5*s*. a qr for 7½ qrs 1 bus., 5*s*. 4*d*. a qr for 6½ qrs, 6*s*. a qr for 19 qrs 3 bus., and 6*s*. 8*d*. a qr for 40 qrs.; 17*s*. 5¾*d*. from 8 qrs ½ bus. of curall sold, at 2*s*. a qr for 4 qrs, and 2*s*. 4*d*. a qr for 4 qrs ½ bus.; £1 1*s*. 3*d*. from 5 qrs 2½ bus. of barley sold, at 4*s*. a qr; £6 13*s*. 10*d*. from 58½ qrs 3 bus. of oats sold, at 2*s*. a qr for 31 qrs, 2*s*. 4*d*. a qr for 7½ qrs, and 2*s*. 8*d*. a qr for 20 qrs 3 bus.; 8*d*. from 2 bus. of peas sold; 4*s*. 3*d*. from 2 qrs 1 bus. of vetches sold, at 2*s*. a qr. Total, £31 13*s*. 2¼*d*.

[East mill]

The same render account for 7*s*. 7*d*. from 1 qr 3 bus. of wheat sold, at 5*s*. 4*d*. for 1 qr, and 9*d*. a bus. for 3 bus.; £3 3*s*. 6*d*. from 18 qrs 1 bus. of maslin sold, at 3*s*. 4*d*. a qr for 7 qrs, and 4*s*. a qr for 8 qrs 1 bus. Total, £3 11*s*. 1*d*.

[Mill outside the gate]

The same render account for 6*s*. 3*d*. from 1 qr 1 bus. of wheat sold, at 7*d*. for 1 bus., 8*d*. a bus. for 4 bus., and 9*d*. a bus. for 3 bus.; 9*s*. 2⌈½⌉*d*. from 2 qrs 5 bus. of maslin sold, at 4½*d*. a bus. for 5 bus., 3*s*. 4*d*. for 1 qr, and 4*s*. for 1 qr; £1 12*s*. 4*d*. from 5 qrs 5½ bus. of coarse-ground corn sold, at 5*s*. 4*d*. a qr for 2 qrs 5½ bus., and 6*s*. a qr for 3 qrs; £1 13*s*. 8*d*. from 13½ qrs of malt sold, at 2*s*. 4*d*. a qr for 5 qrs, 2*s*. 6*d*. a qr for 4 qrs, and 2*s*. 8*d*. a qr for 4½ qrs; 6*s*. 8*d*. from 1 qr of oatmeal sold. Total, £4 8*s*. 1½*d*.

Total of both, £7 19*s*. 2½*d*.

[Entry and] marriage fines

The same render account for 10*s*. from the 2 tithings of Bishops Waltham for tithingpenny at the hundred-court of Martinmas (11 November); 4*s*. from the tithing of Mensingefeld' for the same; 4*s*. from the tithing of Bursledon for the same; 1*s*. 6*d*. from the tithing of Hou for the same; 4*s*. from the tithing of Wa*n*gefeld' for the same; 3*s*. from the tithing of Durley for the same; 2*s*. 6*d*. from the tithing of Wynt*er*shll' for the same; 3*s*. from the tithing of Upham for the same; 3*s*. from the tithing of Wodekot' for the same; 3*s*. from the tithing of Ashton for the same; £1 18*s*. from the same tithings for tithingpenny at the hundred-court of Hockday (1 May); 6*s*. 8*d*. from Mork to have a third of ½ virgate of land which belonged to Agnes his mother; 2*s*. from Robert ate Fryth' to have 2 day-works (*daywrk'*) of land by surrender of the said le Cok*ery*, to build and live on the said holding; 13*s*. 4*d*. from Adam ate Brok to have Laura, who was wife of Roger ate Wynd', with her land; 2*s*. from Alice, relict of John le Duk', to retain 1 ferling of land which belonged to her husband; 1*s*. from Agnes, who was wife of John Shope, to retain 1 cottage and 1 curtilage which belonged to her husband; £9 from Richard Ev*er*ard' to have 1 ferling of land by surrender of Walter Ude; 2*s*. from Alice, relict of Henry Wygayn, to retain 1 cottage and 1 curtilage which belonged to her husband; 6*s*. 8*d*. from Isabel, who was wife of Henry le French', to retain ½ virgate of land which belonged to her husband; 4*s*. from Matilda, relict of Richard Moysent, to retain 1 ferling of land and 2 messuages which belonged to her husband; 6*s*. 8*d*. from Juliana, relict of Richard Boll', to retain 2 messuages 2 acres of land which belonged to her husband; 5*s*. from William Cop*er*ych' to have Joan Walot with 1 messuage and 1 curtilage; 1*s*. from Sibyl, who was wife of Roger Cutel, to retain 1 ferling of land which belonged to her husband; 2*s*. from Henry le Whyte to have 4 acres of purpresture by surrender of Robert Wydecok in la Lygh'; 1*s*. from Lucy, relict of William Edmo*nd*, to retain 1 cottage which belonged to her husband; 2*s*. from Roger, son of William Fab*e*r of Bursledon, to have ½ ferling of land which belonged to his father; 1*s*. from Richard de Farnh*a*m to have 1 messuage with 1 curtilage by surrender of John Bor; 13*s*. 4*d*. from Alexander Brony*ng*' to have ½ ferling of land by surrender of Juliana Bro*n*d; £1 6*s*. 8*d*. from Adam ate Hull' to have 1 messuage ½ virgate of land which belonged to his father; £1 from John le Bor to have ½ ferling of land by surrender of Henry ate Aysse; £1 from Alice, relict of Roginald de Porteslad', to retain 1 messuage and ½ ferling of land and various purprestures which belonged to her husband; £5 from Richard Ywon to have 1 messuage and a third of 1 virgate of land which belonged to Martin de Yulley, father of Margaret, wife of the aforesaid Richard, whose heir she is; 2*s*. from Henry Walewayn for marrying Christina his daughter outside; 2*s*. from Matilda, relict of John ate Fryth', to retain 1 messuage and 1 acre of land which belonged to her husband; 2*s*. from Joan, daughter of Hugh Fab*e*r, to have 1 messuage and 1 curtilage by surrender of Hugh her father; 2*s*. from William Walays to have 1 curtilage by surrender of Hugh Fab*e*r; 3*s*. from Henry Wat*er*boks to have 1 messuage 1 curtilage by surrender of Walter Oxenherde. Total, £25 3*s*. 4*d*.

m.24

Perquisites

The same render account for 3*s*. from Thomas de Bogestok for keeping the lord's wethers badly; £2 from Adam le Palm*ere* because convicted of transgression of labour service; £1 from Adam Austyn, bartoner, for the same; 2*s*. from the Prior of Hamble for licence to agree; 6*s*. 8*d*. from Richard Ude for false complaint against Richard Ev*er*ard; 2*s*. from Geoffrey Frogge because he obstructed a former path to the nuisance of his neighbours; 2*s*. from the tithing of Bishops Waltham for concealment; 2*s*. from Thomas ate Ford' for breaking the assize of ale; 2*s*. from Robert ate Berch' for the assize of bread; 2*s*. from Joan, relict of Robert Cl*e*ric*us* of Upham, because she is not proceeding against Robert ate Bech'; 2*s*. from Guy ate Ford' to have an inquest; 2*s*. from Geoffrey Forc' for transgression against Thomas Banʒ; 6*s*. 8*d*. from Geoffrey Byk' and others because they refused to make a contribution towards the hundred shillings which the hundred paid annually; 6*s*. 8*d*. from the tithing of Wynt*e*shull' because of false presentment; 2*s*. from the tithing of Wodekote for concealment; 2*s*. from Robert Marescall' for trespass done to pasture in wardship; £7 10*s*. 9*d*. from various men for various transgressions; £1 from Richard le Wyte and John Boefs, park-keepers, for selling wood, which they did for their own use. Total, £13 13*s*. 9*d*.

Total of both, £38 17*s*. 1*d*.

Total of all receipts, £230 3*s*. 10¼*d*.

Cost of ploughs

In iron and steel bought for 4 ploughs for the year and 1 plough for ½ year 9*s*. 10*d*. In 4 ploughs made anew 8*d*. In 4 pairs of wheels bought for ploughs 1*s*. 4*d*. In fitting ploughs with iron tyres 5½*d*. In 4 ploughshares bought 3*s*. In 5 plough feet bought 2*s*. 6*d*. In 1 coulter bought for ploughs 1*s*. 4*d*. In 3 halters of hemp bought for the plough-horses 1½*d*. In mending old ploughs 4*d*. In shoeing 4 plough-horses for the year 3*s*., because in between times {when} they were not ploughing they carried the dung. In boon-works of 48 ploughmen from within the hundred 4*s*., and each ploughman will plough 2 acres as they lie. Moreover, within the hundred they are bound to plough 52 acres as they lie for 'landrigh*t*' without the cost of the lord. In winter boon-works of 23 ploughmen from Droxford this year 1*s*. 11*d*., or 1*d*. a ploughman, and each ploughman will plough 2 acres as they lie. In Lenten boon-works of 48 ploughmen from within the hundred 4*s*., or 1*d*. a ploughman, and each ploughman will plough 1 acre as it lies. In stipend of 4 ploughmen for 8 Saturday ploughings at the time of the winter sowing, 11 Saturdays at the summer sowing, and 10 Saturdays at the fallowing, with the stipend of 1 ploughman for 8 Saturday ploughings at the sowing of the barley, 13*s*. 10*d*., or 1½*d*. each when ploughing for sowing, and 1*d*. when fallowing. In stipend of 4 drovers for the year and 1 drover for ½ year 13*s*. 6*d*., or 3*s*. each. In 1 plough-horse bought 9*s*. 6*d*. In 9 oxen bought £5 8*d*., at 9*s*. 6*d*. for 1, 10*s*. 1*d*. each for 2, 11*s*. 6*d*. each for 2, and 12*s*. each for 4. In 4 bus. of peas bought for sowing 1*s*. 4*d*. In 3 qrs 2 bus. of vetches bought 5*s*. 5*d*., at 1*s*. 8*d*. a qr. In forage bought to support the lord's stock £1 4*s*. Total, £10 1*s*. 5*d*.

Cost of carts

In 1 new cart with iron tyres with all equipment bought 14*s*. In mending the old cart 1 ½*d*. In clouts, nails and grease bought 1*s*. 10*d*. In fitting the carts with axles at various times with axles bought for the same 6¼*d*. In 1 cart-rail made anew for the cart 3*d*. In 1 pair of traces bought 5½*d*. In 3 collars and 1 pair of saddle-pads bought 2*s*. 4*d*. In a hemp rope bought 11*d*. In white leather bought 4*d*. In 2 pairs of swingletrees 2*d*. In 1 saddle for the same 2½*d*. In 1 thill-rope (*tilropt'*) bought 1¼*d*. In hooping wooden frets to the hubs of the old cart 2*d*. In forage for 2 cart-horses for the year 3*s*. In stipend of 1 carter for the year 3*s*. In stipend of 1 carter leading the other cart to the dung for ½ year 1*s*. 6*d*., because for the other ½ year he held the horse-plough. Total, £1 9*s*.

Cost of the dairy

In woollen and linen cloth bought for the dairy 8½*d*. In a press bought for the same 6*d*. In 7 bus. of salt bought 10½*d*. In 2 buckets and 1 tub bought anew for the same 9*d*. In earthenware pots and pans 4*d*. In grease bought for greasing sheep 11*s*. 4*d*. In 10 ells of canvas bought for packing wool 2*s*. 11*d*., at 3½*d*. an ell. In castrating 9 piglets 3*d*. In wattling anew the sheepcote at Langeheg' 2*s*. 6*d*. In re-roofing in places the said sheepcote which had been unroofed 3*s*. In roofing in places the sheepcote at Legsted' 6*d*. In 8 cows bought after calving £3 13*s*. 6*d*., at 8*s*. 10*d*. each for 3, 9*s*. 4*d*. each for 3, and 9*s*. 6*d*. each for 2. In a tripod bought 8*d*. In stipend of 1 cowherd for the year 3*s*. In stipend of 1 dairymaid for the year 2*s*. Total, £5 2*s*. 10*d*.

Cost of buildings at Berth'

In re-roofing the barn in places 4*s*. 10*d*. In mending the gate of the same 3*d*. In fencing for the enclosure 3½*d*. Total, 5*s*. 4½*d*.

Cost of buildings in the curia

In rebuilding anew the great barn which had partly collapsed through rotten timber with a carpenter to do this and laths made for the same 14*s*. 8*d*. In large nails to fasten the rafters of the barn 3*d*. In 10,000 nails bought for laths 6*s*. 8*d*. In 15,000 large slates bought for the said barn £1, at 1*s*. 4*d*. a 1,000. In pegs bought for the same 1*s*. 3*d*. In re-roofing the said part of the barn anew and roofing the whole of the barn in places 18*s*. 1*d*. In 13 qrs of lime bought for the same 6*s*. 6*d*. In sand bought 4*d*. In re-roofing the granary in places and the gate inside and re-roofing the great stable in places 1*s*. 11*d*. In 3,000 large slates bought for the same 4*s*. In 2 qrs of lime bought for the same 1*s*. In nails bought for laths 3½*d*. In mending the stable outside the gate with a carpenter for the same 1*s*. 10*d*. In re-roofing the said stable with straw in places 1*s*. 6½*d*. In mending the palisade around the curia in parts 2*s*. In 54 qrs[1] of charcoal made and sent to Wolvesey 6*s*. 9*d*., at 1½*d*. a qr. Total, £4 7*s*. 1*d*.

Cost of the park
In making the palisade of the park anew in places and mending it elsewhere £1 8*s*. 10*d*. Total, £1 8*s*. 10*d*.

Threshing
Nothing for the threshing of peas and vetches because they were threshed by labour service. In 2 sacks bought 1*s*. 1*d*. In 1 basket for corn bought 3*d*. Total, 1*s*. 4*d*.

Hay harvest (*Autumpn'*)
In mowing the meadow of Bitterne according to custom 1*s*. In tossing the hay of the same 1*s*. 6*d*. In mowing the new meadow 2*s*. 6*d*. In tossing the hay 4*d*. In mowing Ballesmed 1*s*. 6*d*. In tossing the hay 2*d*. In mowing the meadow of la M*ere* 1*s*. Total, 8*s*.

Corn harvest (*Autumpn'*)
In bread bought for 347 men at two harvest boon-works 14*s*. 5½*d*., and each has bread worth ½*d*. In 1,041 herrings bought for the same 6*s*. 1*d*., at 8*d*. a hundred, and each has 3 herrings. In bread bought for the great boon-work of 228 men 9*s*. 6*d*., and they have as before. In meat bought for the same 9*s*. 6*d*. In meat bought for the same 6*s*. 10*d*. And they do 1 boon-work at their own cost without food and drink. In mowing 14 acres of vetches 4*s*. 8*d*., at 4*d*. an acre. Total, £2 11*s*. ½*d*.

Cost of mills
In iron bought for mending and lengthening the spindle of the mill outside the gate 5*d*. In steel bought for the bills of both mills 5*d*. In making anew the outer wheel and trough of the east mill 2*s*. 6*d*. In timber sawn for the same 2*s*. 6*d*. In nails bought for the same 8½*d*. In mending the sluice beside the east mill with the digging of earth and carrying of turf for the same and making stakes for the same 3*s*. 4*d*. Total, 9*s*. 9½*d*.

Expenses of the steward
In expenses of the steward for his visits at 2 tourns by 2 tallies £1 2*s*. 11*d*. In expenses of Roger, bailiff from Michaelmas until Christmas, £1 12*s*. 1*d*. In fur bought for the same bailiff 3*s*. In expenses of Robert, bailiff and clerk, for his visits from Christmas until the following Michaelmas £2. In 1 fur bought for the summer livery of Robert the bailiff 3*s*. Total, £5 1*s*.

Wages of the door-keeper
In wages of the door-keeper for the year £1 10*s*. 5*d*. Total, £1 10*s*. 5*d*.

Purchase of stock
In 50 yearlings bought and agisted in the park the previous year, because their sale is answered for in this roll, £17 18*s*. 2¼*d*. Total, £17 18*s*. 2¼*d*.

Foreign expenses
In allowance of the reeve for 80 perches of ditch around the new meadow in the park 10*s*., at 1½*d*. a perch. In obstructing the watercourse so that it does not flow beyond

1 MS omits 'qrs'.

the said meadow 3*s*. 6*d*. In enclosing the said meadow 2*s*. In seedlings collected for the same ditch 1*s*. 8*d*. In 70 perches of new ditch around a certain purpresture beside the cowshed for nurturing calves 8*s*. 9*d*., at 1½*d*. a perch. In seedlings collected for the same 1*s*. 4*d*. In enclosing the said ditch 1*s*. 11*d*. In a sluice for the small fishpond and a new trough for the same with a carpenter for the same 8*s*. In men hired by the day to dig the foundations of the said sluice, dig and carry earth and turfs, and make and put in stakes for the same, 13*s*. In large nails bought for the same 8*d*. In hooping 1 cask of wine 3*d*. In oaks felled and a ditch made for killing foxes by order of the lord £1 3*s*. 8*d*. Total, £3 14*s*. 9*d*.

Total of all expenses, £54 9*s*. ¾*d*.

And he owes, £175 14*s*. 9½*d*.

Cash deliveries
Delivered to Sir G*eoffrey*, treasurer of Wolvesey, by 1 tally, £116 3*s*. 2*d*.

And thus he owes clear, £59 11*s*. 7½*d*.

Issues of the grange

Wheat
{yield: three-fold plus 5 qrs 1½ bus.}
The same render account for 131½ qrs from the whole issue of wheat by struck measure; 6 bus. from churchscot. Total, 132 qrs 2 bus.
Sown over 453 acres as they lie in Rouerigg', la Mere and la Woth', 47 qrs 1 bus.; that is, 5 bus. over 6 acres, less ½ bus. in all. In provision of the steward for his visits by 2 tallies, 1 qr. In provision of Roger, bailiff from Michaelmas until Christmas, 4½ qrs. In provision of Robert the bailiff for his visits from Christmas until Michaelmas, 4 qrs. Delivered to 1 hayward from the Circumcision (1 January) until Lammas (1 August), for 30 weeks, and from the Decollation of St John (29 August) until Michaelmas (29 September), for 4 weeks, 2 qrs 1 bus., because he takes the rest in barley; he takes a quarter every 8 weeks and in between times sits at table. Sold, 73 qrs 4 bus. It balances.

Curall
The same render account for 9 qrs 3½ bus. from the whole issue of curall by struck measure.
Mixed with barley for the liveries of the manorial servants, 1 qr 3 bus. Sold, 8 qrs ½ bus. It balances.

Barley
{yield: four-fold less 4 qrs 5 bus.}
The same render account for 77 qrs 3 bus. from the whole issue of barley by struck measure; 1 qr 3 bus. received above from curall; 1 qr 1 bus. received below from peas; 2 qrs 1 bus. received from vetches. Total, 82 qrs.
Sown over 98 acres as they lie on both sides of la Longehegg' and in Crikelescrofte, 20 qrs; that is, 3 bus. 1 peck an acre, plus ½ bus. 1 peck in all. Delivered to 4 drovers for the year, 26 qrs, taking a quarter every 8 weeks. Delivered to 1 carter for the year, 6½ qrs, who takes as before. Delivered to 1 drover who drove the horse-plough for ½ year and the other cart for the other ½ year, 6½ qrs, and he takes as before. Delivered

to 1 cowherd for the year, 4 qrs 2½ bus., taking a quarter every 12 weeks. Delivered to 1 dairymaid for the year, 5 qrs 1½ bus., taking a quarter every 10 weeks. **{Henceforth the dairymaid should take nothing except a quarter every 12 weeks; also hereafter the dairymaid should answer for the offspring of geese and hens}** In corrody of 1 swineherd and 1 shepherd with the ewes, 4 qrs. In corrody of 1 keeper of lambs for ½ year, 1 qr. Delivered to the same for the other ½ year because he kept the lambs of Bishops Waltham and Droxford, 2 qrs, taking a quarter every 13 weeks. Delivered to 1 hayward from the Circumcision until Lammas, for 30 weeks, and from the Decollation of St John the Baptist until Michaelmas, for 4 weeks, 2 qrs 1 bus., because he takes the rest in wheat; he takes a quarter every 8 weeks and in between times at harvest-time he sits at table. Sold, 5 qrs 2½ bus. Sold at the audit, ½ bus. It balances.

Oats
{yield: two-fold plus 5 qrs ½ bus.}
The same render account for 180 qrs ½ bus. from the whole issue of oats by struck measure; 25 qrs by estimation in sheaves. Total, 205 qrs ½ bus.
Sown over 405 acres as they lie at Langehegg', Hok', Crikelescrofte and at Legsted', 88½ qrs ½ bus.; that is, 1 bus. 1 peck an acre, plus 1 peck in all. In fodder of 2 cart-horses for the year, 15½ qrs. In fodder of the plough-horses at sowing time, 5½ qrs. In fodder of the steward's horses for his visits by 2 tallies, 2 qrs 2 bus. In fodder of the horses of Roger, bailiff from Michaelmas until Christmas, 4 qrs. In fodder of the horses of Robert, bailiff and clerk, for his visits from Christmas until Michaelmas, 5 qrs 2½ bus. In supporting oxen by estimation in sheaves, 25 qrs. Sold, 58½ qrs 3 bus. It balances.

Peas
{yield: three-fold plus 2½ bus.}
The same render account for 3 qrs 2½ bus. from the whole issue of peas; 4 bus. bought. Total, 3½ qrs 2½ bus.
Sown over 20 acres as they lie in la Worth', 2 qrs 3½ bus.; that is, 1 bus. an acre, less ½ bus. in all. Mixed with barley for the liveries of the manorial servants, 1 qr 1 bus. Sold, 2 bus. It balances.

Vetches
{yield: three-and-a-half-fold plus 1 bus.}
The same render account for 8 qrs from the whole issue of vetches by struck measure; 3 qrs 2 bus. bought. Total, 11 qrs 2 bus.
Sown over 59 acres as they lie in la Worth' and beside T*ri*boddestret', 5½ qrs; that is, ½ bus. and 1 peck an acre, less 1 peck in all. Mixed above with barley, 2 qrs 1 bus. In supporting pigs, 1½ qrs. Sold, 2 qrs 1 bus. It balances.

Issues of the mills
Wheat: 1 qr 3 bus. from the whole issue of the east mill; all sold.
Maslin: 18 qrs 1 bus. from the whole issue of the same mill; all sold.

Mill outside the gate
Wheat: 1 qr 1 bus. from the whole issue of the mill; all sold.
Maslin: 2½ qrs 1 bus. from the whole issue of the mill; all sold.
Coarse-ground corn: 5½ qrs 1½ bus. from the issue of the mill; all sold.

Malt: 13½ qrs from the issue of the mill; all sold.
Oatmeal:[1] 1 qr of oatmeal (*gruell'*) from the issue of the mill; all sold.

Stock

Cart-horses: 2 remain from the previous year; 2 remain.
Plough-horses: 3 remain from the previous year; 1 from the heriot of John Thore; 1 from the heriot of Roginald de Porteslad'; 1 bought. Total, 6. 2 sold; 4 remain.
Oxen: 48 remain from the previous year; 3 additions; 1 from the heriot of Henry Frth'; 1 from the heriot of Martin de Yully; 9 bought. Total, 62. 2 in murrain; 6 sold. Total, 8. 54 remain.
Bulls: 1 remains from the previous year; 1 remains.
Cows: 27 remain from the previous year; 8 additions; 1[2] from the heriot of Agnes ate Frith' before calving; 1 from the heriot of Richard Moys*en*t before calving; 1 from the heriot of Richard Boll' before calving; 1 from the heriot of Adam ate Hull' before calving; 8 bought after calving about the feast of St John the Baptist (24 June). Total, 47. 1 in murrain before calving; 6 sold before calving. Total, 7. 40 remain.
Steers: 12 remain from the previous year's bullocks; 1 from the heriot of Roger Kutel. Total, 13. 2 in murrain; 3 added to oxen, 8 to cows. Total, 13. None remain.
Bullocks: 11 remain from the previous year's yearlings; 3 in murrain; 8 remain.
Yearlings: 11 remain from the previous year's calves; 4 in murrain; 7 remain, 3 of them male.
Calves: 19 from the offspring of the said cows because 3 were sterile, 8 bought after calving, 6 sold before calving, and 1 in murrain before calving. 2 in[3] tithe; 6 sold; 11 remain, 6 of them male.
Wethers: 249 remain from the previous year; 58 additions. Total, 307. 7 sold at Martinmas; 18 in murrain before shearing, 11 after shearing. Total, 36. 271 remain.
Rams: 2 remain from the previous year; 6 added from hoggs. Total, 8. 8 remain.
Ewes: 226 remain from the previous year; 50 added from hoggs. Total, 276. 7 sold at Martinmas; 30 in murrain before breeding and shearing, 1 after breeding and before shearing, and 2 after shearing. Total, 40. 236 remain.
Hoggs: 145 remain from the previous year's lambs; 26 sold because feeble; 5 in murrain before shearing; 58 added to wethers, 6 to rams, and 50 to ewes. None remain.
Lambs: 172 produced by the said ewes this year because 17 were sterile. 16 in murrain before weaning, 3 after weaning and before shearing; 16 in tithe; 3 in customary payment to 1 beadle, 1 smith and 1 shepherd; 12 sold before shearing because feeble. Total, 50. 122 remain.
Sows: 2 remain from the previous year; 2 remain.
Boars: 1 remains from the previous year; 1 addition. Total, 2. 1 sold; 1 remains.
Pigs: 12 remain from the previous year; 30 added from hoggets; 1 from the heriot of Henry Wygayn. Total, 43. 3 in murrain; 2 in provision of Roger the bailiff; 5 sold. Total, 10. 33 remain.
Hoggets: 37 remain from the previous year's piglets; 6 in murrain; 1 added to boars, 30 to pigs. None remain.
Piglets: 17 from the offspring of the sows this year. 3 in murrain; 1 in tithe. Total, 4. 13 remain.
Coarse wool {yield of fleece 3¼*d.* less 4¾*d.* in all}: 528 fleeces produced at the shearing this year; 53 in tithe; 375 sent to Wolvesey, which made 2 weys and 12 cloves.

1 MS 'Cur*a*ll''.

2 MS omits '1'.

3 MS 'In ⟨vend'⟩ deci' ij'.

Wool locks: 6 cloves; all sold.
Lamb's-wool {yield of fleece 1¼*d.* plus 8½*d.* in all}: 122 fleeces produced at the shearing this year; all sent to Wolvesey, which made 7 cloves.
Winter cheese: 41 made this year; all sold, which made ½ wey.
Summer cheese {yield of cow 3*s.* and sheep 3*d.* with 4 cheeses in customary payment valued at 2*s.* 8*d.* and 1 cheese in provision of the steward valued at 6*d.*, less 3*s.* 5½*d.* in all}: 162 cheeses made between Thursday the feast of St Alphege (19 April) and Michaelmas (29 September), both days included; 16 in tithe; 3 in customary payment to 1 beadle, 1 smith and 1 shepherd; 1 in customary payment for the mowing of the meadow; 1 in provision of the steward; 141 sold, which made 11 weys.
Butter: 22 cloves made this year; all sold.
Salt: 292½ sesters remain from the previous year; 76 sesters from the rent of Bursledon this year. Total, 368½ sesters. 3 washed away (*decursu*); 365½ sesters sold.
Hens: 172 from churchscot. 1 in default of the land of Peter ate Feld'; 1 in default of the land of William Op*e*rych; 1 in default of the land of Maurice Hudy; 2 in default of the land of Matilda Cha*m*payn; 2 in default of Isabel Walewayn; 2 in default of the land of Henry P*a*rme*nter*; 1 in default of the land of Robert Fab*e*r; 4 in default of the land which belonged to Henry Wrenht, which was leased and which Henry le White now holds; 2 in default of the land of Walter ate Brok'; 2 in default of the land of Walter Ke*m*pe. Total, 18. 154 sold.
Swans: 13 remain from the previous year; 3 from this year's offspring. Total, 16, of which[1]
Peacocks: 6 remain from the previous year; 1 from this year's offspring. Total, 7. 5 in murrain; 5 remain, 2 of them peacocks.
Cider: 60 gallons remain from the previous year; 2 casks from this year's issue; 60 gallons in provision of Roger the bailiff; 2 casks remain.

m.24d
Hides: 2 from oxen, 1 from a cow, 2 from steers, 3 from bullocks, 4 from yearlings dead from murrain. Total, 11. All sold.
Woolskins: 18 from wethers, 31 from ewes and 5 from hoggs dead from murrain before shearing. Total, 53. All sold.
Bare skins: 11 from wethers and 3 from ewes dead from murrain after shearing; all sold.
Lambskins: 16 from lambs in murrain before weaning and shearing, 3 after weaning and before shearing. Total, 19. All sold.
Ornaments: 1 antiphoner, 2 legendaries, 1 missal, 1 alb with a hood, 1 maniple, 1 stole, 1 chasuble, 2 towels, 1 chalice with a paten, 2 cruets of tin, 1 chest for the same, 1 chest which is in the keeping of the reeve for collecting the lord's money, 1 altar frontal of silk, and 1 ell-measure for measuring cloth with a weight for weighing bread remain from the previous year; 1 missal, 1 alb with a hood, 1 maniple with a stole, 1 chasuble, 2 towels, 1 chalice with a paten, 2 cruets of tin, 1 altar frontal of silk, and 1 chest in which to put the aforesaid items sent to Bitterne; 1 antiphoner, 2 legendaries, and 1 ell-measure with a weight for weighing bread remain at Bishops Waltham.
Utensils: 3 brass pots, 1 pitcher, 1 pan, 1 ewer with a basin, 1 lead vessel of 6 sesters, 1 bushel measure, 1 standard gallon measure remain from the previous year; all remain here apart from the bushel and gallon measures.

1 MS omits final phrase.

Carts: 2 remain from the previous year; 1 bought. Total, 3. 1 worn out; 2 carts with iron tyres remain.
Chains: 1 iron chain remains from the previous year; it remains.

Droxford

Arrears

Robert de Froyl*e*, bailiff, and William ate Hatth', reeve, render account for £25 18*s*. 9¾*d*. of arrears from the previous year. All delivered to Sir G*eoffrey*, treasurer of Wolvesey, by 1 tally. They are quit.

Rents of assize

The same render account for £2 18*s*. 5*d*. from ox-gavel (*oxeve*) at the feast of St Thomas the Apostle (21 December); 17*s*. 10½*d*. from wood-gavel (*wodegavel*) at Lammas (1 August); £20 19*s*. 3½*d*. for rents of assize at Michaelmas (29 September). Total, £24 15*s*. 7½*d*.

Quittances

In quittance of 3 ploughmen, 2 shepherds and 1 smith for the year 7*s*. 6*d*., or 1*s*. 3*d*. each; the same for ox-gavel 6*d*.; 1 keeper of lambs from the Nativity of St John the Baptist to Michaelmas, for 1 term, 3¾*d*. Total, 8*s*. 3¾*d*.

Defaults of rent

In default of the land of William de Swanem*ere* for ox-gavel because he is made free 7*d*.; the land of Horn for the same 1*s*.; the land of Thomas de la Steple for the same 2*s*. 4*d*.; the land of Boarhunt which is called Wolfrenelo*nd*' 5*s*.; the chief tenement formerly of John de Mol*endino* for ox-gavel 2½*d*., because it should in fact be put in the increment of rent by charter of the lord; the other tenement which the same John held, which he took on according to custom from St Swithun's whilst the manor was in their hands, for ox-gavel, 3½*d*., for the reason as before; a certain tenement which the same John held which was formerly a relief 7*d*., for the reason as before. Total, 10*s*.

Total of quittances and defaults of rent, 18*s*. 3¾*d*.

Total of rents remaining, £23 17*s*. 3¾*d*.

Farm of the mill

The same render account for £3 for the rent of the mill let at fee-farm. Total, £3.

Annual recognizance

The same render account for 3*d*. from Walter Mol*endinarius* for annual recognizance; 6*d*. from William le Car*eter* for the same; 6*d*. from William; 6*d*. from William le Yl so that he may serve outside the manor, and yet pay suit to his tithing at the steward's tourns as a villein as before. Total, 1*s*. 3*d*.

Cumin

The same render account for 1 lb of cumin from the rent of John, son of Henry le Car*eter*; delivered to Wolvesey.

Bows and arrows

The same render account for 1*s*. from John de Worsted' for 1 bow and 12 arrows for 2 virgates of land which belonged to John Coleman de Shidefeld' and 1 ferling of land which belonged to Richard Crall' in the same vill, which he has by gift of lord John, bishop of Winchester, rendering at Easter according to the contents of his charter which he has from the said bishop and the whole convent of St Swithun's. Total, 1*s*.

Issues of the manor

The same render account for £1 11*s*. 2½*d*. from pannage of pigs at Martinmas, at 2*d*. a pig over a year old, 1½*d*. a pig of 3 terms, 1*d*. a pig of ½ year, and ½*d*. a piglet, and moreover, 1 pig and 1 piglet from pannage this year because each of those who have 10 pigs in the manor will give 1 pig; nothing from winter pasturage this year because it was not able to be sold; 10*d*. from summer pasturage sold there this year; nothing from the pasturage of various places nor from the pasturage in Forcrofte this year for the lord's stock; 3*s*. 9*d*. from 18 geese sold; 3*s*. 10*d*. from 46 hens sold; 3*s*. ¾*d*. from 1,050 eggs sold; 3*s*. from 6 bus. of nuts sold from the wood according to custom; 1*s*. 6*d*. from loppings in Suthwild' sold this year from timber felled for ploughs; nothing from dead trees and dead wood in Haslholte nor from underwood in la Fronches' this year; 8*s*. from the whole hundred for release from carrying the hay of Nutschellyng'; 19*s*. from 9½ virgates of land for release from carrying-service; 6*d*. from John Maynard for 1 piglet; 4*s*. 9¼*d*. from Fyslod'; 12*s*. 4½*d*. from 2 qrs ½ bus. of rye from churchscot sold; 5*s*. 1½*d*. for release from carrying wood felled in preparation for Christmas this year; 14*s*. 3*d*. from transport-service sold this year; 3*s*. 11*d*. from dairy produce sold at the audit. Total, £5 15*s*. 1½*d*.

And for 10*s*. from 1 old cart-horse sold; 9*s*. from 2 old plough-horses sold, at 3*s*. for 1, and 6*s*. for 1; 9*s*. from 1 old ox sold; £1 12*s*. 6*d*. from 4 old cows sold, at 7*s*. 3*d*. each for 2, and 9*s*. each for 2; 6*s*. from 6 late-born calves sold, at 1*s*. each; £1 14*s*. from 34 wethers sold at Martinmas, at 1*s*. each; £2 from 40 ewes sold; £3 3*s*. 4*d*. from 25 pigs sold at Martinmas, at 2*s*. 4*d*. each for 10, and 2*s*. 8*d*. each for 15; 10*s*. from 48 feeble lambs sold, at 2½*d*. each; nothing from coarse wool and lamb's-wool here because it is sent to Wolvesey; 6*s*. 1½*d*. from 7 cloves of wool locks sold, at 10½*d*. a clove; 10*s*. 5*d*. from the skins sold of 18 wethers, 17 ewes and 19 hoggs in murrain before shearing, at 3*d*. a skin of wethers, 2½*d*. a skin of ewes, and 1½*d*. a skin of hoggs; 1*s*. 9*d*. from the skins sold wholesale of 13 wethers and 5 ewes in murrain after shearing; 2*s*. 2*d*. from the skins sold of 26 lambs in murrain before weaning, at 1*d*. a skin; 1*s*. 3¾*d*. from the skins sold of 21 rotted sheep in murrain after weaning, at ¾*d*. a skin; 4*d*. from the skins sold of 12 lambs in murrain after shearing; 2*s*. from the hide sold of 1 ox dead from murrain; 8*d*. from the hide sold of 1 bullock dead from murrain; £1 4*s*.[1] from 2 casks of cider sold apart from the vessels; 3*s*. from 9½ cloves of rowen cheese sold; £2 15*s*. 3*d*. from 6½ weys of summer cheese sold, at 8*s*. 6*d*. a wey;[2] 4*s*. 6½*d*. from ½ wey 1 clove of butter sold. Total, £16 5*s*. 4¾*d*.

Sale of corn

The same render account for £12 1*s*. 3½*d*. from 42 qrs 2½ bus. of wheat sold, at 4*s*. 8*d*. a qr for 5½ qrs, 5*s*. a qr for 17½ qrs 3 bus., and 6*s*. 8*d*. a qr for 18½ qrs; £1 1*s*. 3*d*. from 6 qrs 3 bus. of curall sold, at 3*s*. 4*d*. a qr; 1*s*. 4*d*. from 4 bus. of maslin sold; £1 16*s*. 8*d*. from 11 qrs of bere sold, at 3*s*. 4*d*. a qr; £6 9*s*. 9*d*. from 34 qrs 1 bus. of barley

1 MS omits '*s*.'

2 MS 'p'c' ⌈pond'⌉ ⟨vj d.⟩ viij s.'.

sold, at 3*s*. 4*d*. a qr for 10 qrs 1 bus., and 4*s*. a qr for 24 qrs; £4 3*s*. 2*d*. from 34½ qrs 2 bus. of oats sold, at 2*s*. a qr for 14 qrs 2 bus., and 2*s*. 8*d*. a qr for 20½ qrs; £1 9*d*. from 9½ qrs 1 bus. of peas sold, at 2*s*. a qr for 7 qrs 3 bus., and 2*s*. 8*d*. a qr for 2 qrs 2 bus.; £1 5*s*. 6½*d*. from 14 qrs 3 bus. of vetches sold, at 1*s*. 4*d*. a qr for 8 qrs, and 2*s*. 4*d*. a qr for 6 qrs 3 bus. Total, £27 19*s*. 9*d*.

Entry and marriage fines
The same render account for 10*s*. from Alice, relict of Cuppy*n*g Breto*n*, to retain 1 messuage and ½ virgate of land which belonged to her husband; £1 from John Seyle to have 1 messuage and ½ virgate of land which belonged to Isabel his mother whose heir he is; 2*s*. from William le Yl to have 1 messuage and 1 ferling which belonged to Alice his mother whose heir he is; 4*s*. from Joan la Hore to have 1 messuage and ½ virgate of land which belonged to John, son of her uncle, whose heir she is; 6*s*. 8*d*. from John Chapelay of Hawkley to have Joan la Hore with ½ virgate of her land; 1*s*. from Guy Gamnoky to have 2 day-works of land by surrender of Richard de Seleford', and the said Guy will relieve the said Richard of 1*d*. annual rent for the year. Total, £2 3*s*. 8*d*.

Perquisites
The same render account for 2*s*. from Peter de Brok, overseer of the harvest, for keeping the lord's fields and pastures badly; 16*s*. 3*d*. from various men for various transgressions. Total, 18*s*. 3*d*.

Total of both, £3 1*s*. 11*d*.

Total of all receipts, £80 1*s*. 9*d*.

Cost of ploughs
In iron and steel bought for 2 ploughs for the year and three ploughs for 1 term 6*s*. 10½*d*. In 1 ploughshare bought 9*d*. In 1 plough made anew and others mended 5*d*. In trimming timber 3*d*. In 3 plough feet bought 1*s*. 3*d*. In fitting the said plough with iron tyres 1½*d*. In 3 pairs of wheels bought for the same 1*s*. In 3 halters made from the horses' own hair (*de proprio pilo*) ¾*d*. In shoeing 2 plough-horses 2*s*. 6*d*., because the smith shoes 2 according to custom. In spreading dung 1*s*. 4*d*. In 2 harrows made anew with others mended 4*d*. In stipend of 1 drover for the year 3*s*. In stipend of 1 drover for 1 term 9*d*. In stipend of 2 ploughmen who are sometimes carters for the year 6*s*. In 4 oxen £2 1*s*. 3*d*., at 10*s*. each for 3, and 11*s*. 3*d*. for 1. In forage bought 8*s*. Total, £3 13*s*. 10¾*d*.

Cost of carts
In 1 pair of wheels bought for clearing dung 1*s*. 10*d*. In large nails bought for mending the cart 1*s*. 2½*d*. In fitting the cart with axles with axles bought for the same 7*d*. In 2 collars bought 1*s*. 2*d*. In 1 pair of saddle-pads 6*d*. In clouts, nails and grease bought 9½*d*. In 1 pair of traces bought 4½*d*. In 1 rope bought for tethering horses in the pasture 3*d*. In 2 halters bought 3*d*. In shoeing 2 cart-horses for the year 3*s*. 6*d*. In 1 cart-horse bought 19*s*. 1*d*. In 3 pieces of iron for 3 shovels 6*d*. Total, £1 10*s*. ½*d*.

Dairy
In 7 bus. of salt bought for the dairy, 1*s*. 9*d*. this year, with the expenses of the harvest. In earthenware pots and pans bought for the same 4*d*. In woollen and linen

cloth 9*d*. In a press bought 5*d*. In 1 stall made anew for bullocks 4*d*. In 15 ells of canvas bought for putting wool in 4*s*. 4½*d*., at 3½*d*. an ell. In castrating piglets 1*d*. In 1 tripod bought 8*d*. In 1 tine bought for carrying cider 5*d*. In 3 empty casks bought for putting cider in 7*s*. 2*d*. In hooping and mending 6 casks 2*s*. 2*d*. In stipend of 1 dairymaid for the year 2*s*. In stipend of 1 cowherd for 3 terms 1*s*. 6*d*. Total, £1 1*s*. 11½*d*.

Sheepcote

In 16 hurdles made for the fold 8*d*. In 6 hurdles made for the pen (*lokett'*) with withies collected for the same 2*d*. In re-roofing the ewe-house in places 1*s*. 4*d*. In re-roofing the wether-house in places 8*d*. In wattling the fold with withies and stubble collected for the same 1*s*. 4½*d*. In fat, vinegar and copperas with the stipend of the man greasing the sheep (*ung'*) 16*s*. 1*d*. Total, £1 3½*d*.

Cost of buildings

In building the cow-shed anew with a carpenter for the same by piece-work 10*s*. In making 1,500 laths for the same 1*s*. In 3,000 nails bought 2*s*. 4*d*. In re-roofing the said building by piece-work 2*s*. 8*d*. In re-roofing in places the bailiff's room, small barn, dairy building[1] and cart-house 1*s*. 8½*d*. In stubble collected for the same 10*d*. In hedging to enclose around the garden 9*d*. In pulling down the fencing for the same 8*d*. In mending the walls of the great barn and putting in sills 1*s*. In mending the pig-sty at Haselholte 3*d*. In 1 lock bought for the door of the great barn 3*d*. In building a stack of forage in the curia 1*s*. 1*d*. Total, £1 2*s*. 6½*d*.

Threshing

In threshing and winnowing 49 qrs 1 bus. of wheat, curall and maslin by piece-work 11*s*. 2¾*d*., at 2¾*d*. a heaped quarter. In threshing and winnowing 78 qrs of bere and barley by piece-work 11*s*. 4½*d*., at 1¾*d*. a heaped quarter. In threshing and winnowing 75 qrs of oats 5*s*. 5½*d*., at ¾*d*. a heaped quarter, and ¼*d*. per 2 qrs winnowed. In threshing and winnowing 25 qrs 3 bus. of peas and vetches by piece-work 4*s*. 9*d*., at 2¼*d*. a heaped quarter. In 1 sack bought 5½*d*. In 1 basket bought for corn 2½*d*. Total, £1 13*s*. 5¾*d*.

Harvest-time

In weeding all the corn over and above that weeded by labour service 3*s*. 9*d*. In herrings bought for 6 boon-works of 590 men having two meals a day and 4 herrings each, and for 7 boon-works of 660 men having 1 meal a day and 2 herrings each, 18*s*. 2½*d*. In expenses of the reeve, hayward and other officials of the curia from Lammas (1 August) until the Decollation of St John the Baptist (29 August), for 4 weeks, 5*s*. 4*d*. Total, £1 7*s*. 3½*d*.

Expenses of the steward

In expenses of the steward for 2 tourns by 1 tally 2*s*. In expenses of Roger, bailiff from Michaelmas until Christmas, for his visits 3*s*. In expenses of Robert, bailiff from Christmas until Michaelmas, for his visits 5*s*. 3*d*. Total, 10*s*. 3*d*.

Total of all expenses, £10 19*s*. 9*d*.

And he owes, £68 2*s*.

1 MS 'dom' ⟨b*er*car'⟩ daer''.

[Cash deliveries]
Delivered to Sir G*eoffrey*, treasurer of Wolvesey, by 1 tally, £47 10*s*.

And he owes clear, £20 12*s*.

Issues of the grange

[Wheat]
{yield: . . . 1 qr 5 bus.}
The same render account for 47½ qrs from the whole issue of wheat by struck measure; 10½ qrs 2½ bus. from churchscot. Total, 58 qrs 2½ bus.
Sown over 154½ acres which lie in le Sorelo*nd*', To*n*forlong', le Suthemestecrofte, and Fornden', 14½ qrs; that is, 1½ bus. over 2 acres. In customary payment to 1 sower, 1 bus. In provision of 1 reeve, 1 hayward keeping the woods and pasture, and 1 beadle, from Lammas until the Decollation of St John the Baptist, for 4 weeks, 6 bus. Nothing for the provison of the steward this year. In default of the land of Horn for churchscot, 2 bus.; the land of Tyle, 1½ bus.; the reeve (*le Reve*), ½ bus. 1 peck; the land of the millward (*le Meleward'*) ½ bus. 1 peck. Sold, 42 qrs 2½ bus. It balances.

[Curall]
The same render account for 6 qrs 3 bus. from the whole issue of curall by struck measure. Sold, 6 qrs 3 bus.

[Rye]
The same render account for 2 qrs ½ bus. of rye from churchscot. Sold, 2 qrs ½ bus.

[Maslin]
{yield: two-fold plus . . . 1 bus.}
The same render account for 7½ qrs 1 bus. from the whole issue of maslin by struck measure. Mixed with barley, 7 qrs 1 bus. Sold, 4 bus.

[Bere]
{yield: . . . plus 6 bus.}
The same render account for 25 qrs 2 bus. from the whole issue of bere by struck measure.
Sown over 21 acres as they lie in le Grove, 5 qrs 2 bus. Mixed with barley for the liveries of the manorial servants, 9 qrs. Sold, 11 qrs.

Barley
{yield: 5-fold . . . 1 qr 1 bus.}
The same render account for 73½ qrs 1 bus. from the whole issue of barley by struck measure; 7 qrs 1 bus. received above from maslin; 9 qrs received above from bere; 3 qrs 3 bus. received from vetches for the liveries of the manorial servants. Total, 93 qrs 1 bus.
Sown over 86 acres as they lie in le Harnesgate, le Grove, and Tonforlo*n*g' behind the garden, 16 qrs 1 bus.; that is, 1½ bus. an acre. In customary payment to 1 sower, 1 bus. In customary payment to 1 smith, 3 bus. In customary payment to 1 shepherd of ewes, 3 bus. Delivered to 1 hayward from Michaelmas until Lammas and from the Decollation of St John the Baptist until Michaelmas, because for 4 weeks at harvest-time he was at table, 6 qrs, taking a quarter every 8 weeks. Delivered to 2 ploughmen who were sometimes carters and 1 drover for the year, 17 qrs 2 bus., taking a quarter

every 9 weeks. Delivered to 1 dairymaid from Michaelmas until Lammas and from the Decollation of St John the Baptist until the following Michaelmas, 4 qrs, because she was at table for 4 weeks at harvest-time, taking a quarter every 12 weeks. Delivered to 1 keeper of lambs from weaning until Lammas, 1 qr. Delivered to 1 cowherd for the year, 4 qrs 2 bus., taking a quarter every 12 weeks. In provision of the reeve and officials of the curia for 4 weeks at harvest-time, 2 qrs. In customary provision, that is, in bread at harvest-time on account of the boon-works, 7½ qrs. Sold, 34 qrs 1 bus.

Oats
{yield: three-fold less 8 qrs 6 bus.}
The same render account for 93½ qrs 2 bus. from the whole issue of oats by struck measure; 14½ qrs by estimation in sheaves given to oxen. Total, 108 qrs 2 bus. Sown over 225 acres which lie in Midelcrofte, Suthfeld', and Watcu*m*b', 42 qrs 1 bus.; that is, 1½ bus. an acre, less ½ bus. in all. In customary payment to 1 hayward, 1 bus. In fodder of 2 cart-horses and 3 plough-horses hauling the ploughs, 15½ qrs 3 bus. In supporting oxen by estimation in sheaves, 14½ qrs. In fodder of the steward's horses, 2 bus. In fodder of the horse of the bailiff and clerk for his visits, 5 bus. Sold, 34½ qrs 2 bus.

Peas
{yield: four-fold less 1 bus.}
The same render account for 11½ qrs 3 bus. from the whole issue of peas by struck measure.
Sown over 18 acres which lie in Hynhok', 2 qrs 2 bus.; that is, 1 bus. an acre. Sold, 9½ qrs 1 bus.

Vetches
{yield: three-and-a-half-fold plus 2½ bus.}
The same render account for 9½ qrs of vetches remaining from the previous year in the granary; 10 qrs 3 bus. from the whole issue of vetches this year. Total, 19½ qrs 3 bus.
Sown over 18 acres as they lie in Yforlo*n*g' and Northden', 2 qrs 1 bus.; that is, 1 bus. an acre, less 1 bus. in all. Mixed above with barley, 3 qrs 3 bus. Sold, 14 qrs 3 bus.

m.25

Stock

Cart-horses: 2 remain from the previous year; 1 bought; 1[1] from the heriot of William Cuppyng. Total, 4. 1 delivered to Ernys' de Cnynge by letters of the lord; 1 sold; 2 remain.
Plough-horses: 4 remain from the previous year; 1 from the heriot of Cuppy*ng* Breton; 1 from the heriot of John Will*iam*. Total, 6. 2 sold; 4 remain.
Oxen: 17 remain from the previous year; 4 added from steers; 4 bought; 1 from the heriot of John Serle. Total, 26. 1 in murrain in March; 1 sold. Total, 2. 24 remain.
Bulls: 1 remains from the previous year; 1 remains.
Cows: 21 remain from the previous year; 2 added from steers. Total, 23. 4 sold before calving; 19 remain.
Steers: 6 remain from the previous year's bullocks; 4 added to oxen, 2 to cows; none remain.

1 MS omits '1'.

Bullocks: 6 remain from the previous year's yearlings; 1 in murrain; 5 males remain.
Yearlings: 5 remain from the previous year's calves; 5 remain, 3 of them male.
Calves: 13 from the offspring of the said cows this year because 6 were sterile; 1 in tithe; 6 sold; 6 remain, 4 of them male.
Wethers: 280 remain from the previous year; 22 added from hoggs. Total, 308. 34 sold at Martinmas; 18 in murrain before shearing, 13 after shearing. Total, 65. 243 remain.
Rams: 10 remain from the previous year; 10 remain.
Ewes: 380 remain from the previous year; 34 added from hoggs. Total, 422. 40 sold at Martinmas; 7 in customary payment to 2 shepherds, 3 ploughmen, 1 smith and 1 swineherd at Martinmas; 13 in murrain before breeding and shearing, 4 before shearing and after breeding, and 5 after shearing. Total, 69. 353 remain.
Hoggs: 75 remain from the previous year's lambs; 19 in murrain before shearing; 22 added to wethers, 34 to ewes; none remain.
Lambs: 299 from the offspring of the said ewes because 29 were sterile. 27 in tithe because skins before weaning assessed for tithe separately; 29 in murrain before weaning, 21 after weaning and before shearing, 12 after shearing; 2 in customary payment to 1 reeve and 1 shepherd; 48 sold before shearing because feeble. Total, 139. 160 remain.
Sows: 3 remain from the previous year; 1 in murrain before farrowing; 2 remain.
Pigs: 33 remain from the previous year; 20 added from hoggets; 1 from pannage. Total, 54. 9 in murrain; 25 sold; 20 remain.
Hoggets: 20 remain from the previous year's piglets; all added to pigs; none remain.
Piglets: 25 produced by the said sows this year; 1 from pannage. Total, 26. 4 in murrain; 2 in tithe. Total, 6. 20 remain.
Winter cheese: 39 rowen cheeses made this year; all sold.
Summer cheese {yield of cow 2*s*. 6*d*. and sheep 1½*d*. this year with 5 cheeses in customary payment valued at 2*s*.}: 160 cheeses made between Wednesday the feast of St Mark (25 April) and Michaelmas (29 September), both days included. 16 in tithe; 1 in customary payment to the chaplain on Ascension day (31 May); 2 in customary payment to 1 reeve and 1 shepherd; 2 in provision for harvest-time. Total, 21. 139 sold, which made 6½ weys.
Butter: ½ wey 1 clove made this year; all sold.
Coarse wool {yield of fleece 3½*d*. plus 5*s*. 2½*d*. in all}: 624 fleeces produced at the shearing this year; 2 in customary payment to 2 shepherds; 622 sent to Wolvesey, which made 3½ weys and 3 cloves.
Wool locks: 7 cloves; all sold.
Lamb's-wool {yield of fleece 1¼*d*. less 8*d*. in all}: 172 produced at the shearing this year; all sent, which made 9 cloves.
Woolskins: 18 from wethers, 17 from ewes, and 19 from hoggs in murrain before shearing. Total, 54. All sold.
Bare skins: 13 from wethers and 5 from ewes in murrain after shearing. Total, 18. All sold.
Lambskins: 29 from lambs in murrain before weaning, 21 after weaning and before shearing, and 12 after shearing. Total, 62. 3 in tithe; 59 sold.
Hides: 1 from an ox and 1 from a bullock in murrain; all sold.
Geese: 18 received from Shidefeud' according to custom; all sold.
Hens {henceforth answer for the offspring of geese and hens}: 22 from churchscot; 24 from the wood according to custom. Total, 46. All sold.
Eggs: 1,050 from the wood according to custom; all sold.

Nuts: 6 bus. from the wood according to custom; all sold.
Cider: 2 casks remain from the previous year; 7 casks made from this year's issue. Total, 9. 2 casks sold; 7 casks remain.
Utensils: 1 brass pan, one basin with a ewer, and one brass pot remain from the previous year; all this remains.

Twyford

Arrears

John de Herierd, bailiff, and William Herefyw, reeve, render account for £67 11*s*. 1¾*d*. of arrears from the previous year. Delivered to Sir G*eoffrey*, treasurer of Wolvesey, by 1 tally. They are quit.

Rents of assize

The same render account for £10 2*s*. 8*d*. for rents of assize at Christmas; £10 15*s*. 2*d*. at Easter (22 April); £10 2*s*. 8*d*. at St John the Baptist (24 June); £19 8*s*. 6*d*. at Michaelmas (29 September). Total, £50 9*s*.

Increment of rent

The same render account for 3*s*. from Nicholas Wydeloc for increment of rent for 1 plot containing 12 acres in a certain corner in la Rughehaye, let to him by charter of lord John, now bishop. Total, 3*s*.

Total of rents with increment, £50 12*s*.

Quittances

In quittance of 1 reeve for the year 5*s*.; 1 beadle at Twyford for the year 5*s*.; 1 beadle and 1 bartoner at Marwell for the same time 5*s*.; 1 shepherd of wethers and 1 shepherd of ewes for the same time 6*s*.; 1 shepherd of hoggs from Michaelmas until the feast of St John the Baptist 2*s*. 3*d*.; 1 keeper of lambs for ½ year 1*s*. 6*d*.; 6 ploughmen at Twyford for the year 18*s*., or 3*s*. each; 6 ploughmen at Marwell for the same time 16*s*. 6*d*., or 2*s*. 9*d*. each; 1 oxherd at Twyford for the year 3*s*.; 1 oxherd at Marwell for the same time 2*s*. 9*d*.; 4 workers at Twyford for the year and 4 at Marwell, with their carts every day, £1 4*s*.; 1 swineherd for the year 3*s*.; 2 ploughmen for 3 terms, holding and driving 1 plough at Twyford, 4*s*. Total, £4 16*s*.

Defaults of rent

In default of the land of Allbrook 5*s*., which is now paid at Merdon; the land of Richard de Abynton' at Brambridge £2 6*s*. 10*d*.; the land of Upham drawn into demesne at Bishopstoke 2*s*.; the land of Thurbernd drawn into demesne 5*s*.; the land of Crud' drawn into demesne 1*s*. 3*d*.; the land of W. and N. drawn into demesne 1*s*.; the meadow inundated by the fishpond 1*s*.; the land of Algar drawn into demesne at Bishopstoke 5*d*.; the land of Cok on account of the watercourse in the time of Bishop G*odfrey* 6*d*.; that which belonged to Walter de M*a*rewoll', held of Bishop P*eter*, which Roger Wodelok' now holds by gift of Bishop William and confirmation of his successors and Aymer the Elect, 10*s*. Total, £3 13*s*.

Total of quittances and defaults of rent, £8 9*s*.

Total of rents remaining, £42 3*s*.

Annual recognizance

Nothing from William le Cute because he is dead; 1 lb of wax from Stephen le Ryd' for annual recognizance. Total, 1 lb of wax. All delivered to G*eoffrey*, treasurer, and he is quit.

Issues of the manor

The same render account for £1 6*s*. 2*d*. from pannage of pigs this year; £3 from pannage sold wholesale to the Prior of Winchester in the park; 5*s*. from wholesale pannage of pigs in Prevet this year; £1 17*s*. from the pasturage in la Nython' sold; 15*s*. from the pasturage in la Northmed' sold; nothing from the pasturage in la Estmarle this year for the lord's cows; nothing from the pasturage in la Westmarle this year for the aforesaid reason; nothing from the pasturage of Coukeslo*nd*' this year because it was sown; 6*d*. from the pasturage sold to the chaplain; nothing from the pasturage in la More this year for the lord's stock; 3*s*. 2*d*. from the pasturage of Inhouk' sold; nothing from the pasturage of the field in la Strod' and Lyttlestrod' this year for the lord's stock; 18*s*. 4*d*. from fishing in the water; £3 19*s*. from 7 old oxen sold, at 10*s*. for 1, 11*s*. each for 5, and 14*s*. for 1; £2 6*s*. from 46 wethers sold at Martinmas; £1 3*s*. from 35 ewes sold at the same feast, at 8*d*. each, less 4*d*. in all; 10*s*. from 10 ewes sold at the same time; £1 5*s*. from 62 feeble lambs sold before shearing, at 5*d*. each, less 10*d*. in all; £11 17*s*. 6*d*. from 75 pigs sold, at 3*s*. 2*d*. each; 7*s*. 2*d*. from the carcasses sold of 3 oxen in murrain; 16*s*. 6*d*. from the hides sold of 5 oxen dead from murrain; 2*s*. from the hide sold of 1 cow dead from murrain; 1*d*. from the hide sold of 1 calf in murrain; £1 3*s*. 10*d*. from the skins sold of 16 wethers, 42 ewes, 1 ram, and 25 hoggs in murrain before shearing, at 2*d*. a skin of hoggs, 4*d*. a skin of wethers and ewes; 1*s*. 10½*d*. from the skins sold of 12 wethers and 20 ewes in murrain after shearing; 8*s*. 4*d*. from the skins sold of 100 lambs in murrain before weaning; 1*s*. 10*d*. from the skins sold of 22 rotted sheep after weaning and before shearing; 1*d*. from the skins sold of 4 lambs in murrain after shearing; nothing from coarse wool and lamb's-wool here because it is sent to Wolvesey; 13*s*. 3*d*. from 15 cloves 1 lb of wool locks sold, at 10½*d*. a clove; 8*d*. from 4 capons sold from the rent of Nicholas Wodelok'; £6 3*s*. 9½*d*. from 14½ weys 10 cloves of cheese sold, at 8*s*. 4*d*. a wey; 2*s*. ½*d*. from 7 cloves of butter sold, at 3½*d*. a clove; £4 4*s*. 4½*d*. from 10 weys 3½ cloves of cheese from the issue of the cows of Marwell, sold for the first time this year, at 8*s*. 4*d*. a wey; 6*s*. 5*d*. from 22 cloves of butter from the issue of the said cows there sold this year, at 3½*d*. a clove; 10*s*. from harvest labour services sold; £3 6*s*. 8*d*. from the labour services of 4 carters at Twyford sold this year; £38 11*s*. 2½*d*. from 71 yearlings and 109 wethers, agisted in the pasturage in the park and in the park of Marwell the previous year, sold for various prices; 3*s*. from Walter le Bule for his release from the service of the land which belonged to Alice le Cove; 3*s*. from Alan Mol*endinarius* for release from the service of the land which belonged to John ate Hull'; 3*s*. from John le Palm*ere* for release for him and his from all services of the land formerly of Peter Alfryth' which was the lord's escheat; 3*s*. from Isolda, relict of John Bedell', for release from the service of the land which belonged to Stephen Thurbyrn; nothing from the labour service of the land which belonged to William ate Dell' because it is leased to John Frewyn' who worked for the same; 4*s*. from Maselivia le Swon for release from the service of the land which belonged to her father; 4*s*. from Robert de Exon' for release from the service of the land which belonged to Walter son of Simon; 4*s*. from John de Quercu for his release from the service of the land which belonged to Edith la Smale this year; 4*s*. from Roger Long*us* for his release from the service of the land which belonged to Eve la Lime at the lord's will; 5*s*. 6*d*. from 1 old cart sold; £6 13*s*. 8*d*. from 73 dead trees in la Rughehay sold from a certain purpresture leased to Nicholas Wydelok; 6*s*. 8*d*. from thickets in the same place sold; 5*s*. 6*d*. from the pasturage of 11 acres sold for ½ year to John le Aumon'; 6*d*. from the keeping of 1 ox straying in the park; £1 3*s*. 2*d*. from 2½ weys 8 cloves of cheese and butter of ewes sold at the audit; 9*s*. 8½*d*. from the dairy produce of cows sold at the audit. Total, £96 18*s*. 6*d*.

Sale of corn

The same render account for £26 7*s*. 10*d*. from 87 qrs 6 bus. of wheat sold, at 6*s*. a qr for 83 qrs 6 bus., and 6*s*. 4*d*. a qr for 4 qrs; £4 4*s*. 11*d*. from 18 qrs 6 bus. of curall sold, at 4*s*. 8*d*. a qr for 11 qrs, and 4*s*. 4*d*. a qr for 7 qrs 6 bus.; £28 2*s*. 11*d*. from 120 qrs 5 bus. of barley sold, at 4*s*. 8*d*. a qr; £4 1*s*. 6*d*. from 40 qrs 6 bus. of oats sold, at 2*s*. a qr; £2 18*s*. 4*d*. from 17½ qrs of peas sold, at 3*s*. 4*d*. a qr; £3 2*s*. from 31 qrs of vetches sold, at 2*s*. a qr; 6*s*. 4*d*. from 4 qrs 6 bus. of old vetches from the granary sold, at 1*s*. 4*d*. a qr; 2*s*. 1*d*. from 5 bus. of barley sold at the audit. Total, £69 5*s*. 11*d*.

Farms of mills

The same render account for £2 for the farm of the mill of Brambridge; 1*s*. 6¾*d*. from 5 sticks of eels for the farm of the same mill; £2 15*s*. for the farm of the mill of Compton. Total, £4 16*s*. 6¾*d*.

Mill of North Twyford

The same render account for 8*s*. from the mill of North Twyford according to custom because there is noone there except 1 miller; £1 14*s*. 1½*d*. from 11 qrs 3 bus. of barley sold from the issue of the mill, at 3*s*. a qr; 8*s*. from the portion of meal which the miller was accustomed to have because there is noone there except 1 miller. Total, £2 10*s*. 1½*d*.

Mill of South Twyford

Nothing from the mill of South Twyford because there is noone at the mill.

Mill of Shawford

The same render account for £1 1*s*. from 7 qrs of barley, at 3*s*. a qr; 4*s*. from the portion of meal which the miller was accustomed to have because there is noone there except 1 miller. Total, £1 5*s*.

Total of all the mills without the farms, £3 15*s*. 1½*d*.

Total of all the mills with the farms, £8 11*s*. 8¼*d*.

Entry and marriage fines with tithingpenny

The same render account for 3*s*. from the tithing of North Twyford for tithingpenny at the hundred-court of Martinmas; 6*s*. 8*d*. from the tithing of South Twyford for the same; 6*s*. 8*d*. from the tithing of Owslebury for the same; 16*s*. 4*d*. from the same tithings for tithingpenny at the hundred-court of Hockday; 10*s*. from John de Mol*endino* to have 1 messuage ½ virgate of land which belonged to John de Mol*endino*; 3*s*. 4*d*. from William Frewyn' to have 1 messuage by resignation of John ate Hull'; 5*s*. from Robert Gyll' to have 1 messuage ½ virgate of land which belonged to Ascelyn Gyll'; 5*s*. from Alice Gyll' to have the aforesaid messuage and ½ virgate of land by surrender of the aforesaid Robert; 6*s*. 8*d*. from Richard Cotesne to have 1 cotland which belonged to Alice his mother; £1 from William Jacob and Juliana his wife to have 1 ferling of land by surrender of Walter Beryman and Matilda Maund' his wife; 1*s*. from Walter Buryman for marrying Juliana his daughter within; 6*d*. from Joan ate Hull' for marrying herself within; 2*s*. from Matilda Arvy for marrying Ella her daughter outside; £2 13*s*. 4*d*. from Thomas Dodde to have 12 acres of land by resignation of Ralph le Baker'; £1 from Alice, relict of John Luvesone, to retain 1 messuage and 1 ferling of land which belonged to her husband; 3*s*. from Agnes, who was wife of Thomas Luffyng', to retain 1 messuage 1 acre of land which belonged to her husband; 6*s*. from Henry Wynegod' to have 1 messuage 1 acre of land which belonged to his father; 4*s*. from Thomas le Boys to recover 1 acre of land which was leased to John Frewyn' without licence; 5*s*. from Ivo Galoun to have 1 messuage 1 acre of land which belonged to Matilda his mother. Total, £8 17*s*. 6*d*.

Perquisites
The same render account for ⌈2*s*.⌉ from the tithing of North Twyford because it did not produce in court those it had bailed; 2*s*. from the rector of the church of Upham for trespass of wood in la Rughehay; 3*s*. from the whole vill of Hevelesthy*ng* for finding their livestock in the lord's corn; 2*s*. from William Mol*endinarius* for trespass of pasture; 2*s*. from Walter ate Vise because he received sheaves carried off by the carters at harvest-time; 2*s*. from John Segar because he carried off sheaves without licence; £5 5*s*. 6*d*. from various men for various transgressions. Total, £5 18*s*. 6*d*.

Total of both, £14 16*s*.

Total of all receipts, £231 15*s*. 1¼*d*.

Cost of ploughs
In iron and steel bought for the ironwork of 5 ox-ploughs and 2 horse-ploughs with the stipend of the smith repairing the said ironwork for the year £1 17*s*. 6*d*., at 5*s*. an ox-plough, and 6*s*. 3*d*. a horse-plough, because they ploughed before and after dinner (*prand'*) at the time of the summer sowing. In iron and steel bought for the ironwork of 1 ox-plough from the Purification (2 February) until Michaelmas (29 September) with the stipend of the smith repairing the said ironwork for the same time 2*s*. 6*d*. In 4 ploughshares bought 3*s*. 4*d*. In raising (*levand'*) the same 3*d*. In 4 plough feet bought 1*s*. 4*d*. In new ploughs made and timber felled, trimmed and treated for the same 3*s*. In mending and making harrows 9*d*. In fitting the ploughs with iron tyres 7*d*. In 4 pairs of wheels bought 1*s*. 4*d*. In 11 yokes made 2¾*d*. In shoeing 12 plough-horses hauling the ploughs for the year 16*s*. In shoeing 3 horses harrowing at both sowings 1*s*. 4*d*. In 12 halters made from the horses' own hair 2½*d*. In winter boon-works of 16 ploughmen who ploughed 48 acres as they lie 4*s*.,[1] at 1*d*. an acre. Moreover, they ploughed 34 acres as they lie according to custom. In Lenten boon-works of 20 ploughmen who ploughed 50 acres as they lie 4*s*. 2*d*., at 1*d*. an acre. Moreover, they ploughed 46 acres as they lie according to custom. In quittance of 12 ploughmen for 20 Saturday ploughings between Michaelmas and Easter, because on other Saturdays it was a feast day or raining, £1 10*s*., or 3*d*. a ploughman a Saturday. In quittance of 12 ploughmen for 22 Saturday ploughings between Easter and Michaelmas 16*s*. 6*d*., or 1½*d*. a ploughman a Saturday. In stipend of 2 horse-ploughmen 6*s*. In hiring a plough-holder at the time of the summer sowing when they ploughed after dinner, for 40 days, 3*s*. 4*d*., or ½*d*. a day. In 9 oxen bought £4 16*s*. 3*d*., at 8*s*. 3*d*. for 1, and 11*s*.

1 MS omits '*s*.'

each for 8. In quittance of 2 ploughmen for 10 Saturday ploughings between Christmas and Easter and 22 Saturday ploughings between Easter and Michaelmas 5*s*. 3*d*. Total, £11 13*s*. 10¼*d*.

Purchase of corn

In 18 qrs 3 bus. of barley bought for the liveries of the manorial servants £2 15*s*. 1½*d*., at 3*s*. a qr. Total, £2 15*s*. 1½*d*.

Cost of carts

In 3 pairs of wheels bought for the carts with wooden hoops fitted to the same 9*s*. 10*d*. In 1 new binding bought for 1 pair of the said wheels with clamps and nails for the same and with the stipend of the smith 10*s*. In removing 2 old bindings and putting them on the other two wheels with large nails and clamps bought for the same and with the stipend of the smith 6*s*. 2*d*. In clouts, nails and grease bought for the carts for the year 4*s*. In fitting the carts with axles for the year 1*s*. 4*d*. In mending 1 cart broken with 1 cask of wine on the road to Downton 7*d*. In 2 pairs of traces bought 1*s*. 2*d*. In 2 collars bought 1*s*. 1½*d*. In 1 pair of saddle-pads bought 8*d*. In shoeing 2 cart-horses for the year 5*s*. In stipend of 1 carter for the year 3*s*. In 2 linch-pins and 2 hurters bought 4*d*. In 1 pair of cart-shafts and 1 pair of swingletrees bought 10*d*. Total, £2 5*s*. 6½*d*.

m.25d

Dairy

In woollen and linen cloth bought 1*s*. 2*d*. In earthenware pots and pans bought 1*s*. In 2 qrs of salt bought 4*s*. In assistance for the shepherd at the time of lambing 10*d*. In 36 ells of canvas bought 9*s*. 3*d*., at 3*d*. an ell, plus 3*d*. in all. In 5 sacks with 1 poke made with thread bought for the same and for packing the wool 1*s*. 4*d*. In weeding corn this year 10*s*. In 7 ells of canvas bought for making sacks for the corn 1*s*. 11*d*., at 3¼*d*. an ell, plus ¼*d*. in all. In roofing and mending in places the sheepcotes of Hasely, Colveden' and Hevelestyng' 3*s*. 9*d*. In trimming 4 crucks to prop up the sheepcote of Hasely 4*s*. 6*d*. In 1 new cratch made and other old ones mended with nails bought for same 2*s*. 6*d*. In making and mending doors and cratches for the hogg-house at Colved*en* 2*s*. 6*d*. In grease and copperas for greasing sheep £1 15*s*. 2*d*. In 40 large and small hurdles made for the fold with withies collected for the same 1*s*. 8*d*. In hinges bought for the door of the wether-house 2*d*. In castrating piglets 6*d*. In 71 yearlings bought the previous year to agist in the park and 109 wethers bought to agist in the pasture £28 11*s*. 2½*d*. In 34 lambs bought from the reeve of Merdon 17*s*., at 6*d*. each. In 1 tripod bought 6*d*. Total, £33 11*s*. 11½*d*.

Dairy of Marwell

In woollen and linen cloth bought 8*d*. In a press bought 3*d*. In 3 moulds bought 1*s*. 5*d*. In earthenware pots and pans bought 7*d*. In a tine and 1 tub bought 1*s*. 3*d*. In 1 churn for making butter and a bucket bought 1*s*. 10½*d*. In 1 brass pot bought 9*s*. 6*d*. In 2 brass pans bought 6*s*. 6*d*. In 1 tripod bought 1*s*. In 1 cheese-vat and trough made with boards sawn for the said cheese-vat 2*s*. In stipend of 1 dairymaid from the feast of the Apostles Philip and James (1 May) until Michaelmas (29 September) 2*s*. In stipend of 1 cowherd for the same time 2*s*. Total, £1 10*s*. 1½*d*.

Threshing of corn

In threshing and winnowing 20 qrs of wheat by piece-work 3*s*. 4*d*. In winnowing the same 4*d*., at 1*d*. per 5 qrs. In threshing and winnowing 20 qrs of barley by piece-work

2*s*. 11*d*., at 1¾*d*. a qr. In threshing and winnowing 22 qrs of oats by piece-work 1*s*. 10*d*., at 1*d*. a qr. Total, 8*s*. 5*d*.

Cost of buildings
In building 1 chimney at the southern end of the kitchen at Twyford 11*d*. In mending the stalls in the plough-horses' stable 2*d*. In mending 1 brass pot 10*d*. In constructing fences around the granary of Marwell 6*d*. In mending the boat 2*d*. In 1 lock with a key bought for the door to the bakehouse of Marwell 2*d*. In digging and planting 2 furlongs of ditches around le Breghefeld' £1 1*s*., at 4*d*. a perch for 1 furlong 7 perches, and 2*d*. a perch for 33 perches, less 2*d*. in all. In enclosing 5[1] furlongs and 2 perches around the aforesaid field of Breghefeld' 7*s*. 2¼*d*., at ½*d*. a perch for 3 furlongs 37 perches, and ¼*d*. a perch for 1 furlong 15 perches. In 2 stiles made to have 1 lawful place (*laghepach'*) for crossing 2*d*. In a lock bought for the pinfold of Marwell 2*d*. In 1 lock with a key bought for the door between the dairy and cart stable at Twyford 3*d*. In hedging to enclose around the garden at Twyford 1*s*. In hinges and nails bought for the door to the bailiff's stable at Marwell 10*d*. In re-roofing the said stable in places 3*s*. 4*d*. In plastering and mending a certain building at Twyford in which to keep and fatten the lord's boars 1*s*. 4*d*. In 2 casks bought 6*s*. In mending these and other casks and utensils for cider 10*d*. In stipend of 1 carpenter propping up the walls of the pinfold with 2 crucks 6*d*. Total, £2 2*s*. ¼*d*.

Cost of the park
In planting 61 perches of hedge around the park and garden 5*s*. 1*d*., at 1*d*. a perch. In 2 locks with keys bought for the park-gate of Marwell 8½*d*. Total, 5*s*. 9½*d*.

Cost of meadows
In mowing 12 acres of meadow in Suthwollemed' this year by piece-work 4*s*. 6*d*., at 4½*d*. an acre. In mowing the meadow of Lytlestrod*e*med' by piece-work 2*s*. 8½*d*. Total, 7*s*. 2½*d*.

Cost of the harvest
In bread bought for 15 harvest boon-works of 2,996 men with the officials of the curia who reaped and bound all the corn from 2,370 acres as they lie £4 13*s*. 7½*d*., and the men had 3 farthings of bread. In 5,000 herrings bought for the same work £1 10*s*., at 6*s*. a 1,000. In 2 weys 7 cloves of cheese bought for a want of herrings 18*s*. 9*d*. Total, £7 2*s*. 4½*d*.

Cost of the mill
In repairing the spindle of the mill of North Twyford 8*d*. In hurdles made for the fishery of the mill 2*d*. Total, 10*d*.

Expenses of the steward and bailiff
In expenses of the steward for 1 visit at the tourn of Martinmas, 5*s*. 9*d*. by 1 tally. In expenses of the same at the tourn of Hockday, 2*s*. without tally. In expenses of Simon, clerk, Henry la Gayte and others when the relict of Richard le Warn*er* was given her dower, 2*s*. without tally. In expenses of the bailiff for the year £4 15*s*. In fur for the summer livery of the same 3*s*. Delivered to the keeper of the curia of Marwell, the park and pasture, from Michaelmas (29 September) until Friday after the feast of St Gregory (16 March), 14*s*., at 1*d*. a day for 168 days. Thereafter he took his livery

1 MS omits '5'.

from both wheat and barley, at 1 bus. a week. Also in expenses of Henry la Gayte whilst he was bailiff 3*s*. 6*d*. Total, £6 5*s*. 3*d*.

Total of all expenses, £68 8*s*. 6*d*.

And he owes, £163 6*s*. 7¼*d*.

Allowances
In allowance of the reeve for building 1 new building at Marwell for the dairy there, with all costs and expenses, £4 1*s*. 6*d*. In removing 1 kennel and putting it elsewhere, in all costs and expenses, 16*s*. 9*d*. In pulling down a certain building of 4 cruck bays in the field outside Twyford on the southern side of the vill and raising it at Marwell for the cows there, with 2 bays added with timber felled and sawn for the same, in all costs and expenses, £2. In expenses of 2 carters and 5 horses going to London, Farnham and Downton on 3 occasions carrying wine and other victuals 2*s*. 4*d*. In gifts given by order of Sir G*eoffrey*, treasurer of Wolvesey, 6*s*. 8*d*. Also for 72 qrs of charcoal made and sent to Wolvesey, at 1½*d*. a qr, 9*s*. Also for 41 milch-cows, 13 of them with calf, bought to stock the manor of Marwell, £15 8*s*. 4*d*. Also in allowance of the same for mending the masonry and carpentry of the walls and roofing la Cuppedestable at Marwell £1 13*s*. 6*d*. Total of all allowances, £24 18*s*. 1*d*.

Cash deliveries
Delivered to Sir G*eoffrey*, treasurer of Wolvesey, by 1 tally, £31 4*s*.

Total of all allowances and cash deliveries, £56 2*s*. 1*d*.

And thus he owes clear, £107 4*s*. 6¼*d*.

Issues of the grange

Wheat
{yield: 4-fold plus 11 qrs 6 bus.}
The same render account for 158 qrs 4 bus. from the whole issue of wheat from the grange in the granary by struck measure.
Sown over 148 acres in the field of la Wodelo*nd*', 55½ qrs; that is, 3 bus. an acre. In provision of the steward by 1 tally, ½ qr. In provision of the bailiff for the year, 13 qrs. Delivered to 1 park-keeper of Marwell and Bishopstoke from Friday after the feast of St Gregory the Pope (16 March) until Michaelmas (29 September), for 28 weeks, 1 qr 6 bus., taking the rest in barley, and taking a quarter every 8 weeks. Sold, 87½ qrs 2 bus. Total, 158 qrs 4 bus. It balances.

Curall
The same render account for 18 qrs 6 bus. from the whole issue of curall; all sold. It balances.

Barley
{yield: four-fold plus 15 qrs 6½ bus.}
The same render account for 186 qrs 2½ bus. from the whole issue of barley from the grange in the granary by struck measure; 18 qrs 3 bus. bought. Total, 204 qrs 5½ bus. Sown over 112 acres in the field of Coukeslond', and beside the wether-house at Marwell, and Durfurlong' at Twyford, and in la Nutherfeld', 56 qrs; that is, ½ qr an

acre. Delivered to 1 carter and 2 drivers of horse-ploughs for the year, 15 qrs 4½ bus., taking a quarter every 10 weeks. Delivered to 1 harrower at both sowings, 1½ qrs. In an assistant for 1 shepherd at breeding time, ½ qr. Delivered to 1 dairymaid and 1 cowherd at Marwell from the feast of the Apostles Philip and James (1 May) until Michaelmas, for 21 weeks, 3½ qrs, taking a quarter every 12 weeks, for the raising and building of the cowshed and dairy there, for the first time this year. In provision of the bailiff for the year, 2 qrs 1 bus. Delivered to one park-keeper of Marwell and Bishopstoke from Friday after the feast of St Gregory the Pope until Michaelmas, for 28 weeks, 1 qr 6 bus., taking the rest in wheat, and taking a quarter every 8 weeks. Sold, 120 qrs 5 bus. Sold at the audit, 5 bus. Total, 202 qrs 1½ bus. 2½ qrs remains in the granary.

Oats
{yield: two-and-half-fold plus 5½ qrs}
The same render account for 240½ qrs from the whole issue of oats from the grange in the granary by struck measure; 20 qrs by estimation in sheaves given to oxen. Total, 260½ qrs.
Sown over 173½ acres 1 perch in Netherfeld' and Wottelye, and beside the wether-house, and Colewollehull', 130 qrs 2 bus.; that is, 6 bus. an acre. In fodder of 2 cart-horses for the year, 20 qrs. In fodder of 12 plough-horses from Christmas eve until the Purification (2 February), for 40 nights, 10 qrs, at 2 bus. a day and night. In fodder of the same from the same day until the third day after the Ides of April (16 April), 22 qrs, for 74 days, at 2 bus. 1 peck a day and night, but 1 qr 1½ bus. more because they ploughed before and after dinner. In customary payment to 1 dairymaid at Twyford for pressing, ½ qr. In meal made for the pottage of the manorial servants, 1 qr. In fodder of the steward's horses, 1 qr by tally. In fodder of the bailiff's horses for the year, 15 qrs. In fodder of oxen by estimation in sheaves, 20 qrs. Sold, 40 qrs 6 bus. Total, 260½ qrs. It balances.

Peas
{yield: 7-fold less 1 bus.}
The same render account for 22 qrs 3 bus. from the whole issue of peas from the grange in the granary by struck measure,
Sown over the fields of Shortedan' and Hevelestyng', 2 qrs 7 bus. In supporting pigs, 2 qrs. Sold, 17½ qrs. Total, 22 qrs 2 bus. It balances.

Vetches
{yield: 10-fold less 5½ bus.}
The same render account for 37 qrs 3 bus. from the whole issue of vetches from the grange in the granary by struck measure; 2 qrs by estimation in husks given to ewes and hoggs. Total, 39 qrs 3 bus.
Sown over the fields of la Shortedan' and Hevelestyng', 6 qrs 3 bus. Given to ewes and hoggs in husks, 2 qrs. Sold, 31 qrs. Total, 39 qrs 3 bus. It balances.

Vetches from the previous year
The same render account for 4 qrs 6 bus. of vetches remaining from the previous year; all sold.

Mill of North Twyford
Nothing from wheat this year; 11 qrs 3 bus. of barley from the whole issue of the said mill this year, and all sold.

Mill of Shawford
Nothing from wheat this year; 7 qrs of barley from the whole issue of the said mill, and all sold.

Stock

Cart-horses: 3 remain from the previous year; 3 remain.
Plough-horses: 13 remain from the previous year; 1 from the heriot of John Mol*endinarius*; 1 from the heriot of Walter Wynegod'; 1 addition. Total, 16. 1 in murrain; 15 remain.
Oxen: 66 remain from the previous year; 1 addition; 1 from the heriot of Walter Buryman rendered for his land; 1 from the heriot of John Luveson'; 9 bought. Total, 78. 5 in murrain, of which 2 carcasses worth nothing because they died in March; 7 sold. Total, 12. 66 remain.
Cows: 2 remain from the previous year; 41 milch-cows bought, 13 of them with calf and 28 after calving. Total, 43. 1 in murrain before calving. 42 remain.
Steers: 1 remains from the previous year's bullocks; 1 added to oxen; none remain.
Bullocks: none this year.
Yearlings: 1 remains from the previous year's calves; 1 female remains.
Calves: 1 from the offspring of the said cows because 1 sterile; 13 bought with the aforesaid cows. Total, 14. 1 in murrain; 13 remain.
Wethers: 528 remain from the previous year; 179 added from stock. Total, 707. 46 sold at Martinmas; 16 in murrain before shearing, 12 after shearing. Total, 74. 633 remain.
Ewes: 760 remain from the previous year; 181 added from stock. Total, 941. 45 sold at Martinmas; 13 in murrain before breeding, 29 after breeding and before shearing, and 20 after shearing. Total, 107. 834 remain.
Rams: 14 remain from the previous year; 1 in murrain before shearing; 13 remain.
Hoggs: 385 remain from the previous year's lambs; 25 in murrain before shearing; 179 added to wethers, 181 to ewes. Total, 385. None remain.
Lambs: 655 produced by the said ewes because 28 sterile and 19 aborted; 34 bought from the reeve of Merdon after shearing. Total, 689. 54 in tithe; 5 in customary payment to 1 reeve, 2 beadles, 1 shepherd of Twyford, and 1 shepherd keeping part of the ewes at Bishopstoke; 110 in murrain before weaning, 20 after weaning and before shearing, and 6 after shearing; 62 sold before shearing because feeble. Total, 257. 432 remain.
Coarse wool {yield of fleece 4¼*d.* plus 9*d.* in all}: 466 fleeces from wethers, 13 from rams, 673 from ewes, and 360 from hoggs. Total, 1,512. 151 in tithe; 1 in customary payment to 1 shepherd. Total, 152. 1,360 sent to Wolvesey, which made 9 weys 10 cloves.
Wool locks: 8 lb from wethers and 14 cloves from ewes and hoggs; all sold.
Lamb's-wool {[yield of fleece] 1¼*d.* plus 4*s.* 1*d.* in all}: 404 fleeces produced at the shearing this year; all sent to Wolvesey.
[Woolskins]: 16 from wethers, 42 from ewes, 1 from a ram and 25 from hoggs in murrain before shearing. Total, 84. All sold.
Bare skins: 12 from wethers and 20 from ewes; all sold.
Lambskins: 110 from lambs dead from murrain before weaning, 20 after weaning and before shearing, and 6 after shearing. Total, 136. 10 in tithe; 126 sold.
[Butter]: 20½ weys from the milk of 513 ewes, that is, 4 weys from each hundred according to custom; 2 weys in tithe; 24 cloves in 5 cheeses in customary payment to 1 reeve, 2 beadles, 1 shepherd of ewes, and the ploughmen; 17½ weys 3 cloves sold.

[Butter]: 7 cloves made this year; sold.
Cheese from Marwell {[yield of] . . . 10 cows bought in Lent 3*s*. [each], 18 bought at the feast of St Augustine (26 May) 2*s*. each, and 5 bought about the feast of St John the Baptist (24 June) 1*s*. 6*d*. each}: 150 cheeses produced at Marwell from the issue of the cows bought there this year between Thursday the feast of the Invention of the Cross (3 May) and Michaelmas (29 September), both days included; 15 in tithe; 135 sold, which made 10 weys 3½ cloves.
[Butter]: 22 cloves produced from the issue of the said cows; all sold.
[Pigs]: 77 remain from the previous year; 24 additions. Total, 101. 2 in murrain; 75 sold. Total, 78.[1] 24 remain.
[Boars]: 1 remains from the previous year; 1 remains.
[Sows]: 4 remain from the previous year; 1 addition. Total, 5. 2 in murrain before farrowing, 1 after farrowing; 2 remain.
[Hoggets]: 29 remain from the previous year's piglets. 4 in murrain; 1 added to sows, 24 to pigs. Total, 29. None remain.
[Piglets]: 48 from the offspring of the said sows, of which 18 farrowed in February, 15 in March, and 15 in August. 4 in tithe; 4 in customary payment to 1 reeve, 2 beadles and the swineherd. Total, 8. 40 remain.
[Capons]: 4 from the rent of Nicholas Wydelok'; all sold.
[Hides]: 1 from a plough-horse, 5 from oxen, 1 from a cow, 1 from a calf dead from murrain. Total, 8. 7 sold; 1 whitened; 1 whitened hide remains.
[Sticks of] eels: 5 from the farm of the mill of Brambridge; all sold.
[Swans] of Twyford: 24 remain from the previous year; 2 received from the lord bishop; 12 from this year's offspring. Total, 38. 1 in murrain; 9 delivered for the provision of the lord bishop's house at Wolvesey; 7 sent to London for the provision of the same at the parliament at the feast of St Edward.[2] Total, 17. 21 remain, 8 of them nesting (*herarii*).
Swans of Marwell: 5 remain from the previous year; 5 remain.
Peacocks: 4 remain from the previous year; 1 offspring. Total, 5. 5 remain, 1 of them a peacock.
Cider: 2 casks and 1 pipe made this year from the issue of the garden; they remain.
Carts: 3 remain from the previous year; 3 renewed. Total, 6. 2 worn out; 1 sold; 3 remain.
Utensils: 1 ewer, 1 basin, 2 brass pots, 1 pitcher, 3 pans, 1 of them large, and 1 cooking-pot remain from the previous year; 1 brass pot and 2 brass pans bought; all this remains.
Mares: 4 remain from the previous year; 4 remain.
Colts: 1 remains from the previous year aged 2½ years; 1 added to plough-horses; none remain.
Foals: 2 males remain from the previous year aged 1½ years; 2 remain aged 2½ years.
Also foals: 2 from the offspring of the said mares; 2 remain.
m.26

Bishopstoke

Arrears

John de Herierd', bailiff, and William Aylward, reeve of Bishopstoke, render account for £35 8*s*. 5*d*. of arrears from the previous year. All delivered to Sir G*eoffrey*, treasurer of Wolvesey, by 1 tally. They are quit.

1 Figures add up to 77.

2 Presumably the translation of St Edward the King (13 October). There was a parliament at Westminster on 14 October 1302.

Rents of assize
The same render account for £4 9*d.* for all rents of assize at Christmas; £4 9*d.* at the Annunciation (25 March); £4 9*d.* at the feast of St John the Baptist (24 June); £5 7*s.* 2¾*d.*[1] at Michaelmas (29 September). Total, £17 9*s.* 5¾*d.*

Quittances
In quittance of 1 reeve for the year 4*s.*; 1 beadle for the year 2*s.*; 4 ploughmen for the year 8*s.*, or 2*s.* each; 1 oxherd for the year 2*s.*; 1 cowherd for the year 2*s.*; 1 smith for the year 2*s.*; 1 keeper of the old sheep of Twyford 2*s.* Total, £1 2*s.*

Defaults of rent
In default of the land of Richard de Abynton'[2] drawn into demesne 9*s.*; 12 acres of the long meadow drawn into demesne 7*s.*; 45 acres of land in la Westfeld' drawn into demesne 5*s.*; the land of Pykot drawn into the park 1*s.* 2*d.*; the land of Idrad drawn into the park 2*s.* 6*d.*; the land of Nicholas drawn into the park 1*s.*; the land of Richard Juvenis drawn into the park 1*s.* 4*d.* Total, £1 7*s.*

Total of quittances and defaults of rent, £2 9*s.*

Total of rents remaining, £15 5¾*d.*

Farm of the mill
The same render account for £2 for the farm of the mill for the year; 4*s.* 4*d.* from 400 eels from the farm of the same mill; 2*s.* from the land of Wodye for the year. Total, £2 6*s.* 4*d.*

Annual recognizance
The same render account for 4*d.* from Stephen ate Strode for annual recognizance, so that he remains the lord's villein and does his suit of court at the law-days; 3*d.* from William de Colebroc for the same; 3*d.* from Geoffrey, son of Geoffrey ate Asshe, for annual recognizance; 3*d.* from Thomas, son of Peter ate Quabbe, for the same. Total, 1*s.* 1*d.*

Issues of the manor
The same render account for £2 4*s.* 6½*d.* from pannage of pigs this year; £4 1*s.* 6*d.* from pannage of pigs in the park this year; 13*s.* 4*d.* from the pasturage in la Haycrofte sold this year; nothing from the pasturage in la Fryth' this year because it was sown; 6*s.* 3*d.* from the pasturage in la Brodemed' sold this year; 1*s.* 2*d.* from bracken in the park sold this year; £2 14*s.* from the pasturage of 108 yearlings agisting in the park sold, at 6*d.* a yearling; £3 6*s.* from 6 old oxen sold, at 11*s.* each; £1 15*s.* from 4 feeble cows sold before calving, at 7*s.* for 1, 8*s.* each for 2, and 12*s.* for 1; 14*s.* from 14 feeble and late-born calves sold; 17*s.* 8*d.* from the hides sold at various prices of 6 oxen in murrain; 12*s.* 2*d.* from the hides sold of 6 cows in murrain; 1*s.* 3*d.* from the hides sold of 2 bullocks and 1 yearling in murrain; 1*s.* 10*d.* from the hides sold of 2 plough-horses in murrain; nothing from wood in Brentyng' this year; nothing from cablish in the park and Brentyng' this year; 11*s.* 4*d.* from wood blown down by the wind in the park sold this year; nothing from the loppings and bark of timber felled for the use of the lord here because it was sold by Sir *Geoffrey*, treasurer of

1 MS 'ij d. ⌈ob.⌉ q.'.

2 MS 'Abyn⟨d⟩⌈t⌉on''.

Wolvesey; 4*s*. 8*d*. from ½ wey, 1 clove, 5 lb of rowen cheese sold, at 3½*d*. a clove; £2 18*s*. 4*d*. from 7 weys of cheese made in summer sold, at 8*s*. 4*d*. a wey; 3*s*. 9½*d*. from 13 cloves of butter sold; 11*s*. 8*d*. from 140 hens from churchscot sold; 1*s*. 10*d*. from 550 eggs sold, at 4*d*. a 100; 8*s*. from fishing in the water; 9*s*. from harvest labour services sold **{from now on put the individual labour services which should be better examined}**; 4*s*. from John Cnave*n*hull' for release from the service of the land of Cnavenhull' this year; £19 13*s*. from 53 yearlings in the park the previous year sold at various prices; 1*d*. from the hide sold of 1 calf in murrain; 13*s*. 9½*d*. from dairy produce sold at the audit. Total, £42 16*s*. 3½*d*.

Sale of corn
The same render account for £22 18*s*. from 71 qrs 2 bus. of wheat sold, at 6*s*. a qr for 25½ qrs, and 6*s*. 8*d*. a qr for 45 qrs 6 bus.; 15*s*. from 3 qrs of rye sold, at 5*s*. a qr; 17*s*. 6*d*. from 4 qrs 3 bus. of barley sold, at 4*s*. a qr; £5 3*s*. 10*d*. from 44½ qrs of oats sold, at 2*s*. 4*d*. a qr; £1 4*s*. 11½*d*. from 8 qrs 5 bus. of beans sold, at 2*s*. 8*d*. a qr for 2 qrs 6 bus., and 3*s*. a qr for 5 qrs 7 bus.; £1 4*s*. 3*d*. from 7 qrs 5 bus. of peas sold, at 1*s*. 4*d*. for ½ qr, 3*s*. a qr for 2½ qrs, and 3*s*. 4*d*. a qr for 4 qrs 5 bus.; 12*s*. 3*d*. from 6 qrs 1 bus. of vetches sold, at 2*s*. a qr; 1*s*. 6*d*. from 2 bus. of wheat sold at the audit; 6*d*. from 1 bus. of barley sold at the audit. Total, £32 17*s*. 9½*d*.

Entry and marriage fines with tithingpenny
The same render account for 6*s*. 8*d*. from the tithing of Bishopstoke at the hundred-court of Martinmas for tithingpenny; 6*s*. 8*d*. from the same for the same at the hundred-court of Hockday; 1*s*. from Alexander ate Pyle for marrying Ellen his daughter outside; 6*d*. from Walter Techely for marrying Lucy his daughter outside; 6*d*. from Adam Brigg' for marrying Agnes his daughter outside; 6*d*. from Edith, relict of Richard le Dyeve, to retain 1 messuage which belonged to the aforesaid Richard her husband; 10*s*. from Robert le Coliar' to have 1 house with a curtilage which belonged to Hugh le Coliar'; 10*s*. from Adam ate Broke to have Loretta ate Wynd' with 9 acres of her land; 6*s*. 8*d*. from Thomas le Longe to have Christina ate Cnoll' and 1 ferling of her land; £1 from Robert de Excestr' to have 1 messuage[1] and 11 acres of land which belonged to William de Colebrok'; 13*s*. 4*d*. from Robert Dych to have 1 acre of land by resignation of Robert ate Woll'. Total, £3 15*s*. 10*d*.

Perquisites of court
The same render account for 4*s*. from John, son of Matilda ate Cnolle, because he burnt 1 oak in the lord's park seeking the honey of bees; 2*s*. from William de Duggyngwod' because he struck Stephen Ive, whereupon the hue was raised; 2*s*. from Henry ate Brechlo*n*d' for breaking the assize; 2*s*. from the tithing because it did not produce in court those it had bailed; 2*s*. from Geoffrey Hevedman and 3 of his fellows for transgression against John, son of Matilda Davy; 2*s*. from the tithing of Bishopstoke for concealment; 13*s*. 4*d*. from John ate Cnoll' for trespass of wood in the park of Bishopstoke; £1 6*s*. 8*d*. from Robert Ive for the same; £1 from Stephen Ive for the same; £1 from John Bru*n* for the same; 13*s*. 4*d*. from John le Boys for the same; £1 18*s*. from various men for various transgressions. Total, £6 15*s*. 4*d*.

Total of both, £10 11*s*. 2*d*.

Total of all receipts, £103 13*s*. 1¾*d*.

1 MS 'j ⟨domo⟩ mes''.

Cost of ploughs

In iron and steel bought for the ironwork of 2 ploughs for the year 3*s*. 3*d*. In 2 ploughs made anew and other ploughs and harrows mended at various times 10*d*. In 2 pairs of wheels bought 8*d*. In 1 coulter made anew with iron bought for the same 6*d*. In winter boon-works of 17 ploughmen who ploughed 34 acres of land as they lie 2*s*. 10*d*., at 1*d*. an acre. Moreover, they ploughed 10 acres according to custom. In Lenten boon-works of 28 ploughmen who ploughed 50 acres as they lie 4*s*. 2*d*., at 1*d*. an acre. In quittance of 4 ploughmen for 20 Saturday ploughings between Michaelmas and Easter 10*s*., or 3*d*. a ploughman a day. In quittance of the said ploughmen for 18 Saturday ploughings between Easter and Michaelmas 6*s*., or 2*d*. a ploughmen a Saturday. In cleaning 7 qrs of barley and 26 qrs of oats for sowing 2*s*. In hiring 1 man to doctor (*marschall*and’) the oxen 8*d*. In 8 oxen bought £4 2*s*. 6*d*., at 10*s*. 6*d*. each for five, and 10*s*. each for 3. Total, £5 13*s*. 5*d*.

Cost of carts

In 1 pair of wheels bought 2*s*. In removing 1 old binding and putting it on the said wheels with large nails bought for the same 2*s*. 3*d*. In clamps with small nails bought for the same 9*d*. In a wooden hoop bought 2½*d*. In stipend of the smith fitting the binding to the said wheels and for 2 linch-pins and 1 band of iron 1*s*. 4*d*. In clouts and nails bought for the same 7*d*. In grease bought 4*d*. In fitting the cart with axles at various times 3*d*. In 1 pair of traces bought 4½*d*. In 1 collar bought 7*d*. In white leather bought for harnesses 7*d*. In shoeing 2 plough-horses for the year 2*s*. 8*d*. In stipend of 1 carter for the year 3*s*. In 3 ells of canvas bought for sacks 9*d*. In 4 clouts with nails and grease bought for the wagon 9½*d*. In 1 mare bought 8*s*. 7*d*. Total, £1 5*s*. ½*d*.

Cost of the dairy

In woollen and linen cloth bought 8½*d*. In earthenware pots and pans bought 4*d*. In a press bought 6*d*. In 6 bus. of salt bought 1*s*. 7¼*d*. In mending buckets and 1 lath 3*d*. In mending 1 old cooking-pot and 1 lock 2½*d*. In 1 mould bought 5*d*. In 1 tripod bought 7*d*. In stipend of 1 dairymaid for the year 3*s*. In 53 yearlings bought the previous year for agisting in the park £15 5*s*. 4*d*. In 6 cows bought, 5 of them with calf and 1 after calving, £2 10*s*. ⌈3½*d*.⌉, at 7*s*. 11*d*. each for 2, 8*s*. each for 2, 9*s*. 2*d*. for 1, and 9*s*. 3½*d*. for 1. Total, £18 3*s*. 2¾*d*.

Repair of buildings

In re-roofing the hay-barn in places 1*s*. 8*d*. In enclosing 7 furlongs and 9 perches around Bre*n*tyng’ with hedges 6*s*. ¼*d*. In 4 casks bought for putting cider in 10*s*. In stipend of 3 coopers hooping the said casks and other utensils for 9 days with hoops bought for the same 4*s*. In troughs bought 2*d*. In mending the press with grease bought for the same 8*d*. Total, £1 2*s*. 6¼*d*.

Cost of the meadow

In mowing the long meadow according to custom 6*d*. In mowing the meadow of Brentyng’ according to custom 8*d*. In 1 ox carcass bought for the mowing of the great meadow 5*s*. Total, 6*s*. 2*d*.

Cost of the harvest

In bread bought for 5 boon-works of 576 men who reaped 215 acres as they lie of all corn with 44 customary tenants and the help of 26 cottars, 19*s*., and 2 men had 3 farthings of bread. In herrings and cheese bought for a want of herrings 12*s.* 10½*d.* In supper for 26 cottars reaping the lord's corn for a day 6½*d.*, or ¼*d.* each a day. Total, £1 12*s.* 5*d.*

Cost of the park
In stipend of 2 carpenters repairing and restoring the palisade of the park at la Brodemed' beyond the river-bank for 2 days 1*s.* In 1 lock bought for the east gate of the same park 5*d.* In staples and nails bought for the same gate 1*d.* In staples and hasps bought for the new gate 1*d.* Total, 1*s.* 7*d.*

New building
In raising anew 1 new hay-barn, in all costs and expenses, £3 8*s.* ½*d.* In gifts given for the business of the lord by order of the treasurer 6*s.* 8*d.* Total, £3 14*s.* 8½*d.*

Total of all expenses, £31 19*s.* 1*d.*

And he owes, £71 14*s.* ¾*d.*

Cash deliveries
Delivered to Sir *Geoffrey*, treasurer of Wolvesey, £29 7*s.* 7*d.*

And he owes clear, £42 6*s.* 5¾*d.*

Issues of the grange[1]

Wheat
{yield: 5½-fold plus 2 qrs 5 bus.}
The same render account for 90 qrs 5 bus. from the whole issue of wheat from the grange in the granary by struck measure.
Sown in the field of Parkforlo*ng*' and in la Frithe, 18 qrs 1 bus. In customary payment for the great meadow, 1 qr. Sold, 71 qrs 2 bus. Sold at the audit, 2 bus.

Rye
The same render account for 3 qrs of rye from churchscot; all sold.

Barley
{yield: 4½-fold plus 5 bus.}
The same render account for 18 qrs 5 bus. from the whole issue of barley by struck measure.
Sown in the field of Middelforlong', 7 qrs. Delivered to 1 carter for the year, 5 qrs 1½ bus., taking a quarter every 10 weeks. Delivered to 1 dairymaid from Easter until Michaelmas, 1 qr 7½ bus., or 1 qr every 12 weeks. Sold, 4 qrs 3 bus. Sold at the audit, 1 bus.

Oats
{yield: two-and-a-half-fold less 3 qrs 6 bus.}
The same render account for 81 qrs 2 bus. from the whole issue of oats by struck measure; 1½ qrs by estimation in sheaves. Total, 82 qrs 6 bus.
Sown in the fields of Brentyng', la Fryth' and Herehull', 33 qrs 6 bus. Given to oxen by estimation in sheaves, 1½ qrs. In fodder of 2 mares for the year, 2 qrs. In meal made for the pottage of the manorial servants, 1 qr. Sold, 44½ qrs.

1 MS illustration of a foliated cross; see above, p. x.

Beans
{yield: 6-fold less 1 bus.}
The same render account for 11 qrs 7 bus. from the whole issue of beans from the grange in the granary[1] by struck measure.
Sown in the field of Middelforlang', 3 qrs 2 bus. Sold, 8 qrs 5 bus.

Peas
{yield: 8½-fold plus 1 bus.}
The same render account for 8 qrs 5 bus. from the whole issue of peas from the grange in the granary by struck measure.
Sown in the field of Middelfeld*e*furla*n*g, 1 qr. Sold, 7 qrs 5 bus.

Vetches
{yield: 7½-fold plus 1 bus.}
The same render account for 7 qrs 5 bus. from the whole issue of vetches from the grange in the granary by struck measure.
Sown in the field of Midelfurlo*n*g, 1½ qrs. Sold, 6 qrs 1 bus.

Stock

Plough-horses: 3 remain from the previous year; 1 bought. Total, 4. 2 in murrain before foaling; 2 females remain.
Foals: no offspring this year because the mares sterile.
Oxen: 31 remain from the previous year; 3 additions; 8 bought. Total, 42. 6 in murrain in March; 6 sold. Total, 12. 30 remain.
Bulls: 1 remains from the previous year; 1 remains.
Cows: 38 remain from the previous year; 1 addition; 6 milch-cows bought, 5 of them with calf. Total, 45. 6 in murrain before calving; 4 sold before calving. Total, 10. 35 remain.
Steers: 4 remain from the previous year's bullocks. 3 added to oxen, 1 to cows. Total, 4. None remain here.
Bullocks: 10 remain from the previous year's yearlings; 2 in murrain; 8 remain, 6 of them male.
Yearlings: 9 remain from the previous year's calves; 1 in murrain; 8 remain, 4 of them male.
Calves: 24 from the offspring of the said cows because 5 sterile; 5 bought. Total, 29. 2 in tithe; 1 in murrain; 14 sold because feeble; 12 remain, 5 of them male.
Winter cheese: 42 made this year; all sold, which made ½ wey, 1 clove, 5 lb.
Summer cheese {yield of cow 2*s*. 9*d*. with 2 cheeses in customary payment and 2 cheeses used elsewhere which are valued at 2*s*.}: 163 cheeses made between Friday before the feast of St Mark the Evangelist (20 April) and Michaelmas (29 September), both days included. 16 in tithe; 1 in customary payment for the meadow of Bre*n*tyng'; 1 in customary payment to 1 smith. Total, 18. 145 sold, which made 7 weys.
Butter: 13 cloves from the issue of the dairy; all sold.
Hides: 2 from plough-horses in murrain, 6 from oxen, 6 from cows, 2 from bullocks, 1 from a yearling, and 1 from a calf dead from murrain; all sold.
Peacocks {order to answer henceforth for the feathers}: 2 remain from the previous year; 1 peacock and 1 peahen remains; no offspring this year.
Hens: 147 from churchscot. 2 in default of the land of Eve Algar; 1 in default of the land of John Pynnok; 1 in default of the land of Thomas Pynnok; 1 in default of the

1 MS 'de gr*a*ng' in ⟨gr*a*ng'⟩ in gr*a*nar''.

land of Roger ate Strode; 1 in default of the land of Richard Gimtyr; 1 in default of the land of Henry Aylwyn'. Total, 7. 140 sold.
Eggs: 550 from the beadle according to custom; all sold.
Utensils: 1 brass pot, 2 cooking-pots, 1 posnet, 1 basin remain from the previous year; all this remains.
Cider: 7 casks from this year's issue; 7 casks remain.

East Meon

Arrears

Nicholas de Ychen', bailiff, and Richard Pokepole and Adam de Cu*m*be, reeves, render account for £94 4*s*. 10½*d*. of arrears from the previous year. All delivered to Sir G*eoffrey*, treasurer of Wolvesey, by 1 tally. They are quit.

Rents of assize

The same render account for £23 2*s*. 8½*d*. for all rents of assize at Christmas; £23 2*s*. 8½*d*. at Easter (22 April); £23 2*s*. 8½*d*. at the feast of St John the Baptist (24 June); £27 18*s*. 4*d*. at Michaelmas (29 September). Total, £97 6*s*. 5½*d*.

Increment

The same render account for ½*d*. from John Miles for the increment of rent for a certain purpresture which before he encroached upon without licence of the lord. Total the same.

Total of all rents with increment, £97 6*s*. 6*d*.

Quittances

In quittance of 1 reeve for the year 5*s*.; 8 ploughmen, 3 shepherds and 1 swineherd for the year £1 10*s*., or 2*s*. 6*d*. each; 3 ploughmen for the year who replaced 3 drovers who were at liberty 7*s*. 6*d*. Total, £2 2*s*. 6*d*.

Defaults of rent

In default of the land drawn into demesne, £1 1*s*. 7½*d*. for the year; the land of Reth*e*cu*m*b*e* given to the canons of Newark Priory by Bishop Godfrey, £5 for the year; the pasture and wood of Ballu*n*s which belonged to Thomas de Cu*m*b*e* drawn into demesne, £2 for the year; the mill which Robert Mol*endinarius* sometimes held drawn into demesne, £1 for the year; 8 acres of land which Deodatus (*Deudoenis*) le Hayward sometimes held drawn into demesne, 3*s*. for the year; the land which the Abbot of Durford held drawn into demesne, 3*s*. 5*d*. for the year; the land of Barlych' drawn into the park, 3*s*. 2*d*. for the year; 1 purpresture which belonged to William Gibbe drawn into demesne, 6*d*. for the year; 1 plot beside the marl-pit of Weth*a*m which H. de Borden' held, 4*d*., because it was a nuisance to the neighbourhood. Total, £9 12*s*. ½*d*.

Total of quittances and defaults of rent, £11 14*s*. 6½*d*.

Total of rents remaining, £85 11*s*. 11½*d*.

Cumin

The same render account for ½ lb of cumin from the rent of William ate Bere; 1 lb of cumin from Andrew de Holeweye for annual recognizance. Total, 1½ lbs.

Gloves

The same render account for 1 pair of gloves from the rent of William Gilberd'; all delivered to Wolvesey.

Wax

The same render account for 1 lb of wax from Adam Osmu*n*d' for annual recognizance; all delivered to Wolvesey.

Annual recognizance

The same render account for 3*d*. from John le Espicir for annual recognizance; 6*d*. from Henry de Afford' so that he may come and go within the hundred and pay suit of court for the tithing at the 2 hundred-courts; 6*d*. from William de Stomore for the same; 3*d*. from Robert Judde for annual recognizance so that he need not pay suit of court for the tithing; 3*d*. from Robert Fab*e*r for annual recognizance; 3*d*. from Henry ate Thorn' for the same, plus William ate Churche. Total, 2*s*.

Issues of the manor

The same render account for £2 19*s*. 10½*d*. from pannage of pigs within the hundred this year; nothing from foreign pannage or in the park this year for a want of mast; nothing from the pasturage in the stubble this year; 7*s*. 4*d*. from winter pasturage in Hydon' which is called Blakedo*n* on the west side of Astederod' which is the common land of East Meon, because the other part is enclosed for the lord's profit; nothing from the pasturage in Smaldon' this year on account of the lord's stock; 3*s*. from the pasturage of the meadow below Godeshull' sold in winter; nothing from the pasturage of Innom' in winter or summer this year because it was mown; £1 2*s*. 8*d*. from summer pasturage sold in Hydon' by agistment by the head; 7*s*. from the pasturage beside the sheepcote of Holecu*m*b*e* sold in summer; 4*s*. from the pasturage in la Garsto*n* sold this year in summer; nothing from the pasturage of Wodeueslynch' this year for the lord's lambs; nothing from the pasturage of Bekes this year on account of the lord's sheep; nothing from the pasturage of 1 plot of Hardesco*m*b*e* this year for the lord's lambs; 8*s*. from the pasturage of Lokewell' and Hullyden' sold this year; 7*s*. from the pasturage of Brodemed' sold after mowing; nothing from the pasturage in the park this year on account of the lord's stock; 5*s*. from the pasturage of Oldefiswer' as far as Selecu*m*b*e* and Sabwey sold this year; 2*s*. from the pasturage of the heath beside Hydo*n* sold; 8*d*. from the pasturage beside the sheepcote of Westcre*m*b*e* sold; nothing from the pasturage of the garden this year because it was mown; 3*s*. 6*d*. from the pasturage of 1 parcel of Selescu*m*b*e* sold this year because the rest was sown; nothing from the pasturage of Wodeslynch' this year on account of the lord's lambs; nothing from the pasturage on this side (*cit*ra) of Northebrok' this year because it was fallow; nothing from the pasturage of Litlecu*m*b*e* this year on account of the lord's stock; 2*s*. from the pasturage of la Ford' sold as far as the mill and this side of the chapel; 2*s*. from the pasturage from the mill as far as Holewey and this side of the fishpond sold; 2*s*. from the pasturage from the mill as far as Lymput' sold; 7*s*. from the pasturage of Chalvecroft sold; nothing from the pasturage of Wethull' this year on account of the lord's stock; nothing from the pasturage in Woddon' on account of the lord's lambs; nothing from the pasturage of the quarry as far as Maseco*m*b*e* for the same; nothing from the pasturage of the way to Hullymed' from Pydeh*a*m and Wapseburw this year because it was fallow; 1*s*. from the pasturage of 1 plot ⌈beside⌉ the mill and Drayton' below Garstonmed' and Pykes sold; 2*s*. from the pasturage of 1 plot below Notesburgh' which is called Ynnom' sold; 3*s*. from the pasturage of Godeshull*e*med' sold after mowing; 5*s*. 6*d*. from the pasturage in various places sold this year; nothing from thickets in Holescu*m*b*e*, cablish in la Bornett' and the park and from thickets in Hydon' this year; 3*s*. 7*d*. from pinfolding 18 cows and 2 bullocks in winter and 26 cows in summer, because they are bound to give pinfold twice a year; 8*s*. 5*d*. from pinfolding sheep this year, at 1*d*. per 5 sheep, unless they have 20 sheep, because then they give the twentieth sheep; 2*s*. 2*d*. from 26 customary tenants because the land of William le Fissar' is commuted, each of whom ploughs for 'landriht' and everyone is bound to thresh separately 3 bushels of wheat for sowing over 1 acre in winter or give 1*d*. at the lord's will for the threshing; £3 4*s*. 9*d*. from 448 labour services by the perch sold this year, at 2*d*. each for 329, and 1*d*. each for 119; nothing from Avice de Q*uo*rteslod' separately because she worked with the others; 1*s*. from William Ramwyle for release from labour service for the year; nothing from John de Halewell' because he worked with the others; nothing from coarse wool and lamb's-wool here because it is sent to Wolvesey; 18*s*. 1½*d*. from 20 cloves 5 lb of wool locks sold, at 10½*d*. a clove; £1 3*s*. 10*d*. from 286 hens from churchscot sold; 6*s*. from the hides sold of 9 plough-horses in murrain, at 8*d*. each; 1*s*. from the hides of 2 colts sold; 5*s*. 6*d*. from the hides and flesh sold of 2 oxen in murrain; 6*s*. from the hides sold of 3 oxen in murrain; 1*d*. from the hide sold of 1 calf in murrain; £1 2*s*. 5*d*. from the skins sold of 43 wethers, 28 ewes and 30 hoggs in murrain before shearing, at 3*d*. a skin of wethers, 2½*d*. a skin of ewes, and 1½*d*. a skin of hoggs; 3*s*. from the skins sold of 26 wethers and 10 ewes in murrain after shearing, at 1*d*. a skin; 9*s*. 9¾*d*. from the skins sold of 134 lambs in murrain before weaning, and 23 after weaning and before shearing, at ¾*d*. a skin; 3*d*. from the skins sold wholesale of 9 lambs in murrain after shearing; 4*s*. ¾*d*. from 13 cloves of winter cheese sold, at 3¾*d*. a clove; £6 15*s*. from 15 weys of summer cheese sold, at 9*s*. a wey; 9*s*. from 1 wey of butter sold; nothing from honey this year; £2 2*s*. 8*d*. from 3 casks of cider sold, 1 of them with the wood for 16*s*., and 2 without the wood at 13*s*. 4*d*. each; 1*s*. from the heriot of Gilbert ate Brok' because he did not have 1 beast; 1*s*. from the heriot of Christina Colevil'; 1*s*. from the heriot of William Aylwyn' for the same; 5*d*. from the tails and feathers of 2 peacocks sold; 2*s*. 1¾*d*. from dairy produce sold at the audit. Total, £26 6*s*. 9¾*d*.

m.26d

Sale of stock

10*s*. from 3 old and feeble plough-horses sold, ⌈at 3*s*. 4*d*. each⌉ because nearly dead; £4 2*s*. from 7 oxen sold, at 12*s*. each for 3, and 11*s*. 6*d*. each for 4; 8*s*. from 1 cow sold at Martinmas (11 November); 8*s*. from 8 late-born calves sold, at 1*s*. each; £1 4*s*. 6*d*. from 21 wethers sold at Martinmas, at 1*s*. 2*d*. each; £5 from 100 ewes sold at the same feast, at 1*s*. each; 4*s*. 6*d*. from 9 feeble hoggs sold, at 6*d*. each; £3 6*s*. 6*d*. from 19 pigs sold at Martinmas, at 3*s*. 6*d*. each. Total, £15 3*s*. 6*d*.

Sale of corn

The same render account for £75 10*s*. 5*d*. from 274 qrs 2 bus. of wheat sold, at 4*s*. a qr for 29 qrs 2 bus., 5*s*. a qr for 70 qrs 6 bus., 5*s*. 4*d*. a qr for 82 qrs 3 bus., 6*s*. a qr for 18 qrs 2 bus., and 6*s*. 8*d*. a qr for 73 qrs 5 bus.; £2 6*s*. 8*d*. from 14 qrs of curall sold, at 3*s*. 4*d*. a qr; £5 10*s*. 10½*d*. from 28 qrs 5 bus. of barley sold, at 4*s*. a qr for 25 qrs, and 3*s*. a qr for 3 qrs 5 bus.; £28 8*s*. 4¾*d*. from 275 qrs 3 bus. of oats sold, at 1*s*. 8*d*. a qr for 55 qrs 3 bus., 2*s*. a qr for 86 qrs 3 bus., 2*s*. 2*d*. a qr for 50 qrs 5 bus., and 2*s*. 4*d*. a qr for 83 qrs. Total of all corn sold, £111 16*s*. 4¼*d*.

Farm of the mill

The same render account for £1 15*s*. from the mill let at farm this year. Total, £1 15*s*.

Entry and marriage fines with tithingpenny

The same render account for £3 6*s*. 8*d*. from all the tithings of the hundred for tithingpenny at the hundred-court of Martinmas; £3 6*s*. 8*d*. from the same tithings at the hundred-court of Hockday; £2 10*s*. from Nicholas, son and heir of Nicholas de Langriss', for fine to have all the lands and tenements which belonged to his father in the manor of East Meon; 13*s*. 4*d*. from Cecilia, relict of Gilbert ate Brok', to retain 1 messuage and ½ virgate of land which belonged to her husband; 4*s*. from William de Radesole to have 1½ acres of land by surrender of Richard ate Burgh, and the aforesaid William will relieve the said Richard of 5½*d*. annual rent; 1*s*. from Richard Cl*ericus* to have 1 plot which contains 2 day-works of land by surrender of William ate Church', and he will relieve the said William of 1*s*. annual rent; 3*s*. from Roginald Boll' to have 1 acre of land by surrender of John T*ri*bald, and he will relieve the said John of 6*d*. annual rent; £1 13*s*. 4*d*. from Thomas, son of William de Schireve, to have 1 messuage and 1 virgate of land which belonged to his father; 6*s*. 8*d*. from Richard Corps to have 3½ acres of land by surrender of William ate Wod'; 13*s*. 4*d*. from John Corps to have 1 virgate of land of Martin Waterlyde; 1*s*. from Joan Q*ui*rteflod' to retain 1 acre of land which belonged to Richard Schireve her husband; 2*s*. from Geoffrey ate Garsto*n* to have 1 house and 2 day-works of land by surrender of Andrew de Borden'; 2*s*. from Henry Keppyng to have 1 day-work of land by surrender of John H*er*berd', and he will relieve the aforesaid John of 4*d*. annual rent; 1*s*. from John Miles to retain a certain purpresture, 12 feet long and 4 feet wide at one end and 1½ feet at the other end, which before he encroached upon without licence; £2 from William Colevile to have 1 messuage and 1 cotland which belonged to his father whose heir he is; £1 from Cecilia, relict of Nicholas ate Ock', to retain the lands and tenements which belonged to the same Nicholas her husband; £1 6*s*. 8*d*. from Robert de Borden' to have 1 messuage and 1 virgate of land which belonged to Robert his father; 6*s*. 8*d*. from Emma, relict of William ate Pleystowe, to retain 1 messuage and 1 virgate of land which belonged to her husband; £1 6*s*. 8*d*. from Henry de Pip*ercum*be to have 1 messuage and ½ virgate of land and a purpresture which belonged to Gilbert his father; 6*s*. 8*d*. from Walter Whyte and Matilda his wife to have ½ virgate of land which descended to the same Matilda by the death of Emma Kokenild'; 6*s*. 8*d*. from John, son of Walter le Whyte, to have the aforesaid ½ virgate of land by surrender of the said Walter and Matilda; 13*s*. 4*d*. from John Aylwyn' to have ½ virgate of land which belonged to William his father; £1 from Peter ate Bure to have Christina, who was wife of John Crispyn, with her land; 13*s*. 4*d*. from Walter Schireve to have Cecilia, relict of Gilbert ate Brok', with ½ virgate of her land; 1*s*. from Joan de Quirteflod' to have 1 curtilage which is called Westpark by surrender of Avice de Q*ui*rteflod'; 1*s*. from Adam de Ayford' to have the aforesaid curtilage by surrender of Joan de Q*ui*rteflod', so that the said Adam will relieve the said Avice de Q*ui*rteflod' of 2*d*. of her rent for the year; 1*s*. from Agnes Fermyn for marrying Agnes her daughter outside; £1 from William, son of Walter le Swhyte, to have 1 virgate of land by surrender of Walter his father and Matilda, wife of the said Walter. Total, £23 7*s*.

Perquisites

The same render account for 1*s*. from William Cutep*ri*st for unjustly withholding a debt; 8*s*. 6*d*. from Alice Tapecut' and her fellows for trespass of pasture and default of labour service and other transgressions; 4*s*. 6*d*. from Nicholas ate Pyth' for transgression against his neighbour and trespass of pasture; 4*s*. from Alice, daughter of Richard de Naddeh*am*, Ralph ate Stupe and their fellows for many transgressions;

5*s*. 6*d*. from Richard Crespyn, Robert P*ar*ker and others for transgression against their neighbours, trespass of wood, and other transgressions; 1*s*. 9*d*. from Matilda le Tayllur, John de Halywll' and others for transgression against their neighbours and trespass of wood and pasture; 6*d*. from Alice de Chutesco*mbe* for transgression against her neighbour; 6*s*. 8*d*. from Adam Kay the younger for keeping the plough-horses badly; 1*s*. 6*d*. from Thomas ate Church', John le Kay and their fellows for transgression against their neighbours and false complaint; 2*s*. from Henry le Er for trespass of multure of part of the corn at the lord's mill; 3*s*. from Adam Kay for having his pigs at the barn door; 2*s*. from John Kynho for trespass of herbage in the lord's meadow; 2*s*. from William Fynam*ur* and his sons for transgression against Walter Sweyn; £2 18*s*. 5*d*. from various men for various transgressions; 18*s*. from various men for various transgressions from the 2 courts held after the tourn of Hockday. Total, £5 19*s*. 4*d*.

Total of both, £29 6*s*. 4*d*.

Total of all receipts, £270 1*s*. 11½*d*.

Cost of ploughs

In ironwork of 5 ox-ploughs and 3 horse-ploughs (*caruc' affr'*) for the year and 1 horse-plough (*caruc' equin'*) at the Lenten sowing, 14*s*. 3*d*. this year, on account of the excessive drought. In stipend of the smith forging the ironwork of the said ploughs for the year, 8*s*. by fixed agreement. In 5 ploughshares bought 3*s*. 9*d*. In 2 coulters mended 4*d*. In 7 plough feet bought 2*s*. 11*d*., at 5*d*. each. In a new plough and harrow made and others mended for the year, 7*s*. 4*d*. by fixed agreement, and so much because the worker was not at the bailiff's table. In fitting the ploughs with iron tyres 6*d*. In 6 pairs of wheels bought for the ploughs 2*s*. In shoeing 18 plough-horses for the year 1*s*. 6*d*. In fastening the same 4*d*. In stipend of 1 harrower at both sowings 2*s*. 2*d*. In 16 halters made from the horses' own hair 4*d*. In 1 seed-basket bought 1½*d*. In stipend of 3 drovers for the year 9*s*. In stipend of 2 drovers for the year 10*s*. In stipend of 1 hayward for the year 3*s*. In stipend of 1 cowherd for the year 3*s*. In stipend of 1 keeper of lambs and hoggs for the year 3*s*. In ploughing boon-works in winter or Lent, nothing this year, that is, they are bound to plough 26 acres for 'landriht' in winter and 26 acres in Lent, because the land which William le Fissar' holds is commuted as made clear above, and those who plough for 'landriht' in winter are bound to thresh seed for 1 acre or give 1*d*. for the threshing at the lord's will. In blood-letting of oxen 3*d*. In hiring men for the ploughs when they plough after dinner 1*s*. In 11 plough-horses bought for the ploughs £5 6*s*. 1½*d*., at 9*s*. each for 3, 9*s*. 6*d*. each for 2, and 10*s*. each for 6, plus 1½*d*. in all. In 10 oxen bought for ploughs £6 7*s*. ¼*d*., at 12*s*. ¼*d*. for 1, 12*s*. 6*d*. each for 4, and 13*s*. each for 5. In 2 sacks bought 1*s*. Total, £15 6*s*. 11¼*d*.

Cost of carts

In 1 pair of wheels made from the lord's timber 10*d*. In an old binding fitted to the said wheels, with clamps and large and small nails bought for the same, and with the stipend of the smith, 4*s*. 2½*d*. In hooping the hubs of the cart with iron 2*d*. In fitting the cart with axles for the year 6*d*. In clouts, nails and grease bought for the same, 2*s*. 10*d*. this year, for carrying timber to the chapel. In white leather bought for mending harnesses 6*d*. In 1 pair of traces bought 7*d*. In 1 collar 6½*d*. In 2 halters bought 2*d*. In 1 cart-body and 1 cart-rail made anew 8*d*. In mending the old cart at various times 8*d*.

In doctoring horses 4*d*. In shoeing 2 cart-horses for the year 2*s*. In stipend of 1 carter for the year 3*s*. Total, 17*s*.

Cost of the dairy

In 1 qr 1 bus. of salt bought for the dairy 2*s*. 3*d*. In 5 bus. of salt bought for the pottage of the manorial servants 1*s*. 3*d*. In a press bought 6*d*. In linen and woollen cloth bought 1*s*. In mending buckets and utensils of the dairy 6*d*. In earthenware pots and pans bought 6*d*. In grease, copperas and vinegar bought for greasing sheep 18*s*. 6*d*. In 28 ells of canvas bought for packing wool 7*s*., at 3*d*. an ell. In packing the wool and making sacks with thread bought for the same 1*s*. 2*d*. In 60 hurdles made for the fold 2*s*., at 2*d*. per 5 hurdles. In wattling 80 hurdles 2*s*. 8*d*., at 2*d*. per 5 hurdles. In 30 hurdles made for pens 10*d*., at 1*d*. per 3 hurdles. In mending the walls of the sheepcote of Holecu*m*b*e*, putting in sills, and enclosing, 1*s*. 6*d*. In cratches made for the hoggs 8*d*. In roofing and mending the said sheepcote in places 8*d*. In castrating and spaying pigs 4*d*. Total, £2 1*s*. 4*d*.

Cost of buildings

In roofing and mending the barn beside the pinfold and other buildings 3*s*. 10*d*. In rebuilding the walls of the plough-horses' shed which collapsed and making and mending the great fodder-rack with nails bought for the same 2*s*. 9*d*. In mending the gate of the byre with nails bought 4*d*. In building and mending the walls of the barley-barn which collapsed 1*s*. 7½*d*. In mending and fitting with iron 3 shovels and 1 spade 6*d*. In enclosing 34 perches on this side of the pinfold and elsewhere in the curia with hedges 2*s*. 1½*d*., at ¾*d*. a perch. In hooping and mending 2 cider-casks and making and hooping 2 tubs 6*d*. In making 2 casks of cider 8*d*. Total, 12*s*. 4*d*.

Cost of the park

In enclosing 4 furlongs 8 perches around the park with hedges 10*s*. 8*d*. In making and mending the palisade of the park 5*s*. Total, 15*s*. 8*d*.

Cost of the mill

Nothing this year.

Threshing

In threshing and winnowing 354 qrs 7 bus. of wheat and curall by piece-work £2 19*s*. 1¾*d*., at 2*d*. a struck quarter. In threshing and winnowing 101 qrs 1 bus. of barley by piece-work 10*s*. 1½*d*., at 1½*d*. per 10 struck bushels. In threshing and winnowing 572 qrs 7 bus. of oats by piece-work £1 18*s*. 2¼*d*., at 1*d*. per 10 struck bushels. Total, £5 7*s*. 5½*d*.

Harvest-time

In all costs for the great boon-work with 17 other boon-works of 1,807 men who reaped and bound all the corn, together with 1 boon-work of 160 men without food, £6 12*s*. 4¼*d*., and each had ¼*d*. of bread and 2 herrings or 1 cheese worth ¼*d*., and for the great boon-work they had bread, meat and ale. In mowing and tossing the meadow of Mu*n*nonce 1*s*. In mowing and tossing the garden 1*s*. 4*d*. Total, £6 14*s*. 8¼*d*.

Expenses of the steward

In expenses of the steward at the 2 hundred-courts by 1 tally 11*s*. 8½*d*. In expenses of the bailiff for the year £6 15*s*. 6*d*. In fur for the summer livery of the same 3*s*. Total, £7 10*s*. 2½*d*.

Total of all expenses, £39 5*s*. 7½*d*.

And he owes, £230 16*s*. 4*d*.

Cash deliveries
Delivered to Sir G*eoffrey*, treasurer of Wolvesey, by 2 tallies, £139 2*s*.

And he owes clear, £91 14*s*. 4*d*., of which £36 3½*d*. against Richard de Poukepole, and £55 14*s*. ½*d*. against Adam de Cu*mbe*.

Issues of the grange

Wheat
{yield: 6-fold plus 13 qrs 5 bus.}
The same render account for 14 qrs of wheat remaining in the granary from the previous year; 340 qrs 7 bus. from the whole issue of the grange by struck measure; 3 qrs from churchscot. Total, 357 qrs 7 bus.
Sown over 608 acres as they lie in Selescu*mbe*, Stonyelond', and Pykes, 67 qrs 6 bus.; that is, 1 bus. an acre, less 8 qrs 2 bus. in all. In provision of the steward for his visits by 1 tally, 7 bus. In provision of the bailiff for the year, 10 qrs, because he takes the rest from East Meon Church. Delivered to the vicar for his carrying-service, 5 qrs. Sold, 274 qrs 2 bus.

Curall
The same render account for 14 qrs from the whole issue of curall from the same wheat by struck measure. Sold, 14 qrs.

Barley
{yield: three-and-a-half-fold less 3 qrs 7 bus.}
The same render account for 14 qrs of barley remaining from the previous year in the granary; 101 qrs 1 bus. from the whole issue of barley this year by struck measure. Total, 115 qrs 1 bus.
Sown over 95 acres as they lie in the field of la Chapele, 26½ qrs; that is, 4½ bus. over 2 acres, less 1½ bus. in all. Delivered to 1 carter, 3 stot-keepers, and 1 keeper of hoggs and lambs for the year, 32½ qrs, taking a quarter every 8 weeks. Delivered to 2 oxherds for the year, because 3 customary tenants were drovers for the whole year to the advantage of the lord, 10 qrs 3 bus., taking a quarter every 10 weeks. Delivered to 1 dairymaid for the year, 5 qrs 1½ bus. Delivered to 1 cowherd for the year, who takes a quarter every 12 weeks, 4 qrs 2½ bus. Delivered to 3 keepers of lambs this year, 4 qrs 5 bus. In provision of the bailiff's attendant, 3 qrs. Sold, 28 qrs 5 bus.

Oats
{yield: two-fold less 40 qrs 1 bus.}
The same render account for 572 qrs 7 bus. from the whole issue of oats by struck measure; 42 qrs by estimation in sheaves. Total, 614 qrs 7 bus.
Sown over 685 acres as they lie in the fields of la Chapele, Ponfaldesgore, and Cre*m*be, 190 qrs; that is, 4½ bus. over 2 acres, less 2 qrs 5 bus. in all. In fodder of 2 cart-horses for the year, 18 qrs. In fodder of 18 plough-horses from the feast of the Circumcision (1 January) until Sunday before the feast of St Augustine (20 May), for 140 nights, 52½ qrs, at 3 bus. a night. In fodder of the same when they ploughed after dinner, 5 qrs. In fodder of oxen by estimation in sheaves, 42 qrs. In customary

payment to 8 ploughmen, 3 shepherds, and 3 customary tenants who replaced 3 drovers, who were accustomed to be at liberty, 10½ qrs, or 6 bus. each. In fodder of the steward's horses for his visits by 1 tally, 1½ qrs. In fodder of the bailiff's horses for the year, 20 qrs. Sold, 275 qrs 3 bus.

Stock

Cart-horses: 2 remain from the previous year; 2 remain.
Plough-horses: 18 remain from the previous year; 11 bought. Total, 29. 3 sold; 9 in murrain. Total, 12. 17 remain.
Colts: 2 remain from the previous year aged 2½ years; 2 in murrain; none remain.
Young colts: 1 remains from the previous year aged 1½ years; 1 remains now aged 2½ years.
Foals: 2 remain from the previous year aged ½ year; 1 in murrain; 1 female remains now aged 1½ years. No offspring this year.
Oxen: 57 remain from the previous year; 3 from the heriots of William Schireve, Robert de Borden' the elder, and Gilbert de Pip*er*cu*m*be; 8 additions; 10 bought. Total, 78. 5 in murrain; 7 sold at Martinmas. Total, 12. 66 remain.
Bulls: 1 remains from the previous year; 1 remains.
Cows: 18 remain from the previous year; 4 added from steers; 1 from the heriot of Nicholas ate Ock' before calving. Total, 23. 1 sold before calving; 22 remain.
Steers: 11 remain from the previous year's bullocks; 1 from the heriot of William ate Pleystouwe. Total, 12. 8 added to oxen, 4 to cows; none remain.
Bullocks: 9 remain from the previous year's yearlings; 9 remain, 6 of them male.
[Yearlings]: 6 remain from the previous year's calves; 6 remain, 4 of them male.
Calves: 22 from the offspring of the said cows this year. ⌈1 in murrain⌉; 8 sold. Total, 9. 13 remain.
[Wethers]: 450 remain from the previous year; 129 added from hoggs after shearing. Total, 579. 21 sold at Martinmas; 43 in murrain before shearing, 26 after shearing; 3 in customary payment after shearing for the mowing of the meadow. Total, 93. 486 remain.
[Ewes]: 797 remain from the previous year; 184 added from hoggs after shearing; 6 from the pinfold after lambing and before shearing. Total, 987. 100 sold at Martinmas; 9 in customary payment to 2 reeves, 3 shepherds and 11 ploughmen at Martinmas; 12 in murrain before lambing, 26 after lambing and before shearing, and 9 after shearing. Total, 156. 831 remain.
[Hoggs]: 402 remain from the previous year's lambs; 30 in murrain before shearing; 9 sold at Martinmas; 129 added to wethers, 184 to ewes; 50 delivered to the reeve of East Meon Church; none remain.
[Lambs]: 555 from the offspring of the said ewes this year because 117 were sterile and 4 aborted; 9 from the offspring of strays (*cercia*rum); 29 from the reeve of East Meon Church. Total, 593. 134 in murrain before weaning, 23 after weaning and before shearing, and 9 after shearing; 3 in customary payment to 1 reeve and 2 shepherds before shearing. Total, 169. 424 remain.
[Sows]: 2 remain from the previous year; 2 additions. Total, 4. 2 in murrain; 2 remain.
[Pigs]: 35 remain from the previous year; 28 added from hoggets. Total, 73. 19 sold at Martinmas; 4 in murrain. Total, 23. 50 remain.
[Hoggets]: 50 remain from the previous year's piglets; 10 in murrain; 2 added to sows; 38 males added to pigs; none remain.
[Piglets]: 45 from the offspring of the said sows this year; 8 from the reeve of East Meon Church. Total, 53. 9 in murrain; 44 remain.

[Hens]: 325 from churchscot this year. 5 in default of Henry Coc*us*, Joscelin ate Ligh', William Bouebrok', Robert Kay and Robert de Halsted' because dead; 22 in default of Richard Curton, Elias de Bykedon', Richard Fermyn, Godfrey de Chudescu*m*b*e*, William ate Slade, the relict of Colema*n*, William ate Church', Agnes Eosmu*nd*', Seyld Hery*ng*, Adam Archebold', Emma Joldewyn', William H*er*ber*d*, Adam ate Bur', William de Langhurst, John Purhegg', Henry de Hoggeneslad', Robert de[1] Caldecot', Henry de Bronyngesdon', William Router', William Randolf, Amice de *Qui*rteflod' and Alice de Strethe*nd*' because widowers or widows; 7 in default of Alan Nel for 2 lands, Robert Spurar', the relict of Blakema*n*, William Colevile, William Judde, and Nicholas de Fraxino; 2 in default of the land of Godesm*er*e; 2 in default of the land of the beadle which William Fissar' holds freely of the lord by charter; 2 in default of the land of John de Halywll' at Coombe because he has no wife. Total, 39. 286 sold.
Swans: 3 remain from the previous year; 2 offspring; 1 in murrain; 4 remain.
Peacocks: 6 remain from the previous year; no offspring; 1 in murrain; 5 peacocks and peahens remain.
Coarse wool {yield of fleece 3*d*. plus 2½*d*. in all}: 486 fleeces from wethers, 656 from ewes and 363 from hoggs produced at the shearing this year. Total, 1,405. All sent to Wolvesey, which made 6 weys 22 cloves.
Lamb's-wool {yield 1¼*d*. plus 4*s*. 11*d*. in all}: 433 fleeces produced at the shearing this year; all delivered to Wolvesey, which made 1 wey.
Wool locks: 20 cloves 5 lb; all sold.
Hides: 9 from plough-horses, 2 from colts, 5 from oxen and 1 from a calf in murrain; all sold.
Woolskins: 43 from wethers, 38 from ewes and 30 from hoggs dead from murrain before shearing; all sold.
Bare skins: 26 from wethers and 10 from ewes in murrain after shearing; all sold.
Lambskins: 133 from lambs in murrain before weaning, 23 after weaning and before shearing, and 9 after shearing. Total, 166. All sold.
Winter cheese: 37 made; all sold, which made 13 cloves.
Summer cheese {yield of cow 3*s*. and sheep 2*d*. with 3 cheeses in customary payment valued at 2*s*. 6*d*.}: 176 cheeses made between 8 April and Michaelmas, both days included; 2 in customary payment to 1 reeve and 1 dairymaid; 1 in provision of the great boon-work; 173 sold, which made 15 weys.
Butter: 1 wey from the issue of the dairy this year; all sold.
Cider: 3 casks remain from the previous year; 2 made this year. Total, 5. 3 sold; 2 remain.

m.27
Utensils: 1 cart with iron tyres remains from the previous year; 1 renewed this year; 1 worn out; 1 remains. 4 casks[2] remain from the previous year; 1 worn out and 1 sold with cider; 2 remain. 2 brass pots, 1 posnet, 3 pans, 1 lead vessel, 1 cooking-pot, 1 measure of flax, 1 tripod, 1 tine, 3 padlocks on various doors in the curia, 1 mortar, 1 basin, 2 ewers; all this remains.
Labour services: 748 labour services owed to the curia of East Meon by 13 workers, of whom 4 worked twice a week from Michaelmas until Lammas and 9 once a week; 51 in quittance for the 3 festival weeks, that is, Christmas, Easter and Pentecost; 16 in 'landriht' according to custom; 79 in default of the land which William le Fissar' holds because they are commuted; 273 for carrying dung; 329 labour services sold.

1 MS 'Rob' de ⟨Caldecot⟩ Caldecot''.

2 MS 'iiij ⟨debil'⟩ ⌈doleis⌉ rem''.

Manual labour service: 308 owed to the manor by 7 workers; 10½ released for the 3 festival weeks; 7 in 'landriht' according to custom; 119 for collecting dung; 52½ for spreading dung; 119 sold.
Harvest labour service: 533 owed from Lammas until Michaelmas by the above-mentioned 13 workers, working everyday except Saturdays and Sundays; 91 in quittance of the same for 7 feast days this year; 28 in default of the land of the beadle which William now holds for the same time; 414 for reaping, binding and carrying corn.
Manual labour service: 228 owed by the above-mentioned 7 workers, of whom 5 worked everyday except Saturdays and feast days, and 2 for a second day; all for reaping, binding and collecting corn.

East Meon Church

Arrears
Nicholas de Ychen', bailiff, and Robert Hugh', reeve, render account for £81 6*s*. 8¼*d*. of arrears from the previous year. All delivered to Sir G*eoffrey*, treasurer of Wolvesey. They are quit.

Rents of assize
The same render account for £1 5*s*. for all rents of assize at Christmas; £1 5*s*. at Easter (22 April); £1 5*s*. at the feast of St John the Baptist (24 June); £1 8*s*. ½*d*. at Michaelmas (29 September). Total, £5 3*s*. ½*d*.

Quittances
In quittance of 1 reeve for the year 3*s*.; 1 ploughman for the year 2*s*. 6*d*.; one shepherd for the year 2*s*. 6*d*. Total, 8*s*.

Total of rents remaining, £4 15*s*. ½*d*.

Cumin
The same render account for 1 lb of cumin from Geoffrey Kynhow for annual recognizance; all delivered to Sir G*eoffrey*, treasurer of Wolvesey.

Recognizance
The same render account for 3*d*. from Henry Burrith' for annual recognizance. Total, 3*d*.

Issues
The same render account for 14*s*. 5¼*d*. from the small tithes of lambs this year; 14*s*. 3½*d*. from the small tithes of milk, wool, foals and calves this year; nothing from coarse wool from the demesne or tithes here because it is sent to Wolvesey; 2*s*. 3*d*. from 2 cloves 4 lb of wool locks sold, at 10½*d*. a clove; 18*s*. 7½*d*. from 2 weys 2 cloves of cheese from tithes sold, at 9*s*. a wey; 2*s*. from 2 branches of wood sold; 6*s*. 8*d*. from pigeons sold; 6*s*. 6*d*. from 26 geese from tithes sold; 1*s*. from the pasturage on this side of the field of la Hyde sold, because it was all sown with wheat; 3*s*. from the pasturage of Otlond' sold this year; nothing from the pasturage of Schortebond' because it was fallow; 1*s*. from the pasturage of Wodebrech sold this year; 1*s*. from nettles (*urtic'*) on this side of Bishop's field and the dovecote sold; nothing from the

herbage of the garden this year on account of the calves and other livestock of the lord; 2*s*. from the pasturage of the meadow of Cherchemed sold after mowing; 3*s*. 6*d*. from 1 pair of wheels with iron tyres sold; 4*s*. from 1 old plough-horse sold; 5*s*. from 5 wethers sold at Martinmas (11 November); £1 17*s*. 9*d*. from 121 feeble lambs from tithes sold before shearing, at 4*d*. each for 30, 5*d*. each for 30, and 3*d*. each for 61; nothing from piglets here because delivered to the reeve of the manor; 5*s*. from the skins sold of 20 wethers in murrain before shearing, at 3*d*. a skin; 2*s*. 7½*d*. from the skins sold of 21 in murrain after shearing, at 1½*d*. a skin; nothing from forage this year, because the corn of Steep, Oxshete, Froxfield, Yteden' and Bykeden' was sold wholesale; £2 5*s*. from 3 casks of cider sold, at 15*s*. each without the wood; 2*s*. 11*d*. from 35 hens from churchscot sold; 8*d*. from abandoned timber sold from certain old buildings at Froxefeld'. Total, £8 19*s*. 2¾*d*.

Sale of corn from the demesne
The same render account for £7 4*s*. 5½*d*. from 25 qrs 1 bus. of wheat sold, at 5*s*. a qr for 8 qrs 5 bus., 5*s*. 4*d*. a qr for 6½ qrs, and 6*s*. 8*d*. a qr for 10 qrs; £2 12*s*. 10½*d*. from 18 qrs 7 bus. of bere sold, at 2*s*. 8*d*. a qr for 11 qrs 2 bus., and 3*s*. a qr for 7 qrs 5 bus.; 10*s*. from 2½ qrs of barley sold, at 4*s*. a qr. Total, £10 7*s*. 4*d*.

Sale of corn from tithes
The same render account for £20 3*s*. 7½*d*. from 65 qrs 7 bus. of wheat from tithes sold, at 5*s*. a qr for 9 qrs 1 bus., 5*s*. 4*d*. a qr for 15 qrs 2 bus., and 6*s*. 8*d*. a qr for 41½ qrs; £1 19*s*. 7*d*. from 14 qrs 7 bus. of bere sold, at 2*s*. 8*d*. a qr; £7 13*s*. 6*d*. from 38 qrs 3 bus. of barley sold, at 4*s*. a qr; £5 18*s*. 1½*d*. from 64 qrs of oats sold, at 1*s*. 8*d*. a qr for 44 qrs 7 bus., 2*s*. 2*d*. a qr for 7 qrs 6 bus., and 2*s*. 4*d*. a qr for 11 qrs 3 bus.; £1 12*s*. 4*d*. from 12 qrs 1 bus. of beans sold, at 2*s*. 8*d*. a qr; 4*s*. from 2 qrs of peas sold; 12*s*. 1*d*. from 7 qrs 2 bus. of vetches sold, at 1*s*. 8*d*. a qr. Total, £38 3*s*. 4*d*.

Froxfield, S⌈t⌉eep and Oxeschete
The same render account for £38 from the tithes of corn from the chapels of Froxfield, Steep and Oxeshete sold wholesale. Total, £38.

Bykeden' and Yteden'
The same render account for 14*s*. from the tithes of corn from Bykeden' sold; £1 from the tithes of corn from Yteden' sold; 7*s*. from the tithes of corn from Gerard de Tygehale sold. Total, £2 1*s*.

Total of all the corn from the demesne as well as from tithes sold wholesale, £88 1*s*. 8*d*.

Entry and marriage fines
The same render account for 4*s*. from the tithing for tithingpenny at the hundred-court of Martinmas; 4*s*. from the tithing for tithingpenny at the hundred-court of Hockday; £1 from Alice, relict of William Coc*us* de Pydeh*am*, to retain 1 messuage and 1 virgate of land which belonged to her husband. Total, £1 8*s*.

Perquisites
The same render account for £1 3*s*. 6*d*. from small perquisites from various men this year for various transgressions. Total, £1 3*s*. 6*d*.

Total of both, £2 11*s*. 6*d*.

Total of all receipts, £104 17*s*. 8¼*d*.

Cost of ploughs

In ironwork of 1 horse-plough for the year 1*s*. 8*d*. In stipend of the smith forging the ironwork 1*s*. In 1 ploughshare bought 8½*d*. In 1 plough foot bought 3½*d*. In making and mending ploughs and harrows 8*d*. In 1 pair of wheels bought for the same 4*d*. In 1 coulter made anew with iron bought for the same 10*d*. In 6 halters made from the horses' own hair 1½*d*. In stipend of 1 harrower at both sowings 8*d*. In shoeing 6 plough-horses for the year 9*d*. In fastening the same 1*d*. Delivered to 1 ploughman for ½ ewe at Martinmas according to custom 1½*d*. In stipend of 1 stot-keeper for the year 3*s*. In 1 plough-horse bought 12*s*. 6*d*. Total, £1 2*s*. 9*d*.

Cost of carts

In 1 pair of wheels made from the lord's timber 10*d*. In 1 new binding, with clamps and large and small nails bought for the same, and with the stipend of the smith putting the said binding on the said wheels, 12*s*. 6*d*. In hooping the hubs of the cart with iron 2*d*. In fitting the cart with axles at various times 2*d*. In white leather bought for mending harnesses 1*s*. In grease bought 6*d*. In shoeing 2 cart-horses for the year 2*s*. In stipend of 1 carter for the year 3*s*. 4*d*. In 1 cart-horse bought 16*s*. 7*d*. Total, £1 17*s*. 1*d*.

Sheepfold and sheepcote

In 9 hurdles made for the fold 3*d*. In wattling 22 hurdles 7*d*., at 1*d*. per 3 hurdles. In grease bought for greasing sheep 3*s*. 2*d*. In 13 ells of canvas bought for putting wool in 3*s*. 3*d*., at 3*d*. an ell. In making sacks for the wool with thread bought for the same 6*d*. Total, 7*s*. 9*d*.

Cost of buildings

In re-roofing the bailiff's stable and the cart-horses' stable in places 2*s*. In repairing and restoring the mangers of the said stables 8*d*. In re-roofing and mending in places the unroofed building of the press 2*s*. In re-roofing and mending the granary in places 1*s*. In 100 large nails and other small nails bought for the same 6*d*. In building anew 1 building for stabling the cart-horses and carts, £1 1*s*. 5*d*. for all costs. In making and mending the bench in the great hall 1*s*. In mending the walls of the dairy and the door of the same building 5*d*. In mending the barn-door and likewise the gate of the curia with nails bought for the same 10½*d*. In 9 empty casks bought £1 1*s*., at 2*s*. 4*d*. each. In hooping and mending these and others 1*s*. 6*d*. In hooping and mending tubs and barrows 5*d*. In making 12 casks of cider 4*s*., at 4*d*. a cask. In tallow and soap bought for the press 4*d*. In 1 sieve bought for straining cider ¾*d*. Total, £2 17*s*. 2¼*d*.

Threshing

In threshing and winnowing 38 qrs 5 bus. of wheat from the demesne and 65 qrs 7 bus. of wheat from tithes by piece-work 17*s*. 5*d*., at 2*d*. a struck quarter. In threshing and winnowing 26 qrs 1 bus. of bere and 21 qrs[1] 6 bus. of barley from the demesne, and 14 qrs 7 bus. of bere, 38 qrs 3 bus. of barley and 9 qrs 2 bus. of peas and vetches from tithes, 11*s*. ½*d*., at 1½*d*. per 10 struck bushels. In threshing and winnowing 12 qrs 1 bus. of beans by piece-work 2*s*. ¼*d*., at 2*d*. a struck quarter. In threshing and winnowing 65 qrs 2 bus. of oats from the demesne and 64 qrs of oats from tithes 8*s*. 7¼*d*., at 1*d*. per 10 struck bushels. Total, £1 19*s*. 1*d*.

1 MS omits 'qrs'.

Harvest-time
In bread and herrings, and cheese for a want of herrings, bought for 17 boon-works and 7 carrying-services of 615 men with the customary tenants who reaped, bound and carried all the corn, £1 1*s.* 5*d.* In stipend of 1 hayward at harvest-time 2*s.* Total, £1 3*s.* 5*d.*

Also harvest-time
In stipend of 3 riders this year, of whom 1 stayed for 36 days, 1 for 40 days, and 1 for 45 days, 15*s.* In expenses of the same for the same time 16*s.* In shoeing the horses of the same 9*d.* In expenses of 9 of the bishop's servants (*pedon'*) and 2 stackers £1 15*s.* 6*d.* In stipend of the same 18*s.* 4*d.*, or 1*s.* 8*d.* each. And note that there is 1 servant fewer this year because the corn of Yteden' and Bykeden' was sold wholesale before the harvest. In 3 pairs of wheels made for carrying the corn from tithes 1*s.* 6*d.* In fitting the same with axles 6*d.* In 4 collars bought 2*s.* 2*d.* In clouts, nails and grease bought 1*s.* 10*d.* In shoeing the plough-horses hauling the carts 2*s.* 6*d.* In treating the carts before the harvest 1*s.* In hiring carters this year to help carry the corn at various times 2*s.* 4*d.* In 4 qrs of oats bought for the fodder of the riders' horses 5*s.* 4*d.*, at 1*s.* 4*d.* a qr. Total, £5 4*s.* 9*d.*

Total of all expenses, £14 12*s.* ¼*d.*

And thus he owes, £90 5*s.* 8*d.*

Delivered to Sir G*eoffrey*, treasurer of Wolvesey, by 1 tally, £43.

And thus he owes clear, £47 5*s.* 8*d.*

Issues of the grange

Wheat from the demesne
{yield: six-fold less 1 qr 7 bus.}
The same render account for 38 qrs 5 bus. from the whole issue of wheat from the demesne by struck measure.
Sown over 129 acres as they lie in Lahyd' and Wodebrok', 9½ qrs; that is, 1 bus. over 2 acres, plus 1 qr 3½ bus. in all. In provision of the bailiff, 4 qrs, because he takes the rest from the manor. Sold, 25 qrs 1 bus.

Bere
{yield: three-fold plus 5 bus.}
The same render account for 26 qrs 1 bus. from the whole issue of bere by struck measure.
Sown over 41 acres as they lie in Watcomb*e*, 7 qrs 2 bus.; that is, 1½ bus. an acre, less 3½ bus. in all. Sold, 18 qrs 7 bus.

Barley
{yield: three-and-a-half-fold plus 6 bus.}
The same render account for 21 qrs 6 bus. from the whole issue of barley from the demesne by struck measure.
Sown over 17 acres as they lie at Prusteslad', 6 qrs 2 bus.; that is, 3 bus. an acre, less 1 bus. in all. Delivered to 1 carter and 1 stot-keeper for the year, who take a quarter every 8 weeks, 13 qrs. Sold, 2½ qrs.

Oats
{yield: 3-fold less 5 qrs 3 bus.}
The same render account for 65 qrs 1 bus. from the whole issue of oats by struck measure.
Sown over 105 acres as they lie at Prustehull', Stonyelond', and Watteconb*e*, 26½ qrs; that is, 2 bus. an acre, plus 2 bus. in all. In fodder of 2 cart-horses from Michaelmas (29 September) until Lammas (1 August), for 306 nights, 19 qrs 1 bus., at ½ bus. a night. In fodder of 6 plough-horses from the feast of the Circumcision (1 January) until Sunday before the feast of St Augustine (20 May), for 140 nights, 17½ qrs, at 1 bus. a night. In fodder of the same when they ploughed after dinner, ½ qr. In customary payment to 1 ploughman and 1 shepherd, 1½ qrs. Total, 65 qrs 1 bus. It balances.

Wheat from tithes: 65 qrs 7 bus. from the whole issue of wheat by struck measure; all sold.
Bere: 14½ qrs 3 bus. from the whole issue of bere by struck measure; all sold.
Barley: 38 qrs 3 bus. from the whole issue of barley by struck measure; all sold.
Oats: 64 qrs from the whole issue of oats by struck measure; all sold.
Beans: 12 qrs 1 bus. from the whole issue of beans by struck measure; all sold.
Peas: 2 qrs from the whole issue of peas by struck measure; all sold.
Vetches: 7 qrs 2 bus. from the whole issue of vetches by struck measure; all sold.

Nothing from the corn of the chapels of Ocschete, Steep and Froxfield, and from the tithes of Yteden' and Bykeden' because sold wholesale.

Stock

Cart-horses: 3 remain from the previous year; 1 bought. Total, 4. 1 added to plough-horses; 2 remain.
Plough-horses: 6 remain from the previous year; 1 added from cart-horses; 1 bought. Total, 8. 1 sold; 7 remain.
Oxen: 1 from the heriot of William de Pydeh*a*m; 1 remains.
Wethers: 205 remain from the previous year; 50 received from the reeve of the manor after shearing. Total, 255. 5 sold at Martinmas; 20 in murrain before shearing, 21 after shearing. Total, 46. 209 remain.
Lambs: 150 from tithes this year; 29 delivered to the reeve of the manor; 121 sold.
Wool from the demesne, wool from tithes {henceforth enumerate the fleeces from tithes}: 180 fleeces from wethers produced at the shearing this year; delivered to Wolvesey, which made 3 weys 11 cloves with the wool from tithes.
Cheese from tithes: 2 weys 2 cloves from tithes this year; all sold.
Piglets: 9 from tithes this year; 1 in murrain; 8 delivered to the reeve of the manor; none remain.
Hens: 38 from churchscot. 1 in default of Isabel ate Stupe because a widow; 1 in default of Othyn le Zenghe because he has no wife; 1 in default of John Mile for the same. Total, 3. 35 sold.
Pigeons: 10 dozen from the issue of the dovecote this year; all sold.
Geese: 26 from tithes this year, because the geese from the tithes of the chapels of Steep, Ocshute and Froxfield were sold with the corn from the farms of the same chapels; all sold.
Cider: 3 casks remain from the previous year; 12 made this year. Total, 15. 3 sold without the wood; 12 full casks remain.

Utensils: 1 cart with iron tyres remains from the previous year; 1 made anew this year. Total, 2. 1 sold; 1 remains. 3 casks remain from the previous year; 9 bought. Total, 12. 12 remain. 3 tubs, 1 tine, 3 coffers, 1 of which is for the reeve's tallies, remain from the previous year; all this remains.

Hambledon

Arrears

Nicholas, bailiff, and William Bouelych', reeve, render account for £68 12*s.* 7¼*d.* of arrears from the previous year. All delivered to Sir G*eoffrey*, treasurer of Wolvesey. They are quit.

Rents of assize

The same render account for £6 13*s.* 11¼*d.* for rents of assize at Christmas; £7 9*s.* 1*d.* at Easter (22 April); £6 13*s.* 11¼*d.* at St John the Baptist (24 June); £11 10*s.* ⌈10¾*d.*⌉ at Michaelmas (29 September). Total, £32 7*s.* 10¼*d.*

Increment

The same render account for 1*d.* for the increment of rent from Robert Fab*er* to have 1 plot of land, 12 feet long and 5 feet wide, in the vill of Hambledon. Total, 1*d.*

Total of rents with increment, £32 7*s.* 11¼*d.*

Quittances

In quittance of 1 reeve for the year 2*s.* 6*d.*; 1 bartoner for the year 2*s.* 6*d.*; 3 ploughmen for the year 5*s.*; 2 shepherds and 1 smith for the year 5*s.*; 1 cowherd for the year 1*s.* 8*d.*; 1 swineherd for the year 1*s.* 8*d.* Total, 18*s.* 4*d.*

Defaults of rent

In default of the wood which Herbert[1] de Chidden' holds drawn into demesne, 1*s.* 6*d.* for the year; the land of Shortelond', 6*d.* for the year; 1 grove of Vineys drawn into demesne, 6*d.* for the year; the wood of Mannely which is in demesne through the death of the holder 6*s.* Total, 8*s.* 6*d.*

Quittances and defaults, £1 6*s.* 10*d.*

Total of rents remaining, £31 1*s.* 1¼*d.*

Annual recognizance

The same render account for 3*d.* from Walter ate Greve for recognizance; 3*d.* from Stephen Blaysut to be able to remain in the hundred of East Meon; 3*d.* from William le Boys for annual recognizance; 3*d.* from Henry Fab*er* for the same; 4*d.* from Adam le Cauȝ for the same; 3*d.* from Robert Buly for the same; 3*d.* from William Tassor' for the same and henceforth nothing from the same because he is dead; 6*d.* from Adam Cattefan for the same; 3*d.* from Thomas Sharpe for the same; 6*d.* from Roger Boys for the same; 3*d.* from Jordan Boys for the same. Total, 3*s.* 4*d.*

Cumin

The same render account for 1 lb of cumin from William Sicator' for the year; delivered to Wolvesey.

1 MS repeats 'H*er*berd'.

Wax[1]

The same render account for ½ lb of wax from Philip Visard to have maintenance; ½ lb from William le Ysmo*n*gar' for the same; ½ lb from Thomas Mess*or* for the same. Total, 1½ lb. Delivered to Wolvesey.

Talents

The same render account for 1 talent received from the vicar of Hambledon; delivered to Wolvesey.

Issues of the manor {henceforth mention should be made of the number of animals}

The same render account for £1 18*s*. 4½*d*. from pannage of pigs within this year; £1 1*s*. from foreign pannage; £1 8*s*. 6*d*. from pannage in the park; nothing from William de Chidd*en* from now on because he does the labour service for part of his land; 2*s*. 6*d*. from Robert Coc*us* for release from the labour service for the land of Dimmyng'; 1*s*. 8*d*. from the same Robert for the labour service of the land which belonged to Richard Luce; 6*d*. from the relict of Philip de Furnaeaus for release from the labour service for the land which belonged to Walter Elyot; 2*s*. from cablish sold in the great wood; nothing from underwood in la Brok' this year; 3*s*. from the men of Chidden for the pasturage in Eldecroft and answering elsewhere for 5 sheep for the same pasturage; 3*s*. 3½*d*. from pinfold this year; 3*s*. from the men of Pantolf' for pasturage; 4*s*. 9½*d*. for the pasturage in la Holte sold this year; 6*s*. 8*d*. for the pasturage in the enclosure sold wholesale in winter; £2 7*s*. from the pasturage sold there in summer because the meadow was mown; £2 3*s*. 1*d*. from 4 oxen, at 11*s*. each for 3, and 10*s*. 1*d*. for 1; £1 2*s*. 6*d*. from 3 old cows sold; 1*s*. from 1 feeble plough-horse sold; nothing from the pasturage in la Rugg' this year because it was pastured with the lord's sheep; 1*s*. 6*d*. from the pasturage above the church sold; 1*s*. from the pasturage in la Brok' sold in winter; 5*s*. from the pasturage sold there in summer; £1 4*s*. from the pasturage of 24 animals agisting in the park sold this year; 6*s*. from 6 feeble late-born calves sold; £1 from 16 wethers sold at Martinmas, at 1*s*. 3*d*. each; 13*s*. from 14 ewes sold at Martinmas; 9*s*. 6*d*. from 38 feeble lambs sold; £3 from 19 pigs, at 3*s*. 2*d*. each, less 2*d*. in all; 10*d*. from the hide sold of 1 plough-horse in murrain; 2*d*. from the hide sold of 1 yearling; 3½*d*. from the hides sold of 2 calves dead from murrain; 14*s*. 6*d*. from the skins of 24 wethers, 1 ram and 32 ewes dead from murrain before shearing, at 3*d*. a skin; 1*s*. 6*d*. from the skins sold wholesale of 12 wethers, 7 ewes and 14 hoggs dead from murrain after shearing; 5*s*. 6½*d*. from the skins sold of 57 lambs dead from murrain before weaning, at 1*d*. a skin, and of 19 rotted sheep, at ½*d*. a skin; nothing from coarse wool and lamb's-wool this year because it was sent to Wolvesey; 6*s*. 1½*d*. from 7 cloves of wool locks sold, at 10½*d*. a clove; 5*s*. from 17 cloves of rowen cheese sold; £3 8*s*. from 8½ weys of cheese sold, at 8*s*. a wey; 7*s*. 10*d*. from 1 wey 5 cloves of butter sold; 3*s*. 2*d*. from 38 hens from churchscot sold; 10*s*. from 5 qrs of salt sold; 1*s*. 3*d*. from 15 workers who are bound to thresh 2 bus. of wheat and 4 bus. of oats; nothing from labour services sold this year; nothing from the turbary on la Crith this year; nothing from the pasturage beside P*ar*kgate this year for the lord's animals; 3*s*. 9*d*. from dairy produce sold at the audit; £17 2*s*. 6*d*. from 39 animals sold which were bought to agist in the pasture. Total, £42 3*s*. 4*d*.

Farm of the mill

The same render account for £1 16*s*. for the farm of the mill this year. Total, £1 16*s*.

1 MS omits heading.

Sale of corn

The same render account for £12 14*s*. 3*d*. from 45 qrs 6 bus. of wheat sold, at 5*s*. a qr for 20 qrs 2 bus., and 6*s*. a qr for 25½ qrs; £1 15*s*. from 13 qrs 1 bus. of curall sold, at 2*s*. 8*d*. a qr; £4 13*s*. from 23 qrs 2 bus. of barley sold, at 4*s*. a qr; £3 5*s*. 9½*d*. from 31½ qrs of oats sold, at 2*s*. a qr for 14 qrs 6 bus., and 2*s*. 2*d*. a qr for 16 qrs 6 bus.; 12*s*. 6*d*. from 5 qrs of peas sold, at 2*s*. 6*d*. a qr; 16*s*. 6*d*. from 8 qrs of vetches sold, at 2*s*. a qr; 3*s*. 4½*d*. from 4½ bus. of wheat sold at the audit; 2*s*. 9*d*. from 5½ bus. of barley sold at the audit. Total, £24 3*s*. 2*d*.

m.27d

Entry and marriage fines with tithingpenny

The same render account for ⌈5*s*.⌉ from the tithing of Chidden for tithingpenny at the hundred-court of Martinmas (11 November); 5*s*. from the tithing of Denmead for the same; 5*s*. from the tithing of la Lygh' for the same; 5*s*. from the tithing of Gludden for the same; £1 from the same tithings at the hundred-court of Hockday (1 May); 5*s*. from the relict of Thomas le Cog' to retain 1 cotland which belonged to her husband; 10*s*. from Adam Coker to have ½ virgate of land which belonged to Stephen his father; 2*s*. from William Bouelych' to have 2 acres of land by surrender of Adam Bythewod'; 1*s*. from John Pleyfot to have 1 plot of land in the vill of Hambledon by surrender of Walter le Grev*ere*; 1*s*. from Robert Fab*er* to have 1 plot of land, 12 feet long and 5 feet wide, in the same vill; 4*s*. from Robert le Bole to have 8 acres of land by surrender of William atte Oke; 1*s*. from Walter Rykeby for 1 plot of land, 12 feet long and 10 feet wide, for building in the market; 10*s*. from Peter ate Putte to have Juliana le Burgeys with her land. Total, £3 14*s*.

Perquisites

The same render account for 2*s*. from Thomas ate Brok' for trespass of wood; 2*s*. from Adam G*ra*ndel for keeping the park badly; 6*s*.[1] 8*d*. from William Jolif for keeping the corn badly; £3 5*s*. 9*d*. from other small perquisites. Total, £3 16*s*. 5*d*.

Total of both, £7 10*s*. 5*d*.

Stallage

The same render account for 6*d*. from Joan le Specer and Adam Blachat for holding 1 stall for the year; 6*s*.[2] from Walter Rykeby for holding the other stall; 2*s*. 2*d*. from other small stalls. Total, 3*s*. 2*d*.

Total of all receipts, £107 6¼*d*.

Cost of ploughs {henceforth the ploughs of the customary tenants should not be taken if a profit is able to be made}

In iron and steel bought for 3 ploughs for the year 11*s*. In 3 plough feet bought 1*s*. 3*d*. In 2 ploughshares bought 1*s*. 6*d*. In 5 ploughs made anew and others mended at various times, with timber felled and trimmed for the same, 2*s*. 3*d*. In 2 pairs of wheels bought 6*d*. In 3 harrows made anew 6*d*. In fitting ploughs with iron tyres 1½*d*. In shoeing 6 plough-horses hauling ploughs at the time of both sowings and hauling dung when it was necessary until Lammas, because thereafter they were at the church, 5*s*. 6*d*. In 32 ploughmen in winter and 32 in Lent, £1 according to custom,

1 MS omits '*s*.'

2 MS error for '6*d*.'

of whom each ploughman ploughed and harrowed 1 acre in winter and 1 acre in Lent. In stipend of 3 ploughmen from Michaelmas until Lammas, because thereafter they were at the church, 6*s*. 9*d*. In 1 plough-horse bought 12*s*. 3*d*. Total, £3 1*s*. 7½*d*.

Purchase of corn
In 6½ qrs of barley bought for the liveries of the manorial servants 17*s*. 4*d*., at 2*s*. 8*d*. a qr. Total, 17*s*. 4*d*.

Cost of carts
In 1 pair of wheels made anew from the lord's timber 9*d*. In mending 1 old binding and putting it on the said wheels with the stipend of the smith 2*s*. 6*d*. In clouts, nails and grease bought 1*s*. 9*d*. In mending the axles of the cart at various times 8*d*., on account of the manor of Kilmeston. In shoeing 2 cart-horses 3*s*. 6*d*. In 2 collars bought 10*d*. In 2 pairs of traces bought 9*d*. In 1 rope bought for the cart 1*s*. 2*d*. In 2 halters bought 1½*d*. In stipend of 1 carter from Michaelmas until Lammas, because thereafter he was at the church, 2*s*. 3*d*. Total, 14*s*. 3½*d*.

Repair of buildings
In 2,000 slates bought 3*s*. 4*d*. In re-roofing the hall, lord's chamber, clerks' chamber and kitchen, which had been unroofed several times by the wind, 10*s*. 6*d*. In nails and pegs bought for the same 8*d*. In re-roofing the barn and other buildings in places 4*s*. 4*d*. In laying 100 shingles in places on the barn with nails bought for the same 5*d*. In building anew 1 palisade between the hall and kitchen 2*s*. 8*d*. In building 1 palisade between the hall and dairy and 1 new garden-gate 2*s*. 2*d*. In felling and sawing timber for the same 9*d*. In mending the byre in part and making anew a fodder-rack for the byre 3*s*. 6*d*. In mending the fodder-rack and manger in the stable 6*d*. In making 1 window in the kitchen with hooks and hinges for the same 5*d*. In plastering the walls of the bailiff's room and knights' chamber 10*d*. Total, £1 10*s*. 1*d*.

Cost of the park
In mending 2 gates in the park 2*d*. In making 2 furlongs 2 perches of ditch in the park for the pasture for the calves 10*s*. 3*d*., at 1½*d*. a perch. In completing the hedge along the said ditch 5*s*. 1½*d*., at ¾*d*. a perch. In closing the gaps in the hedge along 8 furlongs 30 perches £1 1*s*. 10½*d*., at ¾*d*. a perch. Total, £1 17*s*. 5*d*.

Dairy
In 1 qr of salt bought 2*s*. In woollen and linen cloth bought 4*d*. In a press bought 3*d*. In earthenware pots and pans bought 4½*d*. In 2 cheese moulds bought 6*d*. In mending the utensils of the dairy 4*d*. In 15 ells of canvas bought 3*s*. 1½*d*. In making sacks with thread for the same and packing the said wool 4*d*. In stipend of 1 dairymaid from the Purification (2 February) until Michaelmas (29 September) 1*s*. 6*d*. In 80 lambs bought before shearing £2 1*s*. 4*d*., at 5*d*. each for 48, and 8*d*. each for 32. In castrating piglets 4*d*. In grease and vinegar bought for greasing sheep 16*s*. 2*d*. In stipend of 1 keeper of lambs for ½ year, 2*s*. this year. Total, £3 8*s*. 7*d*.

Sheepcote
In roofing part of the sheepcote 1*s*. In making anew 1 door to the ewe-house with hooks and hinges for the same 9¼*d*. In a fodder-rack and cratch made for the ewe-house 9*d*. Total, 2*s*. 6¼*d*.

Cost of hay
In fences for an enclosure and enclosing the meadow 3*s*. 1½*d*. In mowing the whole of the meadow 10*s*. In tossing and spreading the hay and making haycocks therefrom 2*s*. Total, 15*s*. 1½*d*.

Threshing
In threshing and winnowing 68 qrs of wheat and curall by piece-work 15*s*. 7*d*., at 2¾*d*. a qr. In threshing and winnowing 55 qrs 2 bus. of barley, 4 qrs of peas and 7 qrs of vetches by piece-work 9*s*. 7½*d*., at 1¾*d*. a qr. In threshing and winnowing 44 qrs of oats by piece-work 3*s*. 2½*d*., at 1¾*d*. per 2 qrs. In 5 sacks bought 2*s*. 6*d*. Total, £1 10*s*. 11*d*.

Harvest-time
In bread bought for 974 men at 15 boon-works with the carters and customary tenants who reaped and bound 222 acres of wheat, 107 acres of barley and 414 acres of oats as they lie £1 19*s*. 8*d*. In relish for the same 12*s*. In allowance of food for the reeve and bartoner at harvest-time 1*s*. 8*d*. Total, £2 13*s*. 4*d*.

Cost of the mill
In iron bought for mending the spindle 8*d*. Total, 8*d*.

Expenses of the steward
In expenses of Simon, clerk, holding the place of the steward at the 2 tourns 9*s*. 6*d*. Total, 9*s*. 6*d*.

Expenses of the bailiff
In expenses of the bailiff for his visits £1 18*s*. In wages of 1 under-servant for the year £2 5*s*. ⌈7⌉½*d*., at 1½*d*. a day, because the bailiff did not stay there. Total, £4 3*s*. 7½*d*.

Purchase of stock
In 39 animals bought for pasturing £13 14*s*. 7*d*. Total, £13 14*s*. 7*d*.

Total of all expenses, £34 19*s*. 7¼*d*.

And he owes, £72 11*d*.

Cash deliveries
Delivered to Sir *Geoffrey*, treasurer of Wolvesey, by 1 tally, £72. And thus he is quit.

Issues of the grange

Wheat
{yield: 4½-fold less ½ qr}
The same render account for 71 qrs 6 bus. from the whole issue of wheat by struck measure; 1½ qrs from churchscot. Total, 73 qrs 2 bus.
Sown over 75 acres which lie in la Garston', Slade and Vyneys, 23 qrs 3½ bus.; that is, 2½ bus. an acre. In provision of Simon, clerk, for 2 tourns, 6 bus. In provision of the bailiff for his visits, 2 qrs 6 bus. Sold, 45 qrs 6 bus. Sold at the audit, 4½ bus.

Curall
The same render account for 13 qrs 1 bus. from the issue of curall by struck measure; all sold.

Barley
{yield: 4-fold less 3 qrs 2 bus.}
The same render account for 69 qrs 2 bus. from the whole issue of barley by struck measure; 6 qrs 5 bus. bought. Total, 75 qrs 7 bus.

Sown over 33 acres which lie at Parkgate and la Rugg', 20½ qrs; that is, 5 bus. an acre, less 2 bus. in all. Delivered to 1 park-keeper for the year, 1 qr according to custom. In customary payment to 1 keeper of lambs until the feast of St John the Baptist, 4 bus. Delivered to 1 carter, 6½ qrs, taking a quarter every 8 weeks. Delivered to 3 ploughmen for the year, 19½ qrs. Delivered to 1 dairymaid from the Purification until Michaelmas, 2 qrs 6½ bus., taking a quarter every 12 weeks. Delivered to 1 keeper of lambs from the feast of St John the Baptist until Michaelmas, for 13 weeks, 1 qr 1 bus. **{Henceforth the keeper of lambs should take for 12 weeks}** Sold, 23 qrs 2 bus. Sold at the audit, 5½ bus.

Oats
{yield: two-fold plus 7 bus.}
The same render account for 160 qrs 7 bus. from the whole issue of oats by struck measure; 18 qrs by estimation in sheaves. Total, 178 qrs 7 bus.
Sown over 131 acres and 1 rood which lie at la Worth', Brechlond' and la Vyneys, 82 qrs; that is, 5 bus. an acre. In fodder of 2 cart-horses from Michaelmas until Lammas, because thereafter they were at the church, 19½ qrs. In fodder of 6 plough-horses from Christmas until the Invention of the Cross (3 May), 16 qrs, at 1 bus. a night. In fodder of the same when they ploughed after dinner, 6 qrs. Given to oxen by estimation in sheaves, 18 qrs. In fodder of the horse of Simon, clerk, for 2 tourns, 2 bus. In fodder of the bailiff's horse for his visits, 3 qrs 2 bus. In threshing and winnowing 129 qrs according to custom, 2 qrs 3 bus., at 1 dish (*discum*) for 12 bus., whereof 6 dishes make 1 bushel. Sold, 31½ qrs.

Peas
{yield: 4-fold plus 2 bus.}
The same render account for 4 qrs 2 bus. from the whole issue of peas by struck measure; 1½ qrs remaining from the previous year in the granary; 1 qr remaining by estimation in the stack. Total, 6 qrs 6 bus.
Sown, 2 bus. Sold, 5 qrs. In fattening pigs for sale, 1½ qrs.

Vetches
{yield: 4-fold}
The same render account for 4 qrs 2 bus. from the issue of vetches remaining in the stack from the previous year; 4 qrs from this year's issue. Total, 8 qrs 2 bus. All sold.

Stock

Cart-horses: 2 remain from the previous year; 2 remain.
Plough-horses: 8 remain from the previous year; 1 bought. Total, 9. 1 in murrain; 1 sold. Total, 2. 7 remain.
Oxen: 26 remain from the previous year; 1 from the heriot of Thomas le Cog; 5 added from stock. Total, 32. 4 sold; 28 remain.
Bulls: 2 remain from the previous year; 2 remain.
Cows: 21 remain from the previous year; 1 from the heriot of Felicia Coker after calving. Total, 22. 3 sold before calving; 19 remain.
Steers: 5 remain from the previous year's bullocks; 39 bought. Total, 44. 5 added to oxen; 39 sold; none remain here.
Bullocks: 5 remain from the previous year's yearlings; 5 remain, 3 of them male.
Yearlings: 7 remain from the previous year's calves; 1 in murrain; 6 remain, 3 of them male.

Calves: 15 from the offspring of the said cows because 3 were sterile. 1 in tithe; 2 in murrain; 6 sold. Total, 9. 6 remain, 3 of them male.

Wethers: 354 remain from the previous year; 77 added from stock; 3 from the men of Chidden before shearing, and they will give 2 in another year. Total, 434. 16 sold at Martinmas; 24 in murrain before shearing, 12 after shearing. Total, 52. 382 remain.

Rams: 13 remain from the previous year; 3 added from stock. Total, 16. 1 in murrain before shearing; 15 remain.

Ewes: 339 remain from the previous year; 94 added from stock; 2 from the men of Chidden after lambing and before shearing. Total, 435. 14 sold at Martinmas; 24 in murrain before lambing and shearing, 8 after lambing and before shearing, 7 after shearing. Total, 53. 382 remain.

Hoggs: 188 remain from the previous year's lambs; 14 in murrain after shearing; 77 added to wethers, 3 to rams and 94 to ewes; none remain here.

Lambs: 255 from the offspring of the said ewes because 46 sterile; 80 bought. Total, 335. 25 in tithe, 5 of them skins; 3 in customary payment to the reeve, shepherd and hayward; 57 in murrain before weaning and 19 after weaning and before shearing; 38 sold before shearing because feeble. Total, 142. 193 remain.

Sows and boars: 1 boar and 3 sows remain from the previous year; 1 boar and 3 sows remain.

Pigs: 43 remain from the previous year; 24 added from stock. Total, 67. 3 in murrain; 19 sold. Total, 22. 45 remain.

Hoggets: 27 remain from the previous year's piglets; 3 in murrain; 24 added to pigs; none remain here.

Piglets {henceforth distinguish the ages of the piglets}: 51 from the offspring of the said sows this year. Total, 51. 5 in tithe; 3 in customary payment to the reeve, swineherd and hayward. Total, 8. 43 remain.

Coarse wool {yield of fleece 3¼*d.* plus 4*s.* 10¼*d.* in all}: 812 fleeces produced at the shearing this year; 81 in tithe; 2 in customary payment to 2 shepherds; 729 sent to Wolvesey, which made 3½ weys 11 cloves.

Lamb's-wool {yield of fleece 1¼*d.* plus 1*s.* ¾*d.* in all}: 193 fleeces produced at the shearing this year; all sent to Wolvesey, which made 11 cloves.

Winter cheese: 30 made; all sold, which made 17 cloves.

Summer cheese {yield of cow 3*s.* and sheep 2*d.* with 1 cheese for customary payment valued at 5*d.*}: 167 cheeses made between Monday after the feast of SS Tiburtius and Valerian (16 April) and Michaelmas (29 September), both days included; 16 in tithe; 1 in customary payment to the reeve; 150 sold, which made 8½ weys.

Butter: 1 wey and 5 cloves; all sold.

Hens {henceforth 5 geese and 1 gander should be reserved and the offspring of geese and hens answered for}: 54 hens from churchscot. 1 in default of the land of Richard le Wop because he has no wife; 1 in default of the land of Alice de C*ru*ce because a widow; 1 in default of the land of Walter Albrech' because he has no wife; 1 in default of Beatrice le Kembort because a widow; 1 in default of the land of Isabel Dau*n*front because a widow; 1 in default of the land of Matilda ate Holte because a widow; 1 in default of the land of Henry le Wanser because a widower; 1 in default of the land of William de C*ru*ce for the same; 1 in default of the land of Lucy Cog because a widow; 1 in default of the land of Walter le Portir because a widower; 1 in default of the land of Juliana Cattefan because a widow; 2 in default of the land of Adam Cattefan which Robert Coc*us* holds freely; 2 in default of the land of Richard Luce which the same Robert holds and which is commuted; 1 in default of the land of Eve le Ryde because a widow. Total, 16. 38 sold.

Peacocks: 7 remain from the previous year; 1 in murrain; 6 remain, 1 of them a peacock.
Salt: 5 qrs from rents; all sold.
Hides: 1 from a plough-horse, 1 from a yearling and 3 from calves dead from murrain; all sold.
Woolskins: 24 from wethers, 1 from a ram and 32 from ewes; all sold.
Skins after shearing: 12 from wethers, 7 from ewes and 14 from hoggs dead from murrain after shearing; all sold.
[Lambskins]: 57 from lambs dead from murrain before weaning; 19 from rotted sheep; all sold.
Utensils: 3 carts with iron tyres with all equipment, 1 standard bushel measure, 2 brass pots, 2 brass pans, 1 posnet and 1 ewer with a basin remain from the previous year; all remain.
[Cider]: 2 casks and 1 pipe made this year; 2½ casks remain.

The Church

[Sale of corn]
The same render account for £14 10*s.* from 54 qrs of wheat sold, at 6*s.* a qr for 20 qrs, and 5*s.* a qr for 34 qrs; 17*s.* 4*d.* from 6½ qrs of curall sold, at 2*s.* 8*d.* a qr; £1 13*s.* 6*d.* from 16 qrs 6 bus. of old and new winter barley sold, at 2*s.* a qr; £13 6*d.* from 65 qrs of old and new barley sold, at 4*s.* a qr; £10 12*s.* 7¼*d.* from 100 qrs 2 bus. of oats sold, at 2*s.* a qr for 27 qrs 5 bus., and 2*s.* 2*d.* a qr for 72 qrs 5 bus.; 6*s.* from 2 qrs of beans sold, at 3*s.* a qr; £1 5*s.* from 10 qrs of old and new peas sold, at 2*s.* 6*d.* a qr; 16*s.* from 8 qrs of vetches sold, at 2*s.* a qr.

Total of all receipts, £43 11¼*d.*

Threshing
In threshing and winnowing 54 qrs of wheat and 6½ qrs of curall by piece-work 11*s.* 1*d.*, at 2*d.* a qr threshed and 1*d.* per 5 qrs winnowed. In threshing and winnowing 52 qrs of barley, 5 qrs of winter barley, 2 qrs of beans, 8 qrs of peas and 6½ qrs of vetches by piece-work 10*s.* 6¼*d.*, at 1¾*d.* a heaped quarter. In threshing and winnowing 80 qrs of oats by piece-work 5*s.* 10*d.*, at 1¾*d.* per 2 qrs. Total, £1 7*s.* 5¼*d.*

[Cost of buildings]
In 1 roofer re-roofing part of the barn for 14 days 2*s.* 4*d.* In 2 men serving him for the same time 2*s.* 4*d.* Total, 4*s.* 8*d.*

[Harvest-time]
In 1 qr of barley bought for the livery of 1 carter 2*s.* 8*d.* In 4½ qrs of oats bought for the fodder of 8 cart-horses and 2 riders 6*s.* 9*d.* In 2 pairs of wheels made from the lord's timber 1*s.* 6*d.* In 1 new binding bought and put on the said wheels with the stipend of the smith 12*s.* 8*d.* In mending the cart at various times 10*d.* In trimming timber for wheels 4*d.* In clouts, nails and grease bought 1*s.* 1*d.* In mending and fitting the cart with axles, and trimming and treating the axles, 2*d.* In white leather bought 5*d.* In 1 collar and 2 pairs of saddle-pads bought 1*s.* 3*d.* In 1 pair of traces bought 4½*d.* In 1 cart-rope bought 1*s.* 3*d.* In stipend of 4 carters at harvest-time 6*s.* In expenses of 2 riders who stayed for 25 days 8*s.* 4*d.* In stipend of the same 10*s.* In shoeing 2 cart-horses and 2 riders 3*s.* 10*d.* In stipend of 2 stackers 6*s.* In food and

drink for 8 of the bishop's servants (*pedon'*) collecting tithes at harvest-time because it was to the lord's advantage that they were at table £1 16*s*. In stipend of the same 13*s*. 4*d*., or 1*s*. 8*d*. each. In hiring carts when it was necessary, 13*s*. this year. Total, £6 5*s*. 9½*d*.

Total of all expenses, £7 17*s*. 10¾*d*.

And thus he owes, £35 3*s*. ½*d*.

Cash deliveries
Delivered to Sir G*eoffrey*, treasurer of Wolvesey, by 1 tally, £8.

And thus he owes clear, £27 3*s*. ½*d*.

Issues of the grange
Wheat: 54 qrs from the whole issue of the grange; all sold.
Curall: 6½ qrs; all sold.
Winter barley: 11 qrs 2 bus. remain from the previous year in the granary; all sold.
New barley: 7½ qrs of new winter barley; 2 qrs for sustenance; 5½ qrs sold.
Barley: 2 qrs remain from the previous year in the granary; 63 qrs 1 bus. from this year's issue; all sold.
Oats: 100 qrs 2 bus. from the whole issue of the grange; all sold.
Beans: 2 qrs from the whole issue of the grange; all sold.
Peas: 10 qrs by estimation from the issues of 3 years which remain in the stack; all sold. Nothing from this year's issue because no issue was made, that is, 8 qrs by estimation remain in the stack.
Vetches: 8 qrs from the whole issue of the grange; all sold.

m.28

Bishops Sutton

Arrears
Nicholas, bailiff, and Walter de Manestrott', reeve, render account for £48 7*s*. 7½*d*. of arrears from the previous year. All delivered to Sir G*eoffrey* de Farh*a*m, treasurer of Wolvesey, and they are quit.

Rents of assize
The same render account for £49 for all rents of assize in the manor of Bishops Sutton for the year: £9 7*s*. 3*d*. at Christmas; £9 7*s*. 2½*d*. at Easter (22 April); £9 7*s*. 3¼*d*. at the feast of St John the Baptist (24 June); £21 17*s*. 1¼*d*. at Michaelmas (29 September). Total, £49 18*s*. 10*d*.

Quittances
In quittance of 1 reeve for the year 5*s*.; 1 beadle who is hayward for the year 3*s*.; 1 smith for the year 2*s*.; 1 shepherd for three terms because there was no threshing in the fourth term 2*s*. 3*d*.; 1 shepherd for the year 3*s*.; 6 ploughmen for the year 18*s*., or 3*s*. each; 6 workers working 2 days a week from Michaelmas until Lammas and everyday at harvest-time 19*s*. 4½*d*.; 1 cowherd for the year 3*s*.; 1 swineherd 3*s*. Total, £2 18*s*. 7½*d*.

Defaults of rent
In default of the[1] land of Philip ⌈Molend*inarius*⌉ drawn into demesne, 2*s*. for the year; the land of Geoffrey Hose given to the canons of Merton Priory for a fishpond

1 MS 'In def' ⟨mol' &⟩ t''.

1*s*.; 1 plot which belonged to John le Poleter, 6*d*. for the year; 1 virgate of land which ⌈belonged⌉ to Adam Bedell' drawn into demesne 10*s*.; 1 messuage pertaining to the mill and 1 plot at the bakehouse pertaining to the same which William Carp*enter* held 3*s*. 3*d*.; 3 acres of land which Guy de Hayden' held at la Leygate 1*s*. 6*d*. Total, 18*s*. 3*d*.

Total of quittances and defaults of rent, £3 16*s*. 10½*d*.

Total of rents remaining clear, £46 1*s*. 11½*d*.

Annual recognizance
The same render account for 3*d*. from William Syniar' for annual recognizance whilst he wishes to remain on the land of St Swithun's; 3*d*. from John le Fode so that he may serve and make his profit outside the liberty of the lord and not be challenged for this by the lord, and that he may come to the law-day and remain a villein as before; 3*d*. from John le Maȝon of Headley not to be prosecuted by the tithing for default at the law-day if he be not present and to be quit of tithingpenny, by the pledge of John ate Brigg'; 3*d*. from Henry Fab*er* for annual recognizance, by the pledge of Richard ate Putte. Total, 1*s*.

Issues of the manor
The same render account for £1 5*s*. 1*d*. from pannage of pigs of the vill this year; 18*s*. 11*d*. from foreign pannage; 10*s*. from pannage of the cottars, at 4*d*. for each working ox, and 3*d*. for a cow of full age; 5*s*. from the herbage of Farnd*on*; 4*s*. from pinfold; 2*s*. 1*d*. from churchscot; 2*s*. from the herbage behind the curia sold; £1 10*s*. from 3 old plough-horses sold; £3 16*s*. 10*d*. from 8 old oxen sold at various prices, that is, 10*s*. each for 7, and 6*s*. 10*d*. for 1; 10*s*. from 1 bull sold; £1 12*s*. from 4 old cows sold, at 8*s*. each; 2*s*. 6*d*. from 3 late-born calves sold; £10 12*s*. 6½*d*. from 29 animals bought for pasturing and sold at various prices; 16*s*. 4*d*. from 14 wethers sold at Martinmas, at 1*s*. 2*d*. each; 14*s*. from 14 ewes sold at the same feast; 12*s*. from 4 pigs sold; 3*s*. 3*d*. from 13 nearly dead lambs sold; 2*s*. 4*d*. from the hides sold of 1 plough-horse and 3 colts dead from murrain; 7*d*. from the hide sold of 1 bullock dead from murrain; 6*s*. 6*d*. from the skins sold wholesale of 7 wethers, 11 ewes and 8 hoggs dead from murrain before shearing, with the skins of 1 wether and 2 ewes dead from murrain after shearing; 1*s*. 10¾*d*. from the skins sold wholesale of 21 lambs dead from murrain before weaning and 14 rotted sheep; nothing from coarse wool and lamb's-wool here because it was sent to Wolvesey; 2*s*. 3*d*. from 2 cloves 4 lb of wool locks sold, at 10½*d*. a clove; 5*s*. from ½ wey 6 cloves of rowen cheese sold; £2 15*s*. from 6½ weys of cheese sold, at 8*s*. a wey for 3½ weys, and 9*s*. a wey for 3 weys; 2*s*. 3½*d*. from 8 cloves of butter sold; 10*s*. 4*d*. from 124 hens from churchscot sold; 2*s*. from 600 eggs sold according to custom; £1 10*s*. from Juliana de Manycr*oft* and 4 of her fellows for release from their harvest labour service, at 6*s*. each; 12*s*. from 1 cask of cider sold apart from the vessel; £1 6*d*. from the pasturage in the park sold; 12*s*. 6*d*. from 100 labour services sold, at 1½*d*. a labour service; 2*s*. from 1 bee-hive (*rusc'*) from the heriot of William le Dudelar' sold; 19*s*. 5½*d*. from dairy produce sold at the audit. Total, £33 1*s*. 2¼*d*.

Sale of wheat
The same render account for £18 3*s*. from 60½ qrs of wheat sold, at 6*s*. a qr; 2*s*. 11*d*. from 5 bus. of curall sold; £1 10*s*. 4*d*. from 6½ qrs of barley sold, at 4*s*. 8*d*. a qr; 1*s*.

6*d.* from 4 bus. of peas sold; 1*s.* from 4 bus. of vetches sold; 3*s.* 9½*d.* from 6½ bus. of barley sold at the audit. Total, £20 2*s.* 6½*d.*

Entry and marriage fines with tithingpenny

The same render account for 5*s.* from the tithing of Bishops Sutton for tithingpenny at the hundred-court of Martinmas; 10*s.* from the tithing of Ropley for the same; 4*s.* from the tithing of Bighton for the same; 3*s.* from the tithing of Bramdean for the same; 2*s.* from the tithing of West Tisted for the same; 8*s.* from the tithing of Headley for the same; £1 12*s.* from the same for the same at the hundred-court of Hockday; 4*s.* from Richard Sutore for 1 plot which came into the lord's hands by the death of William le Dudeler'; 13*s.* 4*d.* from Richard de Graveschate to have the land of his father by surrender of Juliana his mother; 2*s.* from John Gileberd for marrying Agnes his daughter; £1 from Walter P*ar*mehoud to have 1 virgate of land of his inheritance after the death of Seyld his mother; 13*s.* 4*d.* from William le Monek to have Alice de M*er*ton' with her land; 4*s.* from Agnes ate Putte to have the land which belonged to John ate Putte her husband; 1*s.* from William ate Hurn' for marrying Joan his daughter within; £4 from Agnes, who was wife of Roger le Ride, for 1 virgate of land which Roger le Rede her husband held and which formerly belonged to Margery de Zatelink', which virgate of land came into the bishop's hands as his escheat by inheritance because the said Margery had no heirs, to have and to hold for the life of the said Agnes, so that if the said Agnes marries her husband will make a second fine according to the custom of such villeinage. Total, £10 1*s.* 8*d.*

Perquisites

The same render account for 4*s.* from Thomas ate Hok' for trespass of the lord's charcoal; £5 6*d.* from other small perquisites. Total, £5 4*s.* 6*d.*

Total of both, £15 6*s.* 2*d.*

Total of all receipts, £114 12*s.* 10¼*d.*

Necessary expenses of ploughs

In ironwork of 3 ploughs this year 5*s.* In 2 plough feet bought 9*d.* Nothing accounted this year for the shoeing of 2 cart-horses because the smith is bound to shoe 2 cart-horses of Bishops Sutton at his own cost, and he will have 1 acre of wheat as it lies for making the iron of the shoes and 3 trunks for charcoal this year, because there were there three ploughs, and other customs are contained on the dorse of the roll. In 3 ploughs made anew 6*d.* In mending other ploughs 2*d.* In fitting ploughs with iron tyres 2*d.* In 3 pairs of wheels bought 6*d.* Richard de Manicroft' and John de Puteo ploughed 12 acres in winter and 12 acres in Lent, and they will take nothing. In 1 harrow made anew and others mended 3*d.* In 5 yokes made 2½*d.* In 2 oxen bought £1 1*s.* 6*d.* In forage bought to support plough-horses, oxen and cows 10*s.* Total, £1 19*s.* ½*d.*

In 15 qrs of oats bought for sowing and fodder £1 11*s.* 8*d.*, at 1*s.* 8*d.* a qr for 5 qrs, and 2*s.* 4*d.* a qr for 10 qrs. Total, £1 11*s.* 8*d.*

Carts

In 1 pair of wheels made from the lord's timber 9*d.* In clouts, nails and grease bought 1*s.* 4*d.* In fitting the cart with axles 6*d.* In 1 collar bought 6*d.* In 1 pair of traces bought

6*d*. In 1 cart-rope bought 1*s*. 1*d*. In white leather bought for harnesses 10*d*. In shoeing 4 plough-horses 1*s*. 4*d*. In a halter bought 1*d*. In stipend of 1 carter for the year 3*s*. In 1 pair of wheels made for dung 9*d*. Total, 10*s*. 3*d*.

Dairy

In 5 bus. of salt bought 1*s*. 3*d*. In linen and woollen cloth 6*d*. In earthenware pots and pans bought 2½*d*. In a press bought 4*d*. In mending the utensils of the dairy 3*d*. In 9 ells of canvas bought for packing the coarse wool and lamb's-wool 2*s*. 3*d*. In packing the same and making sacks 2*d*. In grease, vinegar and copperas to make well diseased sheep 10*s*. In 30 hurdles made 1*s*. 3*d*. In cratches made anew around the walls in the sheepcote 3*s*. 9½*d*. In tithe of 2 foals 2*d*. In gelding piglets 3½*d*. In stipend of the dairy-keeper who is male 3*s*. In 20 lambs bought 13*s*. 4*d*., at 8*d*. each. In 1 sow and 11 pigs bought 10*s*. 10*d*., at various prices. Total, £2 7*s*. 7½*d*.

Repair of buildings

In thatch bought for roofing the bakehouse and covering the stone walls 2*s*. In thatch bought and roofing the barn in part and the byre nearly anew 6*s*. In hedging to enclose around the curia anew and repairing it where necessary with fencing felled for the same 5*s*. 6*d*. In 3,500 shingles made 6*s*. 5*d*. In laying the same on the hall, room of the steward's clerks, and chapel 5*s*. 10*d*. In roofing and mending the said buildings with old shingles in places where it was necessary 2*s*. In large and small nails bought for the same 2*s*. 6*d*. In sawing boards and felling timber for the walls of the granary 2*s*. 8*d*. In a carpenter making the said walls nearly anew 4*s*. In large nails bought for the same 11½*d*. In roofing the bailiff's room in places 1*s*. 8*d*. In charcoal made 10*s*. Total, £2 9*s*. 6½*d*.

Harvest-time

In 5 qrs of barley bought for the bread of 500 men with the officials of the curia at 3 harvest boon-works 19*s*., and each had 1 loaf a day, of which 100 were made from a quarter. In 1,000 herrings bought to eat with the bread (*companag' eo*rund*em*) 6*s*. 9*d*., and each had 2 herrings a day. In meal bought for the pottage of the same 4*d*. They reaped 288 acres of wheat, barley and oats as they lie; moreover, they are to reap 161 acres which are called gavel-acres (*gavelacr'*) each year according to custom, and this year they reaped all the acres of wheat, barley and oats, and 22 acres are in quittance for the officials of the curia whilst they are in the lord's service. In mending a press 2*s*. 11½*d*. In 5 empty casks bought 10*s*. In timber bought to hoop the said casks 1*s*. 11½*d*. In hooping the said casks 1*s*. 10*d*. In making cider 1*s*. 6*d*. Total, £2 4*s*. 4*d*.

Cost of the park

In stipend of 1 park-keeper for the year according to custom 6*s*. 8*d*. In mending the hedges in the enclosure 1*s*. 4*d*. Total, 8*s*.

Cost of the meadow

In a second mowing of the meadow of Bishops Sutton in parcels 2*s*. 2*d*. In spreading the said hay 3*d*. In tossing the said hay and making haycocks therefrom 10*d*. Total, 3*s*. 3*d*.

Expenses of the steward and bailiff

In expenses of Simon, clerk, for 2 tourns 10*s*. 2*d*. In expenses of the bailiff for the year £5 17*s*. In 1 fur bought for the summer livery of the bailiff 3*s*. In expenses of the sheriff for 1 visit 4*s*. 4*d*. Total, £6 14*s*. 6*d*.

Purchase of stock
In 29 animals bought for pasturing £7 17*s.* 9*d.* Total, £7 17*s.* 9*d.*

Total of all expenses, £26 5*s.* 11½*d.*

And he owes, £88 6*s.* 10¾*d.*

Cash deliveries
Delivered to Sir G*eoffrey*, treasurer, by 1 tally, £52 17*s.* 4½*d.*

And he owes clear, £35 9*s.* 6¼*d.*

Issues of the grange

Wheat
{yield: three-and-a-half-fold less 4 qrs 7 bus.}
The same render account for 64 qrs 6 bus. from the whole issue of wheat from the grange in the granary without heaped measure; 23 qrs 5 bus. from churchscot. Total, 88 qrs 3 bus.
Sown over 43 acres in the fields of Rowele, Mol'[1] and la Rude, 16 qrs 1 bus.; that is, 3 bus. an acre. In provision of Simon, clerk, for 2 tourns, 4 bus. In provision of the bailiff for the year, 11 qrs 2 bus. Sold, 60½ qrs.

Curall
The same render account for 1 qr 2 bus. from the whole issue of curall from the grange in the granary without heaped measure.
Mixed with barley for the liveries of the manorial servants, 5 bus. Sold, 5 bus.

Barley
{yield: three-fold less 5 qrs 2 bus.}
The same render account for 35 qrs 2 bus. from the whole issue of barley from the grange in the granary without heaped measure; 5 bus. of curall received for the liveries of the manorial servants; 1 bus. of vetches received for the same. Total, 36 qrs.
Sown over 23 acres in the field of Bradewey and beside the sheepcote, 11½ qrs; that is, ½ qr an acre. Delivered to 1 carter for the year, 6½ qrs, taking a quarter every 8 weeks. Delivered to 1 man who is in place of the dairymaid and who makes the cheese and keeps the garden and does other work in the curia, 5 qrs 1½ bus., taking a quarter every 10 weeks. Delivered to 1 harrower, 4 bus. In provision of the bailiff's attendant, 2 qrs. Delivered to 1 keeper of lambs on Fobedon' with the lambs of Wield for 23 weeks, 2 qrs 2 bus. In customary payment to the swineherd this year, 6 bus. Sold, 6½ qrs. Sold at the audit, 6½ bus.

Oats
{yield: two-fold less 7½ qrs}
The same render account for 60 qrs from the whole issue of oats from the grange in the granary without heaped measure; 15 qrs by estimation in sheaves given to oxen; 15 qrs bought. Total, 90 qrs.
Sown over 72 acres in the fields of Rowele, Holecu*m*b*e* and la Rud*e*, 36 qrs; that is, ½ qr an acre. In fodder of 3 cart-horses harrowing at both sowings, 18½ qrs. In fodder

1 MS error for 'Hol''; see oats below.

of oxen by estimation in sheaves, 15 qrs. In fodder of the horses of Simon, clerk, for 2 tourns, 4 bus. In fodder of the bailiff's horse for the year, 18 qrs. In fodder of the clerk's horse, 2 qrs until Christmas.

Peas
{yield: 3-fold}
The same render account for 1½ qrs from the whole issue of peas from the grange in the granary without heaped measure. Sown, 1 qr. Sold, 4 bus.

Vetches
{yield: two-fold plus 3 bus.}
The same render account for 2 qrs 5 bus. from the whole issue of vetches.
Sown, 5 bus. Mixed with barley for the liveries of the manorial servants, 1 bus. In supporting pigs and piglets, 1 qr 3 bus. Sold, 3 bus.

Stock

Cart-horses: 3 remain from the previous year; 3 remain.
Plough-horses: 7 remain from the previous year; 1 from the heriot of Roger le Red'; 1 added from stock. Total, 9. 1 in murrain; 3 sold. Total, 4. 5 remain.
Colts: 2 remain from the previous year aged 2½ years; 1 in murrain; 1 added to plough-horses; none remain here.
Colts: 3 remain from the previous year aged 1½ years; 1 in murrain; 2 males remain now aged 2½ years.
Foals: 2 remain from the previous year aged ½ year; 1 in murrain; 1 female remains aged 1½ years.
Foals: 2 from the offspring of the mares this year; 2 remain aged ½ year.
Oxen: 28 remain from the previous year; 1 from the heriot of the relict Seyld; 2 added from stock; 2 bought. Total, 33. 8 sold; 25 remain.
Bulls: 2 remain from the previous year; 1 sold; 1 remains.
Cows {henceforth they should have 20 cows}: 16 remain from the previous year; 4 added from stock. Total, 20. 4 sold before calving; 16 remain.
Steers: 6 remain from the previous year's bullocks;[1] 29 bought. Total, 35. 2 added to oxen, 4 to cows; 29 sold; none remain here.
Bullocks: 5 remain from the previous year's yearlings; 1 in murrain; 4 remain, 3 of them male.
Yearlings: 4 remain from the previous year's calves; 4 remain, 2 of them male.
Calves: 12 from the offspring of the said cows because 2 were sterile and 2 milch-cows did not have calves. 1 in tithe; 3 sold. Total, 4. 8 remain, 7 of them male.
Wethers: 186 remain from the previous year; 24 added from stock. Total, 210. 14 sold at Martinmas; 7 in murrain before shearing, 1 after shearing. Total, 22. 188 remain.
Rams: 6 remain from the previous year; 2 added from stock. Total, 8. 8 remain.
Ewes: 176 remain from the previous year; 30 added from stock. Total, 206. 14 sold at Martinmas; 2 in customary payment to the smith and shepherd at the said feast; 11 in murrain before lambing, 2 after shearing. Total, 29. 177 remain.
Hoggs: 64 remain from the previous year's lambs; 8 in murrain before shearing; 24 added to wethers, 2 to rams, 30 to ewes; none remain here.
Lambs: 126 produced by the said ewes because 23 were sterile; 7 from the shepherd for trespass; 20 bought before shearing. Total, 153. 12 in tithe, 2 of them skins; 3 in

1 MS 'vj bovett' r' anno p' ⟨vitli'⟩⌈bovcl'⌉'.

customary payment to 1 reeve, 1 smith and 1 shepherd; 21 in murrain before weaning, 10 before shearing and after weaning, and 4 after shearing; 13 sold because feeble before shearing. Total, 63. 90 remain.
Sows: 1 remains from the previous year; 1 bought in November. Total, 2. 2 remain.
Pigs: 11 remain from the previous year; 16 added from stock; 1 from strays; 11 bought. Total, 39. 4 sold; 35 remain.
Hoggets: 16 remain from the previous year's piglets; all added to pigs; none remain here.
Piglets: 26 from the offspring of the said sows. 2 in tithe; 3 in customary payment to the reeve, smith and swineherd; 5 in murrain. Total, 10. 16 remain.
Coarse wool {yield of fleece 3¾*d.* less 1*s.* 5½*d.* in all}: 165 fleeces from wethers, 6 from rams, 149 from ewes and 56 from hoggs produced at the shearing this year. Total, 376. 37 in tithe; 1 in customary payment to 1 shepherd. Total, 38. 338 sent to Wolvesey, which made 2 weys 1 clove.
Lamb's-wool {yield of fleece 1¼*d.* less 2½*d.* in all}: 94 fleeces produced at the shearing this year; all sent to Wolvesey, which made 5 cloves.
Winter cheese: 28 rowen cheeses; all sold, which made ½ wey 6 cloves.
Cheese {yield of cow 4*s.* and sheep 3*d.* with 2 cheeses in customary payment valued at 1*s.*}: 162 cheeses made in summer between St Alphegus' day (19 April) and Michaelmas (29 September), both days included, at 1 cheese a day; 16 in tithe; 2 in customary payment to the smith and shepherd; 120 sold, which made 6½ weys.
Butter: 8 cloves; all sold.
Hides: 1 from a plough-horse, 3 from colts and 1 from a yearling; all sold.
Woolskins: 7 from wethers, 11 from ewes and 8 from hoggs dead from murrain before shearing; all sold.
Bare skins: 1 from a wether and 2 from ewes dead from murrain after shearing; all sold.
Lambskins: 21 from lambs dead from murrain before weaning and 14 from rotted sheep; all sold.
Peacocks: 12 remain from the previous year; 2 offspring. Total, 14. 14 remain, 5 of them male.
Hens: 162 from churchscot. 1 in default of the land of Togoud because he has no wife; 2 in default of the land of le Dug; 4 in default of the land of He*n*dyma*n* because churchscot is commuted on free land, 4 in default of the land of Horn for the same; 1 in default of the land of John Horn because he has no wife; 2 in default of the land of Walter le Rideler' because he has no wife; 2 in default of the land of Matilda ate Flod' because a widow; 1 in default of the land of Alice ate Flod' for the same; 2 in default of the land of Cecilia le Hud for the same; 1 in default of the land of Adam de la Huld' because he has no wife; 2 in default of the land of the relict of le Kyng because a widow; 2 in default of the land of Corvesir for the same; 1 in default of the land of Thomas Mol*endinarius* for the same; 2 in default of the land of Richard de Hokkelye for the same; 2 in default of the land of Walter Tostrong for the same; 2 in default of the land of Henry Gileb' for the same; 2 in default of the land of Thomas ate Med for the same; 2 in default of the land of John Belystrong' for the same; 1 in default of the land of Robert Sewade for the same; 2 in default of the land of Margery Mey for the same. Total, 38. 124 sold.
Eggs: 600 received from churchscot according to custom; all sold.
Cider: 1 cask remains from the previous year; 6 casks made this year with 8 qrs of apples from churchscot; 1 sold; 6 casks remain.
Plough feet: 1 from John Fab*er* to have maintenance whilst he wishes to remain in the hundred of Bishops Sutton, for the first time this year; delivered to the ploughs.

Labour services: 875 owed to the curia of Bishops Sutton by 7 workers working twice a week from Michaelmas until Lammas, except Christmas, Easter and Pentecost, that is, 82 labour services each, and 43 each from Lammas until Michelmas; 215 in quittance of 5 workers who gave money for release from their harvest labour service as made clear in the issues of the manor; 106 in threshing and winnowing 53 qrs of wheat and curall, at 1 labour service per ½ heaped qr; 35 in threshing and winnowing 35 qrs of barley; 18 in threshing and winnowing 48 qrs of oats; 8 in threshing and winnowing 4 qrs of peas and vetches, at 1 labour service per ½ heaped qr; 138 in weeding 138 acres of wheat, barley and oats; 78 in harrowing 78 acres; 77 in spreading dung; 10 in carrying the fold; 28 in collecting stubble; 62 in reaping corn; 100 sold.

Cheriton

Arrears
Nicholas, bailiff, and Richard Eme, reeve, render account for £57 12*s*. 3½*d*. of arrears from the previous year. All delivered to Sir G*eoffrey* of Wolvesey. They are quit.

Rents of assize
The same render account for £5 1*s*. 9*d*. for rents of the manor of Cheriton at Christmas; £8 2*s*. 8¾*d*. at Easter (22 April); £5 2*s*. 8¼*d*. at St John the Baptist (24 June); £13 4*s*. 9*d*. at Michaelmas (29 September). Total, £31 11*s*. 11*d*.

Quittances
In quittance of 1 reeve for the year 5*s*.; 1 smith for the ironwork of 5 ploughs for the year 5*s*.; 1 bartoner for the year 2*s*. 6*d*.; 1 keeper of ewes for the year 2*s*.; 1 keeper of wethers for the year 2*s*.; 1 keeper of hoggs for 3 terms 1*s*. 6*d*.; 1 swineherd for the year 2*s*.; 8 ploughmen for the year 16*s*., or 2*s*. each for the year; 2 oxherds until the oxen were put to the stalls 3*s*.; 2 workers working twice a week from Christmas until Lammas (1 August) and everyday at harvest-time 3*s*. Total, £2 2*s*.

Defaults of rent
In default of the land of the wheelwright drawn into demesne, 4*d*. for the year; the land of Hugh and Herbert, 8*d*. for the year; the land of Arnold and Geoffrey drawn into demesne, 8*d*. for the year; the land of Arnold and William ate More drawn into demesne, 8*d*. for the year; the land of Robert and Herbert drawn into demesne, 1*s*. 4*d*. for the year; the land of Richard Fab*er* drawn into demesne, 8*d*. for the year. These defaults are from a certain meadow at Elleford' drawn into demesne for the year. In default of the land which is called la Hyd*e*, 7*s*. for the year; the mill of Clyth' drawn into demesne, £3 10*s*. for the year; the mill of Bergh' because it does not have the multure of the hundred 13*s*. 4*d*. Total, £4 14*s*. 8*d*.

Total of quittances and defaults of rent, £6 16*s*. 8*d*.

Total of rents remaining clear, £24 15*s*. 3*d*.

Annual recognizance
The same render account for nothing from Richard le Clodyere because he is dead; 4*d*. from Robert Wolfonȝ for annual recognizance; 3*d*. from William Pistore for the same. Total, 7*d*.

m.28d

Issues of the manor

The same render account for £1 1*s.* 11½*d.* from pannage of pigs this year; 4*s.* 4*d.* from pannage of the cottars, at 4*d.* an ox and cow; nothing from the pasturage of Eldeford' this year for the lord's livestock; nothing from the pasturage of Perogh' for the same; nothing from the pasturage of Rowele, nor from the pasturage of Gre*n*le, nor from the pasturage of Holeden', nor from the pasturage of Fulele and Fernhull' this year for the same; nothing from the pasturage of Donefore this year for the same; 15*s.* from right of way for carts travelling beyond the lord's pasture; 9*s.* 5*d.* from 113 hens from churchscot sold; 3*s.* 6*d.* from 1,050 eggs sold according to custom; 3*s.* from the relict of le Fiȝ for release from her labour service this year; 2*s.* from Richard Eme for release from his labour service by 1 game of chance (*j hasard'*) at the lord's will; nothing from the entire coarse wool and lamb's-wool here because it was sent to Wolvesey; 4*s.* 1½*d.* from 4 cloves 5 lb of wool locks sold; 4*s.* 6*d.* from ½ wey 4 cloves of rowen cheese sold; £4 7*s.* from 10 weys 7 cloves of cheese made in summer sold, at 9*s.* a wey for 5 weys, and 8*s.* a wey for 5 weys 7 cloves; 8*s.* from 1 wey of butter sold; 19*s.* 8*d.* from 3 feeble plough-horses sold; £1 16*s.* from 3 old oxen sold; 4*s.* from 4 feeble calves sold; £1 1*s.* from 18 wethers sold at Martinmas (11 November), at 1*s.* 2*d.* each; £1 2*d.* from 22 ewes sold at the said feast, at 11*d.* each; 6*s.* 8⌈½⌉*d.* from 23 feeble lambs sold on account of their sickness, ⌈at 3½*d.* each⌉; £2 1*s.* 6*d.* from 15 pigs sold, at 2*s.* 6*d.* each for 7, and 3*s.* each for 8; 2*s.* 6*d.* from the hide sold of 1 ox dead from murrain; 1*s.* 10*d.* from the hides sold of 1 cow and 1 steer in murrain; 2*d.* from the hide sold of 1 calf in murrain; 11*s.* 6*d.* from the skins of 10 wethers, 10 ewes and 30 hoggs dead from murrain before shearing, at 3*d.* a skin of wethers and ewes, and 2*d.* a skin of hoggs, with the skins of 8 wethers, 6 ewes and 13 hoggs dead from murrain after shearing; 2*s.* 9*d.* from the skins of 33 lambs dead from murrain before weaning; 8½*d.* from the skins sold of 13 rotted sheep; nothing from wood this year; 2*s.* from Gilbert le Poller' so that he may take small fry (*menis'*) from the river at Cheriton and Tichborne; £6 9*s.* 4½*d.* from 15 steers sold which were bought for pasturing; 13*s.* from dairy produce sold at the audit; 1*s.* from 1 calf sold at the audit. Total, £23 16*s.* 6½*d.*

Sale of wheat

The same render account for £20 10*d.* from 60 qrs 1 bus. of wheat sold, at 6*s.* 8*d.* a qr; 8*s.* 9*d.* from 1 qr 7 bus. of curall sold; 9*s.* from 3 qrs of winter barley sold, at 3*s.* a qr; £3 15*s.* 10*d.* from 16 qrs 2 bus. of barley sold, at 4*s.* 8*d.* a qr; £3 14*s.* 8*d.* from 32 qrs of oats sold, at 2*s.* 4*d.* a qr; 1*s.* 3½*d.* from 3 bus. of peas sold; 1*s.* 3*d.* from 5 bus. of vetches sold; 7*s.* 6*d.* from 1 qr 7 bus. of barley sold at the audit; 12*s.* 6*d.* from 6 qrs 2 bus. of oats sold at the audit. Total, £29 11*s.* 7½*d.*

Corn from the mill

The same render account for 2*s.* 6*d.* from 4 bus. of wheat from the issue of the mill sold; £2 12*s.* from 14 qrs of barley from the issue of the same mill sold, at 3*s.* a qr for 4 qrs, and 4*s.* a qr for 10 qrs; 1*s.* 6*d.* from 4 bus. of malt from the issue of the same mill sold. Total, £2 16*s.*

Entry and marriage fines with tithingpenny

The same render account for 6*s.*[1] 8*d.* from the tithing of Cheriton at the hundred-court of Martinmas; 6*s.* 8*d.* from the same for the same at the hundred-court of

1 MS omits '*s.*'

Hockday; 3*s*. 4*d*. from Joan la Clodyar' to have 1 cotland which belonged to Richard le Clodyare her brother; 3*s*. 4*d*. from William, son of John Som', to have the said land by surrender of the said Joan Clodiar'; 6*s*. 8*d*. from John ate Med to have 1 cotland with Alveva his wife; 5*s*. from Christina, relict of Gang', to retain 1 cotland which belonged to her husband; 5*s*. from Alice Lovering to retain 1 cotland after the death of her husband; 10*s*. from Robert Jan to have 1 virgate of land, after the mortuary payment for the relict of Cart*ere*, his mother, out of her inheritance; 10*s*. from Simon Crech, son of William Crech, to have ½ cotland which came into the lord's hands as his escheat because a certain Alice la Schinn*ere* who held the said tenement withdrew and noone succeeded to the said land by inheritance, having been waiting for 1 year; 6*s*. 8*d*. from Joan, relict of le Swon, to retain 1 virgate of land which belonged to Henry her husband; £1 from John de Spin' to have the said Joan le Swon with the land; 3*s*. from Luke ate Med to have 1 virgate of land for his lifetime from the inheritance (*ex traditione*) of Nicholas his son. Total, £4 6*s*. 4*d*.

Perquisites
The same render account for 6*s*. 8*d*. from John de Puteo for transgression against the lord; 3*s*. 4*d*. from Thomas de Wichurst because he broke the lord's pinfold; 3*s*. 4*d*. from William Basset for the same; 3*s*. 4*d*. from Richard Jacob for the same; 6*s*. 8*d*. from others of the hundred for the same; 3*s*. from John de Mol*endino* because he received the lord's customary tenants at his mill; £4 19*s*. 2*d*. from other small perquisites. Total, £6 5*s*. 6*d*.

Total of both, £10 11*s*. 10*d*.

Total of all receipts, £91 11*s*. 10*d*.

Cost of ploughs {henceforth the customary tenants should not be made to plough if it is seen that a profit is able to be made}
In ironwork of 4 ploughs for the year and 1 plough at the time of the Lenten sowing 12*s*. 8*d*. In 1 ploughshare bought 9*d*. In 4 plough feet bought 1*s*. 4*d*. In 3 pairs of wheels bought 9*d*. In fitting ploughs with iron tyres 3*d*. In shoeing 8 plough-horses hauling before the oxen 1*s*. 10*d*. In boon-works of 23 ploughmen in winter and 22 ploughmen in Lent 7*s*. 6*d*., and each ploughman ploughed 2 acres in winter and 2 acres in Lent as they lie and will have therefor 2*d*. Moreover, for 5 ploughmen of Ovington 5*d*., and each ploughman ploughed 1 acre in winter and will have therefor 1*d*. In 1 new harrow made and others mended 2*d*. In spreading dung in the fields 1*s*. 2*d*. In 4 oxen bought £2 6*s*., at 11*s*. each for 2, and 12*s*. each for 2. In forage bought for oxen and other animals 10*s*. Total, £4 2*s*. 10*d*.

Purchase of corn
In 1 qr 6 bus. of winter barley bought for sowing 5*s*. 3*d*., at 3*s*. a qr. In 15 qrs of barley bought for the liveries of the manorial servants £2 15*s*., at 3*s*. a qr for 5 qrs, and 4*s*. a qr for 10 qrs. Total, £3 3*d*.

Carts
In 1 pair of wheels made from the lord's timber 9*d*. In iron bought and large nails made and old tyres mended and put on the said wheels with the stipend of the smith 5*s*. In fitting the cart with axles 6*d*. In clouts, nails and grease bought 1*s*. 1*d*. In white leather bought for harnesses 5*d*. In shoeing 2 cart-horses 3*s*. In shoeing 3 plough-

horses helping the cart-horses at the time of the summer sowing to clear dung 10*d*. In 4 halters made 1*d*. In 1 collar and 1 pair of saddle-pads bought 1*s*. In 2 ropes bought for tethering horses in the pasture 2*d*. In stipend of 1 carter for the year 3*s*. Total, 14*s*. 10*d*.

Dairy
In 6 bus. of salt bought 1*s*. 6*d*. In a press bought 4*d*. In earthenware pots and pans bought 5*d*. In woollen and linen cloth bought 8*d*. In 1 mould bought 6*d*. In 1 tine bought 5*d*. In mending other utensils of the dairy 4*d*. In 15 ells of canvas bought 3*s*. 9*d*. In packing wool and making sacks with thread bought for the same 4*d*. In vinegar, copperas and grease to make well diseased sheep £1 1*s*. In 48 hurdles made for the fold 2*s*. In stipend of 1 dairymaid from the Purification (2 February) until Michaelmas (29 September) 2*s*. In 1 cratch made for sheep and others mended 1*s*. In roofing the wether-house in places 1*s*. 6*d*. In 39 lambs bought before shearing £1 4*s*. 6*d*., at 6*d*. each for 9, and 8*d*. each for 30. In 13 pigs bought 9*s*. 9*d*., at 9*d*. each. In gelding piglets 2½*d*. In stipend of 1 cowherd 2*s*. Total, £3 12*s*. 2½*d*.

Repair of buildings
In collecting stubble and roofing the buildings in the curia in places 4*s*. In wattling and mending the walls around the byre 2*s*. In building 1 new bridge over the water 7*d*. In 1 rope bought for the louver in the hall 1½*d*. Total, 6*s*. 8½*d*.

Threshing of corn
In threshing and winnowing 60 qrs of wheat and curall by piece-work 11*s*., at 2¼*d*. a qr. In threshing and winnowing 7 qrs of winter barley and 20 qrs of barley by piece-work 3*s*. 4½*d*., at 1½*d*. a heaped quarter. Know that the workers threshed 36½ qrs 2 bus. of wheat and curall, 16 qrs 1 bus. of barley, 86 qrs of oats, 2½ qrs of peas and 2 qrs 1 bus. of vetches for their labour service. In weeding all the corn except that done by labour service 5*s*. 1½*d*. In wages of 1 attendant who keeps the barn and who threshed at various times 18*s*. 1*d*. Total, £1 17*s*. 7*d*.

Harvest-time
In bread bought for 12½ boon-works of 1,025 men, with the officials of the curia and 14 men of Ovington, who eat twice a day except this year, and 15 workers who are bound, at the choice of the lord, to reap with the boon-works and have food like the others, each reaping either ½ acre of wheat or barley or 1 acre of oats and having 1 sheaf as it falls, £2 2*s*. 8½*d*. In herrings and cheese bought for a want of herrings to eat with the bread 19*s*. 5*d*., and each ought to have 4 herrings a day. They reaped 245 acres of barley and 210 acres of oats as they lie. In stipend of 1 hayward for the year 6*s*. 8*d*. Total, £3 8*s*. 9½*d*.

Expenses of the mill
In iron bought and bands made to hoop the beams 1*s*. In mending the spindle and bills 1*s*. 2*d*. Total, 2*s*. 2*d*.

Expenses of the steward
In expenses of Simon, clerk, holding the place of the steward for the 2 tourns 6*s*. 9*d*. Total, 6*s*. 9*d*.

Purchase of stock
In 15 animals bought for pasturing £3 19*s*. 4½*d*. Total, £3 19*s*. 4½*d*.

Total of all expenses, £21 11*s*. 6*d*.

And thus he owes, £70 4*d*.

Allowances
In 10 cows bought for the stock of the manor £3 14*s*. 4*d*., at 7*s*. 6*d*. each for 6, and 7*s*. each for 4. Total, £3 14*s*. 4*d*.

Cash deliveries
Delivered to Sir G*eoffrey*, treasurer of Wolvesey, by 1 tally, £40 10*s*. 7½*d*.

Total of all allowances and cash deliveries, £44 4*s*. 11½*d*.

And he owes clear, £25 15*s*. 4½*d*.

Issues of the grange

Wheat
{yield: three-fold less 1 qr 6 bus.}
The same render account for 94 qrs of wheat from the whole issue of the grange in the granary without heaped measure.
Sown over 89 acres in the fields of Peregh' and la Slad', 33 qrs 3 bus.; that is, 3 bus. an acre. In provision of Simon, clerk, for 2 tourns, 4 bus. Sold, 60 qrs 1 bus. It balances.

Curall
The same render account for 3 qrs 2 bus. from the whole issue of curall from the grange in the granary without heaped measure.
Mixed with barley for the liveries of the manorial servants, 1 qr 3 bus. Sold, 1 qr 7 bus. Total, 3 qrs 2 bus. It balances.

Bere
{yield: three-fold plus 5 bus.}
The same render account for 7 qrs of bere from the whole issue of the grange in the granary without heaped measure; 1 qr 6 bus. bought. Total, 8 qrs 6 bus.
Sown in the field beside la Hull', 1 qr 6 bus. Mixed with barley for the liveries of the manorial servants, 4 qrs. Sold, 3 qrs. It balances.

Barley
{yield: two-and-a-half-fold less 1 bus.}
The same render account for 36 qrs 1 bus. from the whole issue of barley from the grange in the granary without heaped measure; 4 qrs of winter barley received for the liveries of the manorial servants; 1 qr 3 bus. of curall received for the same; 7 bus. of peas received for the same; 15 qrs bought. Total, 57 qrs 3 bus.
Sown over 33½ acres measured by the perch in the fields of la Hull' and Buttehegg', 16½ qrs 2 bus.; that is, ½ qr an acre. Delivered to the hayward and carter for the year, 13 qrs, taking a quarter every 8 weeks. Delivered to 1 harrower, 4 bus. Delivered to 1 dairymaid from the Purification until Michaelmas, 2 qrs 2 bus. In customary payment to 1 keeper of ewes, 6 bus. In customary payment to 1 keeper of lambs this year, 6 bus. In customary payment to 1 swineherd this year because he was {not} outside the manor during mast, 6 bus. In supporting pigs and piglets, 1½ qrs. Delivered to 1

cowherd from the feast of St Vincent the Martyr (22 January) until Michaelmas (29 September), for 36 weeks, 3 qrs. Sold, 16 qrs 2 bus.

Oats
{yield: two-fold less 2 qrs}
The same render account for 116 qrs 2 bus. from the whole issue of oats from the grange in the granary without heaped measure; 22 qrs by estimation in sheaves given to oxen. Total, ⌈1⌉38 qrs 2 bus.
Sown over 85½ acres which lie in the fields of la Hull' and la Rud', 64 qrs; that is, 6 bus. an acre, less 1 bus. in all. In fodder of 2 cart-horses and 8 plough-horses helping them at the horse-ploughs at the time of the summer sowing because they ploughed before and after dinner and carried dung when they were not at the ploughs, 9 qrs 6 bus. In fodder of oxen by estimation in sheaves, 22 qrs. In fodder of the horses of Simon, clerk, 2 bus. Sold, 32 qrs. Sold at the audit, 6 qrs 2 bus.

Peas
{yield: two-fold plus 2 bus.}
The same render account for 2½ qrs from the whole issue of peas without heaped measure.
Sown, 5 bus. Mixed with barley for the liveries of the manorial servants, 7 bus. In supporting pigs, 5 bus. Sold, 3 bus.

Vetches
{yield: two-fold plus 1 bus.}
The same render account for 2 qrs 1 bus. from the whole issue of vetches. Sown, 1½ qrs. Sold, 5 bus.

Mill
Wheat: 4 bus. from the whole issue of la Clich' put to farm; all sold.
Barley: 14 qrs from the whole issue this year; all sold.
Malt: 4 bus. from the issue of the same mill; all sold.

Stock

Cart-horses: 2 remain from the previous year; 2 remain.
Plough-horses: 13 remain from the previous year. 2 in murrain; 3 sold. Total, 5. 8 remain, 3 of them mares.
Colts: 2 remain from the previous year aged 1½ years; 1 in murrain; 1 male remains now aged 2½ years. No foals this year.
Oxen: 39 remain from the previous year; 1 added from stock; 4 bought. Total, 44. 1 in murrain; 3 sold. Total, 4. 40 remain.
Cows: 10 remain from the previous year; 1 from the heriot of Henry le Swon with calf; 2 added from stock; 10 bought, 4 of them after calving. Total, 23. 1 in murrain before calving; 22 remain.
Steers: 4 remain from the previous year's bullocks; 15 bought. Total, 19. 1 in murrain; 1 added to oxen, 2 to cows; 15 sold; none remain here.
Bullocks: 4 remain from the previous year's yearlings; 4 remain, 1 of them male.
Yearlings: 4 remain from the previous year's calves; 4 males remain.
Calves: 14 from the offspring of the said cows because 3 sterile; 1 from the heriot of Henry Swon with the cow. Total, 15. 1 in murrain; 1 in tithe; 4 sold. Total, 6. 1 sold at the audit; 8 remain.

Wethers: 324 remain from the previous year; 53 added from stock. Total, 377. 18 sold at Martinmas; 2 in customary payment for the mowing of the meadow after shearing; 10 in murrain before shearing, 8 after shearing. Total, 38. 339[1] remain.
Rams: 8 remain from the previous year; 2 added from stock. Total, 10. 10 remain.
Ewes: 288 remain from the previous year; 52 added from stock. Total, 340. 22 sold at Martinmas; 1 in customary payment to 1 shepherd at Martinmas; 10 in murrain before lambing, 6 after shearing. Total, 39. 301 remain.
Hoggs: 150 remain from the previous year's lambs; 30 in murrain before shearing, 13 after shearing; 53 added to wethers, 2 to rams, 52 to ewes; none remain here.
[Lambs]: 236 from the offspring of the said ewes this year because 19 were sterile; 39 bought before shearing. Total, 275. 23 in tithe, 3 of them skins; 3 in customary payment to the reeve, shepherd and smith; 33 in murrain before weaning, 13 after weaning and before shearing, 4 after shearing; 23 sold on account of feebleness. Total, 99. 176 remain.
[Sows]: 2 remain from the previous year; 2 remain.
Pigs: 17 remain from the previous year; 19 added from stock; 13 bought; 1 from the heriot of John Gang'; 1 from the heriot of Thomas Lovering. Total, 51. 15 sold; 36 remain, 1 of them a boar.
[Hoggets]: 21 remain from the previous year's piglets; 2 in murrain; 19 added to pigs; none remain here.
[Piglets]: 31 from the offspring of the said sows this year. 3 in tithe; 1 in customary payment to the swineherd; 3 in murrain. Total, 7. 24 remain.
Coarse wool {yield of fleece . . . plus . . . in all}: 679 fleeces produced at the shearing this year; 2 in customary payment to 2 shepherds; 677 sent to Wolvesey, which made 4½ weys.
Lamb's-wool {[yield of fleece] . . . ¾*d*. less 1*s*. 3*d*. in all}: 180 fleeces; all sent to Wolvesey, which made 13 cloves.
[Winter cheese]: 30 made; all sold, which made ½ wey 4 cloves.
Summer cheese {yield of cow 3*s*. and sheep 3*d*. with 3 cheeses in customary payment valued at 2*s*. this year}: 155 cheeses made between St Alphegus' day (19 April) and Michaelmas (29 September), both days included, at 1 cheese a day; 15 in tithe; 3 in customary payment to the reeve, smith and bartoner; 137 sold, which made 10 weys 7 cloves.
Butter: 1 wey from the issue of the dairy; all sold.
[Hides]: 2 from plough-horses, 1 from a colt, 1 from an ox, 1 from a cow, 1 from a steer and 1 from a calf dead from murrain; all sold.
[Woolskins]: 10 from wethers, 10 from ewes and 30 from hoggs dead from murrain before shearing; all sold.
[Bare skins]: 8 from wethers, 6 from ewes and 13 from hoggs dead from murrain after shearing; all sold.
Lambskins: 33 from lambs dead from murrain before weaning; 17 from rotted sheep; all sold.
[Hens]: 116 from churchscot according to custom; 12 from the hayward, forester and bartoner according to custom. Total, 128. 2 in default of the land of Ponk; 2 in default of the land of John Som' because the land was commuted; 2 in default of the land of Walter le Poller' because a widower; 2 in default of the land of Mabel le Poller' because a widow; 2 in default of the land of Roger le Schin*er*e because a widower; 3 in default of the land of William Fab*er* for the same; 2 in default of the land of Edward Wytegrom for the same. Total, 15. 113 sold.

1 MS 'CCC⟨xxix⟩⟨xxxix⟩'.

[Eggs]: 1,050 from the hayward, forester and bartoner according to custom; all sold.
Ploughshares: 1 from the rent of the relict of William Fab*er*; delivered to the ploughs.
Apples: 8 qrs from the issue of the garden; all sent to Bishops Sutton.
Labour services: 120 owed by 2 workers from Christmas until Lammas, at 2 a week; 129 owed by 3 workers working every day at harvest-time. Total, 249. 64 in threshing and winnowing 29 qrs 6 bus. of wheat and curall by heaped measure; 17 in threshing and winnowing 13 qrs of barley, 2 qrs 2 bus. of peas and 1 qr 5 bus. of vetches by heaped measure; 90 in threshing and winnowing 100 qrs of oats by heaped measure; 38 in spreading and making dung; 40 in weeding corn.

Beauworth

Rents
Nicholas, bailiff, and John Edwyn', reeve, render account for £5 16*s*. 7*d*. for all rents of assize in the manor of Beauworth for the year; all paid at Michaelmas (29 September). Total, £5 16*s*. 7*d*.

Quittances
In quittance of 1 reeve for the year 5*s*.; 1 bartoner for the year 2*s*. 6*d*.; 4 ploughmen for the year 8*s*.; 1 oxherd until the oxen were put to the stalls 1*s*.; 1 shepherd for the year 2*s*. Total, 18*s*. 6*d*.

Defaults of rent
In default of 1 virgate of land which belonged to Richard Gileb' drawn into demesne, 2*s*. 6*d*. for the year. Total, 2*s*. 6*d*.

Total of quittances and defaults of rent, £1 1*s*.

Total of rents remaining clear, £4 15*s*. 7*d*.

Issues of the manor
The same render account for 12*s*. ½*d*. from pannage of pigs of the vill this year; 1*s*. from pinfold this year; 2*s*. from the pasturage of the meadow beside St Catherine's Hill sold after mowing; £1 2*s*. from 2 old oxen sold; 3*s*. 5*d*. from the flesh and hide sold of 1 ox dead from murrain; £1 12*s*. 6*d*. from 26 wethers sold at Martinmas, at 1*s*. 3*d*. each; 1*s*. 8*d*. from 20 hens from churchscot sold; 2*s*. 2*d*. from the skins sold wholesale of 8 wethers dead from murrain before shearing, and 5 after shearing; 1*s*. 1½*d*. from 9 lb of wool locks sold. Total, £3 17*s*. 11*d*.

Sale of wheat
The same render account for £11 17*s*. 6*d*. from 35 qrs 5 bus. of wheat sold, at 6*s*. 8*d*. a qr; 10*s*. 6*d*. from 2 qrs 2 bus. of maslin sold, at 4*s*. 8*d*. a qr; 12*s*. 10*d*. from 2 qrs 6 bus. of barley sold, at 3*s*. 8*d*. a qr; £4 2½*d*. from 34 qrs 3 bus. of oats sold, at 2*s*. 4*d*. a qr; 2*s*. 7½*d*. from 7 bus. of peas sold, at 4½*d*. a bus.; 2*s*. 3*d*. from 1 qr 1 bus. of vetches sold. Total, £17 5*s*. 11*d*.

Entry and marriage fines with tithingpenny
The same render account for 2*s*. from the tithing of Beauworth for tithingpenny at the hundred-court of Martinmas; 2*s*. from the same tithing for the same at Hockday; 5*s*. from William Pykot to have Alveva Pikot with her land. Total, 9*s*.

m.29

Perquisites

The same render account for 2*s*. from Stephen, son of the smith, for trespass of wood; 16*s*. 9*d*. from other small perquisites. Total, 18*s*. 9*d*.

Total of both, £1 7*s*. 9*d*.

Total of all receipts, £27 7*s*. 2*d*.

Necessary expenses of ploughs {henceforth money should be taken from the ploughmen for ploughing and not plough-service if a profit is able to be made}

In steel bought for 2 ploughs for the year 4*s*. 3*d*. In stipend of the smith making the ironwork by piece-work 3*s*. 4*d*., because he is from outside the manor. In 1 plough foot bought 4*d*. In making a new plough and mending many others 1*s*. In boon-works of 7 ploughmen in winter and 7 ploughmen in Lent 2*s*. 4*d*., and each ploughman ploughed 1 acre in winter and 1 acre in Lent and will have therefor 2*d*. In shoeing 4 plough-horses for the year 8*d*. In fitting ploughs with iron tyres 2*d*. In 4 yokes made 2*d*. In 3 wheels bought 6*d*. In 1 harrow made 2*d*. In 1 sack bought for seed 6*d*. Total, 13*s*. 5*d*.

Costs of carts

In mending the cart 3*d*. In fitting the cart with axles 1*d*. In clouts, nails and grease bought 4*d*. In 1 collar bought 3*d*. In a halter made 1*d*. In 1 rope bought for tethering horses in the pasture 1*d*. Total, 1*s*. 1*d*.

Repair of buildings

In roofing the barn and other buildings in places 1*s*. 6*d*. In stalls made anew for the byre 3*s*. In mending the walls of the byre 7*d*. Total, 5*s*. 1*d*.

Expenses towards the fold and sheepcote

In 12 hurdles made 6*d*. In vinegar and copperas to make well diseased sheep 2*s*. 10*d*. In 5 ells of canvas bought for packing wool 3*s*. 4*d*. In sacks made for the wool and packing the wool 4*d*. In 50 wethers bought after shearing £2 14*s*. 2*d*., at 1*s*. 1*d*. each. Total, £2 19*s*. 1*d*.

Threshing

In threshing and winnowing 44 qrs of wheat, 1 qr of curall and 2 qrs 6 bus. of maslin by piece-work 8*s*. 9*d*., at 2*d*. a qr, and 1*d*. per 5 qrs winnowed. In threshing and winnowing 11 qrs of barley 1*s*. 2½*d*., at 3¼*d*. per 2 qrs by heaped measure. In threshing and winnowing 69½ qrs of oats by piece-work 4*s*. 11¾*d*. In threshing and winnowing 1 qr 7 bus. of peas and 1½ qrs of vetches by piece-work 7½*d*. Total, 15*s*. 6¾*d*.

Cost of the harvest

In bread bought for 7½ harvest boon-works of 316 men with the officials of the curia this year 13*s*. 2*d*., each having ½*d*. of bread a day. In cheese and herrings bought to eat with the bread 7*s*. 6*d*., and 2 men had 9 herrings a day. In salt bought 1*d*. In earthenware pots bought 1*d*. They reaped 73 acres of wheat, 18 acres of barley, 142 acres of oats and 4 acres of peas and vetches as they lie. In stipend of 1 carter for the year who is hayward 3*s*. In weeding the corn except that done by labour service 1*s*. 4*d*. In meal bought for the pottage of the reapers 4*d*. Total, £1 5*s*. 6*d*.

Total of all expenses, £5 19*s*. 8¾*d*.

And he owes, £21 7*s*. 5¼*d*.

Delivered to Sir G*eoffrey*, treasurer of Wolvesey, by 1 tally, £20 7*s*. 5¼*d*.

And he owes clear, £1.

Issues of the grange

Wheat
{yield: 4-fold plus 2 bus.}
The same render account for 44 qrs 2 bus. from the whole issue of wheat from the grange in the granary without heaped measure.
Sown over 23 acres in the fields of Rowedell' and Holeden', 8 qrs 5 bus.; that is, 3 bus. an acre. Sold, 35 qrs 5 bus.

Curall
The same render account for 1 qr from the whole issue of curall; all mixed with barley for the liveries of the manorial servants.

Maslin
{yield: two-fold plus 2 bus.}
The same render account for 2 qrs 6 bus. from the whole issue of maslin. Mixed with barley for the liveries of the manorial servants, 4 bus. Sold, 2 qrs 2 bus.

Barley
{yield: three-and-a-half-fold less 6½ bus.}
The same render account for 11 qrs from the whole issue of barley from the grange in the granary without heaped measure; 1 qr of curall received for the liveries of the manorial servants; 4 bus. of maslin received for the same; 5 bus. of peas received for the same. Total, 13 qrs 1 bus.
Sown over 6 acres and 1 rood in the field of Westdo*n*, 3 qrs 1 bus.; that is, ½ qr an acre. Delivered to 1 carter who is hayward, 6½ qrs. In customary payment to 1 shepherd, 6 bus. Sold, 2 qrs 6 bus.

Oats
{yield: two-and-a-half-fold plus 2 qrs 3 bus.}
The same render account for 69½ qrs from the whole issue of oats from the grange in the granary without heaped measure; 13½ qrs by estimation in sheaves given to oxen. Total, 83 qrs.
Sown over 70 acres 1 rood which lie in the fields of Rake and Westdon', 35 qrs 1 bus.; that is, ½ qr an acre. In fodder of the plough-horses and oxen by estimation in sheaves, 13½ qrs. Sold, 34 qrs 3 bus.

Peas
{yield: 8-fold less 1 bus.}
The same render account for 1 qr 7 bus. of peas from the whole issue. Sown, 3 bus. Mixed with barley for the liveries of the manorial servants, 5 bus. Sold, 7 bus.

Vetches
{yield: 6-fold}
The same render account for 1 qr from the whole issue of vetches. Sown, 3 bus. Sold, 1 qr 1 bus.

Stock

Plough-horses: 4 remain from the previous year; 4 remain.
Oxen: 19 remain from the previous year. 2 sold; 1 in murrain. Total, 3. 16 remain.
Wethers: 206 remain from the previous year; 50 bought after shearing; 1 from strays. Total, 257. 26 sold at Martinmas; 1 in customary payment for the mowing of the meadow after shearing; 8 in murrain before shearing, 5 after shearing. Total, 40. 217 remain.
Coarse wool {yield of fleece 4*d*. plus 1*s*. 5½*d*. in all}: 173 fleeces produced at the shearing this year; 1 in customary payment to 1 shepherd; 172 sent to Wolvesey, which made 1 wey 4 cloves.
Hens: 24 from churchscot this year. 2 in default of Gunilda upe Stret' because a widow; 2 in default of the land of Basilia because a widow. Total, 4. 20 sold.
Woolskins: 8 from wethers dead from murrain before shearing; all sold.
Bare skins: 5 from wethers dead from murrain after shearing; all sold.
Utensils: 1 bushel measure, 3 locks, 1 wooden cart with equipment and fittings, 1 basket, 1 sack and 1 seed-basket; all remains.

Alresford

Arrears

Nicholas, bailiff, and William de Haywod', reeve, render account for £86 17*s*. 1½*d*. of arrears from the previous year. All delivered to Sir G*eoffrey*, treasurer of Wolvesey. They are quit.

Rents of assize

The same render account for £4 4*s*. 9½*d*. for rents of assize in the manor of Alresford at Christmas; £9 2*s*. 5½*d*. at Easter (22 April); £4 4*s*. 9½*d*. at St John the Baptist (24 June); £21 16*s*. 5*d*. at Michaelmas (29 September). Total, £39 8*s*. 5½*d*.

Quittances

In quittance of 1 reeve for the year 5*s*.; 1 smith for the year 3*s*.; 1 hayward for the year 4*s*. 6*d*.; 2 ploughmen for the year 6*s*.; 4 workers working 3 days a week from Michaelmas until Lammas (1 August) and every day at harvest-time 12*s*., or 3*s*. each; 8 workers working every day at harvest-time 6*s*., or 9*d*. each. Know that at Alresford there are 3 millers, because the fourth mill is in the lord's hands, each of whom are bound to work 2 days a week from Michaelmas until Lammas, each week with a cart, and everyday at harvest-time, but they do not now work before harvest-time because they are allowed to pay therefor, as made clear in the issues of the manor, but they do work at harvest-time. In quittance of 1 keeper of wethers for the year 3*s*.; 1 keeper of ewes for the year 2*s*. 6*d*.; 1 cowherd for the year 2*s*. 6*d*.; 1 keeper of lambs and hoggs for ½ year 1*s*. 6*d*.; 1 swineherd for the year 3*s*. Total, £2 9*s*.

Defaults of rent

In default of the land and mill which belonged to Nicholas drawn into demesne, £1 10*s*. for the year; 1 cottage which belonged to Harold drawn into demesne, 3*s*. for the year. Total, £1 13*s*.

Total of quittances and defaults of rent, £4 2*s*.

Total of rents remaining clear, £35 6*s*. 5½*d*.

Farm of the mill

The same render account for £1 6*s*. 8*d*. for the farm of the fulling-mill this year. Total, £1 6*s*. 8*d*.

Annual recognizance

The same render account for 3*d*. from Thomas Horn for annual recognizance, by the pledge of Roger Cl*ericus* and Hugh de Cotes. Total, 3*d*.

Issues of the manor

The same render account for £1 3*s*. 3*d*. from pannage of pigs at Martinmas (11 November) this year; nothing from foreign pannage this year; 2*s*. 8*d*. from the herbage of the cottars, at 7*d*. for a fully-grown cow, 3*d*. for a 3 year-old heifer, and 1½*d*. for a bullock; nothing from pinfold this year because the sheep of the cottars are not in the lord's pasture; £1 3*s*. 6*d*. from the pasturage of 26 horses, 9 oxen, 7 cows, 6 bullocks and 9 calves on Porndon' sold this year in winter, at 6*d*. for an ox, horse and cow, 3*d*. for a bullock, and 1*d*. for a foal and calf; 5*s*. 6*d*. from the pasturage of 22 cows and 15 bullocks in Hewod' and Fyncheslye sold this year in winter, at 2*d*. a cow and 1*d*. a bullock; 12*s*. 3*d*. from the pasturage of 29 oxen and 28 bullocks in Fyncheslye sold this year in summer, at 3*d*. an ox and 1*d*. a bullock; nothing from the pasturage in Goslo*n*d' because it was sown; 3*s*. from the pasturage beside the fishpond sold; nothing from the pasturage of Fobedo*n* in winter or summer because it was pastured with the lord's lambs and hoggs, nor from the pasturage of Brokfurlo*ng* for the same, from the pasturage of Beches for the same, nor from the pasturage of Wodefurlo*ng*' for the same; nothing from the men collecting eels in the fishpond this year because it was forbidden by the lord; 5*s*. from the men collecting small fry in the river; 8*d*. from Thomas ate Burgh' for 2 sticks of eels sold; £1 1*s*. from 2 old oxen sold; 15*s*. from 3 oxen sold; 8*s*. 6*d*. from 1 old cow sold; £16 9*d*. from 40 steers sold; 5*s*. from 5 late-born calves sold; £2 6*s*. 3*d*. from 37 wethers sold at Martinmas, at 1*s*. 3*d*. each; £1 12*s*. 6*d*. from 30 ewes sold at the said feast, at 1*s*. 1*d*. each; 7*s*. 6*d*. from 26 nearly dead lambs sold; £2 17*s*. ⌈6*d*.⌉ from 21 pigs sold at various prices; nothing from coarse wool and lamb's-wool here because it was sent to Wolvesey; 7*s*. 7½*d*. from 8 cloves 5 lb of wool locks sold, at 10½*d*. a clove; 3*s*. 9*d*. from ½ wey of rowen cheese sold; £2 16*s*. from 6 weys of summer cheese sold, at 9*s*. a wey; 3*s*. 6*d*. from 11 cloves of butter sold; 15*s*. 8*d*. from the hides sold of 6 oxen dead from murrain; 6*s*. from the hides sold of 3 cows dead from murrain; 1*s*. 6*d*. from the hides sold of 1 steer and 1 bullock dead from murrain; 6*d*. from the hides sold of 1 yearling and 1 calf dead from murrain; £1 3*s*. 3*d*. from the skins of 19 wethers and 27 ewes, at 3*d*. a skin, and 37 hoggs, at 2½*d*. a skin, dead from murrain before shearing, sold wholesale with the skins of 13 wethers and 4 ewes, at 1*d*. each, dead from murrain after shearing; 9*s*. 6¾*d*. from the skins of 141 lambs dead from murrain before weaning, sold with the skins of 18 rotted[1] sheep, at ¾*d*. a lambskin, and ½*d*. a skin of a rotted sheep; 5*s*. from 60 hens from churchscot sold this year; 2*s*. 8*d*. from 800 eggs sold, received from churchscot according to custom; £1 from 3 millers for release from labour service before harvest-time; 3*s*. from the pasturage of Ynlond' sold; 9*s*. 8*d*. from the pasturage sold with the lord's animals, at 10*d*. a head; 7*s*. 2*d*. from dairy produce sold at the audit. Total, £38 5*s*. 8¼*d*.

Sale of corn

The same render account for £7 1*s*. 8*d*. from 21 qrs 2 bus. of wheat sold, at 6*s*. 8*d*. a qr; 4*s*. 1*d*. from 7 bus. of curall sold; £7 from 30 qrs of barley sold, at 4*s*. 8*d*. a qr; 5*s*.

1 MS '*nota*' in margin against line beginning 'roto*rum*' and ending 'Et de ix s. viij d.', in a different hand to the surrounding text.

4*d*. from 2 qrs of dredge sold; £1 13*s*. 3*d*. from 14 qrs 2 bus. of oats sold, at 2*s*. 4*d*. a qr; 13*s*. 1½*d*. from 4 qrs 3 bus. of peas sold, at 3*s*. a qr; 3*s*. from 1½ qrs of vetches sold; 1*s*. 8*d*. from 4½ bus. of beans sold, at 4½*d*. a bus. Total, £17 2*s*. 1¾*d*.

Corn from the borough mill

The same render account for 5*s*. 3*d*. from 7 bus. of wheat from the issue of the mill sold; £4 1*s*. from 20 qrs 2 bus. of barley from the issue of the same mill, at 4*s*. a qr; £3 5*s*. from 19½ qrs of malt from the issue of the mill sold, at 3*s*. 4*d*. a qr; £2 1*s*. 2*d*. from the moiety of meal from the same mill because the miller received the other moiety for service; 10*s*. from eels from the sluice sold. Total, £10 2*s*. 5*d*.

New mill

The same render account for 3*s*. 9*d*. from 5 bus. of wheat from the issue of the same mill sold; £1 18*s*. 6*d*. from 11 qrs of barley from the issue of the mill sold, at 3*s*. 6*d*. a qr. Total, £2 2*s*. 3*d*.

Entry and marriage fines with tithingpenny

The same render account for 6*s*. 8*d*. from the tithing of Alresford for tithingpenny at the hundred-court of Martinmas; 6*s*. 8*d*. from the same for the same at the hundred-court of Hockday; 4*s*. from the tithing of Medstead at the hundred-court of Martinmas; 4*s*. from the same for the same at the hundred-court of Hockday; 6*s*. 8*d*. from Ellen, relict of le Baysar', to have 1 virgate of land which belonged to William le Bayser' her husband; 13*s*. 4*d*. from William de Heywod' to have 1 virgate of land of his inheritance after the death of Agnes his mother; 6*s*. 8*d*. from John le Hayward and Alice his wife to have ½ cotland which is the inheritance of the same Alice; 6*s*. 8*d*. from Edward, son of Roger Cl*ericus*, to have the said land by resignation of John le Hayward' and Alice his wife; 2*s*. from Alice de H*ar*mod' for marrying Alice her daughter outside; 1*s*. from William le Palm*ere* for marrying Alice his daughter within; 6*s*. 8*d*. from Matilda, relict of le Botelyr, to retain 1 virgate of land which belonged to her husband. Total, £3 4*s*. 4*d*.

Perquisites

The same render account for 6*s*. 8*d*. from John ate Pund' for trespass in the curia; £3 16*s*. from other small perquisites. Total, £4 2*s*. 8*d*.

Total of both, £7 7*s*.

Total of all receipts, £111 12*s*. 10½*d*.

Cost of ploughs {henceforth they should not take the plough-service of the customary tenants if it is seen that a profit is able to be made}

In steel bought for the ploughs, nothing, because there is there 1 hayward who maintains the ironwork of 2½ ploughs for the year according to custom. In 3 plough feet bought 1*s*. In ploughs made anew and mended 7*d*. In fitting ploughs with iron tyres 1½*d*. In iron bought and 1 coulter made anew 9*d*. In a harrow made anew and others mended 3*d*. In 1 wheel bought 1½*d*. In boon-works of 23 ploughmen in winter and 25 in Lent 8*s*., and each ploughman ploughed and harrowed 1 acre in winter and 1 acre in Lent and will have therefor 2*d*. Moreover, each will plough and harrow 1 acre in winter for the right to fold on the pasturage of Caddon', but this year they do not have that pasturage and therefore they have ploughed nothing. In a new halter made ½*d*. In stipend of 2 shepherds for the year 6*s*. In 12 oxen bought £7 14*s*., at 11*s*. 6*d*. each for 4, and 13*s*. 6*d*. each for 8. In forage bought to support oxen and other livestock 9*s*. 4*d*. Total, £9 2½*d*.

Purchase of corn
In 31 qrs 2 bus. of barley bought for the liveries of the manorial servants £5 19*s*. 6*d*., at 3*s*. 6*d*. a qr for 11 qrs, and 4*s*. a qr for 20 qrs 2 bus. Total, £5 19*s*. 6*d*.

Carts
In 1 pair of wheels made from the lord's timber 10*d*. In fitting the cart with axles 5*d*. In clouts, nails and grease bought 10*d*. In bands of wood bought for the wheels 2*d*. In white leather bought for harnesses 6*d*. In shoeing 1 cart-horse 1*s*., because the smith shod the other horse according to custom. In stipend of the carter for the year 3*s*. Total, 6*s*. 9½*d*.

Repair of buildings
In roofing the whole of the barn 2*s*. In re-roofing the barn and other buildings in places 2*s*. 4*d*. In a carpenter making a third of the byre anew 3*s*. In wattling, roofing and plastering the said building 6*s*. In collecting withies for the same 2*s*. In repairing the stone walls around the curia in places 1*s*. 5*d*. In digging 2 ditches in the curia 2*s*. 6*d*. Total, 19*s*. 3*d*.

Borough mill
In boards sawn for the mill 1*s*. 7*d*. In mending the mill with these boards and another place outside the mill which is called le Fisbed 1*s*. 11*d*. In iron bought and the spindle lengthened and mended 1*s*. 3*d*. Total, 4*s*. 9*d*.

New mill
In boards sawn for the mill 1*s*. 5*d*. In steel bought and the spindle mended and the bills steeled 1*s*. 1*d*. In 1 millstone bought with its carriage £1 7*s*. 6*d*. Total, £1 10*s*.

Fulling-mill
In boards sawn for the mill 1*s*. 10*d*. In mending the said mill with nails bought for the same 1*s*. 8*d*. Total, 3*s*. 6*d*.

Dairy
In 6 bus. of salt bought 1*s*. 6*d*. In woollen and linen cloth bought 4*d*. In earthenware pots and pans bought 4*d*. In a press bought 4*d*. In 36 hurdles made 1*s*. 4*d*. In 14 ells of canvas bought 3*s*. 6*d*. In making sacks with thread bought for the same and packing the wool 6*d*. In mending the utensils of the dairy 6*d*. In grease, vinegar and copperas bought to make well diseased sheep £1 10*s*. 8½*d*. In stipend of 1 dairymaid 1*s*. 6*d*. In making a new cratch around the walls of the hogg-house 1*s*. 6*d*. In likewise making a cratch in the ewe-house 1*s*. 8*d*. In re-roofing the sheepcotes in places 2*s*. 3*d*. In gelding piglets 4*d*. In vetches and hay bought to support ewes and hoggs in winter 5*s*. 1*d*. Total, £2 11*s*. 4½*d*.

Harvest-time
In bread bought for 4 boon-works of 468 men with the officials of the curia 19*s*. 6*d*., each man having ½*d*. of bread a day. In 1,404 herrings bought to eat with the bread 7*s*., and each had 3 herrings a day. In meal bought for the pottage of the same 7*d*. In

salt bought 1*d*. In stipend of 1 hayward for the year 6*s*. 8*d*. They reaped 332 acres of wheat and oats as they lie. Total, £1 13*s*. 10*d*.

Expenses of the steward
In expenses of Simon, clerk, for 2 tourns, 7*s*. 4*d*. Total, 7*s*. 4*d*.

Purchase of stock
In 40 animals of both sexes bought for pasturing £13. In 187 lambs bought for stock £5 10*s*. 2*d*., at 6*d*. each for 87, and 8*d*. each for 100. In 3 cows bought £1 4*s*. 2*d*. Total, £19 14*s*. 4*d*.

Total of all expenses, £42 10*s*. 10½*d*.

And he owes, £69 2*s*.

Allowances
In expenses made towards sowing the land of Richard Warennari*us* with seed bought for the same for the summer sowing, less a certain rent of 3*s*. 10½*d*. received from the holdings of the same warrener, £3 7*s*. 1¾*d*. In expenses for expediting certain business of the lord, that is, for the collector of the fifteenth, 7*s*. Total, £3 14*s*. 1¾*d*.

Delivered to Sir G*eoffrey*, treasurer of Wolvesey, by 1 tally, £27 9*s*.

Total of all allowances and cash deliveries, £31 3*s*. 1¾*d*.

And thus he owes clear, £37 18*s*. 10¼*d*.

Issues of the grange

Wheat
{yield: two-and-a-half-fold less 1 qr 6 bus.}
The same render account for 42 qrs 3 bus. from the whole issue of wheat from the grange in the granary without heaped measure.
Sown over 55 acres measured by the perch in the fields of Ynlond', Schepelond' and la Co*m*be, 20 qrs 5 bus.; that is, 3 bus. an acre. In provision of the steward for 2 tourns, 4 bus. Sold, 21 qrs 2 bus.

Curall
The same render account for 7 bus. of curall from the whole issue; all sold.

Barley
{yield: two-fold plus 3 qrs 1 bus.}
The same render account for 7 qrs 7 bus. of barley remaining in the granary from the previous year; 51 qrs 1 bus. from the whole issue this year; 31 qrs 2 bus. bought. Total, 90 qrs 2 bus.
Sown over 44 acres in the fields of Goslond', Melecrofte and Heywod', 27 qrs 3 bus.; that is, 5 bus. an acre. Delivered to 1 carter for the year, 6½ qrs. Delivered to 1 hayward for the year, 6½ qrs. Delivered to 2 drovers for the year, 13 qrs. Delivered to 1 harrower, 4 bus. Delivered to 1 dairymaid from the feast of SS Tiburtius and Valerian (14 April) until Michaelmas (29 September), 2½ qrs. In customary payment to 1 keeper of ewes this year, because he kept the lambs from weaning until the feast of St John the Baptist (24 June),[1] 4 bus. In supporting pigs, 2 qrs. Delivered to 1

1 MS 'f*estu*m S*anc*ti ⟨Mich'⟩ Joh*ann*is Bapt*ist*e'.

keeper of lambs from the feast of St John the Baptist[1] until Michaelmas, 1 qr 3 bus., taking a quarter every 10 weeks. Sold, 30 qrs.

Dredge
{yield: 3½-fold}
The same render account for 7 qrs of dredge from the whole issue of the grange without heaped measure. Sown, 5 qrs. Sold, 2 qrs.

Oats
{yield: two-fold plus 6 qrs 5 bus.}
The same render account for 65 qrs 7 bus. from the whole issue of oats from the grange in the granary without heaped measure; 12 qrs by estimation in sheaves given to oxen. Total, 77 ⌈qrs⌉ 7 bus.
Sown over 61 acres at Heywod', Boueto*n* and in la Comb*e*, 38 qrs 1 bus.; that is, 5 bus. an acre. In fodder of 2 cart-horses and 4 plough-horses which came from Bishops Sutton hauling before the oxen at the time of the summer sowing, 13 qrs. Given to oxen by estimation in sheaves, 12 qrs. In fodder of the horses of Simon, clerk, for 2 tourns, 4 bus. Sold, 14 qrs 2 bus.

Beans
{yield: 3-fold}
The same render account for 4½ bus. of beans from the issue; all sold.

Peas
{yield: three-fold plus 1 bus.}
The same render account for 5 qrs 3 bus. from the whole issue of peas from the grange in the granary. Sown, 1 qr. Sold, 4 qrs 3 bus.

Vetches
{yield: 2 bus. less than sown}
The same render account for 4 bus. of vetches remaining from the previous year in the granary; 2 qrs 6 bus. from the whole issue of vetches. Total, 3 qrs 3 bus.
Sown, 1 qr 2 bus. In supporting pigs, 4 bus. Sold, 1½ qrs.

Borough mill
Wheat:[2] 7 bus. from the borough mill; all sold.
Barley: 20 qrs 2 bus. from the whole issue of the same mill; all sold.
Malt: 1 qr 1 bus. remaining from the previous year; 18 qrs 3 bus. from the issue of the same mill this year. Total, 19½ qrs. All sold.

New mill
Wheat:[3] 5 bus. from the issue of the new mill this year; all sold.
Barley:[4] 11 qrs from the whole issue of the same mill; all sold.

Stock

Plough-horses: 2 remain from the previous year; 2 remain.

1 MS 'f*esto* S*ancti* ⟨Mich'⟩ Joh*annis* Bapt*iste*'.

2 MS omits heading.

3 MS omits heading.

4 MS omits heading.

Oxen: 20 remain from the previous year; 12 bought. Total, 32. 5 sold; 6 in murrain. Total, 11. 21 remain.
Bulls: 1 remains from the previous year; 1 remains.
Cows: 12 remain from the previous year; 3 bought before calving; 1 added from stock. Total, 16. 1 sold before calving; 4 in murrain before calving. Total, 5. 11 remain.
Steers: 2 remain from the previous year's bullocks; 40 bought. Total, 42. 1 in murrain; 1 added to cows; 40 sold; none remain here.
Bullocks: 3 remain from the previous year's yearlings; 1 in murrain; 2 males remain.
Yearlings: 4 remain from the previous year's calves; 1 in murrain; 3 remain, 2 of them male.
Calves: 10 from the offspring of the said cows this year because 1 sterile. 1 in tithe for the previous year and this year; 1 in murrain; 5 sold. Total, 7. 3 remain.
Wethers: 454 remain from the previous year; 60 added from stock. Total, 514. 37 sold at Martinmas; 19 in murrain before shearing, 14 after shearing. Total, 70. 444 remain.
Rams: 9 remain from the previous year; 1 added from stock. Total, 10. 10 remain.
Ewes: 338 remain from the previous year; 60 added from stock. Total, 398. 30 sold at Martinmas; 30 in murrain before lambing, 7 after lambing and before shearing, and 4 after shearing. Total, 71. 327 remain.
Hoggs: 158 remain from the previous year's lambs; 37 in murrain before shearing; 60 added to wethers, 1 to rams, and 60 to ewes; none remain here.
Lambs: 258 from the offspring of the said ewes because 20 were sterile; 187 bought before shearing. Total, 445. 25 in tithe, 14 of them skins; 3 in customary payment to the reeve, beadle and 1 shepherd; 141 in murrain before weaning, 5 after weaning and before shearing, and 13 after shearing; 36 sold before shearing on account of feebleness. Total, 223. 222 remain.
Pigs: 27 remain from the previous year; 3⌈2⌉ added from stock. Total, 59. 21 sold; 38 remain, 2 of them sows.
Boars: 1 remains from the previous year; 1 remains.
Hoggets: 34 remain from the previous year's piglets; 2 from strays. Total, 36. 4 in murrain; 32 added to pigs; none remain here.
Piglets: 43 from the offspring of the said sows this year. 4 in tithe; 3 in customary payment to 1 reeve, 1 swineherd and 1 beadle; 3 in murrain. Total, 10. 33 remain.

m.29d
Coarse wool {yield of fleece 3¾*d*. plus 4*s*. 8¾*d*. in all}: 799 fleeces produced at the shearing this year. 80 in tithe; 2 in customary payment to 2 shepherds. Total, 82. 717 sent to Wolvesey, which made 4 weys 11 cloves.
Wool locks: 8 cloves 5 lb; all sold.
Lamb's-wool {yield of fleece 1¼*d*. plus 6*d*. in all}: 235 fleeces produced at the shearing this year; sent to Wolvesey, which made 13 cloves.
Cheese: 27 rowen cheeses; all sold, which made ½ wey.
Cheese {yield of cow 3*s*. and sheep 2*d*. this year because of the especially great sickness of the same}: 168 cheeses made between Sunday before the feast of St Alphegus (15 April) and Michaelmas (29 September), both days included; 16 in tithe; 2 in customary payment to the reeve and dairymaid; 150 sold, which made 6 weys.
Butter: 11 cloves from the issue of the dairy this year; all sold.
Hides: 6 from oxen, 4 from cows, 1 from a steer, 1 from a bullock, 1 from a yearling and 1 from a calf dead from murrain; all sold.

Woolskins: 19 from wethers, 37 from ewes and 37 from hoggs dead from murrain before shearing; all sold.
Bare skins: 14 from wethers and 4 from ewes dead from murrain after shearing; all sold.
Lambskins: 141 from lambs dead from murrain before weaning and 18 from rotted sheep; all sold.
Hens: 104 from churchscot according to custom. 4 in default of the land of Joyce because it is commuted for 5*s*.; 4 in default of that of Robert son of Gilbert which is likewise commuted; 4 in default of the land of Ancel which is likewise commuted; 4 in default of the land of Leveve which is likewise commuted; 4 in default of the land of Bond which is likewise commuted and which Roger Cl*ericus* holds; 4 in default of the land of the skinner which is likewise commuted; 4 in default of the land of the potter (*le Pott*ere) which is commuted; 4 in default of the land of Nicholas Mol*endinarius* which is in the lord's hands; 2 in default of the land of Alice ate Hull' because a widow; 2 in default of the land of Gilbert Vacc*arius* for the same; 2 in default of the land of Ralph de Marnhale for the same; 2 in default of the land of Gilbert atte Mell' for the same; 2 in default of the land of John Swanel for the same; 2 in default of the land of Matilda Walkelyn for the same. Total, 44. 60 sold.
Eggs: 800 received at Easter according to custom; all sold.
Swans: 50 remain from the previous year; 5 offspring. Total, 55. 9 in murrain; 46 remain.
Labour services: 387 owed to the curia of Alresford by 3 workers from Michaelmas until Lammas, each of them working 3 days a week, except for the weeks of Christmas, Easter and Pentecost, because for these three weeks they worked only 2 days a week; 129 owed by the same workers from Lammas until Michaelmas, each of them working everyday for 43 days this year. Total, 516. 387 sold as made clear in the issues of the manor; 76 in reaping 38 acres of wheat and barley, at 1 labour service per ½ acre; 20 in reaping and binding 20 acres of oats; 14 in binding 223 acres of barley, at 1 labour service per 1½ acres; 14 in carrying corn; 5 in making 1 shop (*schoppe*) on the road through Alton (*passu de Awelton'*) with wood for fencing cut for the same.

Alresford Borough

Arrears
Nicholas, bailiff, and Hamo, son of Roger Cl*ericus*, render account for £8 8*s*. 3*d*. of arrears from the previous year. All delivered to Sir G*eoffrey*.

Rents of assize
The same render account for £16 11*s*. 1*d*. for all rents of assize in the borough of Alresford for the year and all paid at Michaelmas (29 September). Total, £16 11*s*. 1*d*.

Quittances
In quittance of 1 reeve for the year 2*s*. Total, 2*s*.

Defaults of rent
In default of the fulling house, 10*s*. for the year; the bakehouse, 3*s*. 8*d*. for the year; the house which belonged to Roger le Blesced' pulled down by Sir S*olomon* de Roff' and his fellow itinerant justices at Winchester because it was a nuisance to the neighbourhood and to those passing through 6*d*.; 1 forge which belonged to Richard

Fab*er* pulled down by the same 1*s*.; 1 plot which belonged to William Sutor' pulled down by the same 8*d*.; 1 plot which belonged to Geoffrey Cl*ericus* vacant for the same 8*d*.; 1 plot which belonged to Walter Som' vacant for the same 8*d*.; 1 plot which belonged to William le Blessed' vacant for the same 6*d*.; 1 forge which belonged to Henry Fab*er* vacant for the same 8*d*.; 1 plot formerly of John March' vacant for the same 1*s*.; 1 plot formerly belonging to Thomas le Blessed' vacant for the same 1*s*.; the house which belonged to Roger le Arblast' pulled down for the same 1*s*. 1*d*.; 1 house formerly of Warin Piscat' pulled down for the same 1*s*. 1*d*.; 1 vacant plot which belonged to Adam Fab*er* 1*s*.; 1 plot which belonged to John Swyft pulled down for the same 1*s*.; 1 vacant plot which belonged to John Godh*a*mme 1*s*. 4*d*.; 1 plot which belonged to John le Lokyar' now vacant for the same 4*d*.; 3 houses formerly belonging to Philip de la Hyde which recently fell down and which plot is vacant 2*s*. 6*d*. Total, £1 8*s*. 8*d*.

Total of quittances and defaults of rent, £1 10*s*. 8*d*.

Total of rents remaining clear, £15 5*d*.

Tolls and stallage
The same render account for £2 from tolls and stallage this year; 7*s*. 10*d*. from the rent of Thomas Cl*ericus* which he was accustomed to get back yearly from his holdings. Total, £2 7*s*. 10*d*.

Perquisites
The same render account for £2 14*s*. 3*d*. from the small perquisites of the court. Total, £2 14*s*. 3*d*.

Total of all receipts, £20 2*s*. 6*d*.

Expenses
In a tumbrel made anew for the visit of the lord king 1*s*. 5*d*. In boards and timber sawn for the bridge, with the carpenter, 3*s*. 4*d*. Total, 4*s*. 9*d*.

And he owes, £19 17*s*. 9*d*.

Delivered to Sir G*eoffrey*, treasurer of Wolvesey, by 1 tally, £17 1*s*.

And thus he owes clear, £2 16*s*. 9*d*.

Wield

Arrears
Nicholas, bailiff, and Thomas Cally, reeve, render account for £19 3*s*. 10¼*d*. of arrears from the previous year. All delivered to the lord of Wolvesey. They are quit.

Rents of assize
The same render account for £1 4*d*. for rents at Christmas; £1 4½*d*. at Easter (22 April); £1 4*d*. at St John the Baptist (24 June); £5 10*d*. at Michaelmas (29 September). Total, £8 1*s*. 10½*d*.

Quittances
In quittance of 1 reeve for the year 5*s*.; 1 smith for the year 3*s*.; 1 granger for the year 2*s*.; 2 ploughmen for the year 4*s*.; 3 workers working every day at harvest-time 1*s*. 6*d*.; 1 cowherd for the year 2*s*.; 1 shepherd 2*s*. Total, 19*s*. 6*d*.

Defaults of rent

In default of the land of the marshal, 4*d*. for the year, because he renders 1 ploughshare in place of the rent; 1 plot of land which belonged to Pagan, 2*d*. for the year; the land which Hugh de la Doune, Simon de Estwald', Walter Bone and William Othin held unjustly from the land formerly of Maurice de Tourevil' drawn into demesne, 6*s*. 8*d*. for the year. Total, 7*s*. 2*d*.

Total of quittances and defaults of rent, £1 6*s*. 8*d*.

Total of rents remaining clear, £6 15*s*. 2½*d*.

Issues of the manor

The same render account for 9*s*. 5*d*. from pannage of pigs this year; 7*s*. from pannage in the park this year; 14*s*. 7½*d*. from the whole vill for release from harrowing for 'dustlo*nd*' because the lord harrows for them; £1 1*s*. 11*d*. from pasturage in the park sold for 19 fully-grown animals and 12 bullocks, at 10*d*. an animal and 6*d*. a bullock; £1 7*s*. 6*d*. from 4 old oxen sold, at 13*s*. 4*d*. for 1, and 14*s*. 2*d*. for 3 nearly dead with the hides and flesh; 8*s*. from 1 old cow sold; £13 9*s*. 6*d*. from 32 animals bought for the lord's pasture sold; 10*s*. from 10 late-born calves sold; 1½*d*. from the hide sold of 1 calf in murrain; £1 2*s*. 8*d*. from 17 wethers sold at Martinmas, at 1*s*. 4*d*. each; 7*s*. from 7 ewes sold at the said feast; 4*s*. 9*d*. from the skins of 8 wethers, 3 ewes and 8 hoggs dead from murrain before shearing, sold wholesale with the skins of 3 wethers, 4 ewes and 3 hoggs dead from murrain after shearing; 1*s*. 1*d*. from the skins of 12 lambs dead from murrain before weaning, sold with the skins of 2 rotted sheep; nothing from coarse wool and lamb's-wool here because it was sent to Wolvesey; 1*s*. 6*d*. from 1 clove 5 lb of wool locks sold; 1*s*. 10*d*. from 22 hens from churchscot sold; 8*d*. from 1 ploughshare sold; 4*s*. from ½ wey 2 cloves of rowen cheese sold; £3 4*s*. 4*d*. from 7 weys 4 cloves of cheese sold, at 9*s*. a wey; 6*s*. 1½*d*. from ½ wey 7 cloves of butter sold; nothing from wood this year. Total, £24 2*s*. ½*d*.

Sale of wheat

The same render account for £17 12*s*. 3*d*. from 55 qrs 3 bus. of wheat sold, at 6*s*. a qr for 25 qrs 3 bus., and 6*s*. 8*d*. a qr for 30 qrs; £1 2*s*. from 5½ qrs of barley sold, at 4*s*. a qr; £5 7½*d*. from 43 qrs 1 bus. of oats sold, at 2*s*. 4*d*. a qr; 1*s*. 6*d*. from 4 bus. of peas sold. Total, £23 16*s*. 4½*d*.

Entry and marriage fines with tithingpenny

The same render account for 2*s*. from the tithing of Wield for tithingpenny at the hundred-court of Martinmas; 2*s*. from the same tithing at the hundred-court of Hockday; 13*s*. 4*d*. from Robert Fab*er* to have ½ virgate of land which belonged to William his father; 10*s*. from William Rolleboys to have ½ virgate of land from the lord's escheat after the death of William le Bon*e* who died without heirs because John le Bone, brother of the said William, who sued to have the said land was not admitted to the same because he holds other land. Total, £1 7*s*. 4*d*.

Perquisites

The same render account for 10*s*. 9*d*. from the small perquisites of the court. Total, 10*s*. 9*d*.

Total of both, £1 18*s*. 1*d*.

Total of all receipts, £56 11*s*. 8½*d*.

Cost of ploughs

In iron and steel bought for the year 5*s*. 8*d*. In 2 plough-irons bought 10*d*. In 1 ploughshare bought 8*d*. In 1 coulter mended 3*d*. In fitting ploughs with iron tyres 1½*d*. In a plough made anew and more mended 11*d*. In 6 yokes made 2*d*. In 2 pairs of wheels bought 6*d*. In boon-works of 6 ploughmen in winter and 6 in Lent 2*s*., and each ploughman ploughed 1 acre in winter and 1 acre in Lent and will have therefor 2*d*. In 4 halters made from the horses' own hair 1*d*. In stipend of 2 oxherds for the year 6*s*. In shoeing plough-horses hauling before the oxen 1*s*. 3*d*. In 5 oxen bought £3 3*s*. 8*d*., at 12*s*. 4*d*. each for 3, and 13*s*. 4*d*. each for 2. Total, £4 2*s*. 1½*d*.

Carts

In 1 new pair of wheels bought 2*s*. 5*d*. In 1 new binding bought and put on the said wheels 10*s*. 9*d*. In clouts, nails and grease bought 1*s*. In a wooden band bought and the cart fitted with axles 3½*d*. In 1 cart-rope bought 1*s*. Total, 15*s*. 6½*d*.

Repair of buildings

In roofing the hall in places 1*s*. 6*d*. In making shingles and laying them on the granary with nails bought for the same 1*s*. 6*d*. In extending the byre by 26 feet with the carpentry, roofing, fencing for the enclosure, and other necessaries, 9*s*. Total, 12*s*.

Cost of the park

In enclosing 7½ furlongs around the park 16*s*. 8*d*., at ¾*d*. a perch. In stubbing up 1 hedge to make ploughland 3*s*. Total, 19*s*. 8*d*.

Dairy

In 5 bus. of salt bought 1*s*. 3*d*. In woollen and linen cloth bought 6*d*. In earthenware pots and pans bought 3*d*. In a press bought 4*d*. In grease, verdigris and copperas bought to make well diseased sheep 12*s*. 8*d*. In stipend of the dairymaid for the year 1*s*. 6*d*. In 21 hurdles made 7*d*. In 6 ells of canvas bought for packing wool 1*s*. 6*d*. In making sacks for wool and packing the wool 3*d*. In 1 new bucket bought 3½*d*. In mending the utensils of the dairy 1½*d*. In a moiety of 1 cow which came from the heriot of Stephen Fab*er* 2*s*. In hay bought to support sheep 5*s*. 6*d*. In stipend of 1 keeper of hoggs on Fobedon' 1*s*. 9*d*. Total, £1 8*s*. 6*d*.

Threshing

In threshing and winnowing 55 qrs 1 bus. of wheat and curall by piece-work 12*s*. 7¼*d*., at 2¾*d*. a heaped quarter. In threshing and winnowing 4 qrs of winter barley and 14 qrs of barley by piece-work 2*s*. 7½*d*., at 1¾*d*. a heaped quarter. In threshing and winnowing 64 qrs of oats by piece-work 4*s*. 8*d*., at 1¾*d*. per 2 qrs. In threshing and winnowing 3 qrs 2 bus. of peas and 1 qr 6 bus. of vetches 10½*d*. Total, £1 9¾*d*.

Harvest-time

In bread bought for 4 harvest boon-works of 163 men with the officials of the curia 6*s*. 9½*d*., each having ½*d*. of bread a day. In cheese bought for a want of herrings 5*s*. 6*d*., and 2 men will have 9 herrings a day when they do not have cheese. In salt bought 1*d*. In meal bought for the pottage of the same 3½*d*. In 221 acres of wheat, barley and oats reaped by piece-work £2 6*s*. ½*d*., at 2½*d*. an acre. In stipend of the bartoner, who was overseeing the reapers for 22 days, 1*s*. 10*d*., at 1*d*. a day. In weeding all the corn 3*s*. 6*d*. Total, £3 4*s*. ½*d*.

Purchase of stock
In 22 animals bought for pasturing £9 9*s*. 6*d*. In expenses made towards improving (*emend'*) the animals 2*s*. 6*d*. Total, £9 12*s*.

Total of all expenses, £21 14*s*. 8¼*d*.

And he owes, £34 17*s*. ¼*d*.

Allowances
In 8 cows bought £3 7*s*., at 9*s*. each for 3, and 8*s*. each for 5. Total, £3 7*s*.

Cash deliveries
Delivered to Sir *Geoffrey*, treasurer of Wolvesey, by 1 tally, £23 11*s*.

Total of all allowances and cash deliveries, £25 18*s*.

And thus he owes clear, £7 19*s*. ¼*d*.

Issues of the grange

Wheat
{yield: 5½-fold plus 1 bus.}
The same render account for 67 qrs 7 bus. from the whole issue of wheat from the grange in the granary without heaped measure.
Sown over 40 acres measured by the perch in the fields of Westbrech and Estbrech, 12½ qrs; that is, 2½ bus. an acre. Sold, 55 qrs 3 bus.

Curall
The same render account for 1 qr from the whole issue of curall from the grange in the granary without heaped measure; all mixed with barley for the liveries of the manorial servants.

Winter barley
{yield: three-fold less 1 qr}
The same render account for 4½ qrs 1 bus. from the whole issue of winter barley from the grange in the granary without heaped measure.
Sown over 5 acres in la Westbroch, 2 qrs. Mixed with barley for the liveries of the manorial servants, 2 qrs 5 bus.

Barley
{yield: 3½-fold less 6½ bus.}
The same render account for 2 qrs 6 bus. of barley remaining from the previous year in the granary; 18 qrs of barley from this year's issue; 1 qr of curall received for the liveries of the manorial servants; 2 qrs 5 bus. of winter barley received for the same; 2 qrs 6 bus. of peas received for the same; 1 qr 2 bus. of vetches received for the same. Total, 28 qrs 3 bus.
Sown over 9½ acres in the field of Estbrech, 4 qrs 6 bus.; that is, ½ qr an acre. Delivered to 2 oxherds for the year, 13 qrs, taking a quarter every 8 weeks. Delivered to 1 harrower at both sowings, 6 bus. Delivered to 1 dairymaid from the feast of the Invention of the Cross (3 May) until Michaelmas (29 September), for 22 weeks, 2 qrs 1 bus. Delivered to 1 keeper of lambs on Fobedon' for 22 weeks, 2 qrs 2 bus. Sold, 5½ qrs.

Oats

{yield: three-fold less 7 qrs 6 bus.}

The same render account for 85 qrs 1 bus. from the whole issue of oats without heaped measure; 10½ qrs by estimation in sheaves. Total, 95½ qrs 1 bus.
Sown over 55 acres in the fields of Hardehyde and Estbrech, 34½ qrs; that is, 5 bus. an acre. In fodder of oxen by estimation in sheaves, 10½ qrs. In fodder of the plough-horses hauling before the oxen, 7½ qrs. Sold, 43 qrs 1 bus.

Peas

{yield: 8-fold}

The same render account for 4 qrs from the whole issue of peas without heaped measure.
Sown, 6 bus. Mixed with barley for the liveries of the manorial servants, 2 qrs 6 bus. Sold, 4 bus.

Vetches

{yield: 4-fold}

The same render account for 2 qrs from the whole issue of vetches from the grange in the granary without heaped measure.
Sown, 6 bus. Mixed with barley for the liveries of the manorial servants, 1 qr 2 bus.

Stock

Plough-horses: 6 remain from the previous year; 6 remain, 3 of them mares.
Foals: 1 from the offspring of the mare this year; 1 female remains aged ½ year.
Oxen: 18 remain from the previous year; 1 added from stock; 5 bought. Total, 24. 4 sold; 20 remain.
Bulls: 1 remains from the previous year; 1 remains.
Cows: 15 remain from the previous year; 2 added from stock; 8 bought before calving; 1 from the heriot of Stephen Fab*e*r which was sterile. Total, 26. 1 sold before calving; 25 remain.
Steers: 3 remain from the previous year's bullocks; 32 bought. Total, 35. 1 added to oxen, 2 to cows; 32 sold; none remain here.
[Bullocks]: 4 remain from the previous year's yearlings; 4 remain, 2 of them male.
Yearlings: 4 remain from the previous year's calves; 4 remain, 2 of them male.
[Calves]: 20 from the offspring of the said cows because 4 were sterile. 1 in tithe because calves which are bought are not tithed; 1 in murrain; 10 sold. Total, 12. 8 remain, 3 of them male.
[Wethers]: 200 remain from the previous year; 35 added from stock. Total, 235. 17 sold at Martinmas; 8 in murrain before shearing, 3 after shearing. Total, 28. 207 remain.
[Rams]: 4 remain from the previous year; 4 remain.
Ewes: 141 remain from the previous year; 32 added from stock. Total, 173. 7 sold at Martinmas; 1 in customary payment to the smith at the said feast; 3 in murrain before lambing, 4 after shearing. Total, 15. 158 remain.
[Hoggs]: 78 remain from the previous year's lambs; 8 in murrain before shearing, 3 after shearing; 35 added to wethers, 32 to ewes; none remain here.
[Lambs]: 102 from the offspring of the said ewes this year because 28 were sterile. 11 in tithe, 1 of them a skin; 3 in customary payment to the reeve, shepherd and smith; 12 in murrain before weaning, 2 after weaning and shearing. Total, 28. 74 remain.

Coarse wool {yield of fleece 3½*d*. plus 2*s*. 4*d*. in all}: 175 fleeces from wethers, 4 from rams, 130 from ewes and 70 from hoggs, produced at the shearing this year. Total, 379. 38 in tithe; 1 in customary payment to the shepherd; 340 sent to Wolvesey, which made 2 weys.
Lamb's-wool {yield 1¼*d*. less 3*d*. in all}: 76 fleeces produced at the shearing this year; all sent to Wolvesey, which made 4 cloves.
Rowen cheese: 31 rowen cheeses; all sold, which made ½ wey 2 cloves.
Cheese {yield of cow 3*s*. and sheep 2*d*. with 3 cheeses in customary payment valued at 1*s*. 6*d*., less 3½*d*. in all this year because a certain cow was bought late}: 154 cheeses made in summer between Monday after the feast of St Vitalis (30 April) and Michaelmas (29 September), both days included; 15 in tithe; 3 in customary payment to the reeve, shepherd and smith; 136 sold, which made 7 weys 4 cloves.
Butter: ½ wey 7 cloves from the issue of the dairy this year; all sold.
Woolskins: 8 from wethers, 3 from ewes and 8 from hoggs dead from murrain before shearing; all sold.
Bare skins: 3 from wethers, 4 from ewes and 3 from hoggs dead from murrain after shearing; all sold.
Lambskins: 12 from lambs dead from murrain before weaning and 2 from rotted sheep; all sold.
Hens: 24 from churchscot this year; 2 in default for 2 widows; 22 sold.
Ploughshares: 1 from the land of the marshal; 1 sold.

Southwark

Arrears
The same render account for £8 4*s*. ¾*d*. of arrears from the previous year. Delivered to Sir G*eoffrey* by 1 tally. They are quit.

Rents of assize
The same render account for £8 1*s*. 10½*d*. for all rents of assize in London and Southwark at Easter (22 April); £8 1*s*. 10½*d*. at Michaelmas (29 September). Total, £16 3*s*. 9*d*.

Decayed rents
In default of the rent of the tenement of Richard de Holebrok', because it is not built upon, nor enclosed, nor is there anything growing on it from which it would be possible to levy a rent, 10*s*. 2*d*.; the tenement which belonged to William Wellyng', 2*s*. this year, because it is not possible to levy a rent; the queen's garden 10*s*. 6*d*.; the tenement of the earl of Lancaster 2*s*.; the tenement of Laurence Hardel 1*s*., because it is not possible to levy a rent this year. Total, £1 5*s*. 8*d*.

Total of rents remaining clear, £14 18*s*. 1*d*.

Nutmeg
The same render account for 3 nutmegs from the rent of Gilbert Coleman this year. Total, 3 nuts.

The same render account for 1 lb of pepper from the rent of 1 seld in Eldefhystrate this year. Total, 1 lb. All delivered to Sir G*eoffrey* by 1 tally. They are quit.

Issues of the manor
The same render account for £3 6*s*. 8*d*. from the herbage in the great field sold; 8*s*. from nettles in la Wild' sold; 5*s*. from 1 garden hired this year to make a curtilage; 9*s*.

from fruit sold this year; 3*s*. from 1 plot behind the kitchen, and not more this year because part of the bishop's hay was stacked there which it was not possible to stack in other buildings because of the sojourn of the count of Savoy there; nothing from hay this year because all was in provision of the bishop's horses; nothing from the pinfold this year because it is submerged. Total, £4 11*s*. 8*d*.

m.30

Sale of corn

The same render account for £2 16*s*. 8*d*. from 10 qrs of wheat sold from the issue of the mill, at 5*s*. 8*d*. a qr; £2 13*s*. 4*d*. from 10 qrs of wheat sold from the same issue, at 5*s*. 4*d*. a qr; £1 8*s*. 4*d*. from 8½ qrs of maslin sold from the issue of the mill, at 3*s*. 4*d*. a qr. Total, £6 18*s*. 4*d*.

Perquisites

The same render account for 6*d*. from John Baldewyn' and his pledges; 6*d*. from Emma, wife of Roginald Pistor'; 3*d*. from John de Wynton' for many transgressions; 3*d*. from Simon de M*er*ton' for the same; 1*s*. from the whole tithing for concealment; 3*d*. from William le Lech' for breaking the assize of ale; 3*d*. from John le Sthalou' for the same; 3*d*. from Roger le Horsdrivare for the same; 3*d*. from Stephen Bost for the same; 3*d*. from John Wynt*er*m*an*; 2*s*. from the whole tithing; 3*d*. from Thomas Seman; 3*d*. from John de Wynton' for false complaint; 3*d*. from the same for bail; 6*d*. from James Copi*n*; 3*d*. from John Wynt*er*m*an* for harbouring; 3*d*. from William de Barton'; 3*d*. from Nicholas de Wynto*n* for his false complaint. Total, 7*s*. 9*d*.

Foreign receipts

The same render account for £1 received from the lord's wardrobe. Total, £1.

Total of all receipts of the year within as well as foreign, £25 15*s*. 10*d*.[1]

Cost of the mill

In 1 measure of steel bought for the mill bills 1*s*. In forging the same 1*s*. In sharpening the bills for the year 2*s*. In repairing the mill spindle this year 5*s*. In shoeing 1 horse for the year 6*d*. In mending 1 saddle-pad and surcingle 8*d*. In cogs and rungs bought 4*s*. In tallow for the same 1*s*. 4*d*. In carrying 224 qrs of corn from London to the mill by boat and from the mill to London 4*s*. 8*d*. In stipend of 1 miller for the year 8*s*. In stipend of 1 man driving 1 mill-horse for the year 6*s*. In 12 qrs of oats bought for the fodder of the mill-horse 16*s*., at 1*s*. 4*d*. a qr. In 10 qrs 6 bus. of oats bought for the same 16*s*. 1½*d*., at 1*s*. 6*d*. a qr. Total, £3 12*s*. 5½*d*.

Cost of hay

In mowing 32 acres of meadow by piece-work this year 16*s*., at 6*d*. an acre. In spreading the said hay 1*s*. 6*d*. In haulage and porterage from the water to the land 8*s*. 6*d*. In tossing the said hay and making haycocks therefrom 16*s*. In carrying the said hay to the curia this year £2 2*s*. 6*d*. In mowing 18 acres of rowen meadow 7*s*. 6*d*., at 5*d*. an acre. In tedding 9*d*. In the haulage and porterage of the aforesaid hay 7*s*. 6*d*. In tossing the said hay and making haycocks therefrom 14*s*. Total, £5 14*s*. 6*d*.

Small expenses

In quittance of tithe of the said meadow next to the chapel of the blessed Margaret 6*s*. 8*d*. In tithe for the garden 2*s*. In removing hay from behind the hall to the palfreys'

1 Figures add up to £27 15*s*. 10*d*.

stable by order of the bishop 9*s*. In 2 weys of lead bought for the guttering of the bishop's chamber 8*s*. In 1 man making the aforesaid gutters for 6 days 3*s*., and for his mate 2*s*. In tin for the same 1*s*. 6*d*. In 3 bus. of charcoal for the same 6*d*. In tallow 1½*d*. In 1 beam (*jupa*) bought for the hall 1*s*. 6*d*. In 1 iron gudgeon for the same 8*d*. In iron for the same 8*d*. In carpentry for the same 1*s*. In 3 locks bought for the bishop's gates 10*d*. Total, £1 16*s*. 9½*d*.

Wages and fees
In fee of the bailiff for the year £5. In wages of 1 door-keeper for the year 15*s*. 2½*d*., at ½*d*. a day. In 2 furs for the bailiff 6*s*. Total, £6 1*s*. 2½*d*.

Payment of rents
The same paid £3 3*s*. 4*d*. to Bermondsey for the rents of assize at Easter; £3 3*s*. 4*d*. at Michaelmas. Total, £6 6*s*. 8*d*.

Total of all expenses, £23 11*s*. 4½*d*.

And he owes, £4 4*s*. 5½*d*. And he owes it all clear.

Issues of the mill of Southwark

Wheat
The same render account for 36 qrs 5 bus. of wheat from the issue of the mill by 1 tally against John le Fennere and John Mol*endinarius*. Total, 36 qrs 5 bus.
In tithe, 3 qrs 5 bus. Delivered to 1 miller and 1 man driving 1 mill-horse for the year, 13 qrs. Sold as noted within (*ut infr*a), 20 qrs. Total as above. It balances.

Maslin
The same render account for 9 qrs 3 bus. of maslin from the issue of the mill by tally against the aforesaid. Total, 9 qrs 3 bus.
In tithe, 7 bus. Sold as noted within, 8 qrs 4 bus. Total as above. It balances.

Oats
The same render account for 22 qrs 6 bus. of oats bought as noted within. Total, 22 qrs 6 bus. All in fodder of the mill-horse. None remains.

Horses: 1 remains. Total, 1. 1 remains.

Esher

Arrears
Richard atte Grove, reeve, renders account for 13*s*. 1¾*d*. of arrears from the previous year. All delivered to G*eoffrey*, treasurer, by 1 tally. He is quit.[1]

Rents of assize
The same renders account for 10*s*. for rents of assize at the Invention of the Cross (3 May) by view of John de Hatfeud'; £5 9*s*. 10½*d*. at Michaelmas (29 September). Total, £5 19*s*. 10½*d*.

Whereof
In quittance of rent of the reeve for the year 1*s*. 10*d*. In default of a certain dwelling-house and land pertaining to the church drawn into demesne £1. Total of quittances and defaults of rent, £1 1*s*. 10*d*.

1 MS 'Et q*u*iet*i* sunt'.

Total of rents remaining, £4 18*s*. ½*d*.

Rent of the hall of Kingston hired for the year
The same renders account for 15*s*. for the rent of the hall of Kingston at Christmas, Easter and Michaelmas. Total, 15*s*.

Issues of the manor
The same renders account for 8*s*. from pannage of 28 pigs and 6 piglets, at 3*d*. a pig and 2*d*. a piglet, and the said right of pannage (*garsevese*) for 6 pigs of Richard atte Barr' this year; nothing from pannage of Esher and Northwod' this year; 4*s*. from 12 animals going to the summer pasturage sold at North*wod* this year, at 4*d*. a head; 3*s*. 6*d*. from the pasturage in la More sold; 6*d*. from the pasturage at la Cru*m*b*e* sold; 8*d*. from the herbage in the garden sold; 9*s*. from fruit from the garden sold this year, the tithe deducted; 8*d*. from the fishery at North*wod*; 10½*d*. from 7 hens from churchscot sold; 2½*d*. from the hide sold of 1 yearling dead from murrain; 5*s*. 6*d*. from the skins sold of 22 wethers dead from murrain before shearing; 1*s*. ½*d*. from the skins sold of 5 ewes dead from murrain before shearing; 5*d*. from the skins sold of 5 wethers dead from murrain after shearing; 2½*d*. from the skins sold of 5 hoggs dead from murrain after shearing; 1*s*. 3*d*. from the skins sold of 20 lambs dead from murrain before weaning; 14*s*. from the milking of 4 cows with calves sold, the tithe deducted, at 2*s*. 6*d*. a cow and 1*s*. a calf; 7*s*. 6*d*. from the milking of 3 cows without calves sold, the tithe deducted, at 2*s*. 6*d*. a cow; 7*s*. from the milking of 56 ewes sold, at 1½*d*. each; 2*d*. from rushes (*ros'*) sold. Total, £3 4*s*. 6*d*.

Sale of stock
The same renders account for 9*s*. from 9 wethers sold before shearing, at 1*s*. a head; 11*s*. 3*d*. from 15 feeble ewes sold before shearing and lambing, at 9*d*. a head. Total, £1 3*d*.

Sale of rye and oats
The same renders account for £3 5*s*. 9¾*d*. from 15 qrs 1½ bus. of rye sold, at 4*s*. 4*d*. a qr; £1 4*s*. 8*d*. from 18½ qrs of oats sold, at 1*s*. 4*d*. a qr; 16*s*. 5½*d*. from 4 qrs 7½ bus. of barley sold at the audit, at 3*s*. 4*d*. a qr. Total, £5 6*s*. 11¼*d*.

Entry fines and perquisites of court
The same renders account for 2*s*. from Matilda de Wexford' for damage done in the lord's wood by 2 cows; 1*s*. from Belotota le Fort for 1 cow in the lord's wood; 3*s*. from Richard ate Wod' for 3 bullocks in the lord's wood; 3*s*. from John Derlyng for 3 bullocks; 3*s*. from Richard ate Barre for 3 bullocks; 1*s*. from Alice Bronnemay for 1 bullock; 2*s*. from John ate Barre for 2 bullocks; 1*s*. from Richard Hamu*n*d for 3 pigs; 8*d*. from Alice Bronemay for 2 piglets; 1*s*. 4*d*. from John Selueyn for 4 pigs; 4*d*. from Richard ate Wod' for 1 pig; 4*d*. from the relict of Fort for 1 pig; 4*d*. from Roger Mol*endinarius* for 1 pig; 8*d*. from William ate Claybrigg' for 2 pigs; 8*d*. from William de Bolewrth' for 2 pigs; 1*s*. from John Derly*ng* for 3 pigs; 1*s*. from the same for 3 piglets; 8*d*. from William de Wexford' for 2 pigs; 4*d*. from Thomas ate Frith' for 1 piglet; 4*d*. from John ate Barre for 1 pig; 8*d*. from William Hereb*erd* for 2 pigs; 2*s*. from Emma Walero*n*d for 6 pigs, because all of these did damage in the lord's wood; 3*d*. from John Derly*ng* for narrowing a certain road too much; 8*s*. from the whole tithing-court for various concealments at the hundred-courts of Martinmas and Hockday; 6*d*. from Matilda de Wexford' for brewing and selling ale against the

assize; 3*d*. from John Durlyng for the same; 6*d*. from William de Bulewrth' for the same; 3*d*. from Richard ate Wod' for the same; 6*d*. from Matilda ate Feld' for the same; 6*d*. from Richard Hamu*n*d for the same; 3*d*. from Thomas Sewyn' for the same; 3*d*. from Alice le Wyn'; 3*d*. from John atte Barre for the same; 3*d*. from Alice Bronnemay for the same; 3*d*. from Agnes ate Mull' for the same; 3*d*. from Roger Mol*endinarius* for the same; 3*d*. from William de Wexford' for the same; 3*d*. from Thomas ate Frith' for the same; 3*d*. from Alexander le Vinerun for the same; 3*d*. from Robert ate Frith' for trespass made by 1 cow in the lord's wood; 1*s*. from John Selueyn for the same by 3 cows; 1*s*. from the same John for transgression against Richard ate Barre; 6*d*. from Richard ate Barre for trespass in the lord's wood by his beasts (*best'*); 6*d*. from John Derlyng' for 2 plough-horses in the lord's wood; 6*d*. from Richard le Rotur for breaking a certain agreement between himself and John Selueyn. Total, £2 3*s*. 1*d*.

Hall of Kingston
The same renders account for 1*s*. 6*d*. from the brewers of Kingston because they sold ale against the assize. Total, 1*s*. 6*d*.

Total of all receipts, £17 9*s*. 3¾*d*.

Cost of ploughs
In 2 plough feet bought and fitted to the ploughs 6*d*. In 1 pair of wheels bought for the ploughs 4*d*. In stipend of the smith repairing the ironwork of the ploughs for the year 4*s*. In 32 herrings bought for 16 harrowers at the sowing of the oats, 3*d*. this year, and each had 2 herrings. In stipend of the ploughman for the year 6*s*. In stipend of the drover for the year 5*s*. Total, 16*s*. 1*d*.

Purchase of barley
In 25 qrs 5 bus. of barley bought for the liveries of the manorial servants and the provision of the harvest £4 5*s*. 5*d*., at 3*s*. 4*d*. a qr. Total, £4 5*s*. 5*d*.

Cost of carts
In 1 pair of wheels bought for the cart 1*s*. 8*d*. In clouts and nails bought for the cart 1*s*. In grease bought for the same 4*d*. In 1 hemp rope bought to tie the cart 8*d*. In 1 saddle with saddle-pads bought for the cart 6*d*. In shoeing the horses, 1*s*. 2*d*. this year. In 1 horse bought 7*s*. 3½*d*. Total, 12*s*. 7½*d*.

Small necessaries
In 1 bus. of salt bought 3½*d*. In 5 ells of canvas bought for packing the wool of Esher 1*s*. 3*d*., at 3*d*. an ell. In expenses for carrying the wool of Esher to Wolvesey 4*d*. In 4 trestles made to support the lord's table 6*d*. Total, 2*s*. 4½*d*.

Repair of buildings
In stipend of 2 carpenters mending the great gate for 1 day 6*d*. In 50 board-nails bought for the same 2*d*. In stipend of 2 carpenters mending the bridge at the kitchen-door for 2 days by piece-work 1*s*., each of them taking 3*d*. a day. In 500 (*di' miliar'*) tiles bought for tiling the hall, chapel and bishop's chamber where it was absolutely necessary 1*s*. 6*d*. In stipend of 1 tiler on the hall, chapel and bishop's chamber for 3 days 1*s*. 6*d*., taking 6*d*. a day. In stipend of 1 carpenter mending the walls of the byre and the walls of the squires' room for 2 days 6*d*. In stipend of 1 roofer with an

assistant roofing the gatehouse for 2 days 8*d*., taking 4*d*. a day. In stipend of 1 carpenter at Nortwod' mending the sheepcote for 4 days 1*s*., taking 3*d*. a day. In stipend of 1 roofer with 1 assistant on the said sheepcote for 5 days 1*s*. 8*d*., taking 4*d*. a day. Total, 9*s*.

Costs for the kitchen of Kingston

In stipend of 1 carpenter felling and quartering timber for 12 working-days 4*s*., at 4*d*. a day. In stipend of 1 carpenter mending the said kitchen for 30 days 10*s*., taking a day as before. In stipend of 1 man assisting the felling of timber in the wood and carrying the timber to Kingston with the aid of the carters for 7 days 1*s*. 2*d*., at 2*d*. a day. In stipend of 1 man pulling down the walls of the said kitchen and making the foundations of the same kitchen for 6 days 1*s*., taking as before. Also for sawing boards to make the wharf next to the water for 6 days 3*s*., at 6*d*. a day. In 1 cart-load of heath for putting in the foundations of the said wharf 5*d*. In 600 oak laths bought for the said kitchen 3*s*., at 6*d*. a 100. In 300 wooden nails (*standifnayl*) bought 1*s*., at 4*d*. a 100. In 2,000 (*ij miliar'*) lath-nails bought 1*s*. 4*d*., at 8*d*. a 1,000. In clay bought for plastering the walls 1*s*. In stipend of 1 plasterer for plastering the said walls, 1*s*. 4*d*. inclusive. In ridge-tiles (*ruggetighelou*) and hip-tiles (*hupetighelou*) bought for tiling the said kitchen 2*s*. In 2,000 tiles bought for the said kitchen 6*s*., at 3*s*. a thousand. Total, £1 15*s*. 3*d*.

Cost of the sheepfold (*ovil'*)

In 18 hurdles bought for the lord's sheepfold 2*s*. 3*d*., at 1½*d*. a hurdle. In 12 lb of grease bought to heal the sheep 1*s*. 6*d*., at 1½*d*. a lb. In verdigris and copperas bought to heal the sheep 10*d*. In washing and shearing sheep besides those done by custom 5*d*. In washing and shearing lambs, 3*d*. this year. In stipend of 1 shepherd for the year 5*s*. In stipend of 1 man keeping the animals at Northwod' and mending fences for the year 3*s*. 6*d*. Total, 13*s*. 6*d*.

Threshing of corn

In threshing 24 qrs of rye by piece-work 4*s*., at 2*d*. a qr. In threshing 4 qrs 5 bus. of barley by piece-work 6¾*d*., at 1½*d*. a qr. In threshing 36 qrs of oats by piece-work 3*s*., at 1*d*. a qr. In winnowing the same corn 1*s*. 4*d*., at 1*d*. per 4 qrs. Total, 8*s*. 10½*d*.

Mowing the meadows, weeding the corn

In weeding the corn this year 6*d*. In mowing the said meadow of Brodemed' by custom, bread from stock and 1 wether with its skin from the said sheepfold. In cheese bought 3*d*. In mowing the meadow of Esher by piece-work besides that done by custom 1*s*. 2*d*. In carrying the hay of Brodemed' to the shed by custom, bread from stock. In herrings bought 4*d*. In mowing the meadow of Northwod' by piece-work, 8*d*. this year. Total, 2*s*. 11*d*.

Cost of the harvest

In 1 boon-work without ale of 23 men who reaped and bound the lord's corn, bread from stock. In 138 herrings bought, 11*d*. this year, at 8*d*. a 100, and each had 3 herrings at noon and 3 at supper. In 1 boon-work with ale of 28 men who reaped and bound the lord's corn, bread from stock. In ale bought 2*s*. 6*d*. In 100 herrings bought for noon 8*d*. In meat bought 2*s*. 2*d*. In wastel-bread bought for mortrel 1½*d*. In milk bought for the same 2*d*. In cheese bought for the whole harvest 1*s*. In candles bought 1*d*. In 27 men hired for 1 day for 2 meals a day at Northwod' who reaped and bound the lord's corn. Also in 26 men hired for 1 day for 2 meals a day at Northwod' who reaped and bound the lord's corn, bread from stock. In ale bought 1*s*. 2*d*. In relish 1*s*. 7*d*. In stipend of the same 4*s*. 5*d*., each of them having for his stipend 1*d*. a day. In expenses of the reeve from Lammas until Michaelmas 2*s*. Total, 16*s*. 9½*d*.

Cost of the vineyard
In expenses for digging around the vineyard of Esher this year £1 3*s*. In collecting vines to make verjuice 3*s*. 10*d*. In 4 bus. of salt bought to salt verjuice 1*s*. 2*d*., at 3½*d*. a bus. Delivered to Peter, the lord's squire, whilst he remains at Esher in order to collect vines and make verjuice, by order of the bishop and by his letters, 3*d*. 6*d*. In stipend of Alexander the vintner for the year 5*s*. In 1 cask bought for putting the verjuice in 2*s*. 2*d*. In 2 barrels bought for the same 1*s*. Total, £1 19*s*. 8*d*.

Payment of outside rents
In rent paid at Michaelmas to the Abbot of Chertsey for the land of Northwod' 6*s*. In 2 ploughshares bought for the same, paid to the same this year, 1*s*. 2*d*. Total, 7*s*. 2*d*.

Foreign expenses
Given for the keeping of a certain ox by the assessor of the fifteenth at Northwod' 1*s*. 10*d*. Total, 1*s*. 10*d*.

Total of all expenses, £12 11*s*. 6*d*.

And thus he owes, £4 17*s*. 9¾*d*.

Cash deliveries
Delivered to Sir *Geoffrey*, treasurer of Wolvesey, by 1 tally, £3.

And he owes clear, £1 17*s*. 9¾*d*.

Issues of the grange

Rye
{yield: four-fold less 1 qr}
The same renders account for 24 qrs of rye from the issue of the grange threshed by piece-work; 6 qrs from the increment. Total, 30 qrs.
Sown over 12 acres at Esher and 13½ acres at Nortwod', 6 qrs 3 bus.; that is, 2 bus. an acre. In bread baked for the harrowers at the sowing of the oats, 1 bus. In bread baked for the mowing of the meadows, 3 bus. In bread baked for the carrying of the hay from the meadows to the manor of Esher, 1 bus. In bread baked for the shearing of the sheep, ½ bus. In bread baked for the provision of the harvest, 1 qr 2 bus. Delivered to 1 vintner for the year, 6½ qrs, taking a quarter every 8 weeks. Sold, 15 qrs 1½ bus. Total, 30 qrs.

Barley
{yield: four-fold less 2½ qrs}
The same render account for 4 qrs 5 bus. of barley from the issue of the grange threshed by piece-work; 1 qr from the increment; 25 qrs 5 bus. bought. Total, 31 qrs 2 ½ bus.
Sown over 2 acres, 1 qr. Delivered to 1 ploughman and 1 drover for the year, 13 qrs, each of them taking a quarter every 8 weeks. **{Henceforth the ploughman and**

drover should take a quarter every 10 weeks and the keeper of animals every 12 weeks} In stipend of 1 vintner digging in the vineyard for 13 weeks, 1 qr 5 bus. Delivered to 1 shepherd for the year, 5 qrs 1½ bus., taking a quarter every 10 weeks. Delivered to 1 man keeping the animals at North*wod* and mending fences, 4 qrs 2½ bus., taking a quarter every 12 weeks. In bread baked for the provision of the harvest by mixing with rye, 1 qr 2 bus. Sold at the audit, 4 qrs 7½ bus. Total, 31 qrs 2½ bus.

Oats
The same render account for 36 qrs of oats from the issue of the grange threshed by piece-work; 9 qrs from the increment; 3 qrs by estimation in sheaves for supporting oxen. Total, 48 qrs.
Sown over 20 acres at Esher and 22 acres at North*wod*, 21 qrs; that is, 4 bus. an acre. In meal for the pottage of the manorial servants, 2½ qrs. In fodder of the cart-horses, 3 qrs. In supporting oxen by estimation in sheaves, 3 qrs. Sold, 18½ qrs. Total, 48 qrs.

Stock

Cart-horses: 2 remain; 1 bought. Total, 3. 1 taken by the assessor of the fifteenth which was sold; 2 remain.
Oxen: 13 remain; 1 addition. Total, 14. 14 remain.
Cows: 8 remain; 1 addition. Total, 9. 9 remain.
Steers: 1 remains from the previous year's bullocks and 1 heifer remains from last year's bullocks. Total, 2. 1 added to oxen, 1 to cows. Total, 2, and thus none remain.
Bullocks: 1 remains from the previous year's yearlings; it remains.
Yearlings: 3 remain from the previous year's calves. Total, 3. 1 in murrain; 2 remain.
Calves: 7 from the offspring of the cows this year and not more because 2 cows were sterile. Total, 7. 4 sold with the milk of the cows; 3 remain.
Wethers: 124 remain; 20 additions. Total, 144. 22 in murrain before shearing, 5 after shearing; 9 sold before shearing; 1 in customary payment for the mowing of the meadows with its skin after shearing. Total, 37. 107 remain.
Ewes: 80 remain; 8 additions. Total, 88. 5 in murrain before shearing and lambing; 15 sold before shearing and lambing. Total, 20. 68 remain.
Hoggs: 33 hoggs and gimmers remain from the previous year's lambs. Total, 33. 5 in murrain after shearing; 20 added to wethers, 8 to ewes. Total, 33. None remain.
Lambs: 56 from the offspring of the ewes this year and not more because 4 ewes were sterile. Total, 56. 20 in murrain before shearing and weaning; 3 in tithe. Total, 23. 33 thus remain.
Coarse wool {yield of fleece 2½*d*. plus 1*s*. 8½*d*. in all}: 186 fleeces produced at the shearing this year. 18 in tithe; 1 delivered to the shepherd by agreement; 167 sent to Wolvesey, which made 19 cloves, at 7 lb a clove. Total, 186. Thus none remain there.
Lamb's-wool {yield of fleece 1¼*d*. plus 4¼*d*. in all}: 33 fleeces produced at the shearing this year; 33 sent to Wolvesey, which made 19 cloves with the coarse wool.
Hides: 1 from a yearling dead from murrain; 1 sold; none remain there.
Sheepskins: 22 from wethers dead from murrain before shearing, 5 after shearing; 5 from ewes dead from murrain before shearing and lambing; 5 from hoggs dead from murrain after shearing; 20 from lambs in murrain before weaning and shearing. Total, 57. Sold within and none remain there.

m.30d
Swans: 1 remains; 5 from this year's offspring. Total, 6. All remain because the lord sent back the same.

Peacocks: 8 remain. Total, 8. 8 remain.
Hens: 10 from churchscot; 3 in quittance of the reeve; 7 sold; none remain there.
Utensils: 1 ewer and 1 basin remain. 6 casks remain from the previous year and 1 bought this year. Total, 7. 2 delivered to the bishop's cellar with wine; 1 made into 2 tubs; 1 delivered to the lord with verjuice. Total, 4. 3 casks and 2 tubs remain.
Cheese: nothing from cows' cheese here because the milk was sold.
Verjuice: 1 cask this year from the vineyard; all sent to the bishop in London.

Soke of Winchester

Arrears[1]
John de Heriyerd, bailiff, John le Portir and Gilbert Horsemayn, sergeants, render account for £7 7*s.* of arrears from the previous year. All delivered to Sir G*eoffrey*, treasurer of Wolvesey, by 1 tally. They are quit.

Rents of assize
The same render account for £8 11*d.* for rents of assize outside East Gate; 3*s.* from John son of Henry in exchange for 3*s.* which the Dominicans were accustomed to render for certain plots in Buck Street within the enclosure of the same; 7*s.* 10*d.* from Ralph de Clayville in exchange for 7*s.* 10*d.* which William le Blu*nt*, G*odfrey* de Berton', the monks of Hyde and Adam Catchelove were accustomed to render for certain plots in Wongar Street and Tanner Street bought to enlarge the site where the Franciscans dwell; 6*d.* from the increment for the year for certain land outside Durn Gate leased to Henry de Dernegat*e* in fee by lord A*ymer*, bishop elect; £3 12*s.* 6*d.* for rents of assize outside the gate on Kingsgate Street; 2*s.* from Richard le Port*er* in exchange for 2*s.* of rent which the Dominicans were accustomed to render for certain plots in Buck Street within the enclosure of the same; 13*s.* 2*d.* for rents of assize in Mullelane; £1 9*s.* 6*d.* for rents of assize in Sevetwichene; £1 8*d.* for rents of assize in Paillardestwichene; 6*d.* from the increment of rent for land which sometime belonged to Henry Prince which was leased to Henry Coc*us* for 1*s.* a year; 3*d.* from the increment for land which belonged to Bernard de Celar' which was leased to Richard le Port*er* for 6*d.* a year; 6*d.* from certain land which was leased to Walter le Blu*nt* on the city ditch; £1 11*s.* 6*d.* for rents of assize outside South Gate; 5*s.* 11*d.* for rents of assize outside the castle gate; 13*s.* 3*d.* for rents of assize outside West Gate; £1 9*s.* ½*d.* for rents of assize outside North Gate; 5*d.* from increment; 4*d.* from the increment for land of Osbert le Maddar', William de Ponte and William, son of Herbert Cap*ellanus*, which was leased to Peter Cl*ericus* for 3*s.* 4*d.* a year; £1 7*s.* 6*d.* for rents of assize in Parchment Street; 15*s.* 6*d.* for rents of assize in Tanner Street; £1 2½*d.* for rents of assize in Wongar Street; 7*s.* 9*d.* for rents of assize in Buck Street; 5*s.* for rents of assize in Colebrook Street; £2 4*d.* for rents of assize in High Street; 1*s.* 4*d.* from the increment of rent for the house of Newbridge; £1 10*s.* 4*d.* for rents of assize in Gar Street; £1 19*s.* ½*d.* for rents of assize in Sparkford; 3*d.* from the increment for land outside East Gate which belonged to Adam Symple which was leased to Henry Prior in fee for 1*s.* 3*d.* a year by lord A*ymer*, bishop elect; 4*d.*[2] from a certain forge built on the street leading to St Giles's Hill; 1*d.* from the increment for a certain plot in Gar Street which belonged to Amice Petyt; 2*d.* from the increment for the year for certain land outside West Gate which was leased to William Carp' in fee;

1 MS omits heading.

2 MS omits '*d.*'

1*d*. from the increment for land which belonged to William Carp' which was leased to Elias Carpent*er* in fee for 10*d*. a year. Total, £28 19*s*. 8½*d*.

Defaults of rent outside East Gate

In default of the land where John Page dwelt 1*s*. 2¼*d*., which was leased to Walter le Paum' for 1*s*. 8*d*. by Bishop G*odfrey*; certain land which was leased to Richard Horsemayn in fee for 1*s*. a year by Bishop W*illiam*, 8*d*.; the land which belonged to Raymond 2*s*. 8*d*., which was leased to Thomas de Chaucu*mbe* in fee for 9*s*. a year; the land of William Swyft 1*s*., which was leased to William le Tukare and Oscar in fee for 2*s*. a year by Bishop G*odfrey*; that leased to Peter son of Raymond there by Bishop R*ichard* £2 13*s*. 5*d*.; the land which Baldric held 2*s*., which was leased to Roger Decan*us* in fee for 2*s*. a year by Bishop G*odfrey*; 1 forge within Barr', 1*s*. a year by Bishop R*ichard*; 1 marsh outside Durn Gate 4*s*., which was leased to the miller of Durn Gate; the land of William Horsemay*n* 3*s*., because it was leased to Payn de Dubbour in fee for 2*s*. a year by Bishop W*illiam*; Godwin 1½*d*.; the land of Hugh Fab*er* 6*d*.; the land which Walter Drappar' held 7*d*.; 1 stone building with a cellar which sometime belonged to Thomas de Chaucu*mb*e 7*s*. 6*d*., because 1*s*. 6*d*. was paid by the almoner of Hyde who leased it for the same rent from Bishop J*ohn* de Pontiss*ara*; Robert le Bal on the water beside le Brottwyn' 4*d*.; the land of Geoffrey le Lung' 6*d*., which was leased to Adam Burgeys for 2*s*. 6*d*. a year by Bishop J*ohn*; the lands formerly of Thomas de Horsemayn 6*d*., which were leased to William de Wandlesworth' for 6*d*. a year by Bishop J*ohn*; the land of Ralph de Gavelacr*e* beyond the bridge 2*s*. 6*d*., this being the third year; the tenement formerly of Ralph de Gavelacr*e* 1*s*., this being the second year. Total, £4 2*s*. 5¾*d*.

Kingsgate Street

In default of the lands of Roger de Insul*a* and Nicholas Cole and Roger 8*d*., because they were leased to Gilbert Flanndr' in fee for 1*s*. 8*d*. a year; the land of the physician which Bishop R*ichard* gave to the church of St Michael 2*s*.; the house where Master Hugh used to live which Bishop H*enry* gave to H., archdeacon of Canterbury, 11*s*. 4*d*.; the land of Rayner which belonged to Henry de Enefond 1*s*.; the land of the keeper of the altar of the blessed Mary within King's Gate because of a widespread fire in the city 10*d*.; the land which William Carbonel held because of the aforesaid fire 2*s*.; the land of William Talon by encroachment of the ditch of the city of Winchester 3*s*.; 1 tenement which the infirmary held 6*d*., this being the ninth year. Total, £1 1*s*. 4*d*.

Mullelane

In default of the land which belonged to Rowland and the almoner of St Swithun's 1*s*. 4*d*., because it was leased to William P*armen*tar' in fee for 1*s*. 8*d*. a year by Bishop W*illiam*. Total, 1*s*. 4*d*.

Sevetwichene

In default of 3 tenements which Richard Med' and Azo held, surrendered to J. son of Peter, infirmarer of Bishop R*ichard*, by the same bishop, 6*s*.; the same Peter 6*d*.; the garden which Henry and Walter Aghtma*n* held 3*s*., because it was leased to J*ohn* Morannd' in fee by Bishop J*ohn* de Pontiss*ara* for 2*s*. a year. Total, 9*s*. 6*d*.

Paillardestwichene

In default of the land which belonged to Jocelyn Pistor 6*s*., because it was leased to Osbert Marescall' in fee by Bishop G*odfrey* for 1*s*. 6*d*. a year; 2 tenements which

Peter Saier held by encroachment of the city ditch 1*s.*; the land of William Hamond which belonged to Ralph de Okebourn' 6*d.*, because it was vacant for this the 15th year; the land of Thomas de Chaucu*mb*e which belonged to Emma Burgeys 6*d.*, because it was vacant for this the 19th year. Total, 8*s.*

South Gate

In default of 2 tenements which Bernard Speciar' and Albred Kay held surrendered to J. son of Peter, infirmarer of Bishop R*ichard*, by the same bishop, 3*s.* 6*d.*; the land which Henry Brian held 4*d.*; the land which Peter de Ponte held consumed by a widespread fire in the city of Winchester 1*s.*; the land of Peter Saier which Richard Hamu*n*d and Peter Short held 6*d.*, this being the 18th year. Total, 5*s.* 4*d.*

Before the castle gate

In default of the land of the watchman (*vigilli*) which formerly belonged to Walter Vigil*us* 4*d.* Total, 4*d.* {Henceforth account for nothing except 3*d.* in default}

Outside North Gate

In default of the land of Alice de la Doun' given to William son of Roginald by Bishop R*ichard* 4*s.* 6*d.*; the land of Henry Juet which William Beaupyn' held 2*s.*, this being the 20th year. Total, 6*s.* 6*d.*

Parchment Street

In default of the land which Simon Cl*ericus* held, surrendered to J. son of Peter, infirmarer of Bishop R*ichard*, by the same bishop, 19*s.* 4*d.* Total, 19*s.* 4*d.*

Wongar Street

In default of the house of Alan de Englefeud', surrendered to the same Alan by Bishop R*ichard*, 5*s.*; the land of the Knights Templar 6*d.*; the land which belonged to John Garland 1*s.* 10*d.*, because Henry Pri*n*ce paid for the same land from his chief house outside West Gate; the land of William Blu*n*t 3*s.* 5*d.*, because Geoffrey de Clayvill' paid for the same land from his chief house outside East Gate; 1*s.* 7*d.* from those totals in chief exceeding the total of receipts and defaults. Total, 12*s.* 4*d.*

Tanner Street

In default of the land of G*odfrey* de Berton', the monks of Hyde and Adam Catchelove 4*s.* 4*d.*, because R*alph* de Clavill' answered for the same land from his chief house outside East Gate, and the same R*alph* has bound himself and all his tenements which he has or by any chance befalling is able to have in the suburb of Winchester to pay the aforesaid rent, by his writing, for himself and his heirs; the land of Juliana David which sometime belonged to Agatha, daughter of Bartholomew de Walyngeford', 6*d.*; 1*s.* from those totals in chief exceeding the total of receipts and defaults. Total, 5*s.* 10*d.*

Buck Street

In default of the land of the Dominicans 5*s.*, because John son of Henry answers for 3*s.* from his chief messuage outside East Gate and Richard le Porter answers for 2*s.* for the same land from certain land which was leased to him outside King's Gate which sometime belonged to Thomas de Tymynges, and the aforesaid John and Richard have bound themselves to pay the aforesaid rent in the same way as the aforesaid Ralph; 4*d.* from those totals in chief exceeding the total of receipts and defaults. Total, 5*s.* 4*d.*

Colebrook Street
In default of 2 tenements there surrendered to Peter son of Raymond 3*s*. Total, 3*s*.

High Street
In default of the land which John Yessyr held and which was in the bishop's hands and is now surrendered to the Hospital of St Cross 13*s*. 4*d*.; the land of Alice de la Bouue which John Messyr held given to William son of Roginald by Bishop R*ichard* 4*s*.; the house at Newbridge leased to Peter le Bal by Bishop R*ichard* 16*s*. 4*d*. Total, £1 13*s*. 8*d*.

Gar Street
In default of the land which Hugh Lov*er*aȝ held 1*s*., because it was leased to Geoffrey de S*anc*ta C*ru*ce in fee for 2*s*. a year by Bishop R*ichard*; Adam Speciar' and 2 acres of land of Silvester Cap*ellanus* 2*s*. 3*d*., because it was leased to Hugh Lov*er*aȝ in fee for 4*s*. a year; the sacrist of St Swithun's in Winchester 4*s*. 1*d*., by encroachment of the ditch; the land which Hugh Puke held 1*d*.; the land which John and Nicholas Keppyng' held 2*s*. 8*d*., because it was vacant for this the 20th year; the land of the subprior of St Swithun's in Winchester 6*d*., because it was leased to John Saladyn for 9*d*. a year by Bishop J*ohn* de Pontiss*ara*; the land of Amice Petyt 9*d*., because it was leased to William le Plum' for 6*d*. a year. Total, 11*s*. 4*d*.

Sparkford
In default of the vacant land which belonged to Walter Pouk' 1*s*. 8½*d*.; a certain garden within the enclosure of the house of St Cross 4*s*. 2*d*. Total, 5*s*. 10½*d*.

Total of all defaults, £11 11*s*. 6¼*d*.

Total of rents remaining, £17 8*s*. 2¼*d*.

Nothing should be found for the quittance of 10*d*. this year because it is not being charged in chief, nor of 2*s*. because before they ran in default.

Payments for the mill-race (*aquaticu*m)
The same render account for £1 from the mill of the Abbess of St Mary's for the mill-race; £1 from the mill of le Bal for the same; £1 from the mill of Andrew Pov*er*ey for the same; £1 from the mill of Andrew Pov*er*ey for the same. Total, £4, paid in equal portions at 4 terms.

'Spengab*ulu*m'
5*s*. from the official of wheels (*ministerio rota*rum) at farm this year. Total, 5*s*.

Brewgable (*Brugab*ul*um*)
The same render account for 5*d*. from William de Beriton' for brewgable; 2½*d*. from William le Lom*er*e; 5*d*. from Henry Doucevyl';[1] 5*d*. from John Huberd; 5*d*. from John Gentyl; 2½*d*. from John de Northwold'; 5*d*. from Adam le Bal; 5*d*. from John Cru*m*pelhorn; 5*d*. from John de Byketon'; 5*d*. from the tenement of Nicholas Dalron; 5*d*. from Walter de Tysted'; 5*d*. from Robert Carnif*ex*; 5*d*. from Simon de Bro*m*ly; 5*d*. from the tenement of Laurence de Ann'; 5*d*. from Alice de Wauth*a*m. Total, 5*s*. 10*d*.

1 MS 'Douce⟨w⟩⌈v⌉yl''.

Kingsgate Street
The same render account for 5*d.* from Thomas Ywon for brewgable; 5*d.* from John de Houlond'; 5*d.* from Robert de Ot*er*burn'; 5*d.* from the relict of Pershore. Total, 1*s.* 8*d.*

South Gate
The same render account for 5*d.* from the tenement of John de Houlond' for brewgable. Total, 5*d.*

North Gate
The same render account for 5*d.* from the brewgable of Robert de Farnh*am*. Total, 5*d.*

Parchment Street
The same render account for 5*d.* from the brewgable of Richard Cury. Total, 5*d.*

Wongar Street
Nothing from Wongar Street this year.

High Street
The same render account[1] for 5*d.* from the house at Newbridge for brewgable. Total, 5*d.*

Total of all brewgable, 9*s.* 2*d.*

Internal perquisites
The same render account for £2 6*d.* from the small perquisites of the court this year; 4*s.* from the rent of the tenement of John de Irmong*ere*; 2*s.* 9*d.* from the tenement of William le Deveneys. Total, £2 7*s.* 3*d.*

Foreign perquisites
The same render account for 5*s.* from the relict of Geoffrey de Wynggeh*am* for release from her suit of court this year; 5*s.* from Joan de Colrych' for the same; 4*s.* from John de Roches for the same; 4*s.* from John Dau*n*dely for the same; 2*s.* from Alan Plukenet for the same; 2*s.* from the Lady of Hunton' for the same; 4*s.* from Andrew de Hautot for the same; 2*s.* from Andrew Payn for the same; 2*s.* from Philip de Exto*n* for the same; 2*s.* from Henry Huse for the same; 2*s.* from Thomas Paynel for the same; 1*s.* from Luke de Brunewych' for the same; 2*s.* from John de Chittheborn' for the same; nothing from Richard le Warnir because he is in wardship; 2*s.* from Mary de Wyntreshull' for the same; 2*s.* from John de Mol*endino* for the same; 2*s.* from John M*e*riet for the same; 4*s.* from John de Syghenhurst because he is not proceeding; 6*d.* from Isabel, who was wife of Richard le Portyr, because she is not proceeding. Total, £2 7*s.* 6*d.*

Total of both, £4 14*s.* 9*d.*

Total of all receipts, £26 17*s.* 1¼*d.*

Expenses
In re-roofing and mending the house formerly of William le Deveneys 3*s.* In wages of the bailiff for the year £3 10*d.* In stipend of 2 sergeants for the year 10*s.* In the

1 MS '⟨de domo⟩'.

oblations of the same 4*d*. In stipend of the clerk 5*s*. In parchment 4*d*. Total, £3 19*s*. 6*d*.

In allowance of the same for gifts made to Alice de Wa⌈u⌉th*am* and Laurence de Ann' 10*d*. Total, 10*d*.

And he owes, £22 16*s*. 9¼*d*.

Delivered to Sir G*eoffrey*, treasurer of Wolvesey, by 1 tally, £11.

And he owes clear, £11 16*s*. 9¼*d*., of which £2 7*s*. 6*d*. are charged to the marshal.

On Wednesday after the feast of St Giles in the year 30 Edward I (5 September 1302) Nicholas Horsemayn and Alice his wife came to the Pavilion and acknowledged themselves to have given, granted and by their charter confirmed to John de Northwold' and Joan his wife and their heirs and also their assigns 3*d*. of annual rent freely and quietly. The contents of the document which follows is to undergo examination:

Know all men present and future that we, Nicholas Horsemayn and Alice, wife of the same, with equal will, have given, granted and by this our present charter confirmed, to John de Northwolde and Joan, wife of the same, threepence of annual rent freely and quietly, to be received yearly at Michaelmas from us and our heirs from a certain tenement in the suburb and Soke of Winchester in the parish of St Michael[1] on the Hill, which is situated between the tenement of John Gentyl on the north side and the tenement of the said John and Joan on the south side. To have and to receive the aforesaid threepence of annual rent with all its appurtenances to the aforesaid John and Joan, their heirs or assigns, freely, quietly, peaceably, by right and inheritance forever. And we the aforesaid Nicholas and Alice, wife of the same, and our heirs will warrant and defend forever against all people the aforesaid threepence of annual rent to the aforesaid John and Joan and their heirs or assigns. For this authority, gift, grant and warrant the aforesaid John and Joan for themselves and their heirs have discharged us and our heirs from the maintenance of a certain gutter and wall, if damage to the same should happen to be incurred, just as is fully contained in that writing, a bipartite indenture, made between us. In witness of which thing, we have affixed our seals to the present charter. These being witnesses, Sir Philip de Hoyvill', knight, Sir Robert de Harewedon', then steward of the bishop of Winchester, John de Westcote, then justice of the Pavilion, Richard de M*ar*well', Adam Pov*er*ay, John de Anne, clerk, Walter le Butelyr, Roger de Wynehale, Adam le Bal, John Gentyl, and Richard Scrilby, and many others.

Also on the aforesaid day and year, the aforesaid Nicholas and Alice for themselves and their heirs, and the aforesaid John and Joan for themselves and their heirs, in the aforesaid court granted and had ratified all agreements and ordinances which were contained in a certain chirograph made between them, to last thereafter forever, in these words:

Be it known to all men by these present that a dispute had been provoked between Nicholas Horsemayn and Alice, wife of the same, plaintiffs, on the one side, and

1 Scribal error for St John.

John de Northwold' and Joan his wife, defendants, on the other, because the aforesaid Nicholas and Alice had claimed to have a part and an easement of a certain wall of the tenement of the aforesaid John and Joan in the suburb of Winchester in the Soke, which wall is indeed of the tenement of the aforesaid John and Joan on the north side of the same, and which formerly was the south wall of a certain cellar, on which wall the aforesaid Nicholas and Alice were bound to maintain a certain gutter at their own cost, so that the same wall might not be damaged by the aforesaid gutter. And if it were damaged, the aforesaid Alice should repair it, just as is more fully contained in a certain writing on this point made by the aforesaid Joan and Alice at the time of the division of the inheritance of the said Alice and Joan and made with their agreement.

Common friends mediated on Wednesday after the feast of St Giles in the year 30 Edward I. It was settled in this way, that is, that the aforesaid wall should remain to the said John and Joan and their heirs, so that henceforth the aforesaid Nicholas and Alice or their heirs should not have any right or claim to the aforesaid wall or be able to sell or make any exaction relating to it. And it is lawful for the said John and Joan and their heirs to make, arrange and dispose of the aforesaid wall and the gutter built on it, or otherwise, according to their free will without condition or any other impediment of the aforesaid Nicholas and Alice or their heirs. And the aforesaid John and Joan granted for themselves and their heirs that the aforesaid Nicholas and Alice should be discharged from the maintenance of the above-mentioned gutter and wall for a 3*d*. annual rent, of which the said Nicholas and Alice enfeoffed the aforesaid John and Joan, to be received at Michaelmas from the tenement of the said Nicholas and Alice, which is between the aforesaid wall of the tenement of the aforesaid John and Joan and the tenement of John Gentyl in the above-mentioned suburb and Soke, by a charter which the said Nicholas and Alice made therefor with the same John and Joan. And the said parties, that is, the said John and Joan in their tenement, and the said Nicholas and Alice in their tenement, will maintain without any dispute, the drain (*hantande*) carrying rainwater or waste (*mundatio*) on their own ground. And the parties have hereupon bound themselves to observe inviolate, faithfully and without deceit, the aforementioned premises, agreement, peace and ordinance, and each and every thing aforementioned, that is, should they be unwilling to fulfil, obey or observe in whole or in part the said agreement, peace and ordinance, it is lawful for the bailiffs of the places and other officials of the king and bishop to distrain the party opposing the full and fullest observation of each and every part of the aforesaid agreement, peace and ordinance. And the party opposing the aforementioned will pay the losses and expenses which the party not opposing them shall sustain on account of the aforementioned. On these matters credence shall be given to the simple word of the party not opposing the aforementioned. Moreover, the aforesaid parties pledge faith mutually to observe each and every part of the aforesaid, so that if either party is reported for a breach of faith in this matter, in whatever manner, then that party concedes that it shall be held over on account of the report and shall sustain on account of the breach of faith corporal punishment imposed by ecclesiastical censure, or will provide or make satisfaction for 40*s*. of the alms of the lord bishop of Winchester, and nonetheless will pay one mark of silver in aid of the Holy Land without power of postponement or objection whatsoever. In witness of which thing the parties have hereupon affixed their seals to this bipartite writing. These being witnesses, Sir Philip de Hoyvill', knight, Sir Robert de Harewedon', then steward of the bishop of Winchester, John de Westcot', then justice of the Pavilion, Richard de M*ar*ewell', Adam Pov*er*ay, John de Anne, clerk, Walter le Botelyr, Roger de Wynehal', Adam le Bal, John Gentyl, and Richard Schull', and many others.

Marshalsea

Arrears
Gilbert Mar*escallus* renders account for £26 6*s*. 4*d*. of arrears from the previous year.

Rents of assize
The same renders account for 3*s*. 4*d*. for the rent of assize at Michaelmas of Thomas Schudd' for 1 messuage 20 acres of land and ½ acre of wood in West Pitt; 3*s*. 4*d*. for the rent of assize at the same term of the heir of John de Brafeld' for 1 messuage 20 acres of land and ½ acre of wood in the same vill; 3*s*. 4*d*. for the rent of assize at the same term of William Bygh' for 1 messuage 20[1] acres of land and ½ acre of wood in the same vill; 6*s*. 8*d*. for the rent of assize at the same term of William Alysanndr' for 2 messuages 40 acres of land and 1 acre of wood in the same vill; 3*s*. 4*d*. for the rent of assize at the same term of Aunger le Drivere and Agnes his wife for 1 messuage 20 acres of land and ½ acre of wood in the same vill; 6*d*. for the rent of assize at the same term of the heir of John de Brayfeld' for 1 cottage in the same vill; 3*s*. for the rent of assize at the same term of Drogo de Celar' and Amice his wife for a certain messuage in Kingsgate Street beside the Carmelite Friars; 2*s*. for the rent of assize at the same term of Robert de la Fermerie for a certain messuage opposite the house of John de Houlo*n*d' in the same place which is of the fee of West Pitt. Total, £1 5*s*. 6*d*.

Rents of assize
The same renders account for 6*s*. for the rent of assize at Michaelmas of the heir of Ralph de Gorhu*n*te in Pendeworth'. Total, 6*s*.

Rents of assize
The same renders account for 13*s*. 8*d*. for the rent of assize at Michaelmas of Andrew Payn for the tenement which he holds in Sparsholt; 3*s*. for the rent of assize at the same term of William Russel for a certain cottage in the same vill; 5*s*. for the rent of assize at the same term of Richard Fromu*n*d for his tenement which he holds in the same vill. Total, £1 1*s*. 8*d*.

Rents of assize
The same renders account for 6*s*. 8*d*. for the rent of assize at Michaelmas of Nicholas de Ychen' for 3 virgates of land in Martyr Worthy. Total, 6*s*. 8*d*.

Total of all rents, £2 19*s*. 10*d*.

Estreat of the total of amercements
Estreat of the Bench beginning at Michaelmas in the year 26, and Hilary, Easter and Trinity in the year 27 (1298-9)
The same renders account for 1*s*. 8*d*. from Martin Mol*endinarius* of South Stoneham and Roger of the same because they did not produce in court Guy de Stonh*am*; 1*s*. 8*d*. from William Raynold de Fal' and John Soudener of the same because they did not produce in court John de la Sale; 1*s*. 8*d*. from William Cuppy*ng* of Droxford and

1 MS '⟨x⟩⌈xx⌉'.

William le Tav*er*nyr of the same because they did not produce in court Richard de Midlington' whom they had bailed; 1*s*. 8*d*. from Gerard le Cornmo*n*gar' of Durley and Thomas Ev*er*ard of the same because they did not produce in court John Ev*er*ard'; 1*s*. 8*d*. from John Crispy*n* of Bighton and John Fab*er* because they did not produce in court Walter Tymb'; 1*s*. 8*d*. from William Marti*n* of West Tisted and Adam ate M*ere* because they did not produce in court Richard de Tysted'; 1*s*. from Richard de Ov*er*ton' and Geoffrey Horn because they did not produce in court John Pilesel the younger whom they had bailed; 1*s*. from Ralph de Sydema*n*ton' and John de Nywenton' because they did not produce in court Roger le Lunt whom they had pledged; 1*s*. from Adam le Mar' and Walter M*er*cat*or* because they did not produce in court Roger le Lu*n*t whom they had pledged; 2*s*. from William Martin, Walter de Cove, Richard de Murifeld' and John Fab*er* of West Tisted because they did not produce in court Richard de Tisted' whom they had bailed; 1*s*. 8*d*. from John Cuppy*ng* of Bighton, William Cl*ericus* of Drayton, John de Solrigg' and John de la Greyn' because they did not produce in court Robert de Weston'; 1*s*. 8*d*. from John Fab*er* of Bighton, Richard le Schep*ur*de, John Sum' and Robert le Bule because they did not produce in court Walter Tymb' whom they had bailed; 2*s*. from Walter ate Forth' of Overton, John Pilesel the elder, John Osebern and John ate Toneshe*n*d' because they did not produce in court John Pilesel the younger whom they had bailed; 1*s*. from Richard le Berch' of Overton, Robert le Hore, John Osebur*n* and Ralph ate Toneshe*n*d' because they did not produce in court Roger le Lu*n*t whom they had bailed in Overton at Easter; 1*s*. 8*d*. from William Fynamur for himself and his pledges because he is not proceeding against Geoffrey le Keu in a plea of land; 1*s*. 8*d*. from William Godrich of Upham and John Goudrich of the same because they did not produce in court Robert ate Bech; 1*s*. from Adam Cissore of Overton and Adam Pukecherl because they did not produce in court John Pilesel. From the amercements of merchants in the county of Southampton in the sixth year (1278): 2*s*. from Henry de Arblaster for false measure. Total, £1 7*s*. 8*d*.

Amercements of the court of J. de Metingh*am* and his fellows of the Bench at Michaelmas in the year 28 (1299-1300) and the following terms

The same renders account for 3*s*. 4*d*. from Jordan le Yunge and his fellows because they did not produce in court Joan de Colrych' whom they had bailed; 3*s*. 4*d*. from Bartholomew Laur*ence* and his fellows because they did not produce in court William, son of Laurence de Lond*on*, whom they had bailed; 1*s*. 8*d*. from William Joye and his fellows because they did not produce in court Walter de Derneford' whom they had bailed; 3*s*. 4*d*. from Robert Wynce*n*t and his fellows because they did not produce in court John de Lynch' whom they had bailed; 3*s*. 4*d*. from Jordan le Yu*n*ge and his fellows because they did not produce in court Joan de Colrich' whom they had bailed; 1*s*. 8*d*. from Thomas Laur*ence* and his fellows because they did not produce in court William, son of Laurence de Lond*on*, whom they had bailed; 1*s*. 8*d*. from Laurence Skyreboth' and his fellows because they did not produce in court Walter de Derneford' whom they had bailed; 1*s*. 8*d*. from William le Duk and his fellows because they did not produce in court John de Lynch' whom they had bailed; 3*s*. 4*d*. from John Wynce*n*t and his fellows because they did not produce in court John de Lynch' whom they had bailed; 1*s*. 8*d*. from William Chaub*er*lain, juror, because he did not come to the afforcement. Total, £1 5*s*.

Court of the Barons of the Exchequer for the pleas of Hilary term in the year 28 (1300)

The same renders account for 6*s*. 8*d*. from Alan Plukenet, son and heir of Alan Plukenet, because he did not come; 6*s*. 8*d*. from William, reeve of Kilmeston, and

Stephen le Rede of the same because they did not produce in court Alan, son and heir of Alan Plukenet, at Easter; 6*s*. 8*d*. from Alan, son and heir of Alan Plukenet, because he did not come; 3*s*. 4*d*. from Stephen le Ryde of Kilmeston and his fellows because they did not produce in court the said Alan. From Trinity term: 3*s*. 4*d*. from Alan Plukenet, son and heir of Alan Plukenet, because he did not come; 1*s*. 8*d*. from Stephen ate Cleye of Kilmeston and his fellows because they did not produce in court Alan, son and heir of Alan Plukenet; 6*s*. 8*d*. from Philip, archdeacon of Winchester, because he did not come. Total, £1 15*s*.

And 1*s*. 8*d*. from Gerard de Tigehal' and his fellows because they did not produce in court William de Tigehal'.

Court of R*oger* Brabaz*o*n and his fellow justices holding the pleas of the king's court for Hilary term in the year 27 Edward I (1299)
The same renders account for 1*s*. 8*d*. from Thomas Tupleyn and his fellows because they did not produce in court Nicholas de Langrissch'.

Court of the same justices in Michaelmas term of the year ending 26 and beginning 27 (1298-9)
The same renders account for 1*s*. 8*d*. from Nicholas de Borden' and his fellows because they did not produce in court Nicholas de Langrissch' whom they had bailed. Total, 5*s*.

King's court for Michaelmas term of the year ending 25 and beginning 26, and for the following Hilary, Easter and Trinity terms (1297-8)
The same renders account for 1*s*. 8*d*. from Nicholas Wynce*n*t and John Wynce*n*t because they did not produce in court William de Lynch'; 1*s*. from John Wynce*n*t, William Wynce*n*t, Nicholas Wynce*n*t and William Pakel because they did not produce in court John de Lynch'; 1*s*. 8*d*. from John de Wyntenesheye of Bradley and Simon Wuwyn' of Wield because they did not produce in court John Bouie; 1*s*. 8*d*. from Hugh son of Elewys and Robert, son of Andrew de Essefeld', because they did not produce in court Thomas Call'; 1*s*. 8*d*. from John Langurend' and John de la Hecch' because they did not produce in court Simon Wuwyn' whom they had pledged; 1*s*. 8*d*. from William le Carpe*n*tyr de Herlefeld' and Thomas Call' of Wield because they did not produce in court Robert de la Doun'; 1*s*. 8*d*. from Simon de la Lye and Benedict le P*ar*me*nter* because they did not produce in court Gilbert Horsemayn; 1*s*. 8*d*. from John le Fughelar', John Cl*ericus* of Long Sutton, William Paghel, William Vince*n*t of Long Sutton because they did not produce in court John de Lynch' whom they had bailed. Total, 12*s*. 8*d*.

From Chancery in the year 28 (1300), from the charge of Robert de H*e*rierd'
6*s*. 8*d*. from Robert Burnel to have the writ 'pone'.

Also from chancery in the year 29 (1301), from the charge of Robert de Herierd'
6*s*. 8*d*. from Richard de Sutton' of Overton to have a writ; ½ mark from Richard le Port*er* to have a writ. Total, £1.

From the eyre of R.[1] de Roff' in the year 8 and the beginning of the year 9 (1280-1)
3*s*. 4*d*. from Adam de Aldewyk' for contempt. Total, 3*s*. 4*d*.

1 MS error for 'S*olomon*'.

From the fines and amercements of Newgate gaol at the court of R. de Sandwyk' and his fellow justices in the years 24, 25, 26 and 27 (1296-9)
The same renders account for[1] Richard de Frilend' because he did not come; 3*s*. 4*d*. from John Bulluk and Nicholas Coc*us* because they did not produce in court the said Richard; 1*s*. 8*d*. from John de Lynch' because he did not come; 3*s*. 4*d*. from John Germayn and John ate Gate because they did not produce in court the said John whom they had bailed; 1*s*. 8*d*. from Richard de Midlin⌈g⌉ton' because he did not come; 2*s*. from Peter le Ryd' and William H*er*berd because they did not produce in court the said Richard; 1*s*. 8*d*. from William de la Den' because he did not come; 2*s*. from Henry Worm*ere* and Thomas Cachefrench because they did not produce in court the said William; 2*s*. from William Houdy and Robert ate Mere because they did not produce in court; 1*s*. 8*d*. from Robert la Beche because he did not come. Total, £1 1*s*.

Money of the king from Chancery in the year 29 Edward I (1301)
The same renders account for 6*s*. 8*d*. from Joan, who was wife of William de Castr', Ralph Will*iam*, and Richard, son of the same Joan, to have the writ 'pone'.

Court of J. de Meting*ham* and his fellow justices of the Bench at Michaelmas term in the year 28, and the fines and issues from the Bench at Hilary term in the year 29 (1300-1)
The same renders account for 3*s*. 4*d*. from the issue of the land of Joan de Colrych' outside the manor (*for'*); 1*s*. 8*d*. from the issue of the land of William, son of Laurence de Lond*on*; 1*s*. 8*d*. from the issue of the land of Walter de Durneford'; 3*s*. 4*d*. from the issue of the land of John de Lynch'; 6*s*. 8*d*. from the issue of the land of Walter de Derneford'. Total, £1 3*s*. 4*d*.

Court of the Barons of the Exchequer for the execution of writs for the king in the year 29 (1301)
The same renders account for 1*s*. from the issue of the land of John Pelrym outside the manor; 1*s*. from the issue of the land of Thomas Laur*ence*; 1*s*. from the issue of the land of William Laur*ence*; 1*s*. 8*d*. from the issue of the land of Thomas Laur*ence* at Hilary term; 6*s*. 8*d*. from the issue of the land of Alan, son and heir of Alan Plukenet. For the execution of writs for the king in the year 29 (1301): 1*s*. from the issue of the land of Richard de Hakeburn'; 3*s*. 4*d*. from the issue of the land of the same Richard; 1*s*. 8*d*. from the issue of the same Richard; 1*s*. 8*d*. from the issue of the land of the same Richard at Easter in the above-mentioned year; 1*s*. from the issue of the land of the same Richard at Easter; 1*s*. 8*d*. from the issue of the land of William Laur*ence*. Also from the same court at Easter term in the year 28 (1300): 1*s*. 8*d*. from the issue of the land of Alan, son and heir of Alan Plukenet.

From the Bench in the year 26 and the beginning of the year 27 (1298-9)
1*s*. from the issue of the land of John[2] atte Lynch'. Total, £1 17*s*. 8*d*.

Court of R*oger* de Brabazun and his fellow justices holding the pleas of the court of king's pleas at Michaelmas term in the year ending 27 and beginning 28, and the following terms (1299-1300)
The same renders account for 3*s*. 4*d*. from the issue of the land of Nicholas de Langrissch' outside the manor; 1*s*. 8*d*. from the issue of the land of Nicholas de

1 MS omits figure.

2 MS '⟨de⟩'.

Lang*r*issch'; 1*s*. 8*d*. from the issue of the land of Philip de Denemed' outside the manor. Total, 6*s*. 8*d*.

Court of the same justices in the year ending 28 and beginning 29 (1300-1)
The same renders account for 1*s*. from the issue of the land of Philip de Denemed' outside the manor; 1*s*. 8*d*. from the issue of the land of Nicholas de Langrissch' outside the manor; 1*s*. 8*d*. from the issue of the land of Philip de Denemed' outside the manor; 1*s*. from the issue of Richard de Frilend'; 1*s*. from the issue of John de Hurselye; 1*s*. from the issue of the land of John de Lynch'; 1*s*. from the issue of the land of Nicholas de Langrissch'.

King's court at Hilary term in the year 27 and the following terms (1299)
The same renders account for £1 2*s*. 8*d*. from the tithing of Ropley and the men of the same vill for the corn of William Gerveys. Total, £1 11*s*.

From the pipe rolls
The same renders account for £10 from John Giffard for relief of 2 knights' fees which belonged to Godfrey Giffard his uncle; 3*s*. 4*d*. from the heir of Braifeud' for relief of a certain tenement in West Pitt; 6*d*. from the same for relief of a certain other tenement in West Pitt. Total, £10 3*s*. 10*d*.

Total of all receipts, £25 12*s*.

Expenses
In wages of the marshal for the year £3 10*s*.

In allowance of the same for a 10*s*. amercement of William le Blesscede which he was being charged for from the previous year, because it was found in the pipe rolls that he paid it before for trespass of wool in the court of J. de Luvetot and G. de Nebaud.

Also in allowance of the same for a 6*d*. amercement of Henry Watsond which he was being charged for from the previous year for a plea of the Pavilion, of which he had the estreat and which he was not able to levy; 1*s*. for John de Northwych; 6*d*. for Nicholas le Keu of Chilbolton. Also in allowance of the same for his fur 2*s*.

Total of all expenses and allowances, £3 14*s*. 10*d*.

And he owes, £21 17*s*. 2*d*. And he owes it all clear.

Warren

Account of Thomas de la Burgh' for the whole of the warren.

Names of those who trespassed against the enclosure (*defens'*)
1*s*. from Richard le Palm*ere*, in mercy for trespass (*de*l*icto*) of animals in the lord's wood, and the same was attached by pledge of William ate M*ar*ssch'; 6*d*. from William ate M*ar*ssch' for the same, attached by pledge of Robert ate Frith'; 1*s*. from Colette atte M*ar*ssch' for the same, attached by pledge of William ate M*ar*ssch'; 6*d*.

from Robert le Mortim*er* for the same, attached by pledge of John de Lyle; 3*d*. from William ate M*ar*ssch' because he did not produce in court the individual whom he had pledged; 6*d*. from Matilda Davy for the same, attached by pledge of William ate M*ar*sch'; 6*d*. from Isabel le Boys for the same, by pledge of Robert le Frithiar'; 1*s*. from Gilbert Mond' because he trespassed in the lord's wood for vert and the same was attached; 6*d*. from John le Mong' for the same, attached by pledge of Nicholas le Withe; 6*d*. from Nicholas le White for the same, the same attached by pledge of Richard ate Mere; 6*d*. from Adam le Hu*n*te for the same, by pledge of Richard Mong'; 6*d*. from Richard ate Mere for the same, attached by pledge of Adam Hu*n*te; 6*d*. from William Mey for the same, the same pledged by Ralph le Cok; 3*d*. from Ralph le Cok because he did not produce in court the individual whom he had pledged; 6*d*. from Ralph le Cok for the same, by pledge of William le Hont'; 6*d*. from William Babeflod', attached by pledge of Richard ate More; 3*d*. from Richard ate More because he did not produce in court the individual whom he had pledged; 6*d*. from Walter True for the same, by pledge of Walter le Kyng; 6*d*. from Richard Simo*n*d for the same, by pledge of William Cl*ericus*; 3*d*. from William le Clerc because he did not produce in court the individual whom he had pledged; 6*d*. from Matilda Arnays for the same, by pledge of Stephen Warn*er*; 1*s*. from William Spur' for the same, by pledge of Stephen Warn*er*; 1*s*. from Richard Bocstok', by pledge of John Waremo*n*d; 3*d*. from John Waremo*n*d because he did not produce in court the individual whom he had pledged; 6*d*. from John Waremo*n*d for the same, by pledge of Richard de Bocstok'; 3*d*. from William Goudrich for the same and the same was attached; 2*s*. from Isabel ate Strod' because she trespassed in the lord's wood and the same was attached; 6*d*. from Elijah Stro⌈u⌉d' for the same; 6*d*. from Richard Sinu*n*d' for the same; 6*d*. from Alice Simond' for the same; 6*d*. from Richard le Pott*ere* for the same; 6*d*. from Richard ate M*ar*ssch' for the same; 1*s*. from Richard Em*ery* for the same; 1*s*. from William Hudy for the same; 3*d*. from Alice Aldon for the same; 6*d*. from John Spur' for the same; 6*d*. from William de Bykebroc for the same; 6*d*. from Henry ate Slegat' for the same; 3*d*. from Robert ate Mere for the same; 6*d*. from William Prut because he trespassed in the lord's wood, by pledge of Henry Truwe; 6*d*. from Matilda ate Mer*e* for the same, attached by surety (*vad'*); 3*d*. from Margaret ate M*ar*ssch' for the same, attached by surety. Total, £1 3*s*. 6*d*.

Attachments for Longewod'

6*d*. from John Wales because he trespassed in the lord's wood and the same was attached by surety, and because he did not come to court; 3*d*. from Richard Peris for having his sows in the wood, attached by surety of the prior's man.

Names of those who trespassed against the enclosure

1*s*. from Thomas de Wycherst for having his animals in the lord's wood, by pledge of James de Wycherst; 6*d*. from James de Wycherst for the same, by pledge of Thomas de Wycherst; 6*d*. from Edward Fab*er* for the same, by pledge of Thomas de Wycherst, and because he did not come; 1*s*. from Richard Jacob for the same, by pledge of Thomas de Wycherst; 6*d*. from William ate Assche for the same, by pledge of R*ichard* Ja[cob]; 1*s*. from William ate Stubb' for the same, by pledge of J*ohn* Wales; 6*d*. from Richard Wawelyn for the same, by pledge of William Bassat, because he did not come; 6*d*. from Robert[1] Clemont for the same, by pledge of William de Sp . . . ; 1*s*. from John Godwyn' because he trespassed in the lord's wood, by pledge of W*illiam* atte Lynch'; 3*d*. from William ate Lynch' because he did not

1 MS '⟨Elyes⟩'.

produce in court the individual whom he had pledged; 6*d*. from Humphrey for the same, by pledge of John Bubbe; 3*d*. from the relict of Jambel for having her sheep in the lord's wood, by pledge of John Bernard', the prior's man; 6*d*. from Thomas Brony*ng* for the same, by pledge of James de Wycherst; 6*d*. from James de Wycherst for the same, by pledge of T*homas* de Wyc[herst]; 6*d*. from William de Aq*ua* because he trespassed in the lord's wood and the same was attached, and because he did not come; 3*d*. from Geoffrey ate Hall' because he trespassed against the prohibition in the lord's wood, by pledge of Thomas Brony*ng*, the prior's man.

Men of the prior
3[*d*. from] Robert le Harre for the same, by pledge of John de Wicherst; 3*d*. from Hugh le Av*er*hurd' for the same, by pledge of Andrew Putsted'; 3*d*. from Godwyn for the same, by pledge of William ate Stubb'; 3*d*. from Godfrey for the same, ⌈by pledge⌉ of Thomas de Wycherst; 3*d*. from Robert Davy for the same, by pledge of John de Wychurst, the prior's men. Total, 1*s*. 9*d*.

And 1*s*. from John Wythelard because he trespassed in the lord's wood and the same was attached. Total, 12*s*.

Attachments for Haseholte
The same renders account for ½ mark from Adam Cauncheler because he trespassed in the lord's wood with hunting nets, attached by pledge of Henry ate M*er*e; 3*d*. from Henry ate M*er*e because he did not produce in court the individual whom he had pledged; 3*d*. from Henry ate M*er*e because he trespassed in his own wood, attached by pledge of John ate Pyle; 3*d*. from Henry ate Samel' for the same, attached by pledge of John ate Pyle; 3*d*. from Robert Wodekoc because he trespassed in his own wood, attached by pledge of William le Bor; 6*d*. from John Car*eter* because he trespassed against the prohibition, attached by pledge of Thomas Russel; 3*d*. from Richard Bige, in mercy for the same, and the same was attached.

m.31d
And 3*s*. from Peter Ysach because he trespassed in his own wood and the same was attached; 6*d*. from John Serle for the same and the same was attached. Total, 11*s*. 8*d*.

Attachments for Holemor
6*d*. from William Comeichho' because he trespassed in his own wood, by pledge of Adam Comichh'; 6*d*. from Thomas le Ryd*e* for having sheep in Holemor against the enclosure, by pledge of Walter Coke; 3*d*. from Richard Lucas for having his horses in H*ol*mle, by pledge of Adam de Holemor; 1*s*. from Banse because he trespassed in his own wood, by pledge of John Strecch'; 2*s*. from William le Frend' for the same, attached by pledge of Richard Werch; 3*d*. from Robert Hogeles for having his horses in the lord's wood, by pledge of Adam de Holemor; 3*d*. from Peter Braban for having his oxen in Hol*emor*, by pledge of Adam Holemor, the prior's man; 3*d*. from Petipas for the same, by pledge of Adam de Hol*emor*, the prior's man; 6*d*. from Isabel ate Pleystowe for the same, attached by pledge of Henry le Scot. Total, 5*s*. 6*d*.

Attachments for la Holte and for Sta*n*cu*m*be
3*d*. from Peter Gosselyn because he trespassed in the lord's wood and the same was attached; 6*d*. from Alexander Kechel for the same and the same was attached; 6*d*. from William ate Pu*n*d' because he trespassed in the wood of Wandsworth; 6*d*. from

Richard Horn for the same and the same was attached; 1*s*. from Thomas ate Houk' for the same and the same was attached; 2*s*. from William le Ragged' because he trespassed in his own wood and the same was attached; 1*s*. from Robelot for the same and the same was attached; 3*d*. from John de Hokkelyele because he trespassed in the lord's wood and the same was attached; 6*d*. from Thomas ate Houk' because he did not come to court; 6*d*. from Richard because he trespassed in the wood of Wandsworth, the same was attached, and because he did not come; 6*d*. from William Keppy*ng* because he trespassed in the lord's wood and the same was attached; 1*s*. from Richard B*e*rccar*ius* for the same. Total, 8*s*. 6*d*.

Total of all receipts, £3 1*s*. 2*d*.

In allowance of the same for transgressions (*trans*gressionibus) by the men of the prior in la Longewod' at the time of the enclosures, for which the prior has the amercements, 2*s*. Also in allowance of the same for transgressions made by the men of the prior in H*o*melie at the time of the enclosures, 1*s*. Total, 3*s*.

And he owes, £2 18*s*. 2*d*.

Delivered to Sir G*eoffrey*, treasurer of Wolvesey, by 1 tally, £1 4*s*. 6*d*.

And he owes clear, £1 13*s*. 8*d*.

Wolvesey

Arrears

Richard Cl*er*icus and Richard Vigil of Wolvesey render account for £26 15*s*. 4¼*d*. of arrears from the last account. All delivered to Sir G*eoffrey*, treasurer of Wolvesey. They are quit.

Rents

The same render account for 1*s*. for the rent of a certain curtilage beyond the bridge beside Segrim's mill; 19*s*. 6*d*. for the rent of a certain house at Durn Gate which Bishop Nicholas bought from King H*enry III*; 13*s*. 4*d*. for a certain meadow leased to Drogo de Celar' on the east side of the Carmelite Friars. Total, £1 13*s*. 10*d*., of which 9*s*. 9*d*. was paid at Easter (22 April) and £1 4*s*. 1*d*. at Michaelmas (29 September).

Farms of the mills

The same render account for £1 for the farm of the fulling mill; £5 for the farm of the mill of St Cross for the year; £5 for the farm of the mill of Priors Barton for the year; £6 for the farm of Segrim's mill for the year; £11 6*d*. for the farm of Durn Gate mill for the year; nothing for the farm of Floodstock mill this year because it was built anew this year; 3*s*. to have a certain watercourse through the middle of the garden of St Cross; 13*s*. 4*d*. from Master Alan Carpentar' for the farm of the mill of Sparkford for the year, granted to him and his heirs by charter of the bishop forever. Total, £28 16*s*. 10*d*.

Issues of the manor

The same render account for 15*s*. 3*d*. from animals remaining in the meadow after St Giles's Fair (29 August to 13 September) until the Purification (2 February); 10*s*.

from the pasturage of fields and ways sold to Roger de Wylehal' because his sheepfold stands on the bishop's land; £1 2*s*. 2*d*. from nettles and the herbage sold in the garden this year; £1 from fines and the pasturage sold on St Giles's Hill; 3*s*. from winter pasturage sold in the meadow of Sewyn' this year; 6*s*. 8*d*. from the herbage of the small meadow outside the gate of Wolvesey sold to John de Sarr' and his fellows for the year because they held Segrim's mill for life of the lord J*ohn*, now bishop, for the above-mentioned farm; 2*s*. 3*d*. from the herbage of the small meadow of Tri*n*tra*m* sold to Roger de Wylehale this year, because 3*d*. was given in tithe; nothing from cut chaff (*minuta palea*) this year because none was sold; 8*s*. from the pasturage of the meadows of Brodemed and Middelmor sold this year to the said Roger for his sheep until the Annunciation (25 March); 4*s*. from the pasturage of the meadows of St Stephen and Crepestr' sold to Henry Goudediw this year for his sheep until the same time, and not more because this year was the first that the chapel in honour of St Elizabeth was being built in the meadow of St Stephen and the pasture there was chalky on all sides; 3*s*. 2*d*. from stubble sold this year, and not more because the rest was used for the timber in the meadow for roofing the said chapel; 2*s*. 6*d*. from vegetables and leeks grown in the garden this year and not more on account of the long stay of the bishop at Wolvesey this year; 4*s*. from the hide sold of 1 ox dead from murrain this year; 3*s*. 6*d*. from the bark sold of rafters felled in Prevet for the repair of the wood-hall, barn and mill of Floodstock; 5*s*. from 1 pipe of cider sold this year. Total, £5 9*s*. 6*d*.

Sale of corn
The same render account for £13 15*s*. 3*d*. from 45 qrs 2 bus. of wheat sold, at 5*s*. a qr for 5 qrs, 5*s*. 6*d*. a qr for 13 qrs, 6*s*. 4*d*. a qr for 6 qrs, 6*s*. 6*d*. a qr for 3 qrs, and 6*s*. 8*d*. a qr for 18 qrs; 12*s*. 8½*d*. from 4 qrs 5 bus. of curall sold, at 2*s*. 8*d*. a qr for 3½ qrs, and 3*s*. a qr for 1 qr 1 bus.; £9 14*s*. from 45 qrs 2 bus. of barley sold, at 4*s*. a qr for 6 qrs 2 bus., and 4*s*. 4*d*. a qr for 39 qrs; £4 3*s*. 8*d*. from 33 qrs of oats sold, at 2*s*. 8*d*. a qr for 20 qrs, and 2*s*. 4*d*. a qr for 13 qrs; £1 13*s*. 9*d*. from 6 acres of green vetches sold wholesale, at 6*s*. 4*d*. an acre, from which the tithe was deducted; 3*s*. from 9 bus. of brew-corn sold, at 4*d*. a bus. Total, £30 2*s*. 4½*d*.

Total of all receipts, £66 2*s*. 6½*d*.

Expenses of ploughs
In 100 pieces of iron for repairing the ironwork of ploughs bought for stock 3*s*. In stipend of the smith making the said ironwork for the year 1*s*. 8*d*. In 2 plough feet bought 1*s*. In 1 wheel bought for the plough 2*d*. In branches felled and put in the field which should not be sown beyond the corn 5*d*. In 2 shovels and 2 dung-forks bought and the same fitted with iron 8*d*. In stipend of 1 man building new stalls for the oxen in the byre for 3 days 9*d*. In building 1 stile in the west field 1*s*. In dung bought this year 11*s*. 4*d*. In hiring an assistant to help the gardener to dig the garden and uproot and clear bad plants (*mal' herb'*) 9½*d*. In stipend of 1 overseer of the harvest for the year 6*s*. 8*d*. In stipend of 1 ploughman for the year 5*s*. In stipend of another ploughman for ½ year 2*s*. Total, £1 14*s*. 5½*d*.

Purchase of corn
In 13½ qrs of wheat bought for sowing £3 16*s*. 6*d*., at 5*s*. 4*d*. a qr for 9 qrs, 6*s*. a qr for 2 qrs 2 bus., and 6*s*. 8*d*. a qr for 2 qrs 2 bus. In 31 qrs 5 bus. of barley bought for sowing and the liveries of the manorial servants £6 4*s*. 10*d*., at 2*s*. 8*d*. a qr for 4 qrs,

4*s*. a qr for 5 qrs 5 bus., and 4*s*. 2*d*. a qr for 22 qrs. In 42 qrs 3 bus. of oats for sowing and the fodder of cart-horses and servants £3 19*s*. 9*d*., at 1*s*. 6*d*. a qr for 12 qrs, 1*s*. 8*d*. a qr for 9 qrs, 2*s*. a qr for 9 qrs 3 bus., 2*s*. 4*d*. a qr for 12 qrs. In 1½ qrs of vetches bought for sowing 3*s*., at 2*s*. a qr. Total, £14 4*s*. 1*d*.

Cost of carts
In 1 pair of wheels bought 3*s*. In fitting the same with iron tyres 1*s*. In 1 new cart-body with 1 cart-rail bought for the cart 2*s*. 6*d*. In fitting 2 wooden bands to the hubs of the said wheels 2*d*. In clamps and ledges (*lurlegg'*) bought for the cart for the year 8*d*. In fitting the cart with axles for the year with axles bought for the same 1*s*. 3*d*. In 1 curry-comb bought 1*d*. In 3 dung-baskets (*dungpott'*) bought for stock 5*d*. In 1 tailored halter bought for the cart-horses 4*d*. In 32 clouts and clout-nails bought for the cart for stock 3*s*. 4½*d*. In shoeing 2 cart-horses for the year and 1 horse which came from the heriot of Richard le Warnir and another horse which belonged to Walter de Preston' for ½ year 6*s*. 6*d*. In stipend of 1 carter for the year 6*s*. 8*d*. In 1 halter bought for the horse which came from the heriot of Richard le Warn*ir* 4*d*. Total, £1 17*s*. 3½*d*.

Threshing of corn
In threshing 45½ qrs of wheat and 4 qrs 5 bus. of curall by piece-work by struck measure 10*s*., at 3*d*. per 10 struck bushels. In threshing 55 qrs 6 bus. of barley by piece-work by the same measure 5*s*. 7*d*., at 1½*d*. per 10 struck bushels. In threshing 47 qrs 6 bus. of oats by piece-work by struck measure 3*s*. 2*d*., at 1*d*. per 10 struck bushels. In winnowing all the aforesaid corn by piece-work 5*s*. 1*d*., at ½*d*. per 10 struck bushels of all types of corn. Given for winnowing at various times 7*d*. Total, £1 4*s*. 5*d*.

Cost of the harvest
In mowing 28 acres of meadow this year 8*s*. 9*d*., and not more because this year was the first that the chapel of St Elizabeth was being built in the meadow of St Stephen and that meadow was entirely mowed for hay for the bishop's horses staying at Wolvesey. In spreading, tossing and gathering all the hay into haycocks, reducing these in size, and carrying and stacking them there, with the hire of carts to carry the said hay, 8*s*. 9*d*. In mowing the meadows of Sewyn', Crepestr', the meadow of St Stephen, and the garden of Wolvesey, this year for a second crop of hay (*rewanno*), and spreading the hay therein, 10*s*. 9¼*d*. In weeding all the corn 1*s*. 11*d*. In reaping, binding and stacking all the corn £3 18*s*. In hiring helpers to carry the same corn 8*s*. 3*d*. Total, £5 16*s*. 5¼*d*.

Cost of buildings
In cleaning the ditches around the castle and meadows 2*s*. In 2 spades bought and fitted with iron 6*d*. In carrying forage from the stack within the curia to the barn 6*d*. In repairing 1 axe 2*d*. In stipend of 1 gardener for the year 6*s*. 8*d*. In planting 11 perches of hedge in the meadow beside Floodstock 3½*d*., at 1*d*. per 3 perches. In cleaning the buildings at Wolvesey in preparation for the visit of the earl of Lincoln and the count of Savoy 8*d*. In hooping all around 1 pipe of cider and repairing other utensils many times during the year 1*s*. 1*d*. Total, 11*s*. 10½*d*.

Total of all expenses, £25 8*s*. 6¾*d*.

And thus he owes, £40 13*s*. 11¾*d*.

Allowances

In allowance of the same for fastening lead which had become detached on the chapel, bishop's chamber and treasury, with nails bought for the same; for hooks and hinges to repair the great door of the hall; for 2 ropes bought for the bell in the chapel; for repairing 1 lock on the door of the prison; for making 2 yards of iron to repair the bishop's seat in the chapel of Wolvesey and other ironwork for the same; for 2 ropes bought to weigh the bishopric's wool; for repairing 1 window in the chamber of the steward's house; for covering the arbour beside the treasurer's chamber with turf; for the stipend of 2 women hired by the day to collect thorns within the curia, and to bear the same to the bakehouse at harvest-time; and for other gifts given to the carters of various manors who often came to Wolvesey during the year with wood, hay and letters, by order of the treasurer, 13*s.* 10½*d.* Also for 2 stones bought to make one porch outside the outer door of the bishop's chamber, with lime and salt bought for the same, 1*s.* 11½*d.* Also for hooks and hinges, large and small nails bought for the postern gate in the garden to Colebrook Street, with 1 lock and key for the same, 7*s.* 10*d.* Also for 1 key bought for the bishop's house in Colebrook Street 2*d.* Also for 1 new lock with a key bought for the postern gate to the priory 1*s.* Also for repairing the glass window in the chapel with ironwork made for the same, and for the ironwork of the previously new table for putting the bishop's books on, 4*s.* 10*d.* Also for 1 tub bought for the bishop to bathe in 2*s.* 6*d.* Also for hose bought for Robert and Nicholas Stak', who cut, stitched and repaired shoes many times during the year, and for Richard le Warnir, 2*s.* 7½*d.* Also for the expenses made for 2 attendants of the household of the count of Savoy, who stayed at Wolvesey for 6 days, 1*s.* Also for the allowance of food for 3 clerks who are in the bishop's prison at Wolvesey for the year £1 2*s.* 9*d.*, at ¼*d.* each a day. Also for the allowance of food for 6 clerks incarcerated in the prison in the town of Winchester for the year £2 5*s.* 6*d.*, at ¼*d.* each a day. Also for the allowance of food for 1 clerk incarcerated in the town of Winchester from Monday before the feast of St Lucy the Virgin (11 December) until Michaelmas, for 41 weeks and 5 days, 6*s.* 1*d.*, at ¼*d.* a day. Also for the allowance of food for 2 clerks incarcerated in the town of Winchester from Friday before Lammas (27 July) until Michaelmas, for 9 weeks, 2*s.* 7½*d.*, at ¼*d.* each a day. Also in allowance of the same to give to the porter when he weighed all the wool of the bishopric of Winchester at Wolvesey this year, 2*s.* Also for 4 oxen bought for the manor's stock £2 11*s.* 11*d.*, at 13*s.* 5*d.* for 1, and 12*s.* 10*d.* each for 3. In allowance of the same for repairing the wood-hall and corn barn, for all costs, just as is made clear from the details, and for repairing the cellar under the chapel, and the chapel, for all costs, £18 18*s.* 3½*d.*

Total of all allowances, £27 4*s.* 11½*d.*

And he owes clear, £13 9*s.* ¼*d.*

No cash deliveries

Issues of the grange

Wheat
{yield: 4-fold plus 3 bus.}
The same render account for 45 qrs 4 bus. from the whole issue of wheat; 13½ qrs bought. Total, 59 qrs.
Sown, 13 qrs 6 bus. Sold, 45 qrs 2 bus.

Curall
The same render account for 4 qrs 5 bus. of curall; all sold.

Barley
{yield: 4-fold plus 2 bus.}
The same render account for 55 qrs 6 bus. from the whole issue of barley; 31 qrs 5 bus. bought. Total, 87 qrs 3 bus.
Sown, 11 qrs 6 bus. Delivered to 1 overseer of the harvest, one carter, one drover and one gardener for the year, each of whom takes a quarter every 8 weeks, 26 qrs. Delivered to one ploughman from Michaelmas (29 September) until the feast of St Dunstan the Bishop (19 May), for 34 weeks, taking a quarter every 8 weeks, 4 qrs 2 bus. Given to the threshers, 1 bus. Sold, 45 qrs 2 bus.

Oats
{yield: five-fold plus 2 qrs 1 bus.}
The same render account for 47 qrs 6 bus. from the whole issue of oats by struck measure; 42 qrs 3 bus. bought. Total, 90 qrs 1 bus.
Sown, 4 qrs. In fodder of 2 cart-horses for the whole year, and 1 horse from the heriot of Richard le Warnir from the eve of the Annunciation (24 March) until Friday after the feast of St Laurence (17 August), and 1 horse which belonged to Walter de P*re*ston' from the feast of the Annunciation (25 March) until Monday after the feast of St Giles (5 September), 48 qrs. In fodder of the horses of the servants of the bishop's household for the year, 5 qrs 1 bus. Sold, 33 qrs.

Stock

Cart[-horses]: 2 remain from the previous year; 1 received from the bishop which was the horse of Walter de Preston'; 1 from the heriot of Richard le Warnir with a saddle. Total, 4. 4 remain, of which 1[1] is at Merdon and the others at Bitterne.
[Oxen]: 11 remain from the previous year; 4 bought. Total, 15. 1 in murrain; 14 remain.
[Cranes]: 2 remain from the previous year; 1 consumed by the bishop; 1 remains.
Cider: 1 cask and 1 pipe remain from the previous year; 3 pipes from the issue of the garden this year; 1 pipe sold; 1 cask was worth nothing and was therefore thrown out; 3 pipes remain.
[Hides]: 1 from an ox dead from murrain; sold below.

St Giles's Fair

[Toll-]gates
South Gate
The first, second, third and fourth day, 1*s.* 2*d.*; the fifth day, 3*s.*; the sixth day, 5*s.* 7*d.*; the seventh day, 17*s.* 4*d.*; the eighth day, 12*s.* 4*d.*; the ninth day, 1*s.* 1*d.*; the tenth day, 2*s.* 6*d.*; the eleventh day, 2*s.* 3*d.*; the twelfth day, 2*s.* 7*d.*; the thirteenth day, 3*s.* 2*d.*; the fourteenth day, 1*s.* 1*d.*; the fifteenth day, 4*s.* 5*d.*; the sixteenth day, 3*s.* Total, £2 19*s.* 6*d.*

East gate
The first, second, third and fourth day, nothing; the fifth day, nothing; the sixth day, 1*s.* 4*d.*; the seventh day, 6*d.*; the eighth day, 1*s.* 2*d.*; the ninth day, 2*s.* 6*d.*; the tenth day, 6*d.*; the eleventh day, 3*s.* 7*d.*; the twelfth day, 1*s.* 9*d.*; the thirteenth day, 6*d.*; the fourteenth day, 9*d.*; the fifteenth day, 6*d.*; the sixteenth day, 11*d.* Total, 14*s.*

West gate
The first, second, third and fourth day, 6*d.*; the fifth day, 2*d.*; the sixth day, 1*s.*; the seventh day, 2*s.* 11*d.*; the eighth day, 3*s.* 3*d.*; the ninth day, 1*s.* 3*d.*; the tenth day, 4*d.*;

1 MS omits '1'.

the eleventh day, 1*s*. 1*d*.; (*m.32*) the twelfth day, 1*s*. 3*d*.; the thirteenth day, 2*s*. 4*d*.; the fourteenth day, 1*s*. 6*d*.; the fifteenth day, 1*s*.; the sixteenth day, 1*s*. 3*d*. Total, 17*s*. 10*d*.

Total of all the gates, £4 11*s*. 4*d*.

From payments for using the tron (*de magno pondere*) this year, £1 8*s*. 5*d*. Total the same.

From ground-rents (*de terragio*) this year, £23 6½*d*.
From toll on cattle (*de boagio*) this year, £1 10*d*.
From the seldage of Ireland this year, that is, for 17 windows, £2 2*s*. 6*d*., at 2*s*. 6*d*. a window.
From the seldage of York this year, £2.
From the seldage of the burellers this year, £4 2*s*.
From the seldage of Lincoln this year, 5*s*.
From the seldage of the French and Cornish, for 13 windows, £1 19*s*., at 3*s*. a window.
Total, £34 9*s*. 10½*d*.

From the entry of the fair this year, 7*s*. 5*d*.
From the Romsey, Redbridge and Crawley roads, £2.
From the Cheriton and Alresford roads, 3*s*.
From the office of reeve of the city this year, £5 13*s*. 4*d*.
From traders in saddles and ladders this year, 10*s*.
From traders in burel this year, 10*d*.
From traders in teasels this year, 2*s*. 2*d*.
From traders in wheels this year, 7*d*.
From animals in the meadows and fields this year, £3
From the official in charge of the animals (*de ministr' animal'*) at the fair this year, 16*s*.
From the pleas and perquisites of the Pavilion this year, £2 1*s*. 4*d*.
For the favour of entering the fair after the day of the Nativity of the blessed Mary (8 September), £1 3*s*. 9*d*.
From the issues of the fair: from the roofing of the toll-house sold, and from hedges, nothing this year.
Total, £15 17*s*. 7*d*.

Total of all receipts, £56 7*s*. 2½*d*.

Expenses
Keeper of the East Gate from the first day for 16 days, William in the Den' of Chidden, 2*s*. 8*d*.
Keeper of the South Gate for 8 days, Hugh de Hurs*ley* and William Kyrie, 2*s*. 8*d*.
Keeper of the West Gate from the first day for 16 days, Richard de Frylend', 2*s*. 8*d*.
Keeper of saddles and ladders, farmed out to John Gentyl and John, sergeant of the Soke.
Keeper of animals at the fair, farmed out to Walter Crud*e*.
Keeper of animals in the meadows, farmed out to Hugh Balehorn.
Keeper of the office of reeve of the city, farmed out to Peter de Portesmuth' and Walter de Tysted'; the minor reeve, John Jackemyson'.

Keeper of the Romsey, Redbridge, Hursley and Crawley roads, farmed out to ⌈John Tothull'.⌉
⌈Keeper of the[1] Cheriton and Alresford roads⌉, Hugh le Forster.
Keeper of the traders in burel, William Sarr' and William de Colbrok'.
Teasels, John Masseday, Laurence de Wilehal', Walter ate Yate.
Wheels, Richard Canon, Adam Burgeys.
Keeper of the tron (*cust' magni pond'*), John de Herierd'.
Weigher, William de Wandlesworth', 6*s.* 8*d.*
Door-keeper of the pavilion, Jordan, the bishop's squire, 2*s.* 8*d.*
Chamberlain of the pavilion, Richard le Palm*ere* of Alresford, 5*s.*
Crier in the fair and city, G. M*a*rescall*us*, 2*s.*
Total, £1 4*s.* 4*d.*

Guardians of the road through Alton (*pass' de Aulton'*), mounted, with arms and their attendants
⌈Mounted guardians of the road through Alton⌉, Hugh de Solrigg', William de Hatfeud, John le Mew, John Dunnyng, John de Hattingely, William Beaumond, Henry Scherewynd', for 16 days, at 6*d.* each a day, £2 16*s.*

Guardians of the same road on foot, Peter Body, William Page, William Reigner, Robert de Langerissch', John Launual, Richard P*arcarius* of Merdon, for 16 days, at 2*d.* each a day, 16*s.*

Total of the road, £3 12*s.*

Armed sergeants guarding the fair, night and day
John Bernard, Nicholas de Lang*r*issch', John de Middelton', Roger Ev*e*rard', William de Stok', Richard de Chalg*ra*ve, John Ev*e*rard.

Collectors of ground-rents, Richard Cl*ericus*, William de Molend*ino*, John Ev*e*rard.

Minor sergeants
Bartholomew de Farh*a*m for 22 days, at 1*d.* a day, 1*s.* 10*d.*; Robert le Taillour for 19 days, at 1*d.* a day, 1*s.* 7*d.*; Richard Pieres for 18 days, at 1*d.* a day, 1*s.* 6*d.*; Robert de Cosh*a*m, Thomas de Kent, John de Alr*esford*, for 17 days, at 1*d.* each a day, 4*s.* 3*d.*; John Freir', William Horn, Robert Mol*endinarius*, for 12 days, at 1*d.* each a day, 3*s.*

Total of minor sergeants, 12*s.* 2*d.*

Total of all the preceding totals, £5 8*s.* 6*d.*

In collecting stubble to thatch the toll-house at South Gate and roofing the same 2*s.* 11½*d.* In re-roofing in places the selds for hire which had been unroofed 2*s.* 8½*d.* In re-roofing the pavilion which had been unroofed by the wind, with nails bought for the same, 3*s.* 11½*d.* In cleaning the pavilion in preparation for the fair and collecting greenwood and spreading it there 3*d.* In rope bought for bearing the measures taken in the town 2*d.* In hiring a certain house at West Gate for collecting tolls there 2*s.* In allowance of the chamberlain for the amercements which he was unable to levy, with 3*d.* pardoned to the prior of Southwick for fixing the treasurer's jurisdiction badly, 3*s.*, as made clear from the details in the chamberlain's account. Total, 15*s.* ½*d.*

1 MS '⟨Romes'⟩'.

In expenses of the aforesaid sergeants guarding the fair and pavilion, as made clear in the chamberlain's account, £1 11*s*. 9½*d*. In expenses of the household at Wolvesey, for 9 days at the time of the fair, £5 13*s*. 10½*d*., and not more because the bishop was at Wolvesey for 8 days at the time of the fair. Total, £7 5*s*. 8*d*.

Total of all expenses, £13 9*s*. 2½*d*.

And he owes, £42 18*s*.

Cash deliveries
Delivered to Sir G*eoffrey*, treasurer of Wolvesey, by 1 tally, £40.

And he owes clear, £2 18*s*., of which 7*s*. 6*d*. are charged to the marshal.

Cams

Arrears
Robert de[1] renders account for 13*s*. 7*d*. of arrears from the previous year. All delivered to Sir G*eoffrey*, treasurer of Wolvesey. He is quit.[2]

Rents of assize
The same renders account for 8*s*. 1*d*. for rents of assize at Christmas; £1 6*s*. 3¾*d*. at Easter (22 April); 8*s*. 1*d*. at St John the Baptist (24 June); £1 7*s*. 10¾*d*. at Michaelmas (29 September). Total, £3 10*s*. 4½*d*.

Increment
The same renders account for 1*d*. for the increment of rent of Thomas Godwyn' to have the moiety of 1 day-work beside his house. Total, 1*d*.

Total of rents with increment, £3 10*s*. 4½*d*.[3]

Issues of the manor
The same renders account for 1*s*. 2*d*. from pannage of pigs; 8*s*. from 1 cart-horse sold; 12*s*. from 2 feeble plough-horses sold; 16*s*. 4*d*. from 14 wethers sold at Martinmas (11 November), at 1*s*. 2*d*. each; 6*s*. 8*d*. from 8 ewes sold at the same feast, at 10*d*. each; £1 from 8 pigs sold at the feast of St Andrew (30 November), at 2*s*. 6*d*. each; 12*s*. from 8 pigs sold at the same feast, at 1*s*. 6*d*. each; 6*s*. from 6 piglets sold, at 1*s*. each; nothing from coarse wool and lamb's-wool here because it is sent to Wolvesey; 8*s*. 10*d*. from 1 wey and 1 clove of summer cheese sold; 10*d*. from the skins sold of 4 ewes in murrain before shearing, at 2½*d*. a skin; 1½*d*. from the skin sold of 1 ewe in murrain after shearing; 3*d*. from the skins sold of 4 lambs in murrain before weaning; ¼*d*. from the skin sold of 1 lamb in murrain after shearing; 2*s*. from the pasturage sold at Alnet'; 2*s*. 6*d*. from the pasturage sold at Ostrewod'; 6*d*. from the pasturage sold in 2 crofts beside the garden; 2*s*. from stubble sold; 2*s*. 6*d*. from 30 men for 1 harvest boon-work; 14*s*. from 7 pigs sold after the harvest; 10*s*. from 8 piglets sold after the harvest, at 1*s*. 3*d*. each; 6*s*. 8*d*. from 8 piglets sold after the harvest, at 10*d*. each; 9½*d*. from 2 cloves 5 lb of butter sold, at 3½*d*. a clove. Total, £6 13*s*. 2½*d*.

1 MS omits surname.

2 MS 'Et q*uieti* s*unt*'.

3 Figures add up to £3 10*s*. 5½*d*.

Sale of corn
The same renders account for £16 12*s*. 10¾*d*. from 57½ qrs ½ bus. of wheat sold, at 4*s*. 6*d*. a qr for 6½ qrs, 5*s*. a qr for 16 qrs ½ bus., 6*s*. a qr for 15 qrs, and 6*s*. 8*d*. a qr for 20 qrs; 18*s*. 11½*d*. from 10 qrs 5 bus. of curall sold, at 1*s*. 8*d*. a qr for 9 qrs 3 bus., and 2*s*. 8*d*. a qr for 1 qr 2 bus.; £1 15*s*. 3*d*. from 8½ qrs 2½ bus. of barley sold, at 4*s*. a qr; 14*s*. 9¾*d*. from 4½ qrs 3½ bus. of dredge sold, at 3*s*. a qr; £3 9*s*. 6*d*. from 30½ qrs 2 bus. of oats sold, at 2*s*. a qr for 14 qrs 6 bus., 2*s*. 4*d*. a qr for 8 qrs, and 2*s*. 8*d*. a qr for 8 qrs; 15*s*. 2½*d*. from 7 qrs ½ bus. of peas sold, at 2*s*. a qr for 3 qrs 6½ bus., and 2*s*. 4*d*. a qr for 3 qrs 2 bus.; 7*s*. 6*d*. from 3 qrs 6 bus. of vetches sold, at 2*s*. a qr. Total, £24 14*s*. 1½*d*.

Perquisites
The same renders account for 6*s*. from the amercements of 2 courts; 13*s*. 4*d*. from Oliver Stak' to receive 4 acres of land whilst the manor of Cams is in the wardship of the lord. Total, 19*s*. 4*d*.

Total of all receipts, £35 17*s*. ¼*d*.

Cost of ploughs
In iron and steel bought for the ironwork of 2 ploughs for the year 6*s*. 8*d*., with the stipend of the smith. In 1 ploughshare bought 9*d*. In 2 plough feet bought 1*s*. In 1 new plough made with the other ploughs mended 10*d*. In 2 pairs of wheels bought 8*d*. In fitting 1 plough with iron tyres 1½*d*. In shoeing 2 plough-horses for 1 term 1*s*. In boon-works of 8 ploughmen in winter and 4 in Lent 2*s*. In hiring 1 man to plough from Easter until Michaelmas, working for 72 days when they ploughed, 3*s*., at ½*d*. a day. In 2 sacks bought 1*s*. In forage bought 14*s*. 7*d*. In stipend of 2 ploughmen for the year 8*s*. In stipend of 1 ploughman from Michaelmas until Easter 1*s*. 6*d*., because thereafter a third ploughman was hired by the day and a fourth ploughman held a plough for his land. In 2 qrs 2 bus. of wheat bought for sowing 11*s*. 3*d*., at 5*s*. a qr. In shoeing oxen 6*d*. Total, £2 11*s*. 10½*d*.

Cost of carts
In 1 cart mended with large nails bought for the same 10*d*. In fitting the cart with axles with axles bought for the same 5*d*. In clouts, nails and grease bought 11*d*. In 1 pair of traces bought 3½*d*. In 1 collar and 1 pair of saddle-pads bought 1*s*. 1*d*. In shoeing 3 cart-horses for the year 4*s*. 6*d*. In 3 halters bought 4*d*. In stipend of 1 carter for the year 5*s*. In stipend of 1 hayward from the Purification (2 February) until Michaelmas (29 September), 6*s*. 8*d*. this year. In hay bought 1*s*. 10*d*. In white leather bought for harnesses 3½*d*. In a crupper and girths bought 2½*d*. Total, £1 2*s*. 4½*d*.

Cost of the dairy
In 3½ bus. of salt bought 10½*d*. In a press bought 1*d*. In 12 hurdles made from their own withies 6*d*. In stubble collected for wattling the fold 2*d*. In grease bought for greasing sheep 2*s*. 6*d*. In meal bought for the pottage of the manorial servants 2*s*. 8*d*. In earthenware pots bought 3*d*. In washing and shearing wethers, ewes and lambs 1*s*. 2*d*. In stipend of 1 shepherd for the year 4*s*. In stipend of 1 attendant making the pottage of the manorial servants, going to the harrowing, and keeping the birds away from the curia and the corn 2*s*. Total, 14*s*. 2½*d*.

Threshing
In threshing and winnowing 91 qrs 3½ bus. of wheat, 10 qrs 5 bus. of curall, 14½ qrs of peas and 19 qrs 2 bus. of vetches by piece-work by struck measure £1 4*s*. 10¾*d*., at

2¾*d*. a quarter of 10 struck bushels. In threshing 38½ qrs 2½ bus. of barley, and threshing and winnowing 8 qrs 1½ bus. of dredge by struck measure, 5*s*. 5½*d*., at 1¾*d*. a quarter of 10 struck bushels. In threshing and winnowing 83 qrs of oats by piece-work 4*s*. 10¼*d*., at ¾*d*. per 10 struck bushels, and ¼*d*. per 20 bushels winnowed. Total, £1 15*s*. 2½*d*.

Harvest-time

In mowing, spreading and tossing the meadows 5*s*. In weeding all the corn 5*s*. In reaping and binding 89 acres of wheat, 16 acres of barley, 5 acres of dredge and 59 acres of oats measured by the perch by piece-work, £4 4*s*. 6*d*., at 6*d*. an acre. In mowing 20 acres of peas and 19 acres of vetches measured by the perch by piece-work, 13*s*., at 4*d*. an acre. In turning and collecting the said peas and vetches 2*s*. 6*d*. In stipend of 1 reap-reeve 2*s*. In stipend of 2 stackers 6*s*. In hiring 1 carter to carry the corn for 14 days 7*s*. In ale, meat, herrings and cheese bought for 1 hayward, reap-reeve and 2 stackers, for 4 weeks at harvest-time, 5*s*. 6*d*. Total, £6 10*s*. 6*d*.

Costs of buildings

In re-roofing in places the buildings within the curia 2*s*. 10*d*. In 2,000 large slates bought for the same 2*s*. 8*d*. In 2 qrs of lime bought 1*s*. In pegs bought 2*d*. In 2 casks bought for putting cider in and hooping the same 5*s*. 4*d*. In making 2 casks of cider 10*d*. In 7 pigs bought 10*s*. 6*d*., at 1*s*. 6*d*. each. In 8 piglets bought 8*s*. In 7 piglets bought 4*s*. 8*d*., at 8*d*. each. Total, £1 16*s*.

Paid at the bishop's court at Fareham for the rent of the land of Harpe 3*d*. Also paid at the aforesaid court for the aforesaid rent from the previous year 3*d*. Also paid there for 1 lb of pepper for this year and for another pound of pepper from the previous year for a rent 2*d*. Paid to the collectors of the fifteenth for the manor of Cams 16*s*. 10*d*. Given to the same collectors for a gratuity 5*s*. Total, £1 2*s*. 6*d*.

Total of all expenses, £15 12*s*. 8*d*.

And he owes, £20 4*s*. 4¼*d*.

Cash deliveries

Delivered to Sir G*eoffrey*, treasurer of Wolvesey, by 1 tally, £16.

And thus he owes clear, £4 4*s*. 4¼*d*.

Issues of the grange

Wheat

{yield: three-fold plus 6 qrs ½ bus.}

The same renders account for 91 qrs 3½ bus. from the whole issue of wheat by struck measure; 2 qrs 2 bus. bought. Total, 93½ qrs 1½ bus.

Sown over 89 acres measured by the perch which lie at Alnetum, Vinecrofte, in burgages, in crofts outside the gate, in Estfeld' in various places, and on Brondesbury, 33 qrs 2 bus.; that is, 3 bus. an acre, less 1 bus. in all. Delivered to 1 hayward from the Purification (2 Febraury) until Lammas (1 August) and from the decollation of St John the Baptist (29 August) until Michaelmas (29 September), for 30 weeks, 1½ qrs 3 bus., because in between times he was at table for 4 weeks, and because he took the rest in barley, taking a quarter every 8 weeks. Consumed by the household at harvest-time, 1 qr. Sold, 57½ qrs ½ bus.

Curall

The same renders account for 10 qrs 5 bus. from the whole issue of curall by struck measure. Sold, 10 qrs 5 bus.

Barley

{yield: two-and-a-half-fold less 3 qrs 3 bus.}

The same renders account for 38½ qrs 2½ bus. of barley by struck measure; 6 qrs received from vetches. Total, 44 qrs 6½ bus.

Sown over 16 acres measured by the perch as they lie in Estfeld' in various places, 9½ qrs 3 bus.; that is, 5 bus. an acre, less 1 bus. in all. Delivered to 1 hayward from the Purification until Lammas and from the decollation of St John until Michaelmas, for 30 weeks, 1½ qrs 3 bus., because in between times he was at table for 4 weeks, taking a quarter every 8 weeks and taking the rest in wheat. **{Henceforth the harrower should not have so great a livery because he is overseer of the harvest and carter there}** Delivered to 1 carter for the year, 5 qrs 1½ bus., and taking a quarter every 10 weeks. Delivered to 2 drovers for the year, 8 qrs 5 bus., and taking a quarter every 12 weeks. Delivered to 1 ploughman from Michaelmas until Easter, for 30 weeks, 2½ qrs, and taking a quarter every 12 weeks. Delivered to 1 shepherd for the year, 4 qrs 2½ bus., and taking as before. Delivered to 1 attendant making the pottage of the manorial servants, going to the harrowing, and keeping the birds away from the curia and the corn for the year, 3 qrs 2 bus., and taking a quarter every 16 weeks. Consumed by the household at harvest-time, 3 bus. Sold, 8½ qrs 2½ bus.

Dredge

{yield: 5-fold plus ½ qr}

The same renders account for 8 qrs 1½ bus. from the whole issue of dredge by struck measure.

Sown over 5 acres measured by the perch which lie in Annerescrofte and in Westfeld', 3 qrs 2 bus.; that is, 5 bus. an acre, plus 1 bus. in all. Sold, 4½ qrs 3½ bus.

Oats

{yield: two-fold less 1 qr 1 bus.}

The same renders account for 83 qrs from the whole issue of oats by struck measure; 10½ qrs 2 bus. by estimation in sheaves given to oxen. Total, 93 qrs 7 bus.

Sown over 59 acres measured by the perch which lie at Alnetu*m*, in 3 crofts beside the garden, in Westfeud' in various places, and in Lambh*a*m, 40 qrs 7 bus.; that is, 5½ bus. an acre, less 2½ bus. in all. In fodder of 3 cart-horses for the year, 11½ qrs. Given to oxen by estimation in sheaves, 10½ qrs 2 bus. Sold, 30½ qrs 2 bus.

Peas

{yield: two-fold plus 1½ qrs}

The same renders account for 14½ qrs from the whole issue of peas by struck measure.

Sown over 20 acres measured by the perch which lie in la Westfeud' and la Estfeld' in various places, 7 qrs 3 bus.; that is, 3 bus. an acre, less ½ bus. in all. Sold, 7 qrs ½ bus.

Vetches

{yield: two-and-a-half-fold plus 4 bus.}

The same renders account for 19 qrs 2 bus. from the whole issue of vetches by struck measure.

Sown over 19 acres measured by the perch which lie in la Westfeld' and Estfeld' in various places, 9½ qrs; that is, ½ qr an acre. Mixed above with barley for the liveries of the manorial servants, 6 qrs. Sold, 3 qrs 6 bus.

m.32d

Stock

Cart-horses: 4 remain from the previous year; 1 sold; 3 remain.
Plough-horses: 2 remain from the previous year; 2 sold; none remain.
Oxen: 20 remain from the previous year; 20 remain.
Wethers: 86 remain from the previous year; 33 added from the stock of hoggs. Total, 119. 14 sold at Martinmas; 105 remain.
Ewes: 71 remain from the previous year; 25 additions; 1 bought before breeding. Total, 97. 8 sold at Martinmas; 4 in murrain before breeding and shearing, 1 after breeding and shearing; 84 remain.
Hoggs: 58 remain from the previous year's lambs; 33 added to wethers, 25 to ewes; none remain.
Lambs: 58 from the offspring of the said ewes because 2 were sterile. 4 in murrain before weaning, 1 after weaning and shearing; 5 in tithe. Total, 10. 48 remain.
Pigs: 8 remain from the previous year, 1 of them a sow; all sold since the feast of St Andrew (30 November).
Young pigs: 8 remain from the previous year; all sold at the aforesaid feast.
Piglets: 6 remain from the previous year; all sold since the aforesaid feast.
Also pigs: 7 pigs, 8 young pigs and 8 piglets bought in preparation for harvest-time; all sold.
Coarse wool {yield of fleece 3¼*d.*}: 190 fleeces produced at the shearing this year; 19 in tithe; 171 sent to Wolvesey, which made 2 weys and 3 cloves with the wool of Fareham.
Lamb's-wool {yield of fleece 1¾*d.* plus 6¼*d.*}: 49 fleeces produced at the shearing this year, which made 4 cloves.
Summer cheese {yield of sheep 2*d.* plus 1½*d.* in all}: 166 cheeses made between Thursday before the feast of St George (19 April) and Michaelmas (29 September), both days included; 16 in tithe; 150 sold, which made 1 wey and 1 clove.
Butter: 2 cloves 5 lb made this year; all sold.
Hides: none.
Woolskins and bare skins: 4 from ewes in murrain before shearing and 1 from a ewe in murrain after shearing; sold.
Lambskins: 4 from lambs in murrain before weaning and shearing and 1 from a lamb in murrain after weaning and shearing; all sold.
Cider: 2 casks produced from the issue of the garden this year; 2 casks remain.
Utensils: 4 ploughs remain from the previous year; 2 ploughs made this year; 2 coulters, 3 ploughshares, 1 cart with iron tyres, 2 cart-bodies, 2 tripods, 1 axe and 2 ropes remain from the previous year; all remains here apart from 2 ploughs which are worn out.

Account of the Bishopric of Winchester for the twenty-first year of the consecration of the lord bishop John[1]

1 Written at the foot of the membrane to serve as a label when the pipe roll was rolled up.

Glossary

The purpose of this glossary is twofold. Firstly, it seeks to define terms which may be unfamiliar to the reader. Secondly, it provides an extended form of the Latin most commonly used in the pipe roll, to serve as a brief guide to the language of the roll. The footnotes indicate works in which a more detailed explanation of a particular term may be found. Where references are not given further explanatory material can often be found in the *OED*.

acre as it lies (*acra sicut jacet*): customary acre, usually smaller than the standard acre but varying in size from manor to manor.[1]

acre by the perch (*acra per perticam*): standard acre.

afforcement (*affortiare*): the reinforcement of a jury by the addition of new members.

to agist (*agistare*): to take in livestock to feed on the demesne at a set price per head.

almoner (*elemosinarius*): official distributor of alms.

annual recognizance (*annua recognitio*): payment made by an unfree male tenant who wished to live outside the manor but who did not wish, or possess the resources, to buy his full freedom.[2]

antiphoner (*antiphonarius*): a book of anthems.

to arraign (*arrationare*): to accuse.

assart (*assarta*): piece of forest land converted into arable by grubbing up the trees and brushwood.

assize (*assisa*): judicial inquest; ordinances of King John and Henry III regulating the weight and price of bread and ale and forbidding the harbouring of strangers.

to attach (*attachiare*): to arrest; to tether.

attendant (*garcio*): often translated as 'boy' or 'lad' or 'groom', etymologically *garcio* implies a man, either young or old, of low status. The pipe roll reveals *garciones* performing a wide range of subordinate duties and has been translated as 'attendant' in all cases apart from those in which the *garcio* served as a workman's 'mate'. On the Taunton manors *garcio* also denoted a **landless man**.[3]

barton (*bertona*): a farm-yard.

bartoner (*bertonarius*): manorial official; duties included supervision of the harvest and haymaking.

1 For the problem of acres on the Winchester estate and conversion tables from customary to standard acres, see Titow, 'Land and Population', pp. 145-64. See also above, p. xiv.

2 Gras and Gras, *Economic and Social History of an English Village*, p. 93.

3 H. S. A. Fox, 'Exploitation of the landless by lords and tenants in early medieval England', in *Medieval Society and the Manor Court*, ed. Z. Razi and R. M. Smith (Oxford, forthcoming).

basnet (*bacinettus*): a basin-shaped helmet.

bast (*bastum*): flexible fibrous bark used to make rope.

beadle (*bedellus*): under-bailiff; duties included supervision of the harvest, ploughing and sowing, and the collection of customary dues.

bench (*banco*): court of Common Pleas, for hearing civil litigation which did not directly involve the crown, such as actions relating to the ownership of land and actions of debt.[1]

bere (*bere*): mixed wheat and winter barley; possibly synonymous with winter barley.[2]

billhook (*bilhok*): a heavy curved knife, used for cutting branches or trimming hedges.[3]

boon-work (*precaria*): additional to customary labour service, demanded whenever necessary to complete the ploughing of the demesne, or the reaping of the corn.

brewgable (*brugabulum*): customary rent due from specific tenements in the city and **soke** of Winchester.[4]

broom (*genecta*): shrub bearing large yellow flowers, it could be used as litter for animals.[5]

bullock (*boviculus*): ox in second or third year, either male or female.

burel (*burellus*): a coarse woollen cloth.

burgage (*burgagium*): area within which borough custom applied; a property held by burgage tenure.

bushel (*bussellus*): dry measure, usually of four **pecks** or eight gallons (36 litres), although at Fareham it was recorded that six pecks made a **struck** bushel.[6]

butt (*boticium*): small, irregular piece of arable land, probably not more than quarter of an acre in size.

byre (*bovarium*): a shed for farm animals.

cablish (*gablicium*): trees or branches blown down by the wind.

capon (*capo*): a castrated cock, used in payment of rents and **recognizances**.

cart (*carrettus*): horse-hauled vehicle, invariably two-wheeled but varying in size.[7]

cart-rail (*scala*): extension fitted to a cart at either the front or the back to increase loading capacity.[8]

chamberlain (*camerarius*): an official of the bishop's household; the chamber may have acted as the bishop's privy purse.[9]

chancery (*cancelleria*): court which heard cases where there was no remedy at common law or which raised special difficulties.[10]

cheese (*caseus*): the production of cheese corresponded with the cycle of milk production. Usually cheeses were made after Michaelmas at the rate of one every

1 A. L. Brown, *The Governance of Late Medieval England 1272-1461* (London, 1989), p. 130.

2 Above, pp. 312-15.

3 J. Langdon, 'Agricultural equipment', in *The Countryside of Medieval England*, ed. G. Astill and A. Grant (Oxford, 1988), pp. 97, 101.

4 Keene, *Survey of Medieval Winchester*, i, p. 185.

5 C. Dyer, 'Documentary evidence: problems and enquiries', in *The Countryside of Medieval England*, ed. Astill and Grant, p. 24.

6 Above, p. 228.

7 Langdon, 'Agricultural equipment', pp. 91-4.

8 Langdon, 'Agricultural equipment', pp. 93-4.

9 Swift, 'Machinery of Manorial Administration', pp. 76-86.

10 Brown, *Governance of Late Medieval England*, p. 133.

other day, but as the milk supply ceased the last few were made at longer intervals, from 'accumulated milk'. Cheese-making began again in April or May, usually at the rate of one a day.[1]

chirograph (*chirographum*): indenture drawn up in duplicate on a single piece of parchment which was then cut, the two halves being taken by the two parties involved.

churchscot (*cherssecto*): contribution demanded for the support of the clergy, usually paid at Martinmas.

clamp (*gropa*): band of iron securing the **strake** of a cart to the **felloe**.

clapper (*clacta*): contrivance in a mill for striking or shaking the hopper so as to make the grain move down to the millstones.

clout (*clutum*): plate of iron fixed to the axle-tree or other part of a cart to prevent wear.

clove (*clavus*): weight used for wool and cheese, 7 lb (3.15 kilogrammes).[2]

coarse-ground corn (*grutum*): possibly a form of high quality malt, perhaps equivalent to **first-grade malt**.[3]

coarse wool (*lana grossa*): wool of all sheep other than lambs.

colt (*pullanus*): young horse to the age of four.

concealment (*concelamentum*): usually a fine for concealing the fact that a man was not a member of a **tithing**.

copperas (*cuprosa*): protosulphate of iron, used as a medicine against sheep scab.

corrody (*corredium*): allowance or provision for maintenance.

cotland (*cotlonda*): a small piece of land, probably with a dwelling-place attached.

cottage (*cotagium*, or *cotellum*): the dwelling-place of a tenant with a piece of land attached.

cottar (*cotarius*): small-holding unfree tenant, often with less than five acres of land.

coulter (*cultura*): iron blade fixed in front of the **ploughshare**; it makes a vertical cut in the soil, which is then sliced horizontally by the share.

cratch (*crecha*): a rack or manger to hold fodder for sheep; a crib.

croft (*crofta*): a small piece of arable land adjacent to a house; a piece of unenclosed ground for tillage or pasture.[4]

cruck (*furca*): one of a pair of curved timbers, forming with other pairs the framework of a building. The Latin *furca* could also signify a straight post, so that the translation is not entirely certain.[5]

crupper (*croparium*): strap buckled to the back of the saddle and passing under the horse's tail, to prevent the saddle from slipping forwards. See also **girth**.

cuisse (*quissera*): armour for protecting the front part of the thigh.

cumin (*cyminum*): plant resembling fennel, used in payment of rents and **recognizances**.

curall (*curallum*): the poorer part of wheat, separated after **threshing** and **winnowing**.[6]

curia (*curia*): central complex of manorial buildings, usually surrounded by a wall.

1 *Accounts and Surveys of the Wiltshire Lands of Adam de Stratton*, ed. M. W. Farr (Wiltshire Archaeological and Natural History Soc., 14, 1959), p. xxxv; above, pp. 20-1, 53, 217.

2 Above, pp. 159, 167-8, 341.

3 See index for entries and compare with prices for first-grade and second-grade malt.

4 Above, pp. 48, 193, 366.

5 L. F. Salzman, *Building in England* (Oxford, 1952), pp. 195-7.

6 Harvey, *Medieval Oxfordshire Village*, pp. 46-7.

curtilage (*curtillagium*): piece of ground attached to a dwelling-house, perhaps about half an acre in size.[1]

customary tenant (*custumarius*): free or unfree tenant holding land according to the customs of the manor.

day-work (*daena*, or *daywork*): measure of land, the amount that could be worked in one day.

defaults of rent (*defectus*): uncollected rent from land which was vacant or had been taken back into demesne; these were recorded year after year, often for centuries on end, and so do not usually refer to the year of the roll in which they appear.

dovecote (*columbarium*): a house for pigeons.

dowel (*douellum*): headless peg of wood or iron used to fasten together two pieces of wood.

to draw into demesne (*trahere in dominicum*): to take land previously leased back into direct management; most common at the beginning of the thirteenth century.

dredge (*dragettum*): mixed barley and oats.

dung-cart: appears in Latin as *scenevector'*, *caretto ad fimos*, *caretto pro fimis*, or as *carm'*. The latter, found on a number of the Taunton manors, is probably a dung-cart although the translation is not certain. However, in 1299-1300 at Staplegrove the reeve recorded *ij carm' ad fym' ax' ij d*. See also **tumbrel**.

ell (*ulna*): measure of length for canvas and cloth, probably 45 inches (1.1 metre).

entry fine (*finis*): paid to the bishop by the incoming tenant of a piece of land on the death or withdrawal of the outgoing tenant.

escheat (*escaeta*): land which reverted to the lord on the death of a tenant without an heir.

estreat (*extractus*): extract or copy of a record, especially relating to fines.

eyre (*itineratio*): visit of royal justices to a locality, at which a wide range of administrative and judicial business was investigated and determined.

farm (*firma*): annual rent for demesne land or resource leased out by the lord.

felloe (*felea*): exterior rim of a wheel, supported by the spokes; in *pl.* the curved pieces of wood which, joined together, form the circular rim of a wheel.

ferling (*ferlingus*): a quarter of an acre.

fifteenth (*quintadecima*): tax of one-fifteenth imposed on personal property; granted by parliament to Edward I in January 1301.

first-grade malt (*brasium capitale*): superior malt made from wheat.

fish-trap (*hiltra*): wooden structure with floodgates and hatches used to catch salmon at Bitterne and apparently unique to Hampshire.[2]

to fit with iron (*ferrare*): hand tools such as spades and forks were made of wood and fitted with iron 'shoes' to protect them from wearing out.[3]

fodder-rack (*rastellus*): a frame made with upright bars of wood to hold food for cattle, horses and sheep, either fixed in a stable or movable.

fotmal (*fotmellum*): weight used for lead, about 70 lb (31.5 kilogrammes).

fret (*fretta*): the iron or wooden hoop about the **hub** of a wheel.

fulling mill (*molendinum fullatorium*): mill used to wash and beat cloth after it has been woven in order to make the weave denser and tighter.[4]

1 Above, p. 237.

2 E. Roberts, 'The salmon fishery at Woodmill near Southampton', *Hampshire Field Club and Archaelogical Soc. Local History Newsletter*, new ser., 21 (1994), pp. 32-3; *DMLBS*, iv, p. 1158.

3 Langdon, 'Agricultural equipment', pp. 97-8.

4 R. Holt, *The Mills of Medieval England* (Oxford, 1988), pp. 152-3.

fur (*furra*): the trimming or lining of a robe granted to the lord's more important officials.
furlong (*quarentena*): measure of land, usually 40 **perches** in length (200 metres).
gavel (*gablum*): form of rent for land.
to geld (*emasculare*): to castrate.
gimmer (*gercia*): a young ewe.
girth (*cingulum*): band of leather drawn round the body of a horse to secure the saddle. See also **crupper**.
to glean (*glanare*): to gather up ears of corn which have been left by the reapers.
gorget (*gorgeria*): armour for protecting the throat.
gradual (*gradalis*): a book of antiphons sung at the altar steps.
granger (*berebretus*): manorial official; duties included supervision of the harvest and **threshing**.
grease (*unctum*): the melted fat of animals, used both as a sheep-salve and as a lubricant.
greave (*jambyrs*): armour for the leg below the knee.
green wax (*viridis cera*): the bishop of Winchester was entitled to collect those fines which the king's justices imposed on his men. 'Green wax' refers to the **estreats** of the justices' rolls in which the fines of those who lived within the bishop's liberties were listed.[1]
grip (*gripa*): a small open furrow or ditch for carrying off water.
gudgeon (*gojonus*): an iron pivot fixed into the end of a beam or on a gate, to provide a fulcrum on which something turns.
hame (*hama*): each of two curved pieces of wood fastened to or forming the collar of a draught horse.
harrow (*hercia*): a rectangular frame of timber set with iron teeth, usually horse-hauled, used to break clods and stir the soil of ploughed land, or to cover in the seed.
hauberk (*lorica*): armour of chain mail in the shape of a tunic to protect the body.
hayward (*haiwardus*): manorial official; duties included supervision of the **curia**, ploughland, pastures and woods.
heifer (*juvencellus*): a young cow that has not had a calf.
heriot (*herietum*): render of the best live beast or chattel of a deceased tenant due by legal custom to the lord of whom he held. By the early fourteenth century some heriots paid in cash were for *inter vivos* land transfers, that is, while both parties were still alive. Heriots do not, therefore, always indicate mortality.[2]
herring (*allecium*): preserved fish given to the **boon-workers** at harvest-time.
hockday (*hockdies*): second Tuesday after Easter; the day when one of the bishop's bi-annual **tourns** was held and when some rents and customary dues were paid. Hockday and Michaelmas divided the year into its summer and winter halves.
hogg (*hoggus*): young sheep in second year, either male or female.
hogget (*hogaster*): young pig of first or second year, either male or female.
hub (*modius*): the central block of a wheel into which the end of the axle-tree is inserted and from which the spokes radiate.
hue (*hutesium*): outcry calling for the pursuit of a felon raised by the party aggrieved.
hundred-court (*hundredum*): bi-annual **tourn** usually presided over by the sheriff, but in those hundreds controlled by the bishop, by his steward.

1 Swift, 'Machinery of Manorial Administration', pp. 108-13.

2 H. S. A. Fox and C. Thornton, 'Arable productivity and peasant holdings at Taunton, 1209-1348' (unpublished ESRC research project no. B0023 2203), p. 11.

hundredpenny (*hundredpany*): annual due payable by all those over twelve on the Taunton manors. On other manors **tithingpenny** was paid.[1]

hurdle (*clata*): a portable rectangular frame, having horizontal bars interwoven or wattled with **withies**; used to form temporary fences and **sheepfolds**.

hurter (*hurtarium*): iron plate to protect the axle of a cart. See also **tack**.

increment of the granary (*incremento granarii*): the amount of grain charged to the reeve when measures were heaped rather than **struck** after threshing.[2]**inquest** (*inquisitio*): a judicial inquiry.

kebb (*kebba*): animal in poor condition put out to graze to improve its condition; sheep 'culled' or rejected from the flock.[3]

kimnel (*cumelinus*): a tub, possibly used for kneading or salting meat.

landless man (*garcio*): used only on the Taunton manors to denote a man without land.[4]

landright (*landriht*, or *landrych*): special ploughing service.[5]

larder (*lardarium*): meat store.

lath (*lata*): a thin narrow strip of wood used to form a groundwork upon which to fasten the slates or tiles of a roof or the plaster of a wall or ceiling.

law-day (*lagheday*): the day on which the **hundred-court** was held.

ledge (*lurlegga*): a band of iron for cart-wheels.

legendary (*legendarius*): a book of legends, especially of saints' lives.

lime (*calcetum*): mixed with sand to produce mortar, with which buildings were pointed.[6]

linen and woollen cloth (*linea tela et laneo panno*): cloth used to wrap cheese and strain milk during cheese-making.

livery (*liberatio*): provision of food granted to **manorial servants** in return for service.

louver (*lovarium*): domed structure on the roof of a building to serve as a smoke-vent and for the admission of light.

mancorn (*mancorn*): mixed rye and winter barley, found only on the Berkshire and Buckinghamshire manors in 1301-2.

manorial servants (*familia*): tenants appointed to fulfil the various offices necessary for the running of the demesne—reeve, **beadle**, **hayward**, shepherd and so on. In return they were remitted a part of their rent and granted **liveries** of grain and stock.

marl (*marla*): a kind of soil consisting principally of clay mixed with carbonate of lime, used as a fertilizer.

marriage fine (*maritagium*): paid when an unfree female tenant of the bishop was married.[7]

marshal (*marescallus*): a keeper of horses; an officer of a court of law answerable for the charge and custody of prisoners, and frequently entrusted with the keeping of a prison.

1 *Medieval Customs of Taunton*, pp. xxxix-xl.

2 Harvey, *Medieval Oxfordshire Village*, pp. 53-6.

3 Titow, *English Rural Society*, p. 117; *Ministers' Accounts of the Manor of Petworth 1347-1353*, ed. L. F. Salzman (Sussex Record Soc., 55, 1955), p. 94.

4 Fox, 'Exploitation of the landless by lords and tenants'.

5 *Medieval Customs of Taunton*, p. liii.

6 Salzman, *Building in England*, pp. 149-52.

7 Above, p. xxiv.

maslin (*mixtura*): mixed wheat and rye.

mast (*pessona*): collective name for the fruit of the beech, oak, chestnut, and other forest trees, used as food for swine.

mattock (*matokkus*): tool used for preparing the ground for sowing.[1]

meal (*farina*, *farina avene*, or *gruellum*): edible part of a grain ground to a powder, especially oatmeal.

messuage (*mesuagium*): portion of land occupied by a dwelling-house and its appurtenances.

mill bill (*billa*): steel adze used for dressing and cracking millstones.

mill-rind (*inka*): iron fitting to support the millstone on the spindle.[2]

missal (*missale*): a mass-book.

mortrel (*mortereles*): a kind of milk soup.

moss (*mossa*): used as a bedding for tiles, to prevent the wind and wet from penetrating between them.

mould (*forma*): wooden cast for cheese.

mowers' sheep (*medsscepe*): payment of grain and cheese on the Oxfordshire manors in lieu of the sheep which the mowers were accustomed to receive.[3]

multure (*tolcorn*): corn retained by the miller as a payment for grinding; a fine for not having ground at the lord's mill.

murder-fine (*murdrum*): fine imposed on a hundred or vill in which a murder had been committed.

murrain (*morina*): unspecific livestock disease; accidental death. Contemporaries lacked a sophisticated means of classifying animal diseases, so that all outbreaks were described as murrain.

oatmeal, *see* **meal**.

oriel (*oriolum*): an antechamber.

overseer of the harvest (*messor*): the leading hand during reaping; his duties also included supervision of the fields, meadows and pastures.

ox-bow (*bogum*): the bow-shaped piece of wood which forms a collar for a yoked ox and has its upper end fastened to the yoke.

palfrey (*palefridus*): a riding-horse.

palisade (*palistrum*): a fence made of stakes fixed in the ground.

pannage (*pannagium*): payment made to the lord for the feeding of swine in a wood.

pavilion (*papillo*): the bishop's court at St Giles's Fair.

pease pottage (*legumin*): **pottage** which contained peas, beans and vetches.

peck (*peccum*): dry measure containing two gallons (9 litres). See also **bushel**.

perch (*pertica*): measure of land, usually 16½ feet (5 metres).

Peter's pence (*denarius Sancti Petri*): annual tax of a penny from each householder having land of a certain value paid to the papal see at Rome.

piece-work (*ad tascham*): hired labour, paid according to the amount of work done.

pillory (*pilloria*): an instrument of punishment, similar to the stocks.

pinfold (*potfalda*): movable pen used to confine livestock in order to manure the land; tenants' animals were often used to manure the lord's land.

pipe (*pipa*): a receptacle for cider, apparently half the size of a cask; possibly contained about 120 gallons (545.5 litres).[4]

1 Langdon, 'Agricultural equipment', pp. 96, 98.

2 Holt, *Mills of Medieval England*, pp. 118, 123-4.

3 H. S. Bennett, *Life on the English Manor 1150-1400* (Cambridge, 1938), p. 111.

4 Above, pp. 181, 303.

pitch (*pice*): resinous substance obtained from the boiling of tar, in the molten state it was used to solder joints and as a substitute for mortar where masonry was particularly exposed to wet.

plank (*planca*): thick oak boards, to be distinguished from the thinner *borda*.

to pledge (*plegere*): to guarantee a person's future good behaviour or specific action.

plough foot (*ferrum pedale*, or *pedale*): in a wheelless plough, an adjustable piece of wood or iron attached to the front of the beam, regulating the depth of the ploughing.[1]

plough-iron (*longum ferrum*): a plate to protect the bottom of the plough.

ploughshare (*vomer*): the large pointed blade, which, following the **coulter**, cuts a slice of earth and passes it on to the mould-board.

plumber (*plumbarius*): a worker of lead.

poke (*poka*): a small sack.

posnet (*pocinettus*): a small metal pot for boiling, having a handle and three feet.

pottage (*potagium*): porridge made from **oatmeal**; **pease pottage** also included pulses.

press (*pressura*): apparatus for pressing the curds in cheese-making or extracting the juice of apples in cider-making.

purpresture (*purprestura*): an encroachment of varying size upon common or demesne land.[2]

to purvey (*providere*): to requisition provisions and horses for the king's use at a price set by the purveyor.

quarter (*quarterium*): dry measure usually containing eight **bushels** (290 litres), but occasionally ten.[3]

quittance (*aquietantia*): a reduction in the rent paid by a tenant who was serving as one of the **manorial servants**.

reap-reeve (*riperevus*): supervisor of the reapers and fields at harvest-time, apparently distinct from the **overseer of the harvest**.[4]

recognizance, *see* **annual recognizance**.

recovery and custody (*warda et forfengium*): reward for rescuing stolen cattle.

refusal to stack (*tasso refutato*): payment in lieu of the obligation to purchase a quantity of the bishop's corn.[5]

to regrate (*regratare*): to buy up victuals in order to sell again at a profit in the same or a neighbouring market.

relict (*relicta*): the widow of a man.

relief (*relevium*): payment made to the lord by the heir of a tenant on taking up possession of the vacant land.

relish (*companagium*): food eaten with bread, usually cheese or **herrings**.

rents of assize (*redditus assissus*): fixed annual money rent, usually paid quarterly, based on the size of the tenant's holding. The rate per **virgate** varied from manor to manor.[6]

to ret (*rodire*): to soak flax or hemp in water in order to soften or season.

1 Langdon, 'Agricultural equipment', p. 89.

2 For examples, see above, pp. 219, 285.

3 Above, pp. 50, 66, 365.

4 Above, pp. 220-1.

5 Titow, *English Rural Society*, pp. 109, 119.

6 Above, p. xxiii.

riddle (*ridellus*): a coarse-meshed **sieve**, used for separating chaff from corn; usually a circular wooden rim with a bottom formed of strong wires crossing each other at right-angles.[1]

rider (*equitator*): employed on certain manors at harvest-time, possibly in a supervisory capacity.

rood (*roda*): measure of land, usually quarter of an acre.

rotted sheep (*rottus*): apparently synonymous with lambs which died after weaning and both before and after shearing.[2]

rowen (*rewaynum*, or *relucrum*): **cheese** made between Michaelmas and the end of November; the second crop of grass or hay in a season.

rundle (*rundellus*): a bar in a mill wheel.

sack (*sacca*): usually made of canvas, used to carry wool and grain; one sack probably contained about 30 stone (192 kilogrammes) of wool.

saddle-pad (*bacium*, or *bargium*): one of a pair of bags laid across the back of a horse behind the saddle.

sale at the audit (*vendicio super compotum*): a fictitious sale of corn or stock charged against the reeve, resulting from the auditors' disagreement with the reeve's claim.[3]

second-grade malt (*brasium cursale*): inferior malt made from barley or dredge.

seed-basket (*seminarium*): almost certainly synonymous with **seed-lip**.

seed-lip (*sedlopum*): wicker basket, sometimes kidney-shaped to fit the contour of the sower's body, from which seed was broadcast.[4]

seld (*selda*): the long rows containing many booths or windows, each let to an individual trader, at St Giles's Fair; elsewhere, a shop, although a more substantial property than that referred to by the Latin *shopa*.[5]

seldage (*seldagium*): rent paid for the hire of **selds**.

sergeant (*serviens*): somewhat inferior official to the bailiff in the manorial hierarchy, taking his place at Bitterne and Havant and the place of the reeve in the **soke** of Winchester; armed guard at St Giles's Fair.

sester (*sexterium*): measure of ale or salt, probably 17 gallons (77 litres).[6]

sheaf (*garba*): measure of grain, variable in size. Often sheaves were measured by the length of a man's limbs or by how much he could carry.[7]

sheepcote (*bercaria*): a permanent structure of timber on stone **sill** walls, usually with a thatched roof, and surrounded by a fence or wall, used to shelter the sheep in winter.

sheepfold (*falda*): a movable structure built with **hurdles**, occasionally with a corner roofed to shelter sheep or shepherd.

shingle (*scindula*): an oak tile, possibly the most expensive form of roof-covering.[8]

sieve (*cribrum*): distinguished from the **riddle** by having a finer mesh.

sill (*sulliva*): a strong horizontal timber serving as the foundation of a wall.

1 Langdon, 'Agricultural equipment', pp. 97, 101.

2 For examples, see above, pp. 86, 91, 250, 259, 261, 266.

3 Above, p. xv.

4 Langdon, 'Agricultural equipment', pp. 95, 99.

5 Keene, *Survey of Medieval Winchester*, i, p. 138.

6 Above, p. 95.

7 A. Jones, 'Harvest customs and labourers' perquisites in southern England, 1150-1350: the corn harvest', *Agricultural History Review* 25 (1977), pp. 14-22.

8 Salzman, *Building in England*, pp. 228-9.

small holding (*bordellum*): a dwelling-place with a small holding attached.
soke (*soka*): jurisdictional liberty created in the thirteenth century in those parts of the city of Winchester where the bishop and St Swithun's Priory were predominant landlords.[1]
spike-nail (*spiknaylum*): especially large nails needed to fasten the thicker **planks**.
spindle (*fusillus*): an iron rod serving as an axis upon which the millstone turned.
stall (*presepia*): division for the accommodation of one animal in a **byre** or cow-shed.
stall (*stallum*): covered stand for the sale of wares at a market.
stallage (*stallagium*): rent paid for the hire of **stalls** in a borough or market.
steer (*bovettus*): ox in third or fourth year, either male or female.
stick (*estika*): measure of quantity of eels, possibly 25 or 26.
stipend (*stipendium*): annual money payment made to manorial workers for service in lieu of daily wages.
stot-keeper (*stottehurd*): official in charge of plough-horses; only found on those manors which specifically employed horse-ploughs.
strake (*strakus*): a section of the iron rim of a cart-wheel.
stray (*estraura*, or *cumelingus*): the lord had the right to impound any animal found wandering on his land or which attached itself to a place of its own accord.
strip of ploughland (*cultura*): area of arable land within an open field, of variable size and quality, which interlocked with other strips in the field.
struck measure (*mensura rasa*): when the grain in the bushel measure was struck level, rather than being heaped, which increased the volume by a quarter, the difference being called the **increment**.
stubble (*stipula*): the remains of corn after reaping, sometimes used for thatching.
suit of court (*secta*): the obligation of a tenant to attend his lord's court.
surcingle (*supercingulum*): similar to a **girth**, to secure a pack on a horse's back.
surety (*vadium*): one who acts as a **pledge**.
swingletree (*paronus*): in a cart, a crossbar, attached at its ends to the horses' **traces** and at its centre to the cart.[2]
tack (*taccum*): iron plate to protect the axle of a cart. See also **hurter**.
talent (*talentum*): a gold coin of uncertain value.
tallow (*cepum*): substance consisting of a somewhat hard animal fat, used as a lubricant and for waterproofing.
tally (*tallia*): a stick of wood marked on one side with notches representing the amount of a debt or payment. The rod was split lengthwise across the notches, the debtor and creditor each retaining one of the halves.
talwood (*talwoda*): wood for fuel.
teasel (*cardo*): plant with prickly leaves and head, used to tease or dress cloth.
temporal (*temporale*): that part of the breviary and **missal** containing the daily offices in the order of the ecclesiastical year, as distinct from those proper for saints' days.
temse (*tamisium*): a **sieve** with a very fine mesh.
tenement (*tenementum*): a built-up property with some open ground attached.
thill-rope (*tilropt*): the rope by which the collar of a draught animal is connected with the cart-shaft.
to thresh (*triturare*): to separate the grain from the straw by beating with a flail.[3]

1 Keene, *Survey of Medieval Winchester*, i, pp. 72-4.

2 J. Langdon, *Horses, Oxen and Technological Innovation: the Use of Draught Animals in English Farming from 1066 to 1500* (Cambridge, 1986), pp. 12-13.

3 Langdon, 'Agricultural equipment', pp. 97, 100.

tie-beam (*copula*, or *lacchea*): a piece of timber, running the width of a building, to connect the rafters of the roof to the principal posts of the wall, in order to steady the structure; in a cart, possibly synonymous with the cart-shaft.

tine (*tina*): a tub or cask for use in the dairy or for carrying cider.

tithe (*decima*): tax of one-tenth levied by the church on harvests and animals for the support of the parish priest.

tithing (*decima*, or *tethinga*): the basic unit of manorial administration; by the thirteenth century both a geographical as well as a social entity, to which each inhabitant over the age of twelve belonged.

tithingpenny (*tethingpeny*): paid by each tithingman at the bi-annual **tourns** to free his tithing from universal attendance.

toll of a sester (*tolsester*): a duty of a **sester** of ale paid to the lord of the manor for the right to brew and sell ale.

tourn (*turnus*): the bi-annual **hundred-court** presided over by the bishop's steward.

trace (*tractio*): the pair of ropes by which the collar of a draught animal is connected with the **swingletree** or plough-beam.

transport-service (*averagium*): a service demanded of **customary tenants** on foot, or with pack-horse, cart, or boat, for the carriage of goods to market.[1]

trapper (*trappa*): a covering, made of metal or leather, put over a horse for the purpose of defence.

tron (*trona*): a weighing machine.

trundle-wheel (*trendellus*): wooden cog-wheel mounted at the inner end of a mill shaft which intermeshed with a lantern-pinion wheel on the vertical spindle that turned the stone.[2]

tumbrel (*tumbrellus*): a cart so constructed that the body tilted backwards to empty out the load, often used as a dung-cart; an instrument of punishment, possibly a cucking-stool.

turf (*turba*): a slab of peat dug for use as fuel; a sod of grass.

verdigris (*viridigresium*): green rust found naturally on copper which was used as a treatment for sheep scab.

verjuice (*viridis succus*): juice of unripe grapes, used in cooking, as a condiment, or for medicinal purposes.

vetch (*vesca*): the bean-like fruit of various species of leguminous plant.

view (*visus*): formal inspection or survey; view of frankpledge was the right of lords to hold private courts in the king's name dealing with the petty crime of their tenants.[3]

villein (*villanus*): unfree tenant, liable to perform labour services and to render such dues as **entry** and **marriage fines** and **heriots**. **Cottars** and virgaters were specific types of villein, and in practice the term is synonymous with unfree **customary tenant**. Villeinage was a hereditary condition.

virgate (*virgata*): measure of land, about 30 acres.

wagon (*carrus*): two-wheeled, ox-hauled vehicle with perhaps double the carrying capacity of a cart.[4]

wain (*plaustrum*): two-wheeled, ox-hauled vehicle, wider than a cart, with heavy solidly-built wheels; similar to the **wagon**.[5]

1 D. L. Farmer, 'Marketing the produce of the countryside, 1200-1500', *AHEW*, iii, pp. 347-50.

2 Holt, *Mills of Medieval England*, pp. 117-18.

3 Titow, *English Rural Society*, pp. 189-90.

4 Langdon, *Horses, Oxen and Technological Innovation*, pp. 152-3.

5 Langdon, *Horses, Oxen and Technological Innovation*, pp. 143, 150-1, 153.

wardrobe (*wardroba*): room attached to the bishop's chamber in which clothes and valuables were kept; a financial office, distributing funds for household expenditure.

warren (*warenna*): an enclosure in which the lord bred and hunted small game, especially rabbits.

wastel-bread (*wastellus*): bread made of the finest flour.

waterlete (*waterleta*): system of irrigation used to improve the pasture of fallow land on a number of the Taunton manors.[1]

water-pipe (*wymond'*): found only at Bitterne and possibly associated with the salmon fishery and **fish-trap** there.[2]

wether (*multo*): a castrated ram.

wey (*waya*): weight used for wool and cheese, 26 **cloves**.

white leather (*corium album*): used to make or mend harnesses; made by softening hides and steeping them in a solution of alum and salt.

wicket (*wikettus*): a small door or gate made in a larger one for use when the large one is closed.

windlass (*windasius*): a mechanical contrivance used for hauling.

to winnow (*ventare*, or *vannare*): to expose grain to the wind so that the chaff is separated from the corn.

winnowing-fan (*ventorium*): a contrivance used to create a breeze for winnowing.[3]

withy (*virga*): a flexible branch of the willow, used for tying or binding and wattling.

wooden halter (*lanna*): probably used in conjunction with the **yoke** as a means of coupling animals together.

woodward (*wodwardus*): official in charge of the woodlands.[4]

woodway (*wodweya*): fixed customary due payable on the Taunton manors.[5]

wool locks (*lana fracta*): clippings left over at the shearing.

yoke (*jugum*): a contrivance by which two oxen are coupled together for drawing a plough; usually consisting of a somewhat curved piece of wood fitted with hoops or **ox-bows** at the ends which are passed round the animals' necks, and having a ring or hook attached to the middle to which is fastened a **trace** extending backward by which the plough is drawn.

1 *Medieval Customs of Taunton*, pp. xxxiii-xxxiv.

2 M. Page, 'The Bitterne "Wymond"', *Hampshire Field Club and Archaeological Soc. Local History Newsletter*, new ser., 24 (1995), pp. 22-3.

3 Langdon, 'Agricultural equipment', p. 101.

4 *Medieval Customs of Taunton*, p. xxvi.

5 The amounts paid in 1301-2 were the same, for example, in 1291-2 and 1311-12: HRO 11M59/B1/51, 67.

Index

HAMPSHIRE RECORD SERIES

SUBSCRIBERS

Subscribers to the Hampshire Record Series do not pay a regular subscription but undertake to buy each book, at a reduced price, when it appears. They are also able to buy earlier volumes at reduced prices. Further details of Hampshire Record Series volumes are available from Hampshire Record Office, Sussex Street, Winchester, Hants SO23 8TH (tel. 01962 846154).

Personal subscribers

Mrs B. Acheson, 19 Dell Road, Bitterne Park, Southampton, Hants, SO2 4QT
Mrs E. Albery, PO Box 71, Penguin, Tasmania, 7316
Miss P. M. Andrews, 45 Hillmead Gardens, Bedhampton, Havant, Hants, PO9 3NN
Mr A. E. Baker, Close Court, The Close, Ringwood, Hants, BH24 1LA
Mr J. T. Balch, 7 Sawyer Crescent, Copmanthorpe, York, YO23 3YA
Mrs D. B. Beckel, 3884 Lewister Road, North Vancouver, BC, Canada, V7R 4C3
Mrs C. Bethune, All Saints Cottage, Queens Road, Alton, Hants, GU34 1HU
Professor M. Biddle, Hertford College, Oxford, OX1 3BW
Mrs S. Bond, 6 Hyde Close, Winchester, Hants, SO23 7TD
Mr J. W. M. Brown, 294 Spring Road, Sholing, Southampton, Hants, SO2 7NX
Mr C. D. Chalmers, 24 Waldens Park Road, Horsell, Woking, Surrey
Mr G. W. Clewer, 5 Mann Close, Whitchurch, Hants, RG28 7LB
Mrs D. K. Coldicott, Mill Pound Cottage, Monxton, Andover, Hants, SP11 8AW
Dr S. J. J. Corcoran, 30 Knowsley Road, Cosham, Portsmouth, Hants, PO6 2PF
Mr C. N. Cornes, 80 Coombe Road, Croydon, Surrey, CR0 5RA
Mr E. G. Crockford, 2 Garden Cottage, Cheriton, Alresford, Hants, SO24 0PT
Mr A. L. T. Davies, Albany Cottage, West Street, Odiham, Hants
Mr C. H. Donnithorne, 3 The Avenue, Alverstoke, Gosport, Hants, PO12 2JS
Mr M. Drummond, Cadland House, Fawley, Southampton, Hants, SO4 1AA
Mr S. R. Dumper, 5 Elder Grove, Crediton, Devon, EX17 1DE
Mr S. Dunford, 140 Crabble Hill, Dover, Kent, CT17 0SA
Mrs J. Hagens, 7 Leybourne Dell, Benenden, Cranbrook, Kent, TN17 4EA
Mr R. H. Hall, Flat 1, Gannet House, 5 Eastern Parade, Southsea, Hants, PO4 9RA
Mr P. H. Hase, Yew Tree Cottage, Sands, Farnham, Surrey, GU10 1LT
Mr M. R. Hickman, 184 Surrenden Road, Brighton, BN1 6NN
Professor M. Hicks, King Alfred's College, Sparkford Road, Winchester, SO22 4NR
Miss C. J. Humphreys, Flat 7, The Weirs, Chesil Street, Winchester, SO23 8HX
Mr and Mrs J. Ide, Karingal, Stewart Road, Emerald, Victoria, 3782 Australia
Mr J. Isherwood, Chalcot, Penton Mewsey, Andover, Hants, SP11 0RQ
Dr T. B. James, King Alfred's College, Sparkford Road, Winchester, SO22 4NR

Mr J. James, 3 Sylvan Close, Hordle, Lymington, Hants, SO41 0HJ
Mrs I. Jeffreys, 18 Roundwood Gardens, Harpenden, Herts, AL5 3AJ
Mr E. Jones, 11 Silwood Close, Winchester, SO22 6EN
Dr J. Lane, Heirweg 27, 6243 AC Geulle, The Netherlands
Miss S. J. Lewin, 21 Greenhill Road, Winchester, SO22 5EE
Mr G. J. Linter, 57 Chantryfield Road, Angmering, Littlehampton, West Sussex, BN16 4DH
Mrs G. M. Lowe, 26 Frankland Road, Croxley Green, Rickmansworth, Herts, WD3 3AU
Mr D. E. Lowman, 6 Cranford Gardens, Millersdale, Chandlers Ford, Hants, SO5 1PU
Mr J. Lunn, 2 Florence Road, Fleet, Hants
Mr G. P. Maidment, Havant Museum, East Street, Havant, PO9 1BS
Mr W. J. Marsh, 68 Mulvagh Avenue, Nepean, Ontario, Canada, K2E 6M6
Mr T. M. Matthews, 18 Mandhill Close, Grove, near Wantage, Oxon, OX12 7HY
Mr R. A. Merson, Tanyard House, 13a Bridge Square, Farnham, Surrey, GU9 7QR
Mr M. Morris, 80 The Butts, Alton, Hants, GU34 1RD
Mr A. Morton, 32 Graham Road, Southampton, SO14 0AW
Mr M. Mugridge, 15 Basingwell Street, Bishops Waltham, Hants, SO32 1AJ
Mr J. Pile, 22 Parkside, Bedhampton, Havant, Hants, PO9 3PL
Mr M. A. Pinhorn, Norman's Place, Newbridge Road, Calbourne, Newport, Isle of Wight, PO30 4QR
Mrs C. Riddell, 48 Common Lane, Tickhill, Doncaster, DN11 9UN
Mrs M. Riglar, 614 Kenton Lane, Harrow, Middlesex, HA3 7LG
Mr P. Roberts, 110 Woodlands Road, Ashurst, Southampton, Hants
Mr J. R. Rogers, Christmas Rose Cottage, Bleak Hill, Harbridge, nr Ringwood, Hants, BH34 3PX
Mrs E. Smith, 5 Hillmead Gardens, Bedhampton, Havant, Hants, PO9 3NL
Mr R. Snudden, 9 Bury Court, Stone Street, Cambridge, CB1 2RX
Mr G. Soffe, 26 Bromsgrove Cottages, Faringdon, Oxon, SN17 7JQ
Mr J. E. H. Spaul, 57 Charlton Road, Andover, Hants, SP10 3JT
Mr D. J. Stagg, 6 Alpine Road, Ashurst, Southampton, Hants, SO4 2AN
Mr P. Stevenage, 16 Wychperry Road, Haywards Heath, Sussex
Mr C. P. Stone, 55 Marlborough Road, Exeter, Devon, EX2 4LN
Mr D. J. Swindell, 9 Laurence Court, Ludgershall, Andover, Hants, SP11 9QN
Mrs J. Thorp, Ridgewood Grange, Chilton Road, Upton, Didcot, Oxfordshire, OX11 9JL
Mr J. Townsend, 95 Arbor Lane, Winnersh, Wokingham, Berks, RG11 5JE
Mr G. Watts, c/o Southern Tours, High Street, Bishops Waltham, Hants
Mr A. Webb, 6 Roseberry Street, Taunton, Somerset, TA2 6NF
Miss P. White, 3 St Mary's Road, Liss, Hants, GU33 7AH
Miss J. A. Williamson, 6 Heather Close, Walkford, Christchurch, Dorset, BH23 5RP

Institutional subscribers

Great Britain

Aberystwyth, National Library of Wales (copyright library)
Birmingham Public Libraries
Birmingham University Library
Cambridge University Library (copyright library)

Colchester, Essex University Library
Edinburgh, National Library of Scotland (copyright library)
Leicester University Library
London, British Library (copyright library)
London, Guildhall Library
London, Institute of Historical Research
London, Lambeth Palace Library
London, London Library
London, Public Record Office
London, Royal Historical Society
London, Society of Antiquaries of London
Newport, Isle of Wight County Reference Library
Oxford, Bodleian Library (copyright library)
Portsmouth City Records Office
Southampton, Hartley Library, University of Southampton
Winchester, King Alfred's College Library
Winchester, Hampshire County Library
Winchester, Hampshire Record Office
York, Borthwick Institute

Overseas

Barr Smith Library, University of Adelaide, Australia
Boole Library, University College, Cork, Ireland
Dalhousie University Library, Nova Scotia, Canada